W9-CDB-750

The Politics of Genocide

Volume 1

THE POLITICS
OF GENOCIDE

The Holocaust in Hungary, Volume 1

RANDOLPH L. BRAHAM

COLUMBIA UNIVERSITY PRESS
New York
1981

Library of Congress Cataloging in Publication Data

Braham, Randolph L
The politics of genocide.

Includes bibliographical references.
CONTENTS: v. 1. The holocaust in Hungary.
1. Jews in Hungary—Persecutions. 2. Holocaust,
Jewish (1939–1945)—Hungary. 3. Hungary—Ethnic relations. I. Title.
DS135.H9B74   323.1'1924'0439   80-11096
ISBN 0-231-04496-8 (the set)
0-231-05208-1 (vol. I)
0-231-04388-0 (vol. II)

COLUMBIA UNIVERSITY PRESS
NEW YORK   GUILDFORD, SURREY
COPYRIGHT © 1981 BY COLUMBIA UNIVERSITY PRESS
ALL RIGHTS RESERVED
PRINTED IN THE UNITED STATES OF AMERICA
Volume I: C 10 9 8 7 6 5 4 3 2
Volume II: C 10 9 8 7 6 5 4 3 2 1

*In memory of my parents
and the other victims
of the Holocaust in Hungary*

Contents

List of Tables

List of Figures

List of Maps

Preface

THE DESTRUCTION of the Jews of Hungary constitutes one of the most perplexing chapters in the history of the Holocaust. It is replete with paradoxes. The Jewish community of Hungary, which enjoyed an unparallelled level of development after its legal emancipation in 1867, was the first to be subjected to discriminatory legislation in post-World War I Europe. Conversely, when the Jewish communities of German-occupied Europe were being systematically destroyed during the first four and half years of World War II, the Jewish community of Hungary, though subjected to harsh legal and economic measures and to a series of violent actions, continued to be relatively well off. But when catastrophe struck with the German invasion of the country on March 19, 1944, it was this community that was subjected to the most ruthless and concentrated destruction process of the war. This took place on the very eve of Allied victory, when the grisly details of the Final Solution—the Nazi drive for the liquidation of European Jewry—were already known to the leaders of the world, including those of Hungarian and world Jewry. The barbarity and speed with which the Hungarian Jews were destroyed has been characterized by Winston Churchill as "probably the greatest and most horrible crime ever committed in the history of the world."

Who must bear the historical responsibility for this catastrophe? In retrospect, it appears that considerable blame falls on those who might be called onlookers—the Allies and the neutral powers for their basic indifference to the plight of the Jews, the International Red Cross and the Vatican for their lack of urgency and insensitivity, and the local Christian population and church authorities for their apathy and passivity. To a lesser extent blame must also be shared by the Hungarian and world Jewish leaders for their shortsightedness and bureaucratic-diplomatic tendencies, though their ineffectiveness reflected primarily the impotence and defenselessness of the Jewish people. Ultimate responsibility, however, must be borne almost exclusively by the Germans and their Hungarian accomplices. It was the concerted and single-minded drive by these two groups that made the effectuation of the Final Solution in Hungary possible: one could not have succeeded without the other. While the Germans were eager to solve the Jewish question, they could not have proceeded without the consent of the newly established Hungarian government and the cooperation of the Hungarian instrumentalities of power. The Hungarian ultra-rightists, in turn, though anxious to emulate their German counterparts, could not have achieved their ideologically defined objectives in the absence of the occupation.

The masses of Hungarian Jewry—the victims—must of course be absolved from any direct responsibility, though questions have occasionally been raised about their failure to escape or resist. Such questions are not only gratuitous but also reflect a fundamental ignorance of the situation in the country at the time. While the Hungarian Jews lived for several years virtually in the shadow of Auschwitz, they had no concrete knowledge about the gas chambers and the mass murders committed in many of the concentration camps. Those among them who had heard talk about these horrors discounted it as rumor or anti-Nazi propaganda. They, like most of their leaders, could not conceive of systematic, assembly-line mass murder in supposedly enlightened twentieth-century Europe. Their reaction, like that of Jews everywhere in the Nazi-dominated continent, was shock and disbelief. Their most prevalent psychological defense mechanism was retreat from reality.

The attitudes and perceptions of the Hungarian Jews were largely shaped by a myopic view of their position in Hungary since 1867. Conscious of the progress they had made during the "Golden Era" of their history (1867–1918) and of the close ties that their central leaders developed with the ruling conservative-aristocratic elite, the Hungarian Jews not only tended to divorce themselves from the concerns of world Jewry, but also developed a basically false sense of security. They continued to delude themselves to the very end, rationalizing that unlike their brethren in the neighboring countries, they would survive the war relatively intact, albeit in an economically depressed position. What happened in Poland, they argued upon hearing some vague accounts of the anti-Jewish excesses there, could not possibly happen in a civilized Hungary where the destiny of the Jews and Magyars had been intertwined for over a thousand years! This optimism was reinforced by the fact that Hungarian Jewry continued for several years to survive almost intact while the other Jewish communities of Europe were being systematically destroyed. During this period of relative tranquillity, the central Jewish leaders, who were acquainted with the Nazis' Final Solution program, unfortunately failed to take any meaningful precautions: they failed to inform the Hungarian political leadership and the Jewish masses or to heed the advice and warnings of the persecution-wise Polish and Slovak Jewish refugees in the country.

Uninformed, unprepared, and basically disunited, Hungarian Jewry consequently became easy prey for the SS and their Hungarian accomplices after the occupation. The Final Solution program—the isolation, expropriation, ghettoization, concentration, and deportation of the Jews—was carried out at lightning speed. In late spring 1944, close to 440,000 Jews from all over Hungary, excepting Budapest, were deported to Auschwitz within less than two months. Time was of the essence, for the Third Reich was threatened by imminent defeat.

Trapped and abandoned by their own government, living in the midst of a basically passive if not hostile Christian population in a country devoid of meaningful resistance, and forsaken by the rest of the world, the Hungarian Jewish leaders—both traditional and Zionist—did everything in their power to save what could still be saved. The traditional leaders, who became the official representatives of the Jewish Council (*Judenrat*) after the occupation and thus an unwilling and unwitting tool in the hands of the SS, relied largely on dilatory tactics. They hoped that the rapid advance of the Red Army would prevent the Nazis from carrying out their sinister designs. The Zionists, while agreeing with the objectives if not always with the tactics of these leaders, generally believed that only by dealing directly with the SS, the unit perceived as holding real power in Hungary, could the maximum be achieved for Hungarian Jewry. In retrospect, it is clear that both of these approaches were doomed to failure. For in defiance of all reason and logic, the German and Hungarian elements involved in the Final Solution program would not allow themselves, their inevitable imminent doom notwithstanding, to be deterred from their determination to make Hungary *Judenrein*.

This study aims to provide a clearer perspective and contribute to a better understanding of the many complex factors that led to the destruction of Hungarian Jewry. It attempts to explain in a rational context the historical, political, communal, and socioeconomic factors that contributed to a greater or lesser extent to the unfolding of this tragedy. Finally, it aims to describe and analyze the Holocaust in Hungary in the context of Hungarian and world history and international politics. The general historical and philosophical framework of the Nazis' biological theories and racial ideology, including the myths about the Jews and the pathology of their proponents, has been omitted, as it has already been adequately treated in a number of scholarly works. In this sphere, the study limits itself primarily to an evaluation of the views and programs of the Hungarian radical Right.

The Chronology (Appendix 5) offers a convenient overview of the events covered in this work. These are described and analyzed on a thematic basis in historical-chronological order. The first ten chapters are devoted to an evaluation of the era before the German occupation. Chapters 11 through 16 cover the antecedents and character of the occupation as well as the policies and measures relating to the implementation of the first steps in the Final Solution program, including the organization and deployment of the instrumentalities of power, the Jewish Council, and the isolation and expropriation of the Jews. The next six chapters describe the last phases of the Final Solution process on a region-by-region basis. Chapters 23 through 31 describe and analyze various aspects of the Holocaust in Hungary, including the attitudes and reactions of the Jews and non-Jews in Hungary, rescue and resistance, the position of the international community, and the fate of the Jews of Budapest during the era of the Nazi puppet Szálasi. Chapter 32 is devoted to an evaluation of the immediate postwar period, covering such issues as rehabilitation, restitution, and retribution.

For convenience and consistency rather than national preference, the geographic names of localities in the territories acquired by Hungary from Czechoslovakia, Romania, and Yugoslavia in 1938–41 are rendered throughout this study in their Hungarian version. Their Romanian, Serbo-Croatian, and Slovak equivalents are given in the Geographic List of Names. Frequently used abbreviations, acronyms, and foreign terms are identified in the Glossary.

Like all studies of its kind, this study contains a number of gaps. Some of these can undoubtedly be attributed to the author's oversight. Others, however, are due to the refusal of several institutions and individuals to make their documents available—35 years after the Holocaust. Thus, for example, I could not gain access to the Saly Mayer files at the AJDC in New York or the archives of Nathan Schwalb, the former *Hehalutz* representative in Geneva. By far the most glaring lacunae are due to the consistent failure of officials associated with various institutions of the Hungarian People's Republic to permit access to the many files relating to war crimes trials and the individual Jewish communities destroyed. Much of the information relating to these topics, consequently, had to be culled largely from secondary sources.

Several chapters of this work were published earlier in abbreviated form in various journals. Chapter 10 was used as the basis for a monograph on the labor service system. For their permission to reproduce these chapters, in a revised and updated fashion, I am indebted to the *East European Quarterly* of the University of Colorado (chapter 10), the Institute of Contemporary Jewry of the Hebrew University of Jerusalem (chapter 23), *Jewish Social Studies* (chapter 7), and *Yad Vashem Studies* (chapters 8 and 14 and parts of chapter 6).

This study could not have been completed without the help and cooperation of several institutions. Their financial assistance for the investigation of archival depositories in many parts of the world, including the United States, the Federal Republic of Germany, Great Britain, Israel, Hungary, and Romania, proved invaluable. For this I am especially thankful to the Memorial Foundation for Jewish Culture and the Research Foundation of The City University of New York. I am also indebted to the World Federation of Hungarian Jews and its officers, Michael Berger, Ervin Farkas, Norman Gati, and Marcel Sand, for their generous contribution. I would like to express my great appreciation to the officers and staff of Yad Vashem in Jerusalem (especially Dr. Erich Kulka and Dr. Chaim Pazner) and the YIVO Institute for Jewish Research (especially Dina Abramowicz) for giving me unhindered access to all their library and archival holdings.

I would also like to express my gratitude to a large number of individuals who were extremely helpful in the course of my research. I am especially indebted to the many *dramatis personae*, including Hansi Brand, Hillel Danzig, the late Fülöp Freudiger, Dezső Hermann, Fábián Herskovits, Oskar (Karmil) Krasznyansky, Miklós (Moshe) Krausz, Georges (Mandel) Mantello, Chaim Pazner (Pozner), Samuel Springmann, and Bruce Teicholz, who graciously consented to be interviewed. I also wish to thank the many individuals who responded to my public appeals for information on the various destroyed Jewish communities. Special thanks are due to Professor Béla Vágó of the University of Haifa for his review of the manuscript, his valuable suggestions, and the transliteration of Hebrew titles. I am indebted to Dr. Andrew Freeman for his critical reading of the first 16 chapters and for valuable contributions to the section on restitution in chapter 32. I am also indebted to Professor L. de Jong, the Director of the Netherlands State Institute for War Documentation in Amsterdam, for archival materials relating to the treatment of Hungarian Jews in German-occupied Holland. I thank Gardenia Hobbs for her secretarial assistance, and Jolie Nanasi and Bruce Teicholz for their efforts toward making the publication of this study possible. For their understanding, expert advice, and cooperation I am indebted to Leslie Bialler, the editor of this work, and Bernard Gronert, the Executive Editor of Columbia University Press. Finally, I must thank my wife Elizabeth and my sons Steven and Robert, who not only provided moral support, but also played an active role in practically all phases of preparing this work for publication.

Randolph L. Braham
July 1980

Reference List of
Selected Geographic Name Changes

Aknasugatag	Ocna Şugatag, Rom.
Alsó Rona	Rona de Jos, Rom.
Alsóvisó	Vişeul de Jos, Rom.
Aranyosmeggyes	Mediaşul Aurit, Rom.
Aranyszentmiklós	Sînnicoara, Rom.
Avasujváros	Negreşti, Rom.
Bácska	Bačka, Yug.
Bácska Topolya	Bačka Topola, Yug.
Bácstopolya *see* Bácska Topolya	
Bánffyhunyad	Huedin, Rom.
Barcanfalva	Bărsana, Rom.
Bárdfalva	Berbeşti, Rom.
Batiz	Botiz, Rom.
Bedőháza	Bedevla, CSR.
Beregszász	Beregovo, CSR.
Beszterce	Bistriţa, Rom.
Bethlen	Bcclcan, Rom.
Bikszád	Bixad, Rom.
Bőd	Beudiu, Rom.
Borsa	Borşa, Rom.
Brusztura	Brustura, CSR.
Budfalva	Budeşti, Rom.
Bustyaháza	Buština, CSR
Coptelke	Pădureni, Rom.
Csáktornya	Čakovek, Yug.
Csata	Čata, CSR.
Cservenka	Crvenka, Yug.
Csikszereda	Miercurea Ciuc, Rom.
Csurog	Curug, Yug.
Dengeleg	Livada, Rom.
Derzse	Dîrja, Rom.
Dés	Dej, Rom.
Desenfalva	Desesti, Rom.
Devecser	Diviciorii, Rom.

Dombó	Dubové, CSR.
Drágomérfalva	Drăgomireşti, Rom.
Dunaszerdahely	Dunajska Streda, CSR.
Élesd	Aleşd, Rom.
Eperjes	Prešov, CSR.
Erdőd	Ardud, Rom.
Érmihályfalva	Valea lui Mihai, Rom.
Érsekujvár	Nové Żamky, CSR.
Farkasrev	Vad, Rom.
Feketelak	Lacu, Rom.
Felsőrona	Rona de Sus, Rom.
Felsővisó	Vişeul de Sus, Rom.
Gánya	Gáňice, CSR.
Glod	Glod, Rom.
Gyergyószentmiklós	Gheorgheni, Rom.
Gyulafalva	Giuleşti, Rom.
Gyurgyevo	Durdevo, Yug.
Halmi	Halmeu, Rom.
Havasmező	Poieni de Sub Munte, Rom.
Hidalmás	Hida, Rom.
Horgos	Horgoš, Yug.
Hosszúmező	Câmpulung la Tisa, Rom.
Huszt	Chust, CSR.
Iklód	Iclod, Rom.
Izakonyha	Cuhea, Rom.
Izaszacsal	Săcel, Rom.
Jod	Jeud, Rom.
Kalinfalva	Kaliny, CSR.
Kápolnokmonostor	Popalnic Mănăştur, Rom.
Karácsonyfalva	Crăciuneşti, Rom.
Kassa	Košice, CSR.
Kecsed	Ghiciud or Miceştii de Cîmpie, Rom.
Kékes	Chiochiş, Rom.
Kérő	Băiţa, Rom.
Királymező	Ustčorna, CSR.
Kis Ida	Malá Ida, CSR.
Kiskalota	Călăţele, Rom.
Kissármás	Sărmăşel, Rom.
Kőkényes	Jrnovo, CSR.
Kolozsvár	Cluj, Rom.

Körtvélyes	Hrušovo, CSR.
Kracsfalva	Crăceşti, Rom.
Kraszna	Crasna, Rom.
Lekér	Lekyr, CSR.
Leordina	Leordina, Rom.
Léva	Levice, CSR.
Losonc	Lučenek, CSR.
Lozsárd	Lajerd, Rom.
Magyarlápos	Tîrgul Lăpuşului, Rom.
Majszin	Moisei, Rom.
Mányik	Manic, Rom.
Máramarossziget	Sighet or Sighetul Marmaţiei, Rom.
Margitta	Marghita, Rom.
Marosvásárhely	Tîrgu Mureş, Rom.
Mezőtelegd	Tiliagd, Rom.
Mindszent	Vise Svatých, CSR.
Mosorin	Mokrin, Yug.
Munkács	Mukačevo, CSR.
Nagybánya	Baia Mare, Rom.
Nagybocskó	Bocicoiul Mare, Rom.
Nagy Ida	Velika Ida, CSR.
Nagyilonda	Ileanda Mare, Rom.
Nagykároly	Carei Mari, Rom.
Nagymagyar	Velky Meder, CSR.
Nagymihály	Michalovce, CSR.
Nagysálló	Velke Šarluhi, CSR.
Nagysomkut	Şomcuta Mare, Rom.
Nagyszalonta	Salonta Mare, Rom.
Nagysármás	Sărmaş, Rom.
Nagyszőllős	Sevluš, CSR.
Nagyvárad	Oradea Mare, Rom.
Nánfalva	Nǎneşti, Rom.
Naszód	Nǎsǎud, Rom.
Nyéresháza	Nerešnice, CSR.
Ördöngösfűzes	Fizeşul Gherlii, Rom.
Oroszka	Oroska, CSR.
Oroszmokra	Ruskámokra, CSR.
Pujon	Pui, Rom.
Remetefalva	Remeţi, Rom.
Retteg	Reteag, Rom.
Rimaszombat	Rimavská Sobota, CSR.

Ronaszék — Costiui, Rom.
Rozália — Rozavelea, Rom.
Rozsnyó — Rožňava, CSR.
Ruszkova — Ruscova, Rom.

Sajkás — Šajkaška, Yug.
Sajófalva — Şieu, Rom.
Sárköz — Livada, Rom.
Sáró — Šaro, CSR.
Sepsiszentgyörgy — Sfîntu Gheorghe, Rom.
Somorja — Šamorin, CSR.
Szabadka — Subotica, Yug.
Szák — Sac, Rom.
Szamosujvár — Gherla, Rom.
Szaplonca — Sapanta, Rom.
Szászrégen — Reghin, Rom.
Szatmárnémeti — Satu Mare, Rom.
Székelyhid — Secuieni, Rom.
Székelyudvarhely — Odorhei, Rom.
Szelistye — Sălişte, Rom.
Szentgothárd — Sucutard, Rom.
Szentmárton — Sînartin, Rom.
Szenttamás — Srbobran, Yug.
Szepsi — Moldava, CSR.
Szerbfalva — Sârb, Rom.
Szilágysomlyó — Şimleul Silvaniei, Rom.
Szlatina — Slatina, Rom.
Szurdok — Strămtura, Rom.

Taracköz — Terešva, CSR.
Tarackraszna — Krasnasora, CSR.
Técső — Tečovo, CSR.
Téhány — Tahanovce, CSR.
Topolya *see* Bácska Topolya
Török Kanizsa — Stara Kanyiža, Yug.

Udvarhely — Odorhei, Rom.
Ujvidék — Novi Sad, Yug.
Ungvár — Uzhorod, CSR.

Váncsfalva — Onceşti, Rom.
Verebély — Vroble, CSR.
Veresegyháza — Strugureni, Rom.
Visk — Viskovo, CSR.
Vulchovec — Vulchovce, CSR.

Zenta   Senta, Yug.
Zombor   Sombor, Yug.
Zsablya   Žabalj, Yug.
Zseliz   Želizovce, CSR.

Hungarian
Military Ranks and Terms

Alakulat: Formation
Alezredes: Lieutenant-Colonel
Altábornagy: Lieutenant-General
Altiszt: Noncommissioned officer
Dandár: Brigade
Ezred: Regiment
Ezredes: Colonel
Főhadnagy: First Lieutenant
Gyalogság: Infantry
Hadaprod: Cadet
Hadaprodőrmester: Sergeant up for promotion
Hadnagy: Lieutenant
Hadtest: Army Corps
Káplár: Corporal
Őrmester: Sergeant
Őrnagy: Major
Őrvezető: Private First-Class
Osztag: Detachment
Parancsnok: Commander
Parancsnokság: Command
Raj: Squad
Szakasz: Platoon
Szakaszvezető: Lance Sergeant
Százados: Captain
Tábornagy: Field Marshal
Tábornok: General
Tényleges szolgálat: Active service
Tiszt: Officer (commissioned)
Tisztes: Noncommissioned officer
Tizedes: Corporal (acting)
Továbbszolgáló: Re-enlistee
Vezérőrnagy: Major-General
Vezérezredes: General
Zászlóalj: Battalion
Zászlós: Ensign; Cornet

Wehrmacht and SS Ranks
with Their U.S. Equivalents

Wehrmacht	*SS*	*U.S. Equivalent*
Leutnant	Untersturmführer	Second Lieutenant
Oberleutnant	Obersturmführer	First Lieutenant
Hauptmann	Hauptsturmführer	Captain
Major	Sturmbannführer	Major
Oberstleutnant	Obersturmbannführer	Lieutenant-Colonel
Oberst	Standartenführer, Oberführer	Colonel
Generalmajor	Brigadeführer	Brigadier General
Generalleutnant	Gruppenführer	Major-General
General der Infanterie, etc.	Obergruppenführer	Lieutenant-General
Generaloberst	Oberstgruppenführer	General
Generalfeldmarschall	Reichsführer	General of the Army

List of
Source Abbreviations

Aşezările evreilor: Aşezările evreilor din România. Memento statistic (The Settlements of the Jews in Romania. Statistical Synopsis). Bucharest: Congresul Mondial Evreesc. Secţiunea din România, 1947.

C. A. Macartney: C. A. Macartney, *October Fifteenth. A History of Modern Hungary, 1929–1945*. Edinburgh: Edinburgh University Press, (Distributed by Frederick A. Praeger), 1957, 2 vols. (493, 519 pp.)

Der Kastner-Bericht: Der Kastner-Bericht über Eichmanns Menschenhandel in Ungarn (The Kasztner Report on Eichmann's Trade in Men in Hungary). Ed. Ernest Landau. Munich: Kindler, 1961, 368 pp.

FAA: "Fegyvertelenül álltak az aknamezőkön . . ." Dokumentumok a munkaszolgálat történetéhez Magyarországon ("They Stood Unarmed on the Mine Fields . . ." Documents on the Labor Service System in Hungary). Comp. and ed. by Elek Karsai. Budapest: A Magyar Izraeliták Országos Képviselete, 1962, 2 vols. (cxxvii + 575, 852 pp.)

HJS: *Hungarian-Jewish Studies.* Ed. Randolph L. Braham. New York: World Federation of Hungarian Jews, 1966–1973, 3 vols. (346, 300, 324 pp.)

IMT: International Military Tribunal. *Trial of the Major War Criminals Before the International Military Tribunal.* Nuremberg: Secretariat of the International Military Tribunal, 1947–1949, 42 vols.

Lévai, *Fekete könyv:* Jenő Lévai, *Fekete könyv a magyar zsidóság szenvedéseiről* (Black Book on the Suffering of Hungarian Jewry). Budapest: Officina, 1946, 320 pp.

Lévai, *Zsidósors Magyarországon:* Jenő Lévai, *Zsidósors Magyarországon* (Jewish Fate in Hungary). Budapest: Magyar Téka, 1948, 479 pp.

Munkácsi, *Hogyan történt?:* Ernő Munkácsi, *Hogyan történt? Adatok és okmányok a magyar zsidóság tragédiájához* (How Did It Happen? Data and Documents Relating to the Tragedy of Hungarian Jewry). Budapest: Renaissance, 1947, 252 pp.

NA: National Archives, Washington.

NCA: Office of United States Chief of Counsel for the Prosecution of Axis Criminality. *Nazi Conspiracy and Aggression.* Washington, D.C.: Government Printing Office, 1946, 8 vols. and 3 supplements.

NMT: Nuernberg Military Tribunal. *Trials of War Criminals Before the Nuernberg Military Tribunals Under Control Council Law No. 10.* Washington, D.C.: Government Printing Office, 1949–1953, 15 vols.

Pinkas ha'kehilot: Pinkas ha'kehilot. Hungaria (Encyclopedia of Communities, Hungary). Jerusalem: Yad Vashem, 1975, 557 pp.

RAH: *Rescue Attempts During the Holocaust.* Eds. Yisrael Gutman and Efraim Zuroff. Jerusalem: Yad Vashem, 1977, 679 pp.

RLB: *The Destruction of Hungarian Jewry. A Documentary Account.* Comp. and ed. Randolph L. Braham. New York: World Federation of Hungarian Jews, 1963, 2 vols., 970 pp.

Tribunalul Poporului Cluj: Tribunalul Poporului Cluj. Complectul de judecată. Şedinţa publică din 31 Mai 1946 (The People's Tribunal, Cluj. Judgment. Public Session of May 31, 1946.

Vádirat: Vádirat a nácizmus ellen (Indictment of Nazism). Ed. Ilona Benoschofsky and Elek Karsai. Budapest: A Magyar Izraeliták Országos Képviselete, 1958–1967, 3 vols.

YIVO: YIVO-Institute for Jewish Research, New York City.

YVS: *Yad Vashem Studies.* Jerusalem: Yad Vashem, 1957–1978, 12 vols.

Zsidó Világkongresszus: Zsidó Világkongresszus (Magyarországi Képviselete) statisztikai osztályának közleményei (Publications of the Statistical Department of the (Hungarian Division) of the World Jewish Congress), Budapest, 1947–1949.

The Politics of Genocide

Volume 1

CHAPTER ONE

PRELUDE TO DESTRUCTION

The "Golden Era" of Hungarian Jewry

THE BREAKUP of the Austro-Hungarian Monarchy in November 1918 brought into focus the anachronisms on which it had been founded in 1867. It revealed the diverse and conflicting forces as well as the fundamental and basically irreconcilable contradictions that underlay the socioeconomic and national-political foundations of the complex and polyglot Dual Monarchy in the age of liberalism. Experiencing during its half-century of existence a large-scale and rapid process of general and industrial development, the state's political and economic structure contained both capitalistic and feudalistic elements whose contradictions unmasked the rhetorical character of its professed liberalism.

The unity and cohesion of the Dual Monarchy were to a large extent maintained by the rapidly developing forces of capitalism. However, unlike the case in the Western democracies, the development of capitalism in the Hungarian part of the Dual Monarchy was spearheaded under the general protection of the state and, in the absence of a politically emancipated and socially self-conscious indigenous middle class, by one that was overwhelmingly German and Jewish in its composition. Though avowedly liberal, the state had in fact retained its basically feudal character throughout the *Ausgleich* (Compromise) period. Its policies reflected the interests of a landed aristocracy whose antiquated tradition and ideology went counter to the social and national aspirations of the masses within the empire. The liberalism it professed was relatively hollow and devoid of any meaningful substance. Formal, legalistic, and rhetorical in character, the liberalism of the ruling class failed to heed either the socioeconomic aspirations of the large masses of landless peasants and of the increasingly large and politically ever more self-conscious industrial proletariat or the longing of the coinhabiting nationalities for self-determination. The *Interessengemeinschaft* between the economically gradually more powerful middle classes led by a group of predominantly "foreign" industrialists and financiers and the politically ruling traditional aristocratic-gentry minority was relatively short-lived and a mixed blessing. While it provided temporary political stability and contributed toward the advancement of their mutual economic interests, it also exacerbated the social and national conflicts underlying the polyglot empire. Unable and unwilling to solve the burning social issues and reluctant to come to grips with the urgent problem of the nationalities, the Dual Monarchy increasingly became an anachronism in the age of liberalism and nationalism.

Yet it was during this period of great social and national upheavals that Hungarian Jewry achieved its greatest successes, experiencing an accelerated and spectacular level of development. Within a few decades, the Jews of Hungary achieved a formidable, if not commanding, position in the country's economic, financial, and cultural life. But it was also during this "Golden Era" that Hungarian Jewry sowed the seeds of its demise after World War I by following a myopic social and national policy. By identifying itself unconditionally and uncritically with a basically reactionary regime whose favors it enjoyed and to which it was indebted, Hungarian Jewry alienated itself from the oppressed classes struggling for justice and equality and from the coinhabiting nationalities fighting for autonomy or national independence.

Evolution and Emancipation of Hungarian Jewry

The Jewish population of Hungary experienced a spectacular growth during the nineteenth century in the wake of the reforms of Joseph II and the concessions of the Diet of 1840.

According to the census of 1700, the Jewish population of Hungary at the beginning of the eighteenth century was only 4,071. The growth of the Jewish population during the remainder of the century was relatively moderate, increasing from 11,621 in 1735 to 80,775 in 1787. By 1805, the number of Jews reached 126,620, representing 1.8 percent of the total population. From this time on, the number and proportion of the Jews increased at a higher rate because of a relatively high birth rate and an increased level of immigration from Eastern Europe, especially the Pale. By 1850, their number reached 339,816 (3.7 percent) and by 1880, 624,826 (4.4 percent). Greater Hungary's Jewish population reached its peak in 1910, when it numbered 911,227 or 5.0 percent of the total population of nearly 21 million.[1]

Full legal equality was first granted Hungarian Jewry during the last weeks of Lajos Kossuth's revolutionary regime in 1849. The liberal era of Hungarian Jewry began with its emancipation on December 22, 1867, under Law No. XVII, which stipulated *inter alia:* [2]

The Israelite inhabitants of the country are declared to possess equal rights with the Christian inhabitants in the exercise of all civic and political functions. All laws, usages, and ordinances contravening this principle are hereby rescinded.

The Jews were subsequently given the right to levy a compulsory tax on members and to establish and maintain religious, educational, health, and welfare organizations. On October 1, 1895, the Jewish faith was legally recognized by the state under Law No. XLII as a "received" religion having a status equal to that of the Christian churches, except the Roman Catholic Church which enjoyed a special status in the Hungarian state.

Following their emancipation, the Jews of Hungary took full advantage of their new opportunities and participated actively in the modernization of Hungary which, its liberal rhetoric notwithstanding, was still in a predominantly pre-capitalist and pre-democratic phase of development. While the historical trend was unmistakably toward further liberalization, and the masses manifested a greater awareness of the political and social conditions prevailing in the country, a tightly knit caste composed primarily of large landowners exercised direct political power[3] and maintained its position of strength by virtue of a narrow franchise and the open ballot and control over the government and all appointments to the administration.[4] The "liberal" regime of Hungary therefore rejected the ideas and hopes associated with the nineteenth-century liberalism of the West, which saw in universal franchise the key to the solution of most, if not all, social problems. Fearful that the expansion of the franchise would open the door to the centrifugal aspirations of the oppressed landless peasants and workers and above all of the coinhabiting nationalities, the aristocratic-gentry regime restricted freedom of expression and kept the franchise to a minimum by establishing stringent property and educational qualifications and by using effective administrative and police pressure during and between elections. The exercise of political rights became in fact more restricted after the establishment of the Dual Monarchy. Whereas 6.7 percent of the population had possessed the franchise in 1848, only 5 percent possessed it in 1874. On the eve of World War I, the figure was still only around 8 percent.[5]

The governmental apparatus and the army were staffed primarily by the déclassé gentry. The gentry can be said to have consisted generally of the class of nobles, former nobles, and their descendants whose landholdings, averaging around 1,000 cadastral yokes, were diminished or lost in the wake of the economic crises of the nineteenth century. Many of these impoverished nobles and their descendants envied and came to oppose the coalition between the large landed aristocracy and the "foreign" representatives of finance and industry. Socially, however, they supported and emulated the aristocracy in clinging to the pursuits and customs of the past. They refused to engage in middle class occupations, looked down upon physical labor and tried desperately to retain at least the outward appearance of their traditional, gentlemanly way of life. In the course of time, they saturated the governmental apparatus at all levels and acquired a leading role in the political and military structure of the state. With the advent of Fascism and Nazism in Europe, they emerged as the most vocal proponents of the new, anti-Jewish policies in Hungary.

Because of Hungary's feudal tradition, the aristocracy and the gentry steadfastly refused to engage in commerce, industry, and other "degrading middle class" occupations, preferring the pursuits of a bygone feudal era. While illiberal in its attitude toward the coinhabiting nationalities and anti-democratic toward the Magyar peasant and laboring masses, the ruling Hungarian aristocracy displayed a consistently liberal attitude toward the Jews and encouraged them to engage in business and industry. In the course of time, a friendly cooperative relationship was established between the Hungarian aristocracy and the Jewish industrialists, bankers, and financiers. Many representatives of the aristocracy were made silent partners in Jewish business enterprises through their enlistment as stockholders and board members. In turn, many of the Jewish economic magnates were ennobled and eagerly assimilated the mores and practices of the aristocracy.[6]

As a consequence of this policy of tolerance, Hungarian Jewry considered itself an integral part of the Hungarian nation, and the Magyars accepted the assimilated Hungarian-speaking Jews as their equals. As such, the Jews not only had a full share in the development of Hungary's economy but also contributed generously to the enrichment of Hungarian culture and science.[7]

The Problem of Nationalities

The Hungarian attitude of benevolent tolerance toward the Jews was motivated not only by economic considerations, but also by the desire to increase the percentage of the Magyars in the polyglot Hungarian

Kingdom through the addition of the "Magyars of the Israelite faith" (*Zsidóvallású magyarok*), as the Jews were referred to in official statistics.

According to the census of 1910, which used language as a basis for the determination of nationality, the Hungarian Kingdom, excluding Croatia-Slavonia, which had been constitutionally affiliated with the Hungarian Crown since 1102, had a total population of 18,264,533. Of these, the Magyars numbered 9,944,627 or 54.4 percent. But even this slim and doubtful majority[8] was achieved only with the aid of the 911,227 Jews who accounted for a little over 5 percent of the population. With the inclusion of Croatia-Slavonia, which had a total population of 2,621,954, of which 105,948 were Magyars, the percentage of the Magyars would have been reduced to only 45.4.

Of the national minorities living in the Hungarian Kingdom, the Romanian was the largest, numbering over 3.5 million or around 20 percent of the population. Next came the Slovaks and Ruthenians with close to 2.5 million, and the Serbs with over 1 million (map 1.1).

Ignoring the multinational character of the state, the Magyar ruling classes were guided by a blind chauvinistic nationalism that barred any meaningful concessions to the coinhabiting nationalities. Pursuing a myopic, antiquated policy, they abandoned the constitutional views of Ferenc Deák, the enlightened Hungarian nationalist leader who shaped the dualistic order, and failed to implement the Nationality Law of 1868, which incorporated the progressive ideas of Baron József Eötvös, the Minister of Cults and Public Education. One of the great Hungarian authorities on the sociological and philosophical questions underlying the national issue, Eötvös endeavored to strike a compromise between the demands of the revolutionary nationalists for administrative-territorial autonomy and the insistence of the Magyar chauvinists for the retention of the unity of the Magyar national state. Eötvös' compromise was based on the idea that the nationalities be allowed to develop their own cultural and national life within the framework of the politically unified multinational Hungarian state and that as individuals they be enabled to enjoy the rights and opportunities associated with Hungarian citizenship. Autonomy was rejected because of the fear that to do so would eventually lead to the demand for secession and independence and the consequent disintegration of the state. Under Eötvös' plans, the nationalities were to have, among other things, their own primary and secondary schools, develop their ecclesiastical institutions, and use their own languages in the administration of local, district, and county governments.[9]

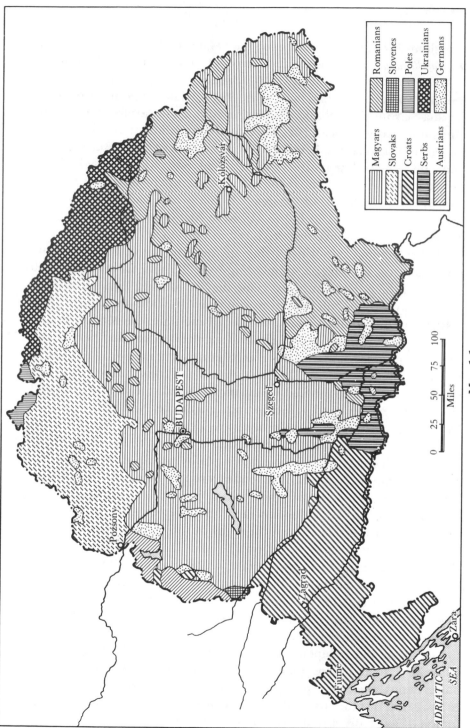

Map 1.1.

The nationalities of the Hungarian Kingdom, 1867–1918.

Mátyás Unger and Ottó Szabolcs, *Magyarország története* (The History of Hungary [Budapest: Gondolat, 1979]).

While the rejection of the principle of territorial autonomy disappointed the nationalities, it was the Magyar chauvinists who prevented the effective implementation of the Nationality Law. Eager to retain Magyar hegemony and resolved to establish a homogeneous Magyar national state, the ruling classes engaged in a process of ruthless magyarization, which not only violated the principles and provisions of the Law, but also exacerbated the domestic national struggles. This process acquired a special momentum after the death of Deák in 1876, a death which symbolized the end of the leadership generation of 1848 and 1867 whose political vision and morality were coupled by an enlightened spirit of toleration.

The new generation of politicians led by Prime Minister Kálmán Tisza (1875–1890) tried to stem the rising tide of nationalism and of the corollary demands for self-determination by unleashing the forces of Magyar chauvinism. It embarked on a ruthless policy of magyarization that aimed at the creation of an exclusively Magyar nation-state through the total assimilation of the nationalities. The provisions of the Nationality Law notwithstanding, the local, district, and county governmental units, like the central political institutions and administrative apparatus, came to be staffed almost exclusively with Hungarian elements primarily associated with the interests of the aristocratic-gentry ruling classes. Most of the leading administrative and army positions were actually held by the gentry, which was impoverished in the wake of the competition of economic liberalism but which still clung to its social status and political power. The Magyar language was increasingly required as a vehicle of instruction in the schools and the press, and the educational and cultural institutions were transformed into effective instrumentalities for the advancement of Magyar national assimilation. The imperialistic doctrine of Magyar nationalism incorporated the political axiom that "either the Magyars would assimilate the nationalities or the nationalities would destroy the Hungarian state." [10]

The Jews played a singularly important role in the process of magyarization. Perhaps no other minority or nationality in the Hungarian Kingdom adopted the Hungarian language and culture with the same "spontaneous eagerness" as the Jews. First the German-speaking Jews of Austrian and Moravian origin and then the Yiddish-speaking Jews of Galician-Polish background gradually shed their "alien" cultural orientation and adapted themselves fervently to Magyar ways of life. While this process of magyarization became intensified after 1867, its beginnings can be traced to 1844, when the leaders of the Jewish youth of Pest launched the *Magyarító Egylet* (Magyarization Society) with the specific objective of magyarizing the predominantly German-speaking Jews of the city.[11] A similar objective was partially pursued by the MIKÉFE (*Magyar Izraelita Kézműves és Földmüvelö Egyesület;* Hungarian Jewish Artisan and Agricultural Association), which was also founded in 1844, under the auspices of the Jewish Community of Pest (*A Pesti Izraelita Hitközség*) at a meeting chaired by Chief Rabbi Löw Schwab. Placed under the leadership of Dr. Fülöp Jakobovits, the head of the Jewish Hospital, MIKÉFE aimed not only at the training and defense of Jewish artisans and agricultural workers, but also at the propagation of the Magyar language and the inculcation of pro-Magyar patriotism among the Jews.[12]

The overwhelming majority of Hungarian Jewry realized that complete assimilation and magyarization was the price they had to pay for their emancipation. In fact, it was the idea of Kossuth, Deák, and Eötvös that the Jews had to earn their emancipation by adopting the Magyar language in their religious instruction and services and by assimilating the traditions, customs, and ideology of the Magyars.[13] While these stipulations were rejected by the Orthodox Jews, they were wholeheartedly embraced by the "liberal" or Neolog majority, which also provided the bulk of the community's official leadership. Although the national government of 1867 tried to overcome the difficulties within the community by convening a congress in December 1868,[14] the conflict between the assimilationist Neolog and the traditional, but equally loyal, Orthodox wings of Hungarian Jewry remained irreconcilable.

Unlike the situation in the West, the emancipation of the Jews was promoted not so much in terms of the liberal philosophy of the enlightenment, but primarily as an aspect of the idea of Hungarian nationalism. One of its basic objectives was to strengthen the precarious numerical position of the Magyars in the polyglot kingdom by absorbing or magyarizing the Jews. Although Hungarian Jewry provided the founder and some of the leading figures of world Zionism, including Theodor Herzl and Max Nordau, it never developed a national consciousness associated with the idea of Zion.[15] In this respect, the Neolog and the Orthodox were of one mind.

The eagerness with which the Hungarian Jews embraced the Magyar cause—the overwhelming majority of them became assimilated and even most of the Orthodox Jews adopted Hungarian as their language of communication—can be explained by a number of factors. They were, of course, grateful for the economic and professional opportunities afforded after emancipation by the feudalistically oriented aristocratic-gentry regime. As a consequence of the *Interessengemeinschaft* between the regime and the Jews, the country experienced an unprecedented level of industrial development and general modernization,[16] while the Jews emerged as the major, if not dominant, factors in the professions and Hungarian capitalism. While the number of all attorneys grew between 1890 and 1900 by 7.2 percent, the number of Jewish attorneys increased by 68.6 percent. Of the 4,807 physicians in 1900, 2,321 or 48 percent were Jewish. In the possession of landed property, too, the advance of the Jews was quite remarkable given the fact that the Jews had not been permitted to own land until their emancipation. In 1884 there were 1,898 Jewish proprietors owning a territory of about 1.75 million cadastral yokes. (A yoke equals 0.576 hectares or 1.42 acres; one hectare equals 2.47 acres.) By 1894, their number increased to 2,788 and the size of their territory grew to 2.62 million cadastral yokes.[17]

The Jews were also cognizant of the protection the regime provided against the threat of anti-Semitism. While anti-Semitic disturbances and demonstrations did, of course, occur even during this period, they were primarily local and sporadic in character rather than concerted or centrally organized. One such was the notorious Tisza-Eszlár ritual murder case (1882). During the trial, the ritual murder charge lodged against a number of Jews for having allegedly killed a Christian girl for the purpose of blood sacrifice was reduced to a simple murder charge. The presiding judge as well as the public attorney courageously denounced the absurdity of the blood myth and the defendants were eventually acquitted. In the wake of the agitations associated with the trial, however, a series of anti-Jewish riots took place in various places, including Pozsony, which the government suppressed promptly and resolutely.

In addition, the anti-Jewish agitations of Győző (Victor) Istóczy and Iván Simonyi[18] drew worldwide attention, but left no major or lasting imprint within the Hungarian Kingdom. The major vehicle of organized, but less virulent, anti-Semitism after 1895 was the newly formed Catholic People's Party (*Katolikus Néppárt*) of Count Nándor Zichy. Supported by the Church, the pro-Hapsburg aristocracy, and the great landowners, this typical clerical-conservative party aimed at combatting the "destructive and anti-Christian" ideas associated with "Jewish" liberalism and socialism.[19]

The prompt and forceful intervention of the government in dealing with these anti-Semitic demonstrations further enhanced the fidelity of the Jews to the Magyar state. Anti-Semitism was of no real consequence in pre-World War I Hungary, not only because of the benevolent attitude of the government, but also because of the generally tolerant character of the Hungarian peasants and the backward political and social structural base of the country. Although the anti-Semitic demonstrations of this period were effectively controlled by the government, the anti-Jewish ideas developed by men like Istóczy and Simonyi or advocated by the Catholic People's Party had a far-reaching effect. The anti-Jewish themes relating to the alleged harmful and corrupting influences of the Jews in all spheres of Christian life were picked up by the Right radicals during the post-World War I period.

The pro-Magyar nationalistic posture of the Jews was, of course, adopted not only because of expediency, or gratitude for the opportunities, and the safety afforded by the aristocratic-gentry regime, but also because of a fervent patriotism that motivated many of them. As Professor Oscar Jászi, a noted sociologist and democratic statesman, correctly observed, "There can be no doubt that a large mass of these assimilated elements adopted their new ideology quite spontaneously and enthusiastically out of a sincere love of the new fatherland."[20] The jingoistic nationalism of many of the Jews was especially manifest in Budapest. Constituting about 20 percent of the population,[21] the Jews of the capital were in the forefront of the process of assimilation. The intellectual elite among them played a creatively active role in the development of the arts, science, and literature. But it was also this assimilationist intellectual elite that provided the primarily Jewish-owned middle-class "liberal" press with the obsequious cadre of journalists and editors that obligingly and uncritically served the cause of Magyar hegemony. This press not only fed the fires of the national chauvinism directed against Austria but also "took the crudest jingoist attitude in the national struggles and was a chief obstacle to a reasonable compromise among the rival nations."[22]

Particularly virulent in this respect were the journalists associated with the daily *Budapesti Hírlap* (Journal of Budapest). They were in the forefront of those advocating the policy of forceful assimilation for the creation of a nation of "thirty million Hungarians." One must also note in this context the ill-conceived activities of men like Béla Grünwald, a historian-sociologist and political figure, who pursued the magyarization of the national minorities, especially in Slovakia, with a missionary zeal. Since most of the Jews who were engaged in the magyarization drive were also the main representatives of the commercial-bourgeois class in the agricultural communities inhabited by the national minorities, they were looked upon as the vehicle of both exploitative capitalism and great Magyar chauvinism. This perception was particularly associated with the Jewish-owned jingoist press, which was identified as "an unscrupulous instrument of feudal and financial class-domination."[23]

The identification of Jewish industrial and financial elements with capitalism and of the Jewish assimilationists with the cause of Magyar chauvinism not only envenomed the social struggle of the disenfranchised and impoverished peasants and workers but also exacerbated domestic conflicts. Even though Jews had also played an important role in the struggle for equality and in the progressive Socialist movement, they also supplied a radical intellectual class in Hungary. Some of them took over the intellectual and political leadership of the leftist parties and movements, including that of the Social Democratic Party and later of the Communist Party.

Many Jews barely eked out a living as artisans, laborers, or small businessmen. The disadvantaged classes, however, tended to look upon them as the sole representatives of capitalism while the oppressed nationalities viewed them as the champions of both capitalism and Magyar chauvinistic nationalism. In the communities of the areas inhabited by the national minorities, including Croatia-Slovenia, Slovakia, Carpatho-Ruthenia, and Transylvania, the Jews spoke almost exclusively Hungarian (Yiddish was also spoken in Carpatho-Ruthenia and to a lesser extent in Transylvania), and were in addition the chief agents of Magyar culture. Economically, they were crowded in the free professions, including law and medicine, and in business and commerce. Shopkeeping, innkeeping, and small trade were almost exclusively in Jewish hands.[24]

During the "White Terror" of 1919 and the early 1920s, which will be discussed below, popular opinion tended—because of the role of a small number of Bolsheviks of Jewish origin—to place the burden of the abortive Communist dictatorship on the Jews as a whole, even though the overwhelming majority of Hungarian Jewry had suffered from and opposed the adventure of Béla Kun. Similarly, during the *Ausgleich* period the Jews as a whole were equated with the Jewish financiers and industrialists and the super-patriotic professionals and intellectuals.[25]

The Jews' historical-political alliance with the Magyars in the polygot state proved a mixed blessing. While the Jews took full advantage of the new opportunities and experienced impressive gains in all walks of life after their emancipation, they later suffered the consequences of their leaders' shortsighted policies. Guided to a large extent by the political and economic interests of the assimilationist Jewish upper middle class, which also provided the bulk of the community's leadership (see chapter 3), they failed to develop a Jewish national consciousness.[26] With their leaders siding unconditionally and uncritically with a socially antiquated and nationally repressive reactionary regime, they never became conscious of their peculiar role and responsibility within a multinational state. Instead of working toward the development of a democratic pluralistic society based upon the toleration of, and respect for, all the coinhabiting nationalities, the Jews of Hungary were misled to "avail themselves of the opportunity to join their interests with those of the privileged classes of the socially and culturally privileged nationality."[27] By doing so, the Jews unwittingly allowed themselves to be politically exploited in the service of an arch-conservative aristocratic-gentry regime, which aimed primarily at preserving its traditional feudal privileges. Little did they realize that this regime raised the specter of the "dangers" represented by the awakening "backward" nationalities in order not only to preserve the unity of the Hungarian national state under Magyar hegemony, but above all to keep in check or suppress the rising demands of the oppressed and exploited social classes for reform, justice, and equality.

The shortsighted repressive social and national policies of Kálmán Tisza were continued with minor variations, but with occasional greater intensity, by all of his successors until the very end of the Compromise Era in 1918.[28] The arch-conservative Magyar nationalist rulers stubbornly refused to contemplate either social reform or compromise with the nationalities. Even at the end, when the war was manifestly lost, these rulers still expected to save Hungary's historic boundaries, and their own dominant position within them, merely by abandoning their alliance with the Central Powers and jettisoning their Austrian constitutional partner. With these formal political-military gestures they hoped to convince the victorious Allies that Hungary had all along been a helpless victim of the German-speaking world.

The Radical Regimes of the Left

The illusions of the aristocratic-gentry rulers were shattered by the disintegration and chaos that followed the military debacle in October–

November 1918. The bold and imaginative measures enacted under the leadership of Count Mihály Károlyi, who was swept into power by a virtually bloodless revolution on October 31, 1918, were outstripped and largely neutralized by the swift unfolding of historical events. The head of one of Hungary's most ancient and wealthy landowning families, Károlyi was an enlightened man of great sincerity and vision. As the leader of the opposition Kossuthist Independence Party since shortly before the outbreak of World War I, Károlyi was committed not only to a reorientation of Hungary's foreign policy from its traditional alignment with Germany to a new understanding with the Entente, and above all France, but also to a true liberalization of Hungary's internal political and social life. He was genuinely concerned with the plight of the oppressed social classes and was sincerely devoted to the idea of reconciliation with the nationalities.[29] But his reform measures were too few and came too late. Károlyi's land reform program came to naught. Although he himself had privately distributed his own lands among his peasants early in 1919, the large estates nevertheless remained basically intact partially because the Socialists, to the great satisfaction of the nobility, had found the land reform measures proposed by the Minister of Agriculture as being "politically reactionary and economically retrogressive." Károlyi also promoted a liberal electoral law on November 22, 1918, but mistakenly decided to postpone elections to a Constituent Assembly until after the departure of the Allied occupation troops. The grave problems inherited from the past were too much for the fragile democratic-socialist coalition government of Károlyi to solve.[30]

The Allies, moreover, compounded the problem by their shortsightedness. They repeatedly reinterpreted the provisions of the Belgrade Armistice of November 13, 1918, to Hungary's disadvantage. They acquiesced, for example, in the decision of Czechoslovakia, Romania, and Yugoslavia to send not only their troops but also their civil authorities into the parts of millennial Hungary they claimed. They also concurred with the repeated shifting of the armistice demarcation lines and maintained an economic blockade to pressure Hungary into compliance. The catalyst that brought about the collapse of the Károlyi government was the memorandum that Lieutenant-Colonel Fernand Vyx, the French officer who served as the military representative of the victor states in Budapest, submitted to the Hungarians on March 20, 1919, calling for the evacuation of further territory in behalf of the Romanians. The chronic domestic turmoil and the bankruptcy of the policy that relied upon the expected generosity of the Allied governments played into the hands of the Communists, who had enjoyed the support of Lenin's Soviet government.[31]

Hapless and betrayed, Károlyi yielded his power to a Hungarian Soviet government headed by Béla Kun, the veteran Communist leader. The son of a lower-middle-class town clerk in Szilágycseh, Transylvania, Kun was born in 1886. As a journalist he was for a while active in Transylvanian social-democratic politics. He embraced Bolshevism after his capture in 1915 and subsequently took an active role in the Revolution. His leadership qualities were soon recognized and on April 14, 1918, he was named head of the Federation of Foreign Groups of the Bolshevik Communist Party. He returned to Hungary on November 16, 1918, using the pseudonym of Colonel (Medical) Sebestyén. After the collapse of the dictatorship of the proletariat, he fled to Vienna and from there, after a short period of internment, to Russia. During the 1920s and early 1930s he was active in Comintern affairs. Caught up in the great Stalinist purges, he was "tried" in 1937 by the Presidium of the Comintern. He disappeared shortly thereafter and, according to some contemporaries, died on November 30, 1939. He was "rehabilitated" in February 1956.[32]

Because of its belligerent "nationalist" position rejecting the Vyx memorandum and condemning the "bourgeois imperialism" of the Allies, Kun's government came into power on March 21, 1919, on a wave of national enthusiasm that transcended class and ideological lines. This was partially based on Kun's defiant resolution to expand the Hungarian forces beyond the limits authorized by the armistice and on the general expectation that Hungary's territorial integrity would be reestablished with the support of the Soviet Republics. This enthusiasm, however, was short-lived. Dedicated as it was to the establishment of a Marxist-Leninist society, the Kun regime instituted, in the course of the "class struggle," a series of radical measures for which the Hungarians were not yet ready. Among other things, it abolished titles and ranks, brought about the secularization of education and the separation of church and state, and decreed the socialization of housing, banking, medicine, transportation, and culture. It nationalized all industrial and commercial enterprises employing more than 20 workers and confiscated all land not personally cultivated by the owners. While the "nationalist" fervor continued to flicker in the wake of the successful military operations against the Czechoslovaks in May–June, these revolutionary measures alienated many strata of the Hungarian population. Rejecting the conciliatory gestures of General Jan Smuts, the South African–British officer who arrived in Budapest on April 4 to ease the impact of the Vyx memorandum, Kun pursued a single-minded policy in line with his preconceived notion of the interests of world revolution.

Acting with chiliastic fervor, he and his revolutionary colleagues recklessly disregarded their own marginality in the country and pursued a rigidly doctrinaire and an increasingly repressive course of action that inevitably provoked a general counterrevolutionary resistance—sparked, *inter alia*, by the harsh measures adopted by the Communists to meet the requirements of their revolution. The peasants were alienated by the refusal of the revolutionary regime to distribute the confiscated lands and by the massive food requisitions for which they were paid in worthless "white" currency. They could buy no industrial products with it, for the factories were inoperative and the country was under a blockade. The shortages of goods, the excessive egalitarianism imposed by an increasingly regimented and bureaucratized regime, the arbitrariness and incompetence of the political neophytes, and the cruelties perpetrated by the new highly motivated idealistic elite for whom the noble ends justified the use of any means, alienated not only the upper strata but also the general urban and rural population of the country.

As a result, the Dictatorship of the Proletariat that was proclaimed on June 25, 1919 (officially known as Hungarian Soviet Republic; *Magyar Tanácsköztársaság*), "in order to bring the bourgeoisie to its senses . . . and if necessary to suffocate its counterrevolution in blood" was short-lived. The terror campaign launched to meet the real and imaginary challenges posed by "internal enemies" and "traitors" to the interests of the working class merely exacerbated the chaos and the tension that gripped Hungary in July 1919. Following the offensive launched by the Romanian Army partially at the request of the Western Allies, the Kun regime, having lost the confidence of the nation and the support of even the most militant members of the industrial working class, collapsed. Kun and his immediate supporters fled to Austria on August 1. A short interregnum ensued. On August 2, Gyula Peidl and Ernő Garami, the two socialists who had refused to go along with the Communist merger on March 21, formed a new government. However, this government was ousted four days later by the traditional ruling elite with the connivance of the Romanians, who entered Budapest on August 4. The new government of István Friedrich remained in power until November 25, 1919.[33] After this, power fell into the hands of the counterrevolutionary forces.

The brief but harsh period of Communist rule left a bitter legacy and had a devastating impact upon the Jews of Hungary. Although the overwhelming majority of Jewry had opposed the proletarian dictatorship and perhaps suffered proportionately more than the rest of the population (for they were persecuted both as members of the middle class and as followers of an organized religion) popular opinion tended to attach the blame for the abortive dictatorship to the Jews as a whole. While this attitude was to a large extent due to the high visibility of Jewish Communists in the Kun government and administration,[34] it was primarily the consequence of the anti-Semitic propaganda and anti-Jewish activities of the counterrevolutionary clericalist-nationalist forces bent on the reestablishment of the *status quo ante.*

These forces ignored not only the losses suffered by Hungarian Jewry at the hands of the Communists, but also the fact that Jewish leaders were among the first to warn the nation about the dangers of Bolshevism. Foremost among these were Vilmos Vázsonyi, the former Minister of Justice, and Béla Fábián, the former member of the Lower House of the Hungarian Parliament and, like Kun, a former inmate of a Russian POW camp.[35]

Counterrevolution and White Terror

Following the overthrow of the social-democratic trade unionist government of Gyula Peidl on August 6, the country was engulfed in a wave of terror which dwarfed in ferocity and magnitude the Red excesses that had preceded and allegedly warranted it.[36] The counterrevolutionary forces were organized under the auspices of the two wings of the Hungarian Right, which had their headquarters in Vienna and Szeged, respectively.

The Vienna group was headed by Count István Bethlen, an astute politician and great landholder of Transylvania, who was to play a leading political role throughout the Horthy era. It encompassed the main representatives of the Hungarian aristocracy and traditional ruling elite, including Count Pál Teleki, a learned geographer; Count Antal Sigray, the leader of the pro-Hapsburg Legitimists; Count Albert Apponyi; Count György Pallavicini; Count Gyula Andrássy; and Count Nándor Zichy, a clericalist. The officers' group first associated with these ultra-conservatives was headed by Gyula Gömbös, the colorful political-military figure whose career reflects to a large extent the origins and history of the fascist movement in Hungary. It was under the auspices of this Vienna group that the Anti-Bolshevik Committee (*Antibolsevista Comité*—ABC), the general staff of the Hungarian counterrevolution, was formed on April 12, 1919.[37]

The Szeged group revolved around the counterrevolutionary government that was formed on May 5 in Romanian-controlled Arad under the leadership of Count Gyula Károlyi, the former Prefect (*Főispán*) of Arad County and a cousin and political enemy of Count Mihály Károlyi. The group included a large number of the disgruntled, war-weary officers, of civil servants from the territories incorporated into the successor states, and of the déclassé gentry elements. This group also organized an executive arm of the Anti-Bolshevik Committee, which included Bishop István Zadravetz, the chief military chaplain, and a rabid counterrevolutionary agitator. Lavishly supported by the Vienna group,[38] the counterrevolutionary government was moved to Szeged on May 29. Shortly thereafter, Károlyi absorbed the Anti-Bolshevik Committee and reorganized his government by including Count Pál Teleki as minister of foreign affairs and Admiral Miklós Horthy, the last commander in chief of the Hapsburg navy who arrived in Szeged on June 6, as minister of war. Gömbös, who recommended Horthy for the ministerial position, was made an undersecretary.

Unable to wrest any meaningful concessions from the French, who controlled Szeged, and who, unlike the British, were alienated by the anti-Semitism and Germanophilism of many of the Hungarian leaders, the counterrevolutionary government was reorganized on July 12. Responding to the demands of the French, a new multiparty government was formed under the leadership of Dezső Ábrahám, which did not include Gömbös. Horthy, who was ostensibly irked by the removal of his mentor, declined the war ministry, but agreed to serve as commander in chief of the new counterrevolutionary "national army" (*nemzeti hadsereg*).

Like the many public organizations and patriotic associations that were formed at the time, the national army was to a large extent composed of the discontented elements that rallied around the counterrevolutionary leaders of Szeged—the disgruntled officers who had lost their positions in the wake of the lost war or of Kun's purges; the fixed-income middle and lower middle classes that were severely hit by the ever steeper inflationary spiral; and the large number of public servants and property owners who escaped from, or were dismissed or expelled by, the authorities of the Successor States. Homeless, property-less, and embittered, many of these elements first placed their hope in the Károlyi and Kun regimes. Disappointed over the violation of their traditional class interests, subsequently they wholeheartedly embraced the counterrevolution. They were easily swayed by the ideologues of the Szeged movement who placed the blame for their suffering on the "alien" Jews and Bolsheviks.

The demagogue-intellectuals of this group claimed to be the authors and embodiments of a philosophy and ideology, which came to be known as the "Szeged Idea" (*A szegedi gondolat*). Devoid of any substantive social and political theoretical content, it was primarily a nebulous amalgam of political-propagandistic views whose central themes included the struggle against Bolshevism, the fostering of anti-Semitism, chauvinistic nationalism, and revisionism. The representatives of this idea often boasted that they had been the forerunners of Fascism and Nazism.

Taking advantage of the protection afforded by the occupation forces of the Allies, the Szeged leaders spared no effort in organizing their national army for use after the expected inevitable defeat of the Kun regime. Their confidence was based primarily on the Allies' vehement opposition to Kun and on the cooperation of the Romanian Army in this endeavor.

Shortly after Peidl's replacement by István Friedrich on August 6, Horthy slipped his national army across the Danube into Transdanubia (*Dunántul*) to establish a foothold for the counterrevolution in western Hungary. Shortly thereafter, having penetrated—if not actually taken over—the Friedrich government, the "Szeged government" dissolved itself (August 22, 1919). Unsurprisingly, Horthy himself was appointed Commander-in-Chief of the armed forces.[39] While Horthy's army avoided any combat with either the Romanian or the Kun forces, it was fully engaged in pogroms and in a White Terror that claimed thousands of victims. As decided upon at Szeged, the people of the "liberated" localities were called upon to organize political meetings and pass "people's judgments" (*népitéletek*) against Communists and Jews. At these mass meetings, the commanders of the national army units often instigated the people to chase the Jews out of their communities. In some places they assured the people that they could do with the Jews whatever they wanted. In others, they posted announcements calling upon the population to "smoke the Jews out."

The first and most bloodthirsty unit to enter Transdanubia was the

PRELUDE TO DESTRUCTION *19*

company led by Pál Prónay, which called itself the "black legion of death" (*fekete halállégió*). This was followed by that led by Gyula Ostenburg and by many others equally eager to eradicate the traces of the Károlyi and Kun regimes, to punish the Communists, liberals, and Jews, and to lay the foundation of a new national Christian order. The so-called Prónay units went from community to community terrorizing the Jews and people suspected of Communist sympathies. They blackmailed and collected large ransom from the "rich" Jews and, to encourage the population to emulate them, they often carried out their executions in public.[40] In some localities, including Siófok, Horthy's headquarters at the time, Veszprém, Sopron, Marcali, Szekszárd, Pápa, and Kecskemét, the Prónay and Ostenburg units had engaged in mass murders.[41]

In addition to the wanton slaughter of thousands of Jews, the counterrevolutionary murder squads killed a large number of leftists, including industrial workers and landless peasants as well as a number of opposition intellectuals. Particularly shocking was the coldblooded murder on February 17, 1920, of Béla Somogyi and Béla Bacsó, Jewish journalists associated with the Socialist organ *Népszava* (People's Voice), by a group of Ostenburg officers that included Ferenc Megay, István Soltész, and Emil Kovarcz. According to the testimony of Ödön Beniczky, then Minister of the Interior, who committed suicide in 1925 in consequence of a trial involving the Somogyi-Bacsó case, the murder was allegedly instigated by Horthy himself, who was irked by the writings of these journalists.[42]

Emil Kovarcz emerged as one of the most vitriolic anti-Semites during the 1930s and 1940s. In February 1939, he was, for example, involved in a grenade attack against Jewish worshippers in Budapest and in 1944, he played a leading role in the deportation of the Jews.

Concerned with the possible effect of the White Terror on the Allies and on the further stiffening of their peace proposals, a number of moderate conservative politicians pleaded with Horthy to put an end to the bloodletting. Count Albert Apponyi, for example, the leader of the Hungarian delegation at the Peace Conference in Paris, had actually warned the government about the impact of the killings abroad. Prime Minister Sándor Simonyi-Semadam read this letter at the March 17, 1920, meeting of the lower house of the Hungarian Parliament and remarked to the deputies that "the hatred of the Jews and the antipathy felt toward the Jews were not worth as much as the territorial integrity of Hungary."[43]

In the fall of 1919, Horthy was approached by a blue-ribbon delegation that included Count István Bethlen, Count Gyula Andrássy, and Count József Károlyi. A memorandum was forwarded to him by István Bárczy, the Minister of Justice, on February 1, 1920.[44] But all of these endeavors to end the terror were of no avail; Horthy and his clique were determined to purify the country of "the danger of Communism."

The goon squads that collaborated with the Prónay, Ostenburg, and many similar units were composed to a large extent of the traditionally apathetic lower middle classes, who were suddenly radicalized by the catastrophic consequences of the lost war. They also included elements of the unskilled proletariat who had only a short while earlier been in the forefront of the Kun revolution. Many were composed of Right-wing ultra-nationalist elements that had just organized a series of "patriotic associations" allegedly to defend the traditional national interests of Hungary.

The Patriotic Associations

The real strongholds of power supporting the Szeged men were the secret and semi-clandestine patriotic associations and paramilitary organizations. The oldest and the most bloodthirsty among these was the Association of Awakening Magyars (*Ébredő Magyarok Egyesülete*), which was founded in 1917 by soldiers discharged during the war. However, by far the most important association to be formed after the war by Right-wing military and civilian elements was the MOVE (*Magyar Országos Véderő Egyesület;* Hungarian Association for National Defense). Originally called into being by a group of officers to replace the officers' association of the Hapsburg era and to fight for Hungary's national integrity and social stability, it was soon transformed into a pronouncedly anti-Legitimist, ultra-reactionary, and rabidly anti-Semitic organization. The radical change in its position came on January 19, 1919, when Gömbös, a co-founder, was elected as its president.[45]

Upon assuming the presidency, Gömbös, who had attracted attention by a strong public attack on Mihály Károlyi and his policies, brought about the establishment of two secret societies to serve as the civilian and military inner rings of the MOVE. The civilian society had two names: one official and public—the Hungarian Scientific Race-Protecting Society (*Magyar Tudományos Fajvédő Egyesület*); the other secret—the Etelköz Association (*Etelközi Szövetség*). The latter was named after the region the Magyars had inhabited around the mouth of the Don before they ventured into Pannonia during the ninth century. This secret society was popularly known by its abbreviated name, EKSz or simply as X. The military counterpart of EKSz was the Society of the Double Cross (*Kettös-Kereszt Szövetség*), named after the Cross of Lorraine on the Hungarian Coat-of-Arms. Both secret societies were organized on the pattern of primitive Hungarian society. The members, who were inducted in a fearful ceremony based upon some early Magyar secret rituals, had to swear absolute allegiance an total subordination to the leader of the society.[46]

Among the other organizations of considerable influence were the Irrendentist Association (*Irredentista Szövetség*), the Order of Heroes (*Vitézi Rend*), and the Christian National League (*Keresztény Nemzeti Liga*). The latter, founded by Dr. Károly Wolff in 1919, also had two secret core groups. One was known as Resurrection (*Feltámadás*), which was led by 50 men identified as Battle Leaders (*Vezérharcosok*). Among these leaders were a number of prominent political and church figures who were to play a dominant role during the Horthy era, including István Bethlen, Pál Teleki, Kálmán Kánya, László Bárdossy, and the Bishops Ottokár Prohászka, Sándor Raffay, and László Ravasz. The other was known as the Szent István group, which was composed primarily of judges and university professors.

The number of the secret and public patriotic and social associations increased phenomenally during the early 1920s. Numbering some 10,000, they constituted an enormous nationwide network covering practically every major group interest, including that of women, students (e.g., the *Turul*), and servicemen. Their activities were first coordinated by a body known as the Association for Territorial Defense (*Területvédő Liga*) and then by its successor organization, the Federation of Social Associations (*Társadalmi Egyesületek Szövetsége*—TESz).[47]

The counterrevolutionary governments not only tolerated and sympathized with the activities of the patriotic associations, but actively encouraged and supported them clandestinely. Their standard response to the occasional protests advanced by the Allies against the excesses of some of these associations was that they were unable to control them because of the limitation imposed upon the official armed forces.

With no active or effective restrictions imposed upon them, many of these patriotic associations arrogated to themselves the power and responsibility to defend the "Magyar cause." They became the chief vehicle for the spread of the virulent seeds of revisionism, irredentism, and, above all, anti-Semitism. The most ferocious among these was the Association of Awakening Magyars, whose members appointed themselves chief executants of the White Terror.

The "patriotic" Association of Awakening Magyars enjoyed virtual immunity for all its activities directed against the Jews and trade union leaders during the counterrevolutionary period. The enormous power and influence wielded by the Association were revealed by Béla Fábián, a Jewish deputy, in his October 8, 1924, statement in the lower house of the Hungarian Parliament. Speaking shortly after a court in Szolnok had acquitted the Association members that were involved in the bombing of a charity ball organized by the Jewish Women of Csongrád in which several people were killed, Fábián declared that the Association was primarily responsible for the cover up of all the murders and crimes committed in Hungary during the previous four years.[48] At the time, the Association was headed by Tibor Eckhardt,[49] who was also a leading member of the Race-Protecting Party (*Fajvédő Párt*).[50]

The patriotic associations remained the strongholds of the reactionary elements associated with the Szeged Idea primarily because of the singular role played in them by Gömbös, their *spiritus rector*.

Gyula Gömbös. From the early days of the counterrevolution until his death in 1936, Gömbös was one of the foremost leaders of the Hungarian radical Right. He was born on December 26, 1886, at Murga, a Swabian township of Transdanubia. His father was a village school teacher and his mother came from a German-speaking Swabian yeoman farmer family. His use of the adjectival predicate "jákfai" as an indication of his noble origin had no basis in fact though it was indicative of his social ambitions. Like many Swabians of the lower middle class, Gömbös entered upon a military career, but in spite of all his efforts he could not attain a rank higher than captain.[51] His political career reflected the ambivalence with which the Right viewed and treated the Jewish question throughout the interwar period. His talents as an anti-Semitic, anti-democratic orator were recognized early by both wings of the counterrevolutionary Right. An anti-intellectual driven by an insatiable ambition, he was a sly and vain individual whose chauvinistic nationalism was perhaps subconsciously motivated by his eagerness to mask his Swabian background. His social views, which appealed to the interests of the gentry, incorporated an opposition to both the great landlords and the financiers—the former because of their association with the Hapsburgs; the latter because of their overwhelmingly Jewish character. He articulated the two major tenets of the social program of the radical Right—agrarianism and the "Christian idea"—the ideological Janus face that characterized most extreme rightist movements. These tenets claimed to express the peasants' demand for land reform and the hatred of the Christian workers and lower middle class for rapacious Jewish capitalism.[52] Although a vocal anti-Legitimist, it was anti-Semitism that constituted the inner core of his political ideology. Like most anti-Semites, he disregarded the important role played by the Jews during the Revolutionary War of 1848–49 and conveniently overlooked their disproportionate sacrifices during the First World War. Rationality notwithstanding, he tended, like the National Socialists in Germany—with whom he had been in close contact since 1921—to look upon the Jews as aliens hostile to the Christian body politic. He helped develop and propagate the Nazi myth about the Jews by depicting them as being at once exploiters and revolutionaries, both plutocrats and Bolsheviks. His anti-Semitism gradually acquired a racial coloration, which was reflected ever more vocally by his "race-protecting" associations. In his vocabulary, "race-protection" was also Janus-faced, for it was designed to focus on the twin danger represented by the Jews as agents of Communism and "Jewish capitalism."[53]

As the leader of the MOVE, Gömbös had acted during the crucial months before the counterrevolutionary victory as the de facto head of a shadow government. Recognizing MOVE's importance, Horthy was glad to accept from Gömbös the title of Honorary President of the association. These two leaders of the counterrevolution developed an intimate partnership in which Horthy provided the prestige and Gömbös supplied the organizational ability as well as the original troops of the national army.

Trianon and Its Impact

Two days after the withdrawal of the Romanian forces on November 14, 1919, Horthy entered "sinful" Budapest with his 12,000-man "heroic" national army. Temporarily quartered at the Gellért Hotel, Horthy was officially welcomed by the representatives of the various larger associations and denominations who assured him of their loyalty. The Jewish delegation paid him a visit on November 20. Led by Jenő Polnay, it assured Horthy somewhat obsequiously that Hungarian Jewry was looking forward to his leadership with an "enthusiastic confidence."[54]

The Friedrich government, which came under pressure by the Allies, who insisted on concluding peace with a reasonably representative and non-Hapsburg regime, gave way on November 25 to a more moderate coalition government headed by Károly Huszár. The Socialists accepted a couple of minor portfolios, but quit the counterrevolutionary government on January 15, 1920—just ten days before the elections for the National Assembly. Although the so-called Friedrich electoral decree of November 17 called for wide, secret, and equal suffrage, the elections were held in the midst of the White Terror in an atmosphere of intimidation, without the participation of the leftist forces. The Communists were, of course, excluded from the elections and the Socialists decided to boycott them.

Under these conditions, the counterrevolutionaries had scored a decisive electoral victory. The new National Assembly, which was composed predominantly of conservative, agrarian, and professedly "Christian" delegates, resolved at its meeting of February 16 to end Hungary's ties with the Hapsburgs as provided by both the Pragmatic Sanction of 1723 and the Compromise of 1867. Having decided to shelve the dynastic issue, the Assembly elected (March 1) Admiral Horthy to serve as Regent by a vote of 131 to 7 (for Count Albert Apponyi). Horthy replaced Archduke Joseph of the House of Hapsburg, whom, shortly after its installation, the Friedrich government had designated to serve as King Charles's Regent for Hungary. The dynastic issue was to remain a problem throughout the Horthy era. Horthy successfully blocked the attempts of Charles and of his heir, Archduke Otto, to regain the throne. The issue remained alive in spite of the adoption by the National Assembly of an Act of Dethronement early in November 1921, and the premature death of King Charles on April 1, 1922, at Funchal, the Madeira Islands.

As Regent, Horthy for all practical purposes wielded "royal" powers, except that he could not create new titles of nobility or exercise the Apostolic Crown's patronage rights over the Roman Catholic Church. As head of state, he could appoint and dismiss the premier; convene, adjourn, and dissolve Parliament; and exercise a suspensive veto of legislative enactments. Much of his power derived from his position as Supreme War Lord (*Legfelsőbb Hadúr*).

It had been Apponyi's unenviable historical task a few weeks earlier to lead a Hungarian delegation to Paris to receive the Allies' peace terms. Their evaluation became the responsibility of the government headed by Sándor Simonyi-Semadam, who succeeded Huszár on March 15, 1920. Composed of the Legitimists (Christian National

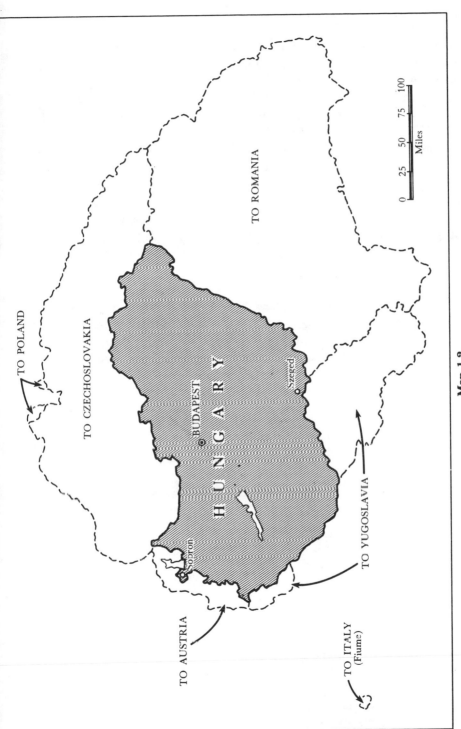

Map 1.2.
Hungary and its losses at Trianon.

Union) and the Free Electors (Smallholder coalition), the Simonyi-Semadam government had no alternative but to accept the extremely harsh peace terms. The treaty was formally signed on June 4 at the Trianon Palace in Versailles and ratified by the National Assembly in a memorial meeting on November 13, 1920; it was registered as Law XXXIII in the Code of Laws of 1921.[55]

Disregarding to a considerable extent the Wilsonian principles on self-determination, the victors dismembered the historic state and redrew its frontiers by ignoring or overlooking the impact of the demographic, topographic, and economic factors involved (map 1.2).

Under the punitive terms of the treaty, Hungary lost two-thirds of its historic territory, one-third of its Magyar people, and three-fifths of its total population. Based on statistics extrapolated from the census of 1910, table 1.1 shows historic Hungary's staggering territorial and population losses.

These losses were accompanied by commensurate losses in its economic resources.[56] In addition, the Trianon Treaty stipulated that Hungary would have to pay reparations and to limit its armed forces to 35,000 officers and men, to be used exclusively for the maintenance of internal order and the defense of its frontiers.

TABLE 1.1.
THE TERRITORIAL AND
POPULATION LOSSES OF HUNGARY
AFTER WORLD WAR I
(PER 1910 DATA)

	Area (Sq. km.)	Population (total)
Historic Hungary (including Croatia-Slavonia)	325,411	20,886,487
Lost to:		
Austria	4,020	292,031
Czechoslovakia	61,633	3,515,351
Italy	21	49,806
Poland	589	24,880
Romania	103,093	5,256,451
Yugoslavia	63,092	4,132,851
Total Losses	232,448	13,271,370
Residual Hungary	92,963	7,615,117

SOURCE: *Magyar statisztikai közlemények* (Hungarian Statistical Publications) Budapest, vol. 83, 1932), map preceding p. 1.

Hungarian domestic and foreign policy between the two world wars was to an overwhelming extent determined by the general desire to undo or revise the Treaty of Trianon. Although revisionism was embraced by practically every stratum of the Hungarian population, there were some differences as to the extent of the revision desired or deemed practical.[57] The ruling classes used the issue of revisionism not only to supplement their repressive measures, to keep social discontent in abeyance, and to divert attention from the injustices at home, but also to promote the reestablishment of the *status quo ante,* including the reacquisition of their estates.

The one positive consequence of the Trianon Treaty was the transformation of Hungary from a conflict-ridden multi-national state into an ethnically integral one. If language is used as a basis of ethnic identification, in 1910, 1920, and 1930 the population of Trianon Hungary was composed as in table 1.2.

The total percentage of those speaking Magyar was in fact much greater than 88.4 in 1910, 89.5 in 1920, and 92.1 in 1930, for many of those whose primary tongue was not Magyar also spoke it as a second language.[58] Since most of the Jews identified themselves as Magyar-speaking, their number and percentage during these years are reflected in table 1.3, which contains the data on the distribution of the population by religion.

TABLE 1.2.
POPULATION OF TRIANON HUNGARY BY ETHNICITY
(LANGUAGE)

	1910		1920		1930	
	Number	Percent	Number	Percent	Number	Percent
Magyar	6,730,996	88.4	7,156,727	89.5	8,001,112	92.1
German	554,594	7.3	551,624	6.9	478,630	5.5
Slovak	165,273	2.2	141,918	1.8	104,819	1.2
Romanian	28,434	0.4	23,695	0.3	16,221	0.2
Croatian	41,979	0.5	36,864	0.5	27,683	0.3
Serbian	26,171	0.3	17,132	0.2	7,031	0.1
Ruthenian	1,133	0.0	23,228	0.3	20,564	0.2
Other	66,537	0.9	39,014	0.5	32,259	0.4
Total	7,615,117	100.0	7,990,202	100.0	8,688,319	100.0

SOURCE: *Magyar statisztikai szemle* (Hungarian Statistical Review) (Budapest, 1941), 2:772; *Magyar statisztikai közlemények* (Hungarian Statistical Publications) (Budapest, 1932), 83:23*–24*.

TABLE 1.3.
POPULATION OF TRIANON HUNGARY BY RELIGION

	1910		1920		1930	
	Number	Percent	Number	Percent	Number	Percent
Roman Catholic	4,785,515	62.8	5,105,375	63.9	5,634,003	64.9
Greek Catholic (Uniate)	165,536	2.2	175,655	2.2	201,093	2.3
Calvinist	1,632,852	21.4	1,671,052	21.0	1,813,162	20.9
Lutheran	485,219	6.4	497,126	6.2	534,165	6.1
Eastern Orthodox	61,427	0.8	50,918	0.6	39,839	0.5
Israelite	471,378	6.2	473,355	5.9	444,567	5.1
Other	13,190	0.2	16,721	0.2	21,490	0.2
Total	7,615,117	100.0	7,990,202	100.0	8,688,319	100.0

SOURCE: *Magyar statisztikai szemle* (Hungarian Statistical Review) (Budapest, 1941), 2: 772; *Magyar statisztikai közlemények* (Hungarian Statistical Publications) (Budapest, 1932) 83:26*–27*.

While the total number of Jews declined to about half of its pre-war size, their percentage in the total population remained about the same. But with the transformation of the country into a basically homogeneous and ethnically integral state, the Jews lost their importance as statistical recruits to the cause of Magyardom. As a consequence, and in contrast to the Compromise Era, when the Jewish question was politically and officially suppressed, the Jews suddenly found themselves exploited as scapegoats for Hungary's disasters. In the atmosphere of the frustrations caused by the consequences of the lost war, an increasingly large percentage of the population became inclined to perceive and judge the Jewish community at large according to the highly visible roles played by its representatives in both Hungarian capitalism and Communism. The climate for anti-Semitism was further aggravated by the fact that the Jews, having taken advantage of the opportunities offered by the Dual Monarchy, by now constituted a large percentage in the free professions (see chapter 3).

The First Anti-Jewish Measures

Following the absorption of historic Hungary's major national minorities into the Successor States, the Jews suddenly emerged as the country's most vulnerable minority group. As in Germany, they were conveniently used as scapegoats for most of the country's misfortunes, including its socioeconomic dislocations. In vain did the Hungarian Jews try to continue to demonstrate their fervent patriotism; in vain did they try to invoke their past services to Magyardom: they were generally considered as basically "alien" and "disloyal." In the politically tense and emotionally volatile climate of the early counterrevolutionary period, the anti-Semitic elements tended to ignore or forget that the official leaders of Hungarian Jewry were also in the forefront of the battle against the "injustices" inflicted upon Hungary.

Shortly after the armistice of October 1918, the Hungarian Jewish leaders were among the first to rally for the protection of the country's integrity. They appealed to the Jews of Europe to use their influence with the politicians of their countries to prevent the dismemberment of Hungary. They also addressed an appeal to the Jews in the territories about to be lost to remain "indomitably . . . and . . . unswervingly" Magyar in their attitude.[59]

The patriotic posture was also shared by the Orthodox leaders. In February 1919, for example, Adolf Frankl, then president of the Orthodox Jewish community of Hungary, addressing the Agudath Yisrael Congress at Zurich, appealed to world Jewry to help in the reestablishment of Hungary's territorial integrity. In January 1920, the leadership of the Neolog community appealed to the Jewish leaders of Britain, France, the United States, Australia, and Switzerland to use their influence upon their corresponding governments to support the position of the Hungarian peace delegation, which, it emphasized, was also its own position. The appeal also included the following statement:

We, Hungarian Jews, want to remain Hungarian. Specifically now, during the most difficult period of need, during the difficult years of reorganization, we do not want to leave our Motherland. We want to take part in the rebuilding of our much beloved Homeland with all our strength, and with the enthusiasm and tenacity of our origin.[60]

These declarations of loyalty and patriotism had, of course, no impact upon the terrorists bent on "settling accounts" with Jewry. Moreover, while the White Terror was venting its fury against the revolutionaries, claiming a disproportionately large number of victims from among the Jews, the Hungarian government emerged as the first one in postwar Europe to begin tackling the "Jewish question."

The Simonyi-Semadam government was replaced on July 19, 1920, by one headed by Count Pál Teleki, who had then hoped to bring about some revision through a rapprochement with France. Teleki had envisioned buying off France's goodwill by having Hungary enter the Polish-Soviet war on the side of Poland, France's protegé and Hungary's traditional ally. This plan came to naught primarily because in August Poland managed to win the battle of Warsaw without additional assistance.

A leading member of the arch-conservative aristocratic ruling hierarchy of Hungary, Teleki was an advocate of a "civilized" form of anti-Semitism (see chapter 5). It was during his tenure as Prime Minister in 1920–21 and again in 1939–41 that Hungary adopted some of the most important anti-Jewish acts. Perhaps it was not an accident that less than one month after his inauguration, László Budavári-Buturescu, a member of the National Assembly, raised the Jewish question and demanded its speedy and institutional solution. He submitted a 10-point proposal which was also supported by István Nagyatádi Szabó speaking in behalf of the government. To substantiate their position, Budavári-Buturescu and Nagyatádi Szabó cited the "large" number of, and "important" role played by, the Jews in the country—the technique resorted to by all anti-Semites during the interwar period. They placed special emphasis on identifying the amount of land owned by the Jews and the high percentage of Jewish students in the institutions of higher learning. According to Budavári, Jews had then owned 4.8 million cadastral yokes which they allegedly acquired by virtue of "speculation" and "usury."[61]

With the influx of a large number of intellectuals and professionals from the territories acquired by the Successor States, Trianon Hungary had found itself with a considerable percentage of unemployed degree holders. It was partially to ease this potentially explosive situation and to decrease the proportion of Jews among these strata of the population that Hungary adopted the first major anti-Jewish law in post-World War I Europe.

Introduced by István Haller, Minister of Cults and Public Education, this so-called *Numerus Clausus* Act, or Law XXV of September 22, 1920, stipulated that Jewish admissions to the institutions of higher learning be reduced to 6 percent. The legislative memorandum in support of the act was prepared by Teleki.[62]

Although the law was only loosely administered and subsequently amended by the Bethlen government, which established a new *modus vivendi* with the Jewish community (chapter 2), it contributed to the radicalization of the institutions of higher learning. As the unemployed Hungarian academic and intellectual elements turned toward the radical Right, these institutions were transformed into hotbeds of anti-Semitism. Particularly vicious was the anti-Jewish agitation in the medical schools, where the anti-Semitic elements insisted that the Jewish students use Jewish corpses for necrotomy, a practice strictly forbidden under Orthodox Jewish law.

Although the *Numerus Clausus* Act was in flagrant violation of the Minorities Protection Treaty, which Hungary had approved rather willingly because of its concern with the fate of its co-nationals in the Successor States, the Hungarian Jewish leadership failed to engage in any vigorous political action against it. The attitude of the Jewish leaders is best characterized by the statement made by Vilmos Vázsonyi, the former Minister of Justice, on October 27, 1924. Speaking before the annual general meeting of the Jewish Community of Pest, Vázsonyi, assuming the patriotic posture of the official leadership, declared that "the Peace Treaty of Trianon, which deprived [the Hungarians] of their rights, cannot be the source of our rights."[63] A Legitimist politician, Vázsonyi's patriotic and anti-Communist credentials were impeccable. In fact, he was highly recommended to Horthy as practically the only political figure in both Szeged and Vienna whose stature and reputation had not been tarnished.[64] The Jewish leadership reflected the same patriotic position when the issue was brought before the League of Nations by Western Jewish organizations. These organizations, including the Joint Foreign Committee of British Jews and the Alliance Israélite Universelle of France, were motivated not only by their concern for Hungarian Jewry, but also by their fear that the Hungarian *Numerus Clausus* Act would serve as a precedent for other states. Publicly, the Hungarian Jewish leaders expressed their resentment against these interventions in what they considered a purely internal matter. They were convinced that they could handle the crisis within the legal and constitutional framework of Hungary. Their attitude was motivated by both patriotism and pragmatism. They were reluctant to have their grievances redressed through foreign intervention, especially since the vehicle for such redress was the minorities provisions attached to the Treaty of Trianon, which was universally regarded as a national disaster. Moreover they were skeptical about the chances of success via the League and above all worried about the possible intensification of the antagonism against the Jews in the wake of "foreign" meddling.

The leaders of Hungarian Jewry issued a declaration of protest against the League's "interventions," which Kunó Klebelsberg, Minister of Cults and Public Education, exploited in Geneva in support of Hungary's position.[65]

In their letter dated November 29, 1925, addressed to the Secretariat, the Hungarian Jewish leaders protested vigorously against the "foreign petitions regarding the academic *Numerus Clausus* in Hungary." Two days earlier they had forwarded a similarly obsequious letter to the Hungarian government.[66]

The anti-Semitic excesses of the first years of the counterrevolutionary period evoked great consternation among the decent strata of the Hungarian population and even stronger reaction abroad. In some Western countries boycotts were even organized against the purchase of Hungarian products. The dire economic conditions under which the country had found itself after Trianon, including a rampant inflation, necessitated a general reassessment of internal policies. The desperate need of massive loans to overcome the economic crisis as well as the pressure of domestic and especially world public opinion induced the dominant Hungarian circles to bring about some major internal changes. It was under these circumstances that Horthy decided on April 14, 1921, to entrust Count István Bethlen, his friend and confidant, with the formation of a new government.

Notes

1. *Hungarian Jewry Before and After the Persecutions* (Budapest: Hungarian Section of the World Jewish Congress, 1949), 25 pp. For further details consult, *Zsidó Világkongresszus,* Nos. 1 through 13–14, published between 1947 and 1949. For an evaluation of the socioeconomic, cultural, and intellectual characteristics of the various major strata of immigrants and for statistical data on the post-World War I period, see chapter 3.

2. For an analytical review of the history of Jewish emancipation in Hungary and its relationship to the assimilation of Hungarian Jewry, see George Barany, "Magyar Jew or: Jewish Magyar?" *Canadian-American Slavic Studies,* 8, no. 1 (Spring 1974):1–44.

3. The party through which the Hungarian landowning aristocracy maintained and exercised its powers since 1875 was the Liberal Party (*Szabadelvü Párt*). With the exception of the 1905–1910 period, when a coalition led by the fiercely anti-Austrian Independence Party (*Függetlenségi Párt*) of Ferenc Kossuth was in power, the Liberal Party continued under different labels and combinations to dominate Hungary's political life until October 15, 1944, under various names. Between 1910 and 1918, it ruled under the name of National Labor Party (*Nemzeti Munkapárt*) and after the collapse of the short-lived revolutionary governments following the debacle of 1918, it ruled under a variety of labels, including the Party of National Unity (*Nemzeti Egység Pártja,* 1920–1939) and the Hungarian Life Party (*Magyar Élet Pártja,* 1939–1944).

4. In the Hungarian Kingdom of the pre-World War I period about 96 percent of all government employees were Magyar. The Magyars also supplied about 92 percent of all high school teachers and about 93 percent of all university instructors. Although they constituted only 54.5 percent of the population, the Magyars held 405 parliamentary seats, while the coinhabiting nationalities constituting the remaining 45.5 percent were represented only by 8 deputies—5 Romanians and 3 Slovaks. Robert A. Kann, "Hungarian Jewry During Austria-Hungary's Constitutional Period (1867–1918)," *Jewish Social Studies,* New York, 7, no. 4 (October 1945):360.

5. C. A. Macartney, 1:11.

6. For a historical-analytical review of this topic see William O. McCagg, *Jewish Nobles and Geniuses in Modern Hungary* (New York: Columbia University Press, 1972), 254 pp.

7. It was during this "Golden Era" that Hungarian Jewish writers like Ferenc Molnár, József Kiss, Jenő Heltai, Menyhért Lengyel, Ernő Szép, and many others left their stamp on Hungarian literature. In 1894, Ignác Goldziher, a world-renowned Orientalist, was the first Jew to be appointed professor at the University of Budapest. This era also saw Ferenc Heltai, a nephew of Theodor Herzl, become Mayor of Budapest (1913), Baron Samu Hazai, a convert, Minister of Defense (1910), János Teleszky, Minister of Finance (1912), Baron János Harkányi, the scion of one of the oldest and influential Jewish families in Pest, Minister of Trade (1913), Vilmos Vázsonyi, Minister of Justice (1917), and Márton Zöld distinguish himself as a general during World War I. In addition, many Jews were elected to, and played important roles in, both houses of the Hungarian Parliament.

8. One must keep in mind that the statistical figures were compiled by the Hungarian authorities which were motivated by a specific national political objective. The spokesmen for the national minorities left no doubt that the census figures were falsified to their disadvantage. Kann, "Hungarian Jewry," p. 359. See also Oscar Jászi, *The Dissolution of the Hapsburg Monarchy* (Chicago: The University of Chicago Press, 1929), pp. 273ff.; and Joseph Rothschild, *East Central Europe Between the Two World Wars* (Seattle: University of Washington Press, 1974), p. 155.

9. For details on the Nationality Law see Jászi, *Dissolution of the Hapsburg Monarchy*, pp. 314–17.

10. *Ibid.*, p. 320.

11. The Society was founded on February 14, 1844, at the Valeró House of Pest with the participation of a number of Jews who came to play a leading role during the Revolution of 1848–49 and in the life of the Jewish community after 1867. Among them were men like Mihály Heilprin, who later became the press chief of Kossuth's Ministry of the Interior; Dr. Fülöp Jakobovits, the founder of the Jewish Hospital of Pest; Lipot Löw, a noted rabbi; Marton Diósy, Kossuth's private secretary; and Dr. Henrik Pollák, who originated the idea of the Society. The governmental authorities in Vienna and Pozsony (Bratislava) delayed the approval of its bylaws until March 24, 1846, because of their fear that the Society would only contribute to the spread of the idea of Hungarian independence. Shortly after the approval of its bylaws, the Society organized a number of schools and kindergartens for the Jewish children. They used Magyar as the language of instruction. It was also under the auspices of the Society that the first Reform congregation was formed in Pest and that the first sermon was delivered in the Hungarian language by Ignác Einhorn, a candidate rabbi, in a makeshift synagogue in Valeró House. In 1847, the Society published its first yearbook, which contained a number of articles imbued with pro-Magyar patriotism. The Society was disbanded by the Austrian authorities after the crushing of the Hungarian Revolution, but was again revived in 1860, through the initiative of Henrik Pollák and Dr. Ignác Hirschler, under the name of Magyar Jewish Society (*Magyar Izraelita Egylet*). It was this new Society that launched the campaign for the translation of the Old Testament into Hungarian. *A Magyar Zsidók Lapja* (Journal of Hungarian Jews), Budapest, February 3, 1944, pp. 3, 7–8.

12. The Association continued to function until the German occupation of Hungary on March 19, 1944, when it was under the direction of Ödön Kertész. *Ibid.*, January 27, 1944, p. 2.

13. Kann, *Hungarian Jewry*, p. 364.

14. The Congress lasted until February 1869. Eötvös and the government were clearly in favor of the Neolog position on centralization and assimilation. For further details on the Congress see Nathaniel Katzburg, "The Jewish Congress of Hungary, 1868–1869," in *HJS*, 2:1–33.

15. For a succinct evaluation of the role and history of Zionism in Hungary see R. L.

Braham, "Zionism in Hungary." In *Encyclopedia of Zionism and Israel*, ed. Raphael Patai (New York: McGraw-Hill, 1971), pp. 523–27.

16. During the 1867–1913 period, the length of the railways increased from 2,285 to 22,084 km (1,417 to 13,692 mi.) while the number of passengers rose from 9 million to 166 million and the number of pieces of mail from 38 million to 828 million. During the same period, the merchandise tonnage increased from 9 million to 87 million and the output of coal production from 7 million to 91 million quintals. (A quintal equals 100 kilograms or 220.46 pounds.) The value of foreign trade increased from 1,763 million crowns in 1882 to 4,174 million crowns in 1912. (A crown equaled 20.26 cents in the decades before World War I.) Between 1869 and 1910, the percentage of those engaged in commerce and industry rose from 4.9 to 25.1 and the percentage of those engaged in agriculture declined to 62.4. Oscar Jászi, *Dissolution of the Hapsburg Monarchy*, p. 170. See also Iván T. Berend *and* György Ránki, *Economic Development in East Central Europe in the 19th and 20th Centuries* (New York: Columbia University Press, 1974), 402 pp.

17. Jászi, *Dissolution of the Hapsburg Monarchy*, p. 320.

18. Győző Istóczy was a member of the Hungarian Parliament representing the Liberal Party. His anti-Semitic campaign was launched in 1874 and was first aimed against the unassimilated Jews. However, by 1880 the campaign, which was also joined by Ónódy, a fellow deputy, was directed against all Jews and attacked the policy of assimilation itself. It was this anti-Jewish campaign by Istóczy and Ónódy that provided the climate for the Tisza-Eszlár case. Istóczy was also active in the international campaign against the Jews. He wrote the "Manifesto to the Governments and Peoples Menaced by the Jews," which was issued by the first International Anti-Jewish Congress, which met in Dresden in 1882.

Iván Simonyi was a parliamentarian associated with the Independence Party. He actively campaigned against the emancipation of the Jews and in 1883 founded an anti-Semitic political club that was instrumental in the election of a number of anti-Semitic deputies. Their activities, however, were of no political consequence and enjoyed little, if any, popular support.

19. For a historical-critical review of anti-Semitism during the Compromise Era see Nathaniel Katzburg, *Antisemiut be'Hungaria, 1867–1914* (Anti-Semitism in Hungary, 1867–1914) (Tel Aviv: Dvir Publishing House, 1969), 294 pp; and Judit Kubinszky, *Politikai Antiszemitizmus Magyarországon, 1875–1890* (Political Anti-Semitism in Hungary, 1875–1890) (Budapest: Kossuth, 1976), 275 pp.

20. Jászi, *Dissolution of the Hapsburg Monarchy*, p. 325.

21. The ratio of the Jews of Budapest remained basically the same until 1944. In 1920, Budapest, with a population of 929,000, contained about 215,000 Jews. Kann, "Hungarian Jewry," p. 367.

22. Jászi, *Dissolution of the Hapsburg Monarchy*, p. 174.

23. *Ibid.*

24. For details on the impact of this cultural and economic position of the Jews on their relations with the non-Magyar nationalities, see Kann, "Hungarian Jewry," pp. 373–86.

25. The tendency of the Jews to gravitate toward finance and the free professions may be partially explained by the fact that until their emancipation they were effectively excluded from virtually all productive activities except the finance-related ones. In Hungary, the local Jewish capitalists were joined by those who migrated from the Western countries after the rise and development of an indigenous competitive middle class there.

26. The economic factor underlying the position of the Hungarian Jews is stressed by Professor S. M. Dubnow, a world-renowned Jewish scholar and author. In agreeing with much of Jászi's thesis, Professor Dubnow wrote *inter alia:* "The feature most noticeable

with the Hungarian Jews was their Magyar hyperpatriotism, fed by fear. . . . The ever more prosperous growing Hungarian Jews, primarily the ones from Budapest . . . feared nothing as much as a new outbreak of antisemitism which might endanger their economic position." S. M. Dubnow, *Weltgeschichte des jüdischen Volkes* (World History of the Jewish People), 10:426, as quoted by Kann, "Hungarian Jewry," p. 368.

27. *Ibid.*, p. 369.

28. After the forced resignation of Kálmán Tisza on March 13, 1890, the governmental changes of Hungary were quite frequent. For the heads of the governments that succeeded each other until the collapse in November 1918, see *Magyarország tiszti cim- és névtára* (Title and Name Register of Hungary). Budapest: A Magyar Királyi Állami Nyomda, 49 (1942):4.

29. Károlyi's nationalities policies were formulated by Jászi, who served in his cabinet as Minister of Nationalities. Jászi's plan called for the establishment of a constitutional-federal arrangement within a democratic Hungary coupled with a general land reform and other social programs. The autonomy granted to the Ruthenians, Swabians, and Slovaks on December 25, 1918, and January 28 and March 8, 1919, respectively, failed however, to impress the border nationalities (Czechs, Romanians, and Yugoslavs) which were eager to acquire total independence from Hungary.

30. For Károlyi's account, see Mihály Károlyi, *Gegen eine ganze Welt* (Against an Entire World) (Munich: Verlag für Kulturpolitik, 1924), 515 pp. See also his *Memoirs of Michael Károlyi. Faith Without Illusion.* (London: Jonathan Cape, 1956), 392 pp.

31. The recruits to the Communist Party came primarily from among the numerically modest but politically important fraction of the approximately half-million Hungarian POW's in Russia. Many of these had taken an active part in the Bolshevik Revolution. At a conference held in Moscow on November 4, 1918, their leaders decided to found the Hungarian Communist Party and to send a few hundred agitators back to Hungary to radicalize the country and prepare it for an eventual takeover. The Party was refounded in Budapest later in the same month and by December 7, the first issue of its journal, the *Vörös Ujság* (Red Gazette), appeared. Its membership increased gradually and by February 1919 the Party could count on 10,000 to 15,000 loyal followers in Budapest and on another 20,000 to 25,000 in the provincial cities. On March 21, 1919, the Socialists were pressured into merger with the Communists and the formation of the "coalition" Soviet-style government. Rothschild, *East Central Europe*, p. 143.

32. For further details on Kun and his regime, see Rudolf L. Tökés, *Béla Kun and the Hungarian Soviet Republic* (New York: Praeger, 1967), 292 pp.

33. For details on the Friedrich regime and on some of its anti-Semitic manifestations, see Eva S. Balogh, "István Friedrich and the Hungarian Coup d'Etat of 1919: A Reevaluation," *Slavic Review*, 35, no. 2 (June 1976):269–86.

34. Of the 45 commissars of the Kun regime, 32, including Kun himself, were Jewish or of Jewish origin. Rothschild, *East Central Europe*, p. 148.

35. For details on their activities, see Samu Stern, *A zsidókérdés Magyarországon* (The Jewish Question in Hungary) (Budapest: A Pesti Izraelita Hitközség, 1938), pp. 15–17.

36. After three years of investigation, the counterrevolutionaries conceded that the Red Terror claimed a maximum of 587 victims, many of whom were, in fact, common criminals or people involved in actual coup attempts. The White Terror, on the other hand, claimed five to six thousand victims, many of whom were innocent Jews. Rothschild, *East Central Europe*, p. 153.

37. Mátyás Unger and Ottó Szabolcs, *Magyarország története* (History of Hungary) (Budapest: Gondolat Kiadó, 1965), pp. 301–3.

Shortly after the establishment of the Anti-Bolshevik Committee, an amateurish anti-Kun plot was organized by Baron Zsigmond Perényi, but was unsuccessful primarily because the workers at the time were still loyal to the revolutionary leader.

38. The Szeged group was partially financed from the 135 million crowns that the counterrevolutionaries had stolen from Kun's embassy in Vienna on May 2. These funds were originally intended to subsidize Communist activities in Austria. Rothschild, *East Central Europe*, p. 151.

39. For Horthy's account of the events of 1919–1920, see his highly slanted memoirs, in which he completely whitewashes the White Terror and speaks positively of Colonel Prónay and Major Ostenburg, the two officers responsible for many of the crimes associated with the counterrevolution. Admiral Nicholas Horthy, *Memoirs* (New York: Robert Speller & Sons, 1957), pp. 99–115.

40. Particularly savage were their activities in Dunaföldvár, Paks, Celldömölk, Balatonfőkajár, Jánosháza, Enying, Mezőszentgyörgy, Berhida, Szilasbalhás, and many other Transdanubian localities. For details see Oscar Jászi, *Revolution and Counter-Revolution in Hungary* (London: P. S. King and Son, 1924), pp. 153–76; and Dezső Sulyok, *A Magyar tragédia* (The Hungarian Tragedy) (Newark: The Author, 1954), pp. 257–76.

41. In addition to Prónay and Ostenburg, a large number of officers were involved in these "heroic" actions. Foremost among these were Count Hermann Salm, Captain Freiszberger, János Piroska, György Sefesik, István Soltész, Miklós Budaházi, First Lieutenant Iván Héjjas, Lieutenant Dénes Bibó, First Lieutenant Emil Kovarcz, and Captain István Babarczy. Horthy had nothing but praise for these officers and rejected any and all requests for their investigation and possible prosecution. In fact, he identified them as his best officers and subsequently promoted most of them. Sulyok, *ibid.*, pp. 254–92, 441.

42. *Ibid.*, pp. 265–66, 282–83.

43. *Ibid.*, pp. 286–88. The White Terror was studied on the spot by a British Labour Party delegation headed by Colonel Josiah C. Wedgwood, which visited Hungary during April–May 1920. For the text of its findings see *Report of the British Joint Labour Delegation for Hungary, May 1920: The White Terror in Hungary.* Edited by Trade Union Congress and the Labour Party, London, June 3, 1920.

44. Sulyok, *ibid.*, pp. 262, 265.

45. After the attack, Vilmos Böhm, Károlyi's Social-Democratic Minister of War, who was also to play a leading role in the Kun government, ordered the dissolution of MOVE and the internment of Gömbös. Gömbös, however, eventually escaped, first joining the Vienna group and then the Szeged group. MOVE was reinvigorated immediately after the overthrow of the Kun regime. One of the first secret organizations to develop strong ties to MOVE was András Csilléry's Hungarian Association (*Magyar Társaság*), which was launched in 1916 in order to maintain "Hungarian supremacy over the extremes of Jewry." For details of the Hungarian Association, see Balogh, "István Friedrich," pp. 275–76.

46. For further details on the MOVE see Rudolfné Dósa, *A MOVE. Egy jellegzetes magyar fasiszta szervezet, 1919–1944* (The MOVE. A Characteristic Hungarian Fascist Organization, 1919–1944) (Budapest: Akadémiai Kiadó, 1972), 228 pp.

47. C. A. Macartney, 1:29–33.

48. Sulyok, *A magyar tragédia*, pp. 270–71, 284, and 288.

49. Eckhardt was elected to head the Association of Awakening Magyars on December 15, 1923. *Ibid.*, p. 270.

50. In addition to Eckhardt, the Race-Protecting Party, which was founded by him and Gömbös in 1923, also included a number of deputies of which Endre Bajcsy-Zsilinszky, Emil Borbély-Maczky, Gyula Gömbös, János Zsirkay, Ferenc Ulain, Menyhért Kiss, and László Budaváry were the most important ones. *Ibid*, p. 421.

Following the death of Gaszton Gaál in 1932, Eckhardt, with his political position changed, became the head of the Smallholders' Party (*Kisgazda Párt*). This party was also joined by Bajcsy-Zsilinszky, who became the most respected liberal of the wartime period and the only true Hungarian hero during the German occupation.

51. For biographical details see C. A. Macartney, 1:33–35; Dezső Szabó "Gyula Gömbös," in *Az egész látóhatár. Tanulmányok* (The Entire Horizon. Studies), vol. 3 (Budapest: Magyar Élet), 1938; Endre Szokoly, . . . *és Gömbös Gyula a kapitány* (And Gyula Gömbös the Captain). (Budapest: Gondolat, 1960); and Dósa, *A MOVE*.

52. György Ránki, "Gondolatok az ellenforradalmi rendszer társadalmi bázisának kérdéséhez as 1920's évek elején" (Thoughts on the Question of the Social Basis of the Counterrevolutionary Regime During the Early 1920s. *Történelmi Szemle* (Historical Review), Budapest, no. 3–4 (1962), pp. 355–56.

53. He crystallized his equation of Jews with Communism in many speeches as well as in his book, *Die Juden in Ungarn* (The Jews in Hungary). In 1920, for example, he declared in a speech: "We do not possess proper racial self-awareness. We have been false Magyars all of us. For, if we had not been divorced from our racial self-knowledge, especially in the last century, then we would not have experienced a Bolshevik Jewish rule." Dósa, *A MOVE*, p. 126. Gömbös was not, of course, opposed to capitalism as such. Like Gottfried Feder, he differentiated between *exploitative*, i.e., Jewish, and *creative*, i.e., Christian, capital. In a 1921 article, for example, he declared himself an advocate of "racially homogeneous capitalism," i.e., one that was divorced from Jewish involvement. *Ibid.*, p. 128.

54. Sulyok, *A magyar tragédia*, p. 285.

55. *Ibid.*, p. 45.

56. Under the provisions of the Trianon Treaty, Hungary lost 58 percent of its railroad mileage and 60 percent of its road mileage; 84 percent of its timber resources and 43 percent of its arable land; 83 percent of its iron ore, 29 percent of its lignite, and 27 percent of its bituminous coal. Hungary also incurred staggering losses in its cattle and other domestic animals, in its light and heavy industrial and commercial enterprises, and banking institutions. Rothschild, *East Central Europe*, p. 156 and Sulyok, *A magyar tragédia*, pp. 42–43.

57. The passion with which the revisionist sentiment was expressed in post-Trianon Hungary is reflected in the following slogans frequently used by orators or in rallies: "Nem, nem, soha" (No, no, never); and "Csonka Magyarország nem ország, egész Magyarország mennyország" (Rump Hungary is not a country; greater Hungary is a paradise). It was especially reflected in the semi-official credo employed during the era: "Hiszek egy Istenben, Hiszek egy hazában, Hiszek egy isteni örök igazságban, Hiszek Magyarország feltámadásában" (I believe in one God, I believe in one homeland, I believe in the Almighty's eternal justice, I believe in Hungary's resurrection).

58. In 1920, there were 575,615 out of 833,475 and in 1930 there were 509,891 out of 687,207 who spoke Hungarian as a second language. With their addition to those who identified Hungarian as their primary tongue, the percentage of those speaking Hungarian was in fact 96.8 in 1920 and 98.0 in 1930. Rothschild, *East Central Europe*, p. 192.

59. Stern, *A zsidókérdés Magyarországon*, pp. 20–21. In 1938, in his apologia written in response to the anti-Jewish measures, Stern emphasized that "everywhere in the occupied territories, the Jews torn from Hungary remain the loyal supporters and protectors of the Hungarian national spirit and of Hungarian culture." *Ibid.*

60. Lévai, *Zsidósors Magyarországon*, p. 12. For details on the Orthodox and Neolog communities, see chapter 3.

61. *Ibid.*, pp. 8–9.

62. The official title of the bill was quite innocent. It read: "The Regulation of Registration to the Universities, Polytechnical Institutes, the School of Political Economy of Budapest, and the Law Academies" (*Tudományegyetemekre, a műegyetemre, a budapesti egye-*

temi közgazdaságtudományi karra és jogakadémiákra való beiratkozás szabályozása). For text see *Magyar Törvénytár. 1920. évi törvénycikkek* (Hungarian Code of Laws. Laws of 1920) (Budapest: Állami Nyomda, 1921), pp. 145–46. For an evaluation of the law's impact, see Thomas Spira, "Hungary's Numerus Clausus, the Jewish Minority, and the League of Nations" in *Ungarn Jahrbuch 1972* (Hungary Yearbook 1972) (Mainz: Hase & Kohler, 1973), 4:115–28.

63. Lévai, *Zsidósors Magyarországon*, p. 9.

64. See letter addressed by Prince Lajos Windischgraetz to Horthy on June 29, 1919, in *Horthy Miklós titkos iratai* (The Confidential Papers of Miklós Horthy), eds. Miklós Szinai and László Szücs (Budapest: Kossuth, 1963), pp. 9–14.

65. Stern, *A zsidókérdés Magyarországon*, p. 20. See also Nathaniel Katzburg, "The Jewish Question in Hungary During the Inter-War Period. Jewish Attitudes," in *Jews and Non-Jews in Eastern Europe.* eds. B. Vágó and G. L. Mosse (New York: John Wiley, 1974), pp. 113–24.

66. Jacob Robinson, et. al., *Were the Minorities Treaties a Failure?* (New York: Institute of Jewish Affairs of the World Jewish Congress, 1943), p. 82.

CHAPTER TWO

FROM CONSOLIDATION TO
PROTO-FASCISM

The Bethlen Era of Consolidation:
1921–1932

THE APPOINTMENT as Premier of Count István Bethlen, the leader of
the Vienna faction of counterrevolutionary exiles, denoted the return
to power of the conservative-aristocratic group of large landholders
and financial magnates that had ruled Hungary before the war. The
scion of a great historic family of Transylvania, Bethlen was a highly
experienced and extremely skillful politician. Rather reserved in his
personal relationships, he was a very cultured and generally respected
figure whose advice on public affairs was eagerly sought by all those in
power during the interwar period, including Admiral Horthy. An arch-
conservative in socioeconomic affairs, he was quite tolerant and broad-
minded on issues relating to intellectual and individual freedom. In
power, Bethlen was dedicated to bringing about the political and economic consolidation of the truncated state in order to be in a better
position to press the issue of revisionism abroad.

The political vehicle through which the traditional ruling elite aimed
at assuring the viability and continuity of the restored system was the
Government Party (*Kormánypárt*).[1] A creation of Bethlen, the Party was
reorganized soon after his acquisition of power to assure a unified,
loyal, and constant support for the twin objectives of Hungary's historic
classes: revisionism in foreign policy and protection of the traditional
feudal-bourgeois social order in domestic affairs. The dominant position of the Government Party in the politics of the interwar period was
practically guaranteed through the revision of the electoral law and the
reorganization of the legislature. Under Bethlen's decree of March 2,
1922, the relatively wide and secret "Friedrich suffrage" was replaced
by Hungary's traditional restrictive franchise, which included the use of
the open ballot in the countryside. The National Assembly, whose two-
year term expired on February 16, was replaced by a new, quinquen-
nial legislature.[2] With the Socialists skillfully and effectively neutralized
at the price of an amnesty, the Government Party had virtually no op-

position in Parliament.[3] The respectability of the Party and the stability of the new political system were further assured through the gradual disarming, if not dissolution, of the extremist factions of the counter-revolutionary Right. The leaders of these factions, including Gömbös, were successfully co-opted into Bethlen's system and the White Terrorists were effectively curbed. Gömbös, in fact, had been entrusted with the preparation of the 1922 elections and had for a while served as the Party's Vice President. Under Bethlen, Gömbös also served first as an Under Secretary and then as Minister of Defense. The international image of Hungary was further boosted by the imaginative cultural and educational policies of Count Kunó Klebelsberg, the innovative and popular Minister of Cults and Public Education. Bethlen's own stature was greatly enhanced as a result of his early diplomatic successes, including the reacquisition of a part of the Burgenland (including Sopron [Ödenburg] and its environs) that had earlier been ceded to Austria,[4] the admission of Hungary into the League of Nations (September 18, 1922), and the securing of a League-sponsored Reconstruction Loan of $50 million (July 1924).

Practical and imaginative as he was in the political-diplomatic sphere, Bethlen was shortsighted and reactionary when it came to social affairs. Although he had frequently shown a sympathetic understanding of the plight of the impoverished peasants and workers and occasionally even manifested a paternalistic benevolence toward them, he pursued basically the same regressive policies characteristic of his pre-war predecessors. The sham agrarian reform act of 1920 hardly alleviated the plight of the landless peasants[5] and was used to a large extent merely to counteract the impact of the more sweeping reforms planned or enacted in the Successor States. Trianon Hungary had in fact reverted back to its pre-war semi-feudal latifundia system. With the virtual reestablishment of the *status quo ante*, the arch-conservative feudal-bourgeois elite did everything in its power to preserve and possibly advance its privileged socioeconomic status. During the Compromise Era, the ruling elite had evoked the specter of the "danger represented by the coinhabiting national minorities" to perpetuate its privileges against the rising demands for the expansion of economic opportunities, freedom, and equality (chapter 1). Now, after the war, this same group—and for the same purpose—used the "injustices of Trianon" and afterward the "nefarious influence of the Jews" as their cardinal pretext. The conservative landowner–financial clique was particularly successful in camouflaging its conscious objective, to maintain and strengthen the nation's traditional feudal-bourgeois institutions, because of the genuinely popular character of the virtually nationwide revisionist-irredentist movement. The economic hardships and social grievances of the oppressed classes were in the course of time given an outlet through the rising tide of nationalism and Fascism.

An ardent nationalist, Bethlen was convinced that in addition to social defusion and political consolidation, economic reconstruction was a precondition for the successful pursuit of revisionism. Although it was deprived of much of its land and its human and natural resources, Hungary still retained considerable agricultural assets and a relatively large industrial base[6] whose exploitation and development required massive capital investments. The reconstruction loan sponsored by the League of Nations and the currency reform of 1925[7] went a long way in easing the pressures of inflation and of the national debt, but were not sufficient to assure the desired economic rehabilitation of the country. Since the development of capitalism in Hungary was intimately intertwined with the role of Jewish financiers and industrialists, who traditionally collaborated with the politically dominant aristocratic-gentry landed and bureaucratic elites, Bethlen had no difficulty in reestablishing the businesslike relationship that had prevailed between the two groups before the war. A highly pragmatic politician, Bethlen realized that Jewish domestic and foreign capital was essential for Hungary's economic reconstruction and for its acquisition he was even ready to subdue, if not permanently discard, his own personal distaste for the Jews.[8] He summarized his position on the Jewish question in his inaugural speech of April 10, 1921, as follows:

I am against all kinds of shrill anti-Semitism. We shall under all circumstances maintain order. Should any of the authorities exceed their jurisdiction, we shall restore them to the jurisdiction specified by law. We do not wish even to touch this subject in a way that interferes with the idea of equality before the law. Equality before the law is guaranteed by the nation and cannot be interfered with. I admit that there is currently a Jewish question in the country, but its solution lies in our becoming economically independent of them. This is also in their own interest, because as soon as they are no longer indispensable, harmony will be reestablished. In this respect, consequently, the government is determined to lay down the premises of a constructive policy.[9]

The mutually advantageous cooperation between the politically dominant aristocratic-gentry class and the economically and financially influential Jewish group led to a series of accomplishments. The rabidly anti-Semitic elements associated with the so-called Szeged clique were, albeit only temporarily, removed from the seats of power. The Jews also, nominally at least, reacquired coequality with their fellow Magyars through the revision of the *Numerus Clausus* Act. In justifying the revision, the sponsors of Law No. XIV of 1928 stated *inter alia:*

Certain circles of Hungarian Jewry have raised the complaint that they felt themselves stigmatized under the provisions of Article 3 of Law No. XXV of 1920. One must pay attention to such imponderables in the world of emotions, for the general satisfaction of the citizens is indispensable for the flourishing of any state. Our Jewish compatriots, however, must not lose sight of the fact that the national catastrophe that befell us led to the shrinking of all of our living conditions and made necessary many painful restrictions.[10]

In spite of the government's tolerant position, the Jewish question continued to remain alive and a source of anguish. During Bethlen's tenure, as during the entire Horthy era, the particular focus of attention was the status of, and the "danger" represented by, the "alien" Jews. The Hungarian leaders, as well as some of the highly assimilated Jewish ones, were gravely concerned about the "infiltration of undesirable Jewish elements from the East." In 1920, the Hungarian government was already providing for the expulsion of the Jews who had infiltrated into the country after January 1, 1914.[11] This provision was amended by a decree initiated by Bethlen in 1925. While the Jews were no longer specifically mentioned as undesirable aliens, the government was given the power to expel for reasons of national security any undesirable alien elements.[12] Early in 1930, all aliens were made subject to registration and careful supervision within the framework of a new state organization, the National Central Alien Control Office (*A Külföldieket Ellenőrző Országos Központi Hatóság*—KEOKH; see chapter 6). The question of Jewish infiltration was the subject of a Crown Council Meeting (*Koronatanács*) early in 1931. After hearing a series of reports from the various ministers about the "dangers" represented by the "alien" Jews, including their alleged involvement in Communist activities, the displacement of citizens from their jobs, and their gobbling-up of real estate, the Council resolved to prevent such infiltration by any and all legal means available. Resolutions were also advanced for the staging of periodic raids for the apprehension of the alien Jews and for measures designed to dismiss them from their jobs.

While apprehensive about the possible implications of the governmental actions taken against the alien Jews, the official leadership of the "Magyars of the Israelite faith" continued to prove its loyalty through declarations relating to its patriotic commitment to the cause of revisionism. In its memorandum addressed to the *Alliance Israélite Universelle* of Paris in 1930, for example, the Hungarian Jews declared characteristically: "The foreign Jews can do most for Hungarian Jewry by cooperating in the improvement of the situation of all of Hungary and by seeing to it that the severe injustice that befell Hungary by being truncated at Trianon is remedied.[13]"

With the Jewish question temporarily neutralized and the political situation consolidated, Bethlen proceeded energetically with the tasks of economic reconstruction. Under his leadership, the Hungarian economy made great strides toward the achievement, and in some sectors the surpassing, of the pre-war levels of agricultural and industrial production. But with the onset of the depression in 1929, much of the economic base created by (and the foundation of) the Bethlen system had suddenly eroded. Within a few years, the economic devastation was of such a magnitude and the political implications so ominous that Bethlen felt compelled to yield his power.[14] The cement between the upper middle class and the large landowners on which the Bethlen system was based suddenly began to dissolve. Bethlen himself became increasingly unpopular, especially among the agrarians who suspected him of favoring mercantile interests.[15]

Within a month after the parliamentary elections of June–July, 1931, in which the Government Party had won 158 of the 245 seats, Bethlen resigned the premiership in favor of Count Gyula Károlyi, the original organizer of the Arad-Szeged counterrevolutionary government-in-exile.[16] Károlyi was an unimpressive, rather colorless, politician, whose policy of financial orthodoxy could neither stem the worsening economic situation nor shore up the political system of the consolidation period. Although associated with Szeged, Károlyi's political and economic views were closer to those of Bethlen (in whose Cabinet he had been serving as Minister of Foreign Affairs since December 10, 1930) than to those of the Right radicals he originally organized. However, his unavoidably orthodox budgetary policies coupled with stringent governmental retrenchments were no help, under the conditions of the depression, to the Bethlen group's efforts to retain power. Political stability was threatened from within and without the circle of the ruling classes represented in the Government Party. In October 1930, a group of deputies led by Gaszton Gaál had already seceded to form the oppositional Independent Smallholders' Party (*Független Kisgazda Párt*).[17] Composed of the more radical agrarians, the new party took an increasingly vocal position against the larger landowning deputies within the Government Party who had constituted themselves as an Agrarian Group.

The disintegration of the ruling coalition was all the more dangerous because of the radicalization that was taking place outside it. Conditioned by their counterrevolutionary past, the aristocratic-gentry rulers were especially concerned with the possible threat from the left[18] even though the Social Democrats and the handful of Communists were politically so weakened and involved in their own internal struggles that they were in no position to take advantage of the discontent among the impoverished peasants and workers.[19] However, more immediate and more threatening to political stability was the revival of the ultra-radical Szeged spirit among the declining middle and lower middle classes, the unemployed high school and university graduates, and most vocally, the lower paid civil servants and junior army officers—Gyula Gömbös' original supporters.[20] Given his background, Gömbös was under these conditions the natural choice of those who were calling for the completion of the historical mission of the national-Christian movement that was started at Szeged.

Swing to the Right: The Gömbös Era, 1932–1936

Gömbös' Anti-Semitism. From the early days of the counterrevolution until his death late in 1936, Gyula Gömbös was the foremost representative and leader of the Hungarian radical Right. His political career clearly demonstrates the ambivalence with which the radical Right treated the Jewish question throughout the interwar period (see chapter 1). A rabid anti-Semite, he was also an opportunist who did not hesitate to admit "loyal and patriotic" wealthy Jews into his movement, and some even into his secret societies. But his opportunism, fostered by his movement's financial insolvency, did not prevent him from exploiting anti-Semitism as a powerful psychological and political weapon in the pursuit of his ideological objectives. Gömbös fostered the demagogic use of anti-Semitism in the recruitment campaign for Horthy's national army, in the White Terror, and in the punishment of "sinful" Budapest. During the debates over the *Numerus Clausus* in 1920, Gömbös called for the expulsion of "surplus Jewry" from Hungary and for the introduction of a general quota system for those allowed to remain in the country. He reiterated the same position in his German-language book—*Die Juden in Ungarn* (The Jews in Hungary)—published during the early 1920s:

The Jewish question must be solved for otherwise there will be no more Hungarian landowners left within 50 to 100 years and [the Jews] will administer the affairs of the country. The thesis is simple: the Jews must not be allowed to succeed in any field beyond the level of their ratio in the population.[21]

Gömbös was in many respects a forerunner of the National Socialist movement. He anticipated many of the policies that were subsequently adopted in the Third Reich. Like the Nazis, he was particularly concerned with the alleged anti-nationalist tendencies of the Jews and saw the partial solution of the Jewish question in the "resettlement" of the "surplus" Jews in cooperation with the "Zionist authorities." Also like the Nazis, during the early phase of his political career he constantly portrayed the Jews as basically and naturally anti-patriotic and prone to internationalist, i.e. Bolshevik, tendencies as a response to anti-Semitism. Gömbös outlined his views in many anti-Semitic publications, including the *Szózat* (Appeal). In the January 1, 1921, issue of the *Szózat*, for example, he wrote as follows:

I find it necessary that the Hungarian Government get in touch with the Zionists' center for the resettlement of the surplus of several hundred thousand Jews of Hungarian citizenship. The fate of the homeless people living scattered all over the world should be studied also from the point of view of the other peoples' tranquility. While the peoples in possession of a homeland are naturally the champions of nationalism, the strongest anti-nationalist tendency stems from the Jews because nationalism almost always goes hand in hand with anti-Semitism. This is the reason why all internationalist movements find a great echo among the Jews. As long as they live scattered, they can have only one aim: the soft-pedaling of national effects through the establishment of a new world order that would denote slavery for us and domination for them. . . .[22]

Gömbös' General Policy. A career officer and a self-proclaimed ardent chauvinist and National Socialist, Gömbös left the army in 1920 to devote all of his time to politics. As the organizer of many of the secret patriotic associations and a deputy of the smallholder faction of the Government Party, Gömbös was in a highly favorable position to galvanize around himself the extremist elements eager to bring about radical changes in the country. He became increasingly disenchanted with Bethlen's moderate approach in domestic and international affairs. The Government Party's apparent loss of vigor after the passing of the Bolshevik menace induced Gömbös and his radical colleagues, including Eckhardt and Endre Bajcsy-Zsilinszky, to form in the fall of 1923 a new, openly racist and pronouncedly Rightist party—the Race-Protecting Party (*Fajvédő Párt*). Emulating Hitler's NSDAP, the Race-Protecting Party was devoted to "active anti-Semitism."[23] By resorting to anti-Semitic demagogy and renewing the demand for land reform, the Race Protectors sought to find or rekindle their following among the urban lower middle class, the radical students, and the landless and small-holders.[24] A few weeks after founding the Party Gömbös, who had been in contact with the Nazi movement since its beginning in 1921, was implicated in a bizarre plot aiming to coordinate a coup in Budapest with Hitler's beer-hall *putsch* in Munich in November 1923. As was typical for the treatment of Right radicals during the interwar period, the plotters were let off with exceedingly light sentences.[25]

However, with the return to "normalcy" during the 1920s, neither the *putschist* nor the demagogic efforts of the Race Protectors met with much success. The party had started with six representatives in 1923; all but Gömbös lost their seats in the election of 1926.[26] Having proved the futility of Gömbös' "independent" efforts, Bethlen managed to bring a tamed Gömbös back into the Government Party, where he served as a useful symbol of the solidarity of the counterrevolutionary camp. In 1928, Gömbös formally liquidated the Race-Protecting Party and accepted an appointment in the Ministry of Defense, first as Under Secretary and then as Minister (1929). From this position, Gömbös began to rebuild his power base within the establishment. Driven by vast ambition and seemingly limitless energy, Gömbös worked out a plan for the expansion of the Hungarian armed forces beyond the limits authorized by the Peace Treaties. He also took advantage of his new position by appointing and promoting his own men in the constantly expanding officers' corps. Before Gömbös became Premier, only officers of somewhat lower ranks were brought in. The higher echelons, including the General Staff, were packed during his tenure as Prime Minister. The radicalization of the army was to prove one of the heaviest millstones around the neck of more moderate elements in Hungary's political life. For the new men brought in by Gömbös were largely of Swabian background, ultra-Rightist and anti-Semitic in their political views and, as subsequent events clearly demonstrated, ready and eager to follow the leadership of the Third Reich irrespective of its potentially catastrophic implications for Hungary.

Within the Government Party, Gömbös was instrumental in mobilizing its rightist faction to advocate a new program. Formulated to a large extent by men like Gábor Baross, Sándor Sztranyavszky, and István Antal, Gömbös' program was launched in May 1932. It was a "respectable" eight-point program, designed to offer something for everybody, which closely approximated the demands of the conservative Agrarian Group.[27] It was designed not only to offer a possible "solution" to the grave social and economic crises brought to the fore by the depression, but also, and perhaps primarily, to demonstrate Gömbös' new respectability and suitability to assume full leadership in guiding the country's destiny.

Gömbös as Premier. Under the dire economic conditions of the depression, many representatives of finance and business, including Jewish ones, responded favorably to this sensible program and offered their support to Gömbös. To assure their continued assistance, Gömbös in turn committed himself to certain moderate positions.[28] Bethlen and his large-landholder aristocratic colleagues became convinced that Gömbös had mellowed and would not alter too drastically the political and social system of the Consolidation Era. Consequently, when Károlyi's financial and budgetary policies failed to bring an improvement in the depression-ridden economy, the momentum for a shift toward the Right built up to such an extent that even Bethlen acceded to Gömbös' appointment as Premier. Coinciding with the spectacular electoral victories of the Nazi Party in Germany, Gömbös' assumption of power on October 1, 1932, began a new chapter in Hungary's history.

Before appointing Gömbös as Premier, Horthy took a number of precautionary measures to limit his freedom of action. Gömbös was made to promise that he would agitate neither for the dissolution of parliament nor for the introduction of land reform or anti-Semitic legislation.[29] Gömbös' choice of ministers was also closely supervised by Horthy, and it bode well for the traditional faction. It included such close collaborators of Bethlen as Miklós Kállay (Agriculture), Ferenc Keresztes-Fischer (Interior), Tihamér Fabinyi (Commerce), and Béla Imrédy (Finance). The most Right-wing member of Gömbös' original cabinet was Bálint Hóman, the Minister of Cults and Public Education. The other leading members of Gömbös' original cabinet were Endre Puky, Minister of Foreign Affairs and Andor Lázár, Minister of Justice. Gömbös also doubled as Minister of Defense. Though the cabinet was composed of the leading members of the Government Party, it was the first one in Hungarian history (excepting, of course, Kun's government) not to include a titled aristocrat. Nevertheless, it was a source of disappointment to many of his earlier associates, including Eckhardt and Ulain, who would have preferred a coalition government composed of the Right radical forces.

Horthy's and the Bethlenites' hopes for a moderate rule were generally satisfied by Gömbös' first acts in office. Particularly heartening was Gömbös' apparent change of heart with respect to the Jewish question and his rapprochement with the Jewish community. The 95-point program published by the new government on October 6 did not even refer to the Jews; it emphasized the emergency economic and financial measures which were felt necessary to combat the depression. Gömbös asked his good friend Baross, whose rightist credentials were impeccable, to establish contact with the official Jewish leadership. A *modus vivendi* was in fact soon reached between the leaders of the Neolog Jewish community and the representatives of the TESz (*Társadalmi Egyesületek Szövetsége;* Federation of Social Associations), the umbrella organization for the secret and patriotic associations. According to Macartney,

A protocol was signed between Baross and J. Szörcsey, respectively President and Vice-President of the TESz, on the one hand, and M. [Samu] Stern and his Vice-President, M. J. Szántó, on the other, under which the Neolog Jews "recognized and approved Gömbös' progressive policy," while Gömbös promised to carry that policy through without violence and without detriment to the Jews' material interests.[30]

To the extent that no anti-Semitic legislation was passed under Gömbös, and in light of the fact that his economic policy was generally quite favorable to the "mercantile" interests, Gömbös in fact kept his part of the bargain. Even more astonishing, if not as convincing, were his references to the Jewish question during his inaugural speech in the lower house on October 11. In an allusion to his notoriously anti-Semitic past, he declared:

To Jewry, in turn, I openly and sincerely declare: I have revised my position. That part of Jewry which throws in its lot with the Hungarian nation I wish to regard as brothers, as I do my Hungarian brothers. I saw Jewish heroes in the war; I know some who earned gold medals for heroism, and I know that they fought bravely and heroically. I know leading Jewish figures who are praying with me for Hungary's future. I know that they will be the first ones to condemn that part of Jewry which does not want or cannot assimilate itself into the nation's social order.[31]

He repeated his assurances to the Jewish community on a number of other public occasions, emphasizing that the Hungarian government wished to protect the legal order and the security of its citizens without regard to denominational differences. The official leadership of Hungarian Jewry, it appears in retrospect, was quite naïve in its evaluation of Gömbös' policies. It tended to accept the Premier's declarations at face value, losing sight of their ideological underpinnings and political motivations. Clinging to its past position, the Jewish leadership aimed to preserve the community's relative well-being by emphasizing its patriotic posture and dissociation from Zionism and similar "alien" movements which were agitating other Jewish national communities. In April 1933, for example, the Hungarian Jewish leaders approached Governor Herbert H. Lehman of New York, requesting that he use his influence with the representatives of the Great Powers then meeting in New York City to rectify the injustices caused through the truncation of Hungary at Trianon. In their telegram, they emphasized that by such an intervention the Governor, himself a Jew, could be of assistance to Hungarian Jewry. As if to justify the legitimacy of their request, they contrasted the positive "consolidation" policies of Gömbös and his government with the open persecution of the Jews in Germany.[32]

The same sentiments were expressed by the Jewish leaders on the occasion of the first anniversary of Gömbös' rule. Typical of such expressions was the reference in the annual report of the Jewish Community of Pest for 1934:

We must recognize that the governmental leadership of Gyula Gömbös has indeed brought for us Jews the further strengthening of consolidation, but it is certain that we are still awaiting the righting of many wrongs, the fulfillment of many of our wishes and desires. Hungarian Jewry is indeed entitled to have Hungary remain an island of peaceful understanding in the midst of the worldwide surge of anti-Semitism, because this Jewry may justly point out that before and during the war, as well as after the débacle, it repeatedly proved its Magyardom and loyalty to the nation not only at home but also in the occupied territories.[33]

The nationalist-patriotic stance of the assimilated official leaders of Hungarian Jewry during Gömbös' rule was also manifested in the debates over the ideas advocated by Gyula Szekfű, Hungary's most renowned historian of the interwar period.[34] Szekfű, like many other outstanding intellectuals, including some sincere friends of the Jews, was more concerned with the "harmful effects" of the numerical preponderance of the Jews in many fields of the economy, science, and the free professions than with the "positive consequences" of their contributions to the modernization and general advancement of Hungary. Szekfű challenged the position of the assimilationists by arguing that it was not they who became Magyarized, but that in fact they "Jewified" the Magyars. He maintained that the only way to ease the burdensome relationship that had existed between the Jews and the Magyars was for the Jews either to accept Zionism, with its implicit commitment to eventual emigration, or to organize themselves as a minority, which would require them to give up their insistence on assimilation. Szekfü firmly believed that the total integration of the Jews was impossible not only because of their religious peculiarities, but also—and this is what he had in common with many of the Jews' critics—because of the continued "immigration of Jews from the East."

The official Jewish leadership, which had never been imbued with a Jewish national consciousness, naturally rejected this indirect call for disassimilation. The naïveté of the Jewish leadership, the lack of perspective with which they judged the anti-Semitism then rampant all over Europe, and the misguided optimism associated with their assimilationist-patriotic stance are best illustrated by the resolution adopted by the trend-setting Jewish Community of Pest, the nation's largest, at its general assembly meeting of January 14, 1934:

We are not interested in this new slogan of disassimilation. We are not animated by any special Jewish national chimera, and we shall resist the attempts either here or abroad, from amongst our own ranks or from the other side, that try to propagate the idea that we should transplant into our midst the currents and movements that have taken root among Jews abroad in various places. . . . We respect the right and freedom of the Jews of all countries to advance their own communal aims and their own denominational life according to their own convictions and conceptions. But just as we cannot proceed in national politics according to foreign examples, and can properly serve the vital national interest only according to our country's development and the traditional constitutional principles of Magyardom, so we cannot follow foreign examples in our denominational life and the faithful service of our Jewry, no matter how praiseworthy they might be. We want to go forward in our own way, and our way is the inseparably interwined route of our Jewry and Magyardom. . . . Our rights may be curtailed temporarily by the storm of the times, but we ourselves will not surrender our rights, we cling indomitably to our Magyardom, and we cannot allow this to be interfered with by foreign international currents, even praiseworthy ones.[35]

Gömbös and his colleagues were quite appreciative of this manifestation of patriotism. As though to reward Jewry for its loyal stand, Gömbös encouraged the hope of the organized Neolog and Orthodox communities that their constitutional status, based as it was on the archaic laws of the pre-World War I period, would be modernized. He even permitted the two communities to hold national congresses in 1935 for the drafting of the relevant legislation.[36] Though both congresses were greeted warmly by the leaders of the Hungarian state and government, including Horthy, Gömbös, and Hóman, and many worthwhile proposals were in fact advanced, nothing substantive materialized: the two communities continued on their separate and occasionally antagonistic paths.

Gömbös' apparent change in tone and rapprochement with the Jewish community were based, as in the 1920s, on opportunistic considerations rather than on a genuine change of heart. As the immediate task was to revive Hungary's economy from the effects of the depression, the aid of Jewish business and finance was highly desirable, if not indispensable. The reduction of Jewish influence in these fields, for which Gömbös had so often called in the past, was impossible to carry out given the grave conditions under which he came to power. That the Race-Protector mentality of the highest officials was still intact during these years can be seen in the minutes of the first Crown Council meeting held under Gömbös on March 18, 1933. The Council, devoted to a general review of domestic and international questions affecting Hungary, also heard a plea from Horthy about the necessity of dealing with the problem of "physical and mental selection" as a means of assuring "the nation's development and the health and strength of the race."[37] He elaborated on these racial views in a special letter drafted for Gömbös later that year. Horthy was particularly concerned about the failure of the desirable elements of the Hungarian race, including the officers, the civil servants, the middle-class intelligentsia, and the well-to-do in general, to reproduce at a faster rate. He showed an equal dedication to bringing about the reduction in the reproduction rate of racially "undesirable elements" such as the infirm, criminals, the mentally weak, and those who shirked work.[38] Jews were not specifically named. Nevertheless, given the apparent belief in eugenics and the precipitous increase in anti-Semitism during the period, it was obvious to most genuine liberals that the Jews could not expect lasting protection from a man with Gömbös' background. By the spring of 1936, the anti-Jewish agitation boiled up to such a high point that a series of anti-Semitic riots erupted, especially in the institutions of higher learning. Assaults on Jewish students took place, for example, at the Péter Pázmány University and at the Polytechnical Institute of Budapest.

Gömbös' opportunistic approach to the Jewish question, based on expediency and temporary tactical considerations, paralleled his handling of general domestic policies. During his first eighteen months in office, when his power base was not yet firmly established, he pursued a cautiously moderate policy that pleased the Bethlenites but did not overtly antagonize his Right radical supporters. While his policies were clearly dictated by the immediate political and economic realities of that period, he did not, of course, permanently abandon the ideological commitments and political expectations that animated his followers. He was still firmly committed to chauvinistic nationalism, racial anti-Semitism, anti-intellectualism, and to a social radicalism, which, while not anti-capitalist per se, aimed to put an end to the inherited privileges of the aristocratic historic classes. Consequently, while during the early phase of his premiership he was still dependent on the Bethlenite forces, including those associated with the Government Party, with the gradual consolidation of his power he became ever more determined to assure his freedom of action from the constraints of the conservative aristocratic forces. Relying for support upon the elements traditionally associated with Right radicalism, including the impoverished lower middle classes, the unemployed academicians and intellectuals, the "humiliated" officers' corps, and the army of civil servants and patriotic refugees from the territories ceded to the Successor States, Gömbös gradually developed a formidable power base by appointing his own protégés into the civil and military bureaucracies of the state apparatus. His chance for packing the upper army hierarchy, including the General Staff, with younger, generally Germanophile officers of Swabian background, came shortly after the resignation of a large number of career officers in the wake of a critical inquest by the League of Nations into Hungarian responsibility for the assassination in Marseilles of King Alexander of Yugoslavia and French Foreign Minister Louis Barthou by a Croat nationalist on October 9, 1934.

Emulating the police practices of Fascist Italy, Gömbös was increasingly effective in dealing with a gradually shrinking and intimidated opposition. By the spring of 1935, he felt so confident in his power that he brought about a purge of the Government Party and called for new parliamentary elections. Held between March 31 and April 11, the indirect elections denoted a new radicalization of domestic politics. Since the elections were held under the provisions of the Bethlen-sponsored electoral law, the results were never in doubt. The now-Gömbös-dominated Government Party won 170 of the 245 seats, of which 154 came from the countryside, where the open ballot prevailed. Of the outgoing Government Party deputies only 25 were returned, as a consequence of Gömbös' reorganization measures. The Bethlenites and Independents, having won only 12 seats, joined the Opposition camp.[39]

Under the new political polarization that followed the 1935 elections, the Opposition emerged as a coalition composed of the traditional

"Conservative-Liberal" ruling classes, the Socialists, the Legitimists, and the Jews.[40] In the early 1940s, it was also joined by the Independent Smallholders. Bethlen, as the leader of, and spokesman for, this coalition, symbolized the opposition of these strata of Hungarian society to tying their country's destiny to that of Nazi Germany, and to the increasingly visible erosion of civil rights and liberties. Unfortunately, the "Opposition Front" was an exceedingly heterogeneous body, and the parties and factions could not always agree on the extent or character of their resistance to nazification at home and pro-Third Reich policies abroad. Their difficulty was compounded by internal social and economic pressures and by the realization that revision required a "realistic" evaluation of the greater opportunities afforded by the forces opposed to the Versailles arrangement.

Gömbös' chief support came from the Right-dominated Government Party, which also enjoyed the backing of the Christian Social League and of the Independent Smallholders. The Right radical opposition, which, in fact, supported Gömbös on many issues, was represented by three deputies: two were elected under the banner of the Hungarian National Socialist Party (Count Sándor Festetics and István Balogh, Jr.) and one under that of the National Radical Party—a party founded by and consisting almost exclusively of Endre Bajcsy-Zsilinszky. In 1937, it fused with the Independent Smallholders' Party.[41]

Viewing the election results as a clear mandate, Gömbös showed a new interest in tackling the grave social issues that plagued the nation. He even renewed the plan for instituting a meaningful agrarian reform, which alarmed Horthy and his traditional conservative large landholder allies. But the plan which Gömbös was particularly anxious to implement was his age-old dream to transform Hungary into a Fascist state. Long frustrated by the political realities of the Horthy-Bethlen–dominated country, he at last felt ready to carry out his ambition. His resolve in this respect is reflected in the top-secret personal agreement he signed with Hermann Göring, Hitler's deputy, during his visit to Berlin on September 30, 1935. Under the agreement, Gömbös undertook to introduce in Hungary, within two years, a system closely resembling that of the Third Reich.[42] He failed in this ambition, primarily because he was shortly thereafter incapacitated by an acute kidney ailment.

The Impact of Nazi Germany. Although Gömbös was not very successful in implementing his domestic program, he was able to tie Hungary's destiny almost irrevocably to Nazi Germany's.[43] Capitalizing on Bethlen's failure to advance the cause of revisionism by relying upon the Western democracies and their instrumentality, the League of Nations, Gömbös brought Hungary's foreign policy into line with that of the Third Reich. Hitler's Germany was the one major power eager to undo the injustices of Versailles, and also the one guided by political and racial principles that were closest to his heart. In fact, Gömbös was the first head of government to pay Hitler a visit after he became Chancellor. The visit of June 17, 1933, resulted in some political compromises under which Hungary was encouraged to pursue its revisionist ambitions against Czechoslovakia (although not yet against Romania or Yugoslavia). However, far more important and more fateful for Hungary were the subsequent penetration and direct involvement of the Third Reich in practically every aspect of the country's life. The political understanding of 1933 was followed by the first major economic agreement under which Hungary was enabled to sell its agricultural surpluses and import the industrial products needed for its modernization and rearmament program.

The German-Hungarian Economic Agreement of February 1934 was to a large extent made possible by the innovative policies of Hjalmar Schacht, the new Economics Minister of the Third Reich. By reversing the autarkic agricultural policies of Alfred Hugenberg, the former Food Minister, Schacht successfully brought about not only an expansion of trade and a greater supply of needed agricultural products, but also Hungary's dependence on Germany for both markets and technical and industrial supplies. In addition to grain and livestock, Germany imported almost the entire Hungarian production of bauxite. Hungary, in turn, imported increasing quantities of finished industrial products, as well as raw materials needed for its developing industries, including coal, coke, and tar derivatives. According to official figures, which do not include secret expenditures on armaments, Hungary's trade with Germany between 1933 and 1937 increased as shown in table 2.1.

In addition to this rapid increase in trade, the virtual interlocking of the country's economy with that of the Third Reich was further enhanced by the penetration of German investment capital. A large number of German firms established branch units or launched new industrial projects in Hungary. While this expansion of German economic interests was particularly resented by the Jews because it brought about the spread of Nazi influence and because it represented a direct challenge to their economic status, it was welcomed by many strata of

TABLE 2.1.
IMPORT-EXPORT TRADE WITH GERMANY:
1933–1937

Year	Imports from Germany (1,000 Pengö)	Percent of Total Imports	Exports to Germany (1,000 Pengö)	Percent of Total Exports
1933	61,507	19.7	43,701	11.2
1934	63,025	18.3	89,866	22.2
1935	91,295	22.7	108,098	23.9
1936	113,393	26.0	115,198	22.8
1937	124,762	26.2	141,586	24.1

SOURCE: C. A. Macartney, 1:141.

Hungarian society. They saw in it a means toward ending the consequences of the depression as well as a way of "freeing them from the tyranny of the Jewish middlemen." The popularity of this position increased with the gradual decrease in unemployment and the commensurate increase in industrial production during the late 1930s, when Hungary was engaged in a massive rearmament program. It was particularly popular with the surplus agricultural and industrial laborers who were periodically employed in Germany and who, having been relatively well-paid and well treated, often returned as converted Nazis.

The economic penetration of Hungary was coupled with the establishment of local bases by the various major agencies of the Nazi State and Party. German youth and student groups as well as "tourists" associated with various Nazi-sponsored organizations, including the Wandervogel ("Bird of Passage") youth movement, entered the country in great numbers, sometimes wearing their Swastika-decorated Nazi uniforms. Their mission was not only to spread their National Socialist ideas among the Hungarians, but also, and above all, to raise the pro-Third-Reich national consciousness of the coinhabiting German Swabian minorities. The Nazis were also able to establish an effective spy network by planting their supporters in various Hungarian agencies, including the police, the gendarmerie and even the Regent's office.[44] They also acquired the support of a large percentage of the higher civil servants and of the Germanophile General Staff, which saw in the Third Reich the only realistic support for revisionism. Perhaps the most successful achievement of the Nazis during Gömbös' period was the radicalization of the press and the establishment and flourishing of a series of ultra-rightist political movements and parties. They were quite generous in supporting the publication of a large number of vitriolically anti-Semitic dailies and weeklies like the *Uj Magyarság* (New Magyardom), *Magyarság* (Magyardom), *Virradat* (Dawn), *Magyar Futár* (Hungarian Courier), *Nemzetőr* (National Guard), *Összetartás* (Unity), and *Pesti Ujság* (Journal of Pest). The journalists and editors associated with these organs, including István Milotay, Ferenc Rajniss, Oliver Rupprecht, Ferenc Fiala, Ferenc Vajta, Gábor Bornemisza, and Károly Maróthy, spewed out an incessant pro-Nazi and anti-Semitic propaganda barrage that poisoned Hungarian public opinion and prepared the ground for the anti-Jewish measures adopted during the German occupation in 1944.[45] They also played a leading role in crystallizing the ideas and in championing the cause of the various Right-radical movements and parties.

Gömbös himself was not destined to see the establishment of the Fascist State, the implementation of his social program, or the full fruition of his pro-German policies. Suffering from an acute kidney disease, he died on October 6, 1936, in a hospital in Munich, where he had gone for treatment on September 3. However, he must have been consoled by the realization that he had taken Hungary a long way toward its association with Right-radicalism at home and with Nazi Germany abroad.

The Rise and Evolution of Ultra Rightist Parties and Movements

The duality that characterized the composition and policies of the rightist forces came once again into focus during the later years of Gömbös' rule. Although the forces originally associated with the so-called Vienna and Szeged groups of counterrevolutionaries (see chapter 1) underwent a gradual realignment during Bethlen's Consolidation Era, they continued to remain basically distinct and, while sharing certain common objectives, fundamentally opposed to each other.

The "liberal-conservative" aristocratic-gentry–dominated Vienna faction managed to acquire and consolidate its ruling position in the state by acquiring the support of the foremost representatives of the Szeged group, including that of Horthy and Gömbös. The ultra-rightist factions of the Szeged group, joined by elements particularly hard-hit by the depression, emerged in the course of time as an increasingly aggressive *opposition* force dedicated to the establishment of a National Socialist society at home and to the firm alignment of Hungary's foreign policy with that of the Third Reich. Although both the ruling and the opposition wings of the Hungarian Right shared certain common objectives, including the pursuit of a "revisionist, nationalist-patriotic, Christian, and anti-Bolshevik" policy, the ruling wing tended to adopt a rather moderate Italian-oriented semi-Fascist position, while the opposition was eager to embrace the German brand of National Socialism in its totality. The ambivalence and inconsistencies in Hungary's policies during the interwar period can to a large extent be traced to this division in the political Right.

Perhaps in no other area was this political ambivalence reflected in a more pronounced and dramatic fashion than in the treatment of the Jewish question. Both wings of the Hungarian Right were, of course, anti-Semitic and both were actively concerned with, and sought an effective solution of, this "burning issue." They differed radically, however, on the scope and means to be used. The aristocratic-gentry–dominated ruling wing of the Right, which had good connections with the Jewish upper middle class, aimed at implementing a "civilized" anti-Semitic program calculated not only to gradually diminish and eventually eliminate the Jews' influence from the country's economic and cultural life, but also to appease the Right radicals at home and the National Socialists abroad. In the pursuit of these objectives, this ruling faction subjected the Jews to great economic pressure, depriving a large percentage of them of their livelihood, and to a cruel and humiliating system of discrimination. Nevertheless, it was consistently opposed to any Nazi-style physical action against the Jews. For example, the atrocities that were committed at Kamenets-Podolsk (August 1941) and Délvidék (January 1942) had neither the approval nor the prior knowledge of the government. Furthermore, it successfully resisted the repeated and ever more insistent demands of the Third Reich for the Final Solution of the Jewish question in Hungary.

In fact, the protection of the Jews through this faction's consistent opposition to any Final Solution program proved quite troublesome for the ruling elite in the early 1940s. For, although dedicated to maintaining the inviolability of Hungary's sovereignty and to retaining, if not further cultivating, Hungary's fragile relations with the Western democracies, it was full cognizant that Hungary's revisionist ambitions and trade interests required the country's alignment with the Third Reich.

Whereas the ruling elite supported the Third Reich for reasons of expediency but was gravely concerned with the dangers of German expansionism, the opposition Right radical wing was politically and ideologically attracted and firmly committed to Nazism. It wholeheartedly embraced the National Socialist program not only because of its anti-Semitism, though this was its most attractive aspect, but also because of its emphasis on the advocacy of social and political reforms. The radicals, consequently, wished to bring about the restructuring of Hungary's antiquated semi-feudal social-political order as well as the total "solution" of the Jewish question.

The backbone of the Right radical movement consisted of the original supporters of the "Szeged Idea," namely the elements associated with the governmental and military bureaucracies. During the 1920s and 1930s, the civil servants and the officers' groups were joined by two additional social strata that at once coveted and challenged the dominance of the landed aristocracy and its alliance with Jewish industry and finance. The first consisted of the middle-sized landowners and the Christian middlemen, who were eager to eliminate their Jewish competitors in agriculture and related fields, including the marketing of produce. In foreign affairs, they were particularly anxious to have Hungary tied to the aggressive policies of Nazi Germany for the restoration of Hungary's historical frontiers, and thereby to assure the reacquisition or expansion of their landholdings. The other stratum consisted of the gradually expanding industrial and commercial "Christian bourgeoisie," which wanted to advance its interests by the expansion of the armaments and other state industries in which they had preference and, above all, by the restriction and eventual elimination of their competitors, the well-established Jewish middle class. This stratum, it appears, not only was one of the pillars of the counterrevolutionary Right, but also in a way owed its emergence to rightist support.

The major support of the Right radical movements came from the impoverished gentry and their heirs, the army officers, and from the increasingly urbanized lower middle class. In the 1930s, these were joined by a sizable number of industrial workers and landless peasants whose socialization these movements were particularly eager to achieve.[46] In the absence of any legal political outlet at the extreme Left, these elements of the working and peasant classes were naturally attracted under the conditions of the depression by the demagogic promises of social and economic reforms that the extreme Right offered them.[47]

Ironically, while the Right radicals represented an increasing threat in the 1930s, they also served as the mainstay of a system dominated by the landed aristocracy. This was especially true of the impoverished gentry, which as civil servants and officers retained the mentality of the aristocracy, and of the new middle classes that aspired to advance their status by challenging the position of the Jews in industry and business rather than that of the aristocratic ruling class. The new, economic basis of anti-Semitism which came to the fore in the wake of the changes brought about by Trianon was further broadened by the consequences of the depression. The anti-Semitism fostered by the identification of Jewish bankers, industrialists, and businessmen as the main causes of the country's economic ills was a convenient vehicle not only for channelizing the discontent of the masses, but also for detracting attention from the inequities of the antiquated semi-feudal regime.

Under these conditions, the ruling aristocracy both welcomed and feared the appearance and development of the Right radical movements. Some of these managed to become formidable political parties; others succeeded merely as pressure groups having considerable political nuisance value. These parties and movements underwent frequent changes and mergers determined primarily by the changing political aspirations of their founders and leaders. Despite the number of their adherents and the character of their leadership, the Right radical parties did not acquire any major influence until the late 1930s, and did not attain power until after the German occupation in March 1944.

Political Organizations of the Right. Almost simultaneously with Gömbös' defection and the consequent dissolution of the Race-Protecting Party in 1928, the first Hungarian National Socialist Party (*Nemzeti Szocialista Párt*) appeared on the scene under the leadership of Béla Szász and Miklós Csomós. Emulating their German counterparts, these leaders adopted the Hungarian Double Cross and Sword as their emblem, the green shirt as part of their uniform, and the watchword *Bátorság* (Courage) as the form of greeting for their followers.

Discounting Endre Bajcsy-Zsilinszky's one-man National Radical Party, the first clearly identifiable indigenous Nazi party of any significance was the National Socialist Hungarian Worker's Party (*Nemzeti Szocialista Magyar Munkáspárt*) of Zoltán Böszörmény, the self-styled adventurer "writer, poet, and folk leader." The forerunner of the Scythe Cross Movement (*Kaszáskeresztes Mozgalom*), the Party attempted to emulate the NSDAP in its entirety. Böszörmény, who liked to boast about his personal acquaintance with Hitler, simply adopted much of the Nazi Party's program and outward trappings, including the greeting *Néptárs* (*Volkgenosse*). The Party, founded in 1931, appealed primarily to the landless rural proletariat of the middle Tisza, the area it kept in social ferment for almost five years.[48] The basic elements of its program were already included in Böszörmény's National Socialist Proclamation (*Nemzeti Szocialista Kiáltvány*) of October 1930. It found the basic cause of the people's misery in the usurious activities of the Jews and called for the destruction of liberalism and of the democratic and socialist movements. Besides its vicious incitement against the Jews, the proclamation, like the program, called for the institution of social and economic reforms similar to the ones then being proposed by Hitler.[49]

In June 1932, Zoltán Meskó, a smallholder member of Parliament and one of Böszörmény's original supporters, founded his own "less radical" and more respectable rival party, the Hungarian National Socialist Agricultural Laborers' and Workers' Party (*Magyar Nemzeti Szocialista Mezőgazdasági Dolgozók és Munkások Pártja*). This party, despite its name, was basically "Christian-bourgeois" in character. Its radicalism consisted mostly of its anti-Jewish racism and its chauvinistic nationalism and revisionism. It even paid lip service to loyalty to Horthy by adopting the slogan "With God for the Fatherland! Loyalty to the Regent." However, its uniform (the brown shirt) and its emblem (the Swastika on a brown field) were perhaps more indicative of its ultimate objectives. In 1933, this party was fused with that of Szász and Csomós. The political coalition, under the general leadership of Meskó, adopted the name of Arrow Cross Party (*Nyilaskeresztes Párt*), the green shirt as part of the uniform, and the crossed arrows as the distinguishing badge (figure 2.1).

With the solidification of Hitler's regime in Germany, the ideas and ideals of National Socialism proved increasingly attractive to an ever larger number of Hungarians, giving rise to a veritable political organization mania. Of the many ultra-rightist parties that mushroomed after 1933, however, only a few were of any significance historically. One of these was the Hungarian National Socialist Party (*Magyar Nemzeti Szocialista Párt*) of Count Sándor Festetics, a member of one of the richest aristocratic families of Hungary. Festetics was converted to National Socialism late in 1933, after years of association with the Government Party—in 1918, he had even served in the government of Count Mihály Károlyi as Minister of Defense. Upon the assumption of the Party's leadership from Aladár Hehs, the original founder, Festetics issued a 26-point program containing Hitler's panaceas for the solution of socioeconomic ills as adapted to the specific conditions of Hungary. It advocated, among other things, that only members of the "Turanian and Aryan race of irreproachable loyalty" could aspire to full citizenship, with the right to hold public office or own real estate.[50]

Figure 2.1.
The Arrow Cross (*Nyilaskereszt*): The emblem of the Hungarian Radical Right Movements.

Another ultra-rightist party of considerable importance was the United National Socialist Party (*Egyesült Nemzeti Szocialista Párt*) of Count Fidél Pálffy, a somewhat impoverished member of Hungary's aristocracy. The program and organizational structure of this party emulated the Hitlerian counterparts, complete with Swastika and Storm Troops and SS, which were subsequently outlawed by the government. This party acquired a considerable number of seats in local government in western Hungary and especially in Zala County, where it enjoyed great popularity.[51]

An attempt to unite the Right radical movement was made in January 1934, when Festetics, Meskó, and Pálffy formed a "Directorate" and adopted the green shirt and the Arrow Cross as their common insignia. Within half a year, however, the conflicting personalities and ambitions of the triumvirate brought an end to the dream of a united rightist movement. Festetics, accused of all things of being insufficiently anti-Semitic,[52] was expelled in June 1934. He thereafter joined the local Hungarian National Socialist Party of István Balogh, Jr., a radical landowner of Debrecen, under the auspices of which both Balogh and Festetics were elected to the lower house of the Hungarian Parliament as the representatives of the extreme Right in the elections of 1935. Meskó and Pálffy continued to collaborate within their newly renamed party, the National Socialist Party of Hungary (*Magyarország Nemzeti Szocialista Pártja*), until September 1935, when Meskó, having been ousted by Pálffy, resuscitated his original party.

But by this time all of the early starters in National Socialist experiments were overshadowed by a new political figure who was to personify the Right radical movement until the end of World War II: Ferenc Szálasi.

Ferenc Szálasi. The character of Hungary's Right radical movement is to a large extent typified by Szálasi's social background, education, and military-political career. He was born in Kassa on January 6, 1897, of mixed Magyar, Armenian, and Slovak stock. Brought up in a strict family, Szálasi, like his father and two brothers, pursued a military career, first at the Military *Real* School of Kőszeg and then at the Military Academy of Wiener Neustadt (Bécsujhely). Following his graduation as a First Lieutenant in 1915, he spent close to three years in the First World War as liaison with the General Staff. Appointed to the General Staff in 1925, Szálasi attracted the attention of his superiors first by his writings on military subjects and then by his political polemics. His career with the General Staff was promising. By 1932, he had become a popular lecturer on political-military subjects and the following year was promoted to the rank of Major.

An ardent nationalist, he was extremely upset by Hungary's dismemberment and devoted most of his energies to the development of a political-ideological program which, he was convinced, would lead to the restoration of the historic state. The basic outlines of this program were worked out while he was a member of the Hungarian Life League (*Magyar Élet Szövetség*), the secret "race-protecting" organization founded by Árpád Taby. He joined the League in 1930 and soon emerged as its chief ideologist and organizer. In August of that year, his political-conspiratorial activities were brought to the attention of Gömbös, then Minister of Defense, who warned him against any further political involvements or the propagation of his "dangerous" views.

Szálasi was not deterred, however, from his single-minded objective, and in 1933 published his first major political-ideological work, the "Plan for the Construction of the Hungarian State" (*A magyar állam felépítésének terve*). Influenced by the ideas and experiences of Italian Fascism, he advocated the restructuring of the Hungarian state along authoritarian lines and the introduction of the corporate system. The book also contains the outlines of his "Hungarist" ideas about the role a restored Hungary would play in the Danube Basin. These latter ideas were further elaborated and crystallized in his *Cél és követelések* (Goal and Demands), published in 1933.

His grandiose, impractical plan for a new historic Hungarian state reflects his idealism and naïveté. Motivated by Great Magyar imperialistic designs, his plan called for the establishment of a new Hungarist state to be known as "The Carpathian-Danubian Great Fatherland" and as the "United Lands and the March of Hungaria." Envisioned to encompass what he called the Ancestral Land (*Ősföld*), i.e., "the area engirdled by the Carpathians and reaching down to the Adriatic," the Hungarist State was to consist of six "Component Lands" (*Részföldek*)[53] in which the Magyars were to play a dominant political role. The supremacy of the Hungarians in the United Lands was to be assured, among other things, by the exclusive use of Magyar as the official language of the "direction and leadership of the state."

A mystic and a practicing spiritualist, Szálasi firmly believed that he was called upon by Providence to save Hungary, and, through Hungarism, Europe. Like Hitler, he was driven by a messianistic ardor and demanded total subordination by his followers:

He who does not identify himself with my doctrine, who does not recognize me unreservedly as leader and will not agree that I have been selected by a higher Divine authority to redeem the Magyar people—he who does not understand me or loses confidence—let him go! At most, I shall remain alone, but even alone I shall create the Hungarist State with the help of the secret force that is within me.[54]

While his *Führer* principles and ultimate political objectives were clearly defined, his socioeconomic views were quite nebulous. Like all ultra-rightists, he advocated the necessity of changing the guard (*őrségváltás*), denoting primarily the replacement of the Jews in the economy. His socioeconomic program was basically a blend of Fascist corporatism and German National Socialism intermingled with some peculiarly Hungarian ideas, including agrarian capitalism, which was particularly supported by the impoverished gentry and their heirs. In contrast to the anti-religious motifs in both Fascism and Nazism, the

Nyilas, as the Hungarian extreme rightists are popularly referred to, emphasized the "Christian idea" as the inner core of their ideology. Undoubtedly this was partially due to the great influence the Christian churches had exerted in Hungary. However, the overriding reason was the politically motivated desire of the *Nyilas* to demonstrate their stand against Jews, Bolsheviks, liberals, and like-minded internationalists.

Szálasi's ideas about the Jews were not fundamentally different from those of the other ultra-rightists. Nevertheless, he was not so pathological in his hatred of the Jews as Hitler or Himmler or László Endre, the nemesis of Hungarian Jewry. Although he is identified with the most horrible period in the history of Hungary (the nearly seven months of terror following the coup against Horthy on October 15, 1944), he was in fact relatively more moderate than many of his contemporaries. While he often referred to the menace represented by the destructive forces of "Judaeo-Bolshevism," he saw the solution of the Jewish question in their voluntary, induced, or forced mass emigration. He was, theoretically at least, even prepared to allow the Jews to take along their movable property. But until such a mass emigration was realized, he sought to regulate the Jewish question in a "constitutional" manner by identifying and treating the Jews as a separate race. As interim solutions, Szálasi advocated the withdrawal of all residence and artisan permits issued after 1900, the permanent halting of all further Jewish immigration, and the "extirpation of the Jewish spirit wherever visible and the practical build-up of the Christian spirit without any compromises."[55]

Although an eccentric and a mystic often quite out of touch with reality, Szálasi was in his own fashion a very patriotic and sensitive man scrupulously dedicated to his beliefs and principles. He was as vehemently opposed to any compromises over his grandiose Hungarist ideas as he was adamant about upholding the sovereignty of Hungary. Perhaps because of these personality traits, Szálasi never actually advocated reliance upon physical means for the Final Solution of the Jewish question along "foreign" (i.e., Nazi) lines. According to some reports, he was opposed to the deportation of the Jews during the German occupation, presumably because of its infringement on Hungarian sovereignty.[56] He never tried, of course, to stop or interfere with the deportations; however, one must admit that these were already taking place before the *Nyilas* acquired power. Although there is no conclusive evidence on whether he actually ordered the draconic measures that were adopted against the Jews during his infamous rule, he undoubtedly influenced them, directly or indirectly, and therefore must share full responsibility for them.

The Szálasi Parties. In Szálasi's scheme of ideas, the instrumentality through which he hoped to achieve his ultimate goal—the restoration of historic Hungary and the concurrent safeguarding of Christian Europe under his divine leadership—was the party. Like almost all his counterparts of the extreme Right and Left, both past and present, he realized the importance of organization, training, and indoctrination under the auspices of a monolithic party. Szálasi's first vehicle on the road to power was the Nation's Will Party (*A Nemzet Akaratának Pártja*), which he organized almost immediately after he resigned his army commission in March 1935. Cooperating with him was Sándor Csia, his life-long friend. Adopting Szálasi's *Goal and Demands* as its program, the Party proved particularly attractive to the former members of the Hungarian Life League and of Böszörmény's movement. At first, the recruitment drive was concentrated in the countryside, especially in the Pest and Sopron areas; later, the Party's attention was focussed on the organization of the workers in the industrial centers, for which purpose a new journal—the New Hungarian Worker (*Uj Magyar Munkás*)—was published. The popularity of the Party was further enhanced by the mass distribution of leaflets, posters, and pamphlets inciting against the Jews, which proved particularly attractive to the disillusioned lower middle class and related traditional "Szegedist" elements associated with the many equally impotent ultra-Rightist factional parties and movements.

The relative success of Szálasi's movement was enhanced not only by the propitious domestic climate, but also, and perhaps even more decisively, by the international successes of Fascism and Nazism. It was during this period that Italy launched its League-of-Nations–defying imperialistic war against Ethiopia and that Hitler scored some of his most spectacular successes. The Führer's vast rearmament program, which not only helped the recovery of the German economy but also rekindled the hope in the possible "imminent" undoing of the "injustices" of Versailles, coupled with the "illegal" remilitarization of the Rhineland, captured the imagination of many of his followers abroad. The hope of revising the Versailles arrangement and the international order sanctified by the League of Nations was further bolstered by the Axis Alliance and the Anti-Comintern Pact and the consequent German-Italian involvement in the Spanish Civil War. In addition to Hitler's modernizing socioeconomic measures associated with his preparations for war, his merciless handling of the Jewish question, including the adoption of the Nuremberg Laws, mesmerized most of the Hungarian Right extremists.

The polarization of Hungary's domestic political life, already clearly discernible during Gömbös' last year in office, was further exacerbated after his death. The rising tide of rightist extremism was increasingly recognized as a clear threat not only to the Jews, but also to the ruling landed magnates. Kálmán Darányi, who succeeded Gömbös to the Premiership on October 10, 1936, at first gave the distinct impression that, under the influence of the Bethlenite forces, he was trying to reestablish the domestic political balance of the late 1920s without, however, jeopardizing Hungary's increasingly close relations with the Third Reich. This was reinforced by his actions not only against the *Nyilas*, whom the Nazis had not yet openly embraced, but also against the Right wing of the Government Party. The latter, under Gömbös and Béla Marton, the Secretary General, was by all appearances striving to transform itself into a dominant "mass party" for the initiation of radical reforms from within. Marton was squeezed out of his position in January 1937. A month later, Miklós Kozma, the pro-Gömbös Minister of the Interior (in charge of the police and gendarmerie), was compelled to resign. However, Darányi's political motivations and objectives were ambivalent and nebulous. While overtly he was firmly associated with the pro-Horthy forces, covertly he sympathized with many of the ideas of the ultra-rightists. He consequently encouraged the reinvigoration of some of the major "national Christian" societies, including the TESz and the MOVE. He was also instrumental in the promotion of new ones, including Marton's Fascist labor organization, the "National Labor Center" (*Nemzeti Munkaközpont—NMK*).

Under the Presidency of János Szeder, the Right-wing Government Party deputy from Csongrád, MOVE suddenly adopted a particularly aggressive posture. In possession of thousands of rifles issued to it by Gömbös, it offered paramilitary training to its members, ostensibly to complement the mission of the *Honvédség.* However, its real designs were more immediate and political. Confident in their new role and increasingly disappointed by the trend of domestic political events, the MOVE leaders, openly encouraged or supported by such rightist figures as Baross, Marton, and Mecsér, decided to oust Darányi in a coup. This overt attempt of early March 1937 brought to the fore the real danger the extremists represented for the integrity of the state and for the stability of the semi-feudalistic social order. Demands for resolute action to curb their power and influence were advanced with increasing frequency and loudness in both houses of the Parliament as well as in the press. Responding to this pressure, József Széll, the new Minister of the Interior, ordered (April 15) the dissolution of the Nation's Will Party and the arrest of its leading officers, including Szálasi. He was at first condemned to three months' imprisonment, but pending his appeal he was released after only ten days in jail.

The government's resolute actions brought only a temporary respite to the country's internal political turmoil. Within a short while, Szálasi in fact managed to turn his legal difficulties into valuable political assets. The regime, too, soon learned that Szálasi's arrest and temporary incarceration[57] merely increased his stature among his followers. Szálasi was very skillful in exploiting his sudden martyrdom for the recruitment of new members[58] and for the acquisition of powerful allies within the political and military establishments. Among the former, he acquired the support of men like András Mecsér, a leader of the Government Party's Right wing, Kálmán Hubay, a journalist and a former staunch supporter of Gömbös, and László Endre and László Baky, two notorious anti-Semites and the later architects of the Final Solution program in Hungary (see chapter 13). Among the military, by far the most important new supporters were General Jenő Rátz, the Chief of the General Staff, and General Jenő Ruszkay. Szálasi also managed to acquire the support of such nonestablishment but influential figures as Ferenc (Franz) Rothen, one of the leaders of the *Volksdeutsche* in the service of the Germans, and Ödön Málnási, the historian, who was destined to emerge as one of the major ideologues of the Party.[59]

Taking advantage of his national appeal and of his newly discovered charisma, Szálasi proceeded with his plans for the unification of the Right radical movement and for its transformation into a powerful and effective political force. In October 1937, he was instrumental in the establishment of a new political party, the Hungarian National Socialist Party (*A Magyar Nemzeti Szocialista Párt*), by fusing his still amorphous movement with Balogh's National Socialist Party and the Race-Protecting Socialist Party (*Fajvédő Szocialista Párt*), which had been founded shortly before by Endre and Lajos Széchenyi. Placed under the leadership of a triumvirate composed of Balogh, Szálasi, and Széchenyi, this party soon came under the *de facto* leadership of Szálasi alone. However, Szálasi's goal, rightist unity, was only partially fulfilled, for his party was still in competition with three other relatively influential ultra-rightist parties—those of Festetics and Pálffy, and János Salló's

"National Front" (*Nemzeti Front*).[60] Nevertheless, the strength and influence of the new party grew sufficiently ominous to elicit the government's almost immediate response. On February 20, 1938, the Political Bureau of the National Police Headquarters in Budapest reminded the government in a lengthy memorandum that the new party advocated the same goals and relied upon the same methods as the dissolved Nation's Will Party.[61] Four days later, the Party was declared illegal and Szálasi and 72 other activists were placed under police surveillance.

But by this time the Right radical movement was too strong and its successes too well known[62] to be effectively controlled exclusively by administrative measures, however prompt and resolute. The difficulty was compounded by the tremendous impact of the Anschluss, which not only transformed the Third Reich into an immediate neighbor of the country but also raised the irredentists' hopes for an imminent realization of their long-awaited territorial revisionist designs. Darányi had hoped to counteract the effects of his administrative actions by adopting some of the policies advocated by the Right radicals. By doing this, he, like many of his successors of the ruling Right, hoped to take the wind out of the radicals' sails and at the same time earn the appreciation of the Third Reich. It was under these circumstances that he announced in his famous Győr speech of March 5, 1938, that Hungary was embarking on a massive rearmament program and that the Jewish question would be solved "in a legal and orderly fashion."[63] Darányi had also hoped to weaken, if not disarm, the extremists by co-opting them into the system. He persuaded Szálasi, who was then under police surveillance and quite anxious to secure parliamentary representation for his party, to collaborate with him within the country's constitutional framework. Szálasi was, of course, never deterred from pursuing his ultimate objective and used this agreement primarily for short-term gains. In the spirit of this understanding, Hubay was enabled to join the lower house by running to all intents and purposes unopposed in the by-elections that were held in Lovasberény on March 27.[64] Darányi apparently also assured the *Nyilas* via Hubay that at the next elections the government would somehow make seven to ten seats available to them. Emboldened by this rapprochement aimed at the "normalization" and "legalization" of the Right radical movement, Hubay launched a new Szálasi-oriented Party, the National Socialist Hungarian Party—Hungarist Movement (*Nemzeti Szocialista Magyar Párt—Hungarista Mozgalom*).[65] In the spirit of the political détente reached between the two wings of the Right, Hubay defined the Party's aims as "The governing of the historic Great Hungarian State on the basis of the world-view of National Socialism without relying upon any illegal or revolutionary means and by upholding the evolutionary Hungarian national historical constitution."[66]

This understanding, which was apparently reached without the full knowledge of the Bethlenite forces, was short-lived, if ever really implemented. The landed aristocracy and their industrial and financial allies rightly feared that such an understanding was bound to become counterproductive and in fact facilitate the expansion of the Right radical movement. Darányi was compelled to resign on May 13 without seeing the fruition of his grand design. His successor, Béla Imrédy, a highly respected financial expert and at the time known for his pro-Western inclinations, was at first quite energetic in curbing the extremists. However, the Right radicals continued to flourish even while Szálasi lingered in prison. This was partially due to the reorganization and reinvigoration of the Hungarist Party,[67] but above all to the radical shift in Imrédy's position (see chapter 4). For the Jews, the political climate had become particularly ominous since Darányi at Győr publicly and officially announced the existence, and the necessity for the solution, of the Jewish question. From that time on, the Jewish question in Hungary was no longer primarily a polemical issue kept in the limelight by the extreme Right;[68] it became the focus of the government's attention, and was to be solved on an institutional basis.[69]

Notes

1. The Government Party was the unofficial name of the ruling coalition that dominated Hungarian politics throughout the Horthy era. It was formed in July 1920 under the leadership of Bethlen through the merger of the Smallholders' Party (Kisgazda Párt) and the Legitimist Christian National Union (A Keresztény Nemzeti Egyesülés Pártja). The diehard Legitimists were excluded in February 1922, when the Government Party was reorganized in the wake of King Charles' attempts to regain the throne. For further details on the Party's background and evolution see chapter 1.

2. The lower house of the new Hungarian Parliament was officially known as the House of Representatives of the Hungarian National Assembly (A Magyar Országgyűlés Képviselőháza). The upper house of the National Assembly (A Magyar Országgyűlés Felsőháza) was reestablished by Bethlen under Act No. XXII of November 15, 1926. It consisted of four types of members: hereditary, ex-officio, elected, and appointed. With a membership of close to 250, the upper house acquired in 1937 (Law No. XXVII) virtual equality with the lower house except in financial affairs. In the 1930s and 1940s, the upper house emerged as a relative bastion of traditional decency against the onslaught of Right radicalism. Some of the most vocal and effective protectors of the rights of the Jews had served in this house.

3. Under an agreement of December 1921, the Socialists, while free to publish their own organ (*Népszava;* the People's Voice) and organize the industrial workers, were prohibited from engaging in political strikes and "antinational propaganda" and from organizational work among the peasants, agricultural workers, and civil servants. They also undertook to support the regime's revisionist ambitions. The Government Party had no difficulty in sweeping all parliamentary elections during the Horthy era. During Bethlen's tenure, the Party, then officially known as the Party of National Unity (*Nemzeti Egység Pártja*), won overwhelmingly in the elections of 1922, 1926, and 1931, acquiring 143, 170, and 158, seats, respectively, out of a total of 245. For detailed electoral data, see Joseph Rothschild, *East Central Europe Between the Two World Wars.* (Seattle: University of Washington Press, 1974), p. 161.

4. A result of the plebiscite of December 14–16, 1921, which was held under the supervision of the Italians.

5. Under Law No. XXXVI of December 7, 1920, only a little over a million cadastral yokes of generally inferior land were distributed to about 700,000 recipients. Moreover, while the original owners were fully compensated, the new ones were burdened with prohibitive redemption payments that soon became ruinous for most of them. Rothschild, *East Central Europe,* p. 159.

6. Hungary, for example, retained the following percentages of her pre-war agricultural assets (excluding Croatia-Slavonia): vineyards, 68.4; arable land, 42.9; pasturage, 30.5; meadows, 25.1; gardens, 25.0; marshlands, 54.0; and uncultivable land, 39.0. Since much of her industry was concentrated in and around Budapest, her industrial assets were even more formidable. Specifically, Hungary retained the following percentages of pre-war industrial capacity (computed on the basis of value of production): machine industry, 90.1; printing, 89.5; clothing, 76.7; electric power, 60.4; leather, 57.8; stoneware and earthenware, 57.7; chemical, 56.8; food processing, 55.7; and iron and metallurgical, 50.3. Rothschild, *East Central Europe,* pp. 167–68.

7. The *Pengő,* equal to 0.26315789 grain of fine gold, was adopted on November 3, 1925, to replace the Crown (*Korona*) as the country's currency. During the 1941–42 period, the official value of the *Pengő* was approximately 20 cents. The black market price of the dollar, however, ranged from about 11 to 13 *Pengős.* Sándor Ausch, *Az 1945–46. évi infláció és stabilizáció* (The Inflation and Stabilization of 1945–46) (Budapest: Kossuth, 1958), pp. 30–31.

8. C. A. Macartney, an admirer of Bethlen, states quite accurately that the Prime Minister was "by temperament allergic beyond most of his class to Jews, and given to expressing his distaste for them to his intimates in free and forceful language." C. A. Macartney, 1:38.

9. Dezső Sulyok, *A magyar tragédia* (The Hungarian Tragedy). (Newark, N.J.: The Author, 1954), p. 512.

10. Lévai, *Zsidósors Magyarországon,* p. 11.

11. Decree No. 20,000 of 1920, which, because of its highly confidential nature, was not even published in the Code of Decrees (*Rendeletek Tára*). For references to it see *Horthy Miklós titkos iratai* (The Confidential Papers of Miklós Horthy), eds. Miklós Szinai and László Szücs. (Budapest: Kossuth, 1963), pp. 82-109.

12. *Ibid.*

13. Lévai, *Zsidósors Magyarországon,* p. 13.

14. By 1931, wholesale agricultural prices had fallen to 78.5 percent of their 1929 level, and by 1933 to 62.7 percent. The value of industrial production in 1933 had fallen to 61 percent of the 1929 level. While some sectors, including textiles, leather, and paper, were less drastically affected, the production of others, like agricultural machinery, virtually ceased. During the corresponding period, average incomes fell by 23 percent, and the unemployment rate among industrial workers and artisans rose from 5 to 35.9 per-

cent. These declines were compounded by the collapse of the Credit Anstalt of Vienna through which the Hungarian banks were connected with the Western credit system causing grave currency difficulties and a scarcity of foreign exchange. Rothschild, *East Central Europe*, p. 170.

15. Bethlen's popularity had already suffered a setback in 1926 in the wake of the scandals relating to the mass counterfeiting of French francs on the premises of the Hungarian Cartographical Institute. The operation involved leading members of the Hungarian and German rightist political and governmental establishments, who pleaded "patriotic" motives. On September 24, 1926, Bethlen, shaken by the impact of the scandals, even offered his resignation to Horthy. For the text of his resignation offer see *Horthy Miklós titkos iratai*, pp. 61–68.

16. For documents on the Bethlen era, see *Bethlen István titkos iratai* (The Confidential Papers of István Bethlen), eds. Miklós Szinai and László Szücs. (Budapest: Kossuth, 1972), 492 pp.

17. Upon Gaál's death in October 1932, the Party came under the leadership of Tibor Eckhardt, the former leader of the Race-Protecting Party and of the Association of Awakening Magyars (see chapter 1).

18. *Horthy Miklós titkos iratai*, pp. 82–109.

19. Miklós Lackó, "Az Új Szellemi Front történetéhez" (Contributions to the History of the New Intellectual Front). *Századok* (Centuries), Budapest, no. 4–5 (1972):920.

20. *Ibid.*

21. Lévai, *Zsidósors Magyarországon*, p. 17.

22. *Ibid.*, p. 18.

23. Rudolfné Dosa, *A MOVE. Egy jellegzetes magyar fasiszta szervezet, 1918–1944* (The MOVE. A Characteristic Hungarian Fascist Organization, 1919–1944) (Budapest: Akadémiai Kiadó, 1972), p. 126.

24. Erik Molnár, *Magyarország története* (The History of Hungary). (Budapest: Gondolat, 1967), 2:382.

25. Dosa, *A MOVE*, p. 137.

26. C. A. Macartney, 1:73.

27. It called for a vague agricultural reform; reduction of taxes; regulation of agricultural indebtedness; credits for industry and agriculture; development of foreign trade; a balanced budget; orientation toward Italy in foreign affairs; and introduction of secret and general suffrage. C. A. Macartney, 1:101.

28. An agreement was reportedly reached between Gőmbős and four members of the upper house under which the latter offered political and financial backing in return for a promise that once in power Gőmbős would not pass laws relating to stocks and bonds and would not extend the conditions relating to "Parliamentary incompatibility" to the upper house. *Ibid.*, pp. 100–101.

29. *Ibid.*, p. 103.

30. *Ibid.*, p. 117.

31. Sulyok, *A magyar tragédia*, pp. 512–13.

32. Lévai, *Zsidósors Magyarországon*, p. 19.

33. *Ibid.*

34. Among Szekfü's most famous books was his controversial *Három nemzedék* (Three Generations), first published in Budapest in 1920. Originally a pro-Hapsburg apologist, Szekfü emerged after World War I as a critic of the dualist era and, by focusing attention on the country's serious socioeconomic problems, a champion of the counterrevolutionary regime. In the 1930s, Szekfü, who taught history at the University of Budapest, crystallized the fear of Nazism and German expansionism. After World War II, he served for awhile as Ambassador to Moscow.

Another prominent Hungarian writer who served the cause of the counterrevolution at first, but later turned against the official leadership for having restored the old order under the camouflage of being "Christian and national," was Dezső Szabó, the author of the influential sociological novel *Az elsodort falú* (The Village That Was Swept Away), first published in 1919. He identified the true cause of racially pure Magyardom with the cause of the Magyar peasantry.

35. Lévai, *Zsidósors Magyarországon*, pp. 20–21.

36. The national convention of the Neolog community started on March 4 and that of the Orthodox community on August 17.

37. *Horthy Miklós titkos iratai*, pp. 131–35.

38. *Ibid.*, pp. 136–38.

39. For the breakdown of the electoral results see Rothschild, *East Central Europe*, p. 174.

40. Interestingly enough, both houses of the Hungarian Parliament continued to include a number of Jews and converts. The upper house, for example, included in addition to the *ex officio* members of the Jewish community (Immanuel Löw and Koppel Reich, representing the Neolog and Orthodox communities respectively) several converts and Jews, including Lajos Láng and Jenő Vida. Among the Jews of various political persuasion who served in the lower house were Ernő Bródy, Manó Buchinger, József Büchler, Imre Győrki, Miklós Kertész, Pál Sándor, and János Vázsonyi. Because of his seniority, Pál Sándor was in fact asked by Gömbős to head the house. Gömbős also placed a number of Jews on his Budapest party list. Among these were Róbert Szurday and Mór Lédermann. See also Lévai, *Fekete könyv*, pp. 18–19.

41. C. A. Macartney, 1:155.

42. *Ibid.*, p. 148.

43. For a detailed review of Gömbös' foreign policy, see *ibid.*, pp. 136–54.

44. Among the major agents of the Third Reich were men like Péter Hain, an influential member of the Hungarian police and of Horthy's circle, and László Baky, who played a leading role in the destruction of the Jews in 1944.

45. For further details, see Robert Major, *25 év ellenforradalmi sajtó, 1919–1944* (Twenty-Five Years of Counterrevolutionary Press, 1919–1944) (Budapest: Cserépfalvi, 1945), 108 pp.

46. The cause of the smallholding and landless peasants was also championed by a number of dedicated, but generally equally ineffective, groups of which by far the most important was that known as the "Village Explorers" (*Falukutatók*). An amorphous group that included journalists, historians, sociologists, and economists as well as novelists and poets, the explorers shared a common disillusionment with Gömbös' social demagoguery and a common desire to bring about meaningful reforms as urgently as possible. For this purpose, these modern-day populists, including Géza Féja, organized themselves in 1937 into a "March Front," historically identifying themselves with the revolutionaries of March 1848. However, in the late 1930s, their dichotomous character was fully revealed: some of them, including the poets József Erdélyi and István Sinka, became associated with the ultra-Right movements; others, including Imre Kovács, Péter Veres, and József Darvas, turned to the Left. The latter were also instrumental in establishing the "National Peasant Party" (*Nemzeti Paraszt Párt*) and were closely associated with the ideas and policies of the so-called "third road" (*harmadik út*) approach first crystallized by the writer László Németh. This approach had called for active resistance against both German and Russian expansionism.

For a critical view of the Populists' policies, see Asher Cohen's "Giz'anut vantishemiut basmol hapopulisti beHungaria. Hasofer vehamedinai Péter Veres" (Racism and Anti-Semitism in the Populist Left in Hungary. The Writer and Politician Péter Veres) in *Dapim lecheker tekufat hashoa* (Studies on the Holocaust Period) (Tel Aviv: Hakibbutz Hameuchad, 1978), 1:176–88.

47. The Hungarian Communist Party was outlawed *de facto* shortly after the victory of the counterrevolutionary forces in 1919. *De jure,* it was declared illegal under Law No. III of 1921 relating to the "More Effective Protection of the Order of the State and Society." The anti-sedition provisions of the law were effectively exploited by the counterrevolutionary as well as the post-World War II regimes. The law prohibited, *inter alia,* agitating or inducing others "to subvert by force or destroy the legal order of the state and society especially by advocating the forcible establishment of the exclusive domination of one particular social class." Particularly pernicious was the provision that called for the punishment of "any person who makes or spreads a false statement calculated to reduce the respect for the Hungarian state and nation or to detract from its good name."

48. On May 1, 1936, Böszörmény launched a quixotic uprising in Nagykőrös with the aim of acquiring power through the conquest of Kecskemét, Cegléd, and ultimately Budapest. It was crushed as soon as it was started. Böszörmény, who pleaded insanity, was sentenced to two and a half years and allowed to escape to Germany. In 1945, following the liberation of Hungary, he appealed to Mátyás Rákosi, then head of the Communist Party, to be admitted as member. C. A. Macartney, 1:159.

49. Miklós Lackó, *Nyilasok, nemzetiszocialisták, 1935–1944* (Arrow-Cross Men, National Socialists, 1933–1944). (Budapest: Kossuth, 1966), pp. 16, 18–19.

50. C.A. Macartney, 1:158; Lackó, *Nyilasok, nemzetiszocialisták,* pp. 16, 20–21.

51. C. A. Macartney, 1:159.

52. Festetics was reproached, among other things, for employing Jewish bailiffs on his large estate. Like many rightists of the early 1930s, when the depression was raging, Festetics also believed that the "Final Solution" of the Jewish question would have to be postponed because of the feared possible further economic dislocations that it might bring about. *Ibid.* See also Lackó, *Nyilasok, nemzetiszocialisták,* p. 56.

53. These were to be the Magyar-Land (*Magyarföld*), Slovak-Land (*Tótföld*), Ruthene-Land (*Ruténföld*), Transylvanian-Land (*Erdélyföld*), Croatian-Slavonian-Land (*Horvát-Szlavonföld*), and the Western Border-Land (*Nyugat-gyepű*). The Magyar-Land was envisioned as encompassing the entire plains, incorporating most of the territories of historic Hungary.

54. C. A. Macartney, 1:160–61.

55. Lackó, *Nyilasok, nemzetiszocialisták,* p. 57. Szálasi's ideas about Hungarism, including its aspect as Pax Hungarica and its moral, spiritual, and material foundations, were also outlined in his *Út és Cél* (Road and Goal), which was originally published in 1936 and reissued by his followers in Argentina in October 1954.

56. C. A. Macartney, 1:165.

57. Shortly after his release, he and Csia visited the Third Reich "to study German revolutionary techniques," but apparently met no one of importance there. He was again tried in July 1937 and was condemned in November to ten months' imprisonment for "seditious conspiracy." In July 1938, the Court reviewed his case and in light of his further seditious activities during the interim period increased his sentence to three years' hard labor and five years' loss of civil rights. On August 16, the *Kuria* (Hungary's Supreme Court) upheld the sentence and ordered Szálasi's immediate arrest. Taken to Szeged Prison on August 27, he was not released until September 18, 1940—shortly after the incorporation of Northern Transylvania.

58. Although there are no official or absolutely reliable membership data available, the evidence provided in secondary sources in recent years demonstrates the dramatic growth in Szálasi's following between 1935 and 1944. Accordingly, the membership of his party grew from around 8,000 in September 1935, to approximately 19,000 in April 1937, to 116,000 at the end of 1940, and to 500,000 in September 1944. These figures do not include the approximately 100,000 members of the various National Socialist factions or parties not under Szálasi's control. In terms of its composition, Szálasi's following was as

follows: industrial workers, from 41 to 50 percent; peasants, from 8 to 13 percent; professionals and self-employed, from 12 to 19 percent; and military officers, about 17 percent. Measured by the election results of May, 1939, Szálasi's influence was even greater. The *Nyilas* acquired approximately 750,000 of the nearly 2 million votes cast. István Deák, "Hungary," in *The European Right*, eds. Hans Rogger and Eugen Weber (Berkeley: University of California Press, 1966), pp. 392, 396–97.

59. Hubay began his journalistic career in a Liberal Jewish-owned paper in Miskolc. He subsequently joined the *Függetlenség* (Independence), the Government Party organ, from which he was dismissed for having attacked Darányi. In November 1937, he first joined Pálffy's Party and then shifted his allegiance to Szálasi. In 1938, Rátz was promoted to Minister of Defense. Partially because of his association with Béla Imrédy, with whom he established the Party of Hungarian Renewal (*A Magyar Megújulás Pártja*), he was appointed Deputy Prime Minister in Sztójay's government of March 1944 (see chapter 13). Originally known as Ranzenberger, Ruszkay was also associated with the General Staff. Because of his linguistic skills he also served in the Hungarian Intelligence service. Rothen had served as Szálasi's expert on foreign affairs until his escape to Germany in 1939. There he served as the *Referent* for East Central Europe in the German Foreign Office. He also doubled as an intelligence agent in close touch with his Hungarian hirelings. Málnási joined Szálasi in the fall of 1937. One of the central theses of his ideology was the close interrelationship between Hungarian Fascism and Christianity in contrast to the paganism found in Hitler's National Socialism.

60. Balogh was expelled soon after the fusion because at a *Nyilas* rally in Debrecen he outlined some "unauthorized" plans for the establishment of a National Kingdom with Horthy to be crowned as King Miklós I. His indiscretion angered both Horthy and Szálasi, but for different reasons.

61. The Chief of the Political Bureau was József Sombor-Schweinitzer, a loyal supporter of the conservative aristocratic regime and basically quite a decent individual. It was primarily because of his political attitude that he was removed soon after the German occupation. Much of what we know about the inner workings and development of the Right radical movement in Hungary is due to his unpublished study prepared in 1943: *A magyar nemzetiszocialista mozgalmak története* (The History of the Hungarian National Socialist Movements). Lackó, *Nyilasok, nemzetiszocialisták*, p. 60.

62. In January 1938, for example, Endre was elected Deputy Prefect of Pest County. The membership and following of the rightist movements grew by leaps and bounds (see note 58, above).

63. Historically, one can identify this speech as the beginning of the anti-Jewish drive in Hungary which culminated in the deportations of 1944. Its immediate impact was the adoption of the First Anti-Jewish Law (see chapter 4).

64. The alliance between Szálasi and Hubay was cemented by a mutual oath taken at the grave of Gömbös.

65. Hubay became the Party President in charge of politics and organization; Szálasi assumed the title of National Leader, reserving for himself the Party's spiritual direction. For the structural and organizational details of the Party see István Deák, "Hungary," pp. 395–96.

66. Lackó, *Nyilasok, nemzetiszocialisták*, p. 106.

67. The *Nyilas* movement and Hungarist Party continued to undergo a series of changes between 1938 and 1944. Following the acquisition of the *Magyarság* (Magyardom), a Hungarian daily, by Oliver Rupprecht (May 27, 1938), who placed it in the service of the Hungarists, the Right radical movement acquired added momentum. Hubay, who became the daily's new editor, was joined by Baky and other extremists of his ilk. In August, Festetics decided to join the bandwagon by merging his party with that of Hubay under the name of the "Hungarian National Socialist Party—Hungarist Movement"

(*A Magyar Nemzeti Szocialista Part—Hungarista Mozgalom*). This new Party operated under the leadership of Hubay and Széchenyi until February 23, 1939, when it was dissolved by Prime Minister Pál Teleki. It reappeared shortly thereafter under the name of the "Arrow Cross Party" (*Nyilaskeresztes Párt*).

68. For a succinct review of the Hungarian ultra-Rightist movements and parties and of their anti-Jewish stand, as well as of the forces of anti-Semitism with emphasis on the British perception of Hungarian domestic politics in the 1930s, see Béla Vágó, *The Shadow of the Swastika. The Rise of Fascism and Anti-Semitism in the Danube Basin, 1936–1939* (London: Saxon House for the Institute of Jewish Affairs, 1975), pp. 17–57.

69. For additional material on Hungarian Fascism or proto-Fascism consult: Deák, "Hungary," pp. 364–407; George Bárány, "Hungary: From Aristocratic to Proletarian Nationalism," in *Nationalism in Eastern Europe*, eds. Peter F. Sugar and Ivo J. Lederer (Seattle: University of Washington Press, 1969), pp. 259–309; Bárány, "The Dragon's Teeth: The Roots of Hungarian Fascism," in *Native Fascism in the Successor States, 1918–1945*, ed. Peter F. Sugar (Santa Barbara: ABC-CLIO Press, 1971), pp. 73–82; György Ránki, "The Problem of Fascism in Hungary," *ibid.*, pp. 65–72; Eugen Weber, *Varieties of Fascism* (Princeton: Van Nostrand, 1964), pp. 88–96, 156–64; Bernard Klein, *Hungarian Politics from Bethlen to Gömbös: The Decline of Liberal Conservatism and the Rise of Right Radicalism*, Ph.D. dissertation, Columbia University, New York, 1962, 258 pp; and Jenő Lévai, *Horogkereszt, Kaszáskereszt, Nyilaskereszt* (Swastika, Scythe Cross, Arrow Cross) (Budapest: Müller Károly, 1945), 124 pp.

CHAPTER THREE

THE JEWISH COMMUNITY
OF HUNGARY BEFORE
THE DESTRUCTION

Demographic Structure

HISTORICALLY, World War I marks a watershed in the evolution of Hungarian Jewry. The 200-year trend of gradual expansion gave way to a decline, in both absolute and percentage terms. Numerically, Greater Hungary's Jewish population reached its peak in 1910, when it numbered 911,227 or 5.0 percent of the total population of nearly 21 million. Of these, 471,355 lived in the territory of Trianon Hungary, where they constituted 6.2 percent of the total population.

The Jewish population of Trianon Hungary continued to decline after World War I to 5.9 percent (473,355) in 1920 and to 5.1 percent (444,567) in 1930 (see chapter 1). During this decade the number of Jews thus declined by 28,788, constituting a net loss of 6.1 percent, while the non-Jewish population increased by close to 700,000, (8.7 percent). The percentage of Jews declined further to 4.9 (400,981) in 1941 and finally, in the wake of the Holocaust, to 1.6 (143,624) in 1946. The decline was particularly noticeable in Budapest, where the number of Jews decreased from 215,560 (23.2 percent) in 1920 to 204,301 (20.3 percent) in 1930 and 184,453 (15.8 percent) in 1941.[1]

Until 1830 the overwhelming majority of the Jews of Hungary (68.1 percent) lived in the countryside, both because of economic factors and, primarily, residency restrictions. With the easing of the restrictions Jews began again to settle in towns and cities, so that by 1890 their percentage in the rural areas declined to 36.2. By 1941 only 18.3 percent of the Jews could be identified as rural.[2]

One reason for the decline in the Jewish population before the catastrophe of 1944 is the losses suffered during World War I (approximately 10,000 of the Hungarian Army casualties were Jewish), the precipitous decline of the birth rate following the wave of anti-Semitism and anti-Jewish excesses after the war,[3] the economic hardships of the depression, the relatively large-scale emigration,[4] and an increasing conversion rate (see chapter 25). The Hungarian-speaking Jews in the

Successor States were much less affected by these factors, although they too suffered the devastating impact of the economic crisis (see chapters 4 and 5).

The census of March–April 1941—the last one before the Holocaust—indicated that Hungary had a total population of 14,683,323 of whom 725,005 or 4.94 percent identified themselves as belonging to the Jewish religion. Approximately 100,000 persons of Christian confession were also regarded as racial Jews under the anti-Semitic legislation of 1938–42.[5]

The geographic distribution of the Jews in 1941 was as shown in table 3.1. In the ceded territories, approximately 146,000 Jews lived in the areas acquired from Czechoslovakia in 1938–39 (68,000 in the Upper Province (Felvidék) and 78,000 in Carpatho-Ruthenia (Kárpátalja)), 164,000 in Northern Transylvania (acquired from Romania in 1940), and 14,000 in the Bácska (Bačka) and other smaller areas acquired from Yugoslavia in 1941.[6]

Rightist and anti-Semitic authors exploited the statistical data of the various censuses, distorting them to substantiate their ideological-political views concerning the alleged danger represented by the Jews.[7] They provided the "documentation" for the anti-Semitic agitators of the interwar period, who prepared the ground for the catastrophe by constantly emphasizing the purportedly dominant and, by definition, harmful role of the Jews in the professions and the economy. The radical rightists, shrewdly exploiting the grave economic crisis of the 1930s, called for a "change of the guard" (*örségváltás*), a slogan which catered to the rapacious instincts of the mob. The traditional anti-Semitism identified with the "national, Christian" ideology of the Hungarian

TABLE 3.1.
NUMBER OF JEWS AND CONVERTS
IN TRIANON HUNGARY
AND THE CEDED TERRITORIES

| | Trianon Hungary | | | Ceded Territories | Total |
	Budapest	Provinces	Total		
Jews	184,453	216,528	400,981	324,026	725,007
Jews of Christian confession	62,350	27,290	89,640	10,360	100,000
Total	246,803	243,818	490,621	334,386	825,007

SOURCE: *Hungarian Jewry Before and After the Persecutions* (Budapest: Hungarian Section of the World Jewish Congress, 1949), p. 2.

Right gradually acquired a Nazi coloration with its emphasis on race and called for a racial solution of the Jewish question.

Economic Position

In contrast to the Compromise Era, when the Jews played an important role in advancing Magyar national interests and when the Jewish question, though present and occasionally publicly identified, was politically and officially suppressed, in the post-World War I period the Jews suddenly found themselves used as scapegoats for most of Hungary's disasters. In the atmosphere of the frustrations caused by the lost war and the consequent disintegration of the Empire, and under the influence of anti-Semitic agitation, an increasingly large percentage of the population tended to perceive and judge the Jewish community as a whole in terms of the important and highly visible role played by a relatively few Jews and converts in both Hungarian capitalism and communism. As in Germany under the influence of the National Socialists, the Jews of Hungary were identified and conveniently blamed as being primarily responsible not only for the country's military disasters but also for its socioeconomic dislocations. Though an overwhelming majority of Hungarian Jewry had opposed Kun's proletarian dictatorship, popular opinion tended to attach the blame for the abortive Bolshevik regime to the Jews as a whole (see chapter 1). By the same token, though the majority of the Jews could hardly eke out a living, the public at large tended to equate the economic status of the Jews with that enjoyed by a relatively small percentage of Jewry, which played a conspicuous, if not dominant, role in the professions and in the major sectors of the economy, including banking, industry, and commerce. It is this small upper-middle-class group that was closely associated with the aristocratic-conservative ruling classes of Hungary. The level of assimilation and acculturation of the members of this group—through money, baptism, and intermarriage—was among the highest in Europe.

Anti-Semitic propaganda tended to disregard the historical factors that had induced the Jews to gravitate toward certain professions in the aristocratic-gentry dominated Hungarian society and denigrate the major contributions the Jews had made to the industrialization and modernization of the country. Disregarding absolute figures, it constantly emphasized the high percentage of Jews in the professions and in industry and commerce. These figures were especially dramatic with respect to Trianon Hungary. In 1930, for example, when Jews constituted 5.1 percent of the population (20 percent of Budapest's), they constituted the following percentages in the various professions: physicians, 55.2; lawyers, 49.2; engineers, 30.4; scientists and writers, 31.71; painters, 14.7; musicians, 25; and actors 26.7. In industry and commerce, the percentages were as follows: independent commercial establishments, 51.3; industrial establishments, 11.0; agents, 75.1; bank employees and officials, 59.4; salesmen, 45.7; bookkeepers, 59.5; and general clerical workers, 19.2.[8]

Anti-Semites were usually silent about the virtual exclusion of Jews from certain fields and professions with which the aristocratic-gentry elements had traditionally been associated. Thus the Jews represented only 0.33 percent in agriculture, 1.6 percent in the civil service and the administration of justice, and an even lower percentage in the army.[9]

Although some Hungarians of Jewish background played a dominant role in the country's heavy-goods industries and in banking, they represented only a minute percentage of the Jewish population. Many of them were in fact converts, and while they had excellent relations with the aristocratic ruling class, most of them had little if anything to do with the Jewish community.

The impressive percentage figures notwithstanding, the fact remains that the general economic status of the Jews tended to decline in the wake of the postwar crises. For example, while in 1920, 28,090 or 12.3 percent of the 227,868 independent arisans were Jewish, in 1930 this category declined to 23,866 or only 11.02 percent of the total of 216,516. In business and finance the number of independent Jewish entrepreneurs declined from 40,275 or 53.7 percent of the total of 75,149 in 1920 to 38,295 or 45.5 percent of the total of 83,995 entrepreneurs in 1930. In the industrial sphere, a relatively few Jews or former Jews owned or controlled a considerable portion of the machine-building and heavy-goods sector, including the large Weiss-Manfréd Works. But 95 percent of the 140,000 Jews employed in the industrial sector were small-scale artisans, factory workers, and apprentices. The same type of situation held in the business sector, in which Jews represented 43.0 percent: the greatest number of Jewish-owned businesses were small, family-operated ones. Even in Budapest, the great majority of the Jewish businessmen lived quite modestly. In 1930, for example, 4,800 (60.0 percent) of the approximately 8,000 Jewish businessmen lived in one- or two-room apartments.

The myth of general Jewish affluence fanned by the anti-Semitic press and based on the wealth and ostentatious behavior of a relatively few Jews was just that—a myth. The proportion of poor among the Jews was in fact higher than for the population at large. According to Samu Stern, then head of the Neolog Jewish community, approximately 401,000, or 90 percent, of the 444,567 Jews (census of 1930) lived at the poverty level. Like 6.9 million other Hungarians in the total population of 8,688,000, they owned neither land nor their own homes. While the Jews constituted 5.1 percent of the population, their proportion among the poor was 5.8.[10]

The economic status of the Jews in the areas acquired between 1938 and 1941 was generally even worse, for the level of economic development in those territories was inferior to that of Trianon Hungary.

Cultural and Sociological Characteristics

The basic cultural and sociological characteristics of Hungarian Jewry evolved under the impact of the various immigration waves, which came to a virtual halt in 1825. They reflect the heritage and the intellectual and cultural differences of the three major layers of immigrants that laid the foundations of the "family tree of Hungarian Jewry": the Austrian-German, the Bohemian-Moravian, and the Galician-Polish.[11]

The first layer of immigrants, relatively small in size, consisted of the Austrian Jews, who settled primarily in the western counties of Hungary following their expulsion from Vienna by King Leopold I in 1670. Joined by immigrants from the German lands, their communities were for several generations led by rabbis especially brought in from their former homelands. These spiritual leaders helped retain and foster the Jewish version of what Marton calls "the German baroque spirit." This was reflected in a closed system of rabbinism, which glorified authority and emphasized the virtues of obedience. Most members of the congregations were artisans and merchants whose income was derived chiefly from the border traffic with Austria. Their income was relatively low, and with a few notable exceptions, their standard of living quite modest.

The second wave consisted of Bohemian-Moravian immigrants. The rate of immigration increased after King Charles III issued a decree in 1726 stipulating that only one male member of each Jewish family would be allowed to marry. In the wake of this edict, obviously aimed at curtailing the Jewish population, eligible Jewish bachelors crossed the Hungarian border en masse and usually settled in the border villages where they married. The flow of immigration gained momentum after 1748, when Maria Theresa added further restrictions to her father's decree by limiting the number of Bohemian and Moravian Jewish families to ten thousand.

The Jewish immigrants from Bohemia and Moravia brought into Hungary a spirit that differed radically from the baroque one brought in by the Austrian-German Jews. These immigrants emerged as the pioneers of enlightenment and religious reform and spearheaded the movement for emancipation and the acquisition of citizenship. In the nineteenth century, their descendants became the most ardent champions of assimilation. It is from this group that some of the greatest figures of the Hungarian progressive movement emerged.

Culturally and socioeconomically, the Bohemian-Moravian Jewish immigrants were of a higher class. In general, those who came to Hungary to marry were financially relatively well off and culturally more advanced that their Austrian-German cousins. In the dawn of the industrial revolution, they were in the forefront of the modernizing process in Hungary. They were among the first to participate in, and enjoy the benefits of, the newly emerging capitalist system. Taking full advantage of the opportunities afforded by the aristocratic-conservative leadership of the country, they played a pioneering role in the development of industry, commerce, banking, and international trade. When the restrictions on higher education were lifted and opportunities for advancement in the professions were widened after the emancipation of 1867–68, the descendants of these immigrants constituted the bulk of the Jewish student body and the overwhelming majority of the Jewish professional elite.

The beginning of the third wave of immigrants, the Galician-Polish Jews, can be traced to the anti-Jewish outbursts associated with the Cossack uprising of Chmelnitzky in 1648. The immigration of these Jews gained momentum after the first dismemberment of Poland in 1772, when Galicia, a province of Poland that was densely inhabited by Jews, became part of the Hapsburg Empire. Most of the immigrants came to Hungary to escape the oppression and above all the nearly unbearable poverty in which they lived. Forced out from almost all branches of economic life, many of them eked out a living by distilling spirits. They settled in the northern and northeastern parts of Hungary in the territories adjacent to Galicia. Poor on arrival, most of them remained, virtually until the Holocaust, near the bottom of the Hungarian-Jewish socioeconomic scale. Their chief occupations were distilling, innkeeping, rural retail business, and especially manual labor. It is from their rank that the bulk of the Jewish proletariat evolved.

The Galician-Polish immigrants were the bearers of a new religious-spiritual movement—Hasidism—that challenged the rigid authoritarian forms of rabbinism. Unlike the cold, anticongregational baroque spirit, Hasidism provided for its believers an intimate relationship between God and the Jewish masses. The new vision of God and the specific ways of life associated with it—reflected, *inter alia,* in the distinct clothing, customs, folklore, and rituals of the Hasidim—provided an ecstatic form of liberation from the yoke of authoritarian leaders and a spiritual escape from the realities of grinding poverty. Aside from this religious impact, the Galician-Polish immigrants also greatly expanded the use of Yiddish and provided a stimulus for the development of Jewish national consciousness. They not only resisted the pressures of assimilation and acculturation, but also provided many of the founders and leaders of Hungarian Zionism. The size of their families was usually much larger than that of the middle class Jewish families of the Great Plains and Transdanubia. To escape the grinding poverty in which they lived, many of their children gravitated in the twentieth century toward the cities and the capital. Some of them succumbed to the temptations of secularism, with the successful ones embracing the virtues of the middle classes and many of the less fortunate ones as well as many of the intellectuals taking up the cause of the Left. Others translated their inherited Jewish consciousness into political action by laying the foundations of various shades of Zionism.

Eventually, the geographic configurations of the three layers of Hungarian Jewry became blurred. By the time of the Holocaust they lived intermixed in all the regions of the country in various proportions. Budapest, the Great Plains, and Transdanubia continued, however, to be dominated by descendants of the Austrian-Germans and Bohemian-Moravians. Composed overwhelmingly of assimilated, patriotic "Magyars of the Israelite faith," they were Neolog in their religious orientation and thoroughly middle class in character, mentality, and class attitude. They were the source of both envy and contempt to many of the Jews in the northeastern parts of the country. Their perception of themselves was similar to the one held of them by the conservative-aristocratic leadership of the country before the occupation. They identified themselves as "Magyarized" Jews as contrasted with the *Ostjuden,* who inhabited the northeastern parts of the country that were held by Czechoslovakia and Romania during the interwar period.

Unlike the "Westernized" Jews, the overwhelming majority of the

Jews of Carpatho-Ruthenia and to a somewhat lesser extent those of Transylvania resisted the temptations of reform and assimilation. Most of the Jews of Carpatho-Ruthenia were Yiddish-speaking and Orthodox in their religious orientation.

The resistance to assimilation in Carpatho-Ruthenia may be gauged from the statistics on mixed marriages in the various regions of pre-World War II Czechoslovakia. While the proportion of Jewish men taking non-Jewish wives was 30 percent in Bohemia, 19 percent in Moravia, and 5 percent in Slovakia, it was only 0.4 percent in Carpatho-Ruthenia. Jewish women who married non-Jewish husbands constituted 26 percent in Bohemia, 16.6 percent in Moravia, 4.8 percent in Slovakia, and 0.9 percent in Carpatho-Ruthenia.[12]

The greater Jewish consciousness of the masses in this area was occasionally matched by a more effective, often Zionist-inspired, local leadership in contrast to the basically undemocratic, assimilationist-oriented national leaderships of both Prague and Budapest. Culturally and religiously akin to the Galician Jews in neighboring Poland, the majority of the Jews of Carpatho-Ruthenia clung tenaciously to their old-fashioned Orthodoxy and Hasidism. In the census of 1930, 92.6 percent of these Jews declared themselves of Jewish nationality and only 5.9 percent considered themselves Hungarians.[13]

The situation in Transylvania was rather unusual, reflecting not only the historical peculiarities of the region, but also the background and traditions of the indigenous Jewish community. From the religious point of view, the majority of the Jews of Transylvania were Orthodox, although most of the larger communities also had Hasidic congregations. The Hasidim were concentrated primarily in the northern and northwestern parts of the region, where cities like Szatmárnémeti and Máramarossziget had become renowned centers of Hasidism. In language and culture, the Jews of Transylvania were fundamentally Hungarian. In the Jewish centers of the north and in the ultra-Orthodox communities elsewhere in the region, the Jews also spoke Yiddish, in some cases exclusively. Romanian was spoken by Jews primarily in Beszterce-Naszod and Máramaros counties and in the predominantly Romanian villages, but here too usually only as the second or third language. The Jewish intellectuals and members of the middle classes spoke almost exclusively Hungarian. Even the generation that was educated in Romanian schools during the interwar period continued to rely on Hungarian as their major language in the home and in everyday life.

The predominant role of Hungarian was also reflected in the cultural and political life of the Transylvanian Jews. The Jewish press and the scientific-cultural life of the province were predominantly Hungarian[14] and Jewish journalists, artists, and writers contributed generously to the development and flourishing of general Hungarian culture.[15]

The cultural and linguistic features of Transylvanian Jewry were the source of many conflicts, to the annoyance of both Romanian and Jewish leaders of Bucharest. It is ironical that at the end the Jews fared far worse under the Hungarians than under the Romanians. For a few years after the Second Vienna Award (August 1940), the Jews of Northern Transylvania, who came under Hungarian rule, ended up in labor camps or Auschwitz; those of Southern Transylvania, left with Romania, survived almost intact. (See chapter 5 for more details on the political and socioeconomic characteristics of Transylvanian Jewry.)

Congregations and Communal Organizations

During the years preceding the Holocaust, Hungarian Jewry had a well-developed network of religious, educational, health, and welfare organizations. These were normally organized by and operated under the auspices of the congregations. Because of its failure to unite at the Congress of 1868–69,[16] Hungarian Jewry came to be identified with three types of congregations:

1. Neolog (also known as Reform or Congressional)—those that adopted the modern, progressive, and innovative ecclesiastical practices spearheaded by the Jewish community of Pest. The Neolog community was drawn primarily from the assimilationist strata of Hungarian Jewry who tended to deviate from the traditional Orthodox practices of Judaism. For example, they used choirs and organ music in the synagogues, permitted decoration in the cemeteries, and emphasized some of the ethical and esthetic aspects in religious instruction. In their synagogues, the *almemar* (the reader's platform) was placed just in front of the holy ark and the sermons and services were usually conducted in Hungarian. The Neologs paid particular attention to the interior and exterior architectural design of the synagogue, which for many was their only link to Judaism. The Neolog congregations were almost always led by lay leaders. The Neologs were predominant in the central leadership as well as in that of most communities of Trianon Hungary.

2. Orthodox—those that clung to the traditional rituals and practices of Judaism. The Orthodox section of Hungarian Jewry, though as patriotic as the Neolog, was anti-assimilationist and insisted on strict adherence to traditional values and practices of Judaism. The Orthodox congregations were usually led by religious leaders. In the course of time, two types of Orthodoxy evolved: a "Western" one which flourished in the northeastern and middle parts of the country and consisted primarily of descendants of the immigrants from Austria, Germany, and Moravia; and an "Eastern" one which developed in the northeastern parts of the country, including some sections of Transylvania, which consisted overwhelmingly of descendants of the immigrants from Galicia. The members of the "Eastern" congregations were predominantly Hasidic. In the course of time, the geographic differences became blurred, and many communities in the eastern and northeastern parts of the country had both types of Orthodox congregations.

3. *Status Quo Ante* (often simply *Status Quo*)—those relatively few who rejected the positions of both major groups.

The Neolog congregations flourished in Budapest and most other regions of Trianon Hungary, especially in its western parts. Orthodoxy retained its hold in the northeastern and eastern regions. The number of congregations tended to change with the mobility of the Jewish population, but the ratio between the Neolog and the Orthodox remained basically the same.

An analysis of table 3.2 reveals that in *number of congregations,* 61.5 percent of the congregations were Orthodox, 30.7 percent Neolog, and 7.8 percent Status Quo (1930). By 1935, while the ratio between the two major groups remained the same, the percentage of Status Quo congregations declined to 3.8. In terms of *membership,* however, the proportion was reversed. In 1930, there were 292,155 members (65.5 percent) in the Neolog, 130,039 (29.2 percent) in the Orthodox, and

TABLE 3.2.
NUMBER OF NEOLOG, ORTHODOX AND STATUS QUO
CONGREGATIONS IN TRIANON HUNGARY:
1930 AND 1935

	Orthodox Congregations		Neolog Congregations		Status Quo Congregations		Total	
	Major	*Branch*	*Major*	*Branch*	*Major*	*Branch*	*Major*	*Branch*
1930	136	300	96	123	24	30	256	453
1935	149	321	104	131	14	13	267	465

SOURCE: *Zsidó Világkongresszus,* No. 8–9, April 1, 1948, p. 10.

22,373 (5.3 percent) in the Status Quo congregations. Approximately 65 percent of all the Neolog members belonged to the four large congregations of Budapest. Outside of the capital, 49 percent of the members belonged to the Orthodox, 46 percent to the Neolog, and 5 percent to the Status Quo congregations. Again excepting Budapest, on the average the Neolog congregations had 470 members each, while the Orthodox and the Status Quo ones had 270 and 415, respectively. By far the largest, richest, and most influential congregation in Hungary was the Jewish Community of Pest (*Pesti Izraelita Hitközség*), a Neolog congregation founded in 1800.[17]

Theoretically, each congregation was associated with and was guided by a central organization. The Neolog congregations were subordinated to the National Bureau of the Jews of Hungary (*Magyarországi Izraeliták Országos Irodája*—MIOI). The Bureau operated in conjunction with the National Council of Hungarian Jews (*A Magyar Izraeliták Országos Tanácsa*). Both the Bureau and the Council were headed by Samu Stern, who was also the President of the Jewish Community of Pest. A Counselor of the Hungarian Royal Court (*Magyar királyi udvari tanácsos*), Stern was a very successful businessman with excellent relations to the aristocratic-conservative elements of Hungarian society. Immediately after the German occupation on March 19, 1944, Stern became the President of the Jewish Council (*Zsidó Tanács*) (chapter 14).

Within the Bureau, Stern was assisted by two Vice-Presidents: Dr. Robert Pap of Szeged and Béla Alapi of Budapest. The Council's executive secretary was Dr. László Bakonyi. Its governing body consisted of Alapi, who served as its Vice-President, three executive officers (Bakónyi, Hugó Csergő, and György Polgár), the heads of the eight permanent and two provisional communal districts (*községkerületek*), and 19 elected members.[18]

The Orthodox congregations operated under the general guidance of the Central Bureau of the Autonomous Orthodox Jewish Community of Hungary (*Magyarországi Autonom Orthodox Izraelita Hitfelekezet Központi Irodája*—MAOIH), which was headed by Samu Kahan-Frankl. Its legal counselor was Dr. Imre Reiner. MAOIH was guided by a national representative body of 100 members—40 rabbis and 60 lay leaders. Its executive committee was composed of 10 to 15 lay leaders and five rabbis. The influential position of the provincial communities in the central leadership of MAOIH is reflected in the fact that none of the rabbis in that leadership came from Budapest.

The Status Quo congregations functioned under the direction of the

National League of the Status Quo Ante Jewish Congregations of Hungary (*Magyarországi Statusquo Ante Izraelita Hitközségek Országos Szövetsége*), which was headed by Jenő Ungár of Debrecen and Béla Bernstein of Nyiregyháza.[19]

As a result of the split, many a community had two and some even three congregations. This was especially true in the larger towns and cities with a relatively high percentage of Jews. Despite their serious religious-doctrinal differences and occasionally conflicting political positions, the congregations usually cooperated in the establishment and operation of communal institutions and in the organization and administration of welfare. The latter became an especially burdensome chore in the wake of the economic crisis and anti-Jewish measures of the 1930s. Until 1938, the system of welfare was organized primarily on a local basis: each community tried to help the needy in its midst within the limits of its own resources.

The tendency toward the centralization of welfare was accelerated by the arrival of Jewish refugees from Germany and Austria following the Anschluss. It was reinforced by the passage in Hungary of the First Anti-Jewish Law in May 1938 (see chapter 4). Much of the burden for the care of the refugees and for aiding Hungarian Jews eager to emigrate was assumed by the Jewish Community of Pest through such institutions as the *Wanderfürsorge* (Travelers' Aid) Society. However, with the addition of a large number of relatively impoverished Jews following the acquisition of the Upper Province (*Felvidék*) from Czechoslovakia early in November 1938, the resources of the Pest community proved inadequate. It was at this time that the American Joint Distribution Committee (AJDC) began its relief operations in Hungary. Deeply aware of the rising tide of Nazism and the exacerbation of the anti-Semitic trend in Hungary, the AJDC took the initiative in urging the three central communal organizations to establish a joint welfare institution. Responding to this challenge, the leaders of the Neolog, Orthodox, and Status Quo communities brought about the establishment of the Welfare Bureau of Hungarian Jews (*Magyar Izraeliták Pártfogó Irodája*—MIPI) in December 1938. Early in 1939, the representatives of the Hungarian Zionist Association (*Magyar Cionista Szövetség*—MCSz) joined the MIPI executive committee at the request of the AJDC.[20] The American agency undertook to contribute up to $25,000 per month to MIPI, providing the Hungarian Jewish community contributed an equal amount.[21] The agreement came about as the result of the discussions held by Samu Stern and Sándor Eppler, the President and Executive Secretary of the Jewish Community of Pest, with the representatives of the international Jewish philanthropic organizations during their June 1939 visit to Paris and London which they undertook with the consent of the Teleki government.[22]

To comply with the stipulation of the AJDC, the community established a fund-raising organization known as the National Hungarian Jewish Assistance Campaign (*Országos Magyar Zsidó Segitő Akció*—OMZSA). Organized in accordance with the recommendations of a committee headed by Géza Ribáry, who became its first head, OMZSA launched its campaign late in the fall of 1939, after it received the necessary authorization from Ferenc Keresztes-Fischer, the benevolent Minister of the Interior. The operations of the OMZSA tended to keep pace with the ever-increasing burdens befalling MIPI.[23] Over half of the OMZSA's income was derived from the Jewish Community of Pest.[24]

The legal and economic status of the Jews worsened considerably after the adoption of the Second Anti-Jewish Law of May 1939, and the increase in the number of impoverished Jews following the acquisition of Carpatho-Ruthenia and Northern Transylvania in 1939–40 (see chapter 5). MIPI's responsibilities were compounded by the arrival of a relatively large number of refugees from neighboring Poland and Slovakia following the adoption of draconic anti-Jewish measures in those countries. In coping with these responsibilities, the organizational structures and functions of both MIPI and OMZSA underwent periodic changes to meet the ever-rising challenges.[25]

The number of Jewish refugees seeking haven in Hungary increased with each passing year of the war. By November 1943, their number reached approximately 15,000. Many of these were interned in special camps supported by MIPI. Some of these camps also held Hungarian Jews who had been interned for failing to prove their Hungarian citizenship or for a variety of political and economic offenses under the existing anti-Jewish and state security legislation.[26]

In the course of the war, the organizational structure of MIPI became increasingly specialized. By 1943–44, it had special sections on legal affairs, refugee matters, emigration, public kitchens, and several other welfare-related functions.[27]

In spite of the ever exacerbating climate of anti-Semitism, the work of both OMZSA and MIPI was to a large extent made possible by the cooperative attitude of the Hungarian authorities, who were naturally content to see the Jews assume the economic burden of helping a considerable portion of the country's population. Keresztes-Fischer extended OMZSA's right to collect money from year to year and the KEOKH (*Külföldieket Ellenőrző Országos Központi Hatóság*—National Central Alien Control Office) and other proper agencies of the Ministry of the Interior made possible the granting of assistance to refugees, the stateless, and the interned. The Hungarian National Bank cooperated by enabling the Jewish organizations to use the dollar funds received from the AJDC for emigration and for aiding Hungarian Jewish emigrants and students living abroad.

After the German occupation, MIPI and OMZSA became appendages of the Jewish Council, which was established under the command of the Nazi authorities.[28] MIPI was transformed into the Social Division (*Szociális Osztály*) of the Association of the Jews of Hungary (*A Magyarországi Zsidók Szövetsége*), as the Council was officially called.[29]

In addition to MIPI and OMZSA, the Hungarian Jewish community had a large network of educational, cultural, religious, and social-welfare institutions, including a number of internationally known centers for Jewish learning (*Yeshivot*). With the exception of the *Yeshivot*, most of these were concentrated in the larger cities, especially Budapest.[30] Many of these institutions came into being after 1938 as the Jewish community's response to the impact of the anti-Jewish laws. Dismissed Jewish artists and musicians, for example, were given an opportunity to work in their fields under the auspices of the National Hungarian Jewish Cultural Association (*Országos Magyar Izraelita Közművelődési Egyesület*—OMIKE), which was organized in 1938. Teachers dismissed from the public school system were hired by the newly established Jewish educational institutions. These institutions functioned relatively undisturbed by the authorities until the German occupation. The OMIKE continued to organize lectures, offer concerts, and stage shows and operas until March 1944.[31] In fact Hungarian Jewry appeared to live in an atmosphere of semi-normality, almost completely oblivious to the suffering of the Jews in the neighboring countries where the Final Solution was in full swing.[32]

The interests of the Jewish veterans and especially of the labor servicemen were represented by the Veterans' Committee of the National Jewish Bureaus (*Országos Izraelita Irodák Hadviseltek Bizottsága*).[33]

The national political consciousness of the Hungarian Jews was relatively low. It is ironic that the community that produced both the founder and one of the great figures of modern Zionism, Theodor Herzl and Max Nordau, was basically opposed to the idea of Jewish nationalism. For reasons of their own, both the Neolog and the Orthodox communities rejected Zionism as a means of solving the perennial Jewish question. The followers of the various Zionist factions were relatively few and consisted primarily of young men and women who had become disenchanted with the policies of the Jewish establishment. Most of them came from the socioeconomically lower strata of Hungarian Jewry. A large proportion of the young Zionist intellectuals was primarily *Galut*-Zionist—i.e., not really interested in emigration. The leadership of the Hungarian Zionist Association was handicapped by the opposition of both the government and the Jewish establishment. It consisted of highly dedicated and well-educated individuals, who were, however, quite deficient in their knowledge of Jewish history or Hebrew. This was especially true of those who lived in Trianon Hungary. In contrast, the Hungarian Jewish communities in the territories acquired between 1938 and 1941 produced a larger number of leaders with a more pronounced national Jewish consciousness. They provided the impetus for the reinvigoration of the Zionist movement during the war. Among their great achievements were the establishment of the Relief and Rescue Committee, which provided assistance for thousands of Jewish refugees in Hungary, and the organization of rescue operations during the German occupation.[34]

The work of the Zionist Association was supplemented by that of the Pro-Palestine Association of Hungarian Jews (*Magyar Zsidók Pró Palesztina Szövetsége*), which, though interested in emigration matters, was primarily concerned with the collection of funds through the *Keren ha'yesod* (Palestine Foundation Fund) and the *Keren Kayemet l'Yisrael* (Jewish National Fund) campaigns.[35]

Whatever the shortcomings of the Hungarian Zionist leaders, their posture during the war was generally much more positive than that of the official leadership of Hungarian Jewry.

The Leadership of Hungarian Jewry

The leaders of Hungarian Jewry, like those of all other officially recognized denominations, had a degree of authority over the communities they administered. The nature and limits of this authority were stipulated by, and were exercised under, the jurisdiction of the Hungarian Royal Ministry of Cults and Public Education (*Magyar Királyi Vallás- és Közoktatásügyi Minisztérium*). Within the Ministry, the denominations were under the direct jurisdiction of the Main Section on Cults

(*Vallásügyi Főcsoport*). In the case of the Jews, the Main Section on Cults exercised direct control over the National Bureau of the Jews of Hungary, the eight major communal districts of the country,[36] the Central Bureau of the Autonomous Orthodox Jewish Community of Hungary, and the two major educational institutions of the community: the Ferenc József National Theological Institute (*Ferenc József Országos Rabbiképző Intézet*) and the National Jewish Teacher Training Institute (*Országos Izraelita Tanitóképző Intézet*).[37]

The composition of the Neolog and Orthodox communal leadership varied greatly. Whereas the Neolog congregations were led primarily by lay leaders, with the rabbis fulfilling almost exclusively ecclesiastical-spiritual functions, the Orthodox ones were guided predominantly by rabbis. The difference in leadership was to a large extent a consequence of the historic development associated with the struggle between the two groups since the 1860s. The Neologs' preference for lay leaders reflected not only their striving for reform, but also their desire to minimize religious tension and controversy with the Orthodox faction. The one major exception was the case of Rabbi Immanuel Löw of Szeged. An outstanding biblical scholar, he was not only a leading member of the local and central Neolog community, but also one of the two representatives of the Jewish community in the upper house of the Hungarian Parliament.

Under the conditions of relative normality that prevailed until the German occupation, the leaders of Hungarian Jewry were quite effective in serving their communities. They maintained a large network of religious, health, educational, and welfare institutions that served not only the indigenous Jews, but also the thousands of refugees that found haven in Hungary (see below). The one grave error in their leadership was their failure to take any precautionary measures against the possibility of a catastrophe similar to the one that befell the Jews in the neighboring countries. Primary responsibility for this must be borne by the central leadership of Hungarian Jewry. For unlike the leaders of most other European Jewish communities, the national leaders of Hungarian Jewry were fully aware of the Nazis' Final Solution program long before it was launched in their country (see chapter 23).

The causes for the lack of preparedness and the absence of any meaningful contingency measures were many and diverse. Among the major ones were the long-standing inability of the various communities to transcend their traditional, ostensibly irreconcilable, differences and bring about transcongregational unity; the failure to adhere to the democratic process in the organization and administration of the Jewish communities in general and of their central organizations in particular; and the aloofness with which the Hungarian Jewish leaders viewed the tragedy of the European Jews caught in the Nazi web, coupled with their blind faith that they would escape the Holocaust.

The sudden occupation of Hungary by the Germans found the Jewish communities as conflict-ridden and disunited as they had been since 1868, when they had tried for the first and last time to overcome their political and religious differences. Even after the White Terror of 1919–20, when some of the illusions of the former "Golden Era" of liberalism (1867–1914) were dissipated, few if any attempts were made to end the constant bickering within and among the three major official communities and between them and the basically ineffective Zionist organization.

The Zionist movement itself was conflict ridden, with each of the four major "parties"—the *Klal* (General), *Mizrachi* (Religious), *Hashomer Hatzair* (Socialist), and *Ichud* (later *Mapai;* United Labor)—competing for preeminence. The conflict was particularly fierce within and between the *Vaada* (see below) and the Palestine Office (*Palesztina Hivatal*) headed by Miklós (Moshe) Krausz. The two "establishment" Zionist organizations, in turn, were often in an ideological and generational conflict with the more activist-oriented *Hehalutz* group, which included a number of young Polish and Slovak refugee Zionist leaders.

Aside from the bickering among the three established communities over the content and form of religious practices, Hungarian Jewry was also plagued by political conflicts between the assimilated group and the Zionists, by the conflicting economic concerns of the rich and the poor, and by the rivalries among the larger and semi-autonomous congregations. All of these were compounded by the jealousy and personal animosity that motivated many of the leaders of these communities in the pursuit of narrow parochial aims.

In terms of the typology of leadership developed by Carl J. Friedrich, a noted American political scientist, the Hungarian Jewish leaders who dominated communal life were of the "maintaining" and "protecting" rather than of the "initiating" type. They rarely if ever initiated any line of action that transcended the estabished system of values. Firmly committed to the values and principles of the traditional conservative-aristocratic system and convinced that the interests of Jewry were intimately intertwined with those of the Magyars, they never contemplated the use of independent political techniques for the advancement of Jewish interests per se. They took pride in calling themselves "Magyars of the Jewish faith" (*zsidóvallású magyarok*). Composed of rich, patriotic, and generally conservative elements, this leadership aimed to contribute to the maintenance of the established order by faithfully obeying the commands of the government and by fully associating itself with the values, beliefs, and interests of Hungarian society in general. At the same time, this leadership did everything in its power to protect the basic interests of the community, from which in return it expected not only acclaim but above all voluntary subservience. Its authority was legitimate in terms of two of Max Weber's three major criteria for legitimacy: it enjoyed the sanctity of *tradition,* however undemocratic and lacking in historical-chronological terms, and it profited from the aura of *legality* provided by both governmental and communal authorization. It lacked, however, *charisma:* none of the leaders had any exceptional personal qualities. While devoted to the welfare and continuing progress of the Jewish community, the leaders of Hungarian Jewry were neither inspirational nor highly intellectual.

The central as well as the local communal organizations and institutions were to a large extent organized and operated in an undemocratic fashion. Franchise was limited by property and other qualifications, with the result that the leadership in practically all the congregations was drawn almost exclusively from the wealthiest strata of the community, joined by a few professionals who played an active role in the general intellectual and political life of the locality. Moreover, in Trianon Hungary, the leadership of the *kehiloth* tended to consist primarily of the patriotic, anti-Zionist, assimilationist elements. Because of their prominence in their communities, these leaders were routinely renominated and reelected. While most of them rendered great service to the masses, they had little organic contact with them.

Most of the Neolog and Orthodox leaders of the central organizations and institutions of Hungarian Jewry in Budapest belonged to the upper middle class and some of the lower echelons of the nobility.[38] This was particularly striking in the case of the Jewish Community of Pest, the country's largest congregation. The 19 leading members of the congregation were lawyers, manufacturers, members of parliament, and bankers. By their rank ten were entitled to be addressed as "Your Honor" and one as "Your Excellency." Though the bulk of the community was composed of small entrepreneurs, artisans, and white-collar workers, not one of their representatives was included in the leadership.[39] This situation was true of the larger congregations in the provinces as well. Reflecting the background of their class and status, the Jewish leaders were basically conservative and tended to identify with the political and socioeconomic views as well as the irredentist-nationalist aspirations of their Hungarian Christian counterparts. Conspicuously absent from this leadership group were the totally assimilated Jewish captains of business and industry like Leó Goldberger and Baron Alfonz Weiss, not to speak of the converted industrial magnates such as Ferenc Chorin. The group also failed to attract or refused to admit the leading artists, intellectuals, and Zionist figures.[40] Also conspicuously absent from the leadership—and this was in accord with the custom of Jewish communities practically everywhere—were women and young people.

Although they were guided by high moral standards and by the desire to advance the religious and social welfare of the Jewish community, the *modus operandi* of the national leaders tended to be largely formal and legalistic, in emulation of the behavior of their gentry counterpart. Unlike many of the Polish and Romanian national Jewish leaders, for example, they shunned the political arena for the protection and advancement of Jewish interests per se, opposing with equal vehemence both the Zionists and the proponents of a Hungarian Jewish Party. Stern summarized this position of the Hungarian Jewish leadership by stating shortly after the adoption of the First Anti-Jewish Law that "in Hungary there is and there was no separate Jewish party and there should be none . . . because the Jews want to remain Hungarian citizens of the Jewish faith."[41] Consequently, the Jewish leaders' response to the ever exacerbating anti-Jewish measures during the interwar period was apologetic and isolated from the general struggle of European Jewry. Their loyalty to the Hungarian nation, like their attachment to the gentry-aristocratic establishment, remained unshaken. Just like the previous generation of leaders who championed the cause of Hungary's territorial integrity after World War I, the leaders of the Nazi era adopted a patriotic stance in dealing with the Jewish question. They consistently refused to confront the issue politically and thereby also raise the national consciousness of the Jewish masses. They opposed an open pro-Jewish stance, lest their loyalty be impugned.

The Hungarian Jewish leaders continued to reflect the historical and theological position taken by the Ferenc József National Theological

Institute on January 13, 1919. This institution, operating under the auspices of the Neolog Jewish Community of Pest, summarized its position as follows:

For over two thousand years Jewry has been only a religion and not a nation or nationality. It is this religious position that the National Theological Institute adopted in the past and continues to adhere to today. We have advocated and continue to advocate that Hungarian Jewry constitutes an organic part of the Hungarian nation; this is what it was, this is what it remains. While guarding the inviolability of their religion, the Hungarian Jews consider themselves the children of the Hungarian nation. It is in this spirit that we shall continue our work in behalf of our denomination and country.[42]

Thus, while the National Socialist movement was gaining power in Germany and the European continent was becoming fertile for anti-Jewish agitation, the Hungarian Jewish leaders, instead of alerting and educating the masses about the new menace, continued to adopt a politically quixotic stance. They tended to view the Jewish question primarily as a legal and constitutional issue confronting the entire nation. Thinking along the ideals of liberal democracy, they saw the anti-Jewish drives as violations of the libertarian and human-rights provisions of the constitution and as such of interest to all the people irrespective of their religious affiliation. They exploited every occasion to obsequiously express the view that the Jews were "loyally intertwined with the totality of the Hungarian nation." This sentiment was poignantly expressed in the "solemn declaration" of the Jewish Community of Pest of 1932:

Our course is the unseparably intertwined course of our Jewishness and Hungarianness. This land, the Hungarian land is our homeland. We watered this land with our blood and sweat and it is our useful work that brought to fruition the blessed fruits of legal equality. The storms of transitional times may shake or tear off the branches of the Hungarian tree of equality, but the tree itself cannot be toppled, because its roots are in the Hungarian Constitution. Our rights may be temporarily curtailed by the storm of the times, but we ourselves will not surrender them; we shall cling unswervingly to our Hungarianness. Here lie the sanctified remains of our ancestors; our past and present bind us here; and we are one with every citizen of this land in the struggle for a happier and more beautiful future of our Hungarian nation.[43]

Like true Hungarian nationalists, they adopted an apologetic stance that tended to equate the love of country with the love of God. This sentiment was expressed most eloquently by a leading figure of the Hungarian Jewish community in the late 1930s:

It is easy to love the homeland when . . . the homeland offers glory and happiness to those who love it; but the homeland must be loved even when it does not bestow upon us the totality of its love. God must be worshiped even when he reduces us to dust . . . ; we worship him whether he rewards or punishes us. We worship him even when he appears to turn his love away from us and we worship our earthly God, our homeland, whatever our fate may be in this homeland.[44]

The Hungarian Jewish leaders tended to a retrospective rather than a contemporary view of national and world Jewish history. Ever since the emancipation, if not much earlier, these leaders had been extremely self-conscious about being identified as Jews. While naturally motivated by self-interest, looking out for the survival and growth of the community as they understood it, they were constantly fearful of being charged with dual loyalty. Partially as a subconscious attempt to negate these charges, they adopted a stance of unqualified patriotism. Conscious of the great strides Hungarian Jewry had made during the "Golden Era," they strove to safeguard those rights that the Jews still enjoyed after the major anti-Jewish laws and to restore, if possible, the *Interessengemeinschaft* that characterized the pre-World War I period. They tended to pursue these objectives, however, without abandoning the traditional operational techniques that were proving increasingly ineffective, if not clearly counterproductive. Inexperienced in militant political struggles for exclusively Jewish causes, having no direct contact with the masses of Hungarian Jewry whose intimate problems and spiritual world they did not adequately represent or understand, and self-isolated from the concerns of world Jewry, these leaders emerged during the German occupation as singularly incompetent to provide the kind of leadership that the extraordinarily perilous times required.[45]

Reaction to the Destruction of the Jews in Nazi-Dominated Europe

The retrospective historical point of view responsible for the Hungarian Jewish leaders' apologetic reaction to the interwar anti-Semitic measures continued to becloud their position even after the hostilities with the USSR and the simultaneous mass murders of Jews began. The official Hungarian Jewish leaders, both lay and religious, held to their shortsighted patriotic stance and formal legalistic posture even during the Holocaust. They persisted in the rejection of a "Jewish line," finding any emphasis on Jewish identity and defense of Jewish interests per se incompatible with their sense of loyalty. This attitude induced them to oppose those advocating the development of a strictly Jewish national consciousness among the masses. To the end, they followed an ostrich-like policy, hoping unrealistically that the aristocratic-conservative Christian leadership of Hungary, with whom they maintained close and mutually rewarding relations, would protect them from the fate of the Jewish communities of the neighboring countries. They did not, of course, expect that this segment of the anti-Nazi Christian leadership would also be among the first to be victimized after a German occupation. Practically until the beginning of the deportations, the Jewish leadership continued to believe that the Hungarian Jewish community, unlike all other large European Jewish communities, would emerge from the war physically relatively intact even if economically generally ruined. The belief that they would escape the tragedy—*megusszuk* (we'll get by), they frequently said in self-assurance—was partially nurtured by the realization that Hungary had been in fact an island of safety in an ocean of destruction for four and a half years of the war. This sense of optimism was sustained by the victories of the Allies. In the West, following the landing in Italy, the invasion was only a matter of time; in the East, the Soviet forces were fast approaching Romania.

The Hungarian Jewish leaders were aware of what the Nazis had wrought in the Jewish communities under their control. The mass exterminations by the *Einsatzgruppen* in Soviet territories, including the massacre of 16,000 to 18,000 "alien" Jews deported from Hungary in July–August 1941 (see chapter 6), and the assembly-line murders in the German concentration camps of Jews deported from all over Europe were known to them (see chapter 23). Nevertheless, and this is one of the great tragedies of the era, they neither kept the Jewish masses fully informed nor did they take any meaningful precautionary measures to forestall or minimize the catastrophe in the event of an occupation of Hungary. Furthermore, while they provided generous assistance to the several thousand refugees that escaped to Hungary, in part with the aid of the Zionists (see below), they often failed to heed the desperate calls for financial help from abroad.

While the central Hungarian Jewish leaders—communal and Zionist—were progressively more accurately informed about the Nazis' Final Solution program (by late April 1944, they even had *prima facie* evidence of the realities of Auschwitz) the masses of Hungarian Jewry had no inkling of the mass murders in the concentration camps and the gas chambers. Those who heard something about the Nazi horrors discounted them as rumors or anti-Nazi propaganda. Like normal people everywhere in the world, they simply could not conceive of the assembly-line murder of millions of human beings in the broad daylight of the twentieth century. While they suspected that the Jews were being terribly maltreated across the borders, they consoled and deluded themselves by thinking that at any rate what happened elsewhere, and especially in Poland, could not possibly happen in "civilized" Hungary. Had not the patriotic Jewish historians and lay and religious leaders convinced them that in Hungary the destiny of the Jews had been intertwined with that of the Christian Hungarians for over a thousand years?

The lay leaders heeded all the censorship regulations in effect and, together with the spiritual leaders, rejected the use of the synagogues for "propaganda" purposes. The sermons from the pulpit, like the communications from Budapest, retained a tone of normality that deceived the masses into believing that they, the Hungarian Jews, would escape the cataclysm. The many small Zionist organizations were preoccupied with recruitment, emigration, and questions relating to *Eretz Yisrael* (Land of Israel). Consequently, while Hungarian Jews were subjected to many restrictions under the anti-Jewish laws (chapters 4 and 6) and tens of thousands of them were massacred near Kamenets-Podolsk and Ujvidék and in the labor service companies in the Ukraine (chapters 6 and 10), organized Jewish life did not change greatly until the German occupation.

The central Jewish leaders and the Jewish organ—*A Magyar Zsidók Lapja* (Journal of Hungarian Jews)—echoed the position of their moderate Christian counterparts in constantly reaffirming their loyalty to the nation and the fatherland without ever publicly noting or warning about the conflagration around them. They failed even to keep the heads of the larger provincial Jewish communities and the governmental leaders of the country confidentially informed about the realities of the Nazis' anti-Jewish drive in Europe, though they had good connections with them. They continued to celebrate the Jewish and national holidays, offer "free university" lectures, stage dramatic and operatic performances, and organize exhibits, concerts, and recitals almost completely oblivious of the threatening storm.[46]

Early in 1942, when the Nazis had already decided on the Final Solution program and the first transports were about to be shipped to Auschwitz, the National Theological Institute restated its January 1919 position that it was operating in the spirit of Hungarian patriotism and Jewish loyalty. In the free university lecture series of the Jewish Community of Pest, Ernő Boda, one of its leading figures, declared that "no theory and no measure whatsoever can sway Hungarian Jewry from its loyalty to its native land, its motherland, and its ancestors.[47] Lectures in this series were also given by Hugó Csergő, Ernő Munkácsi, György Polgár, Ernő Bródy, Nison Kahan, Sándor Eppler, Endre Sós, Ferenc Hevesi, and Jenő Zsoldos, all leading figures of the Jewish community of Budapest; none of them ever publicly identified the scope of the Nazi measures abroad as they knew them at the time.[48] The same conspiracy of silence was also noticeable at the regular and extraordinary meetings of the Jewish Community of Pest.[49]

The public position of the Hungarian Jewish leaders was reflected in an April 1942 editorial of their organ:

The proper and responsible representatives of Hungarian Jewish life have always advocated . . . the Hungarianness of the Hungarian Jews—without missing any occasion to do so. When the Jews gathered around the hearth of their denominational life, they solemnly declared their unbreachable loyalty as often as they expressed their sorrow over the difficulties confronting them; they emphatically proclaimed their common fate with the Magyars of Hungarian Jewry, that Jewry which is fully amalgamated with the Hungarian nation in language, spirit, culture, and feeling.[50]

In September 1943, when many of the European Jewish communities had already been liquidated, the stance of the Jewish leaders remained the same. In commenting about the fact that over 585,000 of the approximately 725,000 Jews had identified themselves as Hungarians in the 1941 census, another editorial stated: "Hungarian Jewry is Hungarian, and it is understood that in its heart and soul it forms an integral part of the Hungarian nation."[51]

The leaders' attitude did not change at all even in early 1944, when Hitler was already making his final preparations for the occupation of Hungary.[52] When tragedy finally struck, the apologetic stance changed to one of rationalization. The leaders took an "understanding" attitude, differentiating between the homeland and its leaders. In the ghetto of Szeged, for example, just before the deportations, the Rabbi of Mohács declared in a sermon that "in spite of all persecution, we must love our country, as it is not the country that has repudiated us, but wicked men." A few weeks earlier, in April 1944, Dr. Ferenc Hevesi, the Neolog Chief Rabbi, urged the Jews "to pray to God for yourself, your family, your children, but primarily and above all for your Hungarian Homeland! Love of Homeland, fulfillment of duty, and prayer should be your guiding light!"[53]

The rationalizations of the Jews continued even in the midst of the ghettoization, concentration, and deportation process. When the Jews were placed into ghettos in the northeastern parts of the country around the middle of April 1944, those in the "assimilated" parts of the Great Plains and Transdanubia expressed "understanding" for the measures taken by an enemy trying to safeguard its security in view of the rapidly approaching Soviet front. The rationalization was reinforced by the rumor that the Jews of Carpatho-Ruthenia—the unassimilated, Orthodox and largely "alien" Jews—had been concentrated merely to prevent them from engaging in sabotage and at worst would be resettled somewhere else in Hungary for the duration of the war. This illusion was fostered not only by the naïve leaders of Hungarian Jewry, but also by the top commanders of the dejewification program. László Endre, one of the radicals primarily responsible for the destruction of Hungarian Jewry, for example, echoed the line that Eichmann had pursued in his dealings with the Jewish leaders. On June 1, 1944, he made the following notation on the back of the petition submitted by the Jewish Council of Budapest on May 26, requesting Andor Jaross, the Minister of the Interior, to put an end to the deportations:

The leaders of the Jewish Council must be called in and informed that deportations are taking place only in the combat zones, where there is a lot of spying and sabotage. These Jews have not assimilated themselves, many have infiltrated from abroad, consequently their temporary removal is in the interest of the brave local Jewry. If the others behave, the resettlements will be discontinued.[54]

The strategy developed by the dejewification squads worked, for the Jews continued their rationalizations to the end. When their turn came to be placed first in so-called Yellow Star houses and later in the ghetto, the Jews of Budapest harbored the same illusions about their safety: "What happened in the countryside cannot possibly happen here in the capital—in this sophisticated city where there are so many foreign diplomats!"

Throughout, the occasional news items about Jewish communities abroad gave the impression that while anti-Semitism in Hitler's Europe was more intense than ever before, the communities themselves were not threatened by extinction. On August 14, 1941, for example, the *A Magyar Zsidók Lapja* reported that German Jews in French labor camps were allowed voluntarily to petition for their transfer to German labor camps "where they wish to work." In one of the extremely rare, if not the only, references to the Warsaw Ghetto, the paper pointed out that "in the midst of the greatest difficulties and deprivations, there are regular cultural performances there."[55] There is no account about the mass starvation and death, and the humiliation and tortures to which the Jews of Warsaw and Poland in general were subjected. There is not even a reference to the Warsaw Ghetto uprising.

The same misleading impression is conveyed by the one report on the Soviet Jewish POWs in German hands. Quoting the *Israelitisches Wochenblatt* (The Jewish Weekly) of Zurich, it states that the Germans transferred the POW's to camps in the Third Reich, where, according to a finding by the Red Cross, their position was not objectionable.[56] The Hungarian Jewish masses could not possibly suspect from this article that many of the Soviet POW's in general and the Jewish POW's in particular were subjected to "special treatment" (*Sonderbehandlung*) by the Germans. A similarly false impression was fostered about the fate of the German Jews. On March 12, 1942, when there were hardly any Jews left in Germany, the paper cited selectively a dispatch from Frankfurt-am-Main to the effect that Dr. Joseph Wohlgemuth, the former rector of the rabbinical seminary of Berlin, had died in the local Jewish hospital. Without any reference to the plight of the German Jews since Hitler's coming to power in 1933, it leaves the impression that the Jews still had their hospitals and implicitly all their other institutions.

Misinformation about the plight of the Jews in the Nazi-dominated parts of Europe extended to inaccurate reporting about the Hungarian Jewish labor servicemen in the Ukraine. While practically every issue of the journal contained appeals to help the labor servicemen with money and clothing, at no time did these appeals include any accounts of the barbarous treatment of the labor servicemen by many of their commanders and guards as well as the SS (see chapter 10). No space was ever allotted to depicting the liquidation of the Jewish communities in all the parts of the Ukraine in which the Hungarian Army and the labor servicemen were stationed and which was witnessed by many of them. Even the personal narratives of labor servicemen used in the appeals for money and clothing refer only to the cold and the lack of adequate clothing and food in the units stationed along the front, without ever mentioning the activities of the *Einsatzgruppen*.

The silence of the Jewish press about the realities of the Nazi persecutions was matched by that of the Social Democratic organ, *Népszava*

(The People's Voice), and the independent and more reliable *Magyar Nemzet* (Hungarian Nation), both read by Jews as well as non-Jews. They were as uninformative about the extermination of the European Jews as the *A Magyar Zsidók Lapja* was. While it is true that the press was censored during the war, the Jewish, like the leftist and liberal-progressive, forces failed to inform the masses even when the domestic climate was relatively propitious for "illegal" activities during the last months of the Kállay era (see chapter 7). The lectures and speeches at the various adult and youth organizations of the political opposition, like the sermons in the synagogues, continued to be as uninformative as before. No attempt was ever made to overcome the censorship regulations through the underground distribution of flyers about either the Nazis' Final Solution program or the mistreatment of the Jewish labor servicemen in the Ukraine and at Bor, Serbia.

The ultra-rightist press, on the other hand, lost no opportunity to inform its readers about the Nazis' "resettlement" program in Europe.[57] They projected a positive image of the new "settlements" in the East, where Jews from all over Europe were allegedly involved in "productive" physical work and no longer depended on "blackmarketeering, swindling, and banking" for making a living. These accounts, which Jews also read, reinforced in many the belief that the extermination rumors were nothing but anti-Nazi propaganda.

The shortsighted legalistic-formalistic and patriotic stance of the national Hungarian Jewish leaders led them not only to withhold the information they had about the realities of the anti-Jewish drive in Europe, but also to deny meaningful help to their counterparts in the neighboring countries. Early in 1943, for example, Gisi Fleischmann, one of the founders and leaders of the Bratislava "Working Group" (*Pracovná skupina*), the illegal body which operated within the framework of the Bratislava Jewish Council, asked the Hungarian Jewish leaders for monetary aid to help the Slovak Jews in labor camps and to bribe Dieter Wisliceny, the SS leader in charge of the deportations from Slovakia, and thus contribute to the rescue effort. The Hungarian Jewish leaders refused, claiming that the prevailing rules did not permit them to spend money outside the local communities. Moreover, they vehemently opposed any "illegal" transfer of funds. They did express readiness to contribute some funds, provided it could be done legally via a bank; but of course this could not be done. Fleischmann was rightfully bitter about the treatment she received in Budapest. She expressed her feelings in a letter of January 14, 1943, addressed to

Nathan Schwalb of the *Hehalutz* in Geneva: "In relation to my stay [in Budapest], I dealt with the leading elements of Jewish life and must note first of all that, in all objectivity, our friends there know neither Jewish solidarity nor social responsibility or charity."[58]

Stern admitted his mistake soon after the German occupation of Hungary, expressing his profound regret for not having sent help to Slovak Jewry in time.[59] Fleischmann and the Working Group, in turn, found some solace in the fact that shortly after the rejection of their request by the official leaders of Hungarian Jewry a new Zionist-led organization was established specifically to help the refugees from Nazi persecutions.

The Treatment of the Jewish Refugees in Hungary

One of the most positive aspects of the Hungarian Jewish community's position during the pre-occupation era was its reaction to the thousands of refugees who escaped to Hungary from the persecutions in their homelands.

The first trickle of refugees began arriving from Germany soon after the adoption of the Nuremberg Laws of 1935. The German refugees were followed by a larger number of Austrian Jews who fled their homeland after the Anschluss of March 1938, which brought the Third Reich to the gates of Hungary. A year later, a considerable number of Jews began arriving from the German-annexed Protectorate of Bohemia and Moravia and from the newly independent puppet state of Slovakia following the dismemberment of Czechoslovakia.

Most of the Jewish refugees from Germany, Austria, and the Protectorate were relatively well off and had either family or business connections in Hungary. Thus they required little, if any, assistance from the Hungarian Jewish organizations.

Some Polish Jewish refugees had entered Hungary even before the outbreak of World War II. These were primarily Jews from Galicia searching for better economic opportunities and attempting to escape the increasingly virulent anti-Semitic climate of Poland. A larger number of Polish Jews began arriving after the Nazis crushed Poland in September 1939. At first, these were almost exclusively anti-Nazi intellectuals and Jewish soldiers who entered Hungary along with members of the Polish armed forces in search of asylum. According to some estimates the approximately 140,000 to 150,000 Poles who entered Hungary after the debacle included from 5,000 to 15,000 Jews.

After they were disarmed, the soldiers, including the Jewish ones, were allowed to leave and join other Polish military units in exile. Until March 1940, most of them left via Yugoslavia and Switzerland to join the forces of General Kopanski in France; after that date, they left to join the forces of General Anders via Turkey and the Middle East. A large number of military and civilian Polish refugees, however, decided to stay in Hungary. The Hungarian authorities were particularly generous to the Christian Poles, to whom they were bound by a long tradition of friendship and cooperation. They also treated the Jewish military personnel with considerable deference. Many of the Polish Jewish officers and soldiers were held in a special camp in Vámosmikola, north of Esztergom, where they enjoyed good treatment until the Szálasi coup on October 15, 1944.[60] The Hungarian authorities were less charitable to the civilian Polish Jewish refugees, whose number increased with each passing month. Many of these had a particularly tough time crossing the Hungarian border since the frontier guards, on instructions from either the central authorities or their own commanders, did everything in their power to keep them out.[61] The overwhelming majority of the Polish Jewish refugees who managed to get across the borders into Slovakia and Hungary were relatively young able-bodied Jews who found the draconic measures in the Nazi-established Jewish ghettos of Poland no longer tolerable.

The reaction of the official Jewish leaders to the arrival of refugees varied. Under pressure by the anti-Semitic press, which constantly dealt with the alleged danger represented by the infiltrating Galician Jews, the leaders adopted throughout the thirties an ambivalent or apologetic position. They consistently felt compelled to defend the loyalty and integrity of the Hungarian Jewish community against the charges that it favored the immigration of the "Eastern" Jews. They emphasized publicly that they had no knowledge of, and were providing no assistance for, such illegal immigration. In their view, the whole issue of refugees was simply a police question to be handled by the authorities: "Hungarian Jewry never desired this type of immigration, let alone assisted it!"[62]

With the beginning of the war against the Soviet Union in June 1941, the problem became increasingly acute. The number of refugees increased with each passing month and the need to adopt more forceful measures to cope with the persecuted Jews became ever more pressing. The initiative for action came from the Zionist leaders, especially the Transylvanian ones. Among the latter was Rezső (Rudolph) Kasztner, the man destined to play a fateful role following the German occupation (see chapter 29). In December 1941, they convened a meeting of some of the most influential figures of Hungarian Jewry, including many current and former members of the Hungarian and Romanian parliaments. Among them were Lajos Láng and Jenő Vida, members of the upper house of the Hungarian Parliament; József Büchler, Miklós Kertész, Imre Györki and Béla Fábián, members of the lower house of the same Parliament; and József Fischer and Ernő Marton, former members of the Romanian Chamber of Deputies. At this first meeting, Kasztner reviewed the status of the Nazis' anti-Jewish drive as he knew it at the time. Specifically, he told them about the mass executions that were taking place in the Ukraine, the Baltic States, and Bessarabia and Bukovina; about the first gassing vans; and about the liquidation of close to 20,000 "alien" Jews near Kamenets-Podolsk in Poland.[63] The participants listened to the report with great skepticism and with little willingness to undertake any initiatives. Láng and Vida, the "captains of industry and banking," and Fábián expressed a readiness to intervene through the Red Cross in behalf of the *Hungarian* Jews deported to Poland.

The refugee problem was rapidly becoming critical. In addition to the escapees fleeing the hopeless conditions of the Polish ghettos, thousands of Jews began arriving from Slovakia, as it became the first country to permit the "resettlement" of Jews soon after the adoption of the Final Solution program at the Wannsee Conference in Berlin in January 1942. The first deportation trains left Slovakia for Auschwitz in March. According to one estimate, approximately 10,000 Slovak Jews entered Hungary during 1942. Most of these were Hungarian-speaking and could more easily adjust to life in Hungary than could the Polish refugees, despite the initial general indifference of the Hungarian Jews.[64] Many of them were interned by the authorities and a few groups were transferred by overzealous ultra-rightists to Kőrösmező, near the Polish border, where they were allegedly shot.[65] The same fate befell many of the Polish Jews who tried to enter Hungary after September 1942.[66]

The material and legal assistance required by the thousands of refugees soon exceeded the resources of those concerned with refugee affairs. The refugees fell into two categories: the "legalized" ones, those who were registered with or interned by the authorities; and "illegal" ones who lived mostly in the capital with false—mostly Christian—identification papers. In 1942, there were approximately 3,500 "legalized"

refugees, most of whom were interned in camps at Columbus, Damjanich, Magdolna, Ó, Páva, Rumbach, and Szabolcs streets in the capital, in the larger multiple-purpose camps of Bácstopolya, Csörgő,
Garany, Kistarcsa, Nagykanizsa, and Ricse, and such smaller internment camps as those of Baja, Balaton-Boglár, Kalocsa, and Szatmárnémeti. The larger multiple-purpose camps also held political prisoners as well as Hungarian and "alien" Jews who were unable to prove
their Hungarian citizenship.

The "legalized" Jewish refugees were in a sense better off than the
others, since they enjoyed the open support of the official leaders of
the Jewish community. Most of the internment camps were wholly or
partially supported by MIPI through funds received from the AJDC or
collected by OMZSA. "Legal" refugees who were not interned in camps
had to report regularly to KEOKH, the agency entrusted with jurisdiction over foreign nationals living in Hungary. It was this agency that
was in charge of the 1941 roundup and deportation of the close to
18,000 "alien," including Polish, Jews to near Kamenets-Podolsk, where
most of them were subsequently slaughtered by the SS (see chapter 6).

The "illegal" refugees presented a greater problem, as they had to be
supplied with false documents, usually identifying them as Polish or
Hungarian Aryans, and provided with homes and financial assistance.
Stern, who articulated the views of the official leaders of Hungarian
Jewry, refused to provide any funds, arguing that he did not want to
jeopardize the interests of Hungarian Jewry for the sake of a few illegal
refugees.[67] In the face of this opposition, a group of Zionist and Orthodox leaders took the initiative to collect the needed funds illegally. The
funds so collected proved insufficient, inasmuch as a considerable proportion had to be diverted to help smuggle Jews hiding in the woods of
Poland and Slovakia across the border. In an effort to tap a foreign
source of funds, contact was established with foreign Jewish organizations, including the Jewish Agency. This move succeeded primarily
thanks to the efforts of Sámuel Springmann, a Polish-born *Poale Tsion*
(Labor) Zionist, who as a watchmaker-jeweler had developed many
good friends among Hungarian officials and foreign diplomats.[68] One
of his achievements was the establishment of a courier service between
Istanbul and Budapest and later between Budapest and Bratislava and
Switzerland.

The first sizable outside contribution came late in 1942 from the Jews
of Palestine via a courier from Istanbul. It was accompanied by a letter
signed by Ruth Klüger, containing the emphatic appeal, "Help the ref-

ugees, help the Polish Jews!" The appeal was indeed a desperate call for help, for the liquidation of the Polish Jewish communities was in full swing at the time.

In response to this appeal, the Zionist leadership of Budapest brought about the establishment of the Relief and Rescue Committee (*Vaadat Ezra ve'Hazalah*)—popularly known as the *Vaada*—in January 1943. Among the founders were Ottó Komoly, the president of the Zionist Association of Hungary, a successful civil engineer and a representative of the *Klal* Zionist faction; Jenő Fränkel, a leader of the *Mizrachi* group; Ernő (Zvi) Szilágyi of the *Hashomer Hatsair* group; and Joel Brand, Kasztner, and Springmann, representing the *Ichud*. The original plans entailed a threefold objective: to save Jewish lives by smuggling operations; to help the refugees within the country; and to prepare for the self-defense of Hungarian Jewry. The nominal leader of the *Vaada* was Komoly, but the *de facto* head was Kasztner, the Executive Vice President. Springmann was in charge of courier matters and finances until his emigration to Palestine in January 1944, and Joel Brand, who achieved world fame the following year in connection with his "blood for trucks" mission authorized by Adolf Eichmann,[69] was in charge of *Tiyul* ("trip"), the code name for the smuggling of refugees across the border.

In the course of time, the smuggling operations involved a well-developed network of daring individuals, who risked their freedom and lives for either humanitarian-idealistic reasons or financial rewards. Among the former were a number of young Hungarian, Polish, and Slovak Zionists, mostly members of the *Hehalutz* (Pioneer) movement;[70] the latter included Ruthenian, Polish, and Slovak peasants, tavern keepers along the borders, railway and frontier officials, and occasionally even soldiers. Until the German occupation, *Tiyul* managed to smuggle approximately 500 Jews out of Poland; around 2,000 other Polish Jews succeeded in getting into Hungary by themselves via Slovakia. Of the close to 2,500 Polish Jewish refugees in Hungary late in 1943, from 800 to 1,200 lived and worked in the provinces, mostly as "Aryans"; the others lived in the capital. The Polish Jewish refugee community also included 114 children, 90 percent of whom were orphans. These were placed in three children's camps: 76 in Vác, 21 in Kassa, and 17 in Budapest. The refugees received through the *Vaada* from 150 to 200 *Pengős* per month and occasional supplements for clothing and medical care.

In addition to the *Vaada*, a Polish-Jewish Refugee Committee headed by Siegfried Moses and Boris (Bruce) Teicholz[71] also looked out for the interests of the Polish Jewish refugees. One of the most difficult tasks of this Committee before the occupation was to free and "legalize" refugees arrested by the police during the frequent raids. The raids were usually organized near the synagogues and Jewish institutional establishments normally frequented by the "Aryan" Jews. Those unable to cross themselves or to recite the Lord's Prayer were arrested, as were those who could but were "betrayed" by their circumcision. Because of the better treatment by the Hungarian authorities of Christian Polish refugees, a number of Jewish ones tried to escape their ordeal by conversion. This, however, proved counterproductive for many: when a number of Palestinian immigration certificates became available through the Jewish Agency late in 1943, they were ineligible because of their newly acquired Christian status.[72]

The plight of the Polish Jewish refugees was the subject of a number of memoranda sent by the Polish-Jewish Refugee Committee to the representatives of the major Jewish organizations in Switzerland via the courier service of the *Vaada*. In response to interventions by these organizations with Ferenc Honti, the Hungarian Consul General in Geneva, the lot of the Polish Jewish refugees improved considerably in the months preceding the occupation. This was in spite of the public position taken on the question of refugees by a number of government officials, including Ferenc Keresztes-Fischer, the benevolent Minister of the Interior. Probably in his endeavor to politically appease the Right, Keresztes-Fischer urged during the budget debate in the Hungarian Parliament late in 1943 that severe measures be taken to halt the infiltration of Jews and "to return those Jews, who crossed the border without permission to the countries from which they came." He also suggested that "those Jews who were already in the country illegally should be sent to concentration camps."[73]

The improved lot of the refugees late in 1943 was due not only to the political climate in the country as a result of Prime Minister Kállay's pursuit of an honorable way out of the war (see chapter 7), but also to the efforts of the Orthodox Jewish leadership, which was more inclined to deviate from the legalistic-formalistic approach of the Neologs. The Orthodox leaders, including Lipót (Leopold) Blau, Miksa (Max) Brick, Adolf Deutsch, József Frank, Fülöp Freudiger, Hermann Stern, and Leó Stern, formed a Relief and Rescue Committee of their own for the "illegal" aid of refugees.[74] On November 16, 1943, the Zionist and the Orthodox committees entered into an agreement that called for:

- The coordination of the work of both committees.
- The joint appropriation of all funds at their disposal.
- The organization of joint campaigns for the collection of additional funds.[75]

At the time of the Zionist-Orthodox agreement, the number of Jewish refugees still in Hungary was estimated at approximately 15,000. Their distribution by country of origin was as follows:[76]

Slovakia	6,000 to 8,000
Germany and Austria	3,000 to 4,000
Poland	1,900 to 2,500
Bohemia and Moravia	500 to 1,000
Yugoslavia	300 to 500

In addition to its work in behalf of the Jewish refugees already in Hungary, the *Vaada* served as a vital communication link between the Jewish organizations of the free world and the oppressed communities of Poland and Slovakia. It maintained close contact with the Jewish Agency office in Istanbul, which was headed by Chaim Barlas,[77] and with Nathan Schwalb, the *Hehalutz* representative in Switzerland.[78] It cooperated very closely with the representatives of the Bratislava "Working Group"[79] as well as with various Jewish underground leaders in Poland. In 1944–45, these contacts were extended to include the representatives of other major Jewish organizations, including the American Joint Distribution Committee, and the American War Refugee Board in Switzerland (see chapters 29 and 31). These contacts involved not only the transfer of funds, but also the exchange of information and the transmission of letters, newspapers, and reports about conditions in the camps and ghettos. They were effectuated through a well-developed courier service that was originally organized by Springmann. By late 1943, it involved elements associated with:

- The official courier service of the Hungarian Ministry of Foreign Affairs.
- The courier service of a neutral European state.
- The intelligence services of the German and Hungarian General Staffs.[80]

Among the most important of the *Vaada*'s intelligence contacts and couriers were: Dr. Schmidt, the head of the Budapest branch of the *Abwehrstelle* III "F," which was headquartered in Vienna; Josef (Józsi) Winninger (alias Duftel), a Hungarian of Jewish background; Dr. Rudi Sedlaczek, Rudi Scholz, and Erich Popescu (alias Werner)—all associated with the *Abwehr,* the German Counter-Espionage Service then under the control of Admiral Wilhelm Canaris; Lieutenant Ferenc Bágyoni, a member of the Hungarian Military Intelligence; and Lieutenant-Colonel József Garzoly, a member of the Hungarian General Staff. By far the most colorful among the couriers was Andor ("Bandi") Grosz, *alias* Andreas or Andre György, *alias* Andreas Grenier. A multiple agent—he served the *Abwehr,* the Hungarian Military Intelligence Service, the SS, the Anglo-Saxons, and the *Vaada*—Grosz came into prominence in 1944, when he accompanied Joel Brand on the much publicized "blood for trucks" mission authorized by Eichmann.[81] Though most of these professed to be opposed to the Nazis, all of them performed their services for pay. In fact, they remained basically loyal to their main employers. The messages transmitted by the *Vaada* leaders were usually also conveyed to the Germans and, in the case of the Hungarian couriers, to the Hungarian authorities.

Thanks to these contacts and couriers, the Budapest *Vaada* played a pivotal role in linking the representatives of Jewry in Bratislava, Istanbul, and Switzerland and in keeping the free world informed about the realities of the Nazis' anti-Jewish drive. It also served as a vehicle for the transmission of correspondence and funds to the Jewish refugees in Hungary and to some of the persecuted Jews in Poland and Slovakia. Because of this special role, the leaders of the Budapest *Vaada* were among the best informed in Europe about the ghastly details of the Nazis' extermination program. They claim[82] that they kept the official leadership of Hungarian Jewry fully and constantly informed about them, only to see them largely ignored. In spite of their close connections with the conservative-aristocratic leadership of Hungary, the official leaders of the Jewish community apparently failed to keep the rulers of the country informed. They continued to follow the same apologetic position that had guided them ever since the end of World War I. Their reaction to the communications by the *Vaada* did not differ from their reaction to the *Numerus Clausus* Act, the anti-Semitic manifestation of Gömbös, and the first anti-Jewish legislative proposals advanced by the Darányi government in 1938: noninvolvement in external Jewish affairs and exclusive reliance upon the Hungarian state and constitution for the protection of Hungarian-Jewish interests.

Notes

1. Ernő László, "Hungary's Jewry: A Demographic Overview, 1919–1945," in *HJS*, 2:158.

2. *Hungarian Jewry Before and After the Persecutions* (Budapest: Hungarian Section of the World Jewish Congress, 1949), p. 15.

3. For example, between 1930 and 1935 the average yearly number of deaths (6,207) exceeded that of births (4,883) by 21 percent for Jews, although between 1931 and 1935 the country as a whole had a 42 percent increase in the number of births over deaths. Samu Stern, *A zsidókérdés Magyarországon* (The Jewish Question in Hungary) (Budapest: A Pesti Izraelita Hitközség, 1938), p. 22. On the postwar anti-Jewish manifestations, see chapter 1.

4. During the two decades after World War I, approximately 25,000 Jews emigrated from Hungary. *A magyar zsidóság uj útja. A Magyar Cionista Szövetség állásfoglalása* (The New Road of Hungarian Jewry. The Position of the Hungarian Zionist Association) (Budapest: A Magyar Cionista Szövetség, 1938), p. 8.

5. For detailed statistical studies on the demography of Hungarian Jewry consult: Ernő László, "Hungarian Jewry: Settlement and Demography, 1735–38 to 1910," *in HJS*, 1:61–136; László, "Hungary's Jewry: Demographic Overview, 1918–1945," *ibid.*, 2:137–82. See also the mimeographed *Zsidó Világkongresszus magyarországi tagozata sta tisztikai osztályának közleményei* (Bulletins of the Statistical Department of the Hungarian Section of the World Jewish Congress) published in Budapest between February 15, 1947, and May 1949.

6. For details on the geographic distribution of the Jews in these territories, see chapters 4 and 5. For a statistical breakdown of the population of Hungary in 1941 by language, nationality and religion, see *Magyar statisztikai szemle* (Hungarian Statistical Review), 19 (1941), part 2, no. 11 (Budapest: Magyar Királyi Központi Statisztikai Hivatal, 1941), pp. 772–73. See also vol. 21 (1943), part 1, no. 5–6, pp. 246–48, 252.

7. See, for example: Stefan (István) Barta, *Die Judenfrage in Ungarn* (The Jewish Question in Hungary) (Budapest: Stádium, n.d.), 201 pp.; Klaus Schikert, *Die Judenfrage in Ungarn* (Essen: Essener Verlag, 1943), 308 pp.; and Alajos Kovács, *A csonkamagyarországi zsidóság a statisztika tükrében* (The Jews of Rump Hungary in the Light of Statistics) (Budapest: Egyesült Keresztény Nemzeti Liga, 1938), 80 pp.

8. Statement by György Polgár as quoted by György Klein, *A magyarországi zsidóság történetének alapvonalai, 1935–1945* (The Basic Outlines of the History of Hungarian Jewry, 1935–1945). Manuscript available at the YIVO-Institute for Jewish Research (New York, Archives File 784).

9. *Ibid.* See also Stern, *A zsidókérdés Magyarországon*, p. 24.

10. Stern, *A zsidókérdés Magyarországon*, pp. 24–26.

11. For details, see Ernő Marton, "The Family Tree of Hungarian Jewry," in *HJS*, 1:1–59.

12. Randolph L. Braham, "The Destruction of the Jews of Carpatho-Ruthenia," *HJS*, 1:224–25. See also Joseph S. Roucek, "Czechoslovakia and Her Minorities," in *Czechoslovakia*, ed. Robert J. Kerner (Berkeley: University of California Press, 1949), pp. 171–92.

13. For a valuable overview of the history of the Jews of Carpatho-Ruthenia, see Livia Rothkirchen, "Deep-Rooted Yet Alien: Some Aspects of the History of the Jews of Subcarpathian Ruthenia," in *YVS*, 12:147–91. See also Louis Rittenberg, "The Crisis in Hungary." *Contemporary Jewish Record* (New York), 2, no. 3 (May–June 1939): 24. For further details on the general background of the Jews of Carpatho-Ruthenia see Aryeh Sole, "Subcarpathian Ruthenia: 1919–1938," in *The Jews of Czechoslovakia* (Philadelphia: The Jewish Publication Society of America, 1968), 1:125–54; Hugo Stransky, "The Religious Life in Slovakia and Subcarpathian Ruthenia," *ibid.*, 2:347–92; and Aryeh Sole, "Modern

Hebrew Education in Subcarpathian Ruthenia," *ibid.*, 2:401–39. For statistical-demographic data, see chapter 5.

14. The Hungarian-language Jewish press of Transylvania included the *Uj Kelet* (New East), the largest circulation daily published in Kolozsvár, the *Népünk* (Our People), the weekly of Nagyvárad, and the *Uj Idők* (New Times), the weekly of Temesvár. Even the Zionist theoretical organ, the *Noár Lapok* (Noár Journals), was published in Hungarian. Béla Vágó, "The Destruction of the Jews of Transylvania," in *HJS*, 1:174. For a general review of the Jewish press in Transylvania see Kálmán Kahán, "Az erdélyi zsidó sajtó története" (The History of the Transylvanian Jewish Press), in *A kolozsvári zsidóság emlékkönyve* (Memorial Book of the Jews of Kolozsvár) by Mozes Carmilly-Weinberger (New York: The Author, 1970), pp. 185–202.

The Jews of Transylvania also had a modest though solid tradition in Hebrew culture. For an evaluation of the Jewish cultural and scientific contributions of Transylvanian Jewry in both Hebrew and Hungarian, see Mózes Carmilly-Weinberger, "Héber kultura Erdélyben" (Hebrew Culture in Hungary). *Ibid.*, pp. 172–85.

15. Jewish journalists were associated with such non-Jewish organs in Transylvania as the *Brassói Lapok* (Brassó Journal), the *Nagyváradi Napló* (Diary of Nagyvárad), and the *Ellenzék* (Opposition) and *Keleti Ujság* (Eastern Newspaper) of Kolozsvár. Among the Transylvanian Jewish writers and poets who distinguished themselves for their contribution to Hungarian culture were Benő Karácsony, Ernő Ligeti, György Szántó, Oszkár Bárd, Sándor Korvin, Illés Kaczér, Ernő Salamon, Rodion Markovits, Viktor Brassai, and Ádám Raffy. Many of these were associated with the *Erdélyi Helikon* (Transylvanian Helikon) literary society. The Hungarian theater of Kolozsvár was founded shortly after World War I by Jenő Janovics. Béla Vágó, "The Destruction of the Jews of Transylvania," pp. 174–75. For a review of Jewish contribution to Hungarian culture in Transylvania, see "Zsidók Erdély magyar kulturájában" (Jews in the Hungarian Culture of Transylvania), in *A kolozsvári zsidóság emlékkönyve*, pp. 202–10.

16. The drive to bring about the unity of Hungarian Jewry was spearheaded after the emancipation of 1867–68 by the assimilationist stratum of Pest, with the support and encouragement of Baron József Eötvös, the Minister of Cults and Public Education. For details on the Congress, consult Nathaniel Katzburg, "The Jewish Congress of Hungary, 1868–1869," in *HJS*, 2:1–33.

17. For details on the history of this congregation and of its many affiliated institutions, see *Magyar Zsidó Lexikon* (Hungarian Jewish Lexicon), ed. Péter Ujvári (Budapest: A Magyar Zsidó Lexikon kiadása, 1929), pp. 701–5.

18. *OMZSA—Évkönyv 5704, 1943–1944* (OMZSA—Yearbook 5704, 1943–1944), eds. Hugó Csergő, Zoltán Kohn, and György Polgár (Budapest: Az Országos Magyar Zsidó Segitő Akció, 1944), pp. 229–30.

19. *OMZSA–Évkönyv 5704.* For an evaluation of the leadership of the Jewish communities with emphasis on the Orthodox one, see Nathaniel Katzburg, "Hanhagat ha'Kehilot" (The Leadership of the Communities), in *Hanhagat Yehudei Hungaria Bamivahan Hashoa* (The Leadership of Hungarian Jewry in the Test of the Holocaust) (Jerusalem: Yad Vashem, 1975), pp. 77–86.

20. The Executive Committee was composed of five Neolog representatives (Samu Stern, chairman, Sándor Eppler, Jenő Szántó, Miksa Krämer, and Emil Zahler), four Orthodox ones (Samu Kahan-Frankl, Fülöp Freudiger, Imre Reiner, and Adolf Deutsch), one Status Quo (Jenő Ungár), and two Zionist ones (Gyula Miklós and Nison Kahan).

21. This was stipulated in the agreement between the AJDC and MIPI dated June 19, 1939. In addition to the AJDC, the Organization for Rehabilitation and Training (ORT) and the HIAS (HICEM), two other major American Jewish organizations, provided assistance for the beleaguered Hungarian Jewish community by establishing vocational

schools and emigration services, respectively. For details on ORT's work in Hungary, see *OMZSA-Évkönyv* 5704, pp. 237–38.

22. See Elek Karsai, "Evian után tizenegy honappal" (Eleven Months After Evian), in *Évkönyv 1971–72* (Yearbook 1971–72), ed. Sándor Scheiber (Budapest: Magyar Izraeliták Országos Képviselete, 1972), pp. 162–80.

23. Most of the expenditures incurred by MIPI in 1939 were met by the AJDC. By 1940, OMZSA was able to match the contributions of the AJDC. The following year, when Hungary joined the Third Reich in the war first against the Soviet Union and then against Britain and the U.S.A., the AJDC was compelled to discontinue its operations in the country. That year, OMZSA covered most of MIPI's budget; from 1942 on, it was the sole contributor. Between November 1938 and the end of 1939, MIPI's expenditures amounted to 1.5 million *Pengős;* they expanded to 2.4 million in 1940, 3.5 million in 1941, and 4.4 million in 1942. *OMZSA-évkönyv 5704*, pp. 198–99.

24. OMZSA's income in 1942 was 4,786,025 *Pengős*. Of this, 2,585,244 *Pengős* was contributed by the Neolog Jewish Community of Pest. The total contributions of the provincial congregations was 1,652,289 *Pengős* or 36.5 percent of the total. In terms of the congregational share, 85 percent of the contributions (3,963,380 *Pengős*) came from the Neolog, 15 percent (730,458 *Pengős*) from the Orthodox, and 2 percent (92,186 *Pengős*) from the Status Quo. *Ibid.*, p. 206.

25. Until the end of 1939, MIPI operated within the framework of the Jewish Community of Pest under the guidance of Sándor Eppler. At that time, it was transferred to its own headquarters at 2 Bethlen Square and its administration was entrusted to Imre Székely. In 1940, György Polgár became its chief executive officer, operating under the joint leadership of Samu Stern and Samu Kahan Frankl. Following the death of Ribáry in May 1942, Polgár also assumed the management of OMZSA. For a listing of the leaders of both MIPI and OMZSA in 1943–44, see *OMZSA-évkönyv 5704*, pp. 231–36.

26. The internment camps established and/or supported by MIPI were located at Columbus, Damjanich, Magdolna, Ó, Páva, Rumbach, and Szabolcs streets in Budapest and in Bácstopolya, Csörgő, Garany, Kistarcsa, Nagykanizsa, and Ricse.

27. For details on the structure and functions of the various MIPI sections in 1943–44, see *OMZSA-évkönyv 5704*, pp. 201–14.

28. For an identification of the MIPI officials and employees who distinguished themselves during the Nazi period, see Lévai, *Szürke könyv magyar zsidók megmentéséről* (Grey Book on the Rescuing of Hungarian Jews) (Budapest: Officina, 1947), pp. 185–86.

29. *Magyarországi Zsidók Lapja* (Journal of the Jews of Hungary), Budapest, July 13, 1944, p. 4. The journal, which was originally known as *A Magyar Zsidók Lapja* (Journal of Hungarian Jews) and published with the permission of the Nazi authorities, aimed to mislead the Jews still left in Hungary by claiming that OMZSA and MIPI were helping the Jews in the provincial ghettos whereas the ghettos had long ago been liquidated. For details on the activities of MIPI and OMZSA in the months preceding the occupation, see *A Magyar Zsidók Lapja* January 5 and 27; February 17 and 24; and March 2 and 9.

30. Budapest, for example, had a large network of institutions for the handicapped, orphans, and destitute children; academic schools; and apprentice schools, some of which were supported by ORT or MIKÉFE. For a partial listing, see *Omzsa-évkönyv 5704*, p. 225. For details on the MIKÉFE, whose background is traced to 1842, see *A Magyar Zsidók Lapja*, January 27, 1944, p. 2 and February 3, 1944, pp. 3–4. For details on the *Yeshivot*, see Abraham Fuchs, *Yeshivot Hungaria* (Hungarian Yeshivot) (Jerusalem: The Author, 1978), 606 pp. See also chapter 1.

31. The performances were in Goldmark Hall, at the Wesselényi Street building of the Jewish community of Pest. The hall was named after Károly Goldmark, a famous Hungarian-Jewish composer.

32. For the 1943–44 season, for example, OMIKE planned a series of eight concerts,

five operas, and a number of plays. Its operatic repertoire included Bizet's *Carmen*, Gounod's *Faust*, Mozart's *Così fan tutte* and *Marriage of Figaro*, Verdi's *Aida*, *Rigoletto*, and *Traviata*, and Strauss' *Fledermaus*. For a complete listing of the 1943–44 program, see *Omzsa-évkonyv 5704*, pp. 243–46.

33. See chapter 10 and Lévai, *Fekete könyv*, pp. 69–77.

34. See chapter 29 and Randolph L. Braham, "Zionism in Hungary," in *Encyclopedia of Zionism and Israel*, ed. Raphael Patai (New York: Herzl Press and McGraw Hill, 1971), pp. 523–27.

35. In 1943–44, the Pro-Palestine Association was headed by Dr. Kornél Kőrösy. For details on the *Keren ha'yesod* and the *Keren Kayemet l'Yisrael*, see *Encyclopedia of Zionism and Israel*, pp. 627–29, 658–60.

36. The eight communal districts did not include the Jewish communities in the territories of Felvidék and Kárpátalja (which were acquired from Czechoslovakia in 1938–39), Northern Transylvania (which was acquired from Romania in 1940), and Délvidék—the Bácska and adjacent areas (which was acquired from Yugoslavia in 1941). These were still in the process of administrative reorganization. *Magyarországi tiszti cim- és névtára* (Title and Name Register of Hungary) (Budapest: A Magyar Királyi Állami Nyomda, 1942), p. 559.

37. *Ibid.*

38. For the role of the ennobled Jews in Hungary, see William O. McCagg, Jr., *Jewish Nobles and Geniuses in Modern Hungary* (New York: Columbia University Press, 1972), 254 pp.

39. Lévai, *Fekete könyv*, p. 35.

40. For a comparative evaluation of the characteristics of the Hungarian and Romanian Jewish leaderships, see Béla Vágó's "Contrasting Jewish Leaderships in Wartime Hungary and Romania," in *The Holocaust—A Generation After* (Jerusalem: Institute of Contemporary Jewry of the Hebrew University of Jerusalem, 1980). See also his "T'murot b'Hanhagat Yehudei Hungaria Biyunei Milkhemet Haolom Hashniya" (Changes in the Hungarian Jewish Leadership During World War II), in *Hanhagat Yehudei Hungaria Bamivahan Hashoa*, pp. 61–76, and his "Hamanhigut hayehudit beHungaria ubeRomaia uteguvoeha limdiniut hanatzit" (Jewish Leadership Groups in Hungary and Romania—Their Reactions to Nazi Politics) in *Dapim lecheker tekufat hashoa* (Studies on the Holocaust Period) (Tel Aviv: Hakibbutz Hameuchad, 1978), 1:25–43.

41. Stern, *A zsidókérdés Magyarországon*, p. 31. See in this context George Barany's " 'Magyar Jew or Jewish Magyar?' Reflections on the Question of Assimilation," in *Jews and Non-Jews in Eastern Europe, 1918–1945*, eds. B. Vago and G. L. Mosse (New York: John Wiley, 1974), pp. 51–98.

42. Stern, *A zsidókérdés Magyarországon*, p. 30.

43. *Ibid.*, p. 31.

44. *Ibid.*, p. 19.

45. Some of these factors that underlay the impotence of the traditional Hungarian Jewish leaders during the occupation were also noted by Ernő Munkácsi, Secretary General of the Jewish Community of Pest and a leading official of the Jewish Council (*Judenrat*). See his *Hogyan történt?* (How Did It Happen?) (Budapest: Renaissance, 1947), pp. 10 and 54–55. For an evaluation of the Jewish leadership after the German occupation of March 19, 1944, see chapter 14.

46. The artistic and cultural programs were organized under the auspices and sponsorship of the OMIKE. They included "cultural afternoons," plays by the leading playwrights of the world, including Racine, Ibsen, and Molière, and operas and operettas. In the month of the occupation, for example, the OMIKE was offering Verdi's Aida. As a matter of fact, the first contact between the SS and the Jewish leadership on the day of the occupation was through László Bánóczi, who was then acting as master of ceremonies

in an OMIKE program at the Jewish community's headquarters at 12, Síp Street (see chapter 14).

47. *A Magyar Zsidók Lapja*, Budapest, January 22, 1942, p. 7.

48. In his February 1942 lecture on the major American Jewish organizations—the AJDC, ORT, HIAS, etc.—Sándor Eppler, who knew the leaders of these organizations, spoke only about their structure and personnel without discussing some of the beleaguered European Jewish communities these organizations were then trying to help. *Ibid.*, February 5, 1942, p. 5.

49. See, for example, the statements by Samu Stern, Nison Kahan, and Géza Ribáry at the special February 1942 meeting of the Jewish Community of Pest. *Ibid.*

50. *Ibid.*, April 30, 1942.

51. *Ibid.*, September 2, 1943. In Trianon Hungary, only 9,764 (0.1 percent) identified their nationality as Jewish in 1941. *Magyar statisztikai évkönyv* (Hungarian Statistical Yearbook) (New Series, Budapest: Stephaneum, vols. 51–54, 1943–1946, 1948), p. 20.

52. See, for example, the appeal for help to the Jewish labor servicemen, which is replete with the same sentiments. *A Magyar Zsidók Lapja*, January 13, 1944, p. 3.

53. Statement by Eugene (Jenő) Ligeti, dated November 21, 1945, available at the YIVO-Institute for Jewish Research, New York, Archives, file no. 768/3555, p. 10, and *A Magyar Zsidók Lapja*, April 13, 1944, p. 2.

54. Országos Levéltár (National Archives), Budapest, P 1434, László Endre File no. 17, as cited by György Ránki, *1944. március 19* (March 19, 1944), 2nd ed (Budapest: Kossuth, 1978), p. 259.

55. *A Magyar Zsidók Lapja*, October 11, 1941, p. 2.

56. *Ibid.*

57. The Nazi-financed *Nyilas* (Arrow Cross) newspapers and anti-Semitic journals never revealed, of course, that "resettlement" was actually "deportation and extermination" in the Nazi dictionary.

58. Yad Vashem, Jerusalem, Archives M-20/93. For further details, see chapter 23. See also Alex Weissberg, *Advocate for the Dead.* (London: Andre Deutsch, 1958), p. 60.

59. Livia Rothkirchen, *The Destruction of Slovak Jewry.* (Jerusalem: Yad Vashem, 1961), p. xxvii.

60. The Poles were accorded many privileges, including government allowances and the right to have their own Polish-language public and secondary schools. Among their patrons were Monsignor Béla Varga, the head of the Smallholders' Party, and Countess Szapáry, the Polish-born wife of Count A. Szapáry. They also had their own self-help organizations, including the Polish Committee (*Polski komitet*) that was headed by General Kollataj-Zrzednicki, Dr. Glasner, and Dr. Wawrzyniak. The Committee was quite aloof to the Polish Jews until 1942, when it changed its position presumably under pressure from the Polish Government-in-Exile in London. Livia Rothkirchen, "Hungary—an Asylum for the Refugees of Europe," in *YVS*, 7:131–32. The situation of the Polish Jewish officers and soldiers changed dramatically after the Szálasi coup. On November 19, 1944, the Vámosmikola camp, which was under the command of First Lieutenant Béla Turcsányi, was dissolved and the internees were, like the many thousands of Budapest Jews, marched toward the Austrian border along the Komárom–Hegyeshalom route. The officers who survived the ordeal filed a protest memorandum in Debrecen on January 14, 1945, indicting the rulers of the *Nyilas* regime for the violation of international conventions relating to the treatment of POWs. The memorandum is available at the University of Haifa, Historical Documentation Center on East Central Europe, H3h19/Arch. M.E.I–12.

61. A number of prominent Hungarian Jews, including Baroness Edith Weiss, did their best to facilitate the border crossings by trying to bribe frontier guards. Their efforts, on the whole, were generally fruitless.

62. Stern, *A zsidókérdés Magyarországon,* pp. 25–26.

63. *Der Kastner-Bericht,* pp. 36–38. Joel Brand contradicts this aspect of Kasztner's account, claiming that nothing came of the attempt to convene a meeting of the Hungarian parliamentarians of Jewish descent. Weissberg, *Advocate for the Dead,* p. 27.

64. Rothkirchen, "Hungary—an Asylum," pp. 134–35.

65. *Ibid.,* p. 134.

66. *Bericht des Leiters des polnisch-jüdischen Flüchtlingskomites in Ungarn* (Report of the Leader of the Polish-Jewish Refugee Committee in Hungary). Yad Vashem, Jerusalem, Archives M-20/99.

67. *Der Kastner-Bericht,* p. 39.

68. For details on Springmann's activities in Hungary, especially in behalf of Polish-Jewish refugees and in connection with the deportation of the "alien" Jews in 1941, see his statement dated January 28, 1958, at Yad Vashem, Jerusalem, Archives 500/41-1.

69. For Brand's account, see Weissberg, *Advocate for the Dead.* For an interesting account of Kasztner's activities in this sphere, see "Kastner's Part in the Smuggling of Refugees—Testimony of Miklós Wesselényi," in *YVS,* 7:143–46. See also chapter 29.

70. One of Brand's closest assistants in these operations was Perez Révész, a Hungarian-speaking Slovak Jewish refugee, who settled in Israel after the war.

71. *Der Kastner-Bericht,* pp. 43, 46–47. For further details on Teicholz's activities in Hungary, see chapter 23.

72. Even the legitimate certificate holders had difficulty emigrating because of the reluctance of the Turkish government to grant transit visas.

73. For a sample of the memoranda and the exchange of correspondence between A. Silberschein and Honti, see Yad Vashem, Jerusalem, Archives M-20/96. Concerning Keresztes-Fischer's remarks, see the dispatch by Burton Y. Berry, the American Consul General in Istanbul, dated December 23, 1943, addressed to the American Secretary of State.

74. Philip Freudiger, *Five Months* (manuscript submitted to this author in 1972), p. 4.

75. *Der Kastner-Bericht,* p. 47. For Freudiger's view of this association, see *Five Months,* p. 5.

76. *Ibid.,* p. 45. The number of Jewish refugees who had found haven in Hungary during the war was much larger. Many of these stayed in Hungary only for a shorter period of time while awaiting the opportunity to leave for Palestine or elsewhere in the free world.

77. In addition to Barlas, the Istanbul delegation of the Jewish agency (referred to hereafter as the section of the *Va'ad ha-Hatzala* or simply as the Istanbul *Vaada*) included A. Lader, the personal representative of Yitzhak Gruenbaum, the head of the central office in Jerusalem; Venya Pomerantz and Menahem Bader, the representatives of the *Ha-Kibbutz ha-Meuchad* and of the *Ha-Kibbutz ha-Artzi,* respectively; and Yaakov Griffel, who represented the *Agudat Yisrael.* For an evaluation of the activities of this section, see Dalia Ofer, "The Activities of the Jewish Agency Delegation in Istanbul in 1943," in *RAH,* pp. 435–50. Its vast correspondence with the Budapest Relief and Rescue Committee may be found in the archives of Beth Lohamei Hagetaot, the Israel State Archives in Jerusalem, and at Moreshet, Israel. For a catalog to the Hungarian files, 1942–44, see *Arkhivon lishkat hakesher be-Kushta* (Archives of the Yishuv Rescue Board in Istanbul). Compiled by Frieda Laster (Haifa: The University of Haifa and The Ghetto Fighters' House, 1977), 117 pp.

78. For unknown reasons, Schwalb refused to make his archival materials available to the public.

79. Much of the correspondence that emanated from the Working Group, including the letters, notes, and memoranda of Gisi Fleischmann, may be found in the Yad Vashem Archives, File M-20/93. For further details, see Livia Rothkirchen, "Kishrei Hamachteret beyn Hamanhigut Hayehudit b'Slovakia u b'Hungaria" (The Underground Relations Be-

tween the Jewish Leaderships of Slovakia and Hungary), in *Hanhagat Yehudei Hungaria Bamivahan Hashoa*, pp. 118–34.

80. *Der Kastner-Bericht*, p. 51.

81. See chapter 29. For biographical data on these agents, consult *Der Kastner-Bericht;* Weissberg, *Advocate for the Dead;* André Biss, *A Million Jews to Save* (London: Hutchinson, 1973); and Béla Vágó, "The Intelligence Aspects of the Joel Brand Mission," in *YVS*, 10:111–28.

82. See their postwar memoirs.

CHAPTER FOUR

THE BEGINNING OF THE END

Darányi's Ambiguous Policies

CONTRARY TO the expectations of the liberal-conservative forces of Hungary, the demagogic proto-Fascist policies of Gyula Gömbös did not prove ephemeral. The emulation of the Third Reich in the pursuit of the overriding revisionist ambitions became an irreversible aspect of the country's domestic and foreign policies. The perpetuation of Gömbös' policies was not only a consequence of the spectacular successes of Hitler's Germany, but also of the ambiguous political position of Kálmán Darányi. A protegé of István Bethlen, Darányi was generally considered a loyal member of the traditional conservative large-land-owning–capitalist group. It was primarily because of this assessment that he was first appointed Minister of Agriculture and then, after Gömbös' illness, Prime Minister.[1]

However, as his subsequent actions clearly revealed (see chapter 2), Darányi was much more sympathetic with the aspirations of the extreme Right and with the policies of the Third Reich than his close friends and political associates had suspected. A basically simple, narrow-minded but generally competent bureaucrat, Darányi had enjoyed the confidence of Gömbös and many other ultra-rightists without having aroused the suspicion of the Bethlenite forces over his apparent duplicity. His politics of "consensus" was aimed at co-opting the *Nyilas* into the traditional governmental system purportedly in order to stunt their revolutionary momentum. Pursued without the knowledge of his mentor, these policies were based not only on expediency, but also on personal conviction.

Darányi's sympathies with the extreme Right and the Reich were reinforced during his several trips to Berlin, where he also met Hitler. While the Bethlenite forces misinterpreted or failed to recognize the realities of Darányi's ambiguous policies, the so-called "respectable" wing of the Right radical movement was quick to take full advantage of them. This faction, which was composed of the more articulate self-appointed political leaders of the gentry-officer group, was quite sympathetic with some aspects of the large-landowning–capitalist ruling classes' program. Furthermore, while sharing the virulent anti-Semitism and irredentist chauvinism of other factions of the Hungarian Right radical movement, composed primarily of the lower middle class and the "misguided" elements of the worker and peasant classes, it did not always share, and occasionally even opposed, the demagoguery and violence of the latter group.

The gentry-officer group, which included a considerable number of military men of Swabian background, was particularly impressed with the achievements of the German National Socialists at home and abroad. These "respectable" leaders were extremely eager to see Hungary involved in the establishment of the "New Order" in Europe and reap the benefits of the Nazi revisionist-revanchist policies as an active member of the Axis Alliance. They were eager to join the bandwagon, for which purpose they felt that Hungary's swift and massive rearmament was both inevitable and desirable.

The Győr Program

Since the ultra-rightist critics of the government's domestic and foreign policies were firmly convinced that the country's inadequate military preparedness was due to the machinations of the Jews, the Socialists, and the other anti-German elements, the issue of rearmament became intertwined with that of anti-Semitism. It was not an accident that the initiative for the emulation of the Third Reich in the handling of both issues came from the higher echelon of the General Staff, which included many Germanophile officers of Swabian background appointed during Gömbös' last two years in office. The leadership had been assumed by the politically oriented officers who were semi-clandestinely though actively involved in ultra-rightist organizations or parties. Foremost among these were General Jenő Rátz and General Jenő Ruszkay.

Admiral Miklós Horthy was generally recognized as the key to the solution of both issues. He was approached almost simultaneously, if not concertedly, by two officers' groups demanding immediate and resolute action. One was headed by Rátz, who articulated his position at a meeting late in December 1937, which was also attended by Minister of Defense Vilmos Rőder and Minister of Finance Tihamér Fabinyi. While the two pro-Bethlen Ministers were not immediately convinced of the merits of Rátz's arguments, Horthy had reassured the General that some solution would somehow be found.[2] The views of the other group of officers were summarized in a memorandum which was prepared at their behest by General Károly Soós, the former Minister of Defense. The contents and objectives of the memorandum were analyzed by General Soós during his private audiences with Horthy and Darányi early in January 1938. In addition to the demands for the swift rearming of Hungary for the advancement of its historic goals, the memorandum also articulated the officers' position on the Jewish question. It demanded, *inter alia:*

- The reduction of Jewish influence in the economy by supporting the economic activities of Christians.
- The enactment of legislation for the exclusion of Jewish influence from the press, theater, movies, and other related cultural activities.
- The "merciless persecution of all left-wing agitation."[3]

The drive of both groups of officers was soon crowned with success, primarily because of the political conversion of Béla Imrédy, the then "liberal-conservative" Governor of the National Bank. His conversion was to a large extent the work of Rátz, with whom he later formed the Party of Hungarian Renewal (see chapter 5). A rather vain though brilliant financier, Imrédy, an Anglophile, suddenly saw himself as the possible savior of Hungary. Acting in collusion with Darányi and Rátz, Imrédy worked out a detailed legislative plan based on the officers' program with primary emphasis on the immediate solution of the rearmament and Jewish issues. The successful implementation of the plan also required the reshuffling of the government. Some of the most vocal pro-Bethlen representatives were replaced.

The details of the plan were revealed in a historic speech made by Darányi in Győr on March 5, 1938. The Prime Minister announced that Hungary was about to embark on a massive rearmament program and prepare for an unrelenting struggle against Bolshevism.[4] To the great shock of the Jews and the decent, liberal Hungarians, he also announced that Hungary was ready to come to grips with the Jewish question by trying to diminish their role in certain sectors of the country's economic and cultural life.

The announcement of the anti-Jewish program was the beginning of the end of this once flourishing Jewish community of Europe. For, while anti-Semitism until that time was the primary public preoccupation of the rightist extremists, its adoption as a government program to be solved on an institutional basis denoted a fundamental departure from the traditions of 1848 and 1867. The immediate impact and ultimate consequences of Darányi's anti-Jewish statements were not mitigated by his rationalization that the planned anti-Jewish law would be "the best guarantee against anti-Semitism and intolerance."

Placing Hungary in the forefront of European countries in the emulation of Nazi Germany's anti-Jewish drive, Darányi had the following to say on the issue:

I believe that it is entirely fruitless to continue an academic discussion on whether or not it is correct to talk about the Jewish question. There is a Jewish question! It is one of our unsolved problems! If it is unsolved, I believe that only a planned and a legal solution of it is possible. I see the essence of the question in the fact that the Jews living within Hungary play a disproportionately large role in certain branches of the economic life, partly owing to their particular propensities and positions and partly owing to the indifference of the Hungarian race. Their position is also disproportionate in the sense that they live to an overwhelming extent in the cities, and above all in the capital. A disproportionately large number of Jews adopted occupational fields in which the possibilities for making a living are better and easier. The penetration of the Jews into the capital had a natural impact upon this city's economic and cultural life, a manifestation which is not always in harmony with the aspirations of the Magyars. The conflict which evolved from this given situation prevents the total unification of the national forces and is a constant source of agitation in the country's public life. The planned and legal solution of the question is the basic condition for the establishment of a just situation—a just situation that will either correct or eliminate the aforementioned social disproportions and will diminish Jewry's influence in the nation's cultural life and other fields to its proper level. Such an arrangement, which will enable the Christian society to acquire its proper place in industry, commerce, credit, and the other fields of the economy, is also in the best interests of Jewry, for it can ease considerably the [danger of] anti-Semitism and, consequently, the spread of extremist and intolerant movements.[5]

The Győr Program, as Darányi's proposals came to be known, was received enthusiastically by the rightist press. The demands for its immediate and total implementation became more frenzied a few days later, when Nazi Germany emerged as Hungary's direct neighbor as a result of the Anschluss. The Jewish question and its proposed solution, having acquired the official imprimatur of the government, were suddenly transformed into a national obsession. Thereafter, it was as if Hungary had no other socioeconomic problem confronting it. To the ruling landowning aristocracy, which had been practicing its own "civilized" form of anti-Semitism, this national preoccupation served as a blessing in disguise, for it helped deter attention from the grave social-agrarian questions. The newspapers and the radio broadcast were full of statistical references to the disproportionate large number of Jews in the press, the arts, the professions, and the various fields of industry, banking, and commerce.[6] These same sources almost always ignored the fact that Jews were almost totally excluded from certain fields, including the civil service and the military, and that a large percentage of the Jews was as destitute as the exploited Christian workers and peasants. They tended to see all Jews in the light of the numerically few, but highly opulent—and occasionally quite ostentatious—Jewish members of the upper middle class.

In accordance with the scenario worked out by Imrédy and Rátz, Darányi restructured his government by replacing a few key Bethlenite ministers with Germanophiles.[7] Shortly thereafter, Darányi introduced the two major government bills, whose text was secretly drafted by Imrédy on the basis of the major recommendations of the officers' groups. These related to the Five-Year Plan for rearmament and economic development and to the restriction of the Jews in certain fields of the country's economic and cultural life.

The First Anti-Jewish Law

With the domestic and international climate conducive to the initiation of anti-Semitic measures, Darányi lost no time in introducing Government Bill No. 616, designed to bring about "the more effective protection of the social and economic balance" of the country.[8] The legislative memorandum relating to this first comprehensive anti-Jewish draft bill, like that for the Second Anti-Jewish Law, was provided by Count Pál Teleki (see chapter 5), a leading member of the conservative aristocratic ruling wing of the Right, who emphasized the danger and detrimental effect of the Jews' encroachment and the necessity of defending the nation against that encroachment. It further stressed that the restriction of the Jews was a national duty.[9]

Though public opinion had been successfully molded by years of vicious anti-Semitic agitation, which was frequently reinforced by repeated disorders and riots caused by the ultra-rightists, the Jews and their liberal friends were shocked by the eagerness with which the "liberal-conservative" government proceeded with the legitimization of anti-Semitism by tackling it officially.

Following their traditional tactic for the redress of grievances, the leaders of the recognized Jewish communities appealed to the government and to the representatives of the various responsible national parties and organizations to help block the adoption of the bill. They expressed their shock and sorrow over the government's action in light of the great services Jewry had rendered Hungary in both war and peace. The Jews were not alone in the struggle against the bill. Some of Hungary's most outstanding writers, journalists, artists, and scientists, including Béla Bartók, József Darvas, Zoltán Kodály, Zsigmond Móricz, and Árpád Szakasits, spoke up eloquently and forcefully against the inequities of the draft bill. They reminded the government in many of their protest declarations that it was the country's constitutional provisions relating to civil rights and liberties, which incorporated the principle of the equality of citizenship, that set Hungary apart from many another contemporary European state. They coupled their reminder with a warning that if the blatantly discriminatory bill were to be enacted into law there would come a time when every Hungarian would look back upon it in shame.[10]

The Jews and their liberal friends had a few supporters in Parliament. In the lower house, the chief opposition came from the few representatives of the Liberal and Social Democratic parties. Among the most eloquent and vocal of these were the Jewish representatives, including János Vázsonyi and Dr. Béla Fábián. The Social Democrats were particularly forceful in their condemnation of the bill.[11] In the upper house, the struggle against the bill was spearheaded by Lajos Láng, György Prónay, and Antal Sigray. They, like their colleagues in the lower house, invoked a series of universally valid moral principles—including liberty, justice, and equality—and reviewed the historical contribution of the Jews to the advancement of Hungary, but to no avail. Their valiant efforts were in vain, for the bill, in tune with the spirit of the times, had the support of the overwhelming majority in both houses.

The cause of the Jews and of their liberal friends was lost when the representatives of the Christian Churches came out in support of the bill. Participating in the debates of the upper house during the second half of May (by which time Imrédy had replaced Darányi as Prime Minister), the leaders of the various Christian denominations, like many other "friends" of Jewry, argued that the adoption of the bill would in fact "prevent the further exacerbation of the Jewish question and assure the disarming of anti-Semitism." They generally demanded only minor adjustments in support of the converts or for the elimination of potential ambiguities in the draft legislation. In his statement of

May 24, for example, Sándor Raffay, the Bishop of the Evangelical (Lutheran) Church, declared emphatically that he fully recognized the necessity for the adoption in the Mountain District of the anti-Jewish bill. Completely ignoring the character and origins of anti-Semitism, he declared self-righteously that the introduction of such a bill could have been avoided if only the Jews had mended their ways and changed their attitude earlier. His only substantive proposal related to the determination of the cut-off date for converts who were to be exempted from the provisions of the bill. Specifically, he proposed that the date of August 1, 1919, i.e., the date Béla Kun was compelled to leave the country, be changed to August 31. He also argued for the possible use of 1868 or 1895, the years when the Jews of Hungary were emancipated and the Jewish religion was recognized as one of the "received" religions of the country, because, in his view, a qualitative difference had to be made between those who converted for whatever reason at the age of 40 or 50 and those who were converted to Christianity at 6 or 7.[12]

It was in a similar vein that Bishop László Ravasz of the Reformed (Calvinist) Church, spoke in the upper house that same day. While he parenthetically expressed a theoretical preference for the use of total assimilation and indigenousness, rather than conversion, as the basic criteria for granting exemptions, he emphasized that Jewry did not constitute a religion, but a distinct race. He supported the bill on the assumption that it would not only assure the peace, tranquillity, and security of the nation, but would also in the long run serve the best interests of those opposing it. He proceeded with an evaluation of the social and historical factors that molded the "undesirable" traits of the Jews and suggested that total assimilation (i.e., assimilation in spirit as well as in outward appearances) or Zionism "practiced outside the borders of Hungary" were the best possible solutions to the Jewish question.[13]

Similar arguments were advanced by Cardinal Jusztinián Serédi, the Archbishop of Esztergom and Prince Primate of Hungary, and Gyula Glattfelder, the Bishop of Csanád. The public statements of the Christian Church leaders contributed not only to the adoption of the bill, but also, and in the long run more importantly, to the legitimization of anti-Semitism and of the many anti-Jewish movements. Their position on this and several other anti-Jewish laws prepared the ground for the effective implementation of the ghettoization and deportation program in 1944. Their public declarations in support of discriminatory laws contributed to the psychological conditioning of the Hungarian people. This explains in part the passivity with which the Hungarian masses witnessed the suffering of their fellow citizens of the Jewish faith and the lack of any meaningful organized resistance in the country following the German occupation in March 1944.

Provisions of the Law. Enjoying the support of the overwhelming majority of both houses of the Hungarian Parliament, Bill No. 616 was enacted into law on May 28 under the signatures of Horthy and Imrédy. Officially known as Law No. XV of 1938,[14] this piece of legislation marked a radical departure from the constitutional evolution of Hungary since 1867, if not 1848. For all practical purposes, the new law amended Law No. XVII of 1868 relating to the emancipation of the Jews. With the exception of the short-lived *Numerus Clausus* Act of 1920, it was the first to draw a legal distinction between Hungarian citizens on the basis of religion.

The declared ultimate scope of the law was to reduce to 20 percent the proportion of the Jews in the professions and in financial, commercial, and industrial enterprises employing more than ten persons. To achieve this goal, the law provided for the establishment of special chambers for the press, the theater, and the movie industry to supplement those already existing for lawyers, physicians, and engineers, and stipulated that no person except members of these chambers could be employed in any capacity in these professions and that Jews could constitute no more than 20 percent of the total membership.[15] The following categories of Jews were to be excluded from the quota:

- War invalids, those who had experienced active combat, and the widows and orphans of war heroes.
- Those who had converted to Christianity on or before August 1, 1919, if they maintained their affiliation with their adopted denomination uninterruptedly.[16]
- The descendants of the above category of converts, if they did not resume their affiliation with the Jewish community.

Until the ratio of 20 percent was achieved in the total membership of the professional chambers, Jews could not exceed 5 percent of the newly admitted members.

It was envisioned that the new law's objectives would be carried out within five years—by June 30, 1943. Exceptions were to be allowed only in a few well-substantiated cases in which the Council of Ministers could, on the recommendation of the particular Minister involved, extend the deadline by another five years.

No sooner was the law enacted than a series of Ministerial decrees were passed for its implementation.[17] According to the original plan, approximately 15,000 Jewish professionals were expected to lose their jobs at a semi-annual rate of 1,500. With the addition of the breadwinners' dependents, the total number of Jews originally estimated to be affected by the law was around 50,000

The chief architects of the law, including Prime Ministers Darányi and Imrédy, argued that since the Jews constituted only a little over 5 percent of the total population it was not unfair to limit their participation in the country's economic and intellectual life to 20 percent.[18] They failed to see in the act any violation of the basic moral and constitutional principles entailed by such a blatant discrimination between Jews and non-Jews and between various types of converts. While some of them insisted, for the moment at least, that the act would solve the Jewish question and stunt the anti-Semitic drive of the Right radicals, most of them, like many of the "friends" of the Jews, failed to realize that it was but the beginning of an avalanche of anti-Jewish measures that would end in disaster. But the national-chauvinist fervor coupled with a magnetic rightist "idealism," fired by the prospects of imminent upward mobility and possible redistribution of wealth at the expense of the Jews, were too overpowering for the relatively few champions of reason, sanity, and decency to overcome. In vain was their effort to draw attention to the many positive contributions the Jews had made to the economic and cultural enrichment of Hungary. Equally in vain was their review of the Jews' pro-Magyar role in the multinational state of the pre-World War I era and of their continued pro-Magyar posture in the Successor States. The enemies of the Jews remembered and wanted only to remember one thing: the disproportionately large number of Jews in the leadership of the short-lived Communist dictatorship of 1919. They were not concerned with the fact that the overwhelming majority of the Jewish masses opposed, and suffered from, that dictatorship as much as the other citizens of the country (not to speak about the horrors of the White Terror which far surpassed those of the Red Terror in scope and intensity). They were, in short, eager to conclude, in the manner of László Ottlik, that anti-Semitism "was the inevitable result of conspicuous Jewish predominance in all the most typical manifestations of intellectual depravity."[19]

Ironically, the Jewish leaders tended to echo the position taken by Darányi and Imrédy by rationalizing the adoption of the law. They acquiesced in the anti-Jewish measure of the government by arguing, in light of the worsening condition of the Jews in the Third Reich and neighboring Romania, that the "reasonable" restrictions imposed upon the Hungarian Jews would not only "take the wind out of the sails of the extremists," but would also prevent the degeneration of the anti-Semitic agitation of the *Nyilas* into outright persecution. In fact, according to some sources, the same rationalization induced the Jewish leaders not only to accept, but also to actually advocate the adoption of such "mildly restrictive" measures.[20] As in the early 1920s, when the *Numerus Clausus* Act was at the center of attention, the Jewish leaders rejected the attempts of the Western Jewish organizations to "interfere" in what they conceived as a purely internal matter.[21]

The introduction of the anti-Jewish bill was Darányi's last major act as Prime Minister. His semi-clandestine dealings with the ultra-Right, including his negotiations with Szálasi proved to be his undoing. For, while the liberal-conservative aristocratic ruling group had few, if any, scruples about the adoption of the anti-Jewish law, it became mortally frightened over the possible rapprochement with the extremists, who were publicly committed to the effectuation of social change.

Imrédy in Power

It is one of the ironies of modern Hungarian history that Béla Imrédy, the man of whom the Nazis became most appreciative in the early 1940s, had been appointed Prime Minister on May 14, 1938, because of his liberal, pro-Western orientation. A devout Catholic, Imrédy was a recognized expert in financial and banking affairs and almost universally believed to be pro-British in his political convictions. This evaluation was reinforced by his first actions in office, including the formation of his government.[22] His policy declarations were in tune with the spirit of the times. They called for a "national-Christian" political line in the pursuit of two great ideals—"social justice and popular, national unity."

Since the primary objective of the large-landowning–capitalist ruling group was the preservation of the state and its traditional social order, Imrédy proceeded with vigorous measures to stem the tide of Right extremism. He was instrumental in issuing Order in Council No. 3400, which forbade state employees from joining any political parties. This measure was directed especially against the civil servants and military personnel, whose sympathies lay with the Right radicals. Shortly after the issuance of the Order, the government's attention was focused on restricting freedom of the press,[23] preventing the increasingly ominous seditious activities of Ferenc Szálasi, who had by then emerged as the symbol of, and a catalyst for, the national Right radical movement. Encouraged and generously supported by the Germans, the *Nyilas* became particularly active in 1938. In addition to an aggressive press campaign, mostly directed against the Jews, they devoted special attention to the mass distribution of propaganda materials in all the major cities of the country. These combined crude anti-Semitism with social demagoguery directed against the ruling conservative aristocratic class. Particularly vicious and upsetting to the Regent and the government was a flyer which bore on one side the familiar "Long Live Szálasi" slogan, and on the other the text "Out with Rebecca from the Palace." This was an allusion to Mrs. Horthy, who was maliciously, though reportedly not totally inaccurately, accused by the *Nyilas* of having some Jewish blood in her family tree. Although Szálasi apparently had nothing to do with this particular flyer, he was tried on a number of charges associated with his subversive activities and condemned on July 7, 1938, to three years' hard labor and five years' loss of civil liberties. Szálasi's incarceration did not, of course, put an end to the flourishing of the *Nyilas* movement. If anything, it helped enhance his stature as a hero and martyr and further the cause of the movement, as reflected in the election results of May 1939.

In foreign affairs, the attention of the Imrédy government was focussed on the possible advancement of Hungary's revisionist ambitions in the context of Germany's increasingly aggressive posture vis-à-vis Czechoslovakia. Ever since the November 1937 visit to Berlin by Darányi and Kánya, when Hitler discussed his plans for Austria and Czechoslovakia, the Germans lost no occasion to dangle before the Hungarians, in the most concrete terms, the possibility of territorial revision. At one time, the Hungarians were offered the return of Slovakia and Ruthenia as a reward for their involvement in the planned war against Czechoslovakia. The Hungarians, however, decided to follow a cautious "free-hand" policy, which rejected any one-sided reliance upon any particular state. Crystallized by Kánya, this policy reflected the interests of the country's conservative forces, which wished to pursue the goals of revisionism by keeping open as many alternatives as possible and by taking advantage of all favorable international developments. This cautious position was determined by many factors, including Hungary's fear of both Bolshevism and German expansionism, its relative lack of military preparedness, and its apprehensiveness about getting involved in a war against the Western democracies and their allies in the Little Entente. Hungary was particularly anxious to involve Great Britain along with the Third Reich and Italy in the settlement of the territorial and national disputes in East Central Europe. The Regent and the civilian, if not the military, leaders of Hungary were at the time convinced that in case of a world war, the Western democracies with their superior naval capabilities were bound to win eventually.

It was in view of these factors that the Hungarian leaders adopted a dilatory position in their negotiations with the Germans in 1938. This was evident in the attitude of the Hungarian delegation during Horthy's state visit to Kiel on August 22[24] as well as in the position of Imrédy during his visit to Hitler at Berchtesgaden on September 20. At Kiel, the Germans were particularly eager to impress Admiral Horthy with their naval power, for they were keenly aware of the Regent's military doctrines. Horthy was obviously particularly aware of the importance of controlling the sea lanes. The Kiel Conference was marred by the Germans' annoyance over Hungary's position at Bled.

Imrédy visited Hitler in the company of Kánya and Lajos Keresztes-Fischer. The Führer was in a particularly aggressive mood, mincing no words about his determination to settle accounts with Czechoslovakia within three weeks even at the risk of war. In spite of the concrete territorial offers, Imrédy, like Horthy at Kiel, opposed Hungary's involvement in a military conflict at the time, citing his country's lack of preparedness.

It was these same factors that had induced the Hungarians to come to terms, however temporarily, with the Little Entente at Bled on August 23. Under the Bled Agreement, Czechoslovakia, Romania, and Yugoslavia recognized Hungary's right to rearm and all parties renounced the use of force for the settlement of disputes. However, shortly after the agreement was signed, a controversy arose over its interpretation. The Hungarians, for example, insisted that since they did not find the position of the Hungarian minority in Czechoslovakia to be satisfactory, they did not regard the nonaggression obligation as binding toward that country. To protect their mutual historical interests, the Little Entente powers apparently signed a secret protocol reaffirming their obligation to provide assistance in case of an attack on any one of them by Hungary. The Germans viewed the Bled Agreement as an attempt to interfere with the anti-Czechoslovak drive of the Führer and were left unconvinced by Kánya's "explanations" about the Hungarian reservations with respect to Czechoslovakia.

Concurrently with its expedient rapprochement with its neighbors,

Hungary was also actively involved in a scheme initiated by the Poles and the Italians for the possible formation of a "Horizontal Axis" composed of Hungary, Italy, Poland, Romania, and Yugoslavia to serve as a "Third Europe" strong enough to resist both German and Russian expansionism.[25] The scheme failed to a large extent because of the appeasement policies of the Western democracies. The Munich Agreement of September 29 had sealed the fate not only of Czechoslovakia, but also of that peace which it purportedly aimed to preserve.[26] The Western powers were obviously more concerned at the time with the long-range dangers of Bolshevism than with the immediate political and military threat of Nazism.

The Acquisition of the Upper Province (*Felvidék*)

Encouraged by the Italian position at Munich, the Hungarians and the Poles insisted that they be given the same rights as the Germans to protect the interests of their compatriots in Czechoslovakia.[27] In contrast with the aggressive posture of the Poles, who were even willing to use force in the disputed Teschen (Cieszyn) area,[28] the Hungarians followed a relatively moderate course. They requested that the issue of the Hungarian-inhabited territories of Czechoslovakia be solved through negotiations on the basis of the principle of self-determination. In accordance with the terms of the Hungarian note of October 3, the negotiations began at Komárom on October 9.[29] The negotiations broke down four days later, as the parties used different census data in support of conflicting historical and political positions.[30] Since England and France were reluctant to fulfill their obligations under the Munich Agreement by participating in another Four Power conference, which Hitler also tried to avoid, the Hungarians decided to submit the issue to German-Italian arbitration. The two Axis Powers accepted this task on October 30, after having been assured by both Hungary and Czechoslovakia that they would treat the award as final.

The terms of the agreement were hammered out in Vienna on November 2 in a series of discussions headed by Ribbentrop and Ciano. Under the terms of the First Vienna Award, as the accord came to be known, Hungary acquired a territory of 4,630 square miles—a strip of land in Southern Slovakia and western Carpatho-Ruthenia which corresponded to the Hungarian-inhabited areas of Czechoslovakia (map 4.1)—with a total population of 1,075,600.[31] Of this, 4,020 square miles with approximately 895,000 people had originally belonged to Slovakia

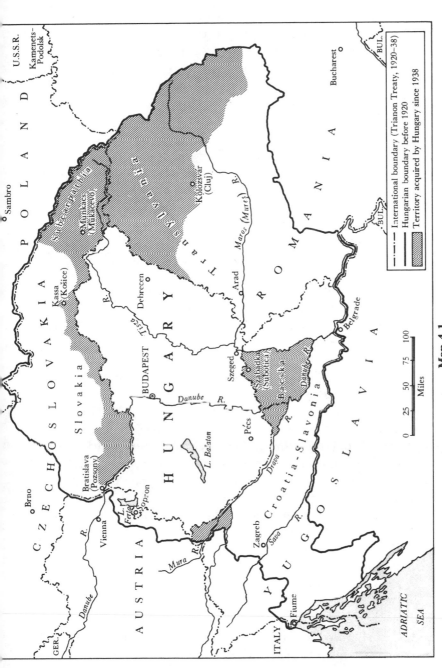

Map 4.1.

Hungary, 1919–1945.

1. Trianon Hungary; 2. Upper Province (*Felvidék*), 4,630 sq. m., acquired from Czechoslovakia in November 1938; 3. Carpatho-Ruthenia or Subcarpathia, 4,257 sq. m., acquired from Czechoslovakia in March 1939; 4. Northern Transylvania, 43,494 sq. m., acquired from Romania in August 1940; 5. The Bačka (Bácska), the Baranya Triangle, the Prekomurje (*Muravidék*), and the Medjumurje (*Muraköz*), 4,488 sq. m., acquired from Yugoslavia in April 1941.

and the remainder—610 square miles with 180,600 people—to Carpatho-Ruthenia.[32] The *Felvidék* (Upper Province), as the Hungarians called this area, included the cities of Kassa, Léva, Losonc, Munkács, and Ungvár, all great centers of Jewish orthodoxy. The Felvidék was occupied between November 3 and 8, and formally incorporated by an Act of Parliament on the 12th.[33]

The Jews of the *Felvidék*

According to the census of 1941, the Felvidék had a Jewish population of 67,876.[34] The major Jewish population centers in the area were as shown in table 4.1.

The 64,841 Jews living in the 26 cities listed in the table constituted 95.5 percent of the area's Jewish population.[35]

Toward the Second Anti-Jewish Law

The Munich Pact of September 29, 1938, constitutes a major milestone in the history of Hungary as well as in the history of the world. While it made possible the first vindication of Hungary's revisionist ambitions, it also induced a fundamental change in the country's domestic and foreign policies. Although the Western Powers and especially Great Britain were quite sympathetic to the Hungarian cause and expressed great satisfaction over the peaceful solution of the Czechoslovak crisis, their appeasement policies had convinced many of their Hungarian friends that only through close collaboration with the Axis Powers could Hungary's national-historical aspirations be fulfilled. Foremost among these political converts was Prime Minister Béla Imrédy. Imrédy's conversion proved fateful not only to himself—he was eventually executed for embracing the Axis cause—but also, and above all, to the Jews of Hungary.

Imrédy's dictatorial ambitions and flirtations with Nazism were first revealed in his Kaposvár speech of September 4, 1938, in which he outlined a new program for Hungary. While there is no doubt that one of the intentions of the speech was to dissipate the impressions caused by an interview he had given the *Daily Telegraph* of London two days earlier,[36] it incorporated a proto-Fascist program which summarized the later concrete demands of the Right radicals.[37] It is interesting to note that in his Kaposvár speech Imrédy did not announce any new anti-Jewish plans, stating that the existing anti-Jewish legislation was

TABLE 4.1.
THE MAJOR JEWISH POPULATION
CENTERS OF THE FELVIDÉK

Locality	Jewish Population	Percent of Local Population
Abauj-Torna County		
Kassa	10,079	15.0
Szepsi	200	8.5
Bars County		
Léva	1,271	10.0
Verebély	223	6.6
Bereg County		
Beregszász	5,856	30.2
Munkács	13,488	42.7
Szolyva	1,432	17.0
Oroszvég	909	31.3
Mezőkaszony	479	18.0
Gömör County		
Rimaszombat	635	9.0
Rozsnyó	388	5.7
Hont County		
Ipolyság	773	15.4
Komárom County		
Komárom	2,743	8.9
Nagymegyer	522	11.8
Nógrád County		
Losonc	1,747	11.7
Nyitra County		
Érsekujvár	2,492	10.7
Nagysurány	563	9.0
Pozsony County		
Dunaszerdahley	2,645	40.2
Galánta	1,216	23.9
Szenc	410	7.8
Nagymagyar	251	14.1
Ugocsa County		
Nagyszőllős	4,264	32.0
Halmi	1,329	32.0
Ung County		
Ungvár	9,576	27.2
Nagykapos	464	17.4
Zemplén County		
Királyhelmec	886	23.6

sufficient. His anti-Jewish plans were articulated shortly after the incorporation of the Felvidék two months later.

Imrédy's incipient bias toward Right radicalism was reinforced by many Hungarian politicians of the Felvidék, who were eager, at the expense of the Jews, to compensate themselves and their compatriots for whatever they had lost as a result of the territorial changes since Trianon. Perhaps no other politician from this region had as much influence upon Imrédy and the shaping of governmental policy as Andor Jaross, the former secretary of the United Hungarian Party (*Egységes Magyar Párt*) of Czechoslovakia and a leader of the 26 deputies who had been assigned to the Felvidék.[38] Jaross' general political views were similar to Imrédy's; his personality, however, was quite different. Jaross was coarse, aggressive, and occasionally brutal. His lack of idealism and erudition was matched by his corruption and anti-Semitism.[39] These were the very qualities that impressed the Germans upon their occupation of Hungary in March 1944. In the German-imposed Sztójay government, Jaross served as Minister of the Interior (chapter 13).

It was under Jaross' sinister influence, among other things, that Imrédy became increasingly impatient with the "slow working" of the parliamentary process and visibly unhappy with the composition of his cabinet. A few days after the incorporation of the Felvidek, Imrédy, enjoying the national euphoria over the first success of revisionism, tendered his resignation convinced that the Regent would entrust him with the formation of a new government. Duly reappointed, Imrédy reshuffled his cabinet on November 15. This involved not only the removal of his potential political rivals, but also the expansion of the power of such Germanophile ministers as Antal Kunder and the inclusion of Jaross as Minister for the Felvidék. These changes, which were clearly designed to strengthen the Right radical forces,[40] were accompanied by personnel changes in several civilian and military agencies. One of the most ominous of these changes was the replacement of Lajos Keresztes-Fischer by Henrik Werth, an openly Germanophile general, as the Chief of the Hungarian General Staff early in October 1938. On December 10, Kánya, the independent-minded foreign minister, was replaced by István Csáky, who did not hesitate to declare that his policy was "quite simply the policy of the Rome-Berlin Axis all along the line."[41]

Imrédy lost no time in advancing his program. On the very day of his reappointment, he outlined his plans before the Council of Ministers and before a meeting of the Government Party leaders. He talked frankly about the necessity of amending the Constitution in order to make possible the streamlining of the parliamentary process[42] and about the desirability of speeding up the land reform program. It was during these meetings that Imrédy delcared that he had "revised" his position on the Jewish question. In contrast to his position taken at Kaposvár, Imrédy now rationalized the necessity of further anti-Jewish legislation. Having received wholehearted support from both his party and the Hungarian Parliament, Imrédy proceeded with the implementation of his program. He lost no time in informing the Third Reich via Döme Sztójay, the Hungarian Minister in Berlin, that Hungary would thenceforth follow an openly more pro-Axis policy. This also entailed the emulation of the Reich in the handling of the Jewish question.

His plans for a second major anti-Jewish law were outlined to a meeting of the Council of Ministers on December 12. The draft of the legislative text was prepared by István Antal, then Secretary of State in the Ministry of Justice, acting in cooperation with Pál Teleki, the Minister of Cults and Public Education, who wrote the preamble in the legislative memorandum relating to the bill. The bill, titled "Concerning the Restriction of the Participation of the Jews in Public and Economic Life," was submitted to Parliament by András Tasnádi Nagy, the Minister of Justice, on December 23, 1938 (see chapter 5). Earlier, on December 7, Bartha introduced the bill for obligatory military service, which also provided the legal basis for the organization and operation of the compulsory military labor service system and for the draconic measures that were adopted against the Jews during the German occupation (see chapter 10).

Imrédy did not survive politically to see the enactment of his draft bills into law. Ironically, it was indirectly the Jewish issue that brought about his downfall. Imrédy's political opponents, fearing his personal dictatorial ambitions as well as the consequences of his pro-Axis foreign policies, took full advantage of the discovery that his ancestry was fractionally Jewish. The genealogical investigation was spearheaded by Károly Rassay and Count Antal Sigray, respectively the leaders of the Liberal and Legitimist parties. There is some evidence that the discovery was used to blackmail Imrédy into either the withdrawal of the second anti-Jewish bill or his resignation from the premiership (this was revealed during Imrédy's trial in 1945–46 in Budapest). When he rejected these offers, the story of his Jewish ancestry, confirmed by a senior police officer who had been sent to Germany by the Minister of the Interior to investigate, was brought into the open. Leaflets about his Jewish ancestry began to appear on the streets of Budapest in January 1939. Admiral Horthy, who began to share the views of Imrédy's political opponents, confronted Imrédy with the documentation relating to his ancestry. Unable to refute the authenticity of the documents,

Imrédy tendered his resignation on February 13, 1939. Three days later, the Regent entrusted Pál Teleki, a representative of the traditional Bethlenite wing of the ruling conservative faction of the Right, with the leadership of the government.

Notes

1. Darányi was appointed Minister of Agriculture on January 9, 1935 to replace Miklós Kállay, who resigned following his disagreement with Gömbös' policies. Shortly after Gömbös fell ill in May 1936, Darányi was appointed Acting Prime Minister and Acting Leader of the Government Party. He was officially named Prime Minister on October 10, 1936.

2. C. A. Macartney, 1:212.

3. The memorandum also included a series of demands for socioeconomic reforms, including the introduction of a steeper progressive taxation, the prohibition of multiple positions, the fairer distribution of land, and the adoption of a new Electoral Law. *Ibid.*, p. 213.

4. The details of the investment program were made public on April 2 by Lajos Reményi-Schneller, the new Minister of Finance. Based on Rátz's proposals, the program called for the allocation of one billion *Pengős* for rearmament and related projects.

5. Lévai, *Zsidósors Magyarországon*, pp. 28–29.

6. These sources normally used the upper statistical figures from the census of 1930. For data on the Jews' proportion in the various fields of occupation, see chapter 3. See also C. A. Macartney, 1:219. The sources most often used by the propagandists of the 1930s and early 1940s were Alajos Kovács, *A zsidóság térfoglalása Magyarországon* (The Expansion of Jewry in Hungary) Budapest, 1922), and his *A Csonkamagyarország zsidósága a statisztika tükrében* (The Jewry of Truncated Hungary in the Light of Statistics) (Budapest, 1940); Klaus Schickert, *Die Judenfrage in Ungarn* (The Jewish Question in Hungary) (Essen, 1937); and Stéfan (István) Barta, *Die Judenfrage in Ungarn* (Budapest, n.d.). See also chapter 3.

7. The major changes were the replacement of Tihamér Fabinyi by Lajos Reményi-Schneller as Minister of Finance and of Andor Lázár by Ödön Mikecz as Minister of Justice. Furthermore, Darányi relinquished his portfolio in the Ministry of Agriculture to Ferenc Marschall. By far the most important of the new appointees was Reményi-Schneller, a vocally Germanophile banker, who became one of the trusted and most valuable confidants of the Nazis during the war years. He kept his portfolio until the end of the Horthy era in October 1944. For further details on Reményi-Schneller's activities, including his dealings with the leaders of the Jewish Council, see chapter 14.

8. The bill was introduced in the lower house of the Hungarian Parliament on April 8, 1938 (session 297), just a little over a month after Darányi's Győr speech. The debates in the lower house lasted from May 5 (session 306) through May 18 (session 315), when the bill, guided through the house by Gábor Baloghy, was adopted after its third reading. See *Országgyülés képviselőházának naplója* (Proceedings of the House of Representatives of the National Assembly) (Budapest: Athenaeum, 1938), vol. 18.

9. Lévai, *Zsidórsors Magyarországon*, pp. 29, 31.

10. *Ibid.*, pp. 29–30.

11. *"A társadalmi és gazdasági egyensuly biztositásáról" szóló törvény-javaslat vitájában elhangzott szocialista beszédek. Peyer Károly, Esztergályos János, Reisinger Ferenc, Malasits Géza, Györki Imre, Kéthly Anna felszólalásai* (Socialist Speeches Delivered During the Debate on the

Draft Law Relating to the "Protection of the Social and Economic Balance." The Remarks of Károly Peyer, János Esztergályos, Ferenc Reisinger, Géza Malasits, Imre Györki, and Anna Kéthly (Budapest: Népszava, 1938) (Szocialista Füzetek, No. 27).

12. *Keresztény egyházfők felsőházi beszédei a zsidókérdésben* (Speeches on the Jewish Question Made in the Upper House by Heads of the Christian Churches), ed. Henrik Fisch (Budapest: The Editor, 1947), pp. 19–24.

13. *Ibid.*, pp. 25–40.

14. For the complete text of the Law see "1938. évi XV. törvénycikk a társadalmi és a gazdasági élet egyensulyának hatályosabb biztositásáról" (Law No. XV for the More Effective Protection of the Social and Economic Balance), in *1938. évi országos törvénytár* (National Code of Laws for 1938) (Budapest: Állami Nyomda, May 29, 1938), pp. 87–89.

15. The law did not apply to strictly Jewish denominational papers.

16. The establishment of, and the differentiation between, two categories of converts became a source of dispute within the various denominations of the Christian Churches and between the Churches and the state.

17. See, for example, *Zsidótörvény végrehajtása. (4350/1938. M.E. sz. rend.)* (The Implementation of the Anti-Jewish Law. Decree No. 4350/1938 of the Council of Ministers) (Budapest: Centrum, 1938). (*Jogi Hirlap*, No. 326); *Zsidótörvény végrehajtása lapok munkatársaira és egyéb személyzetére vonatkozólag (4960/1938. M.E. sz. rend.)* (The Implementation of the Anti-Jewish Law with Respect to Newspaper Correspondents and Other Related Personnel. Decree No. 4960/1938 of the Council of Ministers). (Budapest: Centrum, 1938) (*Jogi Hirlap*, No. 333).

18. For a sample of such apologetic writing designed for Western consumption see László Ottlik, "The Hungarian Jewish Law." *Hungarian Quarterly,* London, 4 (1939):399–412.

19. *Ibid.*, p. 411.

20. In his note of April 8, 1938, addressed to the Bank of England, H. Bruce, the British financial expert and League of Nations Commissioner who served as an adviser to the Hungarian National Bank, claimed that "serious Jews have themselves advocated some such measures. . . ." He was even more specific in his letter to A. Gascoigne, a member of the British Legation in Budapest: "I myself have had prominent Jews come to me to explain to Imrédy that they would welcome a law restricting Jewish employment if only they knew that that would be the end. . . ." Nathaniel Katzburg, "The Hungarian Jewish Situation During the Late 1930's," in *Annual of Bar-Ilan University Studies in Judaica and the Humanities* (Ramat Gan, Israel: Bar-Ilan), 14–15:76.

21. *Ibid.*, pp. 73–83.

22. Imrédy's original cabinet was quite balanced. It included Kálmán Kánya as Minister of Foreign Affairs; Ferenc Keresztes-Fischer as Minister of the Interior; Lajos Reményi-Schneller as Minister of Finance; Pál Teleki as Minister of Cults and Public Education; Ödön Mikecz as Minister of Justice; Sándor Sztranyavszky as Minister of Agriculture; and Jenő Rátz as Minister of Defense. The latter was by far the most controversial appointment. Imrédy doubled as Minister of Trade and Communication until September 22, 1938, when the position was taken over by Antal Kunder, a Germanophile politician.

23. As a result of the 1938 law restricting freedom of the press, close to 400 newspapers and periodicals were suspended. György Ránki, *1944. március 19* (March 19, 1944), 2nd edition (Budapest: Kossuth, 1978), p. 166.

24. The Hungarian delegation included Imrédy, Kánya, Rátz, Sztójay, the then Hungarian Minister in Berlin, as well as large diplomatic and military staffs led by István Csáky and Lajos Keresztes-Fischer, respectively.

25. Following the territorial settlements of October–November 1938 (below) and the consequent collapse of the plans for the "Horizontal Axis," the attention of the Poles and

of the Hungarians was directed toward the possible establishment of a common border. For details on these maneuvers, see Betty Jo Winchester, "Hungary and the 'Third Europe' in 1938." *Slavic Review,* Seattle, 32, no. 4 (December 1973): 741–56.

26. On Hungary's policies prior and after the Munich agreement see Thomas L. Sakmyster, "Hungary and the Munich Crisis: The Revisionist Dilemma." *Slavic Review, ibid.,* pp. 725–40. See also Magda Ádám, *Magyarország és a kisantant a harmincas években* (Hungary and the Little Entente During the 1930's) (Budapest: Akadémiai Kiadó, 1968), 389 pp.

27. The Italians were responsible for the inclusion into the Munich Agreement of two references relating to the question of Hungarian and Polish minorities in Czechoslovakia. According to one provision, the German and Italian guarantee of Czechoslovakia's borders was to depend on the solution of this question. The other stipulated that if this question was not solved within three months, another Four Power meeting would be called into session to effectuate a solution.

28. The Duchy of Teschen (Cieszyn) was divided in 1920, at the height of the Polish-Soviet war, between Czechoslovakia and Poland. The Poles claimed the area on ethnic grounds, while the Czechs did so on historical ones. One day after the signing of the Munich Agreement, the Poles issued an ultimatum to Prague to immediately evacuate the disputed districts. The Czechs had no alternative but to yield.

29. The Hungarian note demanded not only the application of the principle of self-determination, but also the release by the Czechs of all Hungarian political prisoners, the discharge from the Czech Army of Hungarian soldiers, and the token occupation by Hungarian troops of several frontier localities. C. A. Macartney, 1:278.

30. The Hungarians claimed all the areas which had a Magyar majority according to the census of 1910, i.e., 14,106 square miles. The Czechoslovaks, on the other hand, used their own census of 1930 to show that only 678,000 of the 1,346,010 people living in the claimed area were Hungarian and that several of the towns in the disputed territory had non-Magyar majorities. For further details on this dispute see *Ibid.,* pp. 285–304.

31. For the text of the First Vienna Award see *Documents on International Affairs, 1938,* ed. Monica Curtis (London: Oxford University Press, 1943), 2:351. For the Hungarian version see *A müncheni egyezmény létrejötte és Magyarország külpolitikája, 1936–1938* (The Munich Agreement and Hungary's Foreign Policy, 1936–1938), ed. Magda Ádám (Budapest: Akadémiai Kiadó, 1965), Docs. 621, 622 (*Diplomáciai iratok Magyarország külpolitikájához, 1936–1945* (Diplomatic Papers Relating to Hungary's Foreign Policy, 1936–1945, ed. László Zsigmond), vol. 2.

32. Randolph L. Braham, "The Destruction of the Jews of Carpatho-Ruthenia," in *HJS,* 1:223–24. No accurate statistical data are available with respect to demographic distribution in the acquired territory. Cf., for example, C. A. Macartney, 1:302, and Raphael Lemkin, *Axis Rule in Occupied Europe* (Washington: Carnegie Endowment for International Peace, 1944), pp. 146–47. According to an estimate based on the census figures of 1930, the population of the Felvidék was 1,034,463, of which 78,190 (7.6 percent) were Jews. *Magyar statisztikai szemle* (Hungarian Statistical Review) (Budapest: Magyar Királyi Központi Statisztikai Hivatal, 1941):772.

33. For details on the legal and administrative incorporation of the Felvidék into Hungary, see Lemkin, *ibid.,* pp. 146–50.

34. There are no accurate data as to the exact number of Jews in the area at the time of its reacquisition. The estimates range from 52,000 to 78,000. Cf. C. A. Macartney, 1:302 and Randolph L. Braham, "Destruction of the Jews of Carpatho-Ruthenia," p. 225. See also note 32.

35. Ernő László, "Hungary's Jewry: A Demographic Overview, 1918–1945," *HJS,* 2:162–63. For a sociological evaluation of the Felvidék Jews, see chapter 3.

36. In his interview of September 2, Imrédy emphasized that Hungary's foreign policy

aimed at the achievement of peace and justice and that in case of a European conflict Hungary would strive to remain neutral. The interview was reproduced in the Hungarian newspaper *Az Est* (Evening), which emphasized the implicit disagreements between Hungary and Germany. The paper was suspended following an energetic protest by the Germans.

37. In the formulation of his program, Imrédy was apparently influenced by the advice he had received from Mussolini and Ciano during his July 1938 visit to Rome. Speaking from their own experience, the Italian leaders had informed him that if he wanted to prevail over his political opponents he had to come out with more radical social reform programs than the ones they advocated. The Kaposvár program called for the introduction of universal compulsory military service, the reorganization of the *Levente* paramilitary organization, the granting of emergency state powers under certain conditions, the introduction of compulsory labor service for those "unsuited" for regular military service, and the initiation of a series of social reform measures. These included the extension of social services, family allowances, a graduated income tax, land reform, and the settlement of agricultural indebtedness.

38. These 26 deputies had previously represented the reacquired territories in Prague. Their official status was legitimized by virtue of Law No. V of 1939. For the identification of these deputies see *Magyarország tiszti cim- és névtára* (Title and Name Register of Hungary) (Budapest: Magyar Királyi Állami Nyomda, 1942), 49:18.

39. According to Macartney, "it was notorious that Jaross and his political friends enriched themselves largely out of the spoils of confiscated Jewish wealth or, alternatively, by selling 'protection' to Jews." C. A. Macartney, 1:308.

40. The major Cabinet changes involved the replacement of Mikecz by András Tasnádi Nagy as Minister of Justice; of Sztranyavszky by Count Mihály Teleki as Minister of Agriculture; of Bornemisza by Kunder as Minister of Industry (while Bornemisza retained the post of Minister of Trade and Transportation); and of Rátz by Károly Bartha as Minister of Defense. Rátz was replaced primarily because of his inability to get along with the new Chief of the General Staff, General Henrik Werth.

41. Kánya was first provisionally replaced by Imrédy on November 28. Csáky made his declaration in an interview with the *Popolo d'Italia.* C. A. Macartney, 1:318.

42. Imrédy was particularly interested in a legislative reform that would make possible the passing of an "urgent" bill within 48 hours.

CHAPTER FIVE

THE TELEKI ERA

Teleki the Man

THE FORCED RESIGNATION of Béla Imrédy on February 15, 1939, brought the return to active politics and power of one of the most colorful and controversial figures of Hungarian public life, Count Pál Teleki. He was a member of a famous Transylvanian family that had played an active role in shaping the country's political destinies. An experienced politician, Teleki had been elected to the Hungarian Parliament in 1905 and had served for a short while as Prime Minister and Foreign Minister in 1920–21.[1] At heart he was perhaps more of an academician than a politician, having achieved an international reputation as a geographer and cartographer. In fact, after his brief stint in government in the 1920s, he joined the University of Budapest as a Professor of Geography.

Teleki was a typical representative of the conservative, aristocratic gentry portion of the Right that ruled the country. A complex figure, he was dedicated to the preservation of the political supremacy of his class. This, however, did not prevent him from initiating a series of "progressive" measures designed to advance the modernization of Hungary within the context of the Horthyist regime. He sought to reform the state bureaucracy by making it more professional as well as more responsive to the public interest and initiated a series of educational measures that were calculated to raise the general cultural level of the people.[2] These modernizing measures were quite remarkable given the antiquated character of the regime and the absence of a sizable Western-type indigenous middle class.[3]

In foreign affairs, Teleki, like many of his peers, was an ardent nationalist-chauvinist, who devoted much of his energy to the eradication of the "injustices of Trianon" and to the dismemberment of the Little Entente. As a devout Catholic and a declared Anglophile, Teleki feared both Bolshevism and Nazism and recognized the long-range danger that German expansionism represented for Hungary. Nevertheless, while he was convinced that in any world conflict the West was in the end bound to triumph over Germany, his irredentist-revisionist ambitions threw him into the arms of the Axis. However, unlike the radical wing of the Hungarian Right, which was composed primarily of the discontented elements of the military officers' corps, the civil service, and the lower middle class, and which championed the open and unequivocal embracement of the Third Reich, Teleki tried to pursue a foreign policy that was at once in accord with the overall objectives of the Axis and with the requirements of Hungarian national interests. The latter, in his view, required an alliance with the Axis that would assure the alignment of Hungary in the "New Order" of Europe, the satisfaction of Hungary's territorial demands, the advancement of trade, and the flourishing of economic relations, but which would not infringe upon Hungary's independence and sovereignty or require the suspension of contacts and relations with the Western Powers.[4]

Teleki's Anti-Semitism

While not strictly a Nazi-type racist, Teleki was a typical advocate of the brand of anti-Semitism professed by his aristocratic peers. Like his predecessors, Darányi and Imrédy, and his successors, Bárdossy and Kállay, he was a champion of the "civilized" form of anti-Semitism, which aimed at the gradual restriction and eventual elimination of the social and economic influence of the Jews. In his quiet, ascetic, professorial manner, Teleki was one of the most consistently unaccommodating anti-Semitic politicians of the post-Trianon period. While he was inclined to tolerate the assimilated "Magyarized" Jews, he was vitriolically opposed to the so-called "Eastern" ones.

By the late 1930s, Teleki's anti-Semitism had acquired a somewhat racial coloration.[5] Perhaps under the influence of Nazism, Teleki had come to believe that the "Eastern" Jews, who in his view constituted not only a distinct "biological race" but also an "ideological race," represented a grave threat to the Christian Magyars. He traced this threat to the "more than three thousand year-old tradition [and the] more than two thousand year-old seclusion of the Jews." As a consequence of this seclusion, he argued along the line advanced by the Nazis, the Jews had come to form distinct biological groups—that is, a specific race. "You can in eight or nine cases out of ten recognize the Jew," he boasted. He was convinced that as dangerous as the "biological race" of the Jews was, it was less important than their "ideological age-old seclusion." His autocratic, intolerant temperament made him resent the distinctiveness of the Jews in terms of their way of life, dress, customs, and moral-ethical codes. Teleki shared the views of the other anti-Semites in

Hungary, arguing that the Jews were also dangerous because of their relatively large percentage in the population and their influential role in the country's economic and cultural life.

A Machiavellian by political instinct, Teleki did not hesitate to employ the Jewish question in the service of the transitory interests of Hungary. Thus, there was a time when he, like his contemporaries of the pre-1914 period, looked upon the Jews as Hungarians because they were needed for statistical purposes in a polyglot empire in which the Magyars constituted a minority. Typical of this attitude was his remark at the Peace Conference of 1919:

The overwhelming majority of the Hungarian Jews have completely assimilated to the Hungarians. They gave us excellent Hungarian writers, artists, and scientists. Because of their assimilation to the Hungarian national soul and spirit one must recognize that, from a social point of view, the Hungarian Jews are not Jews any more but Hungarians.[6]

Following the conclusion of the Peace Treaties and the consequent establishment of a rump Hungary in which the Magyars became the dominant majority and the Jews were no longer needed to tilt the political scales, Teleki gave vent to his innate anti-Semitic tendencies; he warned the Magyars about the cultural and economic threat of the Jews as a whole and the assimilated, Magyarized Jewish leaders about the danger represented by the "Eastern Jews." He told these leaders in 1920:

You are Jews and you are Magyars. There is a conflict between the Christian Magyars and between the Eastern Jews who came in great masses to our country in the last half-century, and the continual infiltration of which did not stop and does not stop. You have to choose your place in this conflict because it is a serious conflict, it is a problem of life and death for the Hungarian people. You must choose between your Magyar compatriots and between your Eastern co-religionists.[7]

Teleki's animosity toward the "foreign Jews" was also reflected in his lecture to American students during his tour of the United States in 1921. In discussing the anti-Jewish demonstrations during the early phase of the Horthy era, Teleki had the following to say:

I should like to say that it is a mistake to think that the anti-Jewish movement which really existed and which still exists in Hungary is one against the Jewish religion or Jews in general. If I had to characterize it as an historian it would rather have to be with the words "anti-Galician movement." It is much more a question of immigration and antagonism towards a certain group of foreigners who turned against the nation. To prove that let me quote these figures: In 1785 we had 75,000 Jews, who were on the best of terms with the Magyars and with the other peoples, and who began very strongly to amalgamate and fuse with the Magyars and other races. In 1910 we had 912,000 Jews, not counting those who were converted to Christianity who would amount to a few hundred thousand. [These foreigners were granted citizenship] before they had any feelings of loyalty for the land and for their fellow-countrymen. . . .[8]

Teleki, of course, did not bother to inform his student audience that in 1785, when the Magyars were allegedly "on the best of terms" with the Jews, the Jews were in fact living in ghettos with all their restrictive and discriminatory elements. Nor indeed did he bother to enlighten his audience that during the pre-war alliance between capitalism and feudalism under the "liberal" rule of his feudal class, the number of Jews was only a relatively minor concern of certain racially-oriented anti-Semites and that the Jews were looked upon as allies in counterbalancing the other nationalities in the polyglot empire. The "excessive number of foreign Jews" became a major problem only after the antiquated political structure collapsed in 1918.

The consistency of Teleki's anti-Semitism is best illustrated by the two major anti-Jewish laws adopted during his tenure as Prime Minister in 1920 and in 1939. Under his leadership, long before the anti-Jewish legislative program of the Nazi era and in flagrant violation of the principles of equality embodied in the Treaty of Trianon of June 4, 1920, Hungary adopted the first major anti-Jewish law in post-World War I Europe—the so-called *Numerus Clausus* Act of September 1920.

The other major anti-Jewish law intimately connected with Teleki is Law No. IV of 1939 "Concerning the Restriction of the Participation of the Jews in Public and Economic Life" (see below).

The impact of Teleki's policies on the Jewish community of Hungary was not restricted to the legislative sphere. They affected directly or indirectly practically every facet of Jewish life in the country. Blinded by his own anti-Semitism, Teleki failed to accurately assess the extent to which the anti-Jewish laws would arouse the rapacious instincts of his countrymen and to correctly evaluate the real dangers of Fascism.[9]

In the wake of the political and military measures of the Teleki government, the Jewish community underwent a series of demographic and structural changes and came to be confronted with a new set of socioeconomic problems. Of the many factors that influenced the history of the Hungarian Jewish community during this period, perhaps the most determining ones were the acquisition of Carpatho-Ruthenia, the adoption of the Second Anti-Jewish Law, and the incorporation of Northern Transylvania.

The Acquisition of Carpatho-Ruthenia

Contrary to the expectation of many political observers, the replacement of the openly pro-German Imrédy by the ostensibly Anglophile Teleki on February 16, 1939, did not bring about any major changes in the country's domestic or foreign policies. Teleki's cabinet,[10] like his legislative program, was basically the same as Imrédy's. This was also true of Teleki's Jewish policy. In fact, his first weeks in Parliament were devoted to steering through the Second Anti-Jewish Law, which had been introduced by Imrédy.

In foreign affairs, Teleki was dedicated to the advancement of the national interests of Hungary, which he saw as the revision of Trianon by concurrently placating the Germans and reassuring the West. As a realist he recognized the increasing power and influence of the Germans in East Central Europe and realized the importance of Hungary's participation in the imminent liquidation of the Czechoslovak state. At the same time he also deemed it important to assure the West that Hungary, in spite of its "necessary" cooperation with Germany, was dedicated to preserving its national independence and sovereignty.[11]

Upon the absorption of the Upper Province (*Felvidék*)—the Magyar-inhabited part of southern Slovakia and western Carpatho-Ruthenia, which was acquired by virtue of the Vienna Award of November 2, 1938—Hungarian diplomacy was directed toward the acquisition of Carpatho-Ruthenia.[12] Following the Four-Power Munich Agreement of September 29, 1938, and the consequent loss of the Sudetenland to the Third Reich, Carpatho-Ruthenia had been given autonomy within the new short-lived Czechoslovak Federal Republic. The province soon became the center of a Ruthenian-Ukrainian nationalist movement, which was fostered by Monsignor Augustin Vološin, the head of the provincial government,[13] and supported by the Third Reich. The movement was given impetus through the formation of the Ukrainian National Guard, a paramilitary body which was better known under its abbreviated name of Sic.

Partially in gratitude for the Third Reich's support for the acquisition of the Upper Province and partially in anticipation of continued assistance for the incorporation of Carpatho-Ruthenia, Hungary joined the Anti-Comintern Pact on January 13, 1939. It withdrew from the League of Nations on April 11, 1939. Hungary's drive for the acquisition of Carpatho-Ruthenia was motivated not only by its desire to gradually undo the "injustices of Trianon," but also by the expected political-military advantages inherent in a possible common Hungarian-Polish border.[14]

Hungary's political ambition to gain the acquiescence of the Third Reich was crowned with success on March 13, 1939, when it was given the green light for the occupation of the territory. Admiral Horthy expressed his thanks to Hitler in an enthusiastic note in which he promised that "the big attack" would be launched on March 18, following the planned outburst of border incidents two days earlier.[15]

Horthy's plans were somewhat disturbed by the sudden declaration of Slovakian independence on March 14, which was followed immediately by the announcement of the Vološin government that Carpatho-Ruthenia had become an independent state "under the protection of the German Reich."[16]

In accordance with the scenario previously worked out with the Germans, the Hungarians issued an ultimatum to the Prague government the day the Slovaks declared their independence, and a few hours later began their march on Huszt.[17] The occupation of all of Carpatho-Ruthenia was completed by March 18, the Hungarian forces having met only slight resistance from the numerically inferior Sic guard. With it, the long-cherished dream of a common Hungarian-Polish border finally became a reality.[18]

The Jews of Carpatho-Ruthenia

The Carpatho-Ruthenian territory encompassed 12,171 square kilometers (4,257 square miles) with a total population of around 700,000. According to the census of 1941, of these 78,087 were Jews.[19] Many of these lived in the historic territories of Bereg and Ung counties and in the Ruthenian section of Máramaros County. The more important Jewish population centers and settlements are shown in table 5.1.

The 28,142 Jews distributed in the 23 localities listed in the table constituted about 36 percent of the Jewish population of the area. The remainder lived in 445 other smaller localities.[20]

With the incorporation of Northern Transylvania in September 1940, some of the counties, including Bereg-Ugocsa and Máramaros, were reestablished within their pre-World War I boundaries. With the addition of such Jewish centers as Máramarossziget, Borsa, and Felsővisó, these counties emerged once again as those most densely populated by Jews. Interestingly, the increase in the number of the

TABLE 5.1.
IMPORTANT JEWISH POPULATION
CENTERS OF
CARPATHO-RUTHENIA

Locality	Jewish Population	Percent of Local Population
Bereg County		
Bilke	1,103	17.6
Ilonca	887	15.8
Alsóverecke	582	24.7
Máramaros County		
Akna- and Falúszlatina	2,537	28.8
Huszt	6,023	28.5
Nagybocskó	1,708	23.0
Rahó	1,607	12.9
Kőrösmező	1,403	11.0
Felsőapsa	1,289	18.7
Dombó	984	16.4
Alsóapsa	978	11.7
Ökörmező	952	16.1
Kőkényes	914	20.0
Herincse	871	16.1
Irhóc	851	17.7
Majdánka	831	23.3
Szeklence	685	18.6
Gánya	720	21.8
Visk	571	7.5
Urmező	395	13.1
Ung County		
Nagyberezna	1,237	30.7
Szerednye	619	23.6
Szobránc	395	25.5

Jews during the 1910 to 1941 period, both in absolute and percentage terms, was below that of the non-Jewish population. This can be seen from the following data:[21]

	Jewish Population			Percentage of Jews	
			Increase		
County	1910	1941	(In Percent)	1910	1941
Bereg-Ugocsa	45,510	46,621	1.6	13.8	13.1
Máramaros	65,694	78,856	20.0	18.3	16.2
Ung	17,587	20,903	18.8	10.8	9.8

Immediately after the occupation, the Jews of Carpatho-Ruthenia were subjected to the anti-Jewish measures that were already in effect in Hungary. This was quite a shock to most of them, because during the two decades of democratic rule in Czechoslovakia, many of them had been among the chief supporters of Magyar rights and the most vocal champions of the Hungarian language. It was during their reabsorption into the Hungarian Jewish community that the Hungarian Parliament was debating the draft of the second major anti-Jewish law.

The Second Anti-Jewish Law

Scarcely had the Jewish community of Hungary attuned itself to the disaster augured by the First Anti-Jewish Law than it was threatened by a more ominous one. Shortly after the first law went into effect on June 28, 1938, following its adoption a month earlier, anti-Jewish agitation for even more stringent measures became ever more vocal and insistent. The Hungarian Right radicals, spearheaded by the various *Nyilas* (Arrow Cross) elements, exercised increasing pressure on the Hungarian government for the adoption of further anti-Jewish restrictions. During the post-Anschluss period, the efforts of the Right radicals were openly instigated and generously supported by the Third Reich, which also contributed to the financing of the general anti-Semitic propaganda in the country.

The intensification of the Nazis' ideological and propagandist drive was coupled to an ever more clearly discernible German economic penetration of Hungary. With the absorption of the Austrian share of the Hungarian import-export trade, the Reich soon emerged as Hungary's major, and later dominant, trade partner.[22]

If the Anschluss provided the momentum for the adoption of the First Anti-Jewish Law, the acquisition of the Upper Province under the Vienna Award of November 2, 1938, served as the catalyst for the initiation of the drive for the second one. It was during this period that Imrédy's political attitude changed radically. In his speech at Kaposvár on September 4 (i.e., weeks before the Four-Power Munich Agreement), Imrédy was still intimating that the First Anti-Jewish Law was to be the last. However, shortly after the occupation of the Felvidék, Imrédy shifted precipitously toward the extreme Right and became increasingly preoccupied with the "danger" the enlarged Jewish community allegedly represented for Hungary. On November 15, he made the following declaration to a party meeting:

With the reacquisition of the territories of the Upper Province, the proportion of the Jews, which was already unfavorable, became even more so and the infiltration became much wider. We must consequently revise our conception on this question to some extent.[23]

Imrédy elaborated on this theme during the parliamentary debates on the Second Anti-Jewish Law proposal. Early in February 1939, he declared:

The great events that have taken place since the spring of 1938 require the revision of our attitude. Since the adoption by Parliament of the first anti-Jewish law, many countries have taken measures whose tendency and effects have been to induce the Jews whose situation has worsened to look for settlement in countries in which they expect a more favorable climate. Anti-Jewish measures have been adopted above all in Germany and Italy. In the wake of the Anschluss and the incorporation of Czechoslovak territories large areas have again come under German jurisdiction. In Poland also, draft legislation is being prepared to change the status of the Jews. In rump Czechoslovakia, and especially in Slovakia, from where the gravitation of the Jews to Hungary could easily occur, severe measures are also contemplated or in the process of implementation. In Romania, where a special situation arose, many practical measures and decrees have already been adopted making the situation of Jewry there more difficult.[24]

The preparations for the Second Anti-Jewish Law were launched in the midst of anti-Semitic demonstrations, the most serious of which took place in Kisvárda and Mátészalka, two cities with relatively large Orthodox Jewish populations. In the former city, a pogrom was organized after General Alajos Haynal allegedly "discovered" a "secret Jewish radio station." In Mátészalka, the Jews were accused of having secretly collected funds for supplying aircraft to the Czechoslovak armed forces.[25] The draft legislation was prepared by István Antal, Secretary of State in the Ministry of Justice. The preamble, containing the justification for the bill, was written by Teleki, who was then serving as Minister of Cults and Public Education. The bill, "Concerning the Restriction of the Participation of the Jews in Public and Economic Life," was submitted to Parliament by András Tasnádi Nagy, the Minister of Justice, on December 23, 1938.[26]

The text of the legislative proposal clearly reflected the racial views and position of the Nazis, which the Hungarian anti-Semites appear to have assimilated. Following the traditional Manichean attitude of anti-Semites everywhere, the Hungarians began to look upon the Jews not only as a "threat to their national economy and culture," but also as an alien, destructive body that would have to be eliminated from the midst of the nation. The legislative proposal advanced a number of domestic and foreign political arguments and a series of geopolitical and historical rationalizations to "demonstrate" that the Jews had always constituted a distinct and separate racial group with a specific and distinct psychological and spiritual makeup and special lifestyles that separated them from humanity in general and the individual host nations in particular. Reflecting Teleki's line of reasoning, the bill emphasized the particular difficulty of Hungary, which had traditionally relied upon the use of Western methods in dealing with Jews who were primarily of Eastern origin.

In accordance with the policies then in effect in the Third Reich, the bill authorized the government "to promote the emigration of the Jews." The justification advanced in support of the bill, however, emphasized that the Jewish question was international in character and that its solution required an international approach at the proper time and with the proper means.[27]

The bill was opposed and severely criticized by many organs of the Jewish community and their Christian friends. A large number of petitions were submitted and numerous publications were issued with the aim of demonstrating the inequities of the draft bill and the loyalty and contributions of the Jewish community to the advancement of the welfare of Hungary.[28]

In their joint appeal of January 12, 1939, for example, the central offices of the three large Jewish communal organizations emphasized that the bill:

- Was in violation of the Hungarian Constitution and of its basic principles relating to the unitary character of the Hungarian political nation, equality before the law, and the protection of acquired rights.
- Was in conflict with human justice and with the divine commandment of the law.
- Was harming the eminent interests of the Hungarian nation.

The bitterness and disappointment of the Hungarian Jews did not, however, dampen their patriotism—a characteristic they shared with their German counterparts. This is clearly reflected in the concluding paragraph of their petition:

Is this what Hungarian Jewry deserved? The mutilation of our civic rights, the limitation of our private rights, the restriction on our livelihood, the ostracism of our youth? Is this what was deserved by the Hungarian Jewish community, whose only wish in the course of centuries-old history was to keep its religion and remain Hungarian and only Hungarian? Let the battlefields of the war for independence, the marshes of Volhynia, and the Karst rocks speak out on behalf of justice for us; in the trenches no one asked who was of which religion . . . Let it once be permitted for us to state that our creed, honor, and rights are not everybody's prey, at the expense of which one can find the solution of social problems. And let the legislative authorities bring out new laws that will compel every one with means to contribute to the easing of social problems— everyone without respect to religion and origin. This is our respectful request. But should we be disappointed and this bill become law, one of the results would be that hundreds of thousands of us and our children would be compelled to change residence. Residence, but not homeland. Because no human law can deprive us of our Hungarian homeland, any more than we can be deprived of the worship of one God. Just as in the course of the millennial blows of fate, neither fire nor water nor scaffolds or stakes, nor galleon benches or handcuffs could deter us, so with the same determination we will cling to our Hungarian homeland, whose language is our language, whose history is our life. Just as our coreligionists, even after centuries of exile, have preserved the old Spanish language, the culture and love for their old homeland, so shall we keep vigil for our legitimation and for the Hungarian resurrection.[29]

In addition to petitions submitted to the governmental authorities, the central leaders of the Jewish community also commissioned or encouraged the publication of articles and pamphlets designed to enlighten Hungarian public opinion about the falsity of the accusations directed against the Jews. The Jewish Community of Pest (*Pesti Izraelita Hitközség*) actually established a Social Work Committee (*Társadalmi Munkabizottság*) for this purpose. Led by an executive committee composed of Géza Ribáry, Ernő Deutsch, Frigyes Görög, Pál Ligeti, Ernő Naményi, and György Polgár, the Social Work Committee was instrumental in the distribution of pamphlets, flyers, posters, propaganda leaflets, and postcards.[30] The tone of these, like that of the petitions, was typically apologetic, defensive, and patriotic, reflecting the general attitude of the assimilated strata of Hungarian Jewry.

Characteristic of this attitude was the pamphlet published shortly after the adoption of the Second Anti-Jewish Law. It provided a historical review of Jewry's record of loyalty to Hungary and concluded by echoing the position of the Jewish leaders during the Revolution of 1848–49:

"We are Hungarians and not Jews, not different nationals, because we are a different denomination only when we express in our houses of worship our thanks and innermost gratitude to the Almighty for the mercy bestowed on our Homeland and upon us, but in every other aspect of life we are only patriots and Hungarians." (Appeal of the Representatives of the Jews of Hungary and Transylvania, March 17, 1848.)
This is what we are professing even today, in the spring of 1939.[31]

Their patriotic stance notwithstanding, the leaders of Hungarian Jewry showed in one respect a more positive reaction to the Second Anti-Jewish Law than to the first one. In the spring of 1938 they had been inclined to accept the First Anti-Jewish Law—rationalizing that it was basically mild and would "take the wind out of the sails of the extremists"—and above all to reject any interference by foreign Jewish organizations in the internal affairs of Hungary (see chapter 4).

However, by late summer 1938 they in fact took the initiative in appealing for such intervention in order to ease the pressure on the community. On September 8, 1938, Sándor Eppler, the Secretary General of the Jewish Community of Pest, contacted the Joint Foreign Committee of the Anglo-Jewish Association and the Board of Deputies of British Jews, suggesting that one of its members come to Budapest. In March 1939, the Hungarian Jewish leaders, cognizant of the full implications of the Second Anti-Jewish Law, again contacted the British Jewish leaders, pleading for assistance: the provision of emigration facilities for the able-bodied and monetary aid for the aged and the infirm. This plea was repeated and amplified by Samu Stern and Eppler during their visit to London and Paris in May 1939.[32] The problem was indeed acute, not only because of the by-then enacted law but also because of the enlargement of the Jewish population and of the proportion of economically disadvantaged Jews through the acquisition of the Felvidék and Carpatho-Ruthenia. The Jewish population of the latter area especially contained a relatively large proportion of unassimilated, pious, Orthodox Jews living at the brink of poverty. It is fair to assume that the Hungarian government, which authorized the trip, shared, if not actually instigated, the demands of the Jewish leaders for emigration outlets.

The visit by Stern and Eppler was marred somewhat by the concurrent tour of London and Paris by Dr. Gyula (Julius) László, who dramatized not only the special problems of the Jews of Carpatho-Ruthenia, including a number of Polish refugees, but also the negligence manifested toward them by the central Jewish leadership in Budapest.[33] The trip was nevertheless successful in the sense at least that contact was finally established between Hungarian and world Jewry and that some financial help was promised. The suggestions that Britain be induced to exert political influence on Hungary came to naught.

The domestic efforts of the Jews and their friends proved of no avail. In the climate of the anti-Jewish psychosis fomented by the press, the valiant struggle of the bill's opponents in Parliament was doomed to failure. In the debates that lasted from January to May 1939, the cause of the Jews was championed not only by the Jewish representatives, but also by the handful of liberals in the *Polgári Szabadság Párt* (Bourgeois Freedom Party) led by Dr. Károly Rassay, a representative from Budapest and editor-in-chief of the *Esti Kurir* (Evening Courier) and by the few representatives of the Social Democratic Party. The representatives of the Smallholders' Party split: A wing led by Tibor Eckhardt supported the bill, another opposed it, and a third worked for amending the bill by providing as many exceptions and exemptions as possible.[34] In the upper house, the foremost opponents of the bill were István Bezerédj, Count Gyula Károlyi, Count György Prónay, and Count István Bethlen, the former Prime Minister and a confidant of Horthy.

Count Bethlen made a number of speeches both within and outside Parliament against the dangers of blindly emulating Germany on the Jewish question. On February 9, 1939, he warned the nation as follows:

Don't we realize and do not those who flirt with the radical Right see that the solution of the Jewish question along the German model would disturb the economic and monetary order of this country overnight and would result in consequences quite different from those in Germany? Don't you realize that the country could not survive the economic and monetary crisis for a day if such techniques were resorted to? And I dare emphatically warn those among the Hungarian landowners and Hungarian intelligentsia who flirt today with these fashionable slogans that their turn would come first; it is obvious that the landowning class rushing to the support of such a regime would be the first to be destroyed and that the intelligentsia, which has a historical feeling and wants to pursue a Hungarian policy based on Hungarian historical traditions, would be erring and by following this path only make possible its own elimination and replacement by semi-intelligent men without any historical traditions and who would ignore the Hungarian historical traditions in their policies. But I ask you: What are the foreign political implications of this question? I see but one thing clear: If our political life experiences a *Gleichschaltung* along the ideas of the extreme Right, then we shall become not Germany's friends but her servants and in this case the independence of Hungarian foreign policy would come to an end.[35]

While the motives of the various factions of the opposition to the bill varied, they all agreed that the bill: was a flagrant violation of the "constitutional system"; would cause great hardship to hundreds of thousands of people; would, if implemented, inflict serious harm on the economic and intellectual life of the country; and would be a reflection of the government's appeasement of Nazi Germany.

To the great disappointment of the Jews and many liberals in the country, the heads of the Christian churches in the upper house supported the bill, as they had the First Anti-Jewish Law. They objected to the racial aspects of the bill, insisting on amendments to protect the rights and interests of the converted Jews and to advance the cause of assimilationism and conversion among the Jews. Both Sándor Raffay, the Lutheran Bishop, and Jusztinián Cardinal Serédi, the Prince Primate of the Catholic Church, found it necessary to review the historical position of the Jews in Hungary and to emphasize the "threat" that the cultural, political, and economic influence of the Jews represented for the national interests of Christian Hungary.[36]

The debates in the lower house were highlighted by two emotion-laden events. One day the gallery was filled by Jewish reserve officers, who appeared dressed in mourning and wearing numerous military decorations in a solemn but silent protest against the pending iniquitous measure. János Vázsonyi, a Jewish member of the lower house and the son of the famous former Minister of Justice Vilmos Vázsonyi, asked that the bill be amended so as to ensure for Jewish veterans the same treatment that was accorded to their Christian comrades-in-arms.[37]

The other event that shocked the Jewish community as well as the decent strata of Hungarian Christian society took place on February 3. On that day, a group of *Nyilas* hooligans attacked Jewish worshippers who were leaving the Sabbath service at the Dohány Street Synagogue in Budapest. The attack, which also involved the use of hand grenades, wounded 22 Jews, of whom 10 were over 60; several died. One of the chief organizers of the attack was a military officer, Emil Kovarcz, a notorious anti-Semite and leader of the radical wing of the Hungarian Right.[38]

Although the incident aroused considerable sympathy for the Jews and was exploited by those seeking the dissolution of the ultra Right party of Ferenc Szálasi,[39] the anti-Jewish agitation in the press continued unabated, as did the parliamentary debate on the proposed second anti-Jewish act.

Teleki devoted as much, if not more, energy to the passage of the bill as had Imrédy. In fact, in his many speeches after his inauguration, he emphasized time and again that his approval of the anti-Jewish bill was motivated not by tactics but by conviction and that of all the members of the Imrédy cabinet he had been the most radical on the Jewish question.[40]

The bill was adopted and came into force on May 4, 1939.[41]

Provisions of the Act. Unlike the first Anti-Jewish law, the 1939 act provided a detailed and complicated definition of "Jew." While the 1938 act did not specifically stipulate who was to be regarded as a Jew and merely identified the categories of people to be exempted from its provisions, the 1939 act settled the question on explicitly racial grounds. This was made quite specific in the ministerial justification prepared in support of the legislation which stated, *inter alia:*

A person belonging to the Jewish denomination is at the same time a member of the Jewish racial community and it is natural that the cessation of membership in the Jewish denomination does not result in any change in that person's association with the racial community.[42]

Partly because of the strong opposition of the Catholic Church, religion rather than race was the basic criterion employed. Article 1 stipulated that any person who himself belonged or one of whose parents or two of whose grandparents belonged to the Jewish community on or before the promulgation of the law was to be considered Jewish. The law exempted those who were already Christians on the day of their birth or were baptized before their seventh birthday, and whose Jewish parent had converted before January 1, 1939. The law also exempted those Jews who had converted to Christianity before August 1, 1919, if their ancestors had resided in Hungary since January 1, 1849. It further provided for nine categories of Jews who were to be exempted from its provisions, including some categories of war invalids, decorated war heroes, the widows and orphans of war dead, privy councilors, university professors, and olympic champions (article 2).

The law prohibited Jews from obtaining Hungarian citizenship either by naturalization or marriage (article 3) and severely restricted their political and civil rights (article 4). It further prohibited them from holding any government position and provided for the retirement of all Jewish members of the court and prosecution staffs by January 1, 1940, and of all secondary and primary school teachers and of public notaries by January 1, 1943 (article 5). It reestablished the 6 percent provision of the original *Numerus Clausus* Act of 1920 concerning admission of Jewish applicants to institutions of higher learning (article 7) and extended the same percentage quota for Jewish membership in the professional chambers (article 9). Ostensibly to protect the purity of the Christian spirit and Magyar culture, Jews were prohibited from occupying positions as editors, editors-in-chief, or publishers of any periodicals (article 10) or as producers and directors of plays or films (article 11). The law also provided for a series of economic clauses severely restricting the economic opportunities of Jews. The licenses held by Jews for the operation of a variety of types of businesses were to be withdrawn within a limited number of years and no new licenses were to be issued until the percentage of Jews in the local industries was reduced to 6 percent and in certain branches of commerce to 12 percent. Jews were further denied the right to buy or sell land without special permission and could be compelled at any time to sell or lease their agricultural property on terms fixed by the authorities (articles 12–18).[43]

The law stipulated that a firm with fewer than five employees could engage one Jew and those with at least nine employees, two Jews.[44] According to the Hungarian State Insurance Institute, on December 31, 1937, Budapest had 14,817 firms employing 72,494 workers. Of these, 742 had more than 10 employees each, while 14,075 had fewer than 5. It was estimated that the law would affect about 250,000 Jews, of which 65,000 worked in Budapest.[45]

As it turned out, the Second Anti-Jewish Law affected particularly harshly the lower strata of the Jewish population, including salaried workers and the unskilled. Those in business and industry, while severely curtailed in their activities, managed to make ends meet by circumventing its provisions or by taking advantage of the loopholes. They were particularly successful under the so-called "Aladár-system" (*Strohmann* or Aladár *rendszer*) under which Christian "partners" were taken in on a profit-sharing basis. In some cases, Christians played this role out of friendship for their Jewish neighbors.

In the professions, however, the Jews fared less well. This was especially true for those in law and journalism. Soon after the implementation of the Law, 1,863 of the 3,435 applicants for admission to the Press Chamber (*Sajtókamara*) were rejected because of their religion or race.[46] The removal of the Jews from leadership positions in Hungarian society and their restriction or exclusion from the professions were the responsibility of several agencies and professional chambers. A key role in this respect was played by István Kulcsár, Commissioner for Professional Unemployment (*Az Értelmiségi Munkanélküliség Kormánybiztosa*).[47]

Although the Second Anti-Jewish Law had a nefarious effect on the entire Jewish community, it was especially disastrous for the approximately 150,000 Jews in the territories acquired from Czechoslovakia. Many of these had great difficulty in proving their Hungarian citizenship and were the first ones to suffer the evils of racial discrimination. Shortly after Hungary's entry into the war against the Soviet Union on June 27, 1941, many of these "alien" Jews were rounded up and de-

ported to near Kamenets-Podolsk, where most of them were subsequently slaughtered (see chapter 6).

The moderates among the Hungarian clergymen and politicians had
thought, just as they did in 1938, that the passage of the act would appease the anti-Semites. Teleki himself had then believed that the law
would put an end to the Jewish question in Hungary and enable the
country to tackle the many other urgent tasks confronting the nation.[48]
Contrary to their expectations, however, the propaganda campaign
that was launched in connection with the law was not only allowed to
continue unabated, but also permeated public opinion with a virile anti-
Semitism that played into the hands of the Nazis a few years later. As it
turned out, the Second Anti-Jewish Law was merely a prelude to many
more discriminatory and openly racist acts of legislation. On March 11,
1939, Law No. II relating to national defense was promulgated. Under
the emergency powers granted to it under this law, the government
adopted a series of measures relating to the establishment of a new
type of military-related labor service system that was designed for Jews
and other "unreliable" elements within the country (see chapter 10).
This law was also used after the German occupation to provide the
legal basis for the concentration and deportation of the Jews (see
chapter 17). The anti-Jewish legislative program of the Teleki administration came to a climax with the completion of the plans for the adoption of a third, openly racist, anti-Jewish law.

To bolster his bargainining position, especially with respect to the
approaching crisis on the Transylvanian issue, Teleki adopted a
number of measures that were designed, among other things, to please
the Third Reich. Among the most important of these were the ones
relating to the status of the ethnic Germans in Hungary, the dissolution
of Parliament, and the holding of new elections.

The Volksdeutsche

With the gradual rise of militant nationalism among both Magyars
and Swabians, the issue of the German minority in Hungary became
quite problematical. Nazi Germany's expanded interest in the *Ausland-
deutsche* was matched by a commensurate demonstration of sympathy
for and loyalty to the Reich on the part of ever larger sections of the
German minorities. This became particularly evident after the
Anschluss in March 1938. While the Hungarian government was eager
to pursue its revisionist ambitions in conjunction with the Third Reich,

it was reluctant to give the German ethnic minorities any special privileges that might violate the sovereignty of the state. It desired to continue the policies laid down by Professor Jakob Bleyer, the founder (1923) of the *Ungarländisch-Deutscher Volksbildungsverein*—UDV (Hungarian-German Society for Popular Education). Bleyer, who was on the faculty of Budapest University and whose main concern was to obtain cultural concessions, and Gusztáv Gratz, the President of the UDV, were dedicated to maintaining the territorial and cultural unity of Hungary. Under their leadership, the UDV remained a soporific German cultural society. Bleyer died on December 5, 1933, after which (as a result of a reorganization in May 1934), the leadership of the UDV fell into the hands of Bleyer's son-in-law Franz Kussbach, a relatively neutral person, and Franz Anton Basch, a vocal pro-German.

The *de facto* leadership of the German ethnic group in Hungary fell increasingly into the hands of Basch.[49] Encouraged and financially supported by the Third Reich, he organized the young activists, who were eager to embark on Nazi-style radical policies, into the *Volksdeutsche Kameradschaft* (Folk German Fellowship). Basch vehemently opposed the Magyarization process, which had begun in the nineteenth century and which Gyula Gömbös, himself of Swabian background, had wholeheartedly endorsed and pursued. In 1934, Basch suddenly emerged a martyr in the eyes of the ethnic Germans, for he was condemned to three months imprisonment and a year's loss of political rights for "bringing the Hungarian nation into contempt." Disillusioned with the official position of the UDV, Basch, having used the *Kameradschaft* as a pilot group, launched a new, more militant organization in November 1938. By that time, most of the Swabians were electrified by Nazism in the wake of the Anschluss. The new organization, the *Volksbund der Deutschen in Ungarn*—VDU (Folk Union of Germans in Hungary), became increasingly autonomous and was soon transformed into a convenient vehicle for Nazi penetration into Hungary. Its militant posture was not really challenged, for at the time of its founding Hungary itself was in the midst of the euphoria caused by the first success of the revisionist policies pursued in conjunction with the Reich. Under the provisions of the so-called First Vienna Award of November 2, 1938, Hungary had reacquired the Felvidék.

The major elements of the VDU's program were outlined in Basch's inaugural speech, in which he demanded not only cultural autonomy, including special schools, newspapers, and periodicals for the ethnic Germans, but also the recognition of the legal personality of the ethnic community and the establishment of a special party. The objectives of the VDU were fully endorsed by the leaders of the Reich. It was due to their financial and diplomatic support that almost all of these objectives became reality within two years.

The first major breakthrough came during the visit to Berlin of Prime Minister Teleki and Foreign Minister István Csáky on April 10, 1939. The *Volksdeutsche* in Hungary constituted one of the two major issues discussed. The other was Hungary's foreign policy, with specific reference to Poland. The Hungarian leaders reaffirmed their resolve to follow the Axis line, attaching only a single proviso. It concerned Hungary's reluctance to get involved, directly or indirectly, in any attack on Poland. This must have been an agonizing decision, because the Germans had mentioned the possibility of awarding Slovakia to Hungary as a reward. With an eye on Transylvania, Csáky had shown a greater interest in the possible participation in a common war effort by an attack on Romania, Poland's ally.[50]

If the Germans were unsuccessful in persuading the Hungarians to join them in the planned attack against Poland, Hungary's traditional friend, they were more successful in wresting some major concessions from the Hungarians with respect to the treatment of the *Volksdeutsche* in Hungary. In the spirit of the Berlin agreement, the VDU was recognized as a legitimate organization and its statutes were approved by the Hungarian authorities. By that time, it constituted a formidable and coherent political force linking the Swabians with the policies of the Third Reich.

The second major victory of the VDU was won on August 30, 1940, during the signing of the so-called Second Vienna Award, which brought about the partition of Transylvania (see below). Under the provisions of a secret protocol signed by Ribbentrop and Csáky, the members of the German ethnic group received special privileges, including the right to profess National Socialist ideas, to be appointed to local and central governmental positions in proportion to their numerical strength, to readopt their original family names, and to have free cultural relations with the Third Reich. The protocol provisions also authorized the leadership of the VDU to determine who was a *Volksdeutsche* and who belonged to the ethnic group.[51]

With these measures, the Hungarian government undermined the viability of the two approaches it had earlier adopted to counter the effectiveness of the VDU. One was the formation of a counter German ethnic organization known as the *Treuebewegung* (Faithful Movement), placed under the leadership of Msgr. József Pehm, who became famous after World War II as Cardinal Mindszenty. The other was the planned political diffusion of the VDU through the allocation of two parliamentary seats under the aegis of the Government Party.[52]

The German-Hungarian agreement was promulgated on November 28, 1940. Almost immediately, Basch took advantage of its provisions by launching the *Deutsche Zeitung* (German Journal), the VDU's official organ. The constitution of the VDU was adopted in March 1941, and shortly thereafter the Swabian youth were allowed to form their own pro-Nazi paramilitary organizations instead of joining the *Levente*, the Hungarian paramilitary youth organization. These were basically indistinguishable from SS units.

According to the 1941 census, 720,291 identified themselves as belonging to the German ethnic group. Of these, 477,057 lived in Trianon Hungary, 9,054 in the Felvidék, 9,627 in Carpatho-Ruthenia, 47,508 in Northern Transylvania, and 177,045 in the Délvidék (the Hungarian term for the territories acquired from Yugoslavia in April 1941). Keeping pace with the political and military successes of the Third Reich, the pro-Nazi sympathies of these ethnic Germans were matched only by their pro-Reich Great German nationalism. According to the official figures of the VDU, approximately 10 percent of the ethnic Germans played a leading role in the *Volksbund* or were actually members of the SS; 28 percent belonged to the *Volksbund* or the *Hitler-Jugend* (Hitler Youth), 32 percent supported the *Volksbund*, and 30 percent played no role in any of the VDU organizations. Of the latter, however, 28 percent were totally passive and only 2 percent were actively opposed to them.[53]

Under the leadership of Basch, whose official title was *Volksgruppenführer*, the VDU emulated the Nazi organization in all its details, including geographic division and mass organizational structure. The influence and power of the *Volksdeutsche* were formidable not only because of their support by the Reich, but also because they played a leading role in the Hungarian economy and military apparatus. Constituting a major proportion of Hungary's relatively small middle class, they played a leading role in the country's banking, industrial, and commercial life. Their proportion was especially great in the officers' corps, and in the General Staff in particular. They were also influential in the central and local governmental apparatus. In localities where they constituted a majority, they practically supplanted the official Hungarian state authorities. After the deputies from the Délvidék joined the Hungarian Parliament, the deputies of Swabian origin formed a separate "Parliamentary Group."[54] With German as its official language and with the adoption of Nazi paraphernalia including the Nazi salute, the VDU was largely withdrawn from the control of the Hungarian authorities and came under the guidance and control of Himmler—virtually constituting a state within the state.[55] After the launching of the war against the USSR, it also provided many volunteers for the Waffen-SS.[56]

The Elections of 1939

On May 4, the day the Second Anti-Jewish Law was promulgated, Teleki dissolved Parliament and called for new elections to be held under the new ballot system, which was limited although secret. The elections that were held on May 28–29 were disastrous for the center moderate and leftist forces in the country. Although the government had limited the electoral campaign to about three weeks and had earlier suspended for three months the publication of the *Magyarság* (Magyardom), the official organ of the Arrow Cross Party, the parties of the Right scored a spectacular success.[57] The opposition Smallholders' Party and Social Democratic Party were decimated and, what eventually proved even more important, the Imrédy-led Right faction of the ruling Government Party, the Hungarian Life Party, emerged more influential than ever before.[58]

Anti-Jewish agitation in the new Parliament acquired an added momentum with many of the interpellations introduced by the deputies of the radical Right, questioning the government's policies toward the Jews. In fact, the first interpellation was introduced by Kálmán Hubay. He not only criticized Teleki's "insincerity" toward the Germans, but also claimed that the Prime Minister "could not free himself from the suggestive power of world Jewry."[59]

The Rightist Press

The anti-Jewish agitation in Parliament was accompanied by an exacerbation of the anti-Semitic campaign in the press. Capitulating to German pressure, the Teleki government gave free vent to the Rightwing press, which was by now lavishly supported by the Third Reich, to advance the cause of Germany. It also instructed the official governmental organs to support the Nazi position in the international sphere.[60] While the official press proved a bit more subdued in its attack on the Western Allies and more considerate on the Polish-German issue, it frequently echoed the conviction of the Right-wing press on the Jewish question and on the idea of the invincibility of the Third Reich.

The official organs of the MÉP, the *Függetlenség* (Independence) and the *Esti Ujság* (Evening Journal), like those of the Government, the *Pester Lloyd* and the *Magyarország* (Hungary), were consequently often as nauseating as the openly Nazi papers. Of the major opposition papers, only the organ of the Social Democratic Party, the *Népszava* (People's Voice), and the independent *Magyar Nemzet* (Hungarian Nation) were worth reading for their relatively objective and balanced accounts. However, their influence was greatly overshadowed by that of the Right-wing press, which not only had a much larger following, but was also constantly expanding. The *Magyarság* was allowed to reappear on July 12, 1939, to join the many other dailies, including the *Pesti Ujság* (Journal of Pest), *Uj Magyarság* (New Magyardom), and *Virradat* (Dawn), in advancing ever more vitriolically the twin causes of Nazism and anti-Semitism. These were joined during Teleki's first year in office by three equally anti-Semitic weeklies—the *Holnap* (Tomorrow), the *Nép* (The People), and the *Nemzeti Élet* (National Life).[61] Equally rabid and inciting in their pro-Nazism and anti-Semitism were the *Összetartás* (Unity), *Egyedül Vagyunk* (We Are Alone), *Ország* (Country), and the pictorial *Magyar Futár* (Hungarian Courier). The publishers, editors, and journalists associated with these organs, including Ferenc Rajniss (*Magyar Futár*), Oliver Rupprecht (*Magyarság*), György Oláh (*Egyedül Vagyunk*), Ferenc Vajta (*Ország*), Károly (Meisler) Maróthy (*Pesti Ujság*), Gábor Bornemisza (*Összetartás* and *Virradat*), and István Milotay (*Uj Magyarság*), spewed out an incessant Nazi anti-Semitic propaganda barrage that poisoned Hungarian public opinion.[62] Following the split within the Government Party in October 1940, Milotay, Oláh, and Rajniss became the main ideological spokesmen for Imrédy's Party of Hungarian Renewal (see below).

By allowing a free rein to Nazi propaganda, Teleki played into the hands of the Third Reich, for thereby he fostered a public opinion which not only failed to understand his revisionist and basically anti-Nazi objectives, but also made it more difficult, if not totally impossible, to achieve them.

Teleki's Revisionist Policies

In this, as in practically every other respect, the policies of the Teleki government were typical of the position of the ruling conservative-gentry dominated faction of the Hungarian Right throughout the interwar period. Eager to redress the injustices of Trianon, these leaders found it prudent to publicly placate Germany, whose aggressive designs they both favored and feared, and to privately reassure the Western Allies about Hungary's dedication to remain sovereign and independent. This dualism is best illustrated with Hungary's ambivalent position vis-à-vis Poland, its historical ally. Eager to acquire the sympathy and support of the Third Reich for Hungary's envisioned struggle with Romania for the reacquisition of Transylvania, Teleki assured Hitler in July 1939 that in the event of a general conflict Hungary would make its policy conform to that of the Axis. In a second letter, however, he stated that Hungary could not on moral grounds take action against Poland. The German reaction was swift and threatening. Though subsequently (August 8, 1939) Csáky assured Ribbentrop that the Teleki letters would be withdrawn, the Reich continued to mistrust Hungary and decided to hold up the delivery of some war materials. The ban was lifted only after Hungary decided not to issue a declaration of neutrality.[63] Although one of the alleged reasons for the acquisition of Carpatho-Ruthenia was the establishment of a common Hungarian-Polish border as a means to forestall further German expansionism, when Germany pressed the case of Danzig on the eve of World War II, Hungary advised Poland to yield. It is true, however, that when Germany launched World War II by attacking Poland on September 1 (one week after the signing of the Hitler-Stalin Pact), Hungary refused to allow its territory to be used for passage by German troops. While Hungary did not formally declare its neutrality, in accordance with Ribbentrop's advice that "the Hungarian government keep every possibility open,"[64] it maintained a strict hands-off policy during the hostilities and indeed showed its sympathy for Poland by opening its gates wide to some 140,000 incoming refugees most of whom were soldiers.[65] Mindful that Germany would consider such acts unfriendly, Admiral Horthy, who hoped Germany would help in the revision of Trianon, hastened to assure Hitler of Hungary's loyalty and friendship. In his letter, dated November 3, 1939, the Regent reminded the Führer that Hungary had been the only true friend of Germany after the collapse in World War I and pointed out the high esteem enjoyed by the Germans by identifying the high positions men of

German origin held in the Hungarian governmental and military apparatus. To further prove his loyalty, Horthy emphasized the desirability of a campaign against the Soviet Union "in order to free Europe from the menace of Bolshevism" and assured the Führer that the Hungarian nation was "grateful and absolutely reliable" and "conscious of what it owes him and the German nation."[66]

Toward the Second Vienna Award:
The Acquisition of Northern Transylvania

Following the settlement of the territorial issue with Czechoslovakia, the attention of the Hungarian leaders was directed toward the solution of the question of Transylvania with the Romanians. The issue came to a climax shortly after the signing of the Hitler-Stalin Pact. The Soviet involvement in the partition of Poland not only removed the danger of Romania's possible entry into the war on the side of Poland, but also led to a considerable, though temporary, improvement in Soviet-Hungarian relations.[67] In fact, during the year following the Pact, Hungary geared her policies toward the settlement of the Transylvanian issue to the expected advancement of Soviet claims for the return of Bessarabia, which, like Transylvania, had been acquired by Romania at the end of World War I. Under the secret provisions of the Protocol attached to the German-Soviet Nonaggression Pact, the USSR was given a free hand in Estonia, Latvia, and parts of Finland, Poland, and Romania. While the Soviet Union moved against Poland when that state was about to surrender to Nazi Germany, it was more reluctant to press its case against Romania as long as the West, and especially France, was still considered a formidable force. However, the Soviet press began to deal with the Bessarabian issue in a somewhat subdued fashion as early as November 1939. The Hungarians reacted swiftly and began to make contingency plans for the possible synchronization of their demands against Romania.[68] On December 12, General Henrik Werth, the vocally Germanophile Hungarian Chief of Staff, submitted a memorandum in which he argued that in the case of a Russian attack on Romania, Hungary could not remain passive, but had to get involved in a simultaneous attack for the recovery of "the whole of Transylvania."[69]

Mindful of possible Western, especially British, reaction to a move against one of their allies and cognizant of the German desire at the time to maintain peace in southeastern Europe to assure, *inter alia,* the free flow of oil from Romania, the Hungarian government defined its own conditions for possible intervention. According to the government-prepared memorandum, Hungary would intervene if the Romanians massacred minorities, staged a Bolshevik-type revolution, or ceded minority districts without fighting to either Bulgaria or Russia, the two other major claimants.[70]

The diplomatic maneuvers designed to test the attitudes of some of the major powers including Britain and Italy, gained momentum in the spring of 1940.[71] On March 24, Molotov again raised the issue of Romania, and the Third Reich, finalizing its plans for the attack on the West, became fearful of the possible fate of the oil fields. Germany began to make contingency plans for the possible preemptive occupation of the fields, for which it required Hungarian cooperation. Specifically, the Hungarians were asked to permit the crossing of German troops and to cooperate in a possible joint action against Romania, a course highly recommended by Werth. However, prudence and pragmatism restrained the Russians from acting against Romania until the defeat of France.

On June 23, 1940, the very day France signed the armistice agreement, Molotov informed Count Friedrich Werner von der Schulenburg, the German Ambassador in Moscow, that the USSR would demand the cession of Bessarabia and parts of Bukovina. Three days later, the Russians sent an ultimatum to Romania, demanding these territories be vacated within four days. With France defeated and Germany and Italy supporting the Soviet demands, Romania had no alternative but to yield. The Hungarian government now felt justified in pressing its own demands against Romania, which the Russians also apparently found quite legitimate.[72]

Teleki and Csáky met with Hitler in Munich on July 10 to present the Hungarian case on the Transylvanian issue, but left the meeting somewhat dissatisfied because they were told that they could not expect any aid from Germany or Italy if they attacked Romania.[73] Earlier in the month, Horthy had contacted Hitler to press the Hungarian case concerning Transylvania. He reminded the Führer once again that when the whole world had turned against Germany after the defeat in World War I, Hungary had been its only true friend and ally. He suggested that since Transylvania was Europe's only natural fortress and since the eruption of German-Russian hostilities was inevitable, even German interests required that the territory should be in the possession of trusted friends. The Romanians, he argued, were "morally rotten," and "cheated and betrayed all their allies." To further underline his friendship for the Third Reich, Horthy also felt it necessary to give voice to his deep-rooted anti-Semitism. He informed the Führer that the reason why the Jews of Transylvania were satisfied with Romanian rule was the corruption and venality rampant in the country. The Jews, he continued, also caused much mischief in Hungary for "when every decent man was at the front, the Jews had organized revolution and established Bolshevism." [74]

That same month, Romania, which was by then isolated and under great pressure, renounced the Anglo-French guarantee of political independence and tried desperately to acquire such a guarantee from the Third Reich. [75]

Hitler, who was already planning Operation Barbarossa, was eager to assure the cooperation of both Hungary and Romania and offered to mediate. The diplomatic maneuverings involved direct pressure by the Germans [76] as well as the submission by the Hungarians and Romanians of mutually unsatisfactory and unacceptable territorial claims and offers. [77] These maneuvers culminated in the Hungarian-Romanian negotiations which began in Turnu Severin, Romania, on August 16. [78]

The negotiations acquired an acrimonious tone almost immediately and after about ten days of futile wrangling, both parties complained and appealed to the Germans. Ribbentrop, fearing a possible Russian move against Romania, urged the Italians to agree to an invitation of the Romanian and Hungarian foreign ministers to Vienna for some "friendly advice." All parties eventually consented and Ribbentrop and Ciano arrived in Vienna on August 28. With the assistance of their experts, they worked out the details of the arbitration terms, including the drawing of the new frontier lines. These were communicated to the Hungarians and the Romanians on August 30.

The solution was in accordance with Hitler's general guideline that the Hungarians be given about two-thirds of the 60,000 square kilometers they had officially requested. The terms were imposed by arbitration because the Axis foreign ministers had feared that a discussion would become unending. During the signing ceremonies at the Belvedere Palace, the Hungarians reacted enthusiastically upon seeing the map drawn up by the German and Italian experts. Manoilescu, the Romanian Foreign Minister, fainted. [79]

Under the terms worked out by the Germans and the Italians, the Hungarians received an area of 43,591 square kilometers (see map 4.1) with a population of around 2.5 million. [80] The area ceded to Hungary included the northern half of Transylvania, encompassing all of Szilágy, Beszterce-Naszod, Csik, and Sznolnok-Doboka counties, most of Háromszék and Maros-Torda counties, and parts of Kolozs County. The territorial changes also made possible the reestablishment of Mára-maros, Szatmár, and Ugocsa counties within their pre-World War I boundaries.[81]

The Romanians had to vacate the territory within two weeks. The reentry of the Hungarians began on September 5 and was completed by the 13th, and a brief period of military rule followed, during which anti-Jewish measures were introduced.[82] A civilian administration was introduced shortly after the enactment of the law of October 2 that provided for the incorporation of Northern Transylvania into Hungary.[83]

The Hungarian military authorities were, of course, also very hard on the Romanians. Alluding to the possible incorporation of all of Transylvania, the Hungarians began to circulate propaganda leaflets stating "Trianon is dead. Vienna, too will die." The Axis had to take steps to induce the Hungarians to proceed with moderation. On October 18, 1940, Manoilescu complained to the Duce about the insolence of the Hungarians, which was viewed by Ciano as a reaction to twenty years of Romanian oppression "especially as the Magyars are at heart of a savage and harsh temperament."[84]

The population of the ceded territory was composed as shown in table 5.2. The census figures are dubious, for both the Romanians and

TABLE 5.2.
POPULATION OF CEDED PORTION
OF TRANSYLVANIA

	Census of 1910 (Hungarian, by mother-tongue)		Census of 1930 (Romanian, by nationality)		Census of 1941 (Hungarian)
Magyar	1,125,732		911,550		1,347,012
Romanian	926,268		1,176,433		1,066,353
German	90,195	German	68,694	German	47,501
Yiddish		Jews	138,885	Yiddish	45,593
Ruthene	16,284			Ruthene	20,609
Slovak	12,807	Others	99,585	Slovak	20,908
				Romany	24,729
Other	22,968			Others	4,586
Total	2,194,254		2,395,147		2,577,291

SOURCE: C. A. Macartney, 1:423.

the Hungarians used them in their struggle to justify their respective claims to Transylvania. This was particularly true of the statistical treatment of the Jewish minority.

The Jews of Transylvania

The Jews, who suffered the consequences of both Hungarian and Romanian anti-Semitism, became intertwined with the struggle revolving around the national aspirations of the two traditional enemies. We have noted how to bolster their numerical strength in the multi-ethnic empire of the pre-World War I period, the Hungarians classified the Jews for statistical purposes as Hungarian nationals. Since many, if not most, of the Jews had acquired Hungarian as their mother tongue during the post-emancipation "Golden Era" (1867–1918), the number of those still using Yiddish declined radically.

The proportion of Yiddish-speaking Jews in Transylvania[85] was much larger than that in Hungary proper, and the Romanians, following the acquisition of the territory on December 1, 1918, persuaded many of the Jews to identify themselves as Yiddish-speaking—thus Jewish rather than Hungarian nationals.

Before the partition, the total Jewish population of Transylvania was about 200,000. Of these, 164,052 or four-fifths lived in the territories ceded to Hungary. The more important Jewish population centers and settlements of Northern Transylvania, according to the 1941 census, are shown in table 5.3.

The 50 localities listed under the 11 North Transylvanian counties contained a total Jewish population of 111,334, or 67.9 percent of the territory's Jews. The remainder lived in the many neighboring smaller settlements.[86]

The geographic distribution of the Jews in the territories acquired by Romania under the Treaty of Trianon was uneven. A large number of the Jews gravitated toward the western and northwestern areas of Transylvania, which were adjacent to the large Jewish centers in Eastern Hungary and Carpatho-Ruthenia. Many of these settled in the larger cities of the area, including Nagyvárad, Nagykároly, Szatmárnémeti, and Máramarossziget, giving them somewhat of a Jewish character. As a result of the demographic changes brought about during the 1910–1941 period by immigration, internal mobility, and natural and other factors, the percentage of Jews in these counties and cities exceeded the national (4.2 percent) as well as the Transylvanian (3.2 or 3.6 percent) average.

TABLE 5.3.

IMPORTANT JEWISH POPULATION CENTERS OF
NORTHERN TRANSYLVANIA

Locality	Jewish Population	Percent of Local Population	Locality	Jewish Population	Percent of Local Population
Beszterce-Naszód			Máramaros County (con't.)		
County			Alsóvisó	514	10.9
Beszterce	2,370	14.5	Petrova	584	12.3
Naszód	417	13.0	Bárdfalva	508	20.5
Óradna	295	6.7	Barcánfalva	393	9.7
Magyarnemecse	248	14.7	Felsőszelistye	357	8.7
Bihar County			Jód	217	7.2
Nagyvárad	21,133	22.7	Maros-Torda County		
Margitta	1,725	26.1	Marosvásárhely	5,693	12.7
Érmihályfalva	1,662	18.2	Szászrégen	1,635	16.1
Székelyhid	605	10.2	Erdőszentgyörgy	239	6.8
Nagyszalonta	593	3.9	Szatmár County		
Csik County			Szatmárnémeti	12,960	24.9
Gyergyószentmiklós	559	5.1	Nagybánya	3,623	16.9
Csikszereda	299	4.3	Nagykároly	2,255	14.2
Gyergyótölgyes	198	4.4	Nagysomkút	897	27.9
Háromszék County			Szinérváralja	712	12.6
Sepsiszentgyörgy	400	2.8	Aranyosmeggyes	316	7.1
Kolozs County			Sárközujlak	179	4.5
Kolozsvár	16,763	15.1	Szilágy County		
Bánffyhunyad	960	18.7	Szilágysomlyó	1,496	16.5
Hidalmás	301	15.3	Tasnád	752	13.6
Máramaros County			Szilágycseh	531	15.2
Máramarossziget	10,144	39.1	Zilah	394	4.6
Felsővisó	4,269	34.7	Szolnok-Doboka		
Visóoroszi	1,084	29.8	County		
Borsa	2,409	19.6	Dés	3,719	19.3
Majszin	1,067	19.0	Szamosujvár	847	13.4
Szaplonca	920	23.3	Magyarlápos	717	29.7
Tiszakarácsonyfalva	911	46.0	Bethlen	714	20.8
Rozália	737	21.2	Udvarhely County		
Dragomérfalva	684	20.5	Székelyudvarhely	329	2.7

This is best illustrated with the demographic changes in the larger
cities:[87]

	Jewish Population		Increase (Percent)
	1910	1941	
Kolozsvár	7,046	16,763	138.0
Marosvásárhely	2,755	5,693	106.6
Nagyvárad	15,155	21,333	40.8
Szatmárnémeti	7,194	12,960	81.6

As a result of these changes, the cities of Kolozsvár[88] and Nagyvárad emerged as the largest Jewish-inhabited towns in Hungary outside of Budapest. The expansion of the Jewish population of these cities was also reflected in the increase in the percentage of Jews in the respective counties. Thus the percentage of Jews in Bihar County, which includes Nagyvárad, increased from 2.5 in 1910 to 6.1 in 1941. Those of Kolozs County with the city of Kolozsvár, and Szatmár County with Szatmárnémeti, increased during the corresponding period from 4.4 and 7.4 to 7.1 and 8.1 percent respectively.[89]

The ratio of Jews along the eastern and southern slopes of the Carpathians, especially in the so-called Székely lands, and in the Bánát was always relatively low. The decline in the percentage of Jews in these areas was accompanied during the 1910–1941 period by a considerable decrease in the percentage of Jews in some of the counties of central Transylvania as well.

This is reflected by the following figures:

	Percent of Jews	
County	*1910*	*1941*
Beszterce-Naszod	5.7	4.3
Csik	1.6	0.2
Háromszék	0.8	0.6
Szilágy	4.3	2.9
Szolnok-Doboka	5.1	4.3
Udvarhely	1.1	0.7

The historical and cultural heritage that tied the Transylvanian Jews to Hungary and the socioeconomic and political realities that bound them to Romania were the source of many conflicts during the interwar period. It is one of the ironies and tragedies of history that after the division of Transylvania in 1940 the Jews fared far worse in the part allotted to Hungary—the country with which they maintained so many cultural and emotional ties—than in the one left with Romania—the state identified with many anti-Semitic excesses in the course of its history.

Politically, the Jews of Transylvania were less active during the interwar period in the traditional parties (Conservative, Liberal, and Peasant) of Romania than their brethren in the provinces of Old Romania. Many of the activist elements of the Jewish intelligentsia and middle classes supported either the Jewish Party or the Hungarian Party.

Jewish national and political consciousness in Transylvania was fostered to a large extent by the activities of the Transylvanian Jewish National League (*Erdélyi Zsidó Nemzeti Szövetség*), which was founded on November 20, 1918, on Zionist principles, and by the dedicated though not always harmonious efforts of the various Zionist organizations. Partly because of their activities, a number of Transylvanian Jews, including Tivadar Fischer, József Fischer, and Ernő Marton, were elected during the 1930s to serve in the Romanian Parliament.[90]

In the wake of the many anti-Semitic excesses during the Goga-Cuza era (1937–38) and the general upswing of the Romanian brand of Nazism spearheaded by the Iron Guard (*Garda de Fier*), many Jews became enamored with the underground Left, which was unsurprising given the climate of Nazism. A considerable number of Jews in Transylvania as elsewhere had become convinced that Marxism represented the key to the solution of the scourge of anti-Semitism. They were represented in both the local and the national leadership of the illegal Communist Party.[91] The anti-Jewish agitation became violent following the Soviet incorporation of Bessarabia and Northern Bukovina (June 1940). Partly because of this, many of the Jews of Transylvania received the news about the Second Vienna Award with considerable satisfaction. This feeling was reinforced by the older Jews, who still remembered the Hungary of pre-1918, and by Jewish ignorance of the realities of Hungary's anti-Semitic policies at the time.

The Jews of Transylvania were victims of the historical milieu in which they lived. The Romanians resented them because of their proclivity to Hungarian culture and by implication to Hungarian revisionism and irredentism; the Hungarians, and especially the Right radicals, accused them of being "renegades" in the service of the Left. This was one reason why Jewish national consciousness among the Jews of Transylvania was much higher than in Hungary proper. In fact, the Zionist movement in Hungary, though basically illegal, was reinvigorated when the national leadership was joined by the Zionist leaders of Transylvania, including Ernő Marton and Rudolph (Rezső) Kasztner.[92]

The socioeconomic structure of Transylvanian Jewry was similar to that of the Jews in the neighboring provinces. Many were engaged in business or trade and their percentage in the professions and white-collar fields outside of government was relatively high. There were, however, only a handful of Jews associated with mining and heavy industry. While no data on income distribution are available, the many studies on Transylvania reveal that there was a considerable proportion of Jews who could barely make a living; many depended for their survival on the generosity of the community. Most of these impoverished Jews lived in the densely populated Jewish centers of the northwest.

The illusions cherished by many Jews in connection with the replacement of the Romanians by the Hungarians soon gave way to disbelief and despair. Shortly after the completion of the occupation of Northern Transylvania on September 13, 1940, the military authorities implemented many of the anti-Jewish policies that had already been in effect in Hungary proper. The Jewish newspapers were suppressed, as were all nondenominational clubs and associations.[93] The Hungarian democratic, or moderate, press in Transylvania fared no better. The local journals and periodicals were transformed into mouthpieces of the Right, and liberal journalists like Edgar Balogh and Lajos Jordáky were silenced. Periodicals such as *Hitel* (Credit), *Pásztortűz* (Shepherd's Fire), and *Katolikus Status* (Catholic Status) of Kolozsvár, as well as their contributors (many of whom had earlier been known as moderate) became the spokesmen for Fascism. The organs of the smaller communities, such as the *Szamosvölgye* (Szamos Valley) of Dés, the daily *Székely Szó* (Székely Word) of Sepsiszentgyörgy, and the weekly *Gyergyói Lapok* (Gyergyó Papers) of Gyergyószentmiklós, became even more virulently anti-Semitic than their counterparts of Kolozsvár. The swing to the Right was also joined by the various economic and social associations, including the Baross Federation, the Hangya Cooperative, and the Wesselényi Rifle Club, and by such cultural institutions as the *Erdélyi Helikon*. The latter came under the influence of writers like József Nyírő, a "literary representative" of the extreme right.[94]

The heavy hand of the military was felt particularly in the four counties of the Székely area, which the Hungarians considered "holy." The Jews of the area were subjected to a revision of their citizenship; as a result, many of them found themselves in custody because of their "doubtful" citizenship.

The anti-Jewish measures initiated by the military were continued and extended by the civilian authorities. They affected the Jews particularly harshly in their economic and educational pursuits. While those in business and the professions managed to make ends meet by circumventing the laws or by taking advantage of loopholes, the civil servants were with a few exceptions dismissed and students in secondary and higher education found themselves almost totally excluded from the state educational system. The *Numerus Clausus* provision of the laws was so applied as to assure in practice a *Numerus Nullus* in most counties.[95] Whereas the Jewish leadership of Transylvania solved the educational needs of secondary-school Jewish youth by establishing Jewish denominational secondary schools in Kolozsvár and Nagyvárad, the status of Jewish students in higher education was deplorable. During the 1940–41 academic year, for example, the University of Kolozsvár admitted only 10 Jewish students—and they were admitted only because of special connections.[96] At any rate, they were hardly able to attend classes because of Jew-baiting by Christian students.[97]

The *Gleichschaltung* in Northern Transylvania, as in the other territories acquired through the cooperation of the Third Reich in 1938–39, was a clear indication that Hungary was ready to embrace the New Order for Europe envisioned by Hitler.

The Courting of the Reich

The Hungarians naturally greeted the acquisition of Northern Transylvania with great enthusiasm. They viewed it not only as a vindication of their historical position, but also as still another step in the eventual total eradication of the "injustices" of Trianon. They were, of course, cognizant of the fact that their diplomatic successes, which had involved three territorial acquisitions within two years, were due primarily to the assistance they had received from the Third Reich. Gratitude and the expectation of further assistance induced the Hungarian leaders, who were incited by an ever more chauvinistic rightist press, to court the Reich by meeting most of its demands.[98]

Although in Vienna the Third Reich had insisted only on the formalization of the legal status of the *Volksdeutsche*, it let the Hungarians know via Sztójay that it would welcome additional pro-German measures, including possible overfulfillment of economic obligations, the institution of social reforms, the repeal of the measures enacted against the radical Right, and above all, the "solution of the Jewish question."

Given the changed composition of the Parliament, the greater activism of the radicals, and the further swing of public opinion toward the extreme Right, Teleki tried to assure the continued rule of his aristocratic-gentry class by adopting to a large extent the policies of his rightist opponents. Almost immediately after the completion of the reoccupation of Northern Transylvania, Teleki brought about the release from jail of Szálasi[99] and shortly thereafter the repeal of Order 3400, which had prohibited the political involvement of civil servants. The order, which had been adopted in the summer of 1938, was repealed on September 29—the day the Arrow Cross and Hungarian National Socialist parties were merged.

To counter the rumblings of the Imrédy-led Right wing of his own party, Teleki revealed on October 8, 1940, the government's intentions to carry out the Germans' wishes which had been communicated through Sztójay. Among other things, Teleki announced the readiness of the government to institute further land reforms, to launch a new social reform program, and to adopt a third major anti-Jewish law, which was to be "clear, radical, and simple, without the complications and loopholes for evasion of its predecessors."[100]

The radical Right, however, became ever more relentless in its demand for a total solution of the Jewish question along the pattern adopted in the Third Reich. At a meeting of the lower house on November 26, 1940, which discussed some aspects of the labor service system for Jews, Tamás Matolcsy, a representative of the Arrow Cross Front, for example, demanded that the Jews be placed in internment camps rather than in labor service units. His brother and co-party member, Mátyás Matolcsy, a notorious anti-Semitic journalist, insisted, along Hitler's line of reasoning, that the Jews "be removed from the country and from the face of the earth."[101]

While these demands for a radical solution of the Jewish question were not publicly and unequivocally rejected by the government, Teleki found a number of occasions to elaborate upon his own views. In discussing the budget later in the year, for example, he warned that "the key positions of Hungary's economic life must not be left in the hands of Jews, half-Jews, guinea-pigs, or dummies." Like the other responsible leaders of the ruling aristocratic-gentry class, however, he too tried to counterbalance his anti-Semitic program by arguing that it was impossible to take away the livelihood of close to one million people "without giving them an opportunity to move elsewhere." "The Jewish question," he continued, "was a European one and could only be finally settled in a new, organized Europe."[102]

Teleki repeated the same theme on a number of other occasions. In alluding to the government's preparations for a third anti-Jewish law, based upon the Nazi design to separate the Jews from the other citizens of the country, Teleki had the following to say before a session of the Parliament late in 1940:

The radical solution of the Jewish question in our country can be found only within the framework of a European solution. However, until then we have to find some solution. The solution of this problem is a painful process which involves many difficulties; I am aware of the individual tragedies involved. I consider the solution of the problem desirable in the national interest and not for the sake of statistics. In my opinion, we have to prevent large scale intermixing between Jews and non-Jews. A part of our middle and upper classes have already become Jewified. This problem ought to have been solved thirty years ago and not left to us. We must not allow the keys of the country's economy to be left in the hands of Jews, half-Jews, or their strawmen. We must not, however, deprive 800,000 people [1,000,000, if the converts are included] of their livelihood because this is also in the interests of Central Europe. It is not only I who say this [turning toward the noisy *Nyilas* deputies], but also many smarter people whose opinion you also cherish. In other words I am carving out new laws rather than modifying old ones. We must find a sober and proper solution. . .[103]

In his inaugural speech about four months later, Teleki's successor, László Bárdossy, repeated the same arguments almost verbatim (see chapter 6).

Teleki's pronouncements were designed, of course, not only to crystallize his and his peers' position on the Jews, but also to defuse the ever louder criticism of his policies by the ultra Right both at home and abroad. They had, however, relatively little impact on the resolution of the group of representatives led by Imrédy and Jaross to secede from the MÉP and form a new, pro-Reich political party.

The Party of Hungarian Renewal. The crisis that was precipitated by the Imrédy-led Right-wing faction of the Hungarian Life Party in June 1940 came to a climax on October 18, when 18 deputies who had earlier seceded from the Government Party announced the formation of a new party, *A Magyar Megújulás Pártja* (The Party of Hungarian Renewal). Among these were Antal Kunder, Miklós Mester, and György Oláh, who were joined by Ferenc Rajniss, an anti-Semitic journalist and non-Party deputy. Placed under the leadership of Imrédy, who acted as the "National Party leader" (*Országos Pártvezető*), and of an Executive Committee composed of Imrédy, Jaross, and Jenő Rátz,[104] the party adopted a 15-point program, which differed little from that of the Arrow Cross but was more appealing to the lower middle class and the new middle class as well as the rightist-oriented intellectual and civil service groups. It advocated, among other things, Hungary's firm alliance with the Third Reich and the remodeling of its institutions along National Socialist and, especially, Fascist corporate lines.

In connection with the Jews, the program advocated the "settlement of the Jewish question which would free Hungary entirely from the Jews and the Jewish spirit." As an interim measure, Point 14 of the program called for the elimination of Jews from the country's cultural life and the immediate expropriation of their farm lands. Although the Imrédists at first viewed the Jewish question primarily as an urgent economic problem, they soon came to agree with the Arrow Cross elements that the Jewish question would have to be solved within the framework of the overall German-directed anti-Jewish plan covering all of Europe.[105] It was this ideological spirit of the party that was clearly discernible after the German occupation, when the Imrédists wholeheartedly supported the ghettoization and deportation measures.

Although the Party of Hungarian Renewal was relatively small,[106] it quickly gained influence and respectability because it enjoyed the confidence and generous support of the Germans.

The Germans trusted the new party not only because of the composition of its leadership and firm commitment to the ideals of the Third Reich, but also because it offered the best assurance for stability and law and order in an envisioned Nazi-oriented Hungary. At this time they believed the Arrow Cross, with its nebulous Hungarist program, was potentially as dangerous as the disorderly Iron Guard in neighboring Romania, which had just been placed under *de facto* German occupation.

The Germans were quite correct in their assessment of the Imrédists, who consistently challenged the policies of the government and became increasingly vocal in serving the interests of the "New Order" in Europe. Their press organs, including the *Uj Magyarság, Magyar Futár,* and *Egyedül Vagyunk,* edited by István Milotay, Ferenc Rajniss, and György Oláh[107] respectively, kept up a constant propaganda barrage that not only championed the causes of the Reich, including the anti-Jewish drive, but also made the subsequent German occupation more palatable.[108]

Teleki's Maneuvers. There was considerable rivalry between the Imrédists and the various *Nyilas* groups, and although Imrédy and Szálasi met—on Ruszkay's initiative—some time in November, their mutual dislike and animosity could not be overcome. The two factions had in common only their stand against the Jews and opposition to Teleki's leadership. Although Teleki's support in Parliament did not diminish as a result of the withdrawal of the Imrédists—he was more than compensated by the support of the 51 representatives from Transylvania—the government strove to meet the challenge of the extreme Right by deflating it. The aristocratic-gentry rulers were more fearful of the threat to their survival represented by the *Nyilas* than of the country's economic and cultural "domination" by the Jews, whom they both envied and detested. This sentiment was made perfectly clear in Horthy's letter to Teleki, dated October 14, 1940, in which he asked his

Prime Minister to consider steps for the removal of *Nyilas* and Imrédist elements from leadership positions ("the enemy cannot be bought by good positions") and for the easing of the anti-American and anti-British tone of the press. The letter was undoubtedly motivated to a large extent by the strike of the coal miners, which the *Nyilas* had organized a few days earlier as a first step toward a general strike and a possible coup. The Regent's anti-*Nyilas* and anti-Jewish sentiments were synthesized in the following passage:

As regards the Jewish problem, I have been an anti-Semite throughout my life, I have never had contact with Jews. I have considered it intolerable that here in Hungary everything, every factory, bank, large fortune, business, theater, press, commerce, etc., should be in Jewish hands, and that the Jew should be the image reflected of Hungary, especially abroad. Since, however, one of the most important tasks of the government is to raise the living standard, i.e., we have to acquire wealth, it is impossible, in a year or two, to eliminate the Jews, who have everything in their hands, and replace them with incompetent, mostly unworthy big-mouthed elements, for we would become bankrupt. This requires a generation at least. I have perhaps been the first to loudly profess anti-Semitism, yet I cannot look with indifference at inhumanity, senseless humiliations, when we still need them. In addition, I consider, for example, the *Nyilas* to be by far more dangerous and worthless for my country than I do the Jew. The latter is tied to this country by interest and is more faithful to his adopted country than the *Nyilas,* who, like the Iron Guard, with their muddled brains want to swing the country into the hands of the Germans.[109]

While fearing the possible long-range threat that Germany represented for Hungary, Teleki realized that the fulfillment of his country's expansionary ambitions depended upon the support of the Reich. This realization grew with the military successes of the *Wehrmacht* during the first years of the war. Basically a pragmatic politician, Teleki consequently consented early in October 1940 to the granting of transit facilities for German forces entering Romania. These were not only to train Antonescu's Romanian Army, but also to protect the oil fields and serve as a nucleus for the planned joint operations against the Soviet Union.

Meanwhile the Nazi press became increasingly preoccupied with the necessity for the global solution of the Jewish question, highlighting the "positive" measures that had been adopted against the Jews in Romania and Slovakia in contrast with Hungary, "where the Jews continued to exert great economic influence." In his dispatches of early November, 1940, Sztójay was almost panicky in emphasizing the importance of the solution of the Jewish question as part of the continued improvement of German-Hungarian relations. He claimed that the Germans' attitude toward the Hungarians was becoming unfavorable and that the Germans were becoming increasingly impatient over the solution of the Jewish question in Hungary. "I find the evolution of the Jewish question of such far-reaching importance," he argued, "that it may have a decisive impact on German-Hungarian relations, nay . . . I must state in full knowledge of my responsibility that it will in fact become decisive."[110]

Under these pressures Teleki became increasingly eager to show his and his country's loyalty to the Reich. On November 20, he and Csáky went to Vienna, where they saw to it that Hungary was the first country to adhere to the Tripartite Pact concluded by Germany, Italy, and Japan on September 27.[111] In his discussions with Hitler and Ribbentrop relating to the war and the international situation in general, and Hungarian-German relations in particular, Teleki took the initiative in raising the Jewish question and stated that with the conclusion of peace the Jews should be removed from Europe. According to Schmidt's minutes, Hitler considered the solution of the Jewish question in Europe as one of the most important problems of peace. Apparently not yet decided on the Final Solution, the Führer claimed that he would make possible the involvement of all interested states by compelling France to yield some of its colonies[112] for this purpose.[113]

With its adherence to the Tripartite Pact so relatively soon after it had joined the Anti-Comintern Pact and left the League of Nations, Hungary gave up its neutrality and formally linked its fate to that of the Axis.

The Conspiracy Against Yugoslavia

After attaining their military objectives in the West during the first half of 1940, the Axis Powers turned their attention to the Balkans. Although Germany and Italy both aimed at exploiting the area as a primary source of raw materials, their ultimate objective was somewhat contradictory: while the Germans were eager to use the Balkans as a springboard for the planned invasion of the USSR and the British-held territories in the Middle East, the Italians were primarily concerned with the advancement of their goal to transform the Mediterranean into an "Italian Lake." In pursuit of this grandiose objective, they had attacked Greece unilaterally on October 28, 1940. These conflicting military aspirations of the two European powers of the Axis Alliance brought the issue of Yugoslavia, with its Hungarian dimension, again to the fore.

The Hungarians were suddenly confronted with a dilemma. They were increasingly eager to regain the territories they had lost to Yugoslavia after World War I; however, they were becoming considerably apprehensive about the expansion of German power in Central Europe. With the incorporation of Austria, the dismemberment of Czechoslovakia, the defeat of Poland, and the virtual occupation of Romania, Hungary began to look upon Yugoslavia—the last intact member of what had been the Little Entente—as a conduit to the West and also as a possible partner in an envisioned Italo-Hungarian-led bloc designed to prevent the further expansion of the Third Reich.

In response to these historical, military, and political realities, the Hungarians embarked on a contradictory course. Shortly after the incorporation of Northern Transylvania, they began to pressure Berlin to help bring about the territorial revision involving the Magyar-inhabited parts of Yugoslavia.[114] At the same time, they also approached the Yugoslavs, informing them discreetly about their desire to bring about the settlement of the territorial and minorities questions affecting the two nations by direct negotiation—i.e., without the mediation of the Axis Powers. Concurrently with these maneuvers, however, the Hungarians also prepared contingency plans for the possible reacquisition of all the former Hungarian-held territories, including Croatia, in the event of Yugoslavia's disintegration in the wake of an eventual German or Italian attack upon the country.

Hand in hand with these contingency plans, the Hungarians also embarked on a discreet diplomatic campaign to warm up relations with Yugoslavia.[115] The overtures that the Hungarians advanced toward the Yugoslavs in September and October 1940 bore fruit early in December, when a "treaty of peace and eternal friendship" was signed.[116] Under the treaty, the two contracting parties undertook "to consult together on all questions which, in their opinion, affect their mutual relationship." Concurrently, an oral agreement was reached under which the Yugoslavs undertook to provide cultural facilities for the Hungarian minority living in the Voivodina Region. The Germans and the Italians were naturally kept abreast of these developments, since one of the basic objectives of the Axis Powers was to assure Yugoslavia's adherence to the Tripartite Pact. In fact, during the diplomatic crisis of March 1941, when the Hungarians became alarmed about the rumored German guarantee of the integrity of Yugoslavia as a reward for its joining the Tripartite Pact—a move that would have undercut Hungary's revisionist designs—László Bárdossy, the new Hungarian Minister of Foreign Affairs,[117] reminded Berlin that "the Hungaro-Yugoslav Pact had been concluded at the Führer's express wish."[118] Bárdossy was made to acquiesce in the German plan during his courtesy visit with the Führer and Ribbentrop in Munich on March 21, 1941.

The dramatic events of the next few days played into the hands of the Hungarian chauvinist-revisionist elements. In response to German pressure, the Rightist-oriented Yugoslav government yielded and on March 25 Prime Minister Dragiša Cvetković and Foreign Minister Cincar-Marković signed the Tripartite Pact in Vienna. Two days later, however, the rightists were overthrown and a new, Western-oriented government was formed by General Dušan Simović. That very day, Hitler decided to expand the scope of Operation Maritsa—the code name for the military operations planned against Greece—to cover Yugoslavia as well. Hungary was requested via Sztójay to participate in the military operations and to allow the passage of German troops, for which it was offered not only the return of the Bácska and the Banat but also access to the Mediterranean through use of the port of Fiume. The Council of Ministers discussed the offer the following day, after which Horthy delivered his favorable response to Hitler a few hours later. In his letter dated March 28, Horthy expressed his suspicion that the Yugoslav events were influenced by the Soviet Union and looked forward to the meeting between the military experts of the two countries to synchronize their plans.[119] This was accomplished on March 30 during the visit of General Friedrich von Paulus to Budapest.

Teleki himself was at first ambivalent about the plan because he feared the possible negative reaction of the Western powers. His fears were fully corroborated. His note of March 3, outlining Hungary's position for the benefit of London and Washington, and especially his note of March 30, in which he tried to "inform" the West that Hungary's possible intervention in Yugoslavia was motivated not by the desire of conquest but only by the wish to protect the rights of the Hungarian minority, were answered in unambiguous terms. On April 2, György Barcza, the Hungarian Minister in London, informed Teleki that the British would sever diplomatic relations with Hungary if it yielded to German demands for the passage of troops and would declare war if it participated in the hostilities against Yugoslavia. When the Germans attacked Yugoslavia on April 6, using Hungary as a springboard, the British carried out their threat. Teleki, who had not specifically opposed the military preparations or the decision of the Highest Council of Home Defense (*A Legfelsőbb Honvédelmi Tanács*), had committed suicide four days earlier. In his suicide note addressed to Horthy he berated the Governor for Hungary's cowardly breach of word and also blamed himself for not having restrained the Governor from his actions.[120] Horthy tried to explain Teleki's suicide to Hitler and Mussolini on April 3 and ease his and his nation's conscience by rationalizing that since Yugoslavia would disintegrate in the wake of a German attack, the Yugoslavia with which Hungary had a pact would cease to exist. At the same time he assured the Führer that Hungary was proceeding with the military preparations in accordance with the stipulations of his letter of March 28.[121]

The Germans attacked Yugoslavia on April 6, and in accordance with a scenario worked out in advance, Hungary followed suit one day after Croatia declared its independence on April 10. The Hungarians occupied the Bácska, the Baranya Triangle, the Muravidék (Prekomurje), the area surrounded by the Drave, Danube, and Tisza rivers, and eventually the Muraköz (Medjumurje) on the northwestern border of Yugoslavia, the area between the Mura and Drave rivers bordering Austria. Hungary's active role in the war ended on April 14; ten days later Horthy paid his personal homage to Hitler. He was greatly disappointed, however, because Hitler reneged on his promises relating to the Banat. Citing the fierce opposition of the Romanians, the Führer decided to keep the Banat under German control.[122] By virtue of the Hitler-Horthy agreement of April 27, Hungary nevertheless acquired a territory of 11,624 square kilometers, which were formally annexed on December 27, 1941.[123] When Hungarian civilian administration was introduced on July 29, 1941, the Bácska was incorporated into the reconstituted Bács-Bodrog County, the Baranya Triangle was attached to Baranya County, the Muravidék to Zala County, and the Muraköz to Vas County. The Bácska and the Baranya Triangle were known during the time the Hungarians held them (1941–45) as the Délvidék (the Southern Region).[124]

The Jews of the Délvidék: Demographic Data

Of the nearly one million people in the Hungarian-acquired territories of Yugoslavia, only 14,202 were Jewish. The overwhelming majority of these lived in the four major cities of Bács-Bodrog County.

TABLE 5.4.
IMPORTANT JEWISH
POPULATION CENTERS
IN THE DÉLVIDÉK

Locality	Jewish Population	Percent of Local Population
Szabadka	3,549	3.5
Ujvidék	3,621	5.9
Zenta	1,432	4.4
Zombor	1,011	3.1
Ada	326	2.4
Topolya	319	2.3
Ujverbász	302	3.2
Óbecse	234	1.1
Palánka	169	3.1

(The more important Jewish population centers in the county are shown in table 5.4.)

In the Muravidék, by far the largest Jewish community was that of Csáktornya, with 482 members representing 7.0 percent of the total population. The ten localities with a total Jewish population of 11,445 represented 80.6 percent of the Jews in the territories acquired from Yugoslavia.[125] Like the Jews of the Felvidék and Northern Transylvania, most of the Jews of the Délvidék were Hungarian-speaking. They shared the shock of the Jews in the other required territories, who still remembered Hungary before World War I, when they were immediately subjected to the anti-Jewish measures then in effect and which became ever harsher under the new Bárdossy administration.

Notes

1. Teleki served as Prime Minister from July 19, 1920 to April 14, 1921. He served as Foreign Minister from April 19 through September 22, 1920, December 16, 1920 to January 18, 1921, and April 12–14, 1921. He also served in the Imrédy government as Minister of Cults and Public Education from May 14, 1938 to February 15, 1939. *Magyarország tiszti cim—és névtára* (Title and Name Register of Hungary) (Budapest: A Magyar Királyi Állami Nyomda, 1942), 49:4.

2. Charles Gati, "Modernization and Communist Power in Hungary," *East European Quarterly*, 5, no. 3 (1971):342–43.

3. L. Tilkovszky, *Pál Teleki (1879–1941): A Biographical Sketch.* (Budapest: Akadémiai Kiadó, 1974), 70 pp.

4. For details on Teleki's background and foreign policies, see C. A. Macartney, 1:221–26; 329–490. For a leftist view, see Gyula Juhász, *A Teleki-kormány külpolitikája,*

1939–1941 (The Foreign Policy of the Teleki Government, 1939–41) (Budapest: Akadémiai Kiadó, 1964), 368 pp.

5. See his lengthy letter, dated February 13, 1939 (shortly before his appointment as Prime Minister), addressed to John A. Keyser (an Englishman who had various interests and connections in Hungary) quoted in Nathaniel Katzburg, "Paul Teleki and the Jewish Question in Hungary," *Soviet Jewish Affairs,* London, no. 2 (November 1971): 105–11.

6. Nicholas M. Nagy-Talavera, *The Green Shirts and the Others. A History of Fascism in Hungary and Rumania* (Stanford: Hoover Institution Press, 1970), p. 66.

7. Teleki's letter to John A. Keyser.

8. Paul Teleki, *The Evolution of Hungary and Its Place in European History* (New York, 1923), pp. 141ff. as quoted by Robert A. Kann, "Hungarian Jewry During Austria-Hungary's Constitutional Period (1867–1918)," *Jewish Social Studies,* New York, no. 4 (October 1945):383–84.

9. Teleki, for example, reminded the Bethlen politicians who had objected to his policies "that the Hungarian Fascists are as good Hungarians as they, maybe even better ones, because they see more clearly the most important Hungarian problem,"—the Jewish question. Dezső Sulyok, *A magyar tragédia* (The Hungarian Tragedy) (Newark, N.J.: The Author, 1954), p. 368 as quoted by Talavera, *The Green Shirts and the Others,* p. 151.

10. The Teleki cabinet of February 1939 consisted of: Foreign Minister, Count István Csáky; Minister of the Interior, Ferenc Keresztes-Fischer; Minister of Finance, Lajos Reményi-Schneller; Minister of Agriculture, Count Mihály Teleki; Minister of Industry, Antal Kunder; Minister of Trade and Transportation, Antal Kunder; Minister of Cults and Public Education, Bálint Hóman; Minister of Justice, András Tasnádi Nagy; and Minister of Defense, Károly Bartha. *Magyarország tiszti cim- és névtára,* pp. 4–6.

11. Shortly after taking office, Teleki instructed György Barcza, the Hungarian Minister in London, to assure the British Foreign Office that "although Hungary's geographical and political situation compelled her to cooperate loyally with Germany up to a point, he was absolutely determined that such cooperation should never go so far as to impair, much less sacrifice, Hungary's sovereignty, independence, and honor. The Government attached great importance to the understanding and support of the British Government, and would never do anything to injure the interests of Great Britain." C. A. Macartney, 1:331.

12. The territory is also variously referred to as Ruska Kraina, Podkarpatska Rus, Sub-Carpathian Russia, Sub-Carpathian Ruthenia, and Carpatho-Ukraine. Historically, the area, like Slovakia as a whole, belonged to Hungary for around a thousand years. In 1919, it was allotted to Czechoslovakia by virtue of the Peace Treaty of St. Germain. By virtue of the Soviet-Czechoslovak Treaty of June 29, 1945, Carpatho-Ruthenia was ceded to the Soviet Union and incorporated into the Ukrainian Soviet Socialist Republic as the province of Transcarpathian Ukraine.

13. Vološin served as the Prime Minister of the autonomous province from October 26, 1938 to March 14, 1939. Randolph L. Braham, "The Destruction of the Jews of Carpatho-Ruthenia," in *HJS,* 1:234.

14. Because of its adherence to the Anti-Comintern Pact, the Soviet Union broke off diplomatic relations with Hungary, which were established in 1934. Stephen D. Kertesz, *Diplomacy in a Whirlpool: Hungary Between Nazi Germany and Soviet Russia* (Notre Dame, Indiana: University of Notre Dame Press, 1953), pp. 46, 204, 206.

15. *Magyarország és a második világháboru* (Hungary and the Second World War), ed. Magda Ádám, Gyula Juhász, Lajos Kerekes, and László Zsigmond (Budapest: Kossuth, 1961), pp. 211–12.

16. Kertesz, *Diplomacy in a Whirlpool,* p. 45. See also Michael Winch, *Republic for a Day: An Eye-Witness Account of the Carpatho-Ukraine Incident* (London: Robert Hale, 1939).

17. Hungary was anxious to prevent Romania from occupying some or all of the

Romanian parts of Ruthenia and to secure Romania's recognition of its new frontiers. *Documents on German Foreign Policy* (Washington, D.C.: Government Printing Office), series D, vol. 6, pp. xxxviii–xxxix.

18. Following its acquisition, Carpatho-Ruthenia was placed under the administration of a government commissioner, Baron Zsigmond Perényi. The region was represented in Parliament by 10 deputies. (See *Magyarország tiszti cim- és névtára*, p. 18.) For further details on the acquisition of Carpatho-Ruthenia consult C. A. Macartney, pp. 1:329–43 and *Magyarország külpolitikája, 1938–1939* (Hungary's Foreign Policy, 1938–1939), compiled by Magda Adám (Budapest: Akadémiai Kiadó *for the* A Magyar Tudományos Akadémia Történettudományi Intézete, 1970), 809 pp. See also Oscar Jászi, "The Problem of Sub-Carpathian Ruthenia," in *Czechoslovakia,* ed. Robert J. Kerner. (Berkeley: University of California Press, 1949), pp. 193–215; Raphael Lemkin, *Axis Rule in Occupied Europe* (Washington: Carnegie Endowment for International Peace, 1944), pp. 150–53; and Paul Robert Magossi, *The Shaping of a National Identity: Subcarpathian Rus, 1848–1948* (Cambridge, Mass.: Harvard University Press, 1978), 640 pp.

19. For a valuable and thoroughly documented historical overview of the Jews of Carpatho-Ruthenia, see Livia Rothkirchen, "Deep-Rooted Yet Alien: Some Aspects of the History of the Jews in Subcarpathian Ruthenia," in *YVS,* 12:147–91. For additional details, see chapter 3.

20. Ernő László, "Hungary's Jewry: A Demographic Overview, 1918–1945," in *HJS,* 2:163–64.

21. *Ibid.,* pp. 169–70.

22. Germany's share in Hungarian foreign trade increased phenomenally during the 1930s. While in 1930 only 10.3 percent of Hungary's total export went to Germany, by 1939 Germany's share increased to 52.2 percent. The imports from Germany increased from 21.2 to 52.5 percent during the corresponding years. Gati, "Modernization and Communist Power in Hungary," p. 341.

23. Lévai, *Zsidósors Magyarországon,* p. 331.

24. *Ibid.,* pp. 34–35.

25. *Ibid.,* pp. 33–34.

26. Introduced during the 358th session of the lower house, the debates lasted from February 24, 1939 (session 372) through March 27, 1939 (session 388), when the bill, guided through the house by János Makkai, was adopted after its third reading. Changes introduced by the upper house were discussed and ironed out in conference committees on April 21 and 28 and May 3 (sessions 391, 393–94). See *Országgyülés képviselőházának naplója* (Proceedings of the House of Representatives of the National Assembly) (Budapest: Athenaeum), vol. 18.

27. Lévai, *Fekete könyv,* pp. 38–39.

28. See, for example, the following publications: *Apponyi György gróf, Bartok Béla, Berda József (és társaik) tiltakozása a zsidótörvény ellen* (The Protest of Count György Apponyi, Béla Bartok, and József Berda (and Associates) Against the Anti-Jewish Law) (Budapest: Hungaria, 1939); *Hozzászólás a zsidók közéleti és gazdasági térfoglalásának korlátozásáról szóló törvényjavaslathoz tüzharcos szempontból* (Remarks, From the Veterans' Point of View, on the Draft Bill Restricting the Social and Economic Activities of the Jews) (Budapest: Fémes, 1939), 15 pp.; *A második zsidótörvény célja, indokolása, következményei. Néhány szó a magyar zsidó értelmiség nevében a magyar közvéleményhez* (The Aim, Justification, and Consequences of the Second Anti-Jewish Law. A Few Words by the Hungarian Jewish Intelligentsia to Hungarian Public Opinion) (Budapest: Pester Lloyd, 1939), 22 pp.; Endre Sós, ed. *Egyház és társadalom a fajelméletről és a második zsidótörvény javaslatáról. Egyházfők, tudosok, államférfiak, közirok és testületek megnyilatkozásai* (Church and Society on Racial Theory and the Second Anti-Jewish Draft Law. Statements by Church Heads, Scientists, Statesmen, Writers, and Heads of Institutions) (Budapest: Periszkop, 1939), 82 pp.; *Tiszteltelljes*

folyamodása a Magyar Izraelita Vallásfelekezet Törvényes Képviseleti Szerveinek a zsidók közéleti és gazdasági térfoglalásának korlátozásáról szóló 702. sz. törvényjavaslat tárgyában (Respectful Appeal of the "Legal Representatives of Hungarian Jewish Religious Bodies" Concerning Draft Law No. 702 Restricting the Social and Economic Activities of Jews) (Budapest: Pester Lloyd, 1939), 26 pp. For further references relating to the Second Anti-Jewish Law see *The Hungarian Jewish Catastrophe. A Selected and Annotated Bibliography*, compiled by Randolph L. Braham. (New York: YIVO Institute for Jewish Research, 1962), pp. 9–14.

29. Lévai, *Fekete könyv*, pp. 39–40.

30. *Ibid.*

31. *Itéljetek! Néhány kiragadott lap a magyar-zsidó életközösség könyvéből* (You Be the Judge! A Few Pages Torn from the Book on Magyar-Jewish Coexistence), Márton Vida (Budapest: Földes, 1939), 62 pp. For further details on the attitude of the Hungarian Jewish leaders and on the background and contents of the Second Anti-Jewish Law, see Lévai, *Fekete könyv*, pp. 36–56. See also chapter 3.

32. Nathaniel Katzburg, "The Hungarian Jewish Situation During the Late 1930's." *Annual of Bar-Ilan University Studies in Judaica and the Humanities* (Ramat Gan, Israel: Bar-Ilan University, 1977), 14–15: 83–93.

33. *Ibid.*, pp. 94–95. See also Rothkirchen, "Deep-Rooted Yet Alien," pp. 147–91.

34. Lévai, *Zsidósors Magyarországon*, p. 34.

35. *Ibid.*, pp. 35–36.

36. For the text of Raffay's and Serédi's speeches of April 15, 1939, see Henrik Fisch, ed., *Keresztény egyházfők felsőházi beszédei a zsidókérdésben* (Speeches on the Jewish Question Made in the Upper House by the Heads of the Christian Churches) (Budapest: The Author, 1947), pp. 41–63. For further details on the attitude of the Christian Churches toward the Jews see chapter 30.

37. Israel Cohen, "The Jews in Hungary," *The Contemporary Review*, London, November 1939, p. 37. See also *Vázsonyi János országgyülési képviselőnek a második zsidótörvény tárgyalása alkalmából elmondott parlamenti beszéde* (Parliamentary Speech of János Vázsonyi, Member of Parliament, During the Debate on the Second Anti-Jewish Law) (Budapest: Törekvés, 1939), 15 pp.

38. A leading member of Szálasi's Hungarist movement, Kovarcz was elected to Parliament in 1939. He was brought to account for his role in the attack on the Jewish worshippers, but shortly before he was to begin to serve his sentence (in the spring of 1941) he escaped to Germany, where he established close relations with the Gestapo. He returned to Hungary in April 1944, and took part in the anti-Jewish drive. He was in the forefront of the anti-Horthy *Nyilas* coup of October 15 and served the Szálasi regime as Minister of Total Mobilization. Found guilty of war crimes by the People's Tribunal (*Népbiróság*), Kovarcz was executed in 1946.

39. It was finally dissolved on February 24, 1939, but two weeks later, Teleki permitted its reappearance under a new name—the Arrow Cross Party. Miklós Lackó, *Nyilasok, nemzetiszocialisták 1935–44* (Nyilas Men and National Socialists, 1935–1944) (Budapest: Kossuth, 1966, pp. 156–57, 159). See also chapter 2.

40. Lackó, *Nyilasok, nemzetiszocialisták, 1935–1944*, pp. 162–63.

41. "1939. évi IV. törvénycikk a zsidók közéleti és gazdasági térfoglalásának korlátozásáról" (Law No. IV of 1939 Concerning the Restriction of the Participation of Jews in Public and Economic Life), *1939. évi Országos Törvénytár* (National Collection of Laws for 1939) (Budapest: Állami Nyomda, 1939), pp. 91–102. The Law was implemented by Decree 7.720/1939. M.E. of August 22, 1939.

42. Péter Sipos, *Imrédy Béla és a Magyar Megújulás Pártja* (Béla Imrédy and the Party of Hungarian Renewal) (Budapest: Akadémiai Kiadó, 1970), p. 85.

43. For data on Jews in the professions, see chapter 3.

44. For additional data on the Jews' role in the economy, see Levai, *Fekete könyv*, pp. 48–49.

45. Louis Rittenberg; "The Crisis in Hungary," *Contemporary Jewish Record*, 2, no. 3. (May–June 1939):28–30.

46. Lévai, *Fekete könyv*, p. 55. For further details on the Press Chamber see chapter 15.

47. For additional references relating to the Second Anti-Jewish Law consult Braham, *The Hungarian Jewish Catastrophe*, pp. 9–14.

48. Lévai, *Zsidósors Magyarországon*, p. 37.

49. Basch was born in Hatzfeld, in the Banat Region, on July 13, 1901. He was one of the major war criminals tried after World War II and was executed in Budapest on April 26, 1946. For further details on Basch and the *Volksdeutsche* in Hungary consult: G. C. Paikert, *The Danube Swabians* (The Hague: Martinus Nijhoff, 1967), pp. 7–241; C. A. Macartney, 1:69–70, 169–72, 178–79, and 326; and the following works by Johann Weidlein, all published in Schorndorf, by the author: *Der madjarische Rassennationalismus* (The Magyar Race Nationalism), 1961, 131 pp.; *Jüdisches und deutsches Schicksal in Ungarn* (Jewish and German Fate in Hungary), 1969, 84 pp.; and *Geschichte der Ungarndeutschen in Dokumenten, 1930–1950* (The History of the Hungarian Germans in Documents, 1930–1950), 1957.

50. Csáky's idea was communicated on April 27, 1939, to Count Frigyes Villáni, then Hungarian Minister in Rome, for transmission to Ribbentrop. C. A. Macartney, 1:347–48.

51. Paikert, *The Danube Swabians*, pp. 118–19. For the text of the Protocol, see *Magyarország és a második világháború*, pp. 290–93.

52. Joseph Rothschild, *East Central Europe Between the World Wars* (Seattle: University of Washington Press, 1974), pp. 194–95.

53. Dezső Sulyok, *A magyar tragédia* (The Hungarian Tragedy) (Newark, N.J.: The Author, 1954), p. 205.

54. C. A. Macartney, 2:41.

55. *Ibid.*, 1:457.

56. The recruitment was directed by SS-*Gruppenführer* Gottlob Berger and partially financed by the sums collected from Jews as payments for German exit permits. For details, see Lévai, *Eichmann in Hungary* (Budapest: Pannonia Press, 1961), pp. 223–25. See also Loránt Tilkovszky, *SS-toborzás Magyarországon* (SS-Recruitment in Hungary) (Budapest: Kossuth, 1974), 192 pp.

57. The various Hungarian National Socialist parties, including the Arrow Cross Party (then under the leadership of Kálmán Hubay because Ferenc Szálasi was still in prison), the United National Socialist Party (*Egyesült Nemzeti Szocialista Párt*) of Fidél Pálffy and László Baky, and a number of other smaller factions led by Károly Maróthy-Meizler, Mátyás Matolcsy, and Zoltán Meskó, had formed an electoral coalition that won 49 seats as against only 2 in 1935. Of these, 31 had been won by the Arrow Cross Party alone.

58. The Smallholders received only 11 and the Social Democrats only 5 as against the 26 and 14 seats they had held in the earlier Parliament. Because of their small representation, these parties could not really play a meaningful opposition role. In fact, during the pre-occupation period, they often supported the government in its domestic and foreign policies. For example, on January 20, 1940, a representative of the Social Democratic Party expressly supported Teleki's foreign policy and four days later the party-dominated trade unions issued a manifesto repudiating the idea of class domination. The manifesto also emphasized the unions' adherence to "constitutionalism" and to the attainment of the "national objectives of millenary Hungary." The Social Democrats maintained the façade of opposition by formally voting against the government or by abstaining on certain controversial issues. The Smallholders went even further; they often voted with the MÉP. Moreover, the influence of these opposition parties was to a large extent

restricted. The Social Democrats had some influence in the capital and a few other industrial centers; the Smallholders were basically content to rely on the instrumentality of Parliament. C. A. Macartney, 2:378–79.

The Government Party had changed its earlier name of National Unity Party (*Nemzeti Egység Pártja*) at the end of February 1939. It won 183 or 70 percent of the seats, but under the leadership of Count László Vay, a rabid anti-Semite, the party came increasingly under the dominance of its Right wing. Its electoral coalition partner was the Christian Party (*Kereszténypárt*), which had won 4 seats as against 14 in 1935. For further details on the 1939 elections, consult Miklós Lackó, *Nyilasok, nemzetiszocialisták*, pp. 164–83. See also C. A. Macartney, 349–52. For details on the origins and the establishment of the Hungarian Life Party, see Sipos, *Imrédy Béla*, pp. 100–108.

59. Lackó, *Nyilasok, nemzetiszocialisták*, pp. 186–87.

60. C. A. Macartney, 1:353. In April, 1940, the editors-in-chief of all newspapers were warned once again in the Prime Minister's office to heed Germany's interests in international affairs. *Ibid*, p. 395.

61. Lackó, *Nyilasok, nemzetiszocialisták*, p. 184. See also Róbert Major, *25 év ellenforradalmi sajtó, 1919–1944* (25 Years of Counterrevolutionary Press, 1919–1944) (Budapest: Cserépfalvi, 1945), 108 pp.

62. Among the most prolific anti-Semitic agitators were also journalists like Ferenc Fiala, Ferenc (Mischek) Mikes, Árpád Oláh, and Kálmán Hubay. Following the German occupation, the Hungarian *Stürmer*—the *Harc* (Battle)—was launched under the editorship of Zoltán Bosnyák. For further details on the *Harc,* see chapters 14 and 15.

63. *Documents on German Foreign Policy,* Series D, vol. 6, docs. 712, 784; vol. 8, docs. 289, 489, 519, 520, 533, 572.

64. C. A. Macartney, 1:363. When Villáni informed Ciano about Hungary's refusal to allow German troops to cross the country, the Italian Foreign Minister noted in his diary entry for September 11, 1939, "that at some time or other the Hungarians will have to pay for it" because the Germans would not forget it. The following day, Villáni reported that a similar request by the "Glorious Slovak Army" was made and rejected by the Hungarians. Villáni had characterized the Slovaks as "accomplices and pimps" of the Germans. *The Ciano Diaries, 1939–1943,* ed. Hugh Gibson (Garden City, N.Y.: Doubleday, 1946), p. 142.

65. Of these, around 100,000 were allowed to leave by June 1940. Most took up service with the French and British forces. By 1943–44, about 15,000 refugees remained in Hungary, of which 3,000 Jews were cared for by the Jewish community. C. A. Macartney, 1:368–69. See also József Antal, *Lengyel menekültek Magyarországon a háború alatt* (Polish Refugees in Hungary During the War) (Budapest: Rácz Endre, 1946), 94 pp. See also chapter 3.

66. *Horthy Miklós titkos iratai* (The Confidential Papers of Miklós Horthy), eds. Miklós Szinai and László Szücs (Budapest: Kossuth, 1963), pp. 216–20.

67. Under the provisions of the secret protocol attached to the Hitler-Stalin Pact, the Soviet Union began the invasion of Eastern Poland on September 17, 1939, and a few days later met the German forces along the prearranged demarcation line. The resumption of diplomatic relations with the Soviet Union was announced on September 24, and three days later József Kristóffy, the newly appointed Minister to Moscow, presented his credentials to President Mikhail I. Kalinin. Soviet-Hungarian relations continued to improve until Hitler launched Operation Barbarossa on June 22, 1941. In the fall of 1940, Mátyás Rákosi and Zoltán Vas, the two Communist leaders, were freed from prison, given amnesty, and allowed to go to the USSR on November 2. In return, on March 21, 1941, the Soviets returned to Hungary the 58 flags which the soldiers of Czar Nicholas I had captured following the surrender of the Hungarian forces of Artur Görgey at Vi-

lágos in 1849. Aside from these gestures of good will there was a marked improvement in Soviet-Hungarian economic relations as well. See also Macartney, 1:370, 468.

68. Shortly after the Soviet press began to deal with the Bessarabian issue, Antonescu was sent to Rome to inquire about Italy's possible reaction to a Russian attack on Romania. The Romanians urged the Italians to work on the Hungarians "because any Hungarian threat on the Romanian rear would oblige the Romanians to come to an agreement with the Russians." Mussolini agreed to transmit the Romanian demand to Hungary and promised to grant Romania, in case of a Russian attack, the kind of military support Italy had given to Franco's forces in Spain. *The Ciano Diaries*, pp. 182–83.

69. According to a report, Werth instructed General Gábor Faraghó, the newly appointed Military Attaché to Moscow, to contact the Soviet Chief of Staff to arrange for a coordinated action against Romania. C. A. Macartney, 1:386–87 and 389.

70. *Ibid.*, p. 389.

71. At that time the British still believed that the maintenance of Romania was necessary and urged the Hungarians to act in a moderate fashion, preferably not in collusion with either Germany or Russia. *Ibid.*, p. 387. Although Hungary's foreign policy was largely geared to Italy's, Italy was not very enthusiastic about Hungary's revisionist plans, which might disturb the peace in the Balkans. Ciano met with Csáky in Venice on January 5–6, 1940, during which time he tried to convince his Hungarian counterpart that in the light of the Russian menace it was in the interest of Hungary to get along with Romania. He further advised Csáky that if Hungary wanted "to live and even prosper moderately it must avoid becoming . . . a mosaic state." Csáky had assured Ciano that Hungary would "not take the initiative in the Balkans and thus spread the fire." On February 19, Ciano had warned the Hungarians once again via Villáni to be calm and refrain from provoking any conflict.

Hungarian-Italian relations were reviewed anew during Teleki's visit to Rome on March 23–27, at which time Ciano had found Teleki "objective and reasonable." He had assured the Italians he would not move against the Romanians "because he does not want to make himself responsible, even indirectly, for having opened the doors of Europe to Russia." Apparently sensing or knowing of Ciano's own anti-German feelings, Teleki gave him an inkling of his pro-Allied sympathies and of his fears of "an integral German victory." During his meeting with Mussolini, Teleki was informed about the Duce's resolution to enter the war on the side of Germany. *The Ciano Diaries*, pp. 185, 192, 210, and 225–27.

72. On July 7, 1940, Molotov assured Kristóffy that the Soviet government considered the Hungarian claims well-founded and that it would support them. These assurances were repeated during the Hungarian-Romanian negotiations at Turnu Severin on August 16–26. Kertész, *Diplomacy in a Whirlpool*, p. 50.

73. *The Ciano Diaries*, pp. 274–75. For the text of the minutes taken by Paul Otto Schmidt, the official interpreter of the German Foreign Office, see *A Wilhelmstrasse és Magyarország*, pp. 506–9. For additional Foreign Office documents relating to Hungarian-German discussions on the issue of Transylvania see *ibid*, pp. 510–26 and *Documents on German Foreign Policy*, Series D, vol. 10, pp. xxviii–xxxi; vol. 11, p. xlviii. For further documents, including minutes of the meetings of the Council of Ministers, see *Magyarország és a második világháboru*, pp. 259–306.

74. *Horthy Miklós titkos iratai*, pp. 221–25. According to a "secret" revealed by Hitler to Ciano during their meeting at Berghof on November 18–19, 1940, Horthy's nationalistic pretensions also extended to Fiume. Horthy allegedly had asked the Führer to raise the question of Trieste with the Italians. *The Ciano Diaries*, pp. 312–13.

75. Kertész, *Diplomacy in a Whirlpool*, p. 51. Following the territorial concessions to Bulgaria and Hungary and the consequent replacement of King Carol II by a govern-

ment headed by General Ion Antonescu, Romania aligned itself completely with National Socialism. It left the League of Nations and the Balkan Entente and invited in a German "instructor corps" early in October 1940, ostensibly to train the Romanian Army. Eventually an entire Panzer division was allowed in with the permission of the grateful Hungarians, who also permitted the deployment of German military personnel at key Hungarian railroad stations "to maintain the lines of communication between Romania and Germany." *Ibid*, p. 52.

76. Following the Munich discussions with the Hungarians, Hitler approached King Carol II of Romania to bring about a definitive solution of the territorial problems with Bulgaria and Hungary. The King's answer was delivered in person by Prime Minister Ion Gigurtu and Foreign Minister Mihail Manoilescu on July 23 at Salzburg. Hoping that Hitler would be appreciative of Romania's potential contributions to the Axis, King Carol had suggested that Hitler impose and then guarantee a general settlement in southeastern Europe. The Romanians delivered the same message to the Italians on July 27. Ciano had the following to say about the Romanians: "They are simply disgusting. They open their mouths only to exude honeyed compliments. They have become anti-French, anti-English, and anti-League of Nations. They talk with contempt of the *Diktat* of Versailles—too honeyed." The Italians' position was similar to that taken by Hitler. *The Ciano Diaries*, p. 279. See also C. A. Macartney, 1:414. For a succinct account of the negotiations and of the major provisions of the Second Vienna Award, see Béla Vágó, "Le second diktat de Vienne: Le partage de la Transylvanie" (The Second Dictate of Vienna: The Partition of Transylvania), *East European Quarterly*, 5, no. 1 (1971):47–73.

77. In the fall of 1939, the Hungarians had prepared both a maximum claim and a minimum one, which they declared irreducible. Under the maximum claim, the Hungarians asked for 78,000 of the 103,000 square kilometers lost in 1919. According to Hungarian statistics, this territory contained 4.2 million people, of whom 50 percent were Romanians, 37 percent Hungarians, and 10 percent Germans. Under the minimum claim, the Hungarians expected 50,000 square kilometers with a population of 2.7 million, about equally divided between Hungarians and Romanians. The Romanians, in turn, having accepted the Bulgarian demands for the return of Southern Dobrudja, offered the Hungarians only 14,000 square kilometers in the Szatmár and Nagykároly region of Transylvania. C. A. Macartney, 1:387–88, 414.

78. The Hungarian delegation was led by András Hóry and the Romanian one by Valer Pop.

79. *The Ciano Diaries*, pp. 287–89.

80. C. A. Macartney, 1:422–23. The exact territorial and population figures cannot be ascertained. According to Vágó's sources, the Hungarians identified the area received as 43,046 square miles, the Romanians as 42,243 square miles. His census figures also vary slightly, giving 2,388,909 for 1930 and 2,612,102 for 1940. Vágó, "Le second diktat de Vienne: Le partage de la Transylvanie," pp. 65–66. Kertész claims that 43,492 square miles with a population of 2.6 million were returned to Hungary. *Diplomacy in a Whirlpool*, p. 207.

81. Ernő László, "Hungary's Jewry: A Demographic Overview, 1918–1945," in *HJS*, 2:165; 169.

82. The military's involvement in traditionally civilian affairs had begun during the administration of Gömbös. By this time, the military's penetration into the civilian sphere was so advanced that Teleki threatened to resign unless it were stopped. Teleki detailed his dispute with Werth in a letter to Horthy, dated September 1, 1940, to which he attached a lengthy memorandum about the army's increasing influence over the civilian authorities. *Horthy Miklós titkos iratai*, pp. 233–52.

83. Teleki placed the Prefect of Bihar County, A. Hlatky, in charge of civilian administration. Pending the holding of new elections after the emergency period, Northern

Transylvania was allocated 63 seats in the lower house and a proportionate number in the upper house. Of these, 12 were reserved for the Romanians to be filled after Romania granted equivalent representation for the Hungarian minority. The 51 delegates actually appointed consisted of 48 Hungarians and 3 Germans. Most of these aligned themselves with the Teleki faction of the MEP. C. A. Macartney, 1:430. For the list of the Transylvanian deputies see *Magyarország tiszti cim- és névtára*, pp. 18–19.

84. *The Ciano Diaries*, pp. 294 and 302. For details on the treatment of the Romanians during the occupation of Northern Transylvania and during the Horthy era, see Tribunalul Poporului, Cluj. *Complectul de judecată. Hotărîrea no. 1. Şedinţa Publică din 13 Martie 1946* (Judgment. Decision No. 1. Public Session of March 13, 1946), 59 pp. Judgment rendered by the People's Tribunal against 63 individuals accused of war crimes. See also *Horthysta atrocitások Erdély északi részebén (1940). szeptember-1944. oktober)*. (Horthyite Atrocities in the Northern Part of Transylvania, September 1940–October 1944) (n.p., n.d.).

85. For a succinct review of the origin and history of Transylvanian Jewry in general and that of Kolozs County in particular, see Mozes Carmilly-Weinberger, "Zsidók Erdélyben" (Jews in Transylvania), in *A kolozsvári zsidóság emlékkönyve* (Memorial Volume for the Jews of Cluj-Kolozsvár), ed. Mozes Carmilly Weinberger (New York: The Editor, 1970), pp. 7–28; see also pp. 263–68.

86. László, "Hungary's Jewry," pp. 165–67.

87. *Ibid.*, p. 171.

88. For a statistical demographic profile of the Jewish community of Kolozsvár, see "Statisztikai adatok Kolozsvár zsidóságáról az 1919–1936-os években" ("Statistical Data on the Jews of Kolozsvár During 1919–1936), in *A kolozsvári zsidóság emlékkönyve*, pp. 105–13.

89. László, "Hungary's Jewry, p. 173.

90. "Erdélyi Zsidó Nemzeti Szövetség" (Transylvanian Jewish National League), in *A kolozsvári zsidóság emlékkönyve*, pp. 134–37.

91. Prominent among these Communists of Jewish background were men like Béla Breiner, Sándor Jakab, and Hillel Kohn. The "Jewish Communists" fared particularly badly after the Hungarian incorporation of Northern Transylvania. Hundreds of them were arrested in 1940 and kept in such camps as Kistarcsa and Garany. Many of them were "shown off to the public" by the prosecution during the mass trial of 1941, further fanning the flames of anti-Semitism. Many more Jews suspected of Communist leanings were placed in special punitive labor service companies that were deployed in the Ukraine. Very few of these managed to return alive. See also Vágó, "The Destruction of the Jews of Transylvania," pp. 176 and 185.

92. For a succinct review of Zionism in Transylvania, see Livia Bitton, "The Zionist Movement in Transylvania," in *A kolozsvári zsidóság emlékkönyve*, pp. 277–85.

93. In addition to the suppression of the *Uj Kelet, Népünk*, and the other periodicals and the exclusion of Jews from the general press, the authorities also disbanded the *Haggibor* and *Makkabi* Jewish sport organizations of Kolozsvár and Nagyvárad, respectively. Vágó, "The Destruction of the Jews of Transylvania," pp. 179 and 214. The *Uj Kelet* resumed publication in Tel Aviv in 1948 under the editorship of Ernő Marton and Dezső Schön.

94. Vágó, "The Destruction of the Jews of Transylvania," pp. 183–84 and 215–16.

95. No Jewish students were admitted, for example, to the High School of Csikszereda and only four were admitted to that of Gyergyószentmiklós. Of these, one was legally exempted from the anti-Jewish laws and the other three were converts. *Ibid.*, pp. 179; 214.

96. The Jewish High School of Kolozsvár was organized on the initiative of and first headed by Antal Márk, who had personal contacts with Bálint Hóman, the Minister of Cults and Public Education. Upon his death in 1942, he was succeeded by Dr. Endre Bach. For details on the school, including its faculty and student body, consult *A kolozsvári*

zsidóság emlékkönyve, pp. 114–34. For a succinct review of Jewish primary and secondary education in Transylvania between 1840 and 1944, see *ibid.,* pp. 269–76.

97. During the 1932–33 academic year 443, or 11 percent of the 4,158 students enrolled were Jewish. In 1936–37, 67 or 7.59 percent of the graduates were Jewish. Vágó, "The Destruction of the Jews of Transylvania," pp. 179; 214–15.

98. Horthy expressed his gratitude in a personal letter to Hitler, dated September 2, 1940. Both houses of Parliament heard Teleki praise Hitler and Mussolini two days later. The Germanophile Sztójay lost no occasion in Berlin to convey Hungary's gratitude in the most obsequious fashion. See *A Wilhelmstrasse és Magyarország,* pp. 525–31.

99. Szálasi was released on September 18, 1940, and eleven days later became the leader of the newly merged Arrow Cross Party and the Hungarian National Socialist Party. The merger was spearheaded by Jenő Ruszkay, who had only one month earlier joined Baky's and Pálffy's National Socialist Party at the instruction of Franz Rothen, the representative of the German Foreign Office's intelligence service in Hungary. The leader of the new Arrow Cross Party—"the sole repository of National Socialism in Hungary"—was supposed to operate under the guidance of a council consisting of Sándor Csia, Kálmán Hubay, Lajos Széchenyi, and Ruszkay. The program, adopted on October 1, called, among other things, for the elimination of the Jews from Hungary's body politic. Lackó, *Nyilasok, nemzetiszocialisták,* pp. 230–34.

100. C. A. Macartney, 1:436.

101. *FAA,* 1, p. xxxvii.

102. C. A. Macartney, 1:458.

103. Lévai, *Fekete könyv,* pp. 57–58.

104. Lieutenant-General Rátz had served as the Chief of Staff from 1937 to May 14, 1938, when he became Minister of Defense for a half year. In the Sztójay government he served as Deputy Premier and following the Szálasi coup as the president of the upper house. Convicted as a war criminal, he was condemned to forced labor for life.

105. Sipos, *Imrédy Béla és a Magyar Megújulás Pártja,* p. 241.

106. In December 1940, the party had only 20 deputies or 5.9 percent of the representatives. However, with these 20 deputies, the strength of the ultra rightist opposition increased to about 70, or 20.8 percent. Within this opposition, the new party represented 28.5 percent. *Ibid,* p. 203.

107. For a perceptive analysis of the background and role played by these journalists, see *ibid.,* pp. 205–15.

108. For further details on the Party of Hungarian Renewal see *ibid.,* pp. 181–254. See also Lackó, *Nyilasok, nemzetiszocialisták,* pp. 218–47, and C. A. Macartney, 1:435–37.

109. *Horthy Miklós titkos iratai,* pp. 260–65.

110. Sipos, *Imrédy Béla,* p. 183. See also C. A. Macartney, "Hungarian Foreign Policy During the Inter-War Period with Special Reference to the Jewish Question," in *Jews and Non-Jews in Eastern Europe,* eds. B. Vago and G. L. Mosse (New York: John Wiley, 1974), pp. 125–36.

111. For the text of the Tripartite Pact and of the Protocol relating to Hungary's adherence see *Magyarország és a Második Világháború,* pp. 304–6.

112. The Führer obviously referred to the so-called "Madagascar Plan" developed in Section III of *Abteilung Deutschland* of the German Foreign Office in the summer of 1940 and enthusiastically received by the Reich Security Main Office, then under the leadership of Reinhard Heydrich. Under the plan, the island of Madagascar, then under French control, was to be yielded to the Germans and, with the exception of the areas reserved for the German Navy, placed under the jurisdiction of a police governor responsible directly to Himmler. The resettlement of the Jews was to be financed through the utilization of confiscated Jewish property. Madagascar was conceived as an alternative to the settlement of the Jews in Palestine, "which belongs to the Christian and Moslem

worlds," and as a convenient place where the European Jews could be held as hostages to assure the good conduct of their "racial comrades" in America. For further details, see Hilberg, *The Destruction of the European Jews,* pp. 260–61.

113. *A Wilhelmstrasse és Magyarország,* p. 551.

114. The issue of Yugoslavia was raised by Sztójay during the discussions with Weizsaecker on October 15, 1940, concerning Hungary's resolve to join the Tripartite Pact. *A Wilhelmstrasse és Magyarország,* p. 542.

115. In their drive to split the Little Entente and weaken the position of Romania, Hungary's erstwhile enemy, the Hungarians were ready in November 1937 to guarantee the Yugoslav-Hungarian frontier in exchange for a pledge of Yugoslav neutrality in the event of war between Hungary and a third power. The Hungarians, according to German records, did not even ask for cultural autonomy for the Hungarian minority in Yugoslavia. *Documents on German Foreign Policy,* Series D, vol. 2, Doc. 114 and vol. 5, Doc. 178.

116. *Documents on German Foreign Policy,* Series D, vol. 11, Docs. 365, 431, 478, 480, 514. The pact was signed on December 12, 1940, and ratified by the Hungarian Parliament together with that of the Tripartite Pact on February 3, 1941. The exchange of ratifications took place in Budapest on February 27. Baron György Bakách-Bessenyey, the Hungarian Minister in Belgrade, played an important role in the negotiations.

117. Bárdossy became Foreign Minister following the death of Csáky on January 27, 1941. See chapter 6.

118. C. A. Macartney, 1:471.

119. For its text see *The Confidential Papers of Admiral Horthy,* pp. 171–73.

120. For the facsimile of Teleki's letter see *The Confidential Papers of Admiral Horthy,* p. 178ff.

121. *Ibid.,* pp. 176–79.

122. *Documents on German Foreign Policy,* Series D, vol. 12, Docs. 340, 344, 353, 366, 371.

123. For text of the annexation document see Lemkin, *Axis Rule in Occupied Europe,* pp. 631–33.

124. For details on Hungary's involvement in the disintegration of Yugoslavia see C. A. Macartney, 1:385, 446–90; 2:3–14; *Magyarország és a második világháboru,* pp. 307–38; Gyula Juhász, *A Teleki-kormány külpolitikája,* pp. 252–334. For documents on German-Hungarian exchanges on the Yugoslav issue, see *A Wilhelmstrasse és Magyarország,* pp. 552–91 and *Documents on German Foreign Policy,* Series D, vol. 12, pp. xxvi–xxix.

125. László, *Hungary's Jewry: A Demographic Overview, 1918–1945,* pp. 167, 173–74. On the fate of the Jews of the Délvidék, see chapter 20.

CHAPTER SIX

THE BÁRDOSSY ERA

Bárdossy the Man

SHORTLY AFTER Teleki's suicide on April 3, 1941, Admiral Horthy appointed László Bárdossy as Prime Minister. Bárdossy was catapulted into national prominence by the deaths within four months of Hungary's two most prominent governmental leaders. Unlike his predecessor, Bárdossy was of middle-class background; although plagued by chronic ill health, he was endowed with a brilliant mind and an impulsive temperament. His arrogance and impetuosity often irritated both his subordinates and superiors. Having devoted his talents to a career in government service, he first served in the Ministry of Cults and Public Education, then in the Consular Service, and after 1920 in the Ministry of Foreign Affairs. There, he first headed the Press Bureau and in the 1930s he served as the Counselor of the Legation in London and as Minister in Bucharest. Following the death of István Csáky on January 27, 1941, he was appointed Foreign Minister, a position he retained after his nomination as Premier.[1]

Like all the leaders of the Horthy era, Bárdossy was motivated by a mortal fear of Bolshevism and the desire to undo the "injustices of Trianon." With respect to Germany and the Jewish question, he was much closer to Imrédy than to Teleki. His ideological-political outlook was similar to that of Gömbös, to whom he was related by marriage. As a consequence, his ultra anti-Bolshevik, anti-Semitic, and revisionist position led to the adoption of domestic and foreign policies that proved disastrous for Hungary in general and for the Jews in particular. During his tenure as Premier, which lasted less than a year, Hungary participated in the invasion of Yugoslavia, declared war on the USSR and the USA, and became firmly committed to the Third Reich. With regard to Jewish affairs, his premiership is characterized by the extension of the anti-Jewish measures to the Jews of the Délvidék, the adoption of a third major and openly racial anti-Jewish law, the exacerbation of the Jewish military labor service system, and the massacre of Jews at Kamenets-Podolsk and Ujvidék—the only two incidents of mass killing before the German occupation in 1944.

Bárdossy's Jewish Policy

Bárdossy outlined his domestic and foreign political program before the Hungarian Parliament on April 24—ten days after the completion of the military operations in Yugoslavia. He identified the Jewish question as one of the most important, requiring an urgent and far-reaching solution in line with the proposals advanced by Teleki in his budget speech made four months earlier. Specifically, he suggested that:

- Laws be adopted to prevent the intermixing of Jews with non-Jews.
- Jews be removed from social, cultural, political, and spiritual areas affecting the education of future generations, the psychological evolution of the masses, and the psychological, moral, ideological, and political guidance of the nation.
- The key positions in the country's economy be safeguarded from Jews, half-Jews, and their front.[2]

Like Teleki, Bárdossy emphasized that all the proposed measures were to be provisional in the sense that the final solution of the Jewish question had to await the end of the war and be effectuated within a general European framework.

Bárdossy's specific references to the proposed plan for the solution of the Jewish question were obviously made with an eye on the envisioned Third Anti-Jewish Law, the preparations for which were already in full swing. Concurrently, a series of measures were actually adopted against certain categories of Jews. On April 16, less than two weeks after his appointment, Bárdossy's government adopted Decree No. 2870/1941 M.E., regulating the military labor service system for Jews. Together with Decree No. 27300. eln. 8–1941 of the Ministry of Defense (dated August 19, 1941), which implemented it, this drastically altered the status and conditions of service of Jewish men of military service age (see chapter 10).

In connection with the Délvidék, the Bárdossy government did not wait until its formal annexation as required by international law to issue an Order (April 28) requiring that all "Serbs, Bosnians, Montenegrins, gypsies, or Jews who did not (themselves or their parents) have citizenship within the territory of Greater Hungary before October 31, 1918" leave the country within three days. Exemption was granted only to persons married to Hungarians or Germans, women expecting to give birth within two weeks, and persons over 75 years of age. The people affected by the expulsion order were permitted to take along their jewelry, the effects they could carry, and fifty *Pengős* per person. According to one source, 50,000 persons crossed the border at Ujvidék alone during the days immediately following the issuance of the order.[3]

The Third Anti-Jewish Law

The first two major anti-Jewish laws were adopted shortly after the occupation of the Upper Province (*Felvidék*) and of Carpatho-Ruthenia, respectively. They reflected not only the anti-Semitic policies of the Hungarian governments of the period, but also Hungary's symbolic gratitude to the Third Reich for the political and diplomatic assistance received in the reacquisition of these territories. Thus, the adoption of the Third Anti-Jewish Law must be partially viewed as the expression of Hungary's indebtedness to the Reich for the reoccupation of Northern Transylvania and of the Délvidék.

Under an innocuous title which did not even include the word "Jew," the law was by far the most openly and brazenly racist piece of legislation Hungary ever adopted.[4] Signed into law on August 2, 1941, it technically dealt with a variety of matters relating to an earlier general marriage law.[5] However, Part IV (articles 9 and 10) titled "The Prohibition of Marriage Between Jews and Non-Jews" and the punitive provisions of Part V, were clearly based upon the Nuremberg Law of 1935.

The arguments advanced in support of the draft bill aimed to prove the harmful effects of the policies in effect vis-à-vis the Jews since the end of the nineteenth century. The bill, as emphasized in its rationale,

did not aim to pay homage to popular slogans or to thoughtlessly emulate foreign examples, but the process of assimilation that was launched vociferously in 1895 did not yield good results. Mixed marriages had a definitely detrimental effect upon the evolution of our national soul; they brought into a position of influence that Jewish spirit whose harmful effect we have seen. There is no doubt about the failure of the experiment in assimilation. We now want to exchange this for disassimilation.[6]

Having replaced the religious identification by an exclusively racial definition of what constituted a Jew, the law prohibited marriage and extramarital sexual relations between Jews and non-Jews. Radically transcending the provisions of the earlier anti-Jewish laws, the Third Anti-Jewish Law identified as a Jew any person at least two of whose grandparents had been born as Jews, and anyone who was a member of the Jewish denomination irrespective of his origin. A person was not accounted Jewish even if two of his grandparents were Jewish if he himself was born a Christian and his parents were members of a Christian denomination at the time of his birth. By implication, any person who had three or four Jewish grandparents was considered a Jew even though born a Christian.

This time the representatives of the Christian denominations in the upper house unanimously and steadfastly opposed the proposed law. László Ravasz, for example, a leading figure of the Reformed (Calvinist) Church, read a protest note that had been signed by all the bishops and the four superintendents of his denomination.[7] The opposition of the Church leaders was partially due to the fact that the bill directly affected many of their parishioners, both converts and Christian-born ones. As a compromise, the upper house initiated the inclusion of a provision under which the Minister of Justice was given the power to waive the rules under certain exceptional conditions and consider a person a non-Jew if two of his grandparents were Jewish provided that he himself was born a Christian or "converted before his seventh birthday." This compromise solution saved many Hungarians, including members of the aristocracy and of the governmental and political elite group, from being classified as Jews.[8]

The enactment of the law led to a number of so-called criminal miscegenation suits. However, by far the most devastating effect of the law was psychological and propagandistic. Whipping up the hysteria that had been associated with Hungary's entry into the war against the Soviet Union shortly before, the law served as a vehicle for the exacerbation of the anti-Jewish psychosis connected with the "holy crusade against Judaeo-Bolshevism." It prepared the ground for the acceptance by Hungarian public opinion of the draconic measures that were to be adopted during the German occupation.

The War Against the Soviet Union

In foreign affairs, Bárdossy was less ambivalent than Teleki. He was perhaps more realistic about the esteem in which the Western powers held Hungary, and was convinced that Hungary's revisionist ambitions could be achieved only in close cooperation with Italy and the Third Reich. Guided by these convictions, Bárdossy aligned Hungary more firmly than ever before with the policies of the Axis, which, at the time, were geared toward war with the Soviet Union.

Hungary's anti-Bolshevik stand was made clear by Horthy during his visit to Hitler's headquarters at Münchenkirchen on April 24, 1941,[9] and by Bárdossy during his courtesy call to Rome on June 4–5.[10]

The preparations for the attack against the Soviet Union began shortly after the completion of the campaign against France in June 1940. Hitler's original plan was to launch the offensive that very autumn, but it was subsequently amended to begin on May 15, 1941. However, the unexpected turn of events in Yugoslavia late in March and the consequent war in the Balkans forced a further postponement of the anti-Soviet campaign to June 22.[11] Hitler's plans, which had not originally called for Hungary's active military involvement, were communicated to the Hungarians via the military. Initially, the Hungarians were only to have fortified the borders in Carpatho-Ruthenia to prevent a possible Soviet penetration behind German lines, to permit the probable deployment of a part of the German southern army groups (*Heeresgruppe Süd*) on Hungarian soil, and to assure the continued and increased supply of goods and raw materials to the Third Reich.

The Hungarian reaction to these plans was contradictory. On the one hand, they were eager to abstain from involvement in the war because they had no territorial claims against the Soviet Union and wanted to retain the integrity and fighting capacity of their armed forces for the possible war with Romania over the reacquisition of Southern Transylvania. On the other hand, they were concerned with possible disadvantages to Hungary in the event of a German victory which Bartha, the Minister of Defense, Henrik Werth, the Chief of Staff, and other military "experts" expected to occur within six to eight weeks.[12] Hungary's fear of a disadvantageous position was compounded by intelligence reports that the country's surrounding traditional enemies within the Axis camp—Croatia, Romania, and Slovakia—were planning to participate actively in the campaign.

In a series of memoranda, the military leaders, especially Werth, urged the Regent and the government to bring about Hungary's involvement in the war on a "voluntary" basis.[13] While this proposal was rejected by the government at its meeting of June 15, Hungary severed its diplomatic relations with the Soviet Union on June 23—one day after the German attack. But subsequent German hints about the desirability of Hungary's active involvement[14] and the eagerness of the Germanophile officers on the General Staff to share in the expected "imminent" victory against Bolshevism brought about the desired declaration of war on June 27 as the country's response to the alleged

Soviet air attack on a number of Hungarian cities and towns, including Kassa, Munkács, and Rahó, the day before.[15] Almost simultaneously, Hungarian aircraft bombed Stanislav (Stanislawow) in a retaliatory raid. The Hungarian Parliament, whose consent for the declaration had not been previously solicited, was informed by Bárdossy about these developments *ex post facto* that same morning.[16] Having joined the crusade against Bolshevism, Hungary found itself by the end of the year also at war with Great Britain and the United States.[17]

Realizing in the course of the summer that the military campaign against the Soviet Union would not be as swift and decisive as the earlier Nazi campaigns against Poland and France, the Germanophile officers of the General Staff, having previously besieged the government for Hungary's "voluntary" entry into the war, now demanded a substantial "voluntary" increase in the country's contribution to the Axis war effort. In a lengthy memorandum to this effect submitted to Bárdossy, for example, Werth argued that the country's "voluntary" increases in the war effort could be exploited for wresting from Germany political concessions relating to:

- The reestablishment of Hungary's thousand-year-old frontiers.
- The "resettlement" (i.e., explusion) of the Slavic and Romanian populations.
- The resettlement of the Jews.
- The sharing by Hungary of the raw materials of the USSR.

Werth's interference in political affairs upset even Bárdossy, who complained about it to Horthy in a lengthy letter dated August 26, 1941. He accused Werth of ignoring the best interests of the country, which called for the husbanding of its military forces for possible use in the future.[18] Horthy was persuaded and on September 6 replaced Werth with General Ferenc Szombathelyi.

Szombathelyi, like Werth, was of Swabian background (his original name was Knauz). But he believed, unlike his predecessor, that Hungary's national interests required the preservation of its strength; consequently he advocated the possible limitation of the country's commitment to the Axis war effort. The day after his appointment, he, together with the Regent, Bárdossy, Andor Szentmiklóssy of the Foreign Office, and Dietrich von Jagow, who in July had replaced Otto von Erdmannsdorf as German Minister in Budapest, paid a visit to the Führer's headquarters in the pursuit of this objective. The Hungarian statesmen pleaded for the withdrawal of the Hungarian troops "because the losses . . . in equipment had been so heavy as to make it pointless to leave them at the front." They also used the oft-repeated argument that the continued presence of the troops at the front would weaken the country both militarily and economically, depriving it of the ability to keep order in Southeastern Europe—something which was also in the best interests of the Third Reich.[19]

In view of the unanticipatedly stiff Russian resistance and winter counteroffensive, the Axis was not only unwilling to permit the return of the Hungarian troops, but demanded an even greater contribution to the war effort. Visitor after visitor came to Budapest with this purpose in mind.[20] In the end, the Hungarians consented to the dispatch of nine "light divisions" in addition to the seven occupation divisions already committed. The fighting troops together with those in the motorized corps and auxiliary units which were also committed came to a little over 200,000 men. These constituted the Second Hungarian Army, placed under the command of General Gusztáv Jány. The occupation divisions included 40,000 to 50,000 men. To "assist" the Second Hungarian Army in its operations in the Ukraine, a number of auxiliary labor service units were also sent there. Most of these were composed of Jews of wartime military service age, in either regular or punitive labor service companies. In 1942, several tens of thousands of Hungarian Jews had been assigned to front-line duties in the Ukraine, where many of them perished or were captured after the crushing defeat of the Hungarian forces at Voronezh early in 1943 (see chapter 10).

The Worsening of the Anti-Semitic Drive

The entry of Hungary into the Second World War marked a new watershed for the country's Jewish community. During the first few months of the war, the status of the Hungarian Jews worsened considerably. Aside from the implementation of the Third Anti-Jewish Law, the Jews became the subject of a vicious propaganda campaign that associated them not only with the evils of Bolshevism, but also with the economic ills of the country. The nationalistic, patriotic rightist elements demanded that in addition to the expansion of Hungary's military contributions to the war effort, the country also emulate Germany's Jewish policies, including the "resettlement" of the Jews and undesirable nationality groups.

But while the demand for the possible resettlement of the Slavic and Romanian groups was rejected outright as impractical, the arrest and resettlement of the "alien" Jews was pursued with great vigor. During July, from 30,000 to 35,000 were rounded up, and of these close to 18,000 were actually "resettled" near Kamenets-Podolsk, where most were massacred the following month.

Urged on by the venomous anti-Semitic press campaign and the anti-Jewish domestic policies of the government, public opinion took a sharp swing to the Right. The Jews were blamed not only for the country's involvement in the war, but also for all the domestic evils associated with it, including the shortages of goods and the flourishing black market. The Jews were especially vulnerable to these accusations, for they played a very important role in business, industry, trade, and finance. Though hoarding was practiced, as in every country at war, by practically the entire population, the shortages and the consequent price rises were attributed exclusively to the "machinations of the Jews." The traditional anti-Semitism of the Christian middle classes was exacerbated by the commensurate increase in their sympathy with and admiration for Nazi Germany, an attitude which was increasingly shared by ever larger numbers of industrial workers and peasants. In this atmosphere of anti-Jewish hysteria, new measures were constantly demanded and adopted against the Jews. Order after order was issued relating to the Jews serving in the labor service system or to the implementation of the major anti-Jewish laws, further aggravating the situation of the Jews in business and the professions. Toward the end of 1941, a draft law was introduced that eventually reduced the status of the Israelite Confession from a "received" to a "tolerated" one.[21]

But harsh as these measures were, they did not shake the basic confidence of the Hungarian Jews, and especially of the assimilated ones, that they were in no physical danger. However, the two major incidents of mass murder during the Bárdossy era shook the Jewish community as well as the decent strata of Hungarian society to their foundation. These were the massacres at Kamenets-Podolsk and the Délvidék, which in retrospect may be construed as the prelude to the Holocaust in Hungary.

The Kamenets-Podolsk Massacres

Refugees in Hungary. Following the Nazi annexation of Austria, the dismemberment of Czechoslovakia, and the subsequent occupation of

Poland, a large number of people sought refuge in Hungary. Of these, according to various estimates, from 15,000 to 35,000 were Jews, mostly Austrian, German, Polish, and Slovak in origin.[22] Some of these Jews lived in Hungary as Aryans, having acquired false identification papers; others lived at liberty, having obtained official residence permits; still others enjoyed their freedom as "transients" en route to Palestine, a status they acquired through the efforts of the Palestine Office (*Palesztina Hivatal*) of Budapest. A considerable number of the refugees, both Jewish and non-Jewish, lived in internment camps such as those at Csörgő, Garany, and Ricse in Zemplén County. Whatever the basis of their stay in Hungary, all aliens had to register with the National Central Alien Control Office (*Külföldieket Ellenörző Országos Központi Hatóság—KEOKH*), the agency having jurisdiction over foreign nationals living in Hungary.

The National Central Alien Control Office. KEOKH was established by virtue of Law No. XXVIII of 1930. It was modeled after the Swiss alien control system, which was studied and adapted to Hungary by Ámon Pásztóy (his original name was Antal Ferencz Polczer) on the instructions of Béla Scitovsky, Minister of the Interior in the Bethlen government. Pásztóy,[23] a Hungarian rightist of Swabian background, was also responsible for the confidential instructions relating to the implementation of Law No. XXVIII under which the KEOKH was gradually transformed into an oppressive rather than a supervisory agency. Eager to bring the largest possible number of Jews under KEOKH's jurisdiction, the instructions stipulated that only Jews in possession of citizenship papers could be considered as Hungarian citizens. All others, even if born in Hungary, were to be placed under the jurisdiction of KEOKH. As a result of these directives, KEOKH set up a file system which by the late thirties included about 8,000 names. Among these Jews there were many whose parents had been born in Hungary, and many others whose relatives had died for the country during World War I.[24]

Ámon Pásztóy served as the deputy chief of KEOKH until 1937, when he was promoted to head it. He served in this capacity until July 1, 1941, when his place was taken by Sándor Siménfalvy.[25] He continued to play a prominent role in the direction of KEOKH in his new capacity as head of Section VII, the Public Safety Section (*Közbiztonsági Osztály*) of the Ministry of the Interior to which KEOKH was subordinated as subsection VII/c. In addition to Siménfalvy, the chief officers of KEOKH in 1942 were Jenő Sándor and Emil Szentkláray, his deputies; Károly Kéry, chief counsellor; Zoltán Abrudbányay, János Axmann, Enoch Ferenczy, Elemér Glaser, Árkád Kiss, István Kmetty, György Pintér, László Solymosi, Kálmán Szojka, and Dénes Zakariás, counsellors; János Farkas and Tivadar Lehotzky, captains; and Antal Bajóti, Nándor Batizfalvy, László Eltzenbaum, and Sándor Máthé, junior civil servants (*fogalmazók*). The KEOKH had seven branch offices:[26]

Place	Head
Csikszereda	Jenő Mihályi
Esztergom	József Ivánkovich
Kassa	Tamás Pilisy
Kolozsvár	Ernő Elekes
Máramarossziget	Gy. Zoltán Sátory
Nagyvárad	László Sághy
Újvidék	Jenő Szőke

The functions and responsibilities of the KEOKH increased dramatically in the wake of the outbreak of World War II, when ever-larger numbers of refugees began arriving. Following Hungary's entry into the war against the Soviet Union and the subsequent acquisition of military-administrative jurisdiction over a considerable part of Ukrainian territory northeast of Hungary, a plan was devised to resettle the "alien" Jews in the newly "liberated" areas. The plan apparently originated with Ödön Martinides, who also served as chief detective within KEOKH, and Dr. Árkád Kiss, a police counsellor.[27] Both were notorious anti-Semites, who constantly criticized the Minister of the Interior, Ferenc Keresztes-Fischer, for his benevolent attitude toward the Jews, including the Jewish refugees.[28] They were particularly appalled by the Minister's failure through his "pro-Jewish policy" to show sufficient appreciation for the Third Reich's assistance in the territorial acquisitions by Hungary during 1938–41.[29] Martinides and Kiss submitted their plan to Miklós Kozma, a former Minister of the Interior in the Gömbös government (March 4, 1935 through February 3, 1937) and a confidant of Admiral Horthy, who was then Government Commissioner (*Kormányzói Biztos*) in Carpatho-Ruthenia.

The Rounding-Up and Deportation of the "Alien" Jews. The authors of the plan justified the proposal for the expulsion of the "Polish and Russian Jews" on the premise that these Jews, who had found themselves unemployed in the wake of the anti-Jewish measures in Hungary, could start a new life in Galicia. Kozma was enthusiastic about the plan and communicated it to Henrik Werth, the Chief of the General Staff, and Károly Bartha, the Minister of Defense. Both these Germanophile officers shared Kozma's enthusiasm. Werth submitted a memorandum to this effect to Horthy, who, together with Prime Minister László Bárdossy, promptly approved the idea. To implement it, Bárdossy convened late in June a meeting of the Council of Ministers, which was also attended by Werth and Dezső László of the General Staff and by Kozma. The Council apparently agreed "to expel from Carpatho-Ruthenia all persons of dubious citizenship and to hand them over to the German authorities in Eastern Galicia."[30] Overall command for the implementation of the plan, which of course went beyond the framework of Carpatho-Ruthenia, was entrusted to Kozma. The technical details were worked out by Lieutenant Colonel Endre Kricsfalussy-Hrabár and Major Ághy of the gendarmerie and by Arisztid Meskó, the chief of the border police in Carpatho-Ruthenia. The negotiations with the Gestapo were entrusted to Colonel Elemér Sáska of the General Staff.[31]

The protestations of Keresztes-Fischer, allegedly the only member of the Council who opposed the plan, were to no avail. The Council was persuaded by the argument that the Jews were merely being transferred to live and work in an area of Galicia which could no longer be identified as "foreign," for it was under Hungarian administration.

The "legislative" framework for the expulsion of the Jews was provided by Nándor Batizfalvy, a KEOKH officer. Based on the resolution of the Council of Ministers, Batizfalvy worked out the "resettlement" details, which were incorporated in Decree No. 192/1941 issued on July 12. Citing the resettlement opportunities created by the foreign military and political developments, the Decree provided for the registration of all "disqualified aliens" by the appropriate police authorities as a first step toward their eventual removal from the country. The Decree was followed by a secret directive of Sándor Siménfalvy, the new KEOKH chief. According to the directive, the major objective of the Decree was the "deportation of the recently infiltrated Polish and Russian Jews in the largest possible number and as fast as possible."[32] The deportees, according to the Decree, could take along only 30 Pengős,[33] food for three days, and the most essential personal items. The plan called for the Jews to be taken to the border town of Kőrösmező, where they would be handed over to the military authorities.

Some of the local government officials, especially in the counties with large numbers of such "alien" Jews, jumped the gun and began issuing orders to this effect. On July 8, 1941, for example, Dr. Gábor Ajtay, the Deputy Prefect of Máramaros County, issued the following order, which served as model for officials of other counties:

Law No. IV of 1939 Concerning the Restriction of the Participation of Jews in Public and Economic Life, the measures adopted for its implementation, and the Third Anti-Jewish Law now being prepared compel and will compel the Jews living in the country to yield to the Hungarians their position in public and economic life, just as they were compelled to yield their positions in the civil service. In Máramaros County, where the anti-Jewish laws and the license revisions, among other things, were not yet implemented, there live more than 45,000 Jews, who or whose elders infiltrated into the county from Galicia, Bukovina, and Poland. In the city of Máramarossziget alone the number of Jews is over 10,000. The implementation of the anti-Jewish measures, which will begin with the greatest severity in the near future, will affect local Jews at their economic foundation. In view of the fact that a large part of Galicia has been occupied by *Honvéd* troops and in order to bring about an equitable solution of this problem before the implementation of the anti-Jewish measures, I appeal to the Jews living in the county's territory and especially to those who desire to resettle in Galicia to apply within eight days to file the appropriate forms with the designated authorities, namely the Mayor of the city of Máramarossziget or the agents specified by him and the rural authorities in the villages. I would like to draw the attention of those interested in the idea that the resettlement will be organized and carried out on a centralized basis, which is facilitated by the fact that the bulk of the population in the occupied territories either retreated with or were removed by the Russians and for this reason no major difficulty is expected in the settlement of the Jews and the starting of a new life. It will serve the interests of the Jews if they liquidate their uncertain situation in the county by yielding their position and begin a new life on the soil of Galicia with the aid of the authorities.[34]

With the formalities completed, the KEOKH authorities began the roundup of the "alien" Jews, many of whom were of Polish birth or background. Among them, however, were a number of Hungarian Jews who could not prove their Hungarian citizenship simply because their papers were not immediately available. Some Jewish Hungarian citizens were arrested primarily because they were in the way of the local authorities. Thus the entire Jewish community of Putnok, composed almost exclusively of indigenous Jews, was transferred to Kőrösmező—the border town where the Jews were handed over to the German SS and military authorities.[35]

The "alien" Jews who were rounded up in Budapest were concentrated in the Rumbach Street synagogue and in the Jewish community establishments in Magdolna, Páva, and Szabolcs streets. They were normally picked up at night with only a few hours' notice. Exceptions were only made in the case of women in their ninth month of pregnancy, the extremely ill, and men and women over 70 years of age.

By far the greatest cruelties were committed in Carpatho-Ruthenia, where many a Jewish community was uprooted *in toto*. Although the Jews were technically allowed to take along provisions for three days, because of the speed with which they were picked up most of them could take along only the food they happened to have in the house at the time.

To ease the restiveness of the arrested Jews, the police, following the ruse invented by the KEOKH and Ajtay, "assured" them that they would be sent to Poland to take over the homes that had been vacated by the Jews who had retreated with the Soviet forces.[36]

Foreshadowing the mass deportations that were to take place three years later throughout Hungary, the "alien" Jews were crammed into freight cars for the trip to Kőrösmező, near the Polish border, which often lasted from 24 to 48 hours.

From the collection point at Kőrösmező, the Jews were transferred across the border at the rate of about 1,000 a day. By August 10, 1941, approximately 14,000 Jews were handed over to the SS. An additional 4,000 Jews were transferred by the end of the month, when the operation was completed.[37]

From Kőrösmező the Jews were first taken by the SS in trucks to the vicinity of Kolomea (Kolomyya). From there they were marched in columns of 300 to 400 to temporary homes around Kamenets-Podolsk. En route they were often attacked by Ukrainian armband-wearing militiamen, who robbed them of their possessions. Those who refused to yield their valuables were killed.[38]

In the area of Kolomea and Kamenets-Podolsk, which had been vacated by Soviet troops only a few weeks earlier, there were still a few indigenous Jews left. Most of these, however, were women and children, who could offer little besides shelter to some of the deportees from Hungary.[39]

The Massacre of the "Alien" Jews. The Germans were unprepared for the mass arrival of the Jews from Hungary. At first they actually requested that the deportations stop as they "could not cope with all these Jews" and that they constituted "a menace to their lines of communication."[40] The Hungarians naturally refused to take them back and the matter was taken up on August 25 at a conference at the Winnitsa headquarters of the *Generalquartiermeister-OKH,* headed by a

Major Wagner.[41] SS-*Obergruppenführer* Franz Jaeckeln, the Higher SS and Police Leader (who later in the fall brought about the Final Solution of the Jewish question in the Baltic States)[42] assured the conference that he would "complete the liquidation of these Jews by September 1, 1941."[43]

The extermination of the Jews deported from Hungary was carried out during August 27–28.[44] According to an eyewitness account, the deportees were told that in view of a decision to clear Kamenets-Podolsk of Jews they would have to be relocated. Surrounded by units of the SS, their Ukrainian hirelings, and reportedly a Hungarian sapper platoon, they, together with the indigenous Jews of Kamenets-Podolsk, were compelled to march about ten miles to a series of craters caused by bombings. There they were ordered to undress, after which they were machinegunned. Many of them were buried gravely wounded, but still alive.[45]

The involvement of Hungarian troops in the massacres at Kamenets-Podolsk and elsewhere in Galicia is not fully established. In contrast to the reports about the involvement of the Hungarian sapper platoon (presumably composed of Swabian Hungarians) at Kamenets-Podolsk, there were several reports of Hungarian troops actually intervening in behalf of persecuted Jews, both Hungarian and Soviet, in the Hungarian-occupied parts of the Ukraine. Several incidents of this type were reported by the SS, who were disturbed about the attitude of the Hungarians. According to Operational Situation Report USSR No. 23, issued by the Chief of the German Security Police (SIPO—*Sicherheitspolizei*) and Security Service (SD—*Sicherheitsdienst*) on July 15, 1941, "the Honvéd Army . . . seemed to prefer Poles and Jews." The report also complained that the "militia action against Jews has been stopped by the Hungarian Army."[46]

In another report (Operational Situation Report USSR, No. 67) dated August 29, 1941, issued just after the completion of the Kamenets-Podolsk *Aktion*, the SIPO-SD Chief stated triumphantly that "except for the area occupied by the Hungarians, the area from Chotin to Jamol has been made free of Jews."[47] Aside from the anti-Jewish operations in the field, many of the Hungarian officers and soldiers stationed in the Ukraine witnessed the atrocities committed in the occupied parts of the Soviet Union. The Hungarians were particularly upset "by the machine-gunning of men, women, and children" by the *Einsatzgruppen* and the many commandos composed of Ukrainian militia assisting them. They gave vent to their feelings in many letters home and in statements they made while on furlough.[48] Much of this information was collated and sent abroad to enlighten the free world by the Budapest *Vaada* (see chapters 3 and 23).

The number of victims executed at Kamenets-Podolsk cannot be established with any degree of accuracy. In his Operational Report USSR No. 80, dated September 11, 1941, Jaeckeln put the total number of those shot at Kamenets-Podolsk at 23,600[49]—the first five-figure massacre in the Nazis' Final Solution program. Of these, from 14,000 to 18,000 Jews were from Hungary;[50] the remainder were local.[51]

Of the approximately 18,000 deportees from Hungary, around 2,000 survived. About 1,000 Jews who were driven across the Dniester by the 10th Hungarian Pursuit Battalion were turned back on August 28 by *Einsatzgruppe* Tarnopol, which operated under the Commander of the Security Police (*Befehlshaber der Sicherheitspolizei*) of Cracow.[52] Others managed to escape with the aid of Polish peasants or by bribing Hungarian military personnel.

The escapees who returned to Hungary told a harrowing story of suffering and mass murder. One of the survivors by the name of Lajos Stern, Joel Brand's brother-in-law, accompanied a delegation of MIPI members led by György Polgár, which informed Keresztes-Fischer about the details of the Kamenets-Podolsk massacres. The Minister of the Interior was visibly shocked and declared that he had enough of this and ordered Pásztóy to halt all further deportations. In fact, Pásztóy was compelled to recall seven trains en route to the border, two of which had already reached Kőrösmező.[53]

Keresztes-Fischer's reaction was shared by the few Left-oriented Hungarian liberals and by the progressive politicians. Among the most vocal critics of the government's policies was Endre Bajcsy-Zsilinszky, a deputy of the Smallholders' Party, who was executed by the Hungarian Nazis in the winter of 1944.

As the currently available evidence clearly indicates, the 14,000 to 18,000 Jews expelled from Hungary in August 1941 became part of the Final Solution. However, while one cannot condone the forced resettlement of large numbers of people under any conditions, it is safe to assume that when the decision for the "repatriation" of the "alien" Jews was reached late in June 1941, the Hungarian leaders were not yet aware that resettlement meant extermination. News about the mass-killings by the *Einsatzgruppen* in the German-occupied parts of the Soviet Union reached Hungary later in the summer via returning Hungarian soldiers and officers, who had witnessed them. However, it is well nigh impossible to determine whether the Hungarian leadership was apprised of the realities of the "resettlement" program by late August, when most of the "alien" Jews from Hungary were killed, or whether it could have done anything to prevent the massacres.

The Délvidék Massacres

The Campaign Against the Partisans. No sooner had the storm over the Kamenets-Podolsk massacres subsided than a new series of atrocities rocked the nation. This time it involved the "campaign" to clear the Délvidék, as the Hungarian-occupied part of Yugoslavia was called, of the ever-more-active partisans.

Although Yugoslav resistance against the occupants manifested itself soon after the defeat of April 1941, it acquired momentum only after the German attack on the USSR on June 22, 1941. In the northern part of the country, the Chetnik guerrillas were especially active in the German-occupied part of the Banat. Armed primarily with captured German weapons, they used this part of the Banat as a base for raids against the Hungarian-occupied Bácska territory the Hungarians called the Sajkás area (*Šajkaška*), which encompassed the triangle formed by the confluence of the Danube and the Tisza.

The Massacres in the Sajkás Area. According to some rumors, the partisan raids were actually encouraged by the Germans in order to prevent the Hungarians and the Serbs from "getting too friendly" or to induce the Hungarians to occupy Serbia.[54] According to some other accounts, the Hungarian campaign against the partisans aimed at the eventual reacquisition of the formerly Hungarian-ruled but now German-occupied part of the Banat.[55] In response to the increasingly daring forays of the partisans, the Hungarian authorities decided to "smoke out the nest." On January 4, 1942, units of the local gendarmerie staged a house-to-house search in and around the village of Zsablya, in the course of which six gendarmes were killed. The local gendarmerie commander, Colonel Ferenc Fóthy, unable to cope with the situation, called on Dr. Péter Fernbach, the Prefect of Bács-Bodrog County, for assistance. He, in turn, requested Keresztes-Fischer, the Minister of the Interior, to authorize reinforcements. Keresztes-Fischer obtained the concurrence of the Council of Ministers and of the Regent to employ the armed forces.[56]

In accordance with this decision, General Ferenc Szombathelyi, Chief of the General Staff, instructed General Ferenc Feketehalmy-Czeydner, the Commander of the Fifth Army Corps at Szeged, to assist the local gendarmerie and police units. A vocal Germanophile and a rabid anti-Semite, Feketehalmy-Czeydner decided to teach the local partisans a lesson. He was particularly anxious to impress the German and Italian dignitaries who were about to visit Budapest.[57]

Feketehalmy-Czeydner ordered three infantry battalions under the command of Colonel László Deák into the area. The combined gendarmerie-military units were reinforced with the just formed "home guards" (*nemzetőrségek*) consisting primarily of Hungarians and Germans living in the area.

Although order had already been reestablished in Zsablya through the execution of six partisans, Deák and Fóthy reported that pitched battles had taken place. Feketehalmy-Czeydner selected Zsablya and the neighboring villages for revenge. He had these communities surrounded and their population systematically massacred. According to the memorandum prepared by Bajcsy-Zsilinszky, the number of victims in Zsablya alone was around 1,400, including women and children.

They had to perish, according to Feketehalmy-Czeydner, "because they had supported the partisans" and, in the case of the children, might "take revenge when they grew up."[58] In Csurog the number of victims was even higher—1,800.[59] Most of the victims, including about 100 Jews, met their deaths in two warehouses.[60] The "combing campaign" continued with the same ferocity in Boldogasszony, Gyurgyevo Mosorin, Sajkásgyörgye, and Titel. In Titel, 35 of the 36 Jews that lived in the community were slaughtered.[61] Many of the victims were ordered to jump into the frozen waters of the Tisza and kept from surfacing with long clubs. Others were thrown into the river after they had been shot.

The Újvidék Massacres. On the basis of Feketehalmy-Czeydner's official report on the events in the Sajkás area, the Hungarian authorities decided on January 12 to extend the "combing" operations to Újvidék itself. This decision was communicated by Szombathelyi to Feketehalmy-Czeydner on January 17.[62]

On the same day a fuller and more authentic account about the events in the Sajkás area was given to Endre Bajcsy-Zsilinszky by Dr. Rezső Rupert, a fellow deputy. On January 19, both of them were received by Prime Minister László Bárdossy, who informed them that he had already issued instructions for the prevention of atrocities.

It appears that two sets of instructions were issued: one through the military for the continuation of the "raid against the partisans in Újvidék," the other by civilian authorities for the avoidance of atrocities. Needless to say, the latter had no effect on the military's design to clear the area of "hostile" elements.

Immediate command at Újvidék was entrusted to Major-General József Grassy, who entered the city with a detachment of troops on January 20 together with Captain Márton Zöldi leading a detachment of gendarmes from Szekszárd. Around 7 P.M., Feketehalmy-Czeydner held a meeting with the local authorities, including Colonel Lajos Gál and Captain Tabián, the commanders of the local gendarmeric and police, respectively. He informed them that the military were taking over control in the city for three days in order to "clean up." He warned them "against the danger of using arms too late."[63] The city was surrounded and isolated from the rest of the world, the telephonic and telegraphic communications having been cut. Over the signature of Grassy, a 19-point announcement was posted throughout the city establishing for all practical purposes martial law. Among its stipulations were:

- With the exception of civil servants and employees of food stores and public enterprises with permits, no one would be permitted to leave their homes between 6 P.M. and 8 A.M.
- Except in extraordinary cases (e.g., death in the family) no one would be allowed to travel outside the city by rail.
- No one would be allowed to enter the city with the exception of suppliers of food and fuel, who would be given special permits to leave.
- With the exception of food stores, which could stay open between 8 A.M., and 6 P.M., all stores were to be closed.
- All traffic—car, bus, horse-and-buggy—was halted.
- Listening to radio receivers was forbidden.
- All houses of worship were closed.
- Attendance of clubs and special gatherings in private homes was forbidden.
- All windows were to be closed and shaded.[64]

The raid began the following morning at 8 A.M. in a relatively calm manner. The city was divided into eight sectors. About 6,000 to 7,000 "suspects" were brought into the central headquarters and other places and interrogated by so-called "screening committees" (*igazoló bizottságok*), which were set up in the local home of the *Levente*, the Hungarian paramilitary youth organization. Of these, fewer than 100 were detained and from 15 to 50 were shot and thrown into the Danube after the most summary examination.[65] On January 22, the leaders of the raid decided to take hostages from among the "wealthier strata" of the population, which, of course, meant the Jews.

The troops, already indoctrinated in anti-Semitism, were further incited by the possibility of booty, the receipt of extra rations of rum,[66] and the "revelations" by Zöldi that his troops had been fired upon. Zöldi in fact staged the "attack" on his troops and submitted the "evidence" by parading some of his "wounded" and bandaged soldiers before a civilian and military audience.[67] He needed an additional excuse for the intensification of the drive against the partisans and their "allies," for Feketehalmy-Czeydner, dissatisfied with the results of the previous two days, insisted that he wanted to see more bodies. Grassy stated it more crudely when he saw the large number of people called in for investigation: "We have not come here to collect garbage, but to clear the area. The people must be gotten rid of!"

In reprisal for the "shots," Feketehalmy-Czeydner ordered the mass execution of the hostages. Also destined for elimination were residents and passers-by the Hungarian troops and police forces apprehended that day. The thermometer read −30° C (−22° F). The first mass execution took place at Miletić Street, where about 30 to 40 men, women, and children were killed by rifle-fire after having been ordered to lie down on the street. While this was going on, another group of Serbs and Jews was eliminated at the intersection of Miletić and Grčko-školska streets, where the bloodletting continued unabated from 9:30 A.M. to noon. Soon thereafter about 60 people were eliminated at the Belgrade Pier of the city. Large-scale executions were also carried out at the Uspenski Orthodox Cemetery, where about 250 people were massacred, and at the NAK sport stadium. There, the soldiers ordered the naked victims to run, promising to save the lives of the fastest ones; when the running started, the victims were mowed down by machine-gun fire.[68]

By far the most savage atrocities took place at the Danube beach, the so-called Štrand. Force-marched or brought in by truck from various parts of the city, the victims were ordered to strip and stand in rows of four to await their execution. Most of these unfortunate people were shot from the diving board into the Danube, whose ice had been broken by cannon fire. According to eyewitness accounts, many of the victims, including children, begged to be killed because the "cold was unbearable." The execution squad at the Štrand was headed by Gusztáv Korompay (Kronpecher).[69]

Although the full extent of the massacres was revealed only after the thawing waters of the Danube relinquished their victims, news of the atrocities reached Budapest almost immediately. The Prefect of Bács-Bodrog County, Leó Deák,[70] managed to get across the curfew lines during the afternoon of January 23 and telephoned his superiors in Budapest, presumably Keresztes-Fischer. Budapest ordered that all shooting stop immediately. Feketehalmy-Czeydner complied by having an announcement posted around 7 P.M. informing the people of Újvidék that at the request of the prefect the military measures would cease as of 9 P.M. According to some sources, Feketehalmy-Czeydner had been instructed by Szombathelyi to stop the "raids" on January 22, but he went on defiantly for another 24 hours.

The announcement aimed to justify the measures the military had taken during the previous three days and warned the population that if the slightest harm befell any of the soldiers or gendarmes the attacker(s) would be summarily executed; if they were not identified, reprisal would be taken against 20 hostages from among those whose names were kept on record in his office.[71]

Further Atrocities. Although the atrocities had ended in Újvidék, the "raids" continued unabated in Óbecse and Szenttamás. In Óbecse, Jews and Serbs were executed on an individual basis beginning January 10. Mass executions took place January 26–28, when about 200 people were killed, including about 100 of the 200 Jews in the community.[72] The "raids" were finally halted on January 30, 1942.

Statistical Overview. By this time the total number of victims in the Délvidék massacres amounted to 3,309, including 141 children and 299 old men and women. Of these, about 2,550 were Serbs and about 700 Jews. In Újvidék alone 879 people were killed, including 53 women and children and 90 old men. Of the Újvidék victims, 550 were Jews, 292 Serbs, 13 Russians (mostly from the small colony of survivors from the Wrangel Army), and 11 Hungarians.[73]

Reaction to the Massacres. Details about the massacres were revealed only after the lifting of the curfew, when many refugees and visitors from the Délvidék came to Budapest. The gruesome accounts of the atrocities perpetrated by Hungarian soldiers and gendarmes under the order of high-ranking officers who were mostly of Swabian-German background enraged most decent Hungarians. Demands for an inquiry into the affair became increasingly vocal. Questions to this effect were raised in both houses of Parliament on January 29—by János Zichy in the upper house and Bajcsy-Zsilinsky in the lower house. Needless to say, both were abused by the Right for daring to "impugn the honor of the Army."

The government, not to speak of the Minister of Defense and the Chief of the General Staff, took Feketehalmy-Czeydner's report on events in the Délvidék at face value and sided with the Army against the civilians. This attitude apparently extended to the Regency itself. At his trial in Yugoslavia (see chapters 7 and 32) Feketehalmy-Czeydner referred to a letter he had received from General Lajos Keresztes-Fischer, the brother of the Minister of the Interior and head of Admiral Horthy's Military Chancery (*Kormányzói katonai iroda*), according to which he "was being strongly attacked in Jewish circles but that no harm should come to him, because he was a good soldier and a good patriot."[74]

Although the date of this alleged letter could not be ascertained, it is beyond doubt that the Regent was informed in detail about the realities of the Délvidék massacres. He was informed not only by the hearings conducted in the Foreign Affairs Committees of both houses of Parliament, but also by a comprehensive memorandum prepared by Bajcsy-Zsilinszky, which was submitted to him on February 4, 1942. In it the Smallholder deputy reviewed the entire affair, identifying not only the responsibility of the military but also the guilt of the politicians, from Prime Minister Bárdossy down, for not having taken the precautionary measures suggested by those who had alerted them of the impending catastrophe.[75] According to C. A. Macartney, Horthy also received a memorandum to this effect from Géza Szüllő, a Slovak Hungarian leader, who urged that the Regent order an inquiry into the affair.[76]

The government did in fact dispatch a commission of inquiry headed by Judge-Advocate General József Babos. Babos was, however, a secret member of the Arrow Cross Party. The report submitted by this commission simply identified the massacred Jews and Serbs as "partisans." Bárdossy was apparently eager to squash the whole affair for political reasons. He dared not "impugn the honor of the Army" or incur the wrath of the Third Reich.

Shortly after the inauguration of the Kállay government on March 9, 1942, however, a new inquiry was ordered. The new Prime Minister was partially motivated by the desire to establish better relations with the Serbs.[77] This step was all the more remarkable because at that time Kállay was not yet ready to prepare the ground for the establishment of contacts with the Western powers for the possible extrication of Hungary from the war.

Kállay ordered a new investigation of the Délvidék massacres and when the report[78] was ready he arranged for Milán Popovics, a prominent Serb deputy, to raise the question on the massacres in the lower house. During the debates of July 14, Kállay admitted the excesses committed against the Serbs in the Délvidék and promised to initiate legal measures against the culprits. As an immediate step he brought about the transfer of about 250 gendarmes and officials from the Bácska area.[79] The massacres were again debated in the lower house on December 2, 1942, when Endre Bajcsy-Zsilinszky asked, among other things, that the survivors be compensated for their losses.[80]

The Second Hungarian Army suffered a crushing defeat at Voronezh on January 12, 1943, and the tide of the war shifted increasingly in favor of the Allies during that year. With that shift, Hungary's reluctance to participate in the war became ever more discernible, and was matched by Kállay's desire to improve the image and political position of his country. A new investigation of the Délvidék massacres was ordered, this time under civilian leadership, and depositions amounting to over 600 pages were collected. On the basis of the newly gathered evidence, the 15 leading officers involved in the atrocities were brought to trial.[81]

The trial began on December 14, 1943, in Budapest under the chairmanship of Captain Dr. Imre Gazda; József Babos served as prosecutor. The accused were specifically indicted, among other things, for disloyal behavior, for damaging the traditional good name of the Hungarian Army and gendarmerie by misusing the forces under their command, and for having incited them to commit crimes.[82]

Considering that Hungary was, however reluctantly, still a member of the Axis Alliance and at war, the trial was quite fair. Though motivated primarily by politics, it was nevertheless an act of courage and decency for the Hungarians to try high-ranking officers for murdering Jews and Serbs.

The defendants contended that they had acted on direct orders from Minister of Defense Bartha and Minister of the Interior Keresztes-Fischer,[83] but to no avail. The outside world was startled and the Hungarian liberals were gratified by the stiff sentences handed down by the court. Feketehalmy-Czeydner was given 15 years' imprisonment; Grassy 14; Deák 13; and Zöldi 11. Four other leading officers received

10 years each, and a number of minor offenders got summary punishment.[84]

Under the provisions of the Hungarian Military Code the defendants were temporarily paroled on their own cognizance. On January 15, 1944, the four leading defendants fled the country and found refuge in Vienna as guests of the Gestapo. The escape was effectuated with the aid of Archduke Albrecht, the former pretender to the Hungarian throne and a confidant of Heinrich Himmler. He was an active supporter of such ultra-Right Hungarian political movements as the Association of Awakening Hungarians (*Ébredő Magyarok Egyesülete*) and the Hungarian Association of National Defense (*Magyar Országos Véderő Egyesület*—MOVE).[85]

Except for the extreme Right, the escape of the officers and the violation of the age-old military honor code were deplored by both the government and the moderate press. The official communiqué of January 18 issued by the Kállay government identified the escape as "shocking and unprecedented in Hungarian military history." The same day, the matter was also taken up by the Council of Ministers. However, there is no evidence to show that the government undertook any diplomatic or legal measures for the extradition of the criminals, nor did it protest their receipt of political asylum in the Third Reich.[86]

Almost immediately after their escape, the German Foreign Ministry was alerted about the affair by Legation Counselor Karl Werkmeister, who also reported on a conversation he had had with Szombathelyi on a social occasion. Szombathelyi had tried to impress upon Werkmeister the importance of the case, since the Délvidék massacres constituted, in his view, "a national misfortune." When asked why the case had been reopened after being set aside for over a year, Szombathelyi explained it was the decision of the Minister of the Interior. Werkmeister, however, suspected the Ministry of Foreign Affairs and asked Gustav Steengracht von Moyland, the State Secretary of the German Foreign Office, for advice and directives on how to handle the inquiries that were sure to be advanced by the Hungarians.[87] On January 19, 1944, SS-*Brigadeführer* Walther Hewel, Ambassador for Special Assignments and Plenipotentiary of the Foreign Office at the Führer Headquarters, informed Ribbentrop about Hitler's suggestions on how to handle Werkmeister's request. Accordingly, the Hungarians were to be told that the stories about the killing of thousands of women and children should not be believed; the *Honvédség* could not have perpetrated such atrocities. Furthermore, they were to be informed that the massacres were a fabrication of the Jews and that Germany would extend asylum to anyone accused of persecuting Jews.[88] The matter was reviewed for Ribbentrop in a memorandum submitted by Andor Hencke, Chief of the Political Division of the Foreign Office, to Gustav Hilger, Embassy Counselor. Aside from summarizing the background of the trial, the memorandum claimed that the trial had been staged for "foreign political reasons" to please Germany's enemies and that it must be considered as a manifestation of the anti-German attitude displayed "by certain circles in the Hungarian Government."[89] In another document, the main circle was identified as consisting of Kállay, Foreign Minister Jenő Ghyczy, and Interior Minister Keresztes-Fischer.[90]

The German asylum for the four top officers proved short-lived; soon after the occupation of Hungary on March 19, 1944, they returned and resumed their careers. Late in April they appeared "voluntarily" before the now totally Nazi-dominated military tribunal, which promptly withdrew the arrest order, terminated the inquiry, and restored their ranks.[91] They subsequently took an active part in the implementation of the policies of the Sztójay government, including the "solution" of the Jewish question. They achieved prominence after the Szálasi coup of October 15. Feketehalmy-Czeydner, for example, became Deputy Minister of Defense in charge, inter alia, of setting up eight new divisions, including four Hungarian SS divisions. He also exploited his position to settle accounts with his nemesis in the Hungarian Parliament, Endre Bajcsy-Zsilinszky. He had him tried together with ten officers by a military tribunal headed by Lieutenant General Gyula Vargyasy. Bajcsy-Zsilinszky was executed at Sopronkőhida on December 24, 1944.[92]

The Fall of Bárdossy

The massacres at Kamenets-Podolsk and the Délvidék had a shocking effect upon large segments of the Jewish community and Hungarian liberals. They revealed what most people refused to believe: that what had happened in the other parts of Nazi-dominated Europe could also happen in Hungary. To most people, however, these massacres seemed simply "incidents" or aberrations with no ominous implications for the future. While Bárdossy and his government were subjected to severe criticism for their policies and attitudes relating to these massacres, it was the Prime Minister's increasingly pro-Axis and "independent" posture and general political line that irked Admiral Horthy.

Among the political grievances cited by Horthy were Bárdossy's wholehearted engagement in internal and international ideological politics; his search for popularity by building up his position with the support of the Germans and the Hungarian ultra Right; his confrontation of the Regent with one *fait accompli* after another, including the declarations of war against the Soviet Union and the United States; his machinations to oust three pro-Horthy members of the Cabinet (Ferenc Keresztes-Fischer, Dániel Bánffy, and József Varga) and to replace them with "extreme pro-Germans"; and his raising of the question of still another anti-Jewish law, "and even of deporting the Jews."[93]

Bárdossy's political decisions and machinations were undoubtedly important reasons why the Regent resolved to dismiss him. However, it appears that the determining factor was the Prime Minister's consistent opposition to Horthy's plan to assure the election of his Anglophile son, István, as Deputy Regent and heir.[94] Bárdossy, adamant in his position, was compelled to resign on March 7, 1942. Two days later, the Regent appointed Miklós (Nicholas) Kállay to succeed him as Prime Minister.

Notes

1. The Bárdossy government was basically identical with Teleki's at the time. It included Ferenc Keresztes-Fisher as Minister of the Interior; Lajos Reményi-Schneller as Minister of Finance; Baron Dániel Bánffy as Minister of Agriculture; József Varga, who doubled as Minister of Industry and (provisional) Minister of Commerce and Transportation; Bálint Hóman as Minister of Cults and Public Education; László Radocsay as Minister of Justice; and Károly Bartha as Minister of Defense.

2. *FAA*, 1:xlix.

3. C. A. Macartney, 2:13.

4. "1941. évi XV. törvénycikk a házassági jogról szóló 1894: XXXI. törvénycikk kiegészitéséről és modositásáról, valamint az ezzel kapcsolatban szükséges fajvédelmi rendelkezésekről" (Law No. XV of 1941 Supplementing and Amending Law No. XXXI of 1894 Relating to Marriage and to the Necessary Racial Provisions Relating to It). *1941. évi országos törvénytár* (National Code for 1941) (Budapest, August 8, 1941), pp. 95–99.

5. The law dealt, *inter alia*, with premarital medical examinations, marriage loans, and grounds for divorce.

6. Lévai, *Fekete könyv*, p. 59.

7. Munkácsi, *Hogyan történt?* p. 140.

8. For additional references relating to the Third Anti-Jewish Law consult R. L. Braham, *The Hungarian Jewish Catastrophe. A Selected and Annotated Bibliography* (New York: Yivo Institute for Jewish Research, 1962), pp. 9–14.

9. Horthy visited Hitler to thank him for making possible the return of the Délvidék and to plead for the transfer of the Banat to Hungarian jurisdiction. Shortly before his visit, Horthy made his views clear to Hitler in a lengthy letter. He claimed that the great-

est danger confronting mankind was Communism and that the world would experience no peace or tranquillity until the Soviet Union was destroyed. For complete text see *Horthy Miklós titkos iratai* (The Confidential Papers of Miklós Horthy), ed by Miklós Szinai and László Szücs (Budapest: Kossuth, 1963), pp. 296–300.

10. Bárdossy visited Rome in keeping with the tradition of newly appointed premiers. Ciano characterized his visit as "one of the most classically useless" and prognosticated that Bárdossy, too "will pass, like the others, hurriedly and pompously, through the kaleidoscope of Hungarian politics." *The Ciano Diaries, 1939–1943* (Garden City, N.Y.: Doubleday, 1946), pp. 362–63).

11. The complete plans for Operation Barbarossa, the code name for the war against the Soviet Union, were submitted to Hitler by General Franz Halder, the Chief of Staff of the *Wehrmacht*, on December 5, 1940. The final date for the beginning of the campaign was set at a conference on April 30, 1941.

12. Bartha repeated his optimistic assessment about German might during his stay in Rome on June 9. He expressed the conviction that "the Russian Army [could] not resist for more than six or eight weeks because the human element [was] weak." *The Ciano Diaries*, p. 364.

13. Werth had been "kept abreast" about the German military preparations against the Soviet Union by Colonel Sándor Homlok, the Hungarian Military Attaché in Berlin, who also believed and advocated that Hungary had to participate in the campaign. For Homlok's communications and Werth's memoranda see *Magyarország és a második világháború* (Hungary and the Second World War), László Zsigmond et al. (Budapest: Kossuth, 1961), pp. 350–62.

14. Among those who expressed a wish for Hungary's active military involvement was General Kurt Himer, the liaison of the German General Staff in Budapest.

15. According to the testimony of István Újszászy, the chief of the Counter-Intelligence Division of the Hungarian General Staff, at the International Military Tribunal at Nuremberg, the attack was actually carried out by German planes that were painted over with Soviet markings. The provocation, according to Újszászy, was hatched by General Cuno Heribert Fütterer, the German Air Attaché in Budapest, and Major-General Dezső László of the Hungarian General Staff, to bring about Hungary's involvement in the war. In a letter to Bárdossy written shortly after the attack, Colonel Ádám Krudy, the commander of the airport at Kassa, stated that he personally had seen the attack being carried out by German planes. *Magyarország és a második világháború*, p. 345. According to another theory, the attacks were carried out by Czech and Slovak pilots associated with the Soviet air force. See Nandor A. F. Dreisziger, *Hungary's Way to World War II* (Astor Park, Fla.: Danubian Press, 1968), pp. 167–78.

16. After the war, Horthy reproached Bárdossy for allegedly not having informed him about the true background of Hungary's entry into the war. Specifically, Horthy claims that Bárdossy kept him in the dark about the communications of the Soviet Foreign Office on the eve of the war, when the USSR offered its assistance in settling the Transylvanian issue in Hungary's favor should the country decide to remain neutral. The Regent also claims that he was not informed about the realities of the bombing of Hungarian cities that served as the *casus belli* for Hungary's entry into the war. Admiral Nicholas Horthy, *Memoirs* (New York: Robert Speller & Sons, 1957), pp. 190–91.

17. The state of war between Hungary and Great Britain and Hungary and the United States went into effect on December 7 and December 12, 1941, respectively. For a full account of Hungary's involvement in the war, see C. A. Macartney, 2:17–32.

18. *Horthy Miklós titkos iratai*, pp. 300–308.

19. C. A. Macartney, 2:54–55.

20. Ribbentrop visited Budapest on January 6–8, 1942, Ciano from January 15 to 18. Perhaps the most important visit was that of Field Marshal Keitel and his staff of experts

on January 20. The meetings were held in the shadow of Sztójay's warnings from Berlin that the future of Transylvania depended on Hungary's response to these appeals. *Ibid.*, p. 67.

21. The bill was approved by the lower house on December 18, 1941, and on June 19, 1942, went into effect as Law No. VIII. Under it, the representatives of the Jewish denomination in the upper house were deprived of their seats and the payment of dues by Jews to their congregations could no longer be enforced.

22. It is all but impossible to determine the exact number of Jewish refugees in Hungary during the Nazi era. According to some Hungarian officials associated with Kállay, the number of Jewish refugees was 70,000. The *Vaada* of Budapest, however, identified their number in November 1943 as approximately 15,000. Of these, 6,000 to 8,000 were from Slovakia; 1,900 to 2,500 from Poland; 300 to 500 from Yugoslavia; 3,000 to 4,000 from Germany and Austria; and 500 to 1,000 from the Protectorates of Bohemia and Moravia. *Der Kastner-Bericht* p. 45. See also chapters 3 and 27.

23. For his criminal role in the Central Alien Control Office and the deportations, Pásztóy was arrested in the summer of 1945, but for some unknown reason the People's Prosecutor's Office (*Népügyészség*) set him free in January 1946. However, he was rearrested in January 1948 and the People's Tribunal (*Népbíróság*) found him guilty of war crimes for his role in the massacre of 15,000 persons and condemned him to death by hanging. His sentence was upheld by the National Council of the People's Tribunal (*A Népbíróságok Országos Tanácsa*) and Pásztóy was hanged on August 10, 1949. Arthúr Geyer, "Az elsö magyarországi deportálás" (The First Hungarian Deportation), in *Új Élet naptár. 1960–1961* (New Life Calendar, 1960–1961) (Budapest: A Magyar Izraeliták Országos Képviselete Kiadása, 1960), pp. 75, 77, 82.

24. *Ibid.*, pp. 75–76.

25. Siménfalvy was arrested in the summer of 1945 and condemned to five years' imprisonment for his role in the deportation of the "alien" Jews. Geyer, "Az első magyarországi deportálás," p. 82.

26. *Magyarország tiszti cim- és névtára* (Title and Name Register of Hungary) (Budapest: A Magyar Királyi Állami Nyomda, 1942), 49:48. With the advance of the Red Army in the summer of 1944, the branch offices of Kassa, Kolozsvár, Máramarossziget, Nagyvárad, and Újvidék were closed on July 1, 1944. See Decree No. 148.734/1944. B. M. of the Minister of the Interior in *Budapesti Közlöny* (The Gazette of Budapest), no. 139, June 22, 1944, p. 2.

27. Kiss was arrested in 1945 and condemned in 1946 to 15 years at hard labor. Geyer, "Az első magyarországi deportálás," p. 82.

28. Ferenc Keresztes-Fischer, an Anglophile, was one of the most decent members of the Horthy group. As Minister of the Interior he did his best under the circumstances to protect the rights of the Jews until the German occupation on March 19, 1944, when he himself was also arrested and subsequently deported to the Mauthausen concentration camp near Linz. He died in Austria in 1948.

29. Lévai, *Zsidósors Magyarországon*, pp. 40–42.

30. Ervin Hollós, *Rendőrség, csendőrség, VKF 2* (Police, Gendarmerie and the VKF 2) (Budapest: Kossuth, 1971), pp. 235–36.

31. *Ibid.*, p. 236.

32. Geyer, "Az első magyarországi deportálás," p. 77.

33. During the 1941–42 period, the official value of the *Pengő* was approximately 20 cents. The black market price of the dollar, however, ranged from about 11 to 13 *Pengős*. Sándor Ausch, *Az 1945–46. évi infláció és stabilizáció* (The Inflation and Stabilization of 1945–46) (Budapest: Kossuth, 1958), pp. 30–31.

34. Lévai, *Fekete könyv*, pp. 279–80.

35. Lévai, *Zsidósors Magyarországon*, p. 42. According to Geyer, the Jews of Putnok were

returned from Kőrösmező "at the last minute." Geyer, "Az első magyarországi deportálás," p. 78.

36. Statement of Leslie Gordon (Friedmann) given to the Israel Police on May 23, 1961, in connection with the then impending Eichmann Trial. Israel Police, Bureau 06, Document No. 1646.

37. The sources vary on the exact number of Jews deported to Galicia. The President at Bárdossy's trial spoke of 30,000; the indictment against an officer involved in the deportations cited 18,500; a German document used at the Nuremberg trials (PS-1197) places the figure at 11,000. C. A. Macartney, 2:37. At their trials, Siménfalvy put the number of deportees at 18,500, Pásztóy at around 16,000. Geyer, "Az első magyarországi deportálás," p. 81.

38. Statement of Leslie Gordon.

39. For further details on the campaign against the "alien" Jews, see statement by Sámuel Springmann, dated January 28, 1958, at Yad Vashem, Jerusalem, Archives File 500/41-1. A founder and leading member of the Budapest *Vaada*, Springmann, a Polish-born Hungarian, was active in rescuing several of the deportees, including some members of his family.

40. C. A. Macartney, 2:38.

41. PS-197. The document is reproduced in *Nazi Conspiracy and Aggression* (Washington, D.C.: Government Printing Office for the Office of United States Chief of Counsel for the Prosecution of Axis Criminality, 1946), 3:210–13. See also Raul Hilberg, *The Destruction of the European Jews* (Chicago: Quadrangle Books, 1961), p. 520.

42. Jaeckeln was tried by a People's Court in Riga on February 3, 1946, and was hanged the same afternoon. Gerald Reitlinger, *The Final Solution. An Attempt to Exterminate the Jews of Europe, 1939–1945* (New York: The Beechhurst Press, 1953), p. 194.

43. PS-197. See also Hilberg, *Destruction of the European Jews*, p. 520.

44. Elek Karsai, *A budai vártól a gyepűig, 1941–1945* (From the Fort of Buda to the Borderland, 1941–1945) (Budapest: Táncsics, 1965), pp. 30–31.

45. Karsai, *A budai vártol.* See also the statement by Leslie Gordon, who was a member of one of the burial commandos, as well as Izidor Salzer, "Nyitány Kamenetz-Podolszkban. Jegyzőkönyv." (Overture in Kamenets-Podolsk. Minutes), in *Sárga könyv. Adatok a magyar zsidóság háborús szenvedéseiből, 1941–1945* (Yellow Book. Data on the Wartime Suffering of Hungarian Jewry, 1941–1945), compiled by Béla Vihar (Budapest: Hechaluc, 1945), pp. 14–15.

46. NO-4526.

47. NO-2837.

48. See also Arthur D. Morse, *While Six Million Died. A Chronicle of American Apathy* (New York: Random House, 1968), pp. 304–5.

49. NO-3154.

50. Geyer, "Az első magyarországi deportálás," p. 81.

51. For details on the local Jewish community, see *Kamenets-Podolsk u'Sevivata* (Kamenets-Podolsk and Its Surroundings), eds. A. Rosen, Ch. Sharig, and Y. Bernstein (Tel Aviv: Association of Former Residents of Kamenets-Podolsk and Its Surroundings in Israel, 1965), 263 pp.

52. Operational Report USSR No. 66, dated August 28, 1941. NO-2839.

53. Geyer, "Az első magyarországi deportálás."

54. C. A. Macartney, 2:69.

55. Lévai, *Fekete könyv*, p. 281. This assumption is also corroborated by the instructions that Major General István Ujszászy, Chief of the Intelligence Division of the General Staff, sent to Lieutenant Colonel Ferenc Fóthy of the gendarmerie, who was then stationed at Újvidék: "We must create disorder in order to prove to the Germans that public safety in the Banat is bad, since the partisans come into the Bácska regularly from

there. The Germans should yield the administration of the Banat to the Hungarians. In the Bácska, the Hungarian gendarmerie and military authorities can establish order as proven by the activities in the Délvidék, while the Germans in the Banat have greater difficulty in controlling the partisan movement." Hollós, *Rendőrség*, p. 302.

56. According to Hollós, who reflects the postwar Communist regime's interpretation of these events and who relies for their reconstruction largely on the minutes of the People's Tribunal of Budapest, the initiative for the operations came from Keresztes-Fischer, who allegedly sold his plan to Bárdossy, the Minister of Defense Bartha, and Chief of the General Staff Szombathelyi. Hollós further contends that Keresztes-Fischer was kept informed about the operations as they proceeded. Hollós, *ibid.*, pp. 301–5.

57. See note 20.

58. C. A. Macartney, 2:71.

59. According to a memorandum by Endre Bajcsy-Zsilinszky, the Smallholder member of Parliament, the number of victims in Csurog was 3,000. *Ibid.* However, a Yugoslav source (Zdenek-Zdenko Lowenthal) indicates that only about 1,000 people were killed in Csurog.

60. Zdenek-Zdenko Lowenthal, ed. *The Crimes of the Fascist Occupants and Their Collaborators Against Jews in Yugoslavia.* (Belgrade: Federation of Jewish Communities of the Federative People's Republic of Yugoslavia, 1957), pp. 28, 148. For details on the massacre in Csurog, see *Ibid.*, pp. 145–48.

61. *Ibid.*, pp. 29 and 149.

62. Karsal, *A budai vártól*, p. 99. For further details on the tragedy of the Jews of Ujvidék shortly after the city's occupation by Hungarian troops in April 1941 as well as after the German occupation, see chapter 21.

63. C. A. Macartney, 2:72.

64. Karsai, *A budai vártól*, pp. 109–11.

65. C. A. Macartney, 2:72. Macartney and Hollós give different data on the time the raid began, the number of sectors into which the city was divided for this purpose, and the number of persons that were arrested and executed. Cf. Hollós, *Rendőrség*, p. 303.

66. Feketehalmy-Czeydner compelled Dr. Miklós Nagy, the Mayor of the city, under threat of arrest to provide large quantities of rum for the troops. Karsai, *A budai vártól*, p. 112.

67. Lévai, *Fekete könyv*, p. 281; Zdenek Löwenthal, *Crimes of Fascist Occupants*, pp. 29 and 150–51. According to C. A. Macartney, a few shots were actually fired in the city, but no Hungarian soldier or gendarme was killed. C. A. Macartney, 2:72. See also Arthur Geyer, "Az 1942 évi újvidéki 'razzia'," pp. 43–44.

68. Zdenek Löwenthal, *ibid.*, pp. 29 and 150–53. See also Erih Kos, *Novosadski pokolj* (The Massacre at Novi Sad) (Belgrade: Izdanja "Rad," 1961).

69. *Ibid.*, pp. 30, 153–54; Karsai, *A budai vártól*, p. 112. See also Lajos Mandel, "A 'koreszme' magyarorszagi főprobája. Jegyzőkönyv." (The Main Rehearsal of the "Spirit of the Time" in Hungary. Minutes), in *Sárga könyv. Adatok a magyar zsidóság háborús szenvedéseiből, 1941–1945*, pp. 16–20.

70. Leó Deák was shot in 1945 by Tito's men, who mistook him for Colonel László Deák.

71. For the text of the announcement, see Karsai, *A budai vártól*, pp. 113–14.

72. Zdenek Löwenthal, pp. 30 and 154–57. See also Joseph Lewinger's "The Massacre of Jews During the 'Police Raid' in Báçka, January 1942" in *Dapim lecheker tekufat hashoa* (Studies on the Holocaust Period) (Tel Aviv: Hakibbutz Hameuchad, 1978), 1:189–212.

73. Lévai, *Fekete könyv*, p. 282; C. A. Macartney, 2:73. At the trial of the 15 top officers involved in the massacres the total number of those killed was established at 3,309. Of these, according to the indictment, 653 were killed at Zsablya, 869 at Csurog, 168 at Óbecse, and 47 at Temerin between January 4 and 8, 1942; 195 at Mozsor, 32 at Tündéres, and 74 at Dunagárdony between January 9 and 14; and 879 at Újvidék be-

tween January 21 and 23. *Magyarország és a második világháború,* p. 421. For further details on the massacres in Újvidék consult Zoltán E. Szabó, *Ez történt Újvidéken* (This Is What Happened in Újvidék) (Budapest: Müller Károly, 1945).

74. C. A. Macartney, 2:74.

75. For excerpts from the memorandum see Karsai, *A budai vártól,* pp. 116–19.

76. C. A. Macartney, 2:74.

77. In fact Kállay pursued a multilateral approach toward the Serbs. He improved considerably the lot of the Serbs living in the Bácska; Msgr. Csirics, the Serb Orthodox Bishop of Újvidék, was induced to take his seat in the upper house; and Milán Popovics was persuaded to echo his views that "dissension between the local Serbs and Magyars was always sown from outside." Externally, he cultivated friendly relations with both General Milán Nedić, the Premier of the Quisling government, and General Draža Mihailović, the Chetnik leader. C. A. Macartney, 2:145–46.

78. This first report prepared for Kállay was to a large extent a whitewash. Kállay himself mentioned only the 2,250 Serb victims during the parliamentary debates of July 14, 1942. C. A. Macartney, 2:107–8.

79. For excerpts from Popovics's and Kállay's remarks in Parliament, see Karsai, *A budai vártól,* pp. 162–64.

80. For excerpts from his speech, see *Ibid.,* pp. 214–20.

81. Of these, 3 were Army officers—Feketehalmy-Czeydner, Grassy, and Deák—and 12 gendarmerie officers: József Horkay, Lajos Gál, Géza Báthory, Ferenc Fóthy, László Stepán, Imre Kun, József Csáky, Károly Budur, Balázs Kacskovics, Sándor Képiró, Márton Zöldi, and Mihály Gerencsér. *Magyarország és a második világháború,* pp. 418–19. See also *RLB,* Doc. 64.

82. *Magyarország és a második világháború,* p. 421.

83. Karsai, *A budai vártól,* p. 385.

84. C. A. Macartney, 2:201. Geyer claims that the five major criminals, including Feketehalmy-Czeydner, Grassy, Zöldi, and Deák, were condemned to death. Among the five, Geyer also includes the "Strand killer" Gusztáv Korompay, who was not listed among the 15 indicted in the case. Geyer, "Az 1942 évi újvidéki 'razzia'," p. 48.

85. C. A. Macartney, 2:201–2. See also chapter 1.

86. Karsai, *A budai vártól,* p. 390.

87. *RLB,* Doc. 63.

88. *Ibid.,* Doc. 64.

89. *Ibid.,* Doc. 65.

90. *Ibid.,* Doc. 64.

91. Karsai, *A budai vártól,* p. 174.

92. *Ibid.,* pp. 618–23. The perpetrators of the crimes in Délvidék were tried after the war by both the Hungarians and Yugoslavs and many of them were executed in Ujvidék. For details, see chapter 32.

93. Nicholas Kállay, *Hungarian Premier* (New York: Columbia University Press, 1954), p. 8.

94. Horthy had first approached Bárdossy on this issue toward the end of November 1941. Horthy at the time was 73 years old and together with the gentry-aristocratic leadership vehemently opposed the ambitions of Archduke Albrecht who had the sympathy and support of the Germans and the Hungarian radical Right. Horthy managed to have Parliament elect István to the Deputy Regency in February 1942. István left shortly thereafter for the Russian front where he served as a pilot. He died in a plane crash on August 22, 1942. For the background on István's election see *Horthy Miklós titkos iratai,* pp. 309–12; and C. A. Macartney, 274–79. See also Mario D. Fenyo, *Hitler, Horthy, and Hungary. German-Hungarian Relations, 1941–1944* (New Haven: Yale University Press, 1972), pp. 57–60.

CHAPTER SEVEN

THE KÁLLAY ERA

Kállay's General Policy

WITH Kállay's appointment as Prime Minister on March 9, 1942, the political pendulum of the nation began to swing back from Bárdossy's openly pro-German position to Teleki's cautiously Anglophile line. This trend, however, could not be easily ascertained from either the composition of his cabinet[1] or his decisions and public declarations during his first 10 months in office. Jagow, the German Minister in Budapest, submitted the following evaluation of the new Prime Minister to the Foreign Office:

Kállay is basically an apolitical person and has not been active, in the last few years, either in internal or foreign affairs. National Socialism to him is an "alien concept" and he bears no inner sympathy to it. Nevertheless he will no doubt continue the same relations to Germany as his predecessor.[2]

Jagow had good reasons to be pleased with this evaluation, because on March 19, in his first speech as Prime Minister, Kállay reassured the Germans by declaring that the war was "our war" and that Hungary was fighting for its own interests. Shortly thereafter, several hundred left-wing elements, including some Social Democrats, were arrested and imprisoned or sent to the front in punitive labor service units.[3]

Miklós Kállay was the scion of an ancient squirearchy in Hungary. He was born in Kállósemjén, Szabolcs County, in 1887, on the estate his family had owned since the eleventh century. A handsome, typical Magyar country gentleman, Kállay was the personal friend of Admiral Horthy, with whose policies and views he generally agreed. After completing his higher education (he had studied at the universities of Geneva, Paris, and Budapest, earning a doctoral degree in political science), Kállay spent the first 18 years of his political career in local government. Because of his interest and expertise in economics in general and agriculture in particular, he was appointed Minister of Agriculture in the Gömbös government, a position he held from October 1, 1932, through January 9, 1935. In 1937, Horthy's simultaneously appointed him to the upper house and made him Commissioner for Floods and Irrigation, which reflected the Regent's respect and admiration for him.[4]

While definitely not a pro-Nazi and perhaps not even a Germanophile, Kállay was a typical representative of the old, aristocratic-gentry order of Hungary dedicated to the preservation of the status quo. He was a patriot who tended to equate his nationalism with the defense of Hungary's antiquated social order. His position on the Third Reich tended to fluctuate with the fortunes of the war, which prompted many an observer to characterize his policies as the "politics of the swing" (hintapolitika).

Kállay's overall objectives did not essentially differ from those of his predecessors. In addition to preserving the values and character of the social and economic order, Kállay aimed at undoing what the Hungarians had regarded as the injustices of Trianon, protecting the sovereignty and independence of the country, and preserving the military strength of the nation to assure a favorable postwar settlement. In the pursuit of these objectives, he followed a generally pro-German line during his first year in office. Though his course was undoubtedly influenced to some extent by internal political considerations, there is reason to believe that it was essentially based on his belief in the military supremacy of the Third Reich.[5] In spite of temporary setbacks in the winter of 1941–42, Germany was in 1942 at the peak of its military power and conquests. Kállay himself gave vent to this belief upon his return from a meeting with the Führer on June 6–8, 1942. Reporting on his encounter with Hitler to the Government Party meeting of June 11, Kállay emphasized that "his impressions and experiences in Germany reinforced his conviction in the ultimate German victory."[6] The genuineness of Kállay's pro-German policy during the first ten months in office is also emphasized by Dezső Sulyok, one of his contemporaries and a leader of the liberal opposition: "It was only after the breakthrough at Voronezh and General Paulus' catastrophe at Stalingrad that Kállay really changed his evaluation of the war. . . . When he preached a pro-German policy he was deeply convinced that policy was the right one."[7]

During his second year in office, the Second Hungarian Army was destroyed at Voronezh (January 12, 1943) and the Germans were defeated at Stalingrad (February 2, 1943). At this point Kállay began to reorient his policies toward a possible extrication of Hungary from the Axis Alliance. Although not very sophisticated politically, Kállay realized after the military debacles that the immediate major objective in the pursuit of Hungary's traditional interests was to loosen the ties to the Third Reich and to assure a greater degree of maneuverability for a more independent policy. Nevertheless, while eager to free Hungary from its entanglements with the Axis Powers before their ultimate defeat, which was becoming increasingly likely, Kállay, like Horthy and the other representatives of his class, was paralyzed by fear of the Soviet Union and Communism. With the passage of time, this fear was coupled with apprehension about the possibilities of a German occupation and the consequent triumph of Nazism. While opposed to both, the conservative ruling classes of Hungary obviously looked upon Communism as the ultimate evil to which even Nazism, if it proved unavoidable, was preferable.

Following the landing of the Western Allies in Sicily and the subsequent overthrow of Mussolini and Italy's extrication from the war in the summer of 1943, Kállay unrealistically tried to "solve" his dilemma by maneuvering secretly for the possible surrender of Hungary to the Western Powers exclusively. According to Marxist historians of the postwar period, Prime Minister Kállay's feelers and contacts were actually encouraged by Berlin because the Nazis, sensing defeat on the eastern front, aimed at establishing an eventual common cause against Bolshevism with the "Western imperialists." As evidence of such collusion, they also cite the tacit wartime understanding under which the British and American air forces agreed not to bomb Hungary in exchange for Hungary's agreement not to shoot at their planes flying over the country. In the view of these historians, this agreement in practice served the interests of the Reich, because the Hungarian war industry and the rail lines and waterways were *de facto* in the service of Germany.[8]

Kállay's naïveté in overlooking the geopolitical realities of the area, the political bases of the Anglo-American-Soviet relations, and the military implications of the Grand Alliance was matched by his double-dealing opportunism. His policies were designed to safeguard the integrity of the country—including the retention of the territories gained during 1938–41—and preserve the antiquated socioeconomic structure of the gentry-dominated society; but they led to disaster. Preoccupied with the avoidance of a Soviet occupation, Kállay failed to take the necessary precautionary measures to forestall a possible German attack from without and a pro-Nazi coup from within. For example, he could have gradually replaced the openly Germanophile members of the officers' corps with elements loyal exclusively to Hungary and the Regent and kept the armed forces stationed within the country in a state of readiness. Early in 1944, Hungary still had 14 divisions within the country, which, according to Hungarian military experts, could have withstood the relatively poorly armed German forces had the necessary precautionary steps been taken immediately after the first intelligence reports revealed the concentration of German troops along the borders.[9]

However, it is quite possible that even if Kállay had adopted suitable measures, Hungary could not have avoided the feared disaster. For one thing, Kállay could not have been sure that the armed forces, all the precautionary measures notwithstanding, would have followed an anti-German course at the time. This was partially demonstrated in October 1944, when Horthy finally acted to extricate Hungary from the war (see chapter 26). Moreover, the political Right in the country was still very strong. The Germans could count on the support not only of the Arrow Cross and Imrédyist forces, but also on a significant portion of the Government Party. Unlike Italy, Hungary could not, in 1943, have surrendered to the Western Allies who were still very far. Nor for that matter could Hungary have surrendered to the Soviets that year even if it had wanted to, which, of course, was not the case. Any overt attempt at such a surrender would most probably have led to a German military reaction even if Kállay had taken all the precautionary measures. However, it seems in retrospect that in such a case Hungary could have resorted to armed resistance and thereby saved its honor; and, having anticipated Romania in the switchover, could have acquired extra credit for its historical case. This course, however, would have required great sacrifices, which went counter to Kállay's (and his predecessors') objective of safeguarding the physical integrity of the country and preserving the military strength of the nation for any and all postwar contingencies.

In the pursuit of his noble though unrealistic objectives, Kállay embarked on a vacillating policy. As the military successes of the Allies became ever more spectacular in 1943, Kállay's "secret" contacts with the Western Powers became ever more annoying to the Germans. With the inexorable approach of the Red Army to the edge of the Carpathians, the Germans decided to prevent the possibility of Hungary's emulation of Italy; the extrication of Hungary at the time the Soviet forces were already crossing the Dniester would have exposed the *Wehrmacht* forces in the Central and Southern parts of Europe to encirclement and possibly to an immediate crushing defeat. The destruction of Hungarian Jewry, this last surviving large bloc of European Jewry, was to a large extent a concomitant of this German military decision.[10] Ironically, it appears in retrospect that had Hungary continued to remain a militarily passive but politically vocal ally of the Third Reich instead of provocatively engaging in essentially fruitless, if not merely alibi-establishing, diplomatic maneuvers, the Jews of Hungary might possibly have survived the war relatively unscathed.

Kállay's Jewish Policy

During his first year in office Kállay's position on the Jewish question tended to be as ambivalent as his general policy. Although Kállay was consistently opposed to any "physical" solution of the Jewish question, he was not, in 1942 at least, politically averse to the advancement of proposals for the "humane" solution of the question, including the eventual resettlement of the Jews.

Kállay claims that his anti-Jewish statements as Prime Minister were made to appease the Right radicals in the country, including those within his own Government Party. He further asserts that the specific anti-Jewish measures that were adopted during his tenure were calculated to advance the national interests, which even the Jews understood as necessary. For as long as the country remained independent, he argues, the physical survival of the Jews was also assured. Moreover, the restrictive measures that were directed against the Jews were primarily in the economic sphere, and thus could not only have been undone after the war, but also helped channelize the discontent of the masses and indirectly helped save the Jews "at the price of such apparent sacrifices." Kállay, like Keresztes-Fischer, the decent Minister of the Interior, thought of these measures as "concessions which would enable the country to get through the war without losing its independence and moral integrity."[11]

Kállay's first public declaration on the Jewish question took place on the occasion of the Government Party's meeting of March 12, 1942. In a major speech outlining his general program, Kállay had the following to say on the subject:

I, myself, regard the Jewish question simply as a social problem, the most virulent social problem of our day. It has, of course, racial aspects, many economic aspects, and others also, but I should like to treat the whole complex, *sine ira et studio,* on the lines of social justice or social injustice.

The Jew is often an asocial being, individually or collectively. If we draw the balance in any country, we find that in the final implications they were harmful. Let us take the position in Hungary. Often it has been said that Jews, while their activities had often been harmful to Hungary, had also been useful. It is an indisputable fact that Jews were largely responsible for the speed with which our trade and commerce have been built up. But I am certain that we could have done that job ourselves alone. Perhaps not quite so speedily, but so much speed was not necessary, and we have had to pay a heavy price for it. On the other hand, we shall perhaps never recover from the harm Jews did to Hungary in other respects, especially during the revolution of 1918. The problem, therefore, is nothing more than this: rectification of that social injustice which has resulted in Hungary from the disproportionate part played by Jews in Hungarian economic life. My attitude towards this problem is simply this: I regard every measure as proper which would serve the interests of the Hungarian nation as a whole. Neither more, nor less. What is genuinely valuable, what constitutes genuine progress, must be put through mercilessly and without respect of persons. The problem of Hungarian Jewry is a national one, not one of individuals. The nation, through its legislature, can bring and has already brought measures which it is our duty to execute fully. The will of the nation can always assert itself through legislation, and I undertake to execute these measures; but I declare at the same time that I shall protest and fight against individual actions—whether they overstep or whether they fail to reach the limits set by laws and government instructions—because individual action means getting round the law and is a source of abuse.

The restriction of the Jew in the economic field is a basic condition for the economic progress of the Hungarian people, at which none can take offense.[12]

Kállay repeated his position on the Jewish question by using the same arguments in his March 19 speech in Parliament. The speech aimed to emphasize that Hungary was at war because it was its own war and that the country's political orientation involved loyalty to the Axis and their common cause. The historical mission of Hungary, he argued along the lines of the Szeged Idea,[13] was "to shield Christianity against the Asiatic danger of Bolshevism." As before the Party meeting, he discussed the Jewish question in the context of the social problems confronting the nation:

Among the social problems I must point out that our social structure and stratification is not healthy. That social capillarization which keeps a nation's society healthy is defective in our country. This, too, has its good reasons. When the nobles' privileges were abolished, there ought to have started a healthy blending, a seeping upwards of elements from below, while the dead debris of the upper strata vanished where it fell. But at that moment an impermeable stratum intruded, pushed itself in between the lower strata of the population and those above.

The Jews were this impermeable stratum. In this respect, the Jewish problem, too, is a social problem. The fact that so few of the Hungarian peasantry, acknowledged by us all to be gifted and even brilliant, reached the higher social strata is mainly owing to the fact that this impermeable stratum prevented healthy social capillarization.[14]

His speech was well received and many parliamentarians of most political parties, including Béla Lukács, Count Béla Teleki, Béla Imrédy, and Károly Maróthy, echoed his views on the Jews and demanded swift action.[15]

In a policy statement of April 20, 1942, calculated largely to appease the Nazi elements at home and abroad just prior to his scheduled visit to Hitler on June 6, Kállay went beyond the social framework and in fact mentioned the desirability of solving the Jewish question in Hungary by "expelling" the approximately 800,000 Jews. However, he, like his predecessors, merely identified this as a goal to be eventually implemented after the war.[16]

Kállay was an advocate of the "civilized" form of anti-Semitism, which aimed mostly at the gradual elimination of the Jews from the country's economic, social, and cultural spheres. And, in fact, with the exception of the atrocities committed against the labor servicemen in the Ukraine, who were beyond his immediate control, the Jews were not subjected to any mass physical violence during his tenure. However, partially in pursuit of his own political objectives and partially in an attempt to appease the Germans, Kállay exacerbated the legal, social, and economic position of the Jews and tolerated the virulent anti-Semitic propaganda and agitation which played into the hands of the Nazis after the occupation.

Reacting to great domestic and external pressures, including the Right wing of his own party, Kállay initiated the adoption of new anti-Jewish laws,[17] made a series of anti-Jewish policy statements, and authorized the allocation of several thousand Jewish labor servicemen to the Germans for work in the copper mines of Bor, Yugoslavia (see chapter 10), as well as the deployment of tens of thousands of labor servicemen in the Ukraine.

The measures adopted by the Kállay government during the first four months induced Jagow to assure Ribbentrop of Kállay's loyalty to the Third Reich. He emphasized that Kállay had in fact taken "a sharper position on the Jewish question than all of his predecessors."[18]

By June 1942, the systematic extermination of European Jewry was in full swing. The deportation trains from all over Nazi-dominated Europe were rolling toward the extermination camps in Poland. The Nazi master plan also provided, of course, for the inclusion of the "close to one million Jews" of Hungary in the Final Solution program. In response to Jagow's assurances, the Nazis apparently decided to put Kállay's anti-Jewish policy to a test. They almost immediately began a concerted and ever more vocal campaign involving a variety of pressures to bring about their ultimate, ideologically determined goal. At the official political and diplomatic level they demanded that the Hungarian government bring about the quickest possible Final Solution of the Jewish question at home and consent to the inclusion of the Hungarian Jews living abroad in the anti-Jewish measures effectuated in the various affected countries. At the informal, unofficial, political-ideological level, involving the RSHA and certain elements of the Right radicals in Hungary acting without the knowledge of Kállay, they encouraged the initiation of clandestine plans for the phased deportation of all the Jews of Hungary. Whatever the mistakes and shortcomings of Kállay's policies in the midst of the uncertainties of the war, it remains a fact—and this is one of his greatest achievements—that he refused both the major demands of the Nazis.[19] The fact that the Hungarian Jews survived relatively intact until the occupation is the clearest manifestation of Kállay's steadfast opposition to any radical, Nazi-style solution of the Jewish question in Hungary.

German Pressure for the Final Solution in Hungary

German-Hungarian relations concerning the treatment of the Jewish question took an ominous turn in the summer of 1942. The plan for the liquidation of Hungarian Jewry was part of the overall Nazi design for the extermination of European Jewry. The details of this diabolic plan were worked out at Wannsee on January 20, 1942, on the basis of an order of the Führer,[20] under the leadership of SS-*Obergruppenführer* Reinhard Heydrich, head of the RSHA.[21] The "desires and ideas of the Foreign Office in connection with the intended total solution of the Jewish question in Europe" were incorporated in a memorandum prepared for Martin Luther, the Chief of the *Deutschland* Division, who represented the German Foreign Office at the Wannsee Conference. Dated December 8, 1941,[22] the memorandum contains the following provisions relating to Hungarian Jewry:

- Resettlement by the Germans of the Jews handed over by the Hungarian government.
- Declaration of the readiness of the Germans to deport the Jews of Hungary to the East.
- Exertion of pressure on the Hungarian government to introduce anti-Jewish laws along the model of the Nuremberg Law.[23]

Apparently emboldened by Kállay's tough public declarations,[24] the Germans began pressuring Hungary to consent to subjecting the Hungarian Jews living in the Third Reich and in the German-occupied parts of Western Europe to the general anti-Jewish measures and to institute a Final Solution program in Hungary proper.

In his note of June 3, 1942, reacting to Kállay's April 20 speech to the Government Party, Luther emphasized that Germany should strive:

- To acquire the Hungarian government's consent to the subjection of Hungarian Jewish nationals to the "resettlement" program instituted in the Reich.
- To make the wearing of the yellow star compulsory in Hungary.
- To induct the Hungarian government to agree to hand over the Jews of Hungary for resettlement in the East along the models used in Croatia, Romania, and Slovakia.
- To formulate an agreement on the property of the Jewish citizens of the two countries on the basis of the principle of territoriality.[25]

Contrary to the expectations based on earlier assessments of him, Kállay at first ignored the specific demands relating to Hungary and instructed the Hungarian diplomatic representatives in the Reich and the German-occupied countries to protect the lives and interests of the Hungarian Jewish citizens who lived in those territories (see chapter 8).

The Germans, however, kept up their pressure and Kállay had to find some justification for his dilatory tactics. His primary argument was that the Jewish question in Hungary did not lend itself to as easy a solution as it did in Germany because of the proportionately much larger number of Jews in the country and above all because of the important role Hungarian Jewry played in the national economy. Ultimately, he argued, it was also in the best interest of the Germans to recognize this, for much of Hungary's industry was working in the service of the Third Reich. This economic argument against the immediate radical solution of the Jewish question in Hungary was also used by most of the other responsible Hungarian officials contacted by the Germans for this purpose.

Pressure by the Germans was exerted not only through official channels associated with its Foreign Office and Ministry in Budapest, but also through German officials traveling in Hungary on various missions. One of the most familiar German figures in Budapest was Dr. Karl Clodius, the Deputy Chief of the Economic Policy Division of the German Foreign Office. While in Budapest, Clodius discussed the Jewish question with the officials of the Hungarian government as well as with some Right radicals. While the latter, including Major-General József Heszlényi, acting without the knowledge or approval of the government, were eager to conspire in any scheme for the solution of the Jewish question (see chapter 9) the former followed Kállay's line of reasoning. Lipót Baranyai, the director of the Hungarian National Bank, for example, was quite specific in his response to Clodius. According to a confidential report dated July 31, 1942, Baranyai informed Clodius that

. . . an elimination of Jewry and Jewish capital from the Hungarian economy has to be viewed as an impossibility and the Hungarian National Bank has to stand or fall on this question. So long as there is an independent Hungarian government, no responsible Hungarian figure can act upon German initiative to bring about the complete elimination of Jewish capital.[26]

The Germans, however, were not dissuaded. With the Final Solution program in full swing in the other parts of Europe they were resolved more than ever before to extend their net over Hungarian Jewry as well.

The Diplomatic Offensive

On September 24, 1942, Ribbentrop instructed Luther to try to expedite the evacuation of the Jews from the various countries of Europe, including Hungary, because the "Jews were agitating against (the Germans) everywhere and would have to be made responsible for sabotage and assasination acts."[27] In response to these instructions Luther invited Sztójay to see him on October 2. His discussion with the Hungarian Minister was detailed in a lengthy memorandum to Ribbentrop dated October 6. Accordingly, Luther informed Sztójay about the German desires in connection with the treatment of the Hungarian Jews in the occupied territories, in Germany, and in Hungary.

Luther emphasized that in view of the concern for the safety of German troops, the Hungarian Jews in the occupied territories and in Germany could no longer be treated in an exceptional manner. He asked that the Hungarian government either assure their repatriation by December 31, 1942, or consent to their subjection to the general anti-Jewish measures employed in the areas—marking (wearing badges), internment, and resettlement. With respect to the property of the Hungarian Jews, Luther advanced the principles of trusteeship and territoriality. Sztójay, upon being reassured that the same measures would also be applied to Jews of Italian citizenship, encouraged Luthér to believe that the Hungarian government would ask for the return of only a few Jews and consent to the evacuation of most of the Hungarian Jews living abroad because "Hungary would naturally not want to lag behind the other states." As for the Jews in Hungary, Luther impressed upon Sztójay the Germans' desire that the Hungarians bring about the fastest possible solution of the Jewish question in Hungary by:

- The adoption of legal measures for the elimination of all Jews from the cultural and economic life of the country.
- The marking of the Jews.
- The evacuation of the Jews to the East in order to bring about the Final Solution.
- The reaching of agreement on the property of Hungarian Jews on the basis of the principle of territoriality.

Sztójay inquired whether these measures were also being suggested to the Italian government and whether Luther was expressing the official position of the German government. Upon being informed that only the point about the Jews in occupied territories could at the time be considered official, Sztójay suggested that the two other items be communicated to the Hungarian government via Jagow before October 18, because he wanted to take advantage of his stay in Budapest to impress the entire complexity of the Jewish question on Kállay and Horthy. He assured Luther that in view of Horthy's experiences with the Jews and with the Béla Kun regime in 1919, the Regent would have the greatest understanding of the Germans' wishes. He also mentioned the possible economic difficulties that might arise from a hastened Final Solution in Hungary, where from 800,000 to 900,000 Jews lived. Sztójay also revealed Kállay's uneasiness over a "rumor" about the fate of the evacuated Jews, "which he personally did not believe," and conveyed the Prime Minister's concern over whether the Jews could make a living after their evacuation. Sztójay seemed reassured to learn from Luther that "all the evacuated Jews, including of course the Hungarian Jews, are to be used for road construction in the East and later transferred to a Jewish reservation." Before departing, Sztójay assured Luther about Kállay's understanding of the German position on the solution of the Jewish question and expressed his own personal pleasure in these German initiatives because he had "experienced not only in Hungary but also in Germany the devastating undermining influence of the Jews."

Luther concluded his October 6 memorandum by requesting Ribbentrop's authorization to transmit the demands about the Jews in Germany and in Hungary to Jagow for their official presentation to the Hungarian government.[28]

Luther's discussions with Sztójay and his memorandum to Ribbentrop gave rise to a flurry of interdepartmental communications in the Foreign Office involving Emil Rintelen (Ambassador for Special Assignments and member of the Personal Staff of the Reich Foreign Minister), Luther, Ribbentrop, and Ernest Weizsaecker (State Secretary in the Foreign Office). Weizsaecker, who was scheduled to see Sztójay on October 14—just a few days before his return to Budapest—was instructed to impress upon the Hungarian Minister Ribbentrop's desire that the Hungarian government agree to the deportation of the Hungarian Jews to the East.[29] Jagow was instructed to contact the Hungarian government about this on the same day that Weizsaecker met Sztójay in Berlin. The instructions were forwarded by Luther, who repeated the arguments advanced in his memorandum of October 6, and urged Jagow to impress upon the Hungarians the Führer's resolve to bring about an immediate and total solution to the Jewish question.[30]

Confronted for the first time with concrete demands for the solution of the Jewish question, the Kállay government decided to adopt dilatory tactics. Ghyczy, Deputy Foreign Minister, informed Jagow that Kállay would clarify some of the points raised by the Germans in his speech to the Government Party Conference, which was scheduled for October 22.[31] The speech must have greatly disappointed the Germans, for Kállay talked only marginally about some of the questions raised by the Germans and ignored totally the crucial points relating to the marking and resettlement of the Hungarian Jews. Kállay referred to his government's determination to eliminate all Jews from key positions in the country's socioeconomic life and to solve the acute housing shortage. But he also stressed his determination to eliminate those who saw the ills of the country only as an aspect of the Jewish question and recognized no other problem except the Jewish one.

Kállay's remarks on the Jewish question were probably intended not only to prepare the Germans for Hungary's planned response to their relentless pressure on the subject, but also to warn the pro-Nazi ultra Right radical elements within the country, who were exploiting the Jewish issue to promote their own individual "base, private interests" and to "poison and corrupt the atmosphere" at home. Kállay stated:

I must contradict those people who can see no other problem in this country except the Jewish problem. Our country has many problems beside which the Jewish problem pales into insignificance. Those who can see Hungary only through such spectacles are degraded men who must be eliminated from our community. I shall do my utmost, I shall go to the utmost limits everywhere in the country's interest, but I cannot and will not allow anyone to soil the national honor and reputation of Hungary, nor to obstruct the great aim of concentrating the nation's forces, by political extremism and base propaganda.[32]

These were strong words which clearly testify to Kállay's determination to follow an independent domestic policy consonant with Hungary's interests and sovereignty. Kállay's courage is highlighted by the fact that he took this bold stand months before the catastrophic defeat of the Second Hungarian Army near Voronezh. The only concession he made on the Jewish question was with respect to the expansion of the labor service system. Kállay consented to the appeals of the military and ordered that all Jews of military age, regardless of fitness for military service, be drafted "in order to allow for greater effectiveness of the Hungarian Armed Forces."[33]

Two days earlier Sztójay had held an informal confidential discussion with Weizsaecker in the latter's home. Sztójay, who sympathized with the German position on the Jewish question and was consistently undermining his Prime Minister's position in Berlin, was warned that Hungary was not handling the Jewish question in accord with German principles.[34]

Kállay was more specific in his discussions with Jagow on October 27. He told the German Minister that he would soon convey the Hungarian government's attitude toward the treatment of Hungarian Jews in German-controlled areas in the West, but asserted that the handling of the Jewish question inside Hungary was an internal affair. Kállay further explained to Jagow the difficult character of the Jewish question in Hungary in view of the large number of Jews there. Jagow was obviously not persuaded and emphasized the "international" character of the Jewish problem; he suggested that a meeting of German and Hungarian "experts" could overcome and solve the problems noted by the Prime Minister.[35] A few weeks later, Kállay added another argument. He informed Jagow that the solution of the Jewish question in Hungary was a difficult problem because the Hungarian peasants were not anti-Semitic and that, if the Jews were completely eliminated, the Hungarian government would have to enhance the assimilation of the Volksdeutsche (ethnic Germans) in Hungary.[36] Kállay reiterated this position in his speech of November 20, arousing the Germans' fear over the fate of the Saxons and Swabians, most of whom sympathized with the Third Reich and constituted a rich reservoir for the Waffen-SS.[37]

Sztójay communicated the official position of the Hungarian government about the Jewish question to the German Foreign Office on December 2. In a lengthy memorandum, he reminded the Germans that as a sovereign nation Hungary had been the first to initiate anti-Jewish laws aiming at the exclusion of the Jews from the country's economic and cultural life. With respect to the specific demands for the marking and resettlement of the Jews, Sztójay revealed that Hungary did not have the technical means to carry them out. He further emphasized that Hungary, with a population of 14 million had 800,000 Jews (200,000 more than the Third Reich once had among a population of 60 million), and that their elimination would cause great harm to Hungary's economy, adding that the maintenance of production was of interest also to Germany for "80 percent of Hungarian industry" was in the service of the German economy.[38]

In the meantime, Kállay's difficulties in dealing with the Jewish question were being compounded by pressures from the anti-Semitic rightist circles within Hungary. Some of the political and military figures of the extreme Right used the official parliamentary channels to question the government's policies on the Jews. Others acted covertly, communicating directly with the Germans without the knowledge of Kállay.

Responding to two interpellations by Arrow Cross deputies on December 3, Kállay informed the lower house that placement of Jews into labor camps and ghettos could not be justified at the time and under the laws in effect, and emphasized that the economic status of the Jews had been regulated by four major laws during the previous three years.[39]

Concurrently with the pressures exerted officially by the German Foreign Ministry, elements associated with the *Wehrmacht* and the RSHA, Himmler's agency in charge of the Final Solution program, also dealt behind Kállay's back directly with a few representatives of the Hungarian radical Right. By far the most prominent of these were Major-General József Heszlényi, Commander of the Fourth Army Corps, Lieutenant-General Sándor Homlok, Hungarian Military Attaché in Berlin, and Fáy of the Hungarian Ministry of Foreign Affairs. They advanced various schemes for the deportation of the "alien" Jews from Hungary as a first step toward the eventual Final Solution.[40] Another prominent figure who consistently undermined Kállay's position was Prince Albrecht of Hapsburg, a member of the upper house. On December 11, 1942, Prince Albrecht contacted SS-*Gruppenführer* Gottlob Berger, the head of the SS-*Hauptamt* (SS Main Office), to complain about the laxity of the Hungarian government in carrying out the anti-Jewish measures demanded by Germany. According to Berger, Prince Albrecht, who "worked closely with the RSHA," suggested that Hitler summon Horthy and Kállay to "show them how to go further."[41]

The German reaction to the Hungarian government's official response was summarized by Luther in a memorandum of December 18, 1942. Luther found the Hungarians' readiness to eliminate the influence of the Jews from the country's economic and cultural life encouraging but insufficient. He deplored the Hungarian government's insistence that Jews with Hungarian citizenship in the Third Reich and in the German-occupied territories of the West be treated in a preferential manner while other foreign Jews were being evacuated. He also expressed Germany's ire over the way Hungary was proceeding to solve the Jewish question at home and revealed the readiness of the Reich to come to Hungary's aid if the marking and resettlement of the Jews disrupted the economy. Luther stressed that the radical solution of the Jewish question was also in the interest of Hungary and that it had to be completed *before*, rather than after, the end of the war, as had been intimated by Kállay.[42]

Germany's suspicions about the "benevolent" attitude of the Hungarian government toward the Jews were reinforced by a secret memorandum that was based on a discussion with Horthy and other leading Hungarian officials. Citing "an authoritative source," the unidentified author of the memorandum stated that the Hungarians' belief in Axis victory and in the superiority of the Axis armies had been shaken and that Hungary's voluntary participation in the war against the Soviet Union was considered to have been a political mistake. Hungary, according to the memorandum, had decided to "lose cheaply" if the war ended unfavorably; this was proven by the "secret peace of the Hungarian government with Jewry." In light of these developments, the probability for the enactment of further anti-Jewish measures in Hungary was discounted.[43]

On January 15, 1943, Luther had another discussion with Sztójay. He berated the Hungarian Minister for the failure to submit the lists of Hungarian Jews to be repatriated from the Reich and German-occupied Western Europe by December 31, 1942, as originally instructed, and set January 31 as the new "final deadline." He also warned Sztójay that the Führer was determined "come what may, to remove all Jews from Europe while the war is still on" and that the Germans "could not, in the long run, look at the danger [represented by Hungary's shelter-ing of a million Jews] without action." Sztójay, as usual, was apologetic, insisting that he himself did not believe in the communications he was requested to submit by his government.[44]

Luther's warning to Sztójay was complemented by the demand of Fritz Gebhardt Hahn, a legation secretary in the German Foreign Of-fice, that Hungary recognize the full importance of the menace repre-sented by the Jews.[45]

Pressures by the Hungarian
Radical Right

The official position of the Hungarian government on the ever more persistent demands of the Germans was not viewed kindly by Kállay's opponents, including several members of the Right wing of the MÉP. One of the most vocal rabble rousers among these was Baron László Vay, then a member of the upper house.[46] A notorious anti-Semite, Vay was elected early in 1943 to a parliamentary delegation which was scheduled to visit Martin Bormann, the Chief of the Nazi Party Chan-cellery, in Munich on March 12. The delegation was headed by Béla Lukács, the MÉP party leader, and included Professor Dezsó Laky, Pál Thuránszky, and Lajos Huszovszky, all members of the lower house. A few weeks before the departure, a group of Right-wing MÉP deputies handed Lukács a memorandum which called for a "hard, militant, Right-wing policy, based on the Szeged Idea at home, with stern mea-sures against subversive elements and new and effective measures against the Jews."[47] About the same time, Vay sought out Jagow and expressed his hope that the Jewish question would also be discussed in Munich, for there was "much to be done yet in this area in Hungary." He was particularly anxious that Lukács and his colleagues be briefed on this question in depth and in an authoritative fashion. Jagow alerted the Foreign Office that the initiative must not be revealed as having come from Vay.[48]

In response to this initiative, Bergmann, a Minister in the *Inland* sec-tion of the Foreign Office, prepared with Ribbentrop's concurrence a lengthy memorandum dated March 9, 1943, to guide Bormann in his discussion with Lukács and his colleagues. Specifically, and in accord with the Luther memorandum of October 6, 1942, the Hungarian gov-ernment was to be advised:

- To enact legislation to exclude all Jews forthwith and without exception from the country's intellectual and economic life and to dispossess them immediately without compensation.
- To mark all Jews without delay in order to facilitate governmental measures against them and to enable the [Hungarian] people to hold themselves aloof from them.
- To concur with the prompt beginning of the deportation and transportation [of the Jews] to the East by the appropriate German organization.[49]

The machinations of the rightists notwithstanding, the Prime Minister stuck to his political course. In fact, his resolution to pursue a more independent course was strengthened by the military disasters suffered by the Hungarian and German armies in January and February.

Shortly after the military debacles, Kállay and the men around him in the government initiated a series of semi-informal political and diplomatic moves designed to find an honorable way out of the war and reestablish Hungary's nonbelligerent status. Feelers toward this end were extended to the Western Allies through many neutral capitals, including Istanbul, Berne, Lisbon, and Stockholm. In the spring of 1943, Aladár Szegedy-Maszák, the anti-Nazi chief of the Foreign Ministry's Political Department, approached the British during his visit to Stockholm by means of a meeting with Vilmos Böhm, a Social Democratic politician who had played a leading role in Hungary during the immediate post-World War I period; in Stockholm, Böhm was in the employ of the British for whom he prepared periodic reviews of the Hungarian press. In Lisbon, the chief link to the West was Andor Wodianer, the head of the Hungarian Legation. In Berne, the negotiations were conducted by György Bakách-Bessenyey, the Hungarian Minister, whose most important contact was Royall Tyler, a leading official of the American Embassy in Berne, who had served in Hungary in the 1930s as the financial representative of the League of Nations. Perhaps the most significant approaches were those in Istanbul, where a number of leading Hungarians were acting toward the same goal, presumably independently of each other. Among these were András Frey, the foreign correspondent of the *Magyar Nemzet* (Hungarian Nation), an influential Hungarian daily, and professors Albert Szent-Györgyi and Gyula Mészáros. The latter established contact with what they thought were the Western Allies' representatives in Istanbul as early as February–March 1943. (They turned out to have been German agents who were probably tipped off by Mészáros, who apparently was acting as a double agent.)[50] One of the most important contacts in Turkey was László Veress, who shuttled regularly between Istanbul and Budapest. His chief negotiating partner in Istanbul was Sir Hugh Knatchbull-Hugessen, the British Minister in Ankara.[51] The Hungarians also tried to get the Vatican involved in the establishment of contacts with the Western Allies. It was approached toward this end by György Barcza, the former Hungarian Minister in London, during his private visit to Rome in the spring of 1943.[52]

While his "unofficial" emissaries were conducting their "secret" negotiations, Kállay himself embarked on a hectic diplomatic campaign which culminated, on April 1–3, 1943, in his visit to Rome. Apparently anxious to test Mussolini's attitude toward the possibility of a separate peace, Kállay suggested that their countries and possibly Finland "formulate within the Axis a separate common policy, which would not be at variance with our duty of loyalty to our alliance."[53]

With respect to the Jewish question, Kállay claims to have reproached Mussolini for having yielded to Hitler's dictates in contrast to Hungary which, in spite of the numerically and proportionately much larger Jewish population, did "not tolerate outside interference." He found Mussolini's position particularly incomprehensible because Italy had only 60,000 Jews, who played a relatively minor role in the nation's political and economic life, and, unlike Hungary, the country enjoyed a "total absence of popular anti-Semitism." The only apparent concession Mussolini made on this question was that the Hungarian Jews in Italy would not be discriminated against and would enjoy the same treatment as other Hungarian subjects.[54]

During Kállay's stay in Rome, Jagow sent a telegram to Ribbentrop suggesting intervention to change the general political trend in Hungary. He complained that the local political situation was becoming more unfriendly and that the Jews were tending to regain their "negative" influence. He suggested that Germany try to correct the situation by bringing about the establishment of a more broadly based government that would include Béla Imrédy, the Germanophile former Prime Minister.[55]

Kállay's foreign political and diplomatic moves were coupled to a relatively more benign handling of the Jewish question at home. To the great dismay of the Germans, the Hungarians continued to tolerate the small-scale though steady emigration of Jews to Palestine[56] and condoned the presence and the services of a handful of rich assimilated Jews in the upper house.[57]

The Germans were particularly annoyed by complaints from officials of the Hungarian Ministry of Defense against "incidents during the retreat from the Don when members of the . . . Jewish labor service companies were shot by the *Sicherheitsdienst.*" The Germans were warned that unless these incidents stopped, no further labor service units would be sent to the Ukraine.[58] Following the Voronezh debacle, the lot of the Jewish labor servicemen improved considerably under the benevolent leadership of Minister of Defense Vilmos Nagy.[59]

The Schloss Klessheim Meeting
of April 17–18

The Germans were not only frustrated by Hungary's reluctance to accept the suggestions advanced for the solution of the Jewish question, but were also increasingly suspicious of Kállay's moves to decrease gradually Hungary's involvement in the war as a step toward its eventual total extrication. Hungary flatly refused Germany's repeated demands for troops to be sent to the Balkans and on March 31, 1943, decided to request the return of the Second Hungarian Army from the front. These military decisions (as well as the reports received from the German intelligence units in Sweden, Switzerland, and Turkey about Kállay's "secret" negotiations with the Allies and the communications obtained from the Nazi agents in Hungary, including László Baky, about internal political developments) induced Ribbentrop to assign Edmund Veesenmayer, his expert on Southeastern Europe, to make a general on-the-spot survey of the situation. Concurrently an invitation was extended to Horthy to visit Hitler at Schloss Klessheim, near Salzburg, "to discuss the military situation and the question of the Hungarian troops."[60] The meeting, which came to be known as "the first Schloss Klessheim Conference," was held on April 17–18.

In preparation for his discussions with the Führer, Horthy was briefed by a memorandum drawn up by Andor Szentmiklóssy, the head of the Political Division of the Ministry of Foreign Affairs. It provided Horthy with a general orientation concerning Hungary's domestic and foreign political position. It detailed Hungary's contribution to the common war effort and contained a series of arguments as to why a strong Hungary within its historical frontiers would also serve Germany's interest. With respect to the Jewish question, the memorandum contained the standard Hungarian position and emphasized that Hungary had been the first country in Europe to adopt positive anti-Jewish measures after World War I and that Hungarian Jews were greatly restricted in their cultural and economic life. It also pointed out the difficulties inherent in the proportionately larger number of Jews in the country and emphasized that their immediate total exclusion would harm the nation's production, 80 percent of which was geared to the needs of Germany. It rejected the Germans' request for the marking and resettlement of the Jews because the former would make the implementation of the adopted anti-Jewish measures more difficult and Hungary had no legal or technical means to carry out the resettlement at the time.[61]

Hitler complained that the Hungarian soldiers had fought badly and that Kállay was adopting a defeatist attitude aimed at reducing Hungary's involvement in the war to a minimum, if not actually changing sides, as demonstrated by the activities of Hungarian agents in Istanbul and elsewhere. The catalog of accusations also included the charge that Kállay was protecting the Jews. Horthy's defense, that he could not have the Jews killed after they had been deprived of a livelihood, was rejected by Ribbentrop, who also attended the meeting, saying that there was no other way but for the Jews to be either killed or sent to concentration camps. Hitler cited the example of Poland, where "the Jews who did not want to work were shot and those who could not work died." He warned that Jews had to be handled like tuberculosis bacilli in order to prevent them from infecting healthy bodies, because "nations that did not eliminate the Jews perished."

Although unprepared to discuss sensitive political issues, Horthy did his best to defend Hungary's position and rejected Hitler's repeated requests that he dismiss Kállay.

The Germans' dissatisfaction over Horthy's reaction to their demands was clearly reflected in Goebbels' diary note for May 8, 1943:

The Jewish question is being solved least satisfactorily by the Hungarians. The Hungarian state is permeated with Jews, and the Führer did not succeed during his talk with Horthy in convincing the latter of the necessity of more stringent measures. Horthy himself, of course, is badly tangled up with the Jews through his family, and will continue to resist every effort to tackle the Jewish problem aggressively. He gave a number of humanitarian counterarguments which of course don't apply at all to this situation. You just cannot talk humanitarianism when dealing with Jews. Jews must be defeated. The Führer made every effort to win Horthy over to his standpoint but succeeded only partially.[62]

Upon his return to Hungary, Horthy responded to the specific issues raised by Hitler in a lengthy letter to the Führer dated May 7, 1943.[63]

Comprehensive as the letter was, its persuasiveness was undermined by the report which Veesenmayer prepared on his mission to Hungary in March and April.

Veesenmayer's First Mission in Hungary

Veesenmayer drew up his report late in April 1943, and though he was in Hungary at Ribbentrop's request, he sent it first to Himmler —apparently his loyalty as a *Brigadeführer* in the SS overshadowed his duty as an officer of the Foreign Office. The report was passed on only after Himmler had revised it. The report, dated April 30, identified Hungary as an "arrogant nation" with very little "national substance" and a very inefficient ally. Veesenmayer blamed the men who directed Hungarian policy officially or from behind the scenes, including Kállay, Bethlen, Ullein-Reviczky, Chorin, and Leó Goldberger, who he claimed exercised a nefarious influence on the Regent. He lashed out against the Jews whom he found particularly responsible for the defeatist attitude that prevailed in the country and for the "extensive sabotage of the common war aim." Veesenmayer attributed Hungary's sheltering of the Jews to the Hungarians' belief that they would thereby escape serious air raids and would be able to protect "Hungarian interests" after the war by proving "through the Jews that they waged this war on the side of the Axis powers only because they were forced to." In listing the four enemies of Germany inside Hungary, he considered "(a) the Jews, and (b) the aristocracy with family relations to the Jews" as the most dangerous ones.

Veesenmayer very correctly identified Horthy's high standing in Hungary and argued that, despite the "nefarious influence" he was under, he should not be attacked and that the contemplated changes be carried out with him rather than against or without him. Veesenmayer also evaluated the attributes and qualifications of the various national political and military figures who could possibly replace Kállay and concluded that Imrédy and Bárdossy were the two best possible candidates. He felt that the desired changes in Hungary could be brought about only through pressure from the Third Reich and maintained that the "presence of a German SS Division . . . and the initiation of active measures against the Jews" would signify the beginning of the end of the Kállay regime.[64]

The section of the report which dealt with the Jewish question in Hungary apparently made a tremendous impression on Horst Wagner, who had just replaced Luther as the head of the *Inland II* Division. Wagner found that the report corroborated his own views on the Jewish question in Hungary and requested that a copy of that particular section of the report, which he claimed was of "great importance for the foreign affairs point of view of the Jewish question," be sent to Thadden.[65]

The German Foreign Office in High Gear

Ribbentrop summarized Germany's grievances and demands in connection with the Jewish problem in Hungary in an hour-long conversation with Sztójay late in April. In his report on the discussion, dated April 28, 1943, Sztójay informed the Hungarian government that Ribbentrop had emphasized that:

- National Socialism viewed Jewry with infinite contempt and looked upon it as an arch-enemy that could not be appeased.
- Hitler was determined to clear Europe of Jews and had ordered the resettlement of all the Jews of Germany and of the occupied areas to the East by the end of the summer of 1943.
- Germany wished that her allies take the same measures against their own Jews.
- Germany would probably sooner or later take actual measures in respect to Hungary.

Ribbentrop reviewed the many earlier interventions made in this respect, including the one made at Schloss Klessheim, and reiterated the grievances voiced by Hitler to Horthy. Sztójay concluded his report by including Ribbentrop's recommendation that the Jews be interned and by proposing that, in view of the fact that "the German attitude on the Jewish question stiffened and reached the gravest severity," the Jewish question in Hungary "be solved in a way that will avert a third intervention" by the Germans.[66]

The Germans apparently were eager to initiate action against the "close to one million Jews of Hungary" since the general Final Solution program in the rest of Nazi-dominated Europe had already either been carried out or was in full swing. They may also have feared the impact of the Warsaw Ghetto Uprising which was then taking place, for it clearly provided additional evidence about the realities of their "resettlement" program.

The Germans were also becoming increasingly concerned over the failure of their three allies in Central and Southeastern Europe—

Hungary, Bulgaria, and Romania—to implement the Final Solution program. Himmler became particularly eager to prepare the political climate and public opinion in these countries for the elimination of the Jews. In addition to the diplomatic initiatives taken by the Foreign Office, Himmler suggested to Kaltenbrunner in May 1943 that urgent measures be taken for the investigation of ritual murder cases committed by Jews. The trials were to be conducted under the guidance of experts, who would also supervise the dissemination of the related materials "with the aim to ease the evacuation of the Jews from the countries in question." To give credence to the local ritual murder cases, the propaganda services were instructed to distribute copies of Helmuth Schlamm's *Die jüdischen Ritualmorde* (The Jewish Ritual Murders).[67]

On May 21, Sztójay had a discussion with Wagner and informed him that, in the wake of the Hitler-Horthy parley, Kállay was about "to consider seriously the initiation of decisive measures against the Jews." Sztójay also pointed out the difficulties underlying the solution of the Jewish question in Hungary and suggested that the anti-Jewish measures be implemented gradually and at first involve the resettlement of only a part of the Jews who, in order not to alarm "the ones left behind," should be allowed for a short while to carve out a living for themselves.[68]

There is reason to believe, however, that Sztójay did not convey the official position of the government at the time. In responding to a request by the Foreign Office,[69] Jagow in fact informed his superiors on June 2, 1943, that he personally doubted that Sztójay was authorized to make his statement to Wagner. Kállay's position, according to Jagow, was reiterated in his speech of May 29, 1943, in which he stated that he was not inclined to deport the Jews as long as he did not know where to relocate them.[70]

On June 11, Sztójay had another discussion on the Jewish question in the Foreign Office. This time he talked to Otto Erdmannsdorff, the Deputy Chief of the Political Division, to whom he once again cited the economic difficulties that would ensue from a radical solution and expressed his relief over Kállay's alleged expressed desire for a humanitarian solution of the Jewish question in Hungary.[71]

There is little likelihood that the Germans were convinced about the basis of Sztójay's reassurances. Their suspicions, in fact, increased as a result of a report which Himmler's office received some time in July 1943, based on an interview with Horthy. It revealed to the Germans that the Regent largely shared his Prime Minister's views on the Jewish question. The unidentified author of the report claimed that Horthy seemed willing to rid the country of the "little Jews, who originally came from Galicia, but all those Jews who had made contributions in the fields of science, industry, or finance must be regarded as patriots and must remain unharmed." Even the "little Jews," Horthy argued, should be set to do useful work in Hungary proper rather than be removed to the Ukraine.[72]

By this time, around five months after Stalingrad, Kállay's search for a way out of the war intensified. It gathered momentum late in the summer after Italy's surrender and in consequence of the military victories of the Western Allies in Italy, North Africa, and the Far East, and of the Red Army in the East.[73] Nevertheless Kállay, like Horthy on October 15, 1944, failed to take the most elementary military precautions to forestall a possible catastrophe. The General Staff as well as the officers corps in general continued to consist almost exclusively of Germanophile officers, and the national and local press, with a few notable exceptions, continued to feed the anti-Jewish and anti-Bolshevik psychosis that preoccupied the country. Kállay's position was also aggravated by the fact that he did not enjoy the confidence of the right wing of his MÉP party; he was constantly attacked by the opposition rightist parties,[74] and found few supporters among the leftist opposition groups.[75] Among the political leaders of the country he could count only on the friendship of the Regent and the loyalty of a relatively few members of his government, including Ferenc Keresztes-Fischer, Baron Dániel Bánffy, and Jenő Ghyczy. He could expect the support of only a few of the top-ranking military officers, for 21 of the 29 of them were of German (Swabian) background and most of these sympathized with the Third Reich.[76]

A representative of the conservative-aristocratic class interests. Kállay was not inclined to follow the solution offered by the weak but still active group of the center and left-of-center democratic forces of the country. The representatives of this force became ever more vocal in expressing their opposition not only to the continuation of the costly and futile war, but also to the measures that had been adopted against the Jews. In their lengthy memorandum of July 31, 1943, for example, the representatives of the Independent Smallholders' Party (*Független Kisgazda Párt*), the Land Worker Party (*Földmunkás Párt*), and the Bourgeois Party (*Polgári Párt*) demanded that the labor service system be abolished and that the Jews be returned to the regular military units. The memorandum included the following passages:

. . . In the spirit of the Hungarian Constitution no law can come into conflict with the principle of equal rights. If such a law is nevertheless adopted, . . . another legislative act must see to it that this contradiction is eliminated. . . . The two anti-Jewish laws, the new law on national defense, as well as the so-called racial law are in sharp contrast to the fundamental principle of equal rights underlying Hungarian history and the Constitution. . . . The anti-Jewish laws must be rescinded as must all articles in the other two laws that are in conflict with the principle of equal rights. Until this can be implemented, it is in this spirit that the question of the Jewish labor servicemen must be urgently revised and the whole issue dealt with in the most lenient way possible; nay, one must begin the reassignment of the Jews into the Hungarian Army through the purposeful exploitation of all legal avenues available.[77]

The signers of the memorandum also demanded Hungary's withdrawal from the war, the resumption of the status of neutrality, and the dismissal and punishment of officers found guilty of war crimes. Though Kállay was not in a position to accept these bold suggestions, he continued to pursue a course that often irritated and occasionally even alarmed the Germans.

On August 17, 1943, Horthy and Kállay held secret discussions with their trusted anti-Nazi political colleagues, including Count Bethlen, Count Móric Esterházy, Count Gyula Károlyi, Ghyczy, and Keresztes-Fischer, in which they agreed that Hungary was ready in principle to sign a separate peace if the Allies:

- Would guarantee that no Soviet troops would occupy the country.
- Would make a binding declaration concerning the future boundaries of Hungary.
- Would recognize the present regime with the possible inclusion of Social Democrats in a revised government.[78]

This secret meeting, like Kállay's feelers in the neutral capitals, was fully known to the Germans.[79] They lost no time in taking the necessary countermeasures. In his diary entry for September 23, Joseph Goebbels, Hitler's Minister of Propaganda, alluded to them: "As regards the possibilities of treachery by other satellite states, Horthy would like to desert us, but the Führer has already taken the necessary precautions against it. . . ."[80]

And indeed the contingency measures concerning Hungary were taken that very month. Because of the country's important strategic position in Central Europe—important not only for safeguarding the troops in the East and in the Balkans, but also for protecting the Romanian oil fields on which the Nazi war machine depended—and Hitler's well-substantiated fear of another impending Italian-type surrender, the German General Staff, acting in cooperation with Field Marshal Maximilian von Weichs, who was appointed that August as the chief commander of the German forces in Southeastern Europe, completed its plans on September 30, 1943, for the possible occupation and disarming of Hungary.[81] The military contingency plans were reinforced by a new political drive. That same month, Veesenmayer was sent back to Hungary "to study on the spot the practical possibilities of a German influence on the internal political development in Hungary."[82]

Veesenmayer's Second Mission in Hungary

Veesenmayer's second report, dated December 10, 1943, reinforced Hitler's suspicions about Hungary. Veesenmayer presented a very bleak picture of Hungary's performance as an ally and submitted a series of proposals to "correct" the situation. The corrections were to be effectuated by keeping Horthy in power in spite of his weaknesses. Veesenmayer was not far from the mark when he characterized the Regent as basically a good soldier, but "a miserable politician," who "understands nothing about either domestic or foreign policy."

Portending the German occupation, Veesenmayer suggested that "the Hungarian problem would be solved, for all practical intents and purposes," if Horthy were "freed from his entourage" and "made a soldier of the Führer." He called for the replacement of Horthy's advisers by "the Führer, the Reich, and a delegate of the Reich who is up to his mission." In connection with the Jewish question in Hungary, he contended that "the Jews are enemy No. 1 and the 1.1 million Jews amount to as many saboteurs . . . and they will have to be looked upon as Bolshevik vanguards."

The report contained three appendices—one relating to Veesenmayer's discussion with Bethlen, the other to his discussion with Béla Jurcsek, the Germanophile Minister of Supply, and the third to detailed recommendations for intervention in Hungarian affairs. Veesenmayer suggested that the handling of the Jewish question be criticized continuously and with increasing sharpness and that Horthy be assured that his so-called court Jews would be spared; he also stated that "immediate action in the field of the Jewish question after a previously coordinated plan is necessary."[83]

During the time of Veesenmayer's visit to Hungary, the Hungarian government gave the Germans additional reasons for concern. The long-awaited trial of the Germanophile military officers who had been involved in the Délvidék massacres of January–February, 1942 (including General Ferenc Feketehalmy-Czeydner, Major-General József Grassy, and Captain Márton Zöldi) began on December 14, 1943, in Budapest (see chapters 6 and 32). Though largely motivated by *raisons d'état,* this trial of high-ranking officers for murdering Serbs and Jews provoked the Germans.[84]

Although the expected landing of the Anglo-Americans in the Balkans on which Kállay had pinned his hopes did not materialize, the Prime Minister continued his increasingly frantic search for an honorable way out by trying to forestall the equally feared German or Russian occupation. In the pursuit of his principal objective—the reestablishment of "full freedom of action" for Hungary[85]—Kállay took the initiative to induce General Ferenc Szombathelyi, the Chief of the General Staff, and Admiral Horthy to request anew the return of the Hungarian military units from the Ukrainian front to make possible the unilateral defense of the Carpathians against the advancing Soviet forces.[86] Though eager to maintain an independent course and to avoid any occupation, his frequently equivocal and opportunistic position, his understandable mortal fear of Russia and Communism, his failure to consider realistically the political and military ties that bound the members of the Grand Alliance during the war, his and his representatives' ostentatious way of conducting the "secret" negotiations, and his failure to take any precautionary military measures at home brought about first the German and then the Soviet occupation. It is probable that even if Kállay had avoided all shortcomings, he could not have prevented the inevitable Soviet occupation;[87] at best he possibly could have dissuaded the Germans from wasting their desperately needed forces on the occupation of a loyal country—but this, of course, would have made all the difference for the Hungarian Jewish community.

In the last few months before the German occupation, the relative importance of the Jewish problem declined as the Germans became increasingly concerned with the prevention, and Kállay with the promotion, of Hungary's extrication from the war. The shortcomings of Kállay's policies came into focus early in March 1944, when all the signals pointed to an imminent German occupation. Despite the immediate danger that threatened Hungary, the Kállay government failed to take decisive military countermeasures and continued to pursue what many historians judge to have been a "cowardly, weak, and ambiguous" course.[88] While not ultimately fatal for the Hungarian nation, this course unintentionally sealed the fate of Hungarian Jewry.

As for the fate of Kállay: when the Germans finally did occupy Hungary, he found asylum in the Turkish Legation in Budapest. However, he was compelled to leave his refuge following the Szálasi coup on October 15, 1944, and was shortly thereafter deported to Mauthausen. After the war, he first settled in Rome, then came to America in 1951. He died in New York on January 14, 1967, at 79 years of age.

Notes

1. The Kállay government, completed on March 10, was not radically different from Bárdossy's. It consisted of: Minister of the Interior, Ferenc Keresztes-Fischer; Minister of Defense, Károly Bartha; Minister of Justice, László Radocsay; Minister of Trade and Communications and Minister of Industry, József Varga; Minister of Finance, Lajos Reményi-Schneller; Minister of Cults and Education, Bálint Hóman; Minister of Supply, Sándor Györffy-Bengyel; Minister of Agriculture, Baron Dániel Bánffy; and Minister of Propaganda, István Antal. Of these, only Keresztes-Fischer, Radocsay, Varga, and Bánffy were truly loyal to Kállay.

Kállay also doubled as Foreign Minister until July 24, 1943, when the position was taken over by Jenő Ghyczy, another Kállay supporter. At the time of the formation of the government, the Germans feared that the post of Foreign Minister would be assigned to Antal Ullein-Reviczky, the Chief of the Press Office in the Ministry, and lobbied vociferously for the appointment of Bárdossy.

2. Mario D. Fenyo, *Hitler, Horthy, and Hungary* (New Haven: Yale University Press, 1972), p. 61.

3. *Ibid.*, p. 64.

4. C. A. Macartney, 2:82.

5. Kállay claims that the day after his appointment as Premier he met with Béla Lukács, the Chairman of the Government Party, and other leaders, who informed him that unless he followed their policies and accepted their pro-German attitude, he could not count on rank and file support or govern effectively. Specifically, Kállay argues that these leaders threatened to withhold support unless he (1) made concessions to public opinion on the Jewish question; (2) made pro-German declarations; and (3) relieved the anxiety of Gömbös' adherents. Nicholas Kállay, *Hungarian Premier* (New York: Columbia University Press, 1954), pp. 66–69.

6. *A Wilhelmstrasse és Magyarország*, eds. György Ránki, Ervin Pamlényi, Loránt Tilkovszky, and Gyula Juhász (Budapest: Kossuth, 1968), Doc. 488 (Jagow's telegram of June 12, 1942).

7. Dezső Sulyok, *A magyar tragédia* (The Hungarian Tragedy) (Newark: The Author, 1954), p. 477. See also Karl Werkmeister's statement of September 26, 1942, referred to below.

8. See, for example, the work of A. I. Puskás, a Soviet writer of Hungarian origin, *Magyarország a II. világháborúban* (Hungary in the Second World War), translated from the Russian (Budapest: Kossuth, 1971), 333 pp. See especially pp. 158–62.

9. Ferenc Adonyi, *A magyar katona a második világháborúban* (The Hungarian Soldier During World War II). (Klagenfurt, 1954), p. 58, and *Magyarország honvédelme a második világháború elött és alatt* (The National Defense of Hungary Before and During World War II), ed. Lajos Dálnoki Veress. (Munich, 1974), 2:11–13, as cited by György

Ránki, *1944. március 19* (March 19, 1944) 2nd ed. (Budapest: Kossuth, 1978), pp. 109 and 127.

10. For details on Kállay's "secret" dealings with the Western Powers, see C. A. Macartney, 2:162ff.; Fenyo's *Hitler, Horthy, and Hungary,* and Kállay's *Hungarian Premier.*

11. Kállay, *Hungarian Premier,* p. 70.

12. *Ibid.,* pp. 74–75.

13. For an explanation of the Szeged Idea, see chapter 1.

14. Kállay, *Hungarian Premier,* p. 82.

15. Johann Weidlein, *Der ungarische Antisemitismus in Dokumenten* (Hungarian Anti-Semitism in Documents) (Schorndorf: The Author, 1962), pp. 139–42.

16. Kállay claims that before making the declaration relating to the planned expulsion of the Jews he had a discussion "with the official leader of the Jews." Kállay, *Hungarian Premier,* p. 99. For additional information on this and other anti-Semitic statements by Kállay see Weidlein, *Der ungarische Antisemitismus in Dokumenten,* pp. 143–61.

17. One of the most important anti-Jewish acts of the Kállay era was the adoption of Law No. XV:1942 relating to the expropriation of Jewish-owned forest and land holdings. Adopted by Parliament in July, it was signed into law on August 5, and promulgated on September 6. For text see *"1942. évi XV. törvénycikk a zsidók mező- és erdőgazdasági ingatlanairól"* (Law No. XV of 1942 Concerning the Forest and Land Holdings of Jews). *1942. évi Országos Törvénytár* (National Collection of Laws for 1942) (Budapest: Athenaeum 1942), pp. 73–83. For extracts from the speeches in Parliament on the draft law see Weidlein, *Der ungarische Antisemitismus in Dokumenten,* pp. 145–54.

According to one source, at the time of the law's adoption, the Jews owned 1.57 million cadastral yokes, of which 970,000 yokes were farm land and nearly 600,000 yokes forest land. Julius Fischer and Carol Klein, *Reports on the Jewish Situation. A Memorandum on the Situation of Hungarian Jewry* (New York: World Jewish Congress, March 14, 1944), p. 10.

Kállay claims that the expropriation of Jewish-owned land did not hurt the masses of Jewry because the "land in Jewish hands was to an overwhelming extent in large holdings." *Hungarian Premier,* pp. 69–71.

18. Béla Vágó, "Germany and the Jewish Policy of the Kállay Government," in *HJS,* 2:189.

19. In an affidavit dated March 6, 1956, written in support of Jewish restitution demands, Kállay claims that all anti-Jewish measures introduced in Hungary after March 1938 were the consequence of the demands and/or pressures exercised by the Third Reich. For the text of the affidavit, see *Judenverfolgung in Ungarn* (Jewish Persecution in Hungary) (Frankfurt am Main: United Restitution Organization, 1959), pp. 1–5.

20. The instructions for the preparation of concrete plans for the accomplishment of the "desired solution of the Jewish question" were actually issued by Hermann Göring in a letter of July 31, 1941, addressed to Heydrich. PS-710.

21. For details on the Wannsee Conference, see Raul Hilberg, *The Destruction of the European Jews* (Chicago: Quadrangle, 1961), pp. 262–66.

22. The Conference was originally scheduled for December 9, 1941.

23. *RLB,* Doc. 66 (NG-2586).

24. Kállay maintained, rhetorically at least, a tough pro-German and anti-Jewish position throughout 1942. In his report to the Foreign Office, dated September 26, Karl Werkmeister, the Legation Counselor in the German Legation in Budapest, reviewed Kállay's message to the Hungarian soldiers on the Eastern front, reiterating his belief in the sincerity of Kállay's declaration to fight the war alongside the Axis Powers. Werkmeister attributed the air of defeatism noticeable in the Hungarian "upper circles" to the "whisper campaign" of the Jews and suggested that the Germans use pressure to bring about the confiscation of radio receivers owned by Jews. *Ibid.,* Doc. 69.

25. *A Wilhelmstrasse és Magyarország,* p. 660, Doc. 487.

26. *Documents of Destruction. Germany and Jewry, 1933–1945,* ed. Raul Hilberg (Chicago: Quadrangle Books, 1971), p. 188.

27. *RLB,* Doc. 68.

28. *Ibid.,* Doc. 70.

29. *Ibid.,* Docs. 71–73 and 76.

30. *Ibid.,* Doc. 75.

31. *Ibid.,* Doc. 78.

32. Kállay, *Hungarian Premier,* p. 123. This passage from his speech was immediately relayed by Jagow to the German Foreign Office. *RLB,* Docs. 81–82.

33. Kállay, *Hungarian Premier,* pp. 123–24.

34. *RLB,* Docs. 79–80.

35. See Jagow's telegram to the Foreign Office, dated October 27, 1942. *Ibid.,* Doc. 83.

36. See Jagow's note to the Foreign Office, dated November 13, 1942. *Ibid.,* Doc. 84.

37. For a detailed evaluation of the *Volksdeutsche* in Hungary see G. C. Paikert, *The Danube Swabians. German Populations in Hungary, Rumania and Yugoslavia and Hitler's Impact on Their Patterns* (The Hague: Martinus Nijhoff, 1967), 324 pp. For a sympathetic evaluation of the position of the *Volksdeutsche* in Hungary see the following books by Johann Weidlein: *Jüdisches und deutsches Schicksal in Ungarn* (Jewish and German Fate in Hungary) (Schorndorf: The Author, 1969), 84 pp.; *Der madjarische Rassennationalismus* (Magyar Race Nationalism) (Schorndorf: The Author, 1961), 131 pp.; and *Geschichte der Ungarndeutschen in Dokumenten, 1930–1950* (The History of Hungarian Germans in Documents, 1930–1950) (Schorndorf: The Author, 1957). See also chapter 5.

38. *RLB,* Doc. 86. The communications conveyed by Jagow on November 13 and by Sztójay on December 2 were relayed by Luther to Ribbentrop and Weizsaecker on December 3. *Ibid.,* Doc. 87.

39. See Jagow's telegram of December 4. *Ibid.,* Doc. 88.

40. Randolph L. Braham, "The Holocaust in Hungary: An Historical Interpretation of the Role of the Hungarian Radical Right," *Societas,* Oshkosh, Wisconsin, 2, no. 3 (Summer 1972):195–220.

41. *RLB,* Doc. 89.

42. *Ibid.,* Doc. 90.

43. *Ibid.,* Doc. 91.

44. *Ibid.,* Doc. 92.

45. *Ibid.,* Doc. 95.

46. Vay was a leading member of the Right wing of the MÉP, which he headed until November 1940, when Béla Lukács, another member of the same wing, took over the leadership. A former prefect of Debrecen and Hajdu County (1935), Vay was also a member of the Foreign Affairs Committee (*Külugyi Bizottság*) and of the Public Administration Committee (*Közigazgatási Bizottság*) of the upper house. *Magyarország tiszti cim- és névtára* (Title and Name Register of Hungary), 1942 (Budapest: A Magyar Királyi Állami Nyomda for the A Magyar Királyi Központi Statisztikai Hivatal, 1942), 49:9, 13 and 716.

47. C. A. Macartney, 2:209.

48. *RLB,* Doc. 96. Shortly after the German occupation on March 19, 1944, Vay was entrusted (April 5, 1944) by the caucus of the Government Party headed by Lukács to bring about the union of all the rightist forces "which are willing to cooperate with the Government Party" in order to assure national unity. *A Wilhelmstrasse és Magyarország,* p. 814.

49. *RLB,* Docs. 97 and 98.

50. According to German documentary sources, Mészáros was for a long time in the service of the German Intelligence (Vienna Office). *NA,* Microcopy T-120, Roll 688, Frames 311975-976. See also chapter 11.

51. For details on these negotiations and on Kállay's attempts to extricate Hungary from the war, see Ránki, *1944. március 19*, 2nd ed., pp. 7–47 and 58–94.

52. Barcza's activities in Rome were the subject of a bitter complaint by Hitler during his discussions with Horthy at Schloss Klessheim on April 17–18, 1943.

53. C. A. Macartney, 2:147.

54. Kállay, *Hungarian Premier*, p. 151.

55. Vágó, "Germany and the Jewish Policy of the Kállay Government," p. 195.

56. *RLB*, Docs. 99 and 100.

57. The Finance Committee of the upper house included five wealthy Jews or Jewish-Christians: Ferenc Chorin, Aurél Egry, Leó Goldberger, Móric Kornfeld, and Jenő Vida. On April 13, 1943, Chorin and Egry were also elected to the Foreign Affairs Committee of the upper house. In his telegram to the Foreign Office, dated April 15, Jagow claimed that the elections proved that Hungary was not inclined to embark on the Jewish policy that had been suggested and was being pursued by the Germans. *Ibid.*, Doc. 102.

Chorin's role in Hungary's political and economic life including his connections with Admiral Horthy, was detailed in a memorandum by Thadden to Wagner (Inl. II 2464g, dated August 27, 1943) and in a telegram by Manfred Killinger, the German Minister in Bucharest, to the Foreign Office, dated August 28, 1943. *NA*, Microcopy T-120, Roll 4355, Frames K213640-641.

58. *RLB*, Doc. 101. For details on the atrocities committed by the SD and their Hungarian hirelings against the Jewish labor servicemen during the retreat from the Don (Voronezh) front, see chapter 10.

59. Vilmos Nagy served as Minister of Defense from September 24, 1942, through June 12, 1943. For details see chapter 10.

60. C. A. Macartney, 2:149. The invitation was extended by Ribbentrop via Jagow on April 11. See Doc. 56 in *A Wilhelmstrasse és Magyarország*, p. 715.

61. *Horthy Miklós titkos iratai* (The Confidential Papers of Miklós Horthy), eds. Miklós Szinai and László Szűcs. (Budapest: Kossuth, 1963), p. 373–86.

62. *The Goebbels Diaries, 1942–1943*, ed. Louis P. Lochner (Garden City, N.Y.: Doubleday, 1948), p. 357. For the minutes of the Hitler-Horthy meeting, see *RLB*, Doc. 103. For Horthy's version of the conference see his *Memoirs* (New York: Robert Speller and Sons, 1957), pp. 204–6.

63. *Horthy Miklós titkos iratai*, pp. 391–400. In essence, the letter repeated the arguments advanced in Szentmiklóssy's memorandum. Its contents were relayed by Ribbentrop to Jagow on May 26. *A Wilhelmstrasse és Magyarország*, pp. 720–22.

64. *RLB*, Doc. 104 (NG-2192). See also C. A. Macartney, 2:148.

65. Note from Wagner to Veesenmayer dated May 14. *RLB*, Doc. 105. Veesenmayer complied four days later (Inl. II 1297g) requesting that the report be handled extremely confidentially (*NA*, Roll 4355, Frames K213586-590).

66. Jenő Lévai, *Eichmann in Hungary* (Budapest: Pannonia Press, 1961), pp. 55–57.

67. *Ibid.*, pp. 221–22.

68. *RLB*, Doc. 106 (NG-5637). Wagner memorandum to Gustav Steengracht von Moyland, the Secretary of State who succeeded Weizsaecker in May 1943.

69. Jagow was instructed by Ribbentrop to inquire about Sztójay's authorization on May 25, 1943 (*NA*, Roll 4355, Frame K123685). He also received a copy of the Wagner memorandum to Steengracht with the request that he take a position on Sztójay's statements (Inl. II 1378g, Telegram No. 1103, June 1, 1943; *ibid.*, Roll 4355, Frames K213683-684).

70. *RLB*, Doc. 107. On June 3, Thadden sent Wagner a memorandum (Inl. II 1540g) in which he emphasized Kállay's unwillingness to adopt new anti-Jewish measures (*NA*, Roll 4355, Frame K213678). Kállay's position on the Jewish question was also noted by Jagow in his letter to Steengracht, dated May 25, 1943, in which he discussed the revela-

tions by Filippe Anfuso, the Italian Minister in Budapest, about Kállay's policies. According to Anfuso, Kállay had expressed a readiness to satisfy Germany's demands except in the Jewish question because of the large number of Jews in Hungary and their role in the economy. *A Wilhelmstrasse és Magyarország*, pp. 720–21.

71. *RLB*, Doc. 108.

72. *NA*, Microcopy T-120, Roll 1096, Frames 452386-387, as quoted by Fenyo, *Hitler, Horthy, and Hungary*, p. 76.

73. For details on Kállay's "secret" dealings see Fenyo, *Ibid.*, pp. 140ff. and C. A. Macartney, 2:120ff.

74. Shortly after his return from Schloss Klessheim, Horthy received a memorandum signed by 33 ultra-rightist members of the lower house, including Imrédy and Miklós Mester, complaining about Kállay's domestic policies. Dated May 5, 1943, the memorandum emphasized that the Jews had to be extirpated from the nation's body and warned against the dealings with the Western Allies. For text see *Horthy Miklós titkos iratai*, pp. 386–90. Mester shifted his position after the German occupation and dealt closely with some of the leaders of Hungarian Jewry. See chapter 29.

75. His support from the left, which was not a significant force at the time, came primarily from the Social Democrats.

76. Fenyo, *Hitler, Horthy, and Hungary*, p. 171.

77. The memorandum, which also analyzed the domestic and international position of the country and contained specific recommendations for Hungary's adoption of a new course, was handed to the government by Endre Bajcsy-Zsilinszky, the heroic leader of the Smallholders' Party. For excerpts from the memorandum, see *FAA*, 2:383–84. See also C. A. Macartney, 2:169, and Kállay, *Hungarian Premier*, pp. 237–43.

78. Ránki, *1944. március 19*, 2nd ed., p. 30.

79. See Kaltenbrunner's October 26, 1943, communication to Himmler based on an intelligence report that stemmed indirectly from Count Antal Sigray, the leader of the Legitimists. *A Wilhelmstrasse és Magyarország*, pp. 740–42.

80. *The Goebbels Diaries, 1942–1943*, p. 480.

81. Ránki, *1944. március 19*, 2nd. cd, pp. 48–49.

82. Note of Andor Hencke, the Chief of the Political Division, to Franz Sonnleithner, member of Ribbentrop's Personal Staff, dated September 17, 1943. *RLB*, Doc. 109. Hencke also attached a copy of a report by Gerhart Feine, who later replaced Werkmeister as Counselor of the German Legation in Budapest, in which he evaluated the pro- and anti-German political forces in Hungary and reviewed the role of the Regent. Interestingly enough, Feine's report did not mention the Jewish problem in Hungary. For text of the report see *A Wilhelmstrasse és Magyarország*, pp. 733–35.

83. *RLB*, Doc. 110 (NG-5560).

84. The Germans were obviously also annoyed by the continued easing of the government's attitude toward the Jews. Thousands of Jewish labor servicemen, including many who had been maltreated by the *Sicherheitsdienst*, were brought back from the Ukraine. There were few, if any, restrictions on the nonpolitical educational and cultural activities of the Jews. The Ministry of the Interior even permitted the semi-illegal Hungarian Zionist Association (*Magyar Cionista Szövetség*) to establish branch offices in the provincial communities of Hungary. Concerning the latter, see *Magyar Zsidók Lapja* (Journal of Hungarian Jews), Budapest, January 5, 1944, p. 11.

85. Kállay summarized his policies in a personal letter to his trusted ministers abroad dated March 1, 1944. For text see *Hungarian Premier*, pp. 397–406. See also Nicholas Horthy, Jr., "Hungarian Relations with Germany Before and During the War," in *Nazi Conspiracy and Aggression*, vol. 8 (Washington, D.C.: Government Printing Office, 1946), pp. 756–69.

86. The question of the withdrawal of the Hungarian forces was raised by Szom-

bathelyi during his meeting with Hitler and Field Marshal Wilhelm Keitel on January 24, 1944, and by Horthy in his letter to Hitler, dated February 12.

87. One can only speculate whether Hungary would have gotten greater consideration after the war concerning its territorial aspirations had it resolutely preceded Romania in the switch of allies.

88. *Magyarország és a második világháború* (Hungary and the Second World War), eds. Magda Adám, Gyula Juhász, Lajos Kerekes, and László Zsigmond. (Budapest: Kossuth, 1961), p. 395. See also pp. 387–424.

CHAPTER EIGHT

TREATMENT OF HUNGARIAN JEWS IN GERMAN OCCUPIED EUROPE

THE KÁLLAY government's opposition to the persistent and ever harsher demands of the Germans for the introduction of measures leading to the Final Solution in Hungary was matched by an equal resoluteness to protect the interests of bona fide Hungarian Jewish nationals living in the Nazi sphere of influence. And, indeed, until March 19, 1944, when the Germans occupied Hungary, Hungarian Jews stranded in the Third Reich and in the various parts of German-occupied Europe fared far better than the Jewish nationals of many other states, thanks primarily to the protection provided them by the Hungarian government.

Germany, the German-Annexed Areas, and the General Government

The outbreak of World War II and the consequent swift conquest of Poland, Western Europe, and the Balkans saw the introduction by the Germans of a series of draconic anti-Jewish measures, which were preparatory to the mass extermination program that followed the invasion of the Soviet Union in June 1941. These included the introduction of the telltale yellow star, the establishment of ghettos, and the expropriation of property. The Germans were, of course, eager to extend these measures to the foreign Jewish nationals living in the occupied or incorporated territories, including the General Government.[1]

During this early phase of the war, the efforts of the Hungarian government were directed not only at exempting the Hungarian Jews from the general anti-Jewish measures, but also at protecting their rights as Hungarian citizens. The government continued to issue passports for travel abroad, even through Germany,[2] and intervened vigorously against the expropriation by Germany of property belonging to Hungarian Jews.[3]

Following the Wannsee Conference of January 20, 1942, which decided upon the Final Solution, the pressure on the Hungarians to "solve" their Jewish problem and to consent to the application of anti-Jewish measures to Hungarian Jews living in the German sphere became unrelenting. However, the Hungarian government, under Kállay, stood its ground and instructed Döme Sztójay, the Hungarian Minister in Berlin, and its other representatives in the Reich and the Protectorate of Bohemia and Moravia to continue to protect the interests of Hungarian Jewish citizens living or stranded in the German sphere.[4]

Apparently annoyed by the relatively frequent interventions of Sztójay, Martin Luther, who was then Chief of the Germany Section of the German Foreign Office, instructed Dietrich von Jagow, the German Minister to Budapest, to try to persuade the Hungarian Government to accept the German point of view in dealing with Hungarian Jews.[5] Almost concurrently, on August 18, 1942, SS-*Obersturmbannführer* and *Regierungsrat* Friedrich Suhr, the legal expert of Section IV B 4 b of the RSHA, which was headed by Eichmann, contacted Karl Klingenfuss of the Foreign Office requesting clarification of the Hungarian government's attitude toward the possible application against Hungarian Jews of the same measures that had already been adopted against German Jews—marking and deportation to the East.[6] In view of the Hungarian government's adamant position, Klingenfuss advised caution and suggested that the Hungarian Jews be "temporarily exempted."[7] Luther, who was concerned with the overall problem of foreign Jewish nationals in German-occupied territories, suggested in a lengthy memorandum to Ribbentrop that the Hungarian government be informed in no uncertain terms that unless its Jewish nationals were recalled by January 1, 1943, they would be subjected to the same treatment as the local Jews.[8] The deadline was subsequently extended to April 1, 1943.[9] The Germans proceeded with the implementation of the plan without bothering to inform either the Hungarian government or the Hungarian Legation in Berlin. Details of the plan leaked out, and when László Tahy, the Legation Secretary, expressed the Hungarians' grave concern over the matter it was dropped again.[10] Acting in behalf of the German Foreign Office, Fritz Gebhard von Hahn asked Tahy to submit by April 15, 1943, a list of the Hungarian Jews living in Germany, including the Protectorate of Bohemia and Moravia.[11] Concurrently he instructed Eichmann to refrain "for the time being" from arresting Hungarian Jews in the German territories and to free the ones already detained.[12]

It was not until May 31, 1943, that the Hungarian Legation in Berlin submitted the lists requested by the Germans. The lists included the names of 70 Hungarian Jewish nationals residing in the Third Reich, 19 in the Protectorate of Bohemia and Moravia, 16 in the General Government, and 16 in the Netherlands. Among the names were those of individuals whose Hungarian citizenship was verified and who had not been able to be included in the earlier repatriation transports.[13] In a covering letter, the Germans were requested to free Hungarian Jews who were already interned or deported to the East. The letter noted specifically that the Hungarians also had in mind the Jews in the camps of Theresienstadt, Auschwitz, and Sosnowitz.[14] Upon receipt of the lists, Eberhard von Thadden, who headed the Jewish division of the *Inland II* Section of the Foreign Office, immediately assumed that the Hungarian government was no longer interested in the Jews not identified on the lists.[15]

In addition to the efforts exerted with respect to groups of Hungarian Jews, the Germans spent considerable energy on "solving" the problem of individual Hungarian Jews living in Germany and the annexed territories.[16] Among the most interesting cases were those of Edmund Mészáros and Gemma LaGuardia Glück. Mészáros, a converted Hungarian Jew who lived with his Christian wife in Berlin, returned to Budapest for a visit early in the fall of 1943. He was denounced by a professor from the University of Szeged, who claimed that Mészáros had given a negative evaluation of the situation in Berlin during a discussion with an official of the Ministry of Cults and Public Education. The investigation subsequently undertaken by Eichmann's office determined that Mészáros was in fact a Jew whose original name was Ödön Reisz, who had converted to the Roman Catholic faith in 1901.[17]

Gemma LaGuardia was the sister of Fiorello LaGuardia, the Mayor of New York City, and was married to Hermann Glück, a Jew from Budapest. Mrs. Glück taught foreign languages in Budapest, where she was arrested following an exposé in the *Magyar Szó* (Hungarian Word). In view of her special value as a hostage she was first interned in a special camp at Mauthausen and later, at Himmler's specific request, at Ravensbrück.[18]

Paralleling the requests for the repatriation of the Hungarian Jewish citizens in the Third Reich and the annexed territories, the representatives of the Hungarian government also intervened to safeguard or reacquire their property. According to a German-Hungarian agreement, the property of Hungarian Jews living in these territories was considered to belong to the Hungarian state. In accordance with the provisions of the agreement, on June 29, 1943, for example, Spányi of the Hungarian Consulate in Prague submitted to the German Foreign Office Representative with the Reich Protector in Bohemia and Moravia a list of Hungarian Jews that also itemized their movable and immovable property.[19] The question of the property of Hungarian Jewish nationals in the German sphere of influence was raised by Thadden in a letter of April 30, 1943, which was addressed, *inter alia,* to the German Legation in Budapest. The Hungarian government, according to Jagow's response of December 17, 1943, adhered to the principle of territoriality with respect to the property of Jews still in the German sphere and insisted on the return of the property of those Jews who lived in or had already been repatriated to Hungary.[20]

The RSHA, which was eager to make the Third Reich totally *Judenrein* (free of Jews), decided to change its own reluctant concurrence with the tacit and occasionally official postponements of the deadlines set by the Foreign Office for the repatriation of Jews with foreign citizenship. On July 5, 1943, it informed Thadden that the Final Solution required the setting of a definite date for the repatriations. According to its directives, the Jewish citizens of the neutral and Axis-allied countries, including Hungary, would be issued German exit visas up to July 31, 1943. Those found in the German sphere three days after the expiration of the deadline were to be "considered equal to Jews of German citizenship in every respect." Thadden was asked to "put aside any scruples in the interest of finally solving the Jewish problem."[21]

In spite of the RSHA's proposals, however, the Germans continued to employ dilatory tactics in handling the repatriation of foreign Jews. This was particularly true with respect to the Hungarian Jews in the Protectorate of Bohemia and Moravia. In certain cases, the German authorities refused outright to hand over Hungarian Jewish nationals to the Hungarian consular officers in Prague.[22]

On August 12, 1943, Horst Wagner, the head of the *Inland II* Section, issued a memorandum instructing the neutral states and those allied with Germany to arrange for the repatriation of their Jewish nationals by a specific date. The memorandum emphasized that those not repatriated by that date, unless nonrepatriable because of transportation difficulties or illness, would be subjected to the same treatment as German Jews. The deadline for Hungary was August 26.[23] The Hungarians responded on August 23 by submitting six lists of Hungarian Jews living in the German-controlled territories.[24]

By far the most troublesome and potentially embarrassing item for the Germans was the return of nine Hungarian Jews in Theresienstadt, who obviously possessed inside information about the operation of the camp. In accordance with the recommendation of the RSHA, Wagner instructed the Foreign Office Representative with the Reich Protector in Bohemia and Moravia to reject the Hungarian government's request for the repatriation of the Hungarian Jews from Theresienstadt on grounds of "police security."[25] Spányi repeated his request on October 6, 1943, emphasizing that the Hungarian government would take all needed measures to prevent the repatriated Jews from engaging in anti-German propaganda.[26]

That same day, the Foreign Office Representative suggested to Thadden that the nine Hungarian Jews be transferred to the special Bergen-Belsen transient camp.[27] This suggestion, however, was rejected by Eichmann because of "overcrowding" in Bergen-Belsen.[28] The Hungarian General Consulate in Prague remained just as insistent in demanding the transfer of the Jews. On January 11, 1944, it submitted a lengthy memorandum to the Foreign Office representative, reminding him that over a hundred verbal and written communications had been addressed by the Hungarians in behalf of the 1,116 Hungarian Jews identified as living in the Protectorate of Bohemia and Moravia on December 20, 1940. It requested once again that the nine Jews be permitted to leave Theresienstadt.[29] The memorandum was forwarded to the Foreign Office with an urgent request to solve the matter by authorizing the transfer. Thadden consented in principle in order to save Spányi from embarrassment before his own government. According to Thadden, Spányi had earlier agreed to the transfer of the Hungarian Jews from Prague to Theresienstadt, knowing that this meant their ghettoization.[30] The nine Hungarian Jews were finally transferred to the Bergen-Belsen transient camp shortly before the German occupation of Hungary on March 19, 1944.[31]

Following the occupation, however, all interventions ceased, and the question of the repatriation of Hungarian Jews in the German sphere of influence was "solved" together with the whole Jewish question in Hungary proper. With the establishment of the quisling Sztójay government on March 22, 1944, the Germans presumably proceeded to subject the Hungarian Jews living in the Reich and in the Protectorate of Bohemia and Moravia to the same measures they had adopted against their own Jewish nationals. The disinterest of the new Hungarian government in its Jewish nationals living abroad was communicated to the Foreign Office by SS-*Brigadeführer* Edmund Veesenmayer, the new German Minister and Reich Plenipotentiary in Hungary, on June 17, 1944.[32] Thadden relayed this information to Eichmann and the Foreign Office Representative with the Reich Protector in Bohemia and Moravia two days later.[33]

German-Occupied Western Europe

The deportation of the Jews of Western Europe (Occupied France, Belgium, and the Netherlands), began in the summer of 1942. The Germans were, of course, eager to deport not only the indigenous but also the foreign Jews. Among the latter were a number of Jewish citizens of neutral and Axis-allied states, whose planned deportation raised a series of political questions. On July 9, 1942, Eichmann, who was in overall charge of the deportations, requested the German Foreign Office to prepare a comprehensive statement on its attitude toward the possible inclusion of Jews with foreign citizenship in the deportation program planned for these Western European countries.[34] Responding to a similar request dated June 22, Luther informed Eichmann on July 26 that the Foreign Office had no objection in principle to the planned deportation of foreign Jews from the occupied territories in France, Belgium, and the Netherlands "for labor at the Auschwitz camp." For psychological reasons, however, he advised that the stateless Jews be deported first. He further advised Eichmann that "Jews of Hungarian and Romanian nationality can be deported" with the proviso that "care must be taken to secure all property in each case.[35]

The Hungarian government manifested the same concern for the interests of its Jewish nationals in these countries as it did for those in the Third Reich and the Protectorate of Bohemia and Moravia. The Hungarian Legation in Berlin informed the German Foreign Office on September 17, 1942, that the Hungarian government expected to be able to free the interned Hungarian Jews and reminded the Germans that the property of Hungarian Jews in occupied France, Belgium, and the Netherlands constituted a part of the Hungarian national wealth.

The issue of Jewish property became almost as important as that of the Hungarian Jewish nationals. The dispute over its disposition dragged on while the Kállay government was still in power. A Hungarian special committee headed by Andor Schedl, a technical counselor, was dispatched to occupied Western Europe on January 19, 1943, to take inventory of the property of the Jews in the various countries. On January 7, 1944, the Council of Ministers assigned Frigyes Vilmos Krafft to serve as Government Commissioner in the Third Reich and the occupied parts of Western Europe. He was given specific instructions to safeguard and, when appropriate, to take control over such property.[36]

In the fall of 1942, the Germans began an intensive campaign to force the Hungarians not only to abandon their concern for the Hungarian Jews abroad, but also to finally "solve" their own Jewish problem at home in accordance with the Nazi precepts. A directive to this effect was issued by Franz Rademacher, *Amtleiter* of the *Deutschland III* Section of the German Foreign Office, to Luther on October 3. Rademacher was incensed by the Hungarians' demand that the Hungarian Jews in occupied Western Europe be treated in an exceptional manner on the basis of the "most favored" (*Meistbegünstigung*) principle and that the measures already enacted against them be rescinded. Rademacher informed Luther that the German authorities in occupied Western Europe had been instructed to keep the Hungarian Jews interned but not to deport them. He further instructed Luther to inform the Hungarians that the "exceptional treatment" of Hungarian Jews in Germany and the German-occupied territories of the West was no longer possible and that they should undertake the elimination of all Jews from the economic and cultural life of their country by marking and resettling them in the East.[37]

Luther lost no time in instructing Jagow to inform the Hungarian government that the "exceptional treatment" of Hungarian Jews in Western Europe would end on January 1, 1943, when they would be subjected to the same treatment as other Jews—deportation.[38] The Hungarian government adopted a dilatory position, and on October 13 requested clarification as to the countries involved under the term "Western Europe" and as to the handling of the property of Hungarian Jews.[39] Luther instructed Jagow on October 15 that the term denoted the occupied zone of France, Belgium, and the Netherlands.[40]

On December 3, 1942, Klingenfuss informed the RSHA about the information conveyed to the Hungarian government, pointing out that the same communication had also been conveyed to the representatives of the German Foreign Office in Paris, Brussels, and The Hague. Klingenfuss noted that exceptions would be made only in the case of a few Jews in whom the Hungarian government expressed a special interest.[41]

While the Germans were reluctant at this time to officially terminate the "exceptional" treatment of Jewish nationals of allied and neutral states, they nevertheless discreetly deported a large number "for labor to the East." The group included close to 150 Hungarian Jewish nationals from the Netherlands alone. These were deported mostly from the Westerbork camp in September–October 1942.[42] At the official level, the original deadline of January 1, 1943, which, like the subsequent one—August 26, 1943—was established by a German-Hungarian agreement concerning Hungarian Jewish nationals only, was allowed to lapse for political considerations.[43]

In accordance with Sztójay's discussions with Luther on January 14, 1943, the Hungarian Legation submitted to the German Foreign Office an "urgent" note on January 25 requesting that 101 Hungarian Jews named on three appended lists—51 identified as living in France, 23 in Belgium, and 27 in the Netherlands—be allowed to return to Hungary and that their property be safeguarded pending a final decision. The note emphasized that those Hungarian Jews on the lists who were in either internment or labor camps were to be freed so as to be able to repatriate.[44]

The repatriation of the relatively few Hungarian Jews still left in the occupied countries of Western Europe continued at a slow but steady pace during the summer of 1943. However, the attitude of the German authorities toward the Jewish nationals of allied and neutral countries under their jurisdiction changed radically in September. This was due to their eagerness to make Europe *Judenrein* as early as possible as well as to their distress over Italy's extrication from the war.

On September 23, 1943, the Chief of the German Security Police and Security Service addressed a memorandum to the major units under his jurisdiction throughout occupied Europe informing them that although the Jewish nationals of allied and neutral countries in the German sphere of influence[45] could not yet be "relocated to the East for labor," they were to be "temporarily" transferred: males over the age of 14 to the concentration camp at Buchenwald, and women and children to the concentration camp at Ravensbrück. For Hungarian nationals, these measures were to go into effect beginning on October 10.[46]

Belgium. Responding to the Hungarian note of January 25, the Germans at first expressed readiness to cooperate in the repatriation of the 23 Hungarian Jews in Belgium.[47] However, the plan could not be implemented because many of the Jews on the list could no longer be located, following their earlier arrest by the Security Police (*Sicherheits-polizei*—SIPO).[48] The issue was left unresolved, and shortly after October 10, 1943, when the Nazis began to treat Hungarian Jews like German Jews, 11 of these Hungarian Jews were picked up and deported to Mecheln. The Hungarian Consulate in Brussels continued to intervene in their behalf until shortly after the German occupation of Hungary.[49] In view of the changed situation caused by the occupation, the Germans no longer showed any consideration for the fate of the Hungarian Jews remaining in Belgium.[50]

France. Following the introduction of anti-Jewish measures in Occupied France, the German authorities took it for granted that they could extend the same measures to the Jewish citizens of the Axis-allied states as well. Units of the Higher SS and Police Leader in France proceeded to include the Hungarian Jews in their general anti-Jewish measures on the basis of a communication by Luther to SS-*Brigadeführer* Otto Abetz, the German Ambassador in Paris, dated July 2, 1942, according to which the Hungarian government had expressed a disinterest in its Jewish nationals except for a few individual cases.[51]

However, when the Hungarian Jews living in Occupied France were ordered to wear the yellow badge, the Hungarian government immediately instructed Sztójay to protest against the measure, especially since the Italian and the Romanian Jews were not required to do so at the time. In his discussion with Luther on August 11, 1942, Sztójay emphasized that he personally had found the transmission of the protest quite unpleasant because he considered himself a "champion of anti-Semitism."[52]

The Hungarian government clarified its position on September 14, when the General Consul in Paris informed Abetz that the government had neither issued nor authorized anyone to make any statements in Budapest or in Berlin about its alleged disinterest in its Hungarian Jewish citizens. The Hungarian note emphasized that the Hungarian government expected the application of the "most favored" principle to its citizens and demanded that in the interest of the prestige of the Hungarian passport all those interned should be allowed to go free. The note further stated that the Hungarian government viewed the property of Hungarian Jews as part of the Hungarian national wealth and requested that German authorities consult the Hungarian Consulate on these matters.[53]

Shortly thereafter, Himmler instructed SS-*Gruppenführer* Heinrich Müller, the head of Section IV of the RSHA and Eichmann's immediate superior, to place about 10,000 Jews still in France, including Hungarian and Romanian Jews with rich relatives in America, into a special camp for possible use as "valuable hostages."[54]

According to a report by Rudolf Schleier, the German Minister in Paris, the Hungarian Consulate estimated that there were around 1,600 Hungarian Jews in Occupied France early in 1943. Of these, 65 were on a Hungarian repatriation list of 90 Jews whose citizenship had been proven and who were allowed to return to Hungary on February 24, 1943. Of the remainder, around 1,000 were having their citizenship status investigated. The Security Police were told that the Hungarian government had no interest in the remaining 500, whose citizenship had not been confirmed.[55] According to the French Police, there were 2,065 Hungarian Jews in Occupied France. It submitted the list to the Hungarian authorities, requesting them to arrange for a speedy repatriation of those in whom they had an interest in order that anti-Jewish measures might then be applied against the others.

The Hungarian Jews in Occupied France, and especially in Paris, had a benevolent mentor in the person of Dr. Antal Uhl, a Roman Catholic priest. Until his recall by the Hungarian government following his arrest by the Gestapo for pro-Jewish activities, Father Uhl served as a savior for many persecuted Hungarian Jews. He provided them with false papers, including cards certifying their membership in the Hungarian Catholic Mission (*Magyar Katolikus Misszió*). Together with Irén Tergina and Berta Kipper, two of the nuns associated with the Mission, Dr. Uhl intervened on behalf of Jews in the Hungarian Consulate General and provided food for those interned in the Tourelle in Paris.[56]

In addition to their interventions in behalf of the Hungarian Jewish citizens in Occupied France, the Hungarian authorities also intervened for the repatriation or freeing of Hungarian Jews in Vichy France and in the camps or prisons of Drancy,[57] Beaune-La-Rolande, and Fresnes. The German Security Service (*Sicherheitsdienst*—SD) was at first inclined to free the interned Hungarian Jews if the Hungarian government showed no further interest in the other Hungarian Jews living in France. The Hungarians, however, continued to pressure Berlin to intervene against the arrest of Hungarian Jews in Vichy France and to free those already interned. Thadden rejected the request for the repatriation of the Hungarian Jews in Vichy France on "police security grounds," but intimated that the German Embassy in Paris might "review" the cases of the interned Jews. He insisted, however, that the interned Jews would be granted freedom only if they left the German sphere within fourteen days. The Hungarians accepted the proposals in principle and suggested that the proper authorities in Paris and Vichy be instructed to facilitate the issuing of exit permits and transit visas for the Hungarian Jews cleared. Eichmann was fully informed about these developments and was assured by Thadden on February 16, 1944, that the German Foreign Office intended to give no concrete answer to the Hungarians.[58] Thadden presumably was already aware of the forthcoming occupation of Hungary. On May 25, 1944, Veesenmayer informed the Foreign Office that the new Hungarian government headed by Sztójay renounced its claim for the repatriation of the Hungarian Jewish nationals in Vichy France.[59]

The Netherlands. The Hungarian government's representatives also intervened to protect the interests of the Hungarian Jewish nationals in the Netherlands. On instructions from his government, Sztójay intervened in Berlin in December 1942 to stop the liquidation of the property of Hungarian Jews in the Netherlands until a Hungarian trustee was appointed.[60] The chosen trustee was Kálmán Kollar of Amsterdam, the owner of the Pantheon Publishing House of Amsterdam and Leipzig. Details about Kollar's background were supplied on February 3, 1943, by SS-*Brigadeführer* Otto Bene, the German Foreign Office Representative with the Reich Commissioner for the Occupied Netherlands, to von Hahn.[61]

Close to 150 Hungarian Jewish nationals were included in the deportations from the Netherlands in September–October 1942. This evoked a strong reaction in Hungary, especially among the Jewish leaders, and led to the initiation of demands for the repatriation of Hungarian Jews still in the Netherlands.

Acting on instructions from his government, Arthur Jäger, the Director General of the Hungarian Consulate in Amsterdam, submitted to Bene's office on January 16, 1943, a list of 14 Hungarian Jews whose citizenship had been proven, requesting their speediest repatriation.[62] Bene assumed that these would be repatriated within 14 days, if they had not in the meantime been deported to the East.[63] Bene's assumption proved optimistic, for the repatriation of Jews required clearance from both the SIPO and SD authorities in the Netherlands and from Eichmann's office in Berlin. Eventually 15 Hungarian Jews were authorized to repatriate on March 15. This was followed by four other smaller transports in 1943, all before the implementation of new instructions issued on September 23 by the Chief of the Security Police and Security Service.[64]

On March 30, 1943, Benc transmitted to the Foreign Office five lists of Hungarian Jews of which one pertained to those still living in the Netherlands,[65] another to those interned at Westerbork,[66] two to those "transported to the East," and one to those already repatriated.[67] He also requested instructions on what to do with the Jews still remaining in the Netherlands in whom the Hungarian government ostensibly showed no interest.[68]

In the meantime, the *Reichssicherheitshauptamt,* acting in parallel with but independently of the Foreign Office, took the initiative in reacting to the pressures exerted by the Kállay government. On March 31, Otto Hunsche, one of Eichmann's closest collaborators in the office, instructed SS-*Sturmbannführer* Willi Zöpf, the *Befehlshaber der SIPO und des SD* and head of Section IV B 4—the Eichmann office branch—in the Netherlands, that the approximately 80 Hungarian Jews in Westerbork at the time should not be deported to the East until the question of their possible repatriation was settled with the Hungarian representatives. Zöpf dutifully transmitted this communication to SS-*Obersturmführer* Albert Konrad Gemmeker, the Commander of Westerbork, on April 10.[69]

Shortly after the repatriation deadline for Hungarian Jews set by the SIPO and SD chief's memorandum of September 23 expired, a number of Hungarian Jewish nationals were in fact arrested and their apartments looted almost immediately thereafter.[70] The mass relocation of the Jews, however, did not begin until early in February 1944, when Hitler had already made up his mind to occupy Hungary. On January 23, 1944, Zöpf alerted Gemmeker about the imminent implementation of the memorandum under which males over 14 were to be transferred from Westerbork to Buchenwald and women and children to Ravensbrück. Four days later, the transfer to Buchenwald was established for February 2 and that to Ravensbrück for February 3. In fact 27 Jews (one of Spanish citizenship) were transferred to Buchenwald on February 1 and 63 women and children (among them a few of Spanish citizenship) to Ravensbrück on February 5. According to Zöpf's February 8 note to Eichmann's office, those transferred to the German concentration camps included a number of Jews whose repatriation the Hungarian government subsequently authorized.[71] Following the completion of these two major transfers, a small number of Hungarian Jews were relocated to German camps on an individual basis. In the period following the occupation of Hungary on March 19,

1944, Hungarian Jews apprehended in the Netherlands and elsewhere in Western Europe were mostly transferred to Bergen-Belsen.[72]

Greece and Italy

There were relatively few Hungarian Jews in Greece and Italy, and until the occupation their personal safety and property were safeguarded. In the case of Italy, which treated the Jewish question in a relatively benevolent fashion, offering haven to many foreign Jews who had fled Nazi persecution,[73] the Hungarian government cooperated in the repatriation of Jews who were in possession of valid passports issued after September 1, 1939, and of Jews whose Hungarian citizenship was cleared by the Hungarian Consulate in Milan or Trieste.[74] During his visit to Rome on April 1–3, 1943, Prime Minister Kállay was assured by Mussolini that the Hungarian Jews in Italy would not be discriminated against and would enjoy the same treatment as other Hungarian subjects.[75]

The Hungarian Jews in Greece, like several other categories of foreign Jews, were spared the ordeal of the Greek Jews in 1943. However, following the occupation of Hungary and the consequent application of anti-Jewish measures, the Hungarian Jews in Greece were also included in the Final Solution program. According to a telegram by Veesenmayer to the Foreign Office, dated June 27, 1944, the *Sicherheitsdienst* in Greece decided on the deportation of the Hungarian Jews living there without bothering to consult the new Hungarian authorities, assuming that the "Hungarian government will show no interest" in its Jewish nationals. With respect to the property confiscated from the Hungarian Jews in Greece, Veesenmayer advised the Foreign Office that it be safeguarded pending a final decision concerning the problem of the "property of Hungarian Jews living in the German sphere of influence."[76]

Slovakia

The Jews of Slovakia were among the first ones to be subjected to the Final Solution program following the Wannsee Conference. The deportations from Slovakia began in March 1942, and by the end of October close to 58,000 Jews—75 percent of the Jewish community—were "resettled."[77] Thousands of Slovak Jews, many of whom spoke Hungarian, escaped and found haven in Hungary. While it is very difficult if not impossible to determine whether there were any Jews of Hungarian citizenship among the deportees, the currently available evidence indicates that the Hungarian Jewish nationals were subjected to the same discriminatory economic measures of the Jewish Code (*Židovský kodex*) promulgated on September 9, 1941, as the Slovak Jews. The Hungarian government intervened quite frequently against this inequity, arguing that the economic activities of Hungarian Jews were left unhindered in Germany itself. An embarrassing inquiry to this effect was submitted to the German Foreign Office on March 26, 1942, by Hanns Elard Ludin, the German Minister in Bratislava.[78] On May 12, Rademacher informed Ludin confidentially, and with the specific request that he not inform the Slovak government, that while Germany was trying to eliminate foreign Jews from the economic life of the country, it could not proceed with the Aryanization of the wealth and similar anti-Jewish measures against the Jewish citizens of those states that might employ reprisals against the Third Reich. He emphasized that the cases involved Jewish citizens of England, the Americas, and the Soviet Union and noted that the involvement of Hungarian Jews in the economic life of the Reich was not worthy of mention.[79]

As a result of pressure exerted by the Hungarian government to conclude an agreement relating to the treatment of Hungarian Jews in Slovakia, the Slovak Legation in Berlin approached the German Foreign Office for advice on June 23, 1942. Since the Slovaks operated on the assumption that, with respect to Aryanization, no distinction was to be made between Slovak Jews and Jews of Hungarian citizenship, the questions raised by the Hungarians involved sensitive and fundamental political considerations which had to be cleared with the Germans. Consultation of the Germans was also required by article 4 of the German-Slovak Security Treaty, in which Slovakia undertook to coordinate its foreign policy with that of the German Reich.

With respect to the questions raised by the Hungarians, the Slovak Legation requested clarification on the following:

- Does the Hungarian state have the right to request the Aryanization of the property of Jews of Hungarian citizenship by Hungarian Aryans, and should it be by Hungarian or Slovak citizens or by juridical persons (corporations) of Hungarian ownership in Slovakia or by such entities in Hungary?
- Should the Aryanization take place via a Hungarian trustee company or the Slovak authorities?

- Do agreements already exist between the German Reich and Hungary concerning questions of this nature?
- What regulations are to be applied to those making requests against this property and for the appraisal of the property? [80]

The answers were not easily forthcoming. The questions raised by the Slovaks were discussed in a number of departments in the German Foreign Office.[81] On November 30, 1942, Ludin's office again approached the Foreign Office requesting clarification on whether there existed a secret Hungarian-German agreement relating to the treatment of the Jews in the Reich because, according to Prime Minister Vojtech Tuka, the Hungarians kept on referring to it in pressing their case in Slovakia.[82]

Following the clarification of the political implications of the various questions asked by the Slovaks, Klingenfuss contacted the German Legation early in December, 1942, and provided the official German response, but requested that it be used "only if needed." Ludin was urged to assure the Slovak government that its suspicions were unfounded and that the anti-Jewish policy of the Reich was uniformly applied. There were differences in the application of anti-Jewish measures primarily because the agreements with the various governments involved had not been concluded at the same time.

With respect to the specific questions raised, Klingenfuss emphasized that the Hungarian Jews in the Reich were not treated in an exceptional fashion, meaning that:

- The Hungarian Jews in the Reich were subject, without exception, to the anti-Jewish laws.
- The Hungarian Jews were to be subjected to marking and resettlement in the Reich as well as in the occupied territories, and these measures had partially already been carried out.
- The property of the resettled Hungarian Jews was being safeguarded for the Hungarian state pending final legal arrangements.
- The question of property rights was to be settled on the basis of the principle of territoriality, and discussions to this effect would be held with the Hungarian government.

Klingenfuss further noted that the Hungarian government had expressed certain reservations about the handling of the property of Hungarian Jews in occupied Western Europe, requesting that it be represented by a trustee in any disposal of such property.[83]

In the meantime Slovak-Hungarian relations concerning the treatment of Hungarian Jews in Slovakia continued to be tense. On December 15, 1942, Dr. Malis, the Counselor of the Slovak Legation in Berlin, contacted Luther anew, complaining about the "great difficulties" the Slovaks were having in their negotiations with the Hungarians. He informed Luther that in accord with the German line the Slovaks had told the Hungarians either to repatriate their Jewish nationals or to agree to their subjection to the anti-Jewish measures adopted by Slovakia, including "resettlement." Since the Hungarians did not agree to the latter proposal and showed an unwillingness to repatriate the Jewish nationals, Malis expressed the fear that should the Slovaks unilaterally decide on the "resettlement" of the Hungarian Jews, the Hungarian government might take countermeasures against Slovak citizens in Hungary. "In this connection," Malis emphasized, "one could not take race into consideration, since for measures of this kind Hungarian law does not provide for such a differentiation." Luther brought Malis up to date concerning the German position on the Hungarian Jews in the Reich as expressed by Klingenfuss' note to the German Legation in Bratislava and suggested that the Slovaks follow the same course "in order to assure a generally uniform implementation of the settlement of this question in Europe."[84]

The Hungarian Jews in Slovakia continued to enjoy the protection of the Kállay government until it was replaced in the wake of the German occupation in March 1944. Since by that time the situation in Slovakia was relatively stabilized and the Jews were treated much better than in Hungary, where the SS and their Hungarian hirelings had embarked on a draconic ghettoization, concentration, and deportation program, the flow of refugees was reversed, with many Hungarian Jews seeking haven in Slovakia. However, the refuge proved temporary, for in October the deportation of the remaining Slovak Jews was resumed in the wake of the Banska Bystrica uprising late in August, and many of the refugees suffered the fate of their compatriots in Hungary.

The Kállay government was as resolute in protecting bona fide Hungarian Jewish nationals living in Nazi-dominated Europe as it was in opposing the insistent and ever growing pressure of the Germans to bring about the Final Solution in Hungary itself. Unfortunately, Kállay did not enjoy the support of all of his subordinates in this endeavor. A number of high-ranking diplomatic and military officials, acting in collusion with ultra-rightist politicians, conspired with the RSHA representatives toward the initiation of mass deportation plans that were to culminate in the German-suggested Final Solution program.

Notes

1. The "General Government" (*Generalgouvernement*) was one of the administrative areas of German-occupied Poland, which was administered by *Generalgouverneur* Hans Frank. Its establishment led to a minor German-Hungarian dispute over its borders with Hungary, which was eventually solved in the wake of lengthy negotiations in 1942. For details on the issues involved and on the German and Hungarian delegations participating in the negotiations consult *NA*, Microcopy T-120, Roll 2561, Frames E310873-927. (All subsequent references pertain to Microcopy T-120.)

2. In 1940, Adolf Eichmann was opposed to the granting of transit visas to Hungarian Jews because of his fear that that might limit the chances of emigration of Jews from Germany. *RLB*, Doc. 1.

3. See, for example, Ernst Wörmann's memorandum of October 19, 1940. *RLB*, Doc. 2.

4. The legal rights and interests of the Hungarian Jews living or stranded in the Third Reich were protected by the Hungarian government through the activities of Dr. Ernst (Ernő) Katinszky, a German lawyer, apparently of Hungarian background, who was appointed as a legal counselor of the Hungarian Legation in Berlin on May 12, 1926, to "represent the legal interests of the Hungarian representative bodies in the German Reich." For details on his appointment and activities in behalf of Hungarian Jews during the war see *NA*, Roll 4665/4, Serial K1509/K350109-.

5. For Luther's note of August 17, 1942, see *RLB*, Doc. 4.

6. *Ibid.*, Doc. 5.

7. *Ibid.*, Doc. 6.

8. *Ibid.*, Doc. 7.

9. See Bergmann's note of February 18, 1943, addressed to the German Legation in Budapest. *Ibid.*, Doc. 8.

10. *Ibid.*, Doc. 9. According to Luther, there were more than 530 Hungarian Jews left in the Reich, not including those in the Protectorate of Bohemia and Moravia, in October 1942, and of these 250 lived in Berlin. *Ibid.*, Doc. 73.

11. According to a note of the German Foreign Office Representative with the Reich Protector in Bohemia and Moravia, dated January 8, 1941, 1,116 Hungarian Jews lived in the Protectorate on December 20, 1940. *NA*, Roll 4664, Serial K1509/K350291-.

12. *RLB*, Doc. 10.

13. For the lists consult *NA*, Roll 4664, Serial K1509/K350960-.

14. *RLB*, Doc. 11.

15. See Thadden's letter (Inl. II A 4579) to Eichmann dated June 2, 1943. *NA*, Roll 4664, Serial K1509/K350960-.

16. See, for example, the correspondence relating to the status of a Cäcilie von Hencz, née Pordis, in *NA*, Roll 4664, Serial K1509/K350354-.

17. *Ibid.*

18. *Ibid.*

19. *RLB*, Doc. 12.

20. For the correspondence between the German Foreign Office and the German Legation in Budapest on this subject see *NA*, Roll 4355, Frames K214290-295.

21. NG-2652-E.

22. On August 7, 1943, the Hungarian Legation in Berlin lodged a complaint with the German Foreign Office to this effect (*RLB*, Doc. 13). On August 18, Thadden informed the Hungarian Legation (Inl. II A 6510) that, before any further action could be taken, specific information was needed about the cases in which the Reich Protector had allegedly refused exit visas. *NA*, Roll 4664, Serial K1509/K350792-.

23. *RLB*, Doc. 14.

24. *Ibid.*, Doc. 15. The lists may be found in *NA*, Roll 4664, Serial K1509/K350960-.

25. *RLB*, Doc. 16.

26. *NA*, Roll 4664, Serial K1509/K350960-. The document also includes the names of the nine Hungarian Jews in Theresienstadt.

27. *Ibid.* Rolf Günther, Eichmann's deputy in Berlin, intimated the possibility of the transfer in a letter to Thadden of July 10, 1943. For text of the letter see *ibid.*

28. See Eichmann's letter of November 15, 1943, in *RLB*, Doc. 17.

29. *RLB*, Doc. 18.

30. *Ibid.*, Doc. 19.

31. *NA*, Roll 4664, Serial K1509/K350291-.

32. See Veesenmayer's telegram 173 (Inl. II A 2100), *ibid.*

33. *Ibid.*

34. *RLB*, Doc. 20.

35. *Ibid.*, Doc. 27.

36. *Ibid.*, Doc. 21. See also Jenő Lévai, *Szürke könyv magyar zsidók megmentéséről* (Gray Book on the Rescuing of Hungarian Jews). (Budapest: Officina, n.d.), p. 100.

37. *Ibid.*, Doc. 22. The points outlined by Rademacher were probably formulated by Klingenfuss, whom Rademacher had asked on October 2 to prepare a position paper on the subject in anticipation of Luther's scheduled meeting with Sztójay on October 5, 1942, "to discuss the Jewish question." *NA*, Roll 4355, Frame K213392.

38. See Luther's telegram of October 8, 1942, in *RLB*, Doc. 23.

39. *Ibid.*, Doc. 24.

40. *NA*, Roll 4355, Frame K213335.

41. *RLB*, Doc. 25.

42. For the list of the Jews deported from the Netherlands in September-October 1942, see Records of Section IV B 4 (189 h) The Hague in the archives of the *Rijksinstituut voor Oorlogdocumentatie*, Amsterdam. (Cited hereafter as *Rijksinstituut.*)

43. *Ibid.*

44. *NA*, Roll 4664, Serial K1509/K350792-.

45. The countries listed in the memorandum were: Italy, Switzerland, Spain, Portugal, Denmark, Finland, Hungary, Romania, and Turkey. For the text of the memorandum, see *Rijksinstituut.*

46. *Ibid.*

47. See Luther's teletype to the German Legation in Brussels dated January 28, 1943. *RLB*, Doc. 26.

48. See von Hahn's note to G. K. Diel of February 8, 1943, in *NA*, Roll 4664, Serial K1509/K350792-.

49. See telegram of Mayr-Falkenberg of the German Legation in Brussels dated March 25, 1944, *Ibid.*, Roll 4664, Serial K1509/K350109-.

50. An instruction to the effect that the cases of Hungarian Jews in Belgium be treated in dilatory fashion was issued by Thadden on April 19, 1944. *Ibid.*

51. *RLB*, Doc. 29.

52. *Ibid.*, Doc. 28.

53. *Ibid.*, Doc. 29.

54. *Ibid.*, Doc. 30.

55. *Ibid.*, Docs. 31–32.

56. *Ibid.*, Docs. 33–34. See also Lévai, *Szürke könyv*, pp. 98–100.

57. According to a preliminary list submitted by the Hungarian Legation in Berlin on December 27, 1943, there were 13 Hungarian Jews in Drancy. *NA*, Roll 4664, Serial K1509/K350960-.

58. *Ibid.* See also *RLB*, Doc. 36.

59. *NA*, Roll 4665, Serial K1509/K350109-. Notification to this effect was sent by Rolf Günther, Eichmann's deputy in Berlin, to all interested German police agencies on June 7 with the specific instruction that the Hungarian Jews be shipped to Auschwitz. *Rijksinstituut.*

60. *RLB*, Doc. 39.

61. *Ibid.*, Docs. 40–41.

62. This list was followed by a number of smaller supplementary lists. For example, on January 25, Jäger submitted another list with the names of nine Hungarian Jews. A combined and somewhat enlarged list was submitted by both Jäger in Amsterdam and Sztójay in Berlin at the end of the month. In a note dated February 20, 1943, Eichmann's office, which received a copy of the lists, noted that seven of the people named had already been sent "for labor in the East" at the recommendation of Bene's office. *Rijksinstituut.*

63. *RLB*, Doc. 42.

64. All in all, 78 Hungarian Jews were repatriated from the Netherlands. Of these, 15 were in the transport of March 18, 7 left on May 13, 32 on August 18, 16 on August 16, and 8 on October 23. *Rijksinstituut.* For the list of the 78 Hungarian Jews, see *ibid.*

65. For the list of the 103 Hungarian Jews still living in the Netherlands early in 1943, see *NA*, Roll 4664, Serial K1509/K350792-. It is also available in *Rijksinstituut.*

66. For the list of the close to 80 Hungarian Jews in Westerbork at the time, see *ibid.*

67. For the lists of the close to 150 Hungarian Jews deported to the East and of the 78 repatriated from the Netherlands in 1943, see notes 42 and 57. See also *NA*, Roll 4664, Serial K1509/K350792-.

68. *RLB*, Doc. 43. Especially difficult was the case of 17 Jews whose Hungarian citizenship could not be immediately established. The list of these was forwarded by Bene to SS-*Sturmbannführer* Zöpf in The Hague on June 9, 1943, for action. A few of these were eventually cleared and appeared on a list forwarded by Jäger's office on August 21 with a request for the granting of repatriation permits. *Rijksinstituut.*

69. *Ibid.* For further details on the activities of the various Nazi officials in German-occupied Netherlands, see Jacob Presser, *The Destruction of the Dutch Jews* (New York: E. P. Dutton, 1969), 556 pp.

70. See Jäger's protest note of October 18, 1943, addressed to Bene. *Rijksinstituut.*

71. *Ibid.* For the lists of the Jews transferred to Buchenwald and Ravensbrück, see *Ibid.*

72. *Ibid.*

73. See Leon Poliakov and Jacques Sabille, *The Jews Under the Italian Occupation* (Paris: Centre de Documentation Juive Contemporaine, 1955), 207 pp. Also available in French, Italian, and Yiddish editions.

74. *RLB*, Doc. 44.

75. Nicholas Kállay, *Hungarian Premier. A Personal Account of a Nation's Struggle in the Second World War* (New York: Columbia University Press, 1954), p. 151.

76. *RLB*, Doc. 45.

77. Livia Rothkirchen, *The Destruction of Slovak Jewry* (Jerusalem: Yad Vashem Institute, 1961), pp. xxiii, xxv.

78. *NA*, Roll 4666, Frame K348233.

79. *Ibid.*, Frame K348237.

80. *Ibid.*, Frames K348239–240.

81. *Ibid.*, Frames K348241–248.

82. *Ibid.*, Frames K348249–250.

83. *Ibid.*, Frames K348253–255.

84. *Ibid.*, Frames K348251–252.

CHAPTER NINE

THE FIRST MASS DEPORTATION PLANS

The Initial Objective

EMBOLDENED BY the successful campaign of July–August 1941, in which some 14,000 to 18,000 "alien" Jews—including many Jewish refugees in Hungary—were forcibly "resettled" in Galicia (where most of them were subsequently slaughtered near Kamenets-Podolsk) some elements of the Hungarian radical Right had decided to try to rid the country of all its "alien" Jews. Encouraged by the Third Reich's ever greater pressure for the Final Solution, and impressed with the dejewification measures in the Nazi-occupied parts of Europe, these Right radical elements—apparently disgruntled by the failure of the official Hungarian leaders to act forcefully against the Jews—decided to take matters in their own hands.

Although these elements of the radical Right were relatively unknown and played only a secondary role in the country's military and political establishment, their position on the Jewish question had been accepted by the Nazis immediately concerned with the Final Solution as the position of "Hungarian statesmen." Notwithstanding the Hungarian government's opposition to the Final Solution, these Nazis saw the "statesmen" as the vehicle to implement their sinister designs.

The category of "alien" Jews which the Hungarian radical Right wanted to eliminate consisted basically of the following three groups: (1) The refugees, who had found a haven in Hungary from persecution in Nazi-occupied Europe and Slovakia; (2) the Jews of foreign background—mostly Galician Jews who had fled to Hungary during World War I—who had lived in Hungary for several decades but had been refused naturalization; and (3) a large percentage of the Jews inhabiting the territories acquired by Hungary during the 1938–41 period.[1] Unlike many of their brethren of Trianon Hungary, who tended toward assimilation and acculturation, a large percentage of these Jews refused to identify themselves as "Magyars of the Israelite faith" (*Izraelita-vallású magyarok*) and continued to cling to Jewish tradition.

In addition to suffering the consequences of the discriminatory anti-Jewish laws which had affected all of Hungary's Jewry since 1938, many of these "alien" Jews also suffered the crushing burden of poverty and the special police measures that were enacted against them. Nevertheless, they continued to live in relative physical safety until shortly after Hungary's entry into the war against the Soviet Union on June 27, 1941.

However, the ambiguously anti-Semitic policies of Admiral Miklós Horthy's regime led logically and inevitably toward the open, though at first only partial, adoption of the Nazi solution. Soon after the outbreak of hostilities, the idea was born to emulate the Third Reich by transcending the legal solution of the problem of the alien Jews by a physical one, which would involve their arrest, internment, and "resettlement."

This solution, at first designed for and successfully employed against only the alien Jews, came to be applied three years later against the entire provincial community with almost equal success.

The Leading Hungarian Rightists Behind the Plan

Although it is not totally clear who originated the idea for the physical solution of the question of the alien Jews, the currently available evidence reveals the prominent role played by a few high-ranking officers and political figures in the initiation of steps that led to this solution. Among the most prominent of these Germanophile high-ranking officers were Major-General József Heszlényi, Commander of the Fourth Army Corps, and Lieutenant-General Sándor Homlok, the Hungarian Military Attaché in Berlin.

There is very little verifiable biographical information on Heszlényi. In 1942, he was the head of Section III of the Ministry of Defense—in charge of supplies and procurement.[2] In this capacity he established good relations with the economic experts of the *Wehrmacht* and of the German Foreign Office, including Dr. Karl Clodius, the Deputy Chief of the Economic Policy Division. In June–July 1942, Heszlényi, as the commander of the Fourth Army Corps, which had its headquarters in Pécs, was assigned to the Second Hungarian Army, which had just been deployed in the Ukraine. His units were stationed along the Don, near Voronezh, where they were destroyed in January 1943 together with the rest of the Second Hungarian Army. After the German occupation, he was recognized by Edmund Veesenmayer, the new German Minister and Reich Plenipotentiary, as the best possible candidate for the position of Deputy Minister of Defense. Veesenmayer identified him as "one of the best officers, enjoying great prestige in the army." He emphasized the fact that Heszlényi was "unimpeacheable from the political point of view."[3]

With the deterioration of the military situation in 1944, Heszlényi was placed at the helm of the newly formed Third Army. In connection with the Jewish question, he came into prominence again in September 1944, when as commander of the Hungarian forces which occupied a part of Southern Transylvania, including Arad, he issued a series of anti-Jewish edicts. A month later, he became one of the chief supporters of Ferenc Szálasi, the leader of the Arrow Cross Party, in the coup that ousted Admiral Horthy (chapter 26). According to one account, he committed suicide on the frontier when the beaten Hungarian troops withdrew into Austria.[4]

Homlok shared Heszlényi's political views and aspirations. Born in Késmárk, near Kassa, he attended the Ludovika Military Academy and served on the Hungarian General Staff. From 1927 to 1934 he served as the Hungarian Military Attaché in Paris. In 1934, Homlok was reassigned to the General Staff, where for a while he was entrusted with the leadership of Section 5, which dealt with the military-political implications of issues before the Staff. In this capacity, he played a leading role in 1938–39 in the Hungarian drive against Carpatho-Ruthenia. In 1941, he was appointed Hungarian Military Attaché in Berlin. In his dispatches, he warned about the imminence of the Russo-German war and insisted on the necessity of Hungary's military participation on the side of the Third Reich. Following the collapse of Germany, Homlok fled to Austria, where he was liberated by the Americans. Unaware of his activities in Hungary, the Americans found him employment with the International Refugee Organization of the United Nations in Austria. In 1951, he came to the United States. From 1952 to 1956 he worked for the Hungarian National Committee (*Magyar Nemzeti Bizottmány*) in New York. He retired in 1956 and died in New York in April 1963.[5]

As the head of Section III of the Ministry of Defense, Heszlényi was in charge of supplies and procurement for the Hungarian Armed Forces. It was in this capacity that he went to Berlin early in January 1942 to discuss with the appropriate organs of the *Wehrmacht* and of the German Foreign Office Hungary's wish to acquire a share of that year's harvests in Galicia and to participate in the exploitation of the occupied territories of the Soviet Union.

The time and scope of Heszlényi's mission in Berlin were communicated to Dr. Karl Clodius. In the communication the *Wehrmacht* suggested that Hungary should not be permitted to participate in the Galician harvests and that the question of Hungary's involvement in the exploitation of the Soviet Union be treated in a dilatory fashion.[6]

Clodius himself was quite a familiar figure in Budapest, for he tended to visit Hungary frequently in connection with trade relations between the two countries.

Heszlényi's negotiations with the Germans, Clodius and Major Radtke and General Becker of the *Wehrmacht,* began on January 7. Seeing the negative attitude of the Germans toward Hungary's economic interests in the occupied areas, Heszlényi appealed to the "comradely help" of the military. This was to no avail either.[7] However, according to the summary prepared by General Becker, Heszlényi also brought up the question of the "alien" Jews in Hungary. He asserted that "Hungary wants to transfer back to Russia 12,000 Jews who have come to Hungary from Galicia during the war." Since the appropriate local German authorities refused permission for the transfer, General Becker stated that Heszlényi would be given an opportunity to discuss this matter with the appropriate authorities in Berlin.[8] Heszlényi's proposal was taken up shortly thereafter at a meeting of the "competent section of the OKW," which was also attended by the representatives of the SS and of the Foreign Office in Occupied Eastern Territories.

Though Heszlényi had acted in the name of Hungary, there is no evidence that his proposal was advanced with the knowledge or the concurrence of the Hungarian government.[9] The Germans themselves acted quite cautiously at the time. Attractive as the proposal must have appeared to the Germans, they had to shelve it for a few months—"until later in the spring—because of transportation difficulties."[10]

In the interim the Bárdossy government was replaced by the one headed by Miklós Kállay (on March 7, 1942) and the extreme-Right–inspired deportation project was temporarily allowed to lapse. But whereas Kállay followed an increasingly cautious policy, some of his military and political subordinates showed greater impatience on the Jewish question and worked clandestinely for an immediate solution. They planned to effectuate "resettlement" of the Jews in several phases, with the first installment designed to include 100,000 alien Jews.

The Revival of the Plan

About four months after the inauguration of Kállay, the initiative undertaken by Major-General Heszlényi was revived. In the interim, the new Hungarian government had crystallized its general and to a lesser extent its Jewish policies, while the Germans had decided on the Final Solution at their Wannsee Conference in Berlin; in fact, many Hungarian-speaking Jews had already perished together with their Slovakian brethren in Auschwitz.[11]

The initiative for the "resettlement" of the alien Jews was now assumed by Sándor Homlok. In a letter dated July 2, 1942, he reminded the OKW about the request submitted by Heszlényi and demanded a definitive solution.[12] Toward the end of the same month, Karl Klingenfuss, Legation Counsellor in the *Deutschland* (later *Inland*) section of the German Foreign Office, expressed his section's concurrence with Hungary's desire to get rid of its unwanted Jews and promised to look into the problem of transportation, which had prevented the implementation of the plan by the OKW in January. He also promised to investigate the feasibility of using Transnistria, the Romanian-annexed Soviet territory between the Dniester and the Bug, as the destination for the deportations from Hungary.[13] Early in August, he informed the OKW that the entire matter was being transferred for a final decision to the RSHA, Himmler's agency in overall charge of "resettlements."[14] The Romanians, who were at the time under great German pressure to solve the Jewish question in their country—pressures they courageously decided to resist—opposed the idea of transferring Hungarian Jews to the area between the Bug and Moldavia.[15] Klingenfuss, who saw in this a blessing in disguise, hastened to inform Eichmann (August 5, 1942), the man in charge of directing of transports to Auschwitz and other death camps in German-occupied Poland.[16]

The issue gathered momentum, and on September 17 Klingenfuss again communicated with Eichmann, informing him that the *Wehrmacht* representative, Major Wiesner, was anxious to have the response of the RSHA since the case was to be taken up at a conference toward the end of the same month.[17] In a letter of September 25, 1942, Eichmann, citing technical reasons, rejected the idea of mobilizing the entire deportation apparatus merely for the deportation of the Jewish refugees. He contended that it would be better to delay this action until Hungary was ready to effect the Final Solution.[18] Klingenfuss relayed this answer to the OKW on September 30.[19]

The scheme to bring about the "resettlement" of 100,000 Jews as a first installment in the solution of the Jewish question in Hungary was known not only to the higher German authorities and Generals Hesz-lényi and Homlok, but, as the evidence clearly shows, also to a number of leading Hungarian political figures. György Ottlik, a member of the influential Foreign Affairs Committee (*Külügyi Bizottság*) of the upper house and the chief editor of the German-language *Pester Lloyd* of Budapest, the semi-official organ of the government, visited Germany in the course of his West European tour of August–September 1942. Upon his return he submitted a lengthy memorandum dated October 10, 1942, to the Foreign Ministry, at the time headed by Prime Minister Kállay. Based on a three-hour conversation Ottlik had with Sztójay, the Hungarian Minister in Berlin, during the first day of his visit to the German capital, the memorandum reveals that Sztójay knew about the German decision to "solve" the Jewish question "radically" in the course of the war. Ottlik further contended that according to Sztójay only two elements were straining Hungarian-German relations: one was the Hungarian attitude toward the German *Volksgruppe* living in Hungary—a problem which was being solved. The other, to quote Sztójay's statement to Ottlik, was "the incomparably graver one, the great influence and role played by the Jews in Hungary.

The memorandum continues;

As long as this is condoned, one cannot trust the Hungarians. Sztójay consequently would find it appropriate if Hungary did not wait until [the Germans] raised this issue sharply, but would expedite the tempo of the changing of the guards and resettle a sizable portion of our Jewish population in occupied Russia. Our Minister first spoke of about 300,000[20] but then bargained himself down to 100,000. On my interjected remark he did not keep it a secret that "resettlement" meant execution.[21]

Wisliceny's Visit in Budapest

In early October 1942, *SS-Hauptsturmführer* Dieter Wisliceny, then attached to Bratislava and in charge of the deportations of the Slovak Jews, visited Budapest. In his report to Hanns Elard Ludin, the German Minister in Bratislava, dated October 8, 1942, Wisliceny states that two days earlier he was introduced to a certain Fáy, whom he identified as Kállay's personal secretary.[22] The introduction was made possible by Dr. Szarka, the Secretary of the Hungarian Chamber of Foreign Trade in Bratislava.[23]

Being involved with economic matters, Dr. Szarka probably knew and dealt with Augustín Morávek, the head of ÚHÚ (*Ústredný Hospo-*

darský Úrad; The Central Office for Economy). ÚHÚ was founded in 1940 and operated under the immediate jurisdiction of the Prime Minister of Slovakia. This agency had complete authority over the elimination of the Jews from the economic and social life of the country and the transfer of their property to Aryans. It was in Morávek's office, moreover, that the negotiations for the resettlement of the Jews of Slovakia were launched in May 1941 with the participation of Wisliceny, who was officially appointed by the Slovak authorities as "Adviser for ÚHÚ," and of Dr. Erich Gebert, the adviser to the Ministry of Economy and Finance.[24]

By the time Wisliceny paid his visit to Budapest, close to 58,000 Slovak Jews, or about 75 percent of the Jewish community, had already been deported to Auschwitz.[25] He by then clearly deserved to be called an expert on the Final Solution. Concerned with the "unsolved" question of the Jewish problem in Hungary, Dr. Szarka must have been impressed with Wisliceny's accomplishments when he introduced him to Fáy.

In his report to Ludin, Wisliceny states that immediately after lunch at the Golf Club in the Svábhegy section of Budapest on October 6, 1942, Fáy inquired about the solution of the Jewish question in Slovakia and solicited his views on the Jewish question in Hungary. Wisliceny continues:

Fáy mentioned that the existing laws were inadequate and that the concept of Jews was also not specified in sufficiently clear form. The economic dejewification was also said not to have led to the desired results. The problem was very difficult, since the Jews represented an enormous economic factor and their large number also was important. A resettlement of the Jews from Hungary, as was being carried out at this time in all Europe, could be realized only in stages [in Hungary]. Fáy asked me whether it was a fact that the Jews were being resettled out of Romania as well. I answered him that to my knowledge preparations to that effect were being made. Suddenly Fáy asked if Hungary would also be considered in a resettlement program. It was a matter of about 100,000 Jews in Carpatho-Ukraine and the territories acquired from Romania, whom Hungary would like to resettle. As a second stage, one would have to handle the [Jews in the Hungarian Plains], and finally [those in] the capital city of Budapest. I then told told him that I was in Budapest merely for private reasons and that I could not answer this question. I had no clear picture whether there were reception facilities for Hungarian Jews in the Eastern Territories.

I had the impression that Fáy had tried to make my acquaintance through Szarka and that he asked these questions on higher orders.[26]

This document is extremely important, for it not only identifies for the first time the intended composition of the first 100,000 Jews to be resettled—i.e., Jews from Carpatho-Ruthenia and Northern Transylvania—but also reveals that it was designed merely as the first of several phases of the "resettlement" program, which would ultimately lead to the Final Solution.

It is not clear whether the "resettlement" idea originated with Fáy or Szarka or some other Hungarian Nazis such as the notorious Jew-baiters László Baky, László Endre, or Baron László Vay, acting singly or in concert with the military establishment. It is safe to assume, however, that it was advanced without the knowledge or consent of Prime Minister Kállay. Wisliceny's statement to the effect that it was his impression that Fáy asked his questions "on higher orders" cannot be accepted as hard-core evidence.

Himmler's Interest in the Plan

Ludin dutifully forwarded Wisliceny's report to the German Foreign Office with a cover letter dated October 13, 1942.[27] It must have reached the RSHA shortly thereafter, for Himmler himself suddenly took a personal interest in the affair. He approached Ribbentrop in a lengthy letter dated November 30, 1942, in which he reviewed the Heszlényi offer to the OKW as expressed in the name of the Hungarian government. He further reminded him of the recent demands advanced by Hungarian statesmen for the solution of the Jewish question. Almost paraphrasing Fáy's assertion as stated in Wisliceny's report, Himmler informed Ribbentrop· that the Final Solution was envisioned to be carried out in several phases, with the first phase to involve the "evacuation" of 100,000 Jews from the eastern part of the country. He stressed that although at first he had been against a partial solution of the Jewish question in Hungary, he was now ready to assign Wisliceny, the expert responsible for clearing Slovakia of its Jews, to the German Legation in Budapest, where he could act as a "scientific adviser." Himmler further claimed that the "solution" of this "burning problem" in Hungary would undoubtedly also affect the Bulgarian and Romanian governments, inducing them to solve their respective Jewish questions as well.[28]

At Ribbentrop's request,[29] Martin Luther, then chief of the *Deutschland* Section of the German Foreign Office, instructed Dietrich von

Jagow, the German Minister in Budapest, to inquire whether the Hungarian authorities were ready to effectuate the deportation of the 100,000 alien Jews or perhaps all of the Jews of Hungary.[30] In his answer of February 18, 1943, Jagow informed the Foreign Office that he had instructed the German Military Attaché in Budapest to contact the Hungarian General Staff and ascertain whether Heszlényi and Homlok were actually empowered by the Hungarian government to make the request for the deportation of the alien Jews. Jagow's final report remains a mystery, for the archives of the German Foreign Office contain no trace of it.[31]

Although the efforts of the few elements of the extreme Right remained unsuccessful during the Kállay era, their secret dealings with the *Wehrmacht* and the RSHA and their "unauthorized" offer of 100,000 alien Jews served as a basis of the Hitler-Horthy agreement of March 18, 1944, under which 100,000 to 300,000 Hungarian Jews were made available to the Third Reich "for war production purposes."

Notes

1. Hungarians and their sympathizers understandably resentful of the Trianon and other post-World War I agreements insist that these territories were *reacquired* rather than *acquired*, since they had been part of Hungary before the war.

2. *Magyarország tiszti cim- és névtára* (Title and Name Register of Hungary) (Budapest: A Magyar Királyi Állami Nyomda for the A Magyar Királyi Központi Statisztikai Hivatal, 1942), 49:628.

3. *A Wilhelmstrasse és Magyarország. Német diplomáciai iratok Magyarországról, 1933–1944* (The Wilhelmstrasse and Hungary. German Diplomatic Papers About Hungary, 1933–1944), compiled and edited by György Ránki, Ervin Pamlényi, Loránt Tilkovszky, and Gyula Juhász. (Budapest: Kossuth, 1968), p. 847. (Referred to hereafter as *A Wilhelmstrasse és Magyarország.*) See also István Nemeskürty, *Requiem egy hadseregért* (Requiem for an Army) (Budapest: Magvető, 1974), p. 37.

4. C. A. Macartney, 2:340. However, his name was listed in 1946 among the Hungarian war criminals held by the American authorities in Germany. See letter of Major General William S. Key to Lieutenant General Sviridov, Chairman of the Allied Control Commission in Hungary, dated June 12, 1946, in *Criminals at Large*, eds. István Pintér and László Szabó (Budapest: Pannonia Press, 1961), pp. 298–99.

5. For further details on Homlok consult the index pages of the following works: *Magyarország és a második világháború* (Hungary and the Second World War), edited and compiled by László Zsigmond, Magda Ádám, Gyula Juhász, and Lajos Kerekes (Budapest: Kossuth, 1961); *A Wilhelmstrasse és Magyarország;* Elek Karsai, *A budai Sándor palotában történt* (It Happened in the Sándor Palace of Buda) (Budapest: Táncsics, 1963); and C. A. Macartney.

6. *NA*, Microcopy T-120, Roll 2563, Frames E312577-578.

7. *Ibid.*, Frames E312569-570.

8. *Ibid.*, Frames E312575-576.

9. Neither Admiral Horthy nor Prime Minister Kállay made any reference to Hesz-

lényi in their memoirs. During an interview with this author (January 26, 1956) Kállay asserted that he never even heard of Heszlényi.

10. See letter of Alfred Jodl, Chief of the OKW, addressed to the German Foreign Office (July 21, 1942). *RLB,* Doc. 46.

11. The round-up of the Jews of Slovakia began in March 1942. The first transport of 999 girls was taken to Auschwitz on March 26. By late May 1942, about 40,000 Jews had been deported from Slovakia. Livia Rothkirchen, *The Destruction of Slovak Jewry* (Jerusalem: Yad Washem, 1961), pp. xxii–xxiii.

12. *RLB,* Doc. 46.

13. *NA,* Microcopy T-120, Roll 4355, Frame K213390. For the provenance of this and subsequent references to *Inland* documents, see also *RLB,* p. xxix.

14. *NA,* Microcopy T-120, Roll 4355, Frame K213391.

15. *Ibid.,* Frames K213388-389.

16. *Ibid.*

17. *Ibid.,* Frames K213385-386.

18. *RLB,* Doc. 47.

19. *NA,* Microcopy T-120, Roll 4355, Frames K213381-382.

20. Roughly the total number of Jews in the territories acquired by Hungary during 1938–41. See chapters 4 and 5.

21. Elek Karsai, *A budai vártól a gyepűig, 1941–1945* (From the Fort of Buda to the Borderland, 1941–1945) (Budapest: Táncsics, 1965), pp. 203–6.

22. Wisliceny did not identify Fáy's first name. In a letter addressed to this author on August 25, 1971, Jenő Lévai asserted that it was Gedeon. There was in fact a Gedeon Fáy-Halász who had served in the Ministry of Foreign Affairs when Prime Minister Kállay was its head. This Fáy served in "The Minister's Cabinet" (*A miniszter kabinetje*) and his title was identified in the official register of the government as "dr. min. s. titk." (*Dr. Minisztériumi segéd titkár;* Dr. Ministerial Assistant Secretary). *Magyarország tiszti cím- és névtára,* 49 (1942):36. In 1943, he was promoted to head the Minister's Cabinet. *Magyarország és a második világháború,* p. 498.

In a letter dated November 3, 1971, Dr. Aladár Szegedy-Maszák, the former head of the Political Section of the Hungarian Foreign Ministry (1943–44), asserts that as attached to the Minister's Cabinet Fáy "was technically and administratively the personal secretary of Kállay in his capacity as Foreign Minister." According to Lévai (letter dated October 26, 1971), Fáy was transferred to the Political Section (*Politikai Osztály*) of the Foreign Ministry in March 1944. The Ministry was then headed by Prime Minister Sztójay, but was in fact led by Dr. Mihály Jungerth-Arnóthy, the Deputy Foreign Minister. Gedeon Fáy-Halász came to the United States after the war, but moved to Munich in the late 1960s.

Nicholas Nagy-Talavera claims, and Raul Hilberg assumes without providing any evidence, that the Fáy mentioned by Wisliceny was the notorious anti-Semite Baron László Vay whose name Wisliceny may have misspelled (Nicholas Nagy-Talavera, *The Green Shirts and the Others. A History of Fascism in Hungary and Rumania* [Stanford; California: Hoover Institution Press, 1970], p. 184; Raul Hilberg, *The Destruction of the European Jews* [Chicago: Quadrangle, 1961], pp. 522–23). Baron László Vay was involved with the Final Solution, but his German contact was not Wisliceny, but indirectly Martin Bormann.

A Secretary of State Fáy is also mentioned without any further identification by Lévai in his *Fekete könyv* (p. 211) as having been a member of the "Kaláka," the secret society headed by László Baky, the notorious Gendarmerie Major and Hungarian Nazi leader, who, as Secretary of State in the Ministry of the Interior in the Sztójay government, was one of the few figures chiefly responsible for the destruction of Hungarian Jewry. This society continued to meet once a week even after Baky was removed from office on September 5, 1944, partially for his role in the coup attempt against Horthy on July 7–8. The information about the "Kaláka" was provided by Baky himself in his testimony written in the Markó Street prison in Budapest in 1945.

23. Gábor Szarka served as a section head (*Főelőadó*) in the Bratislava mission of the Royal Hungarian Foreign Trade Office (*A Magyar Királyi Külkereskedelmi Hivatal*). *Magyarország tiszti cim- és névtára*, p. 323. According to Lévai (personal letter dated October 26, 1971), Szarka was transferred to Copenhagen in 1944.

24. Rothkirchen, *The Destruction of Slovak Jewry*, pp. xiv and xx.

25. *Ibid.*, p. xxv.

26. *RLB*, Doc. 74

27. *Ibid.*

28. *Ibid.*, Doc. 48.

29. The request was forwarded on December 10, 1942, by Franz Sonnleithner, a member of the Foreign Minister's personal staff. *Ibid.*, Doc. 49.

30. *Ibid.*, Doc. 50.

31. This author at least was unsuccessful in locating the document in the archives of the German Foreign Office in Bonn.

CHAPTER TEN

THE LABOR SERVICE SYSTEM

DURING THE Second World War Hungary operated a military-related labor service system with unique characteristics and objectives. This system encompassed hundreds of thousands of men of military age classified as "unreliable" and thus deemed unfit to bear arms. These men were organized into military formations under the command of Hungarian Army officers, were supplied with tools, and were employed primarily in construction, road building, and fortification work for the military within Hungary and in many Hungarian and German-occupied parts of the Ukraine and Yugoslavia. Although the system was originally intended for all "unreliables" (including Romanians, Serbs, Slovaks, and Communists) it was used primarily as an anti-Jewish measure.

Antecedents

The labor service system (*munkaszolgálat*) in Hungary can be traced back to the practices of the counterrevolutionary regime that was established soon after the crushing of the proletarian dictatorship of Béla Kun in 1919. The idea of establishing special labor service units for those deemed politically "unreliable" for regular military service originated with a group of officers headquartered in the then French-occupied city of Szeged. Led by Admiral Miklós Horthy, who later became the Regent of Hungary, this group was motivated by the so-called "Szeged Idea" (chapter 1) and supported by the many superpatriotic and secret organizations that flourished in the 1920's.

As early as August 21, 1919, when Budapest was still under Romanian occupation, Horthy, who was then the commander-in-chief of the counterrevolutionary "national army" (*nemzeti hadsereg*), recommended that the organized workers be excluded from the newly planned army as "unreliable" elements. By November, this restriction was suggested for the Jews as well.[1]

During the fall of 1919, elements associated with both the Supreme

Command (*Fővezérség*) and the Ministry of War (*Hadügyminisztérium*)[2] proposed plans to establish special units, variously referred to as "labor detachments" or as "labor formations" (*munkásalakulatok*) for politically unreliable men of military age. The "unreliables," it was envisioned, would perform their military duty as labor servicemen without the right to bear arms. The proposals also anticipated many of the practices that were actually put into effect during World War II, including the wearing of civilian clothes instead of uniforms and of special arm bands to distinguish the men from the other recruits.

The first labor detachments were set up, under the instructions of Horthy, on December 6, 1919. He decreed the initial establishment of 40 labor detachments with 6,000 "interned political prisoners" to be employed under the command of "suitable and energetic" officers. The labor detachments were envisioned to include from 100 to 200 men each and employed in "an orderly and competent manner on public projects of urgent national interest."[3]

Hungary was the first country in interwar Europe in which the Jewish question was handled in an institutional fashion. Preceding the anti-Jewish legislative program of the Nazi era, Hungary adopted in September 1920 a flagrantly discriminatory act (the *Numerus Clausus* Act), whose impact transcended its original objectives. Purportedly designed to decrease the proportion of Jews in higher education, it indirectly led to the initiation of anti-Jewish measures in other fields as well. Within the military establishment, the Jewish question was first raised by Minister of Defense Sándor Belitska at the February 8, 1921, meeting of the Teleki government. The major issue that he put before the Cabinet was whether the Jews should perform their military obligations in separate detachments or intermixed with the other troops. His personal view was that the Jews be placed in separate detachments, but within the framework of the regular military units.[4]

The Jewish question was not officially raised during the premiership of Count István Bethlen (April 14, 1921–August 24, 1931) or that of Count Gyula Károlyi (August 24, 1931–October 1, 1932), though Jews were subtly and consistently discriminated against in a series of fields, including the higher echelons of the civil service and the military. The openly rightist orientation of Hungary began with Károlyi's successor, Gyula Gömbös. It was during his era (October 1, 1932–October 6, 1936) that Hungary's policies were oriented toward the Third Reich, through which the Hungarian revisionists had hoped to vindicate the injustices of Trianon. Although Gömbös was one of the chief authors and representatives of the Szeged Idea, the fruition of his policies was not clearly discernible until 1938.

The Legal Basis for the Labor Service System

The dramatic political and diplomatic maneuvers and military actions undertaken in 1938 reflected not only the ascendancy of the Nazi influence in Europe, but also the beginning of the frontal assault on the Versailles Treaty and its corollary arrangements. Almost simultaneously with the Anschluss, Hungary began to openly emulate the Third Reich both in the military and the anti-Jewish spheres. The systematic drive for the modernization and expansion of the Hungarian armed forces and for the restriction of the rights of the Jews was launched by Prime Minister Kálmán Darányi in his Győr speech of March 5, 1938 (chapter 4). The first major anti-Jewish law "for the more effective balancing of the social and economic life" of the country was adopted two months later and with it there began the systematic, institutionalized restriction of the rights of the Jews as citizens, a process which six years later culminated in their destruction.

Hungary's drive for revising the "injustices of Trianon" and for modernizing and expanding its armed forces received a boost later in August. During his state visit to Germany, Admiral Horthy was alerted about the Führer's plan to "solve" the Czechoslovak issue and was presumably also encouraged to make certain military contingency plans, including the modernization of the army.[5] Concurrently with Horthy's visit in Germany, Hungary also signed an agreement with the members of the Little Entente under which the signatories agreed not to use force as a means for settling disputes and Hungary was given the right to rearm (chapter 5). A little more than two months later, Hungary was enabled to incorporate the Magyar-inhabited southern parts of Slovakia—the Upper Province (Felvidék)—under the First Vienna Award (chapter 6).

Since it soon became apparent that the Munich Agreement had not really ended the Czechoslovak crisis by "solving" the issue of the Sudetenland, and had in fact made the oncoming war inevitable by encouraging Nazi aggression, the revisionist forces in Hungary began to implement their plans for marshaling the country's military and economic resources. In was in pursuit of this objective that on December 7, 1938, Minister of Defense Károly Bartha introduced into the lower house a comprehensive draft law relating to national defense (*honvédelem*). The justification for the law emphasized that as a matter of general principle, in times of war or threat of war, every citizen was obliged to defend the homeland through his personal service and property.

Adopted as Law No. II:1939,[6] the legislation regulated all facets of the national defense system, including the structure and functions of the Highest National Defense Council (*Legfelső Honvédelmi Tanács*), the paramilitary *Levente* system, and the military service and air defense systems. Although it was obviously not specifically directed against the Jews (the Second Anti-Jewish Law was then being drafted), some of its provisions were subsequently used as the legal basis for the introduction of the compulsory labor service system and as judicial justification for the draconic measures that were adopted during the German occupation. Among the more important provisions in this respect were those included in Article 141, which gave the government extraordinary emergency powers in times of war or threat of war, and in Articles 87–94, which stipulated that all persons between the ages of 14 and 70 were liable to work for the defense of the nation to the limit of their physical and mental capacities.

The legal basis for the labor service system was provided by Article 230. According to its first paragraph, all Hungarian citizens of 21 years of age who were classified as permanently unsuitable for military service could be compelled to engage in "public labor service" (*közérdekű munkaszolgálat*) in special labor camps for a period not exceeding three months at a time. The original intent and scope of the labor service system could not be immediately discerned. On the surface, they were not exclusively or even necessarily discriminatory in nature, for those conscripted into this service were envisioned to receive the same pay, clothing, and rations as those in the armed forces. As it turned out, however, they reflected the practices of the early Horthy era, when the "unreliables," including of course the Communists and the Jews, had been systematically excluded from the military. This was, indeed, one of the primary though unstated objectives of the law. It was used for the exclusion from the military of all potentially "unreliable" elements, which in the late 1930s also included some of the national minorities (Romanians, Serbs, and Slovaks), and, in the case of the Jews at least, for their gradual elimination from the country's socioeconomic life. The strictly military goals of the system were basically of only secondary importance.

The Attitude of the Ministry of Defense

The details for the implementation of Article 230 were left to be worked out by the Ministry of Defense. The work of the Ministry was complicated by the fact that the Hungarian Parliament was at the time discussing the draft of the Second Anti-Jewish Law. Article 5 of this piece of legislation prohibited Jews from occupying any official position at either the central or the local state level. The provision also pertained, of course, to the officials and officers associated with the armed forces, however small their number at the time.

The Ministry of Defense was eager to clarify the impact of the Second Anti-Jewish Law on the armed forces and to crystallize its own position on the Jewish question. A meeting on this matter was held on March 31, 1939. Participating in it were the leading figures of the military establishment. The agenda was identified on the invitation sent out two days earlier and included the following items:

- Who was to be considered a Jew in principle?
- Who was to be considered a Jew individually, i.e., among the officers, cadets, those in active service, and in the reserves?
- What would be the procedures for the determination of the identity of the Jews?
- What would be the procedures for the establishment of lists of Jews arranged by categories in the armed forces? [7]

The participants accepted the definition of a Jew provided by the draft of the Second Anti-Jewish Law with the proviso that it would be made further restrictive for career officers. They failed, however, to deal with the question of reserve officers and could not agree on the evaluation of high military decorations or on whether or not to retain Jews in regular military service. With respect to the latter, three major ideas were aired. Colonel Imre Németh, the head of the Presidential Section of the Ministry, proposed that Jews be grouped in separate companies and assigned to the fighting troops under strict supervision and command. Colonel Dezső László of the General Staff suggested that the Jews be placed into special units and deployed in front of the Christian detachments. The Minister of Defense argued that the Jews be placed in special labor companies. Although the overwhelming majority of those present were inclined to retain the Jews in fighting units as envisioned under the first two proposals, the ultimate decision was postponed until a statistical breakdown could be prepared on the Jews in the armed forces, especially the officers' corps. There was general consensus about the necessity of checking the background of each com-missioned and noncommissioned[8] officer and to dismiss from active service all those identified as Jews under the anti-Jewish laws in effect. Exception was to be made only for those who had earned certain high medals or decorations for bravery in battle during World War I.[9]

On April 4, 1939, the Presidential Section of the Ministry prepared its own proposals. In addition to the recommendations listed above, it proposed that no Jews be admitted into the officers' training schools and that Jewish recruits be allowed to bear arms, for otherwise Jewish blood would be saved at the expense of the Christians. These troops were to be intermixed with the Christian units, because if they were to be placed into segregated units, "they could surrender more easily, es-cape to the enemy, or commit treason."

The position paper of the Presidential Section also included the sta-tistical breakdown on the proportion of Jews in the armed forces. There were absolutely no full Jews in the active, professional commis-sioned officers' corps. The armed forces as a whole, which at the time numbered 102,007, included 2,292 Jews, or 2.24 percent. There were 9 Jews among the 6,153 noncommissioned career officers, 2 Jews among the 5,415 reenlisted noncommissioned officers, 30 Jews among the 10,669 regular noncommissioned (*sortisztes*) officers, 1,101 Jews among the 31,594 draftees without rank serving their second or third year, and 1,150 Jews among the 48,176 new recruits.[10]

Finally, the position paper specified the procedures to be employed in the determination of the racial and religious background of those as-sociated with the armed forces, and identified the documents required for submission for this purpose. It was envisioned that each member of the armed forces would submit not only his birth or baptism certificate, but also those of his parents and four grandparents.[11]

The Ministry of Defense held its second meeting on the solution of the Jewish question within the armed forces on April 5. Once again, the participants could not agree on the status of the Jews in the armed forces. Henrik Werth, the Chief of Staff, suggested that they be al-lowed to bear arms, but in separate closed units under the command of Christian officers—"they should not receive any indulgent assign-ments." Hugó Sónyi, the commander-in-chief of the Hungarian Armed Forces, argued that the Jews be placed in separate and closed labor units and not be allowed to bear arms—or "they would for decades have the opportunity to corrupt" members of the Christian community. János Pruzsinszky, the head of the Civilian Section, stated that the German pattern of total exclusion was inapplicable in Hungary because it might induce Christians to convert to Judaism to avoid the draft. He further claimed that the general national interests demanded that the Jews be required to bear arms, for otherwise only Christians would spill their blood in times of war. The Minister of Defense retorted that "diseases can also cause losses" and suggested that the Jews be placed in labor units. Those unfit for labor, the Minister continued, were to be placed under strict supervision and discipline in special internment camps.

There was also a voice of civility and reason among the participants. General Árpád Ambrózy, the judge-advocate, pointed out in response to the above positions that in the course of his career as a judge he had not come across a single case in which Jews had actually neglected their duties. He reminded the participants that if the Jews were not permitted to serve in the armed forces, the Christians would not tolerate this inherent injustice.[12]

On the basis of these discussions, the Presidential Section on April 12 prepared its own specific proposals for the implementation of the anti-Jewish laws within the armed forces, which were adopted with minor changes by the Leadership Conference (*Vezetőségi Értekezlet*) of the Ministry on May 15. Accordingly, commissioned officers and their spouses were required to prove that all four of their grandparents had been Christians. Noncommissioned officers had only to prove their parents were Christian. Jewish retired officers were allowed to retain their rank, but could not receive combat assignments when recalled to service or in times of mobilization.[13] No agreement was reached on whether or not Jews were to be permitted to bear arms. The issue was discussed in a series of other meetings in the Ministry and the General Staff during the summer of 1939.

A decision on the implementation of the anti-Jewish laws in the armed forces was finally reached late in the summer and detailed in the instructions of the Minister of Defense dated September 23, 1939. Referring to Article 5 of the Second Anti-Jewish Law, the instructions stated that no Jews could from that time on acquire the rank of commissioned or noncommissioned officer. The Jews found suitable to bear arms were to be distributed proportionately among the combat troops. Those found unfit to bear arms were to be placed in special labor service units. In neither case could they be assigned to intelligence units, hold any desk or office jobs, or be employed as messengers or warehouse workers. Moreover, no concessions or special allow-

ances for Jews in the armed forces or the labor service system were to
be authorized by the lower echelons without the prior approval of the
Ministry.[14]

Organization of
the Labor Service System

The general principles underlying the objectives of the labor service
system as well as the provisions relating to its organization, structure,
and administration were incorporated in Decree No. 5070/1939. M.E.
of the Council of the Ministers which was signed by Prime Minister Pál
Teleki on May 12.[15]

Based upon the provisions of Article 230 of Law No. II:1939, the
Decree stipulated that the primary objectives of the labor service system
were to:

- Train or retrain the youths recruited for labor service in accordance with their aptitudes.
- Employ those in the service to satisfy the needs of the armed
forces and to meet the requirements of defense work.
- Utilize them for any other work of public interest with the approval of the Ministry.

Under the Decree, the recruitment agencies had the responsibility of
determining whether the recruits were fit for armed service, labor service, or neither. Those selected for labor service were to serve for a period not exceeding three months at a time in special labor camps which
were identified as "militarily organized worker units." The number, character, and internal organization and supply of the camps were to be determined by the Minister of Defense, who (through the particular army
corps command) also had jurisdiction over matters of command, discipline, training, and specific organizational details. He exercised supreme command over the labor camps through the National Superintendent of the Public Labor Service System (*A Közérdekű Munkaszolgálat Országos Felügyelője—KMOF*). The latter was appointed by the
Head of State from among the generals of the armed forces upon
the recommendation of the Minister.[16]

The labor service system went into effect on July 1, 1939. Among the
first to be called up for labor service were those born in 1916 who had
previously been classified as unfit to bear arms. From the operational
point of view, it was not very different from the system in effect in the
Honvédség as a whole. The labor servicemen (*munkaszolgálatosok*)[17] had

to report to their local recruitment centers. Following the usual check-up and classification, they were assigned to camps which operated within the framework of labor battalions (*közérdekű munkaszolgálatos zászlóaljak*) under the jurisdiction of the eight army corps commands (*hadtest parancsnokságok*) in existence at the time. The recruits were grouped into companies (*századok*) which usually consisted of 200 to 250 men, and within each company they were subdivided into platoons (*szakaszok*). In many cases the platoons were divided into squads (*rajok*). The companies, in turn, were functionally grouped into, and operated under the immediate control of, the battalions. Instead of rifles, the labor servicemen acquired the shovel and the pickax as their "standard weapons."

They had to address their officers in the traditional fashion, using their rank. Guards had to be addressed as "Mr. Instructor" (*Oktató Úr*). The labor battalions that were set up in July 1939 are as shown in table 10.1.

Following the reacquisition of Northern Transylvania from Romania (August–September 1940) and of the Bácska and Baranya regions from Yugoslavia (April 1941), the number of army corps was increased to nine (see map 13.1) and the headquarters of some of the labor battalions were shifted. In March 1943, the headquarters of Labor Battalions III and VI were in Kőszeg and Püspökladány, respectively. Labor

TABLE 10.1.
LABOR BATTALIONS, JULY 1939

Army Corps No. and Headquarters	Labor Battalion No. and Headquarters	
I. Budapest	I. Budapest	Invalids' House (Soroksár Street)
	IX. Esztergom	Kenyérmező camp
II. Székesfehérvár	II. Komárom	Fort No. II.
III. Szombathely	III. Pápa	Cavalry barracks
IV. Pécs	IV. Mohács	
V. Szeged	V. Hódmezővásárhely	
VI. Debrecen	VI. Hajdubőszőrmény	
VII. Miskolc	VII. Pétervásár	
VIII. Kassa	VIII. Kassa	Zrinyi Miklós Street Barracks

SOURCE: *Magyarország tiszti cim- és névtára* (Title and Name Register of Hungary). (Budapest: A Magyar Királyi Állami Nyomda, Vol. IL, 1942), p. 631, and *FAA*, 1:84–85.

Battalion X, with headquarters in Nagybánya, was attached to the new Army Corps IX, with headquarters in Kolozsvár. Finally, Labor Battalion XI, with headquarters in Rimaszombat, was attached to Army Corps VII; and battalion XII, headquartered in Tasnád, was attached to Army Corps IX.[18]

The labor service system operated under the central control and guidance of KMOF as the head of a special division in the Ministry of Defense. Specifically, KMOF was empowered to:

- Deal with all matters of principle relating to the system.
- Assure the central administration of the labor camps.
- Prepare the draft legislation relating to the effective operation of the system.
- Deal with matters relating to the mobilization of the labor force.
- Study the labor service system of other countries.
- Handle all personnel matters affecting the system.
- Prepare the budget for the effective operation of the system.[19]

According to the estimates of the Ministry of Defense, annually about 20,000 of the 90,000 recruits would be selected for labor service. Of these, only about 6,000 would, by virtue of their training and experience, be fit for industrial labor; the remainder, it was envisioned, would be used for "mass labor" in the fields and forests or in road building.

Although the military labor service system differentiated between two types of draftees, with one group clearly if not explicitly viewed as composed primarily of "unreliable" elements, in 1939 the system was not exclusively anti-Jewish or even totally discriminatory in character. At the time, the treatment of both groups in terms of pay, discipline, and board was basically the same. They were also on a par in terms of family assistance and welfare benefits for the disabled. The only difference in uniform was that those assigned to labor service (*munkaszolgálat*) had an "M" made of green fabric sewn on their lapel. Moreover, the labor servicemen deployed in the summer and fall of 1939 were in fact allocated by KMOF to various useful military and civilian public projects.[20]

The Transitional Phase

Although the instructions issued by the Minister of Defense on September 23, 1939, were designed to enforce the anti-Jewish laws within the armed forces, the status of the Jews in both the military and the labor service systems remained fundamentally unchanged until April 1941. The pressures that were periodically advanced by the General Staff and by the radical rightist elements for the further exacerbation of the anti-Jewish measures within the armed forces remained basically unheeded. It was only after Hungary's involvement in the war against Yugoslavia that the labor service system was revamped and the status of the Jews changed radically.

The successes of the *Wehrmacht* in Poland in September 1939 and in Western Europe in April–May 1940 apparently convinced the Germanophile General Staff that the Third Reich was bound to win the war. Not by accident, in the midst of these military triumphs Henrik Werth, the Chief of Staff, urged Bartha to bring about further restrictions against the Jews. In a memorandum of April 18, 1940, Werth raised a number of questions concerning the status of the Jews in the military and the attitude to be adopted toward them in the case of a general mobilization. He then summarized his earlier recommendations, emphasizing that:

- The Jewish question should be solved within the armed forces in a radical and urgent manner by internal administrative means and independently of the political line of the government.
- The Jews should be compelled to do military and technical labor in areas where the losses of blood were the greatest.
- Jews should be prevented from acquiring the status of commissioned or noncommissioned officers in the reserve.
- Jews, with the exception of family heads, should not be classified as special, second-line reservists.
- Jews should not be assigned to home units or noncombat units abroad, or be employed in offices or as messengers.
- Jewish reserve officers, with the exception of those who had earned certain high decorations, should be deprived of their rank.
- The Jews qualified to bear arms should be distributed proportionately in all service units with the exception of the air force, the intelligence services, and the armored and border units.
- Jews should not be permitted to retain their civilian occupations lest they take all the profits away from Christians, and in the military they should be assigned so as to prevent the possibility of their minimizing their losses.[21]

Although these proposals had fallen on many sympathetic ears in the Ministry, they could not be implemented; at the time Hungary was concerned with the possibility of imminent open conflict with Romania over the issue of Transylvania. The Jews represented a considerable proportion of the physicians, veterinarians, pharmacists, engineers, and licensed motor vehicle drivers desperately needed by the armed forces. The General Staff itself complained on April 15 that many of the military and labor service units were unfit for deployment because of the lack of professionals. These problems were discussed in the Ministry of Defense on April 12 and July 9. At the latter meeting, it was decided that the Jewish professionals would be assigned to military positions commensurate with their civilian status, but could acquire no leadership position as commanders. The Jewish drivers were to be employed in an auxiliary capacity as driver aides. All Jews who were not used or found unsuitable for service in the armed forces were to be placed in "special labor companies" (különleges munkásszázadok).[22] These exclusively Jewish companies, like the regular public labor service companies, were placed under the command of Christian officers and staff. Jewish officers assigned to these labor companies could serve until the middle of 1941 as platoon or squad commanders only.

Consonant with the general rearmament and mobilization program that was pursued in the summer of 1940, the special labor service companies were also brought up to war strength. By July 17, there were 60 such companies in operation and the plans called for their increase to 90 to 100 within a short time.[23]

The mobilization of the Jews for labor service was urged particularly by the General Staff. Such mobilization, in its view, would not only serve the interests of the military, but would also "preclude the Jews from engaging in any nefarious activities in the hinterland" and reassure the Hungarian population about Jewry assuming its share in the war or the burdens of mobilization.[24]

The general deployment of the Jews for labor was regulated by the Ministry of Defense on August 23, 1940, at the height of the Hungarian-Romanian crisis. Based upon an earlier decision of the Highest National Defense Council, the secret decree of the Ministry[25] stipulated that all Jews—not only veterans—were to be called up for labor, classified, and assigned in terms of their age and health. Those in the lower age groups and the healthy were to be placed in "Jewish field labor companies" (tábori zsidó munkásszázadok); older and weaker Jews, suitable only for auxiliary service, were to be placed in "inland Jewish labor companies" (honi zsidó munkásszázadok).[26] Those who might fall ill in either of these companies were to be placed in "Jewish convalescent hospital labor companies" (*lábbadozó korházi zsidó munkás-századok*). Under the secret decree, those in the 25 to 42 age group were to be called up first and to be followed by those between 43 and 48, and eventually by those of 49 to 60.

In 1940, the Jewish labor companies were employed in a series of projects of interest to the military. Many of them were sent to clear the woods—especially along the frontier with Romania. Others were employed in road construction, the dredging and clearing of rivers, the unloading of freight at train yards, and the building and maintenance of airfields. Jewish labor servicemen were occasionally also allocated for work on large estates. The conditions of labor were still quite tolerable and a considerable number of labor servicemen enjoyed certain privileges that were quite remarkable given the general anti-Semitic climate at the time. For example, Jews working in labor companies stationed near their homes or those of friends and relatives were permitted to eat and sleep away from the company. Many of the richer Jews, moreover, managed to either "buy" their way out of the service or, if recruited, to free themselves of "dirty work" by paying poorer comrades.

The status of the labor service system changed for the worse shortly after the reannexation of Northern Transylvania. The domestic and foreign policies of the Teleki government took a sharp turn to the right in response to internal political pressure and the general realization that the country's further revisionist ambitions could be achieved only in close cooperation with the Third Reich. The need for closer alliance with the Germans and emulation of their anti-Jewish policies was articulated persuasively by the new Party of Hungarian Renewal (*Magyar Megújulás Pártja*), which was formed by Imrédy and his close followers who seceded from the Government Party. Reacting to these pressures, Teleki announced on October 8, 1940, that he would soon introduce a new anti-Jewish draft law which would be "clear, radical and simple, without the complications and loopholes for evasion of its predecessors." The following month, Hungary became the first country to adhere to the Tripartite Pact.

These policies were bound to affect the status of the Jews in the labor service system as well. One of the first measures adopted during this period was the dismissal of a large number of Jewish soldiers who had participated in the reoccupation of Northern Transylvania. Many of these were subsequently assigned to the labor service companies. Horthy's original idea was to demobilize and dismiss the Jewish soldiers and officers from the armed forces. However, the Council of Ministers apparently overruled him, and the Jews of military age were subsequently placed in labor camps, where at first they were mostly employed in lumber exploitation.²⁷ Others, especially the professionals and those with technical expertise, were reassigned within the various branches of the armed forces, according to their age and skills.²⁸ However, in accordance with an earlier instruction of the Minister of Defense dated September 14, they could not be assigned to certain positions or units which were identified as "protected" (*védett*), i.e., restricted to Christians only.²⁹

Shortly after Teleki's announcement about the planned third, openly racial, anti-Jewish law, the Ministry of Defense began to deliberate its possible contribution to the formulation of the final provisions of the draft legislation and their application within the armed forces. At a meeting on November 5, the representatives of the various divisions in the Ministry adopted the following major guidelines:

- Jewish youth should be removed from the *Levente* paramilitary organization and assigned to perform "preparatory field labor service." (*tábori munkaszolgálatos előképzés*).
- Jews of draft age should be used within the armed forces, but not for military service.
- Means should be found for advancing the emigration of the Jews.
- Preferably, Jews should not be allowed to continue in their civilian professions.
- Upon discharge from labor service, Jews should be rehired by their former employers only to the extent that this would not cause the firms to exceed the maximum employment of Jews allowed by the laws in effect.
- The military criminal code should be applicable to Jews in most cases even when they were not formally associated with the armed forces.³⁰

The representatives of some of the ministerial sections—and especially those of the General Staff—suggested the adoption of even sterner measures, including the total dejewification of the armed forces and the restriction of the Jews to labor service exclusively. As an immediate measure Werth advocated that the status of the reserve officers and officials be settled in an administrative fashion within the Ministry. He suggested that they be dismissed from the services, including the gendarmerie, by March 31, 1940, and be transferred to the labor service units. His views were generally supported by the heads of the various other divisions in the Ministry. Lieutenant Colonel Ferenc Bardóczy, the head of Section 8, for example, championed the position of the Chief of Staff by arguing in "ethical" terms that the retention of Jews as officers or officials was in conflict with the provisions of the Second Anti-Jewish Law, which demoted the Jews to second-class citizenship. Since under the law the Jews were now of low social status, it was all but impossible "ethically" to allow them to retain their rank. Neither the military nor the civilian population could extend them the honor that was normally due to officers and people of rank.[31] Concurrently, the various sections of the Ministry were also discussing a series of other issues raised by the planned third anti-Jewish act. On these, too, it was the General Staff which took the most extreme position, advocating the sternest measures possible. While Bartha suggested that the legislative proposals of the Ministry be formulated so as to make certain exemptions possible for Jewish veterans who had earned high awards and decorations, Colonel Iván Hindy, head of the ministerial section dealing with matters of discipline and honor, insisted that no differences be made between one Jew and another. He argued against any exemptions and insisted that the only way to solve the Jewish question within the armed forces was by following the total dejewification approach.[32]

The views advocated by the military extremists were echoed by the representatives of the Right radical parties during the parliamentary debates of November 1940. Particularly vicious in their demands were the deputies of the Arrow Cross Party. Jenő Szőllősi, for example, urged that the Jews be kept in camps removed from the villages to protect the rural population from being morally corrupted. Sándor Gosztonyi suggested that unemployed Christians be employed on public works projects and that the Jews be made responsible for their remuneration. He apparently aimed at solving the two major social issues confronting the nation—umemployment and "the privileged positions of the Jews"—in a complementary fashion. Tamás Matolcsy demanded that the Jews be placed in internment rather than labor camps, while his younger brother, Mátyás Matolcsy, a rabid anti-Semitic journalist, insisted that "Jewry must leave this country and this earth."[33]

Szőllősi's demands were echoed by László Endre in his letter of November 5 addressed to Prime Minister Teleki. The Deputy Prefect of Pest-Pilis-Solt-Kiskun County, who was later to emerge as the person chiefly responsible among the Hungarians for the destruction of Hungarian Jewry, echoed the Nazi racial views about the necessity of preserving the purity of Christian blood. He warned the Prime Minister about the danger represented by the Jewish labor servicemen in the villages who were "seducing" the Christian girls and called for appropriate precautionary measures. Endre's letter was forwarded to the Ministry of Defense where the appropriate action was taken. László Baky, the other Hungarian official chiefly responsible for the destruction of Hungarian Jewry, also advanced Nazi-type racial theories in the lower house, arguing that the separation of the Jews was necessary because they were harmful to the body politic.[34]

During the November 1940 session of Parliament the first demands were advanced to have the Jewish labor servicemen wear a yellow arm band rather than the national colors.[35] Such a proposal was also advanced by the General Staff. But since many of the 52,000 Jews in the 260 special labor service companies in existence at the time were scheduled for demobilization, this scheme was temporarily shelved.[36]

Although the specifically discriminatory character of the Jewish labor service system was not formally decreed until the middle of April 1941, there were clearly visible signs by the end of 1940. At this time many of the Jews in the labor service companies were illegally deprived of their uniforms and compelled to perform their duties in their own civilian clothes. On December 2, the Jews were placed in so-called "mixed"—exclusively Jewish—labor companies (*vegyes munkásszázadok*), separated from other, mostly leftist, "unreliable" elements unfit to bear arms.[37] Most of these discriminatory measures had no legal basis and were enacted as "internal administrative measures."

The New Regulation of the Jewish Labor Service System

Since the Ministry of Justice, which was in charge of the preparation of the Third Anti-Jewish Act, could not be specific about its legislative timetable, the Ministry of Defense decided to proceed on its own to provide a definitive "legal" basis for the regulation of the Jewish labor service system under its jurisdiction. It relied on Article 141 of Law No. II:1939, which gave the government emergency powers in times of war or threat of war. Early in 1941, it prepared a draft decree which aimed to clarify the status of Jewish career officers. Another major objective of the draft was to provide a legal framework for the draft-aged Jews not in active service at the time (*nemhivatásos állományú zsidók*) to fulfill their military obligations in exclusively auxiliary units without ranks or the right to bear arms. The authors of the draft used the provisions of the Second Anti-Jewish Law to define who was a Jew.

Following the concurrence of the Ministry of Justice, the draft was accepted by the Council of Ministers and issued on April 16 as Decree No. 2870/1941. M.E. over the signature of Prime Minister László Bárdossy.[38]

The implications of the brief Decree were immediately recognized by the leaders of the Jewish community, who urged Bárdossy and the government not to implement it. In their memorandum of April 23, they argued that the Decree not only deprived Jews of the right to fight with weapons in their hands, but also hurt the self-esteem of all those who had attained a rank in their military career. They reminded the governmental leaders that 20,000 Jews had fought with honor in the 1848–49 war for independence and that 10,000 Jews had died for the fatherland during World War I. The memorandum also included a number of affidavits from Hungarian dignitaries and high-ranking officers testifying to the positive attitude of the Jews during World War I.[39] Needless to say, in the anti-Semitic climate of the time, the appeal of the Jews went unheeded.

The country was in the midst of the euphoria associated with the successful military campaign against Yugoslavia and the reacquisition of the Bácska and Baranya region. The gratitude felt for the assistance of the Germans was expressed by demands for the emulation of the Third Reich in the adoption of further anti-Jewish measures. In the course of time, these became ever louder and more insistent. In fact, one day after the Jewish leaders submitted their memorandum, Bárdossy made his maiden parliamentary speech as Premier, in which he outlined the plans for a new and more radical anti-Jewish program. Shortly thereafter the drive began against the so-called "alien" Jews, which culminated in their deportation and destruction by the end of August (chapter 6).

The forebodings of the Jewish leaders about the implications of the Decree were fully substantiated on August 19, when the Ministry of Defense issued an order (No. 27 300. eln. 8.-1941) for its implementation. It was under the provisions of this order that the Ministry regulated all aspects of the new "auxiliary service" (*kisegitő szolgálat*) system, which affected all Jews of military age.[40] Like the soldiers in uniform, the recruits assigned to the auxiliary labor service units were obliged to serve for two years. Only those who were exempted under the existing laws were excluded.[41]

The Jewish officers were finally deprived of their rank[42] and practically all of those still liable for service were compelled from that time on to serve as ordinary auxiliary labor servicemen.[43] Their "officer's discharge certificates" (*emléklapok*) were recalled and replaced with new ones which no longer identified their ranks. These new certificates, like the corresponding sections of the military registers in which they were entered, were stamped, in clear emulation of the Nazi practice, with the letters "Zs" (*Zsidó:* Jew). Interestingly enough, however, in spite of the many legislative and administrative measures enacted against Jewish officers, there were still 129 officers in active service in May 1942. These were identified as of Jewish background under the existing laws and were mostly serving at the headquarters of the army corps.[44]

The Labor Service in Wartime

When the order was issued, Hungary had already been at war with the Soviet Union for almost two months. During these first few months of hostilities, many of the field labor service companies were assigned to repair and maintain the roads and bridges connecting the inland with the Hungarian-occupied parts of the Ukraine. Much of the work was along the Carpathian passes.

The condition of the Jewish labor servicemen changed from bad to worse in the course of the war. This was reflected not only by the more aggressive anti-Semitic attitude of many of the commissioned and non-commissioned officers and guards attached to the field companies, but also by the increasingly blatant discriminatory treatment of the Jews as servicemen. They were, among other things, gradually deprived of their uniform and compelled to wear the discriminatory yellow and white arm bands, which identified them as open targets for abuse.

Uniforms and Clothing. The Jewish labor servicemen were still permitted to wear their military uniforms, but without any insignias or signs of rank. In fact, during the first years of the labor service system, practically all of the labor servicemen—including those sent to the Ukraine soon after the outbreak of hostilities in June 1941—wore military uniforms and army boots. Like the regular personnel—and this was true throughout the war—they had to carry standard documents and identification on their persons at all times, including the pay-book (*zsold-könyv*), which also served as an identification document, (see fig. 10.1), and the dog tag (*dögcédula;* fig. 10.2). The armed forces used the same forms for both arm-bearing and labor servicemen for all service-related functions, including call-up, discharge, and furlough.

In the general anti-Jewish climate of the time, the sight of uniform-wearing Jews evoked great consternation not only among the Germans,

Figure 10.1.
Front and first two inside pages of the paybook and identification document (*zsoldkönyv*).

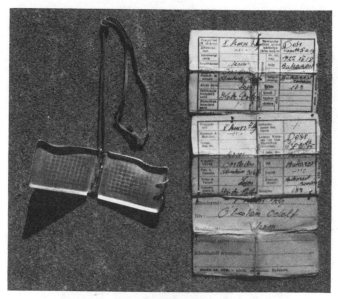

Figure 10.2.
Dogtag (*dögcédula*) normally worn around the neck.

but also among the anti-Semitic Hungarian officers and soldiers. On December 18, 1941, after he had seen uniformed Jewish labor servicemen in Vinnitsa, the Chief of Staff himself complained to the Minister of Defense. In his view, the practice spoiled the good reputation of the armed forces and irritated the Germans. However, in several internal and field units, the Jewish labor servicemen had already been deprived of their uniforms and compelled to wear their own civilian clothes. The excuse used by the local military authorities in these cases was a shortage of uniforms.

Citing this excuse and the standard arguments against Jews wearing uniforms, some elements in the military urged, shortly after Hungary's entry into the war, that all Jewish labor servicemen be compelled to wear civilian clothes. The leadership in this, as in most other anti-Semitic initiatives within the armed forces, was again taken by the General Staff. On February 6, 1942, when it was preparing for the deployment of the Second Hungarian Army in the war against the Soviet Union, the General Staff recommended that the Jews serving in the KMOF and in the field units be compelled to wear their civilian clothes or, if that was impossible at the time, to have their good uniforms replaced by substandard ones normally used for military exercises. Its recommendations were accepted by the Minister of Defense on March 17, when an order was issued to the effect that the "uniform" of the Jews in the field units consist of civilian clothes, a yellow arm band, and an insignia-free military cap (see fig. 10.3). In theory, Jews not in possession of good civilian clothes were to be supplied with uniforms captured from the Czechoslovaks and Yugoslavs.[45] In theory, too, the Jews were also entitled at first to military boots and basic utensils, but the allocation of boots became the exception rather than the rule.[46] By early 1942, practically all of the labor servicemen served in their own civilian clothes and footwear.

The clothing situation of the Jewish labor servicemen was quite tolerable until the fall of 1942. By that time, however, many of the labor companies that were stationed in the Ukraine and later on in Bor, Yugoslavia, had been engaged in heavy physical activities and in long marches that weakened and/or destroyed their clothes. Moreover,

Figure 10.3.
Jewish labor servicemen in their "uniform" before their departure for Galicia or the Ukraine.

many of these companies were under the command of especially sadistic officers and guards that subjected the servicemen to so-called "calisthenics" (frog leaping, somersaulting, crawling, etc.) after their heavy work. Frequently, these officers deprived the servicemen of their officially allotted food rations, which were already very low in relation to the hard labor expected of, and in fact exacted from, them. To survive, many servicemen were consequently driven to sell their clothes either to the more fortunate ones or to the local population for food. Others used whatever hidden valuables they still had for this purpose. The rations stolen from the labor servicemen, especially in the Ukraine, were often sold back to the richer Jews for "coupons" (*bonok*)—written statements about the value of goods received which the officers and/or guards would later redeem from the families of these unfortunates. These were in fact ransom notes which many of the emaciated and ill-clothed Jews were driven to write in their desperate effort to alleviate their plight, however temporarily. As a result of the extremely deplorable conditions that prevailed in the Ukraine, many labor servicemen died during the winter of 1942–43 in spite of the efforts of the Jewish relief organizations to collect and ship warm clothes to the frontlines.

The Yellow Arm Bands. The order requiring the wearing of a yellow arm band was not generally enforced until the spring of 1942. Until then, practices varied according to the attitude of the company commanders. Most of the servicemen deployed in the Ukraine removed the arm band from their jackets during the early phase of the war. In some units, the Jewish labor servicemen, like the other national minorities, wore an arm band featuring the national colors. In others, however, they had been made to wear the yellow arm band (illegally) since May 1941, to satisfy the demands of anti-Semitic elements both within and outside the armed forces.[47]

The question of the arm bands was regulated shortly after the return of General Ferenc Szombathelyi, the Chief of Staff,[48] from an inspection tour of the front. Noting that many of the Jews were working in their uniforms without any marks clearly distinguishing them from the soldiers, Szombathelyi urged the Minister of Defense (December 18, 1941) to order that the Jewish labor servicemen wear "a wide arm band that would be recognized from a distance." The color was presumably not specified, because the General Staff had come to realize that certain German units also used yellow arm bands for specific military purposes in the field. The General Staff consequently suggested that instead of the yellow arm bands, which it feared would only upset and confuse the German units, the Jews wear a white arm band bearing a yellow Star of David. KMOF offered a remedy for assuring the implementation of the compulsory and continuous wearing of the arm bands by suggesting that they be sewed on permanently. At the end, it was decided to retain the yellow arm bands because they had already been ordered and because the Germans had been persuaded that the Jews would be clearly distinguished from them by having their uniforms replaced with civilian clothes.

The Christians of Jewish background, i.e. the converts who were identified as Jews under the laws then in effect—most of them were serving in separate "Christian Labor Service Companies" (*Keresztény Munkaszolgálatos Századok*)—were compelled to wear a white arm band as distinguishing mark.[49]

Clearly identified by their arm bands, the Jewish labor servicemen became an easy target for abuse by Hungarian and German anti-Semites. The labor service companies were deployed both within the country and along the frontlines. Many of them were stationed in Northern Transylvania along the Romanian border, building roads and fortifications. The ones most subjected to abuse were those stationed in the Ukraine and at Bor, Serbia.

The Jewish Labor Servicemen
in the Ukraine

Originally the Minister of Defense and the General Staff had expected that the campaign against the USSR would end within six to eight weeks with the complete victory of the Germans and their allies. By September 1941, however, the Hungarians came to realize that the war would be long and costly. Consequently, the government tried, to the great dismay of the General Staff, to limit Hungary's participation in active combat and to save as much of the armed forces and resources as possible to assure a favorable position for the country during the postwar settlements. However, the Germans had other plans. They were able to persuade the Hungarians, who were then still awed by the Nazis' military prowess and greedily eager to fulfill all their revisionist ambitions, to rearm and deploy the Second Hungarian Army in the struggle against the Soviet Union.[50] This decision also affected the Jews of military age, for the General Staff had decided at an earlier date that in the case of mobilization up to 10 percent of all those mobilized would be Jews.[51] This decision was reiterated by the Minister of Defense in his order (No. 15 802) of March 17, 1942, which also stipulated that all the Jewish labor companies would be utilized in the military operation zones.[52]

The number of Jews serving in the labor battalions subordinated to the nine army corps was still relatively small at the end of 1941. According to the statistics compiled at the request of the Ministry of Defense on December 11, 1941 (allegedly to determine the clothing needs of the labor servicemen) there were 14,413 Jews among the 23,018 labor servicemen on active duty on December 15. Their distribution is shown in table 10.2.

TABLE 10.2.
LABOR SERVICEMEN ON ACTIVE DUTY,
DECEMBER 1941

Army Corps	Christian Guards	Christian Labor Servicemen	Jewish Labor Servicemen	Total
I	149	628	1,984	2,761
II	65	622	3,154	3,841
III	66	504	782	1,352
IV	62 (2286) [a]	322	612	3,282
V	97	2,349	2,887	5,333
VI	36	35	617	688
VII [b]	64	530	789	1,383
VIII	69	714	2,531	3,314
IX	64	615	1,057	1,736
Total	672 (2286)	6,319	14,413	23,690

SOURCE: *FAA* 1:422.
[a] Probable number of those not on active duty, which was not identified by Army Corps IV.
[b] Army Corps VII reported that it did not include those not on active duty.

Shortly after the decision on the deployment of the Second Hungarian Army, which was placed under the command of General Gusztáv Jány, the number of Jewish labor servicemen destined for service along the front lines increased tremendously. Most of the tens of thousands of Jews recruited for service were called on an individual basis rather than by age group. They were issued so-called "SAS" (*Siess, Azonnal, Sürgös;* Hurry, Immediately, Urgent) notices which required them to report to the specified labor battalion headquarters or recruitment centers, normally within less than one week. By this practice, the Hungarian authorities apparently aimed not only to satisfy the labor requirements of the military, but also to "solve" some of the fundamental social and economic problems confronting the nation as they perceived them. Another motivating force was to satisfy the ideological objectives of the anti-Semites.

Among the Jews called up individually were those who had played a prominent role in their communities. Special attention was devoted to calling up the rich, the prominent professionals, the leading industrialists and businessmen, the well-known Zionist and community leaders, and above all those who had been denounced by local Christians as "objectionable" elements. Many of these denunciations had been made by the greedy and morally bankrupt individuals who were eager to take over the businesses or practices of the mobilized Jews. Others were volunteered by the local *Baross Szövetség* (Baross Association)—the anti-Semitic business organization—the counterintelligence services, and chapters of the professional organizations.

In fairness, one must also record the fact that there were a number of occasions, however few and isolated, when the Ministry of Defense or the Regent were petitioned in behalf of individuals or smaller groups of Jews. The overwhelming majority of these requests for exemptions or transfers were submitted in behalf of converts and professionals, especially physicians. Requests of this kind were, for example, submitted by the Hungarian Holy Cross Society (*Magyar Szent Kereszt Egyesület*)—the organization of converts to Catholicism—and by the Medical Association of Lipótváros in Budapest (*Budapesti Lipótvárosi Orvostársaság*).[53]

In response to the "pressures by the local patriotic citizens and organizations," the Ministry of Defense issued a secret decree on April 22, 1942, ordering KMOF and the commanders of the nine army corps to see to it that 10 to 15 percent of the field labor companies were composed of Jews "well-known by their wealth or reputation." The Decree also authorized the recruitment of Jews in these categories even if they were above 42 years of age, the limit specified by law for frontline service.[54]

The individual SAS recruitment notices were sent out directly by the army corps commands. The recruitment centers were merely supplied with lists which enabled them to check compliance by those who were called up.[55] These lists were normally prepared on the basis of data received from the Ministry, which, in turn, compiled them on the basis of "complaints" received from various sources. Many of these complaints (i.e., denunciations) were forwarded by "anonymous individuals" or "patriotic groups" that provided details about the background, status, and "harmful activities" of the Jews identified on their lists. There were special lists of Jewish physicians who had been ousted from the medical association under the major anti-Jewish laws, of prominent and rich Jews, and of "unreliable" Jews. One of the stated objectives for this selective recruitment was the desire to put an end to the "whispering propaganda" of the Jews.

Many of the Jews recruited on the basis of these lists were totally unfit for labor or any other service. A number of them were quite old or suffered from a variety of illnesses. Some were crippled or insane.[56]

Another group singled out for special punitive labor service consisted of individuals (both Jews and non-Jews) deemed "risky" or dangerous from the point of view of national security. These included, of course, a large number of Communists and other leftists—many of whom were also of Jewish background—who at the time were in special escape-proof internment camps for political detainees. Most of these were subsequently placed in "special" (*különleges*), i.e. punitive, companies that were dispatched to the frontlines. There they were clearly identified by yellow arm bands with large black dots denoting their "criminal past."

According to the figures compiled by the General Staff, there were 14,269 "unreliable" individuals ready to be placed in special companies as of March 24, 1942. Of these, 1,485 were in internment camps administered by the Ministry of the Interior;[57] 100 were on a special list; 11,484 were so classified by the recruitment units of the nine army corps; and 1,200 were identified as unreliable elements employed in industrial enterprises, mostly around Budapest.[58] The procedures for the identification, classification, and registration of the "unreliable" elements were regulated by General Ferenc Szombathelyi, the Chief of Staff, on May 30. According to him, the primary objective of the special punitive labor service companies was to enable society to get rid of the elements found harmful to the interests of the nation, whenever and wherever they might be. These were ordered to the front lines as soon as they reached company strength.[59]

The first units of the Second Hungarian Army, which consisted of close to 250,000 men, left the country under the command of Gusztáv Jány[60] on April 11, 1942.[61] There were approximately 50,000 Jewish labor servicemen in the different types of labor companies attached to the Second Hungarian Army.[62] Participating in the general summer offensive of the Germans, many of these units reached the Don, south of Voronezh, by July 10.[63]

German-Hungarian Frictions. Upon their entry into the Ukraine, including the former territories of Polish Galicia, many of the Hungarians—officers, enlisted men, and Jewish labor servicemen alike—had an opportunity to see or indirectly learn of the massacres perpetrated by the German *Einsatzgruppen* against the Jews.[64] The victims of the mass exterminations were not only the indigenous Jews, but also the Jews that had been deported to the East—including the so-called "alien" Hungarian Jews, who were slaughtered at Kamenets-Podolsk in late August 1941.[65] The precautionary measures of the Nazis notwithstanding, the killings were on too massive a scale to be totally concealed. Many of the Hungarians who witnessed the massacres were appalled by the machinegunning of the innocent men, women, and children. They were among the first sources of information about the realities of the Nazis' anti-Jewish drive, as they wrote their nightmarish eyewitness accounts to their families or recounted them in person while on furlough. Many such accounts were brought to the attention of the Jewish leaders, and some were even reported in the American press.[66]

While a number of Hungarians participated in some of the atrocities committed against the Jews and maltreated the labor servicemen under their command, there were also Hungarians who intervened in support of the Jews and of the local Polish or Ukrainian population. This became the source of occasional friction between the German and Hungarian military and political authorities.

The Hungarians' activities in Eastern Galicia were particularly annoying to the Germans. There, according to some reports by German agents, the Hungarians were not only coddling the Jews, but were also trying to influence the local Polish and Ukrainian population to pursue their own territorial ambitions. This is expressed clearly in a lengthy report, dated November 23, 1943, submitted by Kloetzel, the representative of the German Foreign Office in Cracow, to his superiors. Kloetzel was especially incensed by the fact that the members of a labor service company stationed around Stanislav were wearing Hungarian uniforms. He dismissed the explanation that this was necessary because the civilian clothes of the Jews had been torn in the course of the hard labor performed by them and that the uniforms were in fact reject items in the military arsenal. He characterized the attitude of the Jews by the statement a labor serviceman allegedly made to a German policeman. The policeman was allegedly told in a Yiddish jargon: "Sergeant, I am a Jew, [but] you can't to anything to me [because] I am a Hungarian soldier." Kloetzel also asserted that the labor company became ever smaller as the partisan groups in Galicia became proportionately ever larger. Last but not least, he complained that Hungarian officers were showing great interest in the solution of the Jewish question and were taking pictures of the Jewish mass graves around Stanislav.[67]

There were other sources of friction between the Germans and the Hungarians involving the Jewish labor servicemen. The Germans objected vehemently to the retention of Jews in the *Honvédség* and to the stationing of labor service companies close to the borders of the Third Reich. With regard to the former, the Germans believed that the Hungarians permitted a larger number of Jews to serve in the armed forces. These Jews, in their view, had a detrimental effect upon the *Wehrmacht* units stationed near them. It turned out that the Hungarians had, in fact, retained only a very limited number of Jews or technicians of Jewish background in the armed forces, either because under the existing laws they were not characterized as Jews or because they possessed certain technical skills of great interest to the military.[68]

The Germans' fear over the possible "detrimental" effect of Jews upon the *Wehrmacht* in the Ukraine was matched by their nervousness over the deployment of labor companies around Hegyeshalom in the northwestern part of Hungary near the Third Reich. Rolf Günther, Eichmann's deputy in Berlin, was particularly upset over a company that was engaged in a railway construction and maintenance project. The members of the company were allegedly mostly intellectuals and professionals, including former lawyers and manufacturers, and were feared not only for their ability to "observe" traffic along the border, but also for their unavoidable contacts with German military and civilian personnel in Hegyeshalom, where they frequented the same restaurant.[69]

Still another source of friction involved the atrocities committed against the emaciated Jewish labor servicemen by some German military, police, and security units, unilaterally or in collusion with ultra Rightist Hungarians, during the retreat following the military debacle at Voronezh and Stalingrad in January–February 1943.

The Work and Plight of the Labor Servicemen

In the Ukraine, the labor service companies were employed on a variety of projects specified by the Hungarian and the German military authorities.[70] Among their tasks were the construction, clearing, and maintenance of roads and railroads (including snow removal), the loading and unloading of munitions, provisions, and other materials, and the performance of war-related technical tasks such as the building of trenches, tank traps, bunkers, and gun emplacements, and the removal of mines from the fields (see fig. 10.4). The various types of fortification work were extraordinarily demanding in winter, when the soil was frozen and the shovels and pickaxes wielded by the emaciated labor servicemen could hardly penetrate it. The clearing of the mine fields, which sometimes involved marching over them, exacted large numbers of casualties. Often the men were made to assist in propelling the horse-drawn supply trains, especially along the passes and the rain-soaked mud roads, and on many occasions they were actually compelled to replace horses that collapsed or died of exhaustion. Some especially sadistic commanders made them pull the heavily laden wagons "to save the energy of the animals."

The conditions under which the Jewish labor servicemen lived and worked in the Ukraine were especially bad, primarily because of the viciously anti-Semitic attitude of most of the company commanders and guards—not to speak of the SS and military police units that were rampaging in the area. The behavior of these commanders and guards reflected not only their own anti-Semitic attitude, but also the instructions of their immediate superiors back home or at the frontlines that went counter to the official governmental guidelines.

The official guidelines relating to physical punishment were applicable to everyone under the jurisdiction of the Ministry of Defense—arms-bearing soldiers and labor servicemen alike. Because of certain abuses in a company stationed in Hungary in 1941, KMOF felt compelled to remind all officers associated with the ten labor battalions at the time that the procedures stipulated in the Service Regulation (*Szolgálati Szabályzat*) also applied to labor servicemen. In fact, his orders to this effect had to be acknowledged in writing by every officer newly appointed to any of the labor battalions.[71] However, most of the officers and guards deployed in the Ukraine acted in accordance with the oral instructions they had received from their superiors in the various recruitment centers before departure. Thus, for example, Lieutenant-Colonel Lipót (Metzl) Muray, the notorious "hangman of Nagykáta," who put together and dispatched from the recruitment center at Nagykáta 10 to 12 labor service companies, allegedly instructed the company commanders not to bring the men back home

Figure 10.4.
Jewish labor servicemen at work on various projects in the Ukraine.

alive, since they were the enemies of the state. While in Nagykáta, as in many other recruitment centers, most of the labor servicemen had a chance to learn what was awaiting them in the Ukraine. They were maltreated and subjected to dehumanizing torture while still in Hungary.[72] Muray claimed that his position merely reflected the instructions he and the other recruitment officers in the area had received from Major-General Artúr Horvay early in March 1942. Horvay had allegedly informed the participants at an orientation session that:

- It was prohibited for anyone to talk with Jews; guards could talk with them only at a distance of three feet in the presence of a witness.
- Jews could walk only on the middle of the road, while the guards patrolled on the sidewalk.
- Jews could be visited only once a month by their closest relatives.[73]
- Jews were not entitled to receive packages.
- The correspondence of the Jews was to be strictly censored.
- Jews were prohibited from shopping in stores.
- Jews could have a maximum of fifty *Pengős*.
- Jews were not permitted to smoke, especially since they were not entitled to cigarette rations.[74]

In the Ukraine, far removed from the scrutiny of the central authorities, the officers and guards often gave vent to their sadistic inclinations by abusing the labor servicemen entrusted to them. They cruelly maltreated the labor servicemen, withheld or stole their already low rations, and often and for long periods of time made them quarter under the open skies. Some of them, like Lieutenant György Kaucsky, were resolved to have their companies exterminated. By October 1, 1942, 96 of the labor servicemen under Kaucsky's command were killed; of these, he personally shot more than 30.[75] Others amused themselves by having the Jews for "five o'clock tea" or subjected to a "lakeside vision" (*tóparti látomás*), named after a famous Hungarian movie. The former involved the beating of the Jews in the guards' quarters, while the latter consisted of their being forced to somersault in the nearby marshes. The Jews were often made to climb the ice-covered trees and crow, in imitation of a rooster, that they were "dirty Jews." Some of the guards amused themselves by hosing the Jews in winter until they became "ice statues" or by tying them onto tree branches with their hands tied against their backs. These, and many other similarly cruel "amusements" were normally carried out after the Jews had returned from their work.[76]

The conditions of labor were almost always intolerable. The labor servicemen were generally ill-equipped, ill-clothed, and inadequately fed. According to the information forwarded to Minister of Defense Nagy, the Jewish labor servicemen in some companies were marched to work from place to place in extremely cold weather while still clothed in their summer garbs or bundled in rags. Some of them had bare skin showing through the rags. Their daily ration consisted of scraps of bones and vegetables. They were not permitted to have farinaceous products.[77]

Emaciated and disease-ridden, the labor servicemen were often subjected to corporal abuse not only by their own guards, but also by the members of the German or Hungarian military units for or under which they worked. Particularly cruel in this respect were the Hungarian sappers' units, many of which were composed of anti-Semitic Hungarian-speaking *Volksdeutsche*, mostly Swabians from the Dunántul and the Bácska and Banat areas.

The treatment of the Jews within the armed forces was aptly summarized by Szombathelyi in his defense statement written after the war:

The Jewish question had a catastrophic effect upon the armed forces. It had a terrible corrupting effect. Every value underwent a revaluation. Cruelty became love for the fatherland, atrocities became acts of heroism, corruption was transformed into virtue; under such conditions we, well-thinking individuals, could not understand the events. There emerged two types of discipline. One was applied to the Jews against whom any action was permissible. . . .[78]

The reaction of the Jewish labor servicemen to the horrors inflicted upon them varied. Most of them tried to the limit of their abilities to maintain their mental equilibrium and physical strength and to stay out of trouble. Driven by their instinct of survival and the burning desire to be eventually reunited with their loved ones, they endeavored to survive from day to day. They suffered in silence or shared their sorrow with their comrades. Many found solace in prayer and meditation. Others, admittedly few and mostly of middle class background, became demoralized and, driven by hunger, sold all their belongings, sometimes even their clothes and shoes, and eventually perished.

However, many of the labor servicemen engaged in active resistance to the blatantly unjust measures adopted against them. In May–June 1941, before Hungary's entry into the war, a relatively large number escaped into the Soviet Union. For example, from the six labor service companies that were stationed near Kőrösmező, where they were employed on the building of invasion routes along the Soviet border,

123 labor servicemen escaped between May 25 and June 6. According to the Hungarian officials in charge, the escapes were the consequence of the very harsh physical labor and the humiliation associated with it as well as of the Jews' fear that the then impending Third Anti-Jewish Law would deprive them of a livelihood upon demobilization.[79] Following Hungary's declaration of war against the Soviet Union, a number of Jewish labor servicemen escaped to the partisans, with whom they fought against the common enemy. Their knowledge of Hungarian was especially valuable to the partisans, since they were able to lure Hungarian military units into traps.[80] In some cases, their association with the partisans was quite unhappy, for a number of units, especially among the Bandera-led Ukrainian partisan detachments, while anti-German, were also anti-Soviet and anti-Semitic.

The calvary of the Jewish labor service companies, like that of the Second Hungarian Army as a whole, began in the wake of the Soviet breakthrough at the Hungarian-held Uriv bridgehead near Voronezh on January 12, 1943.[81] The losses of the Hungarians were staggering. Nagy claims that only 60,000 to 70,000 of the 200,000 frontline forces survived, while only 6,000 to 7,000 of the 50,000 labor servicemen were eventually returned to Hungary.[82] Many of the remainder were captured by the Red Army and placed in POW camps. The surviving units were regrouped and during the spring months supplemented by fresh troops and labor servicemen.[83]

Citing the figures of the Hungarian Ministry of Defense, Macartney identifies the losses of the regular and labor service units between June 27, 1941 and December 31, 1943 as shown in table 10.3:

TABLE 10.3.
HUNGARIAN MILITARY LOSSES

	Regular Forces	*Auxiliary Forces*	*Total*
June 27, 1941–December 31, 1942			
Killed or died	8,506	1,628	10,134
Wounded	23,736	318	24,054
Missing or POW	3,224	202	3,426
January 1–December 31, 1943			
Killed or died	6,560	2,158	8,718
Wounded	15,781	716	16,497
Missing or POW	59,436	20,434	79,870
TOTAL	117,243	25,456	142,699

SOURCE: C. A. Macartney, 2:100.

It is safe to assume that the official figures revealed by the Ministry of Defense, like most official casualty reports, were calculated to minimize the losses suffered in battle and to make the war more palatable to public opinion. The actual figures relating to casualties suffered by the Hungarian regular and auxiliary forces cannot be ascertained. In the chaos that followed the Voronezh debacle, many of the companies simply disintegrated. Thousands upon thousands were killed during the battle of the Don, and tens of thousands more were captured by the victorious Soviet forces. Tens of thousands retreated in panic. The commanders of many of the labor service companies deserted their posts, leaving the Jews either under the control of a handful of subordinates or to their own fate. The straggling labor servicemen, bundled in their lice-infested rags and blankets, were subjected to unbelievable humiliation and torture during the long and tortuous retreat. With the logistics in disarray, they were deprived even of the meager food rations they had received while their companies were still relatively intact. Occasionally, when they were driven out of their warm shelters by intruding German or Hungarian soldiers, they felt compelled to walk throughout the night to avoid freezing to death.

In spite of the unbelievable hardship under which they straggled westward, the remnant of the labor service companies maintained on the whole a much better discipline and manifested a better spirit of comradeship than the withdrawing Hungarian troops. The latter, according to most accounts, withdrew in panic having been thoroughly beaten by the Red Army within a few days. This was recognized not only by General Gusztáv Jány, the Commander of the Second Hungarian Army,[84] but also by other officers. Lieutenant-Colonel Béla Vécsey, commander of the 35th Infantry Regiment, for example, stated that he was

compelled to determine that these Jews are much more disciplined than our *Honvéds;* their readiness to work and their productivity are also better than those of the *Honvéds.* The Jews brought out the wounded and the dead *Honvéds* in the midst of the greatest fire. A Jewish company had about fifty dead and twice as many wounded.[85]

On another occasion, Vécsey stated:

The Jewish companies at the front behave very bravely; they leave no Hungarian dead or wounded behind. We shall live to see the day when they will become heroes, while our infantry is constantly on the run.[86]

In the course of the epic retreat, elements of the withdrawing armies not only plundered and killed the helpless labor servicemen, but were also feuding among themselves. The Germans often vented their anger and frustrations over their defeat by harassing the demoralized Hungarians, whom they blamed for the original Soviet breakthrough at the Don. The SIPO and SD units and occasionally even some *Wehrmacht* elements were particularly vicious in their attack on the Jews, which incensed the decent elements among the Hungarian officers and soldiers.[87] General Gusztáv Jány himself, upon learning of the atrocities perpetrated by the various German units,[88] felt compelled to file a protest with the Commander of the Second German Army. He substantiated his protest note by stating among other things:

The Jews are organized within the Hungarian Army into labor companies within whose framework they perform important operations (for example, maintenance of roads, construction of fortifications, etc.). We cannot permit that these operations be made impossible by units not associated with the Hungarian Army.[89]

Many of the lower rank Hungarians who witnessed the barbarities committed against the Jews forwarded their observations to their superiors in Budapest. Many others gave detailed oral reports upon being hospitalized following their return to Hungary. These reports and the subsequent order of Minister of Defense Nagy that the officers and enlisted men treat the Jewish labor servicemen correctly and with civility merely increased the Germans' anger at the Hungarians.[90]

The feuding between the withdrawing Germans and Hungarians had little or no effect upon the status of the Jewish labor servicemen in the Ukraine, especially since the order of the Minister of Defense was hardly heeded there. Far from the scrutiny of the central authorities, the malevolent anti-Semitic elements in the Hungarian army continued to harass the Jews. Emaciated by hunger and the numbing cold and infested with lice, many of the labor servicemen, having lost their resistance, succumbed to a variety of diseases of which typhoid fever was the most prevalent. In the absence of hospital facilities or medication many of these died by the wayside. In some cases, the labor servicemen suffering from typhoid, together with the healthy ones, were ordered to run for fifteen minutes, then "bathe" in the ice-cold river and stand undried afterwards in the blowing wind for inspection by the sadistic guards.[91]

Thousands of labor servicemen actually or thought to be suffering from typhoid were directed toward a makeshift quarantine "hospital" at Doroshich (Dorosics), a *kolkhoz* village located between Zhitomir and Korosten west of Kiev. The hospital consisted of a few rooms in a brick building, but most of the servicemen were placed in open barns. The quarantine area was surrounded by a barbed-wire fence. The disease claimed dozens of victims every day; the corpses were stacked by the wall of a nearby stable. On April 30, 1943 (the last day of Passover), the authorities decided to attack the disease in a decisive fashion. One of the barns, which housed around 800 labor servicemen, was set afire. The living torches that jumped out of the flaming barn were machinegunned by waiting guards. Nevertheless, a handful of labor servicemen, though wounded, managed to escape and survive.[92]

Upon hearing about the horrors of Doroshich, Minister of Defense Nagy immediately ordered a military commission to investigate the background of the fire and to identify the persons responsible. According to the report that was submitted shortly thereafter, nobody could be charged with responsibility or even negligence since the "fire had been inadvertently set by smoking Jews." The report was silent about the decision to concentrate the diseased Jews under such inhuman conditions or about the massacre perpetrated by the guards that surrounded the barn.[93]

The Era of Vilmos Nagy

Ironically, the most intense suffering of the labor servicemen stationed in the Ukraine took place during the tenure of General Vilmos Nagy, the benevolent Minister of Defense, who did everything in his power to ameliorate their plight. Nagy was sworn in on September 24, 1942 and served until June 12, 1943. The boisterously Germanophile Bartha was dismissed not only because he presumably demanded, consistent with his traditional position, a more active involvement in the war, but primarily because he got increasingly involved in domestic politics and tolerated the scandalous treatment of the labor servicemen.

Upon assuming his responsibilities Nagy noted the vicious anti-Jewish spirit that prevailed in the Ministry. Many of the section heads and their subordinates did everything in their power to sabotage or circumvent his instructions, which were designed to improve the lot of the labor servicemen. Especially adamant in their anti-Semitic attitudes were the heads of the personnel and mobilization sections of the Ministry.[94]

In October, during a visit to Hitler's headquarters near Vinnitsa, Nagy also toured the front, where he met with a number of labor service companies. He reminded the commanders to treat the men under them well if they wanted to extract good work. He even talked to a number of labor servicemen personally to show the officers and guards that he considered these "unfortunate pariahs" as "soldiers and human beings."[95]

On October 27, shortly after his return from the tour, Nagy informed the Council of Ministers about his findings. In connection with the labor servicemen he stated: "If we wish to obtain good work from the labor servicemen we must treat them well and supply them with good clothing and food."[96]

Nagy repeated these ideas in his appearance before the Hungarian Parliament. Speaking at a session of the upper house, for example, he stated:

I changed the labor service system and since service in the national defense cannot be construed as punishment for the citizen, I have terminated [any practice] that could be useful to anyone who would look upon this service as a punishment. In order to protect the national wealth, I also saw to it that everybody in possession of technical skills valuable for the *Honvédség* and useful in military service should, upon their call-up . . . be employed in fields relating to their technical expertise. It is my conviction that my current and future actions, based on the above principles, will serve on the one hand the protection of the nation's morality and the proper use of its wealth and will contribute, on the other, to the unity of the nation by following the path of humanity, righteousness, and honor.[97]

Participating in the debate on the budget in the lower house, Nagy discussed the question of the Jewish labor servicemen in the same vein. Speaking on November 19, 1942, he stated among other things:

For my part, I stand on the side of law and humaneness, because I need workers for the performance of technical tasks which I do not want performed by the troops. And if I demand work I must care about the working capacity of these men. The recruits should not consider their recruitment into the labor companies as humiliation. This is service in the national defense, which is binding for all and which has a legal basis. However, they should also be convinced that their commanders consider them recruits whom they are bound to take care of humanely and honorably.[98]

In his endeavor to ameliorate the plight of the labor servicemen, Nagy issued a series of instructions stipulating that:

- The labor service companies no longer be treated like POW's.
- Ill and unsuitable servicemen be discharged.
- The food rations be improved to enable the men to work.
- Corporal punishment and other forms of maltreatment be discontinued.

- Individuals responsible for the brutal treatment and black-mailing of labor servicemen be punished.[99]

The instructions of the Minister of Defense had a generally positive effect upon the status of the labor servicemen stationed within Hungary. However, the commanders and guards of most field units stationed along the frontlines failed to heed either the instructions or the warnings of their superiors back home. There were, of course, many notable exceptions in which commissioned and noncommissioned officers and rank-and-file guards did everything in their power to protect and care for the labor servicemen placed in their charge. Some of them succeeded in returning their companies almost intact. Others failed, but for reasons beyond their control.[100]

On December 11, 1942, Nagy appointed Major-General Jenő Rőder as his special assistant in charge of ascertaining whether his instructions, both oral and written, were being carried out in the units stationed within the country.[101] It was also his responsibility to investigate and if possible remedy complaints relating to the treatment of labor servicemen. The person in charge of similar functions for the labor service units stationed in the Ukraine was Major-General Béla Tanitó, who, according to Rőder, had been appointed to this position by Szombathelyi.[102]

Apparently in response to recommendations made by Rőder, Nagy issued a new set of orders on March 9, 1943, concerning the treatment of the labor servicemen stationed within Hungary. Decree No. 110 160 eln. KMOF. 1943 contained detailed provisions relating to the general principles underlying the treatment of the labor servicemen, the procedures to be employed in disciplining them, and their supervision and employment.[103]

Law No. XIV of 1942. Ironically, it was Nagy's fate to also have to issue the Decree relating to the implementation of Law No. XIV of 1942, which incorporated the provisions of the major decrees relating to the labor service system then in effect. Law No. XIV:1942 was adopted on July 31, following its enthusiastic support by the rightist elements in both houses of Parliament.[104] Technically, it merely amended Law II of 1939 and provided a fundamental legal basis for the labor service system. In fact, however, it further aggravated the status of the Jews in the armed forces, for it used the provisions of the openly racial Third Anti-Jewish Law as a basis for the definition of "Jew."

The Decree (No. 55 000. eln. oszt.-1942 of the Ministry of Defense) implementing Law No. XIV:1942 was issued over Nagy's signature on December 21, 1942. It contained detailed provisions relating to the determination of who was and who was not a Jew in terms of the new racial law, to the responsibilities of all Jews of military age, irrespective of their former ranks in the *Honvédség*, as rank-and-file members of the auxiliary labor service units, and to the procedures for the determination of exemptions and disqualification from labor service. It also provided for the recall of all military-related documents issued to Jews and their replacement by new auxiliary-service identity cards with the letters "Zs" (*Zsidó*; Jew) marked prominently on the front page (see fig. 10.5).[105]

Nagy claims that while he inherited the responsibility for issuing the

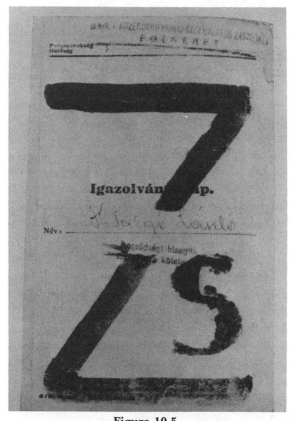

Figure 10.5.
Sample of a Jewish labor serviceman's paybook and identification document
(*zsoldkönyv*) marked with the letters "Zs" (*Zsidó:* Jew).

Decree from his predecessor, he did everything in his power to ameliorate some of its provisions. He states that he insisted, among other things, that Jews be called up by age groups rather than by the haphazard and inequitable SAS system and that the Service Regulation used in the armed forces be applicable to the labor servicemen as well.[106]

Reorganization of the Labor Service System

Shortly before Nagy was sworn in as Minister of Defense, KMOF issued new regulations relating to the organization of the labor service units and to the classification and training of the labor servicemen. Technically, the regulation of September 11, 1942,[107] affected only the labor companies associated with battalions II–VI and IX–XIII.[108] It also specified in detail the daily routine to be followed and the types of training to be employed in the system, differentiating between the various types of technical or construction projects and the service record of the recruits.

In the fall of 1942, the Germans began a systematic drive to pressure Hungary for a Final Solution along the model followed in most of the other countries in the Third Reich's sphere of influence. The Hungarian government resisted these demands, but felt compelled to show some gesture of understanding and good will. This was manifested in the realm of the labor service system. The Kállay government felt that, the labor service notwithstanding, the Jews were in fact enjoying a privileged position by not being permitted to serve in the armed forces. Consequently, to assuage the feelings of the Germans and to satisfy the manpower requirements of the country, Kállay instructed that "all Jews of military age, whether suitable for military service or not," be directed into labor camps.[109] The general call-up of the Jews was coupled to a resolution to bring about the gradual replacement and eventual demobilization of those over 42 years of age doing hard physical labor, especially on the frontlines.

Presumably influenced by his observations at the front, where he met Jews over 42 doing hard physical labor, Nagy issued a secret decree on November 6, 1942, providing for the call-up of Jews between 24 and 33 years of age and for the gradual replacement and eventual demobilization of those over 42. The call-up of the 24 through 33 age groups was to be effectuated through public posters.[110] The Decree also stipulated the categories of Jews to be excluded, including exempted Jews and foreign Jews. The Decree further stressed that only Jews suitable for labor should be recruited for the service. In connection with the Jews deemed risky from the point of view of national security, the Decree provided for the establishment of a special company in each labor battalion.[111]

To systematize the call-up and recruitment system, the Ministry of Defense provided for the registration of all Jews between 18 and 48. The announcement of November 14, 1942, stipulated that in addition to the standard documents, each affected Jew had to bring along two snapshots, one of which, after it was stamped by both the recruitment center and the local bureau for vital statistics, was to serve as a "registration certificate."[112] Following the completion of the registration process, a number of age groups were called up in 1943 for shorter or longer periods of service.[113]

Further Reform Measures. The conditions for the employment of the labor servicemen, including their remuneration, quartering, and feeding and the corresponding financial responsibilities, were regulated on June 23, 1943, by a decree of General Lajos Csatay,[114] the former head of Army Corps IV, who succeeded Nagy on June 12, when the latter was asked to resign by the Regent and Kállay, who were under great pressure from the Germans.[115] A staunch opponent of Communism

Figure 10.6.
Sample of a photograph "registration certificate."

and of the Left in general, Csatay was more sympathetic to Germany than his predecessor. But he was basically a professional soldier loyal to Horthy and to the system he represented. Ironically, under his energetic leadership and because of his basically correct though stern attitude toward the labor servicemen, the Ministry of Defense became a major source of rescue during the German occupation. Many ablebodied Jewish men of all ages were called up for special duty in 1944, rescuing them from the ghettos and certain deportation.[116]

The regrouping and partial reorganization of the companies deployed in the Ukraine took place a few months after the Voronezh debacle. Only the companies in charge of road maintenance were left jurisdictionally unchanged. The remnants of the other "technical units" were regrouped under the commands of Lieutenant-Colonel Sellyey, Colonel Kolthay, and Major Szentkatolnay.[117]

Since the reform measures instituted by Nagy were not being heeded and Jewish labor servicemen were continuously subjected to inhuman treatment, especially in the units stationed outside of Hungary, Csatay felt compelled to reissue Nagy's March 9 directives relating to the treatment of labor servicemen. He coupled this with a warning that he would not tolerate any abuse and that he would have the culprits courtmartialed.[118]

By this time (October 1943), the Kállay government was trying to extricate Hungary from the Axis Alliance. The weak but still active center and left of center democratic opposition headed by Endre Bajcsy-Zsilinszky had urged earlier in the summer the adoption of a new course that would reestablish Hungary's neutrality. In their lengthy memorandum of July 31, the members of this opposition demanded the reassignment of the labor servicemen into the armed forces (see chapter 7).

Several members of the government, including Kállay, sympathized with this position. However, they were eager to effectuate meaningful changes and above all to extricate Hungary from the war without bringing about either a German or a Soviet occupation. Therefore, the government adopted a series of measures calculated to show its disenchantment with the Axis and with some of the policies that had been adopted in the spirit of National Socialism. Prominent among these policy changes in the Jewish sphere were the measures relating to easing the plight of the labor servicemen and to the prosecution of a number of individuals accused of anti-Jewish excesses. In addition to prosecuting the leading officers associated with the Bácska massacres of

February 1942, including General Ferenc Feketehalmy-Czeydner, the Hungarian authorities indicted a number of army officers and labor company commanders and guards that had abused the Jews under their command.[119] Most of these, however, were freed or merely temporarily discharged pending their appeal. All of them were rehabilitated a few months later following the German occupation of Hungary.

Further Reorganizational Measures. The "provocative" actions of the Hungarian authorities were not viewed kindly by the leaders of the Third Reich, who followed the internal developments of their Allies very closely. The Germans were fully aware of Kállay's intentions and of his "secret" negotiations with the Western Powers. They were particularly incensed over the failure of the Hungarian government to bring about the demanded Final Solution. In the fall of 1943, they became particularly apprehensive about the possibility that Hungary might follow the leadership of Italy and abandon the Axis Alliance and consequently resolved not only to forestall this possibility, but also to bring about Hungary's total involvement in the war. They were eager to see not only the deployment of additional troops, but also the expansion and intensification of Hungary's industrial and agricultural production to supplement the needs of the Reich. The latter requirement, coupled with Hungary's own needs to satisfy the demands of the military and of the civilian population, necessitated an expansion and centralization of the various types of labor service units that operated within and outside the country. The organizational and administrative centralization of these units became imperative because, as a consequence of mobilization, the industrial and agricultural enterprises lacked the skilled manpower required for the fulfillment of the demands imposed upon them. Many of these enterprises turned to the armed forces for help, requesting the allocation of labor servicemen. Eager to assure domestic tranquility and to satisfy the steadily increasing demands of the military and of the Third Reich, the *Honvédség* eventually allocated a large number of labor service companies to enterprises operating under the auspices of a number of ministries.[120] These companies remained under the ultimate jurisdiction of the military, but their operations were placed under the control of the various enterprises.

By the summer of 1943, over 800,000 individuals, both Jews and non-Jews, were in the military labor service. Organizationally, these individuals served within the framework of the following three major labor service systems:

- Military labor companies (*Katonai munkásszázadok*), composed of Hungarians and national minorities of Trianon Hungary.
- Public labor service battalions (*Közérdekű munkaszolgálatos zászlóaljak*).
- Auxiliary, i.e., Jewish, labor service companies (*Kisegitő* (*zsidó*) *munkásszázadok*).

Under a decision of Governor Horthy dated November 4, 1943, the three major labor service systems were centralized to assure their more effective and economical operation and to bring about greater labor discipline. They were placed under the central command of the newly established Labor Organization for National Defense (*Honvédelmi Munkaszervezet*), which was entrusted with the

- Establishment, training, and equipment of military, public, and auxiliary labor service companies for use both within and outside the country.
- Mobilization and allocation of skilled and unskilled workers to enterprises engaged in military production.
- Mobilization and allocation of workers to replace those called up for military service.
- Supervision of the way in which the labor servicemen were being housed, supplied, employed, and compensated.[121]

Under the new set-up, the state organizations as well as the enterprises engaged in military-related production were required to present all their requests for labor to the Ministry of Defense. Ultimate decision-making power was vested in the Minister, who was expected to act in conjunction with certain sections of the Ministry and with the Labor Organization for National Defense.[122]

The operational tasks were entrusted, according to Jenő Rőder, to the Labor Division (*Munkaügyi Csoport*) of the Ministry, which was placed under the command of Lieutenant-General Gusztáv Hennyey.[123] The Division was composed of two sections. One consisted of KMOF under the leadership of Horny; its primary tasks included the evaluation of requests for labor and the submission of recommendations relating thereto, the supervision of the distribution, and the assignment to specific locations of the labor service companies. The other section was headed by Colonel Egon Gátföldi (Spanner) and was in charge of the organization of the labor service units and of matters relating to logistics and discipline.[124] The organizational structure was altered again in 1944 in the wake of the German occupation.

The reorganizational measures, like the ministerial decisions relating to the treatment of the labor servicemen, had only minor effects on the realities of the labor service system. Csatay's warnings, like the earlier admonitions of Vilmos Nagy, remained largely unheeded. This was again especially true for the many companies deployed far from the immediate scrutiny of the central governmental authorities in the Ukraine and in Bor, Serbia.[125]

Labor Servicemen at Bor

The treatment of the Jewish labor servicemen in the copper mines of Bor and their tortuous odyssey during the Axis retreat from the Balkans in the fall of 1944 constitute one of the saddest chapters in the catastrophe of Hungarian Jewry. With the war going from bad to worse in 1943, the Germans became increasingly concerned with assuring the continued supply of their war industries with vitally important raw materials, including ferrous and nonferrous metals. As a consequence of the defeat and withdrawal from Soviet territory—the source of much of these materials—the Germans decided to intensify their mining operations in the areas nearer to the Third Reich. The munitions industry was especially interested in the expansion of copper production.

The Bor mines, which are situated about 200 kilometers (124 miles) southeast of Belgrade, supplied about 50 percent of the copper requirements of the German war industry. They were acquired by German interests following the subjugation of Yugoslavia in April 1941. Originally owned by the Société des Mines de Bor, which was controlled by the Mirabeau Bank of Paris, they were taken over by the Prussian National Bank (*Preussische Staatsbank*) on the pretext that the mines were supplying war materials to Britain.[126] They were placed under the overall supervision of Franz Neuhausen, the Trustee-General for Economic Affairs in Serbia, and were operated jointly by Siemens and the *Organisation Todt,* Albert Speer's construction agency.[127]

The Deployment Agreement. The idea of deploying Hungarian Jewish labor servicemen in the copper mines at Bor originated with Gerhard Fränk, Vice President of *Organisation Todt* (OT) and Speer's collaborator in the Ministry for Armament and War Production.[128]

In a note of February 20, 1943, Fränk established the number of workers needed by the mines at 13,000, of which only about 3,000 were already at work. He argued against the employment of Serbs, for they tended to "engage in passive resistance" or "go over to the partisans." The Bulgarians, on the other hand, were either unwilling to work in Serbia or were needed for fortification work in their own country.[129]

Since the Jews of Yugoslavia had been killed the year before, Fränk decided to solve his labor shortage problem by the acquisition of 10,000 Hungarian Jewish labor servicemen, for which purpose he got in touch with *SA-Obergruppenführer* Dietrich von Jagow, the German Minister in Budapest. Jagow had no difficulty in immediately obtaining the concurrence of "certain influential gentlemen" in the Hungarian Ministry of Defense, but the transfer required the agreement of the Hungarian government, which was a political question. Fränk, with Speer's blessing, got in touch with the German Foreign Office to bring about the effectuation of the deal, which had the approval of the *Reichsführer-SS*.[130]

Fränk's request was relayed by Bergmann, Minister in the *Inland* Section of the German Foreign Office, to Ribbentrop on February 23. He promptly approved it.[131] Thereupon Bergmann instructed Jagow to proceed with negotiations over the details of conditions of employment and remuneration. These were to be settled in consultation with Wilhelm Neyer, OT-*Hauptfrontführer* and OT representative in Budapest, and a certain Captain Leitner.[132]

Neyer was very influential in Budapest, especially in matters relating to the labor service system. He was the official liaison of the OT to the Ministry of Defense, especially KMOF. As a matter of fact, his office was adjacent to Horny's, and his close relationship with Horny, who spoke perfect German, guided much of KMOF's activities. He was constantly kept informed about all matters relating to the labor service system and was instrumental in the decisions pertaining to the call-up and deployment of the servicemen.[133] Neyer was also the exclusive link between OT and the Hungarian Ministry of Industry.[134]

Shortly after Bergmann's instructions had been relayed to Jagow, Neyer approached KMOF requesting that the Hungarian government authorize the allocations of Jewish labor service companies for work on German war-related projects. Specifically, he demanded the deployment of 20 labor service companies with 4,000 men for work at the German shipyards at Reval, Estonia, and of 10,000 men for the copper mines at Bor.[135] In addition, he demanded the replenishment of the labor service companies with the Second Hungarian Army in the Ukraine.

Horny immediately relayed the German demands to Vilmos Nagy, who was aware of the brutal conditions at Bor. Nagy was vehemently opposed to granting the demands, and the Hungarian Council of Ministers went along with his recommendations.[136] In the meantime, however, the "influential gentlemen" in the Ministry of Defense and the General Staff, including General Ferenc Szombathelyi, the Chief of Staff, continued to encourage the Germans by promising them the necessary manpower. When informed about these dealings with the Germans behind his back, Nagy was upset not only because Szombathelyi and the others had no political authority to make such promises, but also because of his awareness of the slave-labor conditions that prevailed in the mines.[137]

The Germans, of course, did not give up and continued to exert great pressure, which was soon accompanied by a demand for the replacement of the Minister of Defense. Aware of Nagy's opposition to the extradition of Hungarian citizens, both Prime Minister Kállay and Minister of Industry Géza Bornemissza apparently tried to convince him on June 12, 1943, to change his position and to allow at least the assignment of 2,000 labor servicemen to Serbia. Nagy remained steadfast in his opposition, especially since he was by then convinced that the Germans would lose the war.[138]

With the resignation of Nagy there was no further obstacle to the granting of the Germans' request. On June 23, Jagow informed the Foreign Office that the Hungarians had made a firm commitment for the deployment of 6,000 labor servicemen in companies under the command of Hungarian officers.[139] The final agreement was hammered out on July 1, and was signed on July 2 by Neyer for OT and by General Imre Ruszkiczay-Rüdiger, Hungarian Deputy Minister of Defense.[140] The agreement provided that

- The Hungarian government would place at the disposal of OT 3,000 Jewish workers organized into military companies. They would be handed over to the Germans at the Prahovo Danube station, with the first installment of 1,000 men to be delivered no later than July 15, 1943.
- The Jewish companies were to remain under Hungarian military control; in case of difficulties, the commander of the Jewish battalions was to prepare duplicate written reports—one for the Hungarian Ministry of Defense and one for OT.
- In compensation for the work force, the Germans would deliver monthly to the Hungarians 100 tons of copper ore containing at least 30 percent copper in a form usable by Hungarian foundries. The shipments were to be handed over to the Hungarians against payment at Prahovo.

- The details on the deployment, feeding, and housing of the work force were to be the ones worked out by the mixed commission which made an on-the-spot check in behalf of the Hungarian Ministry of Defense between May 26 and June 1, 1943.
- The Hungarian Ministry of Defense would place at the disposal of OT additional Jewish manpower if further copper shipments were offered by the Ministry of Supplies of the Third Reich.[141]

The agreement was hailed by most Germanophile elements in the Ministry of Defense and the country as beneficial for Hungary. The people associated with KMOF—including, of course, Horny—emphasized that the agreement was beneficial and necessary to assure the expansion of Hungarian industrial production, since part of the copper ore produced by the labor servicemen in Bor was promised to the Hungarians.[142] These proponents, however, conveniently neglected to mention that the Hungarian war industry itself was to a large extent working in the service of the Third Reich.

Although the agreement was signed on July 2, it appears that the Hungarian Ministry of Defense had earlier already authorized the transfer of some Hungarian Jewish servicemen. According to a survivor of the Bor ordeal, his company arrived at the copper mines on June 15, 1943.[143]

The detailed instructions for the implementation of the Hungarian-German agreement were spelled out in a decree (No. 111 470 eln. KMOF-1943) of the Minister of Defense signed by Ruszkiczay-Rüdiger on July 6.[144] The labor services companies readied, under the agreement, for deployment in July 1943 are listed in table 10.4.

The labor servicemen scheduled for deployment in the mines were given a short furlough to enable them to acquire the necessary clothing and equipment. They were required to return to duty two days before their scheduled departure.[145] The Hungarian authorities assumed the financial costs of these labor service companies until they reached Prahovo in Serbia. From that point on, these burdens were assumed by OT. Overall immediate command over these companies was entrusted to Lieutenant-Colonel András Balogh. Just before their departure, the labor servicemen and the members of their families who came to bid them farewell in Hodmezővásárhely heard a spirited and encouraging speech by Neyer, who apparently was eager to quell the anxieties of the Jews and of the decent strata of Hungarian society.[146]

Conditions of Labor. In accordance with the flexibility provided by Ar-

TABLE 10.4.
LABOR SERVICE COMPANIES
DEPLOYED IN BOR, SERBIA
IN JULY 1943

Labor Company	Stationed at:	To Be Readied for Deployment by:
Labor Battalion No. V	Szeged	
Company No. V/1	Páhi	July 11, 1943
Company No. V/2	Szeged	
Company No. V/3	Páhi	
Company No. V/4	Szeged	
Company No. XII/5	Tasnád	
Company No. 101./62		July 20, 1943
Company No. 101./63	Szentkirály-	
Company No. 101./64	szabadja	
Company No. 101./68		
Company No. 110./59		
Company No. 103./4	Székesfehérvár	July 30, 1943
Company No. 108./81	Zombor (Bükkszállás)	
Company No. 108./84	Zombor (Bácsszentiván)	
Company No. 108./90	Zombor (Bácskertes)	
Special Company No. 801 (Jehovah's Witnesses)	Jászberény	

SOURCE: *FAA*, 2:378.

ticle 5 of the German-Hungarian agreement, the total number of Hungarian Jewish labor servicemen at Bor increased steadily. By the time the Germans were compelled to evacuate the Balkans in September 1944, their number reached 6,000.[147] In addition to the Hungarian Jewish servicemen, the Germans also employed at the mines a small number of Hungarian Seventh Day Adventists (*Szombatisták*) and Jehovah's Witnesses, (who were also classified as "enemies" ot the Third Reich), Serbian convicts, Russian prisoners, and, after the withdrawal of Italy from the Axis Alliance, a number of Italians.[148]

Although under Hungarian military control and discipline, the Hungarian Jewish servicemen worked under the immediate supervision of German foremen. They worked under grueling conditions for around

11 hours a day, receiving 7 *Dinars* and half a pound of bread and a portion of watery soup per day in compensation.[149]

Some of the labor servicemen were employed in building the Bor–Žagubica railway line; others were engaged in road repair work. The majority, however, worked in the mines. Especially hard and exhausting was the lot of those building the access tunnel, which was 5 kilometers long and several hundred meters deep. The labor servicemen had to work in knee-deep water breathing air filled with suffocating dust and explosive gas.[150]

During their leisure time, including Sundays, they were often ordered out for "household" chores—cutting wood for the kitchen or doing repair work on the buildings. Some of the company commanders and the guards were especially sadistic. On the slightest excuse they would hang the "culprits" by their hands, which were tied behind their backs. On some occasions the guards would bang against the rope or hit the victims until they lost consciousness.[151]

Each company had its own commander and guards. Overall command was exercised first by András Balogh and then by Lieutenant-Colonel Ede Marányi.[152]

Despite the deplorable living and working conditions in the camp and mines, the losses in life were relatively negligible.[153] Tragedy befell the draftees during and after their withdrawal in September–October 1944, when the Axis Forces were compelled to evacuate the Balkans under Red Army and Yugoslav partisan pressure.

The Road to Disaster. The Germans decided to evacuate the Bor area in mid-September. The first contingent of Hungarian Jewish servicemen, numbering about 3,600, left Bor on September 17 under the escort of about 100 Hungarian guards. A few of them escaped or were rescued by the Yugoslav partisans.[154] The bulk of this first group, however, was marched under the most inhuman conditions through Belgrade, Ujvidék, and Zombor to Mohács.

From Mohács they were transferred to Szentkirályszabadja in Veszprém County, and from there they were deported to Germany. They eventually ended up in the camps of Flossenburg, Sachsenhausen, and Oranienburg. Only a handful of the former Bor inmates survived the German concentration camps.[155]

An even more cruel fate befell the second group of Jewish evacuees, numbering about 2,500, who left Bor on September 19 under the command of First Lieutenant Sándor Pataky and Second Lieutenant Pál Jóhaz.[156] The road to Belgrade led through Žagubica, Petrovac, Mala

Krsna, and Smederevo. They reached Belgrade on September 25. While the men were driven mercilessly with little or no food and water, only a few were shot during this stretch. The Serbs along the road tried to help them and urged them to escape, but few dared.[157] Three days later they left for Pančevo toward the east, where eight of the starving servicemen were killed for having picked some corn or having begged for water. This area was inhabited by Swabians, most of them pro-Nazi, who denounced the "plundering" Jews. Exhausted and emaciated, some of the servicemen tried to escape here. The Germans caught 147 and executed 146 of them (one was able to escape) on the road to the village of Jabuka.[158]

From Pančevo the column of servicemen was taken northwest toward Perlez, Titel, and Ujvidék under German supervision and accompanied by local members of the German militia, who wore black uniforms with armbands marked "DM" (*Deutsche Miliz*). Along the way the column came across a heap of rotten melons. The Jews had been given permission to pick them, but the Germans shot about 250 when they did so. When the column reached the then Hungarian-held territory of Yugoslavia near Titel, control was again resumed by the Hungarians. At Ujvidék, the column was kept in strict confinement near the railway station for about three days and then continued to march to Szenttamás on the way to Zombor. Near Szenttamás about 20 of the Jews were killed for an attempt to drink water and 10 more were murdered near Novi Vrbas for being unable to walk.[159] The column reached Cservenka on October 6; the following day about 800 of the servicemen were moved to Zombor and the others were taken over by the SS.[160]

The Slaughter of October 7–8, 1944. At Cservenka the Jewish servicemen were quartered in the Glaeser Welker Rauch brickyards. Rumors were rampant on October 7 that the Hungarian commander's request for supplies had been rejected by the Germans at Zombor and that the Germans had decided to eliminate the Jews in order to free the roads for the withdrawing Axis forces. The day was spent in terror and great agony, for the SS, in preparation for the executions, decided to first destroy the Jews' spirit and tire them out totally. The Jews were tortured and made to run from place to place all day. At 9:00 P.M. they were allowed back to their quarters only to be awakened 90 minutes later.

The SS made them surrender all their remaining valuables, including wedding bands, and then took them in groups of 20 to 30 to the huge pit that was used as a source of raw materials for the manufacturing of bricks. Here is how one of the three survivors of the massacre described the executions:

The pit was about 40–50 meters long and 8–10 meters wide. Its depth was about 1½ meters. . . . On either side of the pit four SS-men were standing. Two of them brought up the victims, and two shot them. They would take 20 to one side and 20 to the other. . . . They were firing from a range of three meters. . . . I saw all this. Then they did the same to me. He (the SS-man) came up to me, prepared me and then stepped aside. Thus I also received the present, the bullet. . . .[161]

The shooting ended around 4:00 A.M. on October 8, by which time from 700 to 1,000 Jews had been massacred.[162] The survivors of the column left Cservenka at 5:00 A.M. toward Zombor, only to be exposed to further bloodshed. Near Stari Sivac, for example, a German soldier on a motorcycle killed several Jews who had been resting by the roadside. The column was also fired on by Hungarian soldiers from a train withdrawing them along the Sivac–Krnja railway line. Several casualties were suffered in Zombor itself and along the road between Zombor and Gjakovo. The column finally reached Baja from where the servicemen were transferred three days later to Szentkirályszabadja. Here, Lieutenant-Colonel Marányi, the former commander of Bor, executed seven of them "to reestablish order and discipline."[163]

In Baja the survivors were subjected to the same fate as the one that befell the Jews of the Hungarian provinces—deportation. Most of them ended up in Buchenwald and Flossenburg, from where only a handful returned.

Among the Jewish labor service victims who were withdrawn from Bor was Miklós Radnóti, a noted Hungarian poet and literary translator. He was killed by an SS-man sometime between November 6 and 10, 1944, and was buried in a mass grave at Abda, near Győr. When his body was exhumed after the war, his last poems were found in his raincoat.[164] They reflect the agony and martyrdom of the Jewish labor servicemen who served at Bor.

The Labor Service System During the German Occupation

The Sztójay Era. Following the German occupation of Hungary on March 19, 1944, and the establishment of the pro-Nazi Döme Sztójay government, the labor service system turned out to be a source of rescue for many thousands of Jewish men threatened by deportation. While the Jewish labor servicemen in the Ukraine and in Bor continued to suffer from the harsh and often cruel treatment of their superiors, those called up or volunteering for duty in the labor service companies stationed within the country fared comparatively well, at least until the *Nyilas* era.

It is one of the ironies of history that the Ministry of Defense, which had been viewed as one of the chief causes of suffering among Jews during the previous four to five years, suddenly emerged as the major governmental institution actively involved in the saving of Jewish lives. The motivations behind the Ministry's actions are not absolutely clear. It is safe to assume that many national governmental and military leaders, as well as many local commanders, aware of the realities of the ghettoization and deportation program and motivated by humanitarian instincts, did everything in their power to rescue as many Jews as possible. One of the most praiseworthy of these military figures was Colonel Imre Reviczky, the Commander of Labor Battalion No. X of Nagybánya. Under his direction, all Jews who appeared for service at his headquarters were immediately inducted and provided with food and shelter, irrespective of their age or state of health.[165]

These Hungarians were also probably motivated to save able-bodied Jews because of the manpower shortage from which the country was suffering at the time. This shortage also affected projects that were of great interest to the Germans. At a meeting of May 1, 1944, attended by the representatives of OT, the *Wehrmacht,* and the *Sicherheitspolizei* in Budapest, it was agreed that all requests for labor, Jewish and non-Jewish alike, were to be submitted to and handled exclusively by Neyer, the OT's representative in the Hungarian Ministry of Defense.

The Hungarian and German authorities apparently agreed that in order to meet the manpower shortage and to assure the continued production of the industrial and agricultural goods required by the military, about 150,000 able-bodied Jews would be exempted from the "evacuation" measures that were about to begin. Under this plan, the number of Jewish labor service companies was to be increased from 210 to 575.[166]

The agreement did not enjoy the support of the Eichmann-*Sonderkommando,* which was eager to make Hungary *Judenrein.* Its position was clarified by SS-*Hauptsturmführer* Theodor Dannecker, who argued that the able-bodied labor servicemen could be better employed for the common war effort in Germany and in consequence would be neither subjected to a special selection process nor gassed.[167] However, the Minister of Defense, Lajos Csatay, remained adamant and proceeded with the implementation of the agreement. He had an instruction issued, calling on Jewish males aged 18 to 48 to report to their recruiting stations for induction into the labor service system.[168] The pertinent announcements, posted in many parts of the country, could not possibly have been read by all those affected by the call-up order, for the Jews, with the exception of those of Budapest, had already been placed in ghettos and many of them had in fact been already deported. In view of this reality, the Ministry of Defense and the headquarters of the labor service battalions issued an unusually large number of so-called SAS call-up notices with instructions that they were to be forwarded to the ghettos or internment camps in case the named Jews had already been removed from their residences. Some army commanders even decided to effectuate the recruitment of eligible Jews in the ghettos themselves. This was, for example, the position adopted by Colonel Dezső Újvárossy of Army Corps No. III, which had its headquarters in Szombathely. In a secret note of June 6, he instructed the chief executive officer of Körmend that since the Jews had been placed in ghettos he was going to carry out the instructions of the Ministry of Defense within the ghetto walls. He requested that the Jewish Councils instruct all affected Jews to appear on June 12 at a place designated by them and to guide the recruitment committees to this place. Újvárossy instructed the executive officer to assign police and physicians to assist the recruiting officers.[169]

These activities became a source of great annoyance to the German and Hungarian officials involved in the Final Solution program. Lieutenant-Colonel László Ferenczy, who was in charge of the ghettoization and concentration of the Jews, was particularly upset. He complained about it not only to his immediate superiors, including Endre, but also to his SS colleagues directly involved in the ghettoization, concentration, and deportation process. During the ghettoization of the Jews of Transylvania early in May, Ferenczy consulted the SS representative in Kolozsvár, Dieter Wisliceny, who informed him, on instructions received from the Eichmann-*Sonderkommando* in Budapest, that on the basis of an alleged agreement with the Hungarian Ministry of Defense no Jews could be called up for labor service from the areas in which ghettoization was taking place. Ferenczy thereupon prohibited the further delivery of call-up notices.[170] Lieutenant-General Hennyey, who was at the time in charge of the Mobilization Division of the Ministry, appears to have concurred in this, declaring at a conference held on May 25 that the issuance of call-up notices had been halted as of May 15. While such notices were issued even after the conference, by that date most of them could be delivered only in the concentration centers where the Jews were awaiting entrainment for Auschwitz.

Ferenczy's disappointment was accompanied by anger that in many places the labor servicemen were permitted to walk freely, without the escort of Christian guards, and that their passes had not been withdrawn.[171] Indeed, the labor servicemen did not have to wear the Yellow Star. They continued to be identified by a yellow or white arm band, depending upon their religious affiliation.[172]

Ferenczy was particularly distressed over the actions of some officers associated with Labor Battalion No I, which had its headquarters in Jászberény. These officers, including Lieutenant Sándor Body, the battalion physician, had authorized a 10-day leave for about 400 labor servicemen. Four of these were arrested early in June by the German Security Police. Upon learning the details of the leave, the Germans decided to stage a general "preventive" raid at the railway station of Hatvan, a major rail link between Budapest and Jászberény, on June 7, the day the labor servicemen were expected to return to duty.[173]

The staging of the raid for that day was not an accident. It was during June 5–10 that the Jews of Northern Hungary were being concentrated prior to deportation. When the train with the labor servicemen returning from furlough stopped at Hatvan, a Hungarian deportation squad headed by Captain Márton Zöldi, who had earlier distinguished himself in the Délvidék massacres of January–February 1942, saw to it that the cars with the labor servicemen were attached to a deportation train that had just halted at the station.[174] They ended up in Auschwitz. However, the Ministry of Defense was not deterred from its course and continued to issue call-up notices for Jews in the areas of Hungary which were not yet fully *Judenrein.*[175]

On June 7, the Minister of Defense issued a secret decree under which the labor servicemen were to be treated like POW's. On the surface, the Decree was punitive in character (and it was so implemented in many companies), but in fact it was most probably designed to protect the Jews from the danger of arrest by the SS and their Hungarian hirelings and from subsequent deportation. The Decree stipulated, among other things, that the new labor servicemen as well as the mobilized skilled workers, engineers, and technicians were to be placed in special POW-like camps in the vicinity of the plants or factories in which they were to be employed. The camps were to be surrounded by barbed-wire or planks and guarded on a permanent basis. The Jews were not allowed to leave the camps except in the company of Christian escorts, and they were even forced to spend their leaves within the confines of the camps.[176] During the summer of 1944, the armed forces emerged as a partial source of rescue for the civilian Jews as well. Many of the Jews of Budapest—men and women alike—were employed together with the regular labor servicemen on projects of great interest to the military. With the periodic bombing of Budapest and other targets in Hungary following the country's occupation by the Germans, the Jews were often used to clear the rubble caused by the air-raids.[177]

With the shortage of labor getting progressively acute, the government resorted increasingly to the recruitment of women into the labor service system. In 1943, the women served under the central administration of the National Superintendent of Labor Service for Women (*a Női Munkaszolgálat Országos Felügyelője*).[178] Following the reorganization of the labor service system in 1944, (Appendix 1), they were placed, like all other labor service personnel, under the jurisdiction of the Labor Organization for National Defense.

During the recruitment drive of 1944, priority was given to the call-up of women between 18 and 30, who had been employed in Jewish enterprises.[179] Concurrently with the easing of the deportation threat in Budapest, the Ministry of Defense also found it timely to re-regulate the system for the assignment and remuneration of the labor service companies employed by enterprises operating under the auspices of the various ministries.[180]

The situation of the Jews continued to improve relatively during August and September following the replacement of Sztójay by General Géza Lakatos, the former Commander of the First Hungarian Army. To forestall the anticipated German pressure for the "evacuation" of the Jews of Budapest, the leaders of the remnant community, including Ottó Komoly, the Zionist leader, worked out a scheme with some of the Hungarian officials to place the remaining Jews into special work camps in the provinces. The scheme, which was also communicated to some of the Hungarians opposing the regime, including Reverend Albert Bereczky of the Reformed Church,[181] was never implemented because it was overtaken by the fast-moving historical events. By early fall, even Governor Horthy became fully convinced of the hopelessness of the struggle and decided to extricate Hungary from the war. His ill-prepared attempt at an armistice failed on October 15, when Ferenc Szálasi and his Arrow Cross Party staged a coup with the assistance of the Germans. With the *Nyilas* in power, the status of the labor servicemen, like that of Jewry as a whole, became once again intolerable.

The Nyilas Era. The coup brought to power the ultra-Right radical elements that were vehemently opposed not only to the Jews, but also to the aristocratic-conservative part of the Hungarian ruling class.

In the Szálasi government, the position of Minister of Defense was held by Lieutenant-General Károly Beregfy, the former Commander of Army Corps VI with headquarters in Debrecen. A notorious anti-Semite, Beregfy did everything in his power to exacerbate the position of the Jews. Less than a week after the seizure of power, Beregfy ordered the call-up "for national defense service" of all Jewish men between the ages of 16 and 60 and of Jewish women between the ages of 16 and 40. The recruitment was to be effectuated within two days.[182] On October 26, Beregfy authorized the transfer of a large number of labor service companies to the Germans (Appendix 2) allegedly to work on the construction of fortifications along the borders of the Third Reich and Hungary for the defense of Vienna. The companies were ordered to proceed to Mosonmagyaróvár via Tata and Győr and from there they were directed to Hegyeshalom, the Hungarian checkpoint on the road to Vienna.[183] The transfer of the labor service companies began on November 2.

Jewish women were the subject of two additional call-up decrees issued on November 2 and 3. The first related to the call-up of women between 16 and 50 years of age who knew how to sew;[184] the other was a repeat of the order of October 26 and involved the call-up of all Jewish women between 16 and 40 years of age for "national defense-related labor service."[185]

Shortly after their "recruitment," thousands of these Jewish women were marched together with the regular labor servicemen along a highway of death leading to the borders of the Reich. There, they were deployed for the building of the "Eastern Wall"—trenches, tank traps, and other fortifications—for the defense of Vienna (see chapter 26).

With the inexorable advance of the Red Army toward the Hungarian capital, the *Nyilas* decided to transfer the labor service companies to Transdanubia (Dunántul) along the Hegyeshalom, Sopron, and Kőszeg line in Western Hungary to build fortifications and perform other military-related work for the defense of Vienna. Many of the labor servicemen, including those in the so-called "protected" (*védett*) companies—those that enjoyed the protection of neutral countries, especially Sweden and Switzerland—were entrained at the Józsefvárosi Railway Station in Budapest under conditions reminiscent of the deportations from the provinces. The number of Jewish labor servicemen handed over to the Germans was estimated at around 50,000.[186]

The lot of these servicemen was not very different from that of the Jews in the most notorious concentration camps. Particularly tragic was the situation of the labor servicemen stationed in and around Fertőrákos, Balf, and Hidegség near Sopron and in Kőszeg. In Kőszeg—the seat of the Szálasi government since the beginning of the evacuation of Budapest in November—there were around 8,000 labor servicemen, who had been directed there via Hegyeshalom and Zürndorf.[187]

Poorly housed and more poorly fed, they were required to work for long hours during the winter months of 1944–45. Those who became exhausted and could no longer work were simply shot and buried in mass graves. The *Nyilas* and their SS friends went on a rampage with the approach of the Red Army. Hundreds upon hundreds of labor servicemen were killed in cold blood. The exhumations conducted after the liberation found, for example, the bodies of 790 labor servicemen in a mass grave in Hidegség. Approximately 400 bodies were found at Ilkamajor, 814 at Nagycenk, 350 at Sopron-Bánfalva, 300 at Mosonszentmiklós, and 220 near Hegyeshalom.[188] At Kőszeg, the labor servicemen were even subjected to gassing. This took place during the evacuation of the city on March 22–23, 1945, when 95 ill and emaciated labor servicemen were locked in a sealed barrack and gassed by three German commandos especially equipped for this purpose. They were buried next to the other 2,500 labor servicemen who died or were killed in the area.[189] Large-scale atrocities against labor servicemen also took place at Kiskunhalas and at Pusztavám in Fejér County.[190]

The surviving labor servicemen were herded toward the Third Reich. Many of them ended up first in the Mauthausen concentration camp and then in the Günskirchen camp. Along the way they were continuously abused and subjected to the murderous whims of the SS. It was in the course of this ordeal that László Fenyő, a noted poet, lost his life near Burgeisenberg.

The lot of the labor service companies left in Budapest was just a shade better than that of those in Western Hungary. One of them, Company No. 101/359, the so-called Clothes-Collecting Company (*Ruhagyüjtő Munkásszázad*) was under the command of László Ocskay, a very decent and humane officer. The company was originally assigned to work under the jurisdiction of the Jewish Veterans' Committee with headquarters at 12 Síp Street, the seat of the Jewish Council. After the establishment of the ghetto in Budapest early in December 1944, the company was designated to provide police protection within the ghetto. After the *Nyilas* rejected the plan, the company was transferred to the facilities of a high school on Abonyi Street, outside the ghetto, where the men worked for, and ironically enjoyed the protection of, the SS. With the aid of Adorján Stella, a highly decorated reserve officer, about 25 of these labor servicemen led by Dr. György Wilhelm organized themselves into a special service unit acting for and in cooperation with the International Red Cross. This unit, known as Section T of the International Red Cross, was engaged in the relief and rescue of the persecuted Jews and also took part in some resistance activities (see chapter 29).

Although an Allied victory was only a question of time, the Szálasi government continued to act as if no catastrophe were impending. It continued to deal seriously with various aspects of the Jewish question, including the labor servicemen. On January 15, 1945, for example, the *Nyilas* Ministry of Defense was still interested in determining the exact number, location, and character of the labor service companies that were in existence.[191] Six days later, the High Command issued a decree prohibiting contact between the Jewish labor servicemen and Christian Hungarians, whether military or civilian.[192] But these were merely the cries of the mortally wounded *Nyilas* and Nazi forces. For while the labor servicemen, like all other Jews in captivity, continued to suffer at their hands, the ring drawn around them by the victorious Allies was getting ever smaller. Hungary was finally liberated on April 4. Most of the other Jews in the Nazi sphere of influence, including of course the Hungarian Jewish labor servicemen and deportees, had to wait for another month, when the Third Reich collapsed with the unconditional surrender of its remaining leadership.

Jewish Self-Help to Labor Servicemen
A few months after the organization of the labor service system in 1939, the central Jewish organizations began to devote serious attention to the rights and interests of Jewish veterans and servicemen. In the forefront was the Jewish Community of Pest (*a Pesti Izraelita Hitközség—*

PIH), the country's largest and most prosperous communal organization. Early in November 1939, they established under the aegis of the PIH a Communal Veteran's Section (*Hadviseltek Hitközségi Ügyosztálya—*HHU). The HHU acted in close cooperation with the charity and fundraising organizations of the community that had been established shortly before. By far the most important of these were the Welfare Bureau of Hungarian Jews (*Magyar Izraeliták Pártfogó Irodája—*MIPI) and its fund-raising arm, the National Hungarian Jewish Assistance Campaign (*Országos Magyar Zsidó Segítő Akció*, OMZSA—see chapter 3).

Within a short while, the HHU was transformed into a veterans' organization subordinated to and supported by both the MIOI and the MAOIH. It adopted a new name, the Veterans' Committee of the National Jewish Bureaus (*Országos Izraelita Irodák Hadviseltek Bizottsága—*OIIHB) better known simply as Veterans' Committee (*Hadviseltek Bizottsága—*HB). Its offices were located at the headquarters of the Jewish community of Budapest, 12 Síp Street. It operated under the leadership of Dr. Béla Fábián.[193]

The interests of the converted labor servicemen were protected by the War Veterans' Comradely Group (*Hadviseltek Bajtársi Csoportja*), which was organized in November 1941 under the auspices of the Holy Cross Association (*Szent Kereszt Egyesület*). It was led by József Cavallier, the head of the Association. Before Hungary's entry into the war on June 27, 1941, the HB was primarily concerned with fighting the inequities of the laws that called for the separation of servicemen on the basis of race and religion.

When the Jews were forced to wear their own clothes, their situation in the field companies became particularly distressing—especially after the deployment of the Second Hungarian Army along the Don during the late spring of 1942. By fall, many of the Jews no longer had adequate clothes to survive the cold Russian winter. In September 1942, the Ministry of the Interior authorized MIOI and MAOIH to organize a campaign among Jews for the collection of winter clothes for the labor servicemen.[194] Immediately thereafter, a massive campaign was launched on a nationwide basis under the general direction of the HB. In addition to the central Jewish organs and organizations, every local communal organization and congregation was mobilized for the campaign. In addition to personal appearances and appeals from the pulpits, the call for donations was frequently carried on the pages of *A*

Magyar Zsidók Lapja (The Journal of Hungarian Jews).[195] As a result of the 1942 fall campaign, 28 freightcars laden with winter clothes for the Jewish labor servicemen were shipped to the front lines.[196]

Eventually the specific needs of the labor servicemen serving in the Ukraine were identified by the Ministry of Defense and communicated directly to the HB for action. The shipments of such goods collectively as well as individually continued until the deportation of the Jews in 1944.

Although the HB issued periodic reports about the successful transmission of packages, there is no conclusive evidence whether such aid actually reached the labor servicemen stationed in the Ukraine and in Bor. There were many reports of such packages having been stolen by the guards and their contents sold at high prices. According to Lieutenant-General Jenő Rőder, the clothing collected during 1943 was forwarded to the front in the fall by rail. The freight cars were guarded by Hungarian soldiers up to the frontier, when they were replaced by Germans. Of these shipments, Rőder claims, the Jewish labor servicemen received nothing.[197]

The HB was also actively involved in solving problems relating to these servicemen and their families. It often acted as an intermediary for the transmission of specific grievances to the proper governmental authorities and above all to KMOF. Among the grievances most often voiced were those related to the "illegal" call-up or retention in service of men over 42 years of age, pensions for veterans, supplementary allocations for the families of labor servicemen (including their widows and orphans), and the equipment and treatment of the men in active service.[198] In the course of time, the HB became the major source of information relating to the clarification of laws affecting the labor servicemen and the recognized conduit to the Ministry of Defense. It was through its articles in the *A Magyar Zsidók Lapja* that the public at large learned about the details and implications of the laws and regulations relating to pensions, war supplements and relief, and many other related matters.[199]

The competence of the HB in these matters was also recognized by KMOF, which on September 9, 1943, announced that all individual and private appeals and inquiries relating to the labor servicemen were to be submitted to HB.[200] However, as a consequence HB was so overwhelmed by inquiries and petitions even in areas where it clearly had no competence (e.g., those relating to the possible demobilization, location, and movement of labor service companies) that it was compelled to issue a statement emphasizing that it was not a government agency. The statement stressed that the HB was performing primarily a social mission and that it had no knowledge of and could exercise no influence in matters relating exclusively to the military.[201]

The activities of the HB were expanded after the German occupation to include matters relating to the employment of the Jews of Budapest on war-related projects specified by the German and Hungarian authorities. Toward the end of the war, its primary concerns revolved around the safe and speedy return of the deportees and of the labor servicemen in Soviet POW camps.

Hungarian Jews in Soviet POW Camps

The number of Hungarian Jews in Soviet captivity during the war cannot be accurately determined. The estimates vary from 20,000 to 30,000.[202] There were basically two types of Jewish labor servicemen in Soviet POW camps: those who escaped from their units in search of liberation from their terrible oppression; and those (and these were the overwhelming majority) who were captured by the Red Army following the offensive around Voronezh in January 1943. Their treatment was generally the same, although many with good "political credentials" were given preferential status. In most cases, the labor servicemen, though formerly oppressed and severely persecuted by the Hungarians and the Germans, were kept in camps that also included the captured elements of the *Wehrmacht* and the *Honvédség*. Often they shared their captivity with their own former officers and guards. And, in fact, in some cases the labor servicemen were treated much worse than the Hungarian officers because the camp commanders normally accorded officers the special treatment that was due to those with military ranks.[203]

In their approach to the Jewish labor servicemen the Soviet authorities followed basically the same approach that the United States followed toward the Japanese Americans but in a much more primitive and brutal fashion. In the midst of war they had neither the time nor the inclination to differentiate between those POW's who might be pro-Soviet and those who might be anti-Soviet. Moreover, from the Soviet point of view, the labor servicemen had been engaged in operations that were of great use to the enemy. In fairness, it must be noted that the Soviet authorities were no more generous with their own subjects who had "allowed themselves to fall into enemy hands." After their liberation by the Red Army, they, too, were placed in various types of "re-habilitation" or "retraining" camps which were not basically different from the POW camps in which the labor servicemen were held.

The attitude of the Soviet officers and officials directly involved in the capture and the subsequent placement of the labor servicemen into POW camps varied. There were many among them who were anti-Semitically inclined and who desired to make absolutely no differentiation between the Jews and the other POW's, whether the latter were Nazis or *Nyilas*. On the other hand there were also a large number of understanding officers and officials, who were aware of the realities of the anti-Jewish persecutions in Nazi-dominated Europe and of the character of the Hungarian labor service system. Many among these were Jewish and some of them spoke Yiddish. It was through their generosity that many a captured labor serviceman was enabled to "escape" from the temporary front-line camps and avoid being transferred to the POW camps in the Soviet Union. Many who ended up in Soviet POW camps were helped by the leaders of the Hungarian Communist Party and their sympathizers in exile in the Soviet Union. Foremost among these leaders, who subsequently played a leading role in the postwar evolution of Hungary, were Mihály Farkas, Ernő Gerő, Béla Illés, and Zoltán Vas. It was partially through their intervention that many of the emaciated labor servicemen captured by the Red Army were saved from almost certain death by being placed and treated in the Davidovka Hospital.[204] It was also through the good offices of the Hungarian exiles in the Soviet Union that the Hungarian-language Kossuth-Radio broadcasts from Moscow periodically informed listeners in Hungary about the status of individual labor servicemen in POW camps. Most of the captured labor servicemen, however, were not so lucky. They ended up in a variety of camps all over the Soviet Union, including the area close to the Arctic Ocean, Siberia, the Ural Mountain communities, and the Caucasus. The larger POW camps in which the Hungarian Jewish labor servicemen were held were as follows:

Arkhangelsk (Camps No. 211/1, 211/2, and 221/1); Asbest; Asha (130); Beltsy (103); Bogorodsk (437); Borisov (183 and 425); Chelyabinsk (8, 9, and 68/5); Cherepovets (437); Gomel (189/13); Gorki (30/0, 117/1, and 242); Kalinin (7381); Karaganda (99); Kharkov (7149/2); Kiev (62/4 and 62/16); Kimry (384/7); Kirov (307/3, 307/8, 7303/3, 7307/2, and 7307/8); Krasnogorsk (27/1 and 27/3); Krasnokamsk (207/8); Magnitogorsk (30); Minsk (168/15); Moscow (27/1 and 435);

Nizhnij Tagil (153/1, 153/2, 153/3, 153/4, and 153/6); Odessa; Petrovenka (256/13); Rostov (251/1); Rudnichnyy (3171); Rustavi (182/3); Saratov District (157); Sevastopol (245/16); Shakhty (182/3 and 182/7); Stalingrad (108/2); Stalino (280/14 and 280/26); Stryy; Sverdlov District (523/5); Talitsa (165); Volsk (137/1); Vorkuta; and Zaporozhye (100/1).[205]

Shortly after the end of the hostilities, the surviving remnant of the Hungarian Jewish community, including the returnees from the liberated German concentration camps, organized a campaign for the speedy repatriation of the labor servicemen from Soviet POW camps. Among the most important Jewish organizations newly established for this purpose as well as for the rehabilitation of the victims of Nazism and Fascism were the National MUSZ Organization (*Országos MUSZ Szervezet*), the National Anti-Fascist Union of Labor Servicemen (*A Munkaszolgálatosok Országos Antifasiszta Szövetsége*), the National Jewish Aid Committee (*Az Országos Zsidó Segitő Bizottság*), and the National Committee for the Care of Deportees (*A Deportáltakat Gondozó Országos Bizottság*—DEGOB). The former two were composed of and were primarily dedicated to the protection and advancement of the interests of the former labor servicemen. DEGOB also had a historical documentation center to collect the accounts of the survivors, deportees and labor servicemen alike.[206]

In the pursuit of their objectives, the leaders of these associations organized a number of mass meetings and bombarded the Hungarian and Soviet authorities with petitions and appeals urging the speedy return of the labor servicemen. One such mass meeting, for example, was held in the Royal Café in Budapest on April 14, 1946.[207] The Soviet authorities were approached, via Gyula Szekfű, a noted Hungarian historian who was then serving as Minister in Moscow.[208] But all of these efforts remained basically fruitless until after the signing of the Peace Treaties in February 1947.[209] Although a few individuals managed by some means to get home before that date,[210] the bulk of the labor servicemen were not returned until the repatriation of all Hungarian and Romanian nationals in the Soviet Union. The first list of repatriated labor servicemen was published on June 19, 1947.[211] From that date on, ever larger numbers of labor servicemen were repatriated.[212]

Notes

1. *FAA,* pp. vii–viii.

2. The ministry was subsequently renamed the Ministry of Defense (*Honvédelmi Minisztérium*).

3. *FAA,* p. xi.

4. *Ibid.,* p. xiii.

5. The visit to Kiel began on August 22, 1938, and was used by the Germans to impress not only Horthy and his entourage, including Prime Minister Béla Imrédy, Foreign Minister Kálmán Kánya, and Minister of Defense Jenő Rátz, but also the Western Powers.

6. Following its adoption by the lower house on January 27, 1939, and by the upper house on February 4, the Law was promulgated on March 11. For text see "1939. évi II. törvénycikk a honvédelemről" (Law No. II of 1939 on National Defense), in *1939. évi Országos Törvénytár* (National Code of Laws for 1939). (Budapest, March 11, 1939).

7. The invitation had been sent out in the name of the Minister over the signature of Lieutenant-General Emil Zách. For text see *FAA,* 1:3–5.

8. In Hungary, the noncommissioned officers were of two types: *altiszt* and *tisztes* (or *sortisztes*).

9. *FAA,* 1:17.

10. *Ibid.,* p. 18. The paper also provided statistical data on the proportion of Jews among physicians, veterinarians, military judges, and other types of professionals in the armed forces.

11. *Ibid.,* p. 20. The procedures for the screening of the identity of the officers and of their wives were first established under Order No. 47 988 of the Ministry of Defense dated September 23, 1939. See below.

12. *Ibid.,* pp. 21–24.

13. *Ibid.,* pp. 24–32, 42–48. The resolution on Jewish retired officers was probably adopted as a result of the comments made by Lajos Szentgyörgyi, the head of the section in the Ministry that was in charge of legislative matters. Szentgyörgyi argued that if the recommendation of the Presidential Section were adopted and the retired officers were deprived of their uniforms, the spirit of the anti-Jewish laws would be violated, because the sponsors of these laws consistently emphasized that the motivating force behind these laws was necessity and not hatred. *Ibid.,* p. 37.

14. Order No. 47 988. *Ibid.,* pp. 102–3. The Order also established the procedures to be followed in screening the identity and background of all members of the armed forces (in the case of officers, of their wives as well) to assure eventual dejewification. The screening procedures were first reformulated under Decree No. 27 500 of the Ministry of Defense dated May 16, 1942, and following the adoption of Law No. XIV of 1942, which regulated the labor service for Jews, under Decree No. 47 530 dated September 3, 1942. Decree No. 27 500 also contains for the benefit of the screeners a succinct history of the Jews in Hungary and the processes involved in their Magyarization, including the changing of names. For text of these decrees, see *Ibid.,* 2:8–24, 90–94.

15. The decree was promulgated on May 17, 1939, when it was published in the *Budapesti Közlöny* (Budapest Gazette), No. 111. It was based on the draft proposals prepared by the Ministry of Defense on April 24 which were discussed by the Council of Ministers on May 12. The Council adopted a number of changes and adhered, *inter alia,* to the wishes of the Ministry of Cults and Public Education in upholding the independence of the National Voluntary Labor Service System of University and College Students (*Egyetemi és Főiskolai Hallgatók Önkéntes Nemzeti Munkaszolgálat*) which had been in operation for some time. *FAA,* pp. 52–63.

16. The first Superintendent of the labor service system was General Dániel Fábry. He

was succeeded in 1940 by Colonel László Stemmer and in 1941–43 by Colonel Ernő Horny. Following the reorganization of KMOF in the fall of 1943 (see below), the leadership was assumed in 1944 by Lieutenant-General Gusztáv Hennyey. *Ibid.*, 2:837.

17. In the course of time, the labor servicemen came to be identified or better known simply as "Muszos" or "Muszosok" the condensed singular and plural version of *munkaszolgálatos(ok)*.

18. *FAA*, 2:309. The commanders of these corps and their chiefs of staff (in 1942) are listed in *Magyarország tiszti cim- és névtára.*

19. *FAA*, 1:75. KMOF underwent a jurisdictional change in 1943. In response to German pressure for more labor service assistance, the Ministry of Defense set up a Labor Section (*munkaügyi csoport*) in the fall of 1943. Placed under the leadership of Lieutenant-General Gusztáv Hennyey, it had two subdivisions. One consisted of KMOF under Horny, which had power over the allocation of and control over the labor service units, while the other, under the leadership of Colonel Egon Gátföldi (Spanner), was in charge over personnel, logistics, and organizational matters. *Ibid.*, 2:204.

20. For documents relating to the details of the labor service system in operation during the early phase, including recruitment, demobilization, equipment, clothing, and benefits, see *FAA*, 1:90–102, 108–48.

21. *Ibid.*, 1:128–31.

22. *Ibid.*, pp. xxvi, 137–42.

23. *Ibid.*, p. 143. The raising of the labor companies to war strength was ordered by the Ministry of Defense in Decree No. 12,508/M. lb.-1940. *Ibid.*, p. 138.

24. *Ibid.*, pp. 145–47.

25. Decree No. 441/Om. biz. lb.-1940. For text see *ibid.*, 1:281–83.

26. Following the entry of Hungary into World War II, it was mostly the field labor service companies that were sent to the war zones in the Ukraine. The inland Jewish labor service companies were employed primarily within the country on projects initiated or supervised by the various army corps commands. In some cases, the allocations were based on the request of factories in need of skilled or unskilled labor. For information on the kind of projects on which Jewish labor servicemen were employed within Hungary in 1942 and on the procedures used for their allocation see *Ibid.*, 1:547–75; 2:108–15.

27. See the telegrams by Otto von Erdmannsdorff, the German Minister in Budapest, dated September 12 and September 19, 1940.

28. This instruction of the Ministry of Defense (HIL. HM. cln. lb.-1940-1-111 119), dated October 25, 1940, was based upon an earlier Decree of the Ministry (507 706.10.-1940), which stipulated that all nonprofessional Jewish personnel of the armed forces were to be transferred to the labor battalions. *FAA*, 1:234–36.

29. See Decree No. 44 710. eln.-1940, which identified 109 such positions or units, *Ibid.*, pp. 219–21.

30. *Ibid.*, pp. xxxii–xxxiii.

31. *Ibid.*, pp. 246–62.

32. *Ibid.*, pp. xliii, 281–95.

33. *Ibid.*, pp. xxxv–xxxviii.

34. *Ibid.*, pp. cvii, 237–42.

35. The demands for the introduction of the yellow arm band were made in response to the protests of János Halmai, a *Nyilas* deputy, in the lower house (November 14) against allowing the Jews to wear the national colors. *Ibid.*, p. xxxvi.

36. *Ibid.*, pp. 243–46. The compulsory wearing of the yellow arm band was introduced in August 1941. See below.

37. The separation of the Jews from others serving in the "public labor service companies" was effectuated by transforming the companies numbered 3 and 4 of the labor battalions into "mixed," i.e. exclusively Jewish, ones. *Ibid.*, p. xxxviii.

38. The draft was adopted by the Ministry of Defense on April 4. The Ministry of Justice made only a few stylistic changes, and Horthy insisted that exemptions be provided for those officers who had been decorated for exceptional heroism during World War I. The Decree was published in the *Budapesti Közlöny* of April 19, 1941. Within the armed forces it was distributed as General Order No. 25 252. eln. 15. sz.-1941 as published in *Honvédségi Közlöny* (The Gazette of the *Honvédség*), 68, no. 18 (April 22, 1941). *Ibid.*, pp. 296–303, 763.

39. Among those who submitted affidavits were Archdukes József and Ferdinand, Baron Géza Lukachich, General Gusztáv Say, former Minister of Defense Baron Sándor Szurmay, Lieutenant-General Dezső Molnár, and Baron József Gaudernák. *Ibid.*, p. 303.

40. The Order was amended on December 11, 1941, and on March 19, 1942. For the original text and its amendments see *ibid.*, 1:309–26.

41. To substantiate their claim for exemption, the applicants had to submit documents proving their citizenship, affirming their "positive" attitude during the revolutionary period of 1918–19, and substantiating their awards and medals for bravery and/or claims as invalids. The exemption qualifications and procedures were revised on February 28, 1942. *Ibid.*, 2:274–86.

42. Upon their recall to auxiliary service in 1941, these officers were still addressed, as required under the Order, by their rank, prefixed by the word "former." Under Decree No. 55 000 of the Ministry of Defense dated December 21, 1942, the ranks could no longer be used, even with the prefix. *Ibid.*, p. 495.

43. *Ibid.*, p. 4.

44. Their distribution by rank was as follows: 34 Lieutenant-Colonels; 23 Majors; 56 Captains; 15 First Lieutenants; and 1 Second Lieutenant. *Ibid.*

45. *Ibid.*, 1:400, 404, 412, 421–23, 425, 542–43; 2:77–79.

46. By late 1942, the Jews had to provide their own shoes as well. However, by 1943, many of the Jewish labor servicemen were shoeless. Some of the military commanders suggested late in 1943 that these Jews be supplied with boots no longer usable by the *Honvédség*. A special effort to correct the situation was made by the Jewish welfare organization. *Ibid.*, 2:474–78.

47. The introduction of the yellow arm bands was demanded by the General Staff early in May 1941 after some Hungarians in the then just reoccupied parts of the Bácska and Baranya allegedly complained about seeing Jews wearing arm bands with the national colors. *Ibid.*, 1:333–36.

48. Szombathelyi, the former commander of Army Corps VIII, replaced Werth as Chief of Staff on September 6, 1941.

49. *FAA*, 1:404, 407, 412, 421–23, 426, 493.

50. The agreement to deploy the Second Hungarian Army was reached after the visits to Hungary by Ribbentrop and Field Marshal Keitel early in 1942.

51. *FAA*, 1:422.

52. *Ibid.*, pp. 509–10.

53. *Ibid.*, 2:61–67.

54. Decree No. 23 123. eln. 1b.-1942 of the Ministry of Defense. *Ibid.*, 1:524–25.

55. Lieutenant-Colonel Lipót Muray (Metzl), the chief of the recruitment centers of Nagykáta and Tápiósüly, claimed that he received slips of paper with the names of Jews to be called up from Lieutenant-Colonel Béla Hajós of the mobilization section of Army Corps I. *Ibid.*, pp. 155–74.

56. *Ibid.*, 1:178, 181–82, 184, 189, 190, 514–25, 545; 2:70–72, 125, 349–52.

57. Of these, 16 were in jail in Budapest; 104 in the jails or prisons administered by KEOKH; 166 in the jails of Kolozsvár; and the remainder in the internment camps of Kistarcsa (302), Garany (293), Nagykanizsa (450), Szabadka (30), and Bácstopolya (124).

Ibid., 1:512. For the March 24, 1942, memorandum of the Chief of Staff relating to the establishment of the special companies, see *ibid.*, pp. 510–13.

58. *Ibid.* In the spring of 1942, three punitive companies were sent to the frontlines together with the Second Hungarian Army. On November 16, 1943, the Council of Ministers went along with the proposal of the Minister of Defense that the "unreliable" elements left in the industrial enterprises be apprehended and dispatched to the front in similar companies to assure "labor discipline and the termination of enemy propaganda." *Ibid.*, 2:443–44.

59. Decree No. 34 411. eln. 2. Vkf.D.-1942. *Ibid.*, 2:42–51. For the account of the experiences of such a company, see István Kossa, *A Dunától a Donig. Riport* (From the Danube to the Don. Report) (Budapest: Athenaeum, 1948), 383 pp.

60. General Gusztáv Jány was arrested after the war and accused of responsibility for the misfortunes of the Army on the eastern front. Following a three-month trial in 1947, Jány was condemned to death on October 4. He was executed by a firing squad on November 28, 1947. Elek Karsai, *Itél a nép* (The People Judge) (Budapest: Kossuth, 1977), pp. 275–92.

61. C. A. Macartney, 2:93.

62. The exact number of Jewish labor servicemen and of different types of labor service companies deployed in the Ukraine cannot be ascertained. The 50,000 figure is mentioned, *inter alia*, by Vilmos Nagy, the former Minister of Defense. See his *Végzetes esztendők, 1938–1945* (Fatal Years, 1938–1945) (Budapest: Körmendy, 1946), p. 107. Citing official figures, C. A. Macartney states that 37,200, mostly Jewish, labor servicemen were deployed in the Ukraine in 1942 (2:100). Without citing any references, Lévai gives the number of Jews serving at the Don and the other parts of the Ukraine during the winter of 1942–43 as 40,000. See his *Fekete könyv*, p. 272. For an incomplete listing of the various types of labor companies stationed in the Ukraine in January 1943—i.e., just prior to the destruction of the Second Hungarian Army—see *FAA*, 1:cxxii–cxxiii.

63. C. A. Macartney, 2:97.

64. For details on the activities of the *Einsatzgruppen* in the East, see Raul Hilberg, *The Destruction of the European Jews* (Chicago: Quadrangle, 1961), pp. 242–56.

65. Randolph L. Braham, "The Kamenets-Podolsk and Délvidék Massacres: Prelude to the Holocaust in Hungary," in *YVS*, 9:133–56. See also chapter 6.

66. Arthur D. Morse, *While Six Million Died. A Chronicle of American Apathy* (New York: Random House, 1967), pp. 304–5.

67. *NA*, Microcopy T-120, Roll 688, Frames 311981-985. The document was also used in the war crimes trials in Nuremberg (NG-3522). See also 3012-PS as reproduced in *IMT*, 31:493–95.

68. The Germans complained specifically about the Jews in Hungarian Railway Pioneer Battalion No. 101. The correspondence between the *Oberkommando der Wehrmacht*, the German Foreign Office, and the German Legation in Budapest during February–June 1943 reveals that the Battalion actually employed two Jews—a technical draftsman and an office worker. *Judenverfolgung in Ungarn* (The Persecution of Jews in Hungary) (Frankfurt am Main: United Restitution Organization, 1959), pp. 129, 131, 139, and 155. In addition to technicians, the *Honvédség* also retained a number of motor vehicle mechanics and drivers. See, for example, *FAA*, 1:429.

69. *RLB*, Doc. 53.

70. The Second Hungarian Army was subordinated to *Heeresgruppe Süd*, which was under the command of Field Marshal Maximilian von Weichs. According to Szombathelyi, the Hungarians' only responsibility was to assure the supply of men and materiel and to maintain discipline in the ranks. *FAA*, 1:276:77.

71. Order No. 112 025. eln. KMOF-1941, dated December 23, 1941, and addressed to the commanders of the labor battalions. *Ibid.*, pp. 415–17. In response to the abuses com-

mitted, both Minister of Defense Nagy and his successor, Lajos Csatay, issued new instructions relating to the treatment of the Jewish labor servicemen. See below.

72. Muray was arrested on March 16, 1945, and tried together with a number of other officers associated with the labor service system, including Tibor Herczegh, Tibor Molnár, and Rudolf Sponer. He was convicted by the National Council of the People's Tribunals (*Népbiroságok Országos Tanácsa*) on April 30 (NOT 25/1945/21.) and executed on May 1, 1945. For details on the trial and the text of his statement, see *FAA*, 1:148–201.

73. This point was academic, for the Jews were normally dispatched to the front within a few weeks, if not days.

74. *FAA*, 1:156.

75. *Ibid.*, 2:125–26. A similar resolution was made and carried out by Colonel Alajos Haynal, the commander of the 22nd Infantry Regiment. István Nemeskürty, *Requiem egy hadseregért* (Requiem for an Army) (Budapest: Magvető, 1974), p. 184.

76. *FAA*, 2:193.

77. *Ibid.*, 1:279–80.

78. *Ibid.*, pp. lxv–lxvi.

79. *Ibid.*, pp. 337–45.

80. *Ibid.*, 2:61–63.

81. The Red Army began its winter offensive by smashing through the Hungarian units, which were flanked to the left by the German Second Army, and to the right by the Italian Eighth Army and the Third and Fourth Romanian armies. C. A. Macartney, 2:97.

82. *FAA*, 1:278, and Nagy, *Végzetes esztendők*, pp. 107, 128. For a detailed though somewhat journalistic and slanted account of the destruction of the Second Hungarian Army see Nemeskürty, *Requiem egy hadseregért*, 244 pp. For his description of the plight of the labor servicemen, see pp. 179–94.

Ironically and tragically many of those who were repatriated late in 1943 and 1944 were shortly thereafter, in the wake of the German occupation, placed into ghettos and subsequently deported to Auschwitz together with their families.

83. The specific army units and labor service companies that were dispatched to the Ukraine during the spring and early summer of 1943 are identified in *FAA*, 1:lxxx–lxxxii.

84. On January 24, 1943, shortly after the defeat near Voronezh, General Jány issued an order of the day in which he stated that "the Second Hungarian Army had lost its honor because with the exception of a few men faithful to their oath and duty it did not do what everybody rightly expected of it." Nemeskürty, *Requiem egy hadseregért*, p. 134.

85. *Ibid.*, p. 189.

86. *Ibid.*

87. The shooting of Hungarian Jews along with other "enemies" in the Ukraine, including children, was admitted to by SS-*Sturmbannführer* Christensen in his memorandum of March 19, 1943, addressed to all SD *Kommando* leaders. 3012-PS, reproduced in *IMT*, 31:493–95.

88. For specific examples of atrocities perpetrated by the German units see *FAA*, 1:lxxv–lxxvi.

89. *Ibid.*, p. cxxiii.

90. *RLB*, Docs. 55, 57.

91. This was the case, for example, of the labor servicemen in Company No. 101/35 and other companies stationed early in 1943 in Horcsik, the Ukraine, under the command of Sergeant György Zsoldos. Zsoldos was condemned to 15 years of hard labor after the war. *FAA*, 2:194.

92. The chief doctor of the hospital was Dr. Emil Menyász, a gynecologist from Kolozsvár; he was assisted by Dr. János László, a surgeon from Budapest. They were both labor servicemen themselves. Zoltán Singer, "A 110/34-es munkásszázad története" (The

History of Labor Company No. 110/34) in *Volt egyszer egy Dés* . . . (There Was Once Upon a Time a Dés . . .) (Tel Aviv: A Dés és Vikékéről Elszármazottak Landsmannschaftja, n.d.) pp. 245–80. Singer is one of the survivors of Doroshich.

93. Nagy, *Végzetes esztendők,* pp. 106–7. The idea that the Jews were themselves responsible for the fire was also included in a telegram of July 1943, sent by the camp commander, Dezső Szentkatolnay-Reintz, to the Ministry of Defense. Lévai, *Fekete könyv,* p. 277.

94. Nagy, *Végzetes esztendők,* p. 83. The heads of the personnel section (*1b. osztály*) were: Lieutenant-Colonel Miklós Nagyőszy, 1939–1941; Colonel Mihály Cseke, 1942; Colonel Ágoston Gecsányi, 1943; and Lieutenant-Colonel Aladár Gál, 1944. The head of the mobilization section (*1. om. osztály*) in 1942–44 was Lieutenant-Colonel Dénes Dobák. *FAA,* 2:836.

95. Nagy, *Végzetes esztendők,* pp. 99 and 105. See also *FAA,* 1:277–78.

96. *Ibid.,* 1:lxxi.

97. Lévai, *Fekete könyv,* p. 272.

98. *FAA,* 1:172–74.

99. Nagy, *Végzetes esztendők,* pp. 83, 140. His instructions were incorporated in Order No. 121 480. eln. KMOF-1942, dated December 19, 1942. *FAA,* 2:178–84.

100. Outstanding among these were men like Sergeant Sándor Májer of Field Company No. 110/34; Dr. Attila Juhász, the humane commander of a company in the Ukraine, who was hanged by the *Nyilas* in the fall of 1944; First Lieutenant Elek Szerdahelyi and Nándor Tosch of Internal Company No. 101/14; László Seress of Field Company No. 110/60; Antal Kőrössy, the commander of Company No. 108/15, László Ócskay, the commander of Company No. 101/359, and First Lieutenant Barna Kiss, the commander of Company No. 101/2.

One must mention in this context Colonel Imre Reviczky, the commander of Labor Service Battalion No. X of Nagybánya, who saved thousands of labor servicemen throughout his tenure and especially during the German occupation, as well as Minister of Defense Nagy himself. The decent and humane attitudes of Barna Kiss, Reviczky, Kőrössy, and Nagy were recognized by Yad Vashem, which bestowed upon them its highest honours as Righteous Gentiles: the Medal of Honour, the Certificate of Honour, and the right to plant a tree on the Avenue of the Righteous at Yad Vashem in Jerusalem. For references on the specific actions of these individuals consult: Zoltán Singer, *Volt egyszer egy Dés* . . . (regarding Juhász and Májer); *FAA,* 2:51–56 (Szerdahelyi and Tosch); Elemér Salamon, *Mozgó vesztőhely* (Rolling Perishing Place) (Budapest: Athenaeum, 1945), 115 pp. (Barna Kiss); and László Szilágyi-Windt, *Az ujpesti zsidóság története* (The History of the Jews of Ujpest). (Tel Aviv: Lahav Printers for the Author, 1975), pp. 221–23 (Seress).

101. *FAA,* 2:175–76.

102. Recollections by Rőder dated March 1959. *Ibid.,* pp. 202–6. No information has yet been unearthed concerning Tanitó's activities.

103. *Ibid.,* pp. 286–304.

104. The draft law was submitted to Parliament by the Ministry of Defense on June 10, 1942, on the basis of the discussions that had been held within its various sections since March 3. For excerpts from the statements made in both houses of Parliament during June and July, including those by László Baky, Zoltán Meskó, and Károly Bartha, see *ibid.,* 1:431–99.

105. *Ibid.,* pp. 490–99. The Decree was published in *Honvédségi Közlöny,* no. 58 (December 28, 1942). The Germans, of course, were fully informed about these measures. See *RLB,* Doc. 52.

106. Nagy, *Végzetes esztendők,* pp. 109–10. Nagy probably referred to the Secret Decree of November 6, 1942, which is discussed below.

107. Decree No. 120 780. eln. KMOF-1942. *FAA*, 2:96–106.

108. The only reference in the Decree to Labor Battalions No. I, VII, and VIII pertains to the identification of the labor servicemen transferred from these battalions for training. Accordingly, these were to be referred to as "labor servicemen" (*munkaszolgálatosok*) while the others were to be termed "auxiliary laborers" (*kisegitő munkások*).

Labor Battalions XI, XII, and XIII were set up late in the summer of 1943. Little information is available about these battalions, the number of companies under their commands, or their deployment. See *FAA*, 1:lxxxvi; 2:97, 103, 153, 157, 328, 370–76, 402, 639.

109. Kállay first announced his intentions about the general call-up of the Jews at the Government Party meeting of October 22, 1942. Nicholas Kállay, *Hungarian Premier* (New York: Columbia University Press, 1954), pp. 122–24.

110. For the sample text of these posters, see *FAA*, 2:144–46 and Appendix IV in the same volume.

111. Decree No. 5600: M. 1b.-1942. *Ibid.*, 2:130–35.

112. *Ibid.*, 2:148–49. For related documents, see pp. 149–72, 255–74.

113. On March 28, 1943, for example, men aged 25 through 37 were called up. This was followed on July 1 by the special call-up for a three-month period of certain categories born*between 1906–1918, and 1919–1922. On July 19, men in the 38 to 42 age groups were called up. *Ibid.*, pp. 308–12, 367–69, and 379–83.

114. Decree No. 97 Om. KMOF.-1943. *Ibid.*, pp. 363–67. This decree was most probably formulated during Nagy's tenure. Among the other measures adopted during the Nagy era calculated to improve the status of the Jewish labor servicemen, one must cite the plans (April–June, 1943) for the assignment of rabbis to the companies stationed within the country and the decree of April 7, 1943, which provided for the allocation of war benefits to the immediate family (wife, children, and parents) of Jewish labor servicemen. These benefits were expanded on November 23, 1943. *Ibid.*, pp. 320–28, 330–37, 445–46.

115. During the *Nyilas* era, Nagy was first imprisoned at Sopronkőhida and, following the advance of the Red Army, he was taken to Germany, where he was eventually liberated by the Americans. For Nagy's account of the circumstances leading to his resignation and of his ordeal during the *Nyilas* era see his *Végzetes esztendők*, pp. 133–54, and 263–68. He died in June 1976 at Klotildliget near Budapest (where he lived after his retirement) at the age of 92.

116. During the deportations of 1944, Csatay was one of the few (if not the only one) who objected to the wholesale removal of able-bodied Jews "on grounds of military necessity." Loyal to Horthy to the end, Csatay and his wife committed suicide during the Szálasi era. C. A. Macartney, 2:283, 463.

117. See order of the commander of the Second Hungarian Army, dated April 7, 1943. *FAA*, 2:328–30.

118. Decree No. 180 475. eln. KMOF.-1943, dated October 9, 1943. *Ibid.*, pp. 415–16.

119. On October 22, 1943, for example, the authorities indicted 22 officers and guards, including Brunó Tövisváry, Zoltán Szalkay, László Hajdú, and Konrád Galgóczy for barbarous actions committed against Jewish labor servicemen. *FAA*, 2:417–30. See also pp. 384–93 for material on István Palotás, the commander of Labor Service Company No. 101/83.

120. According to Csatay, in November 1943 there were 72,000 workers assigned to satisfy the lumber requirement of the nation. The enterprises operating under the auspices of the Ministry of Industry were assigned 95 labor companies, while those of the Ministries of Agriculture and Commerce were allocated 16 and 53 companies respectively. *Ibid.*, p. 449.

121. *Ibid.*, pp. 456–64.

122. The enterprises and the state organs and organizations were required to apply through the authorities having jurisdiction over them to either section 17a, 43, or 45 of the Ministry. *Ibid.*, pp. 459–60.

123. Major-General Lajos Fábián was appointed as Hennyey's deputy. During the Lakatos era in 1944, Hennyey served as Foreign Minister.

124. *FAA*, 2:204.

125. In addition to the personal narratives cited in the text, there are a large number of other testimonies describing the ordeal of the labor servicemen in the Ukraine, including the territory of Polish Galicia. See, for example, Docs. 13, 23, 67, 72, 78, and 84 in *FAA*. See also docs. 768/3660, 769/855, 769/1147, 769/1529, 772/2339, 774/2984, and 775/3057 at the YIVO Institute for Jewish Research in New York. Of particular historical interest is the German-language report that Hillel Danzig, the Zionist leader of Kolozsvár and a survivor of a labor service company stationed in the Ukraine, submitted to the Jewish Agency in April 1945. The report is one of the first exposés of the labor service system in general and of the Ukrainian ordeal in particular that reached the Geneva and Jerusalem offices of the Agency. It is available in the Central Zionist Archives in Jerusalem (S26/1190). The Hebrew version (*B'tzel susim;* In the Shadow of Horses) was published in Tel Aviv in 1976. Most of these documents were prepared on the basis of personal testimonies recorded by DEGOB (*a Deportáltakat Gondozó Országos Bizottság;* National Committee for the Care of Deportees) in Budapest shortly after the end of hostilities in 1945.

126. Nathan Eck, "The March of Death From Serbia to Hungary (September 1944) and the Slaughter of Cservenka," in *YVS*, 2:255.

127. *Ibid.*, p. 256.

128. Interestingly, Speer does not discuss the employment of Hungarian Jewish labor at the Bor copper mines in his memoirs. See Albert Speer, *Inside the Third Reich* (New York: Macmillan Company, 1970), 705 pp.

129. *RLB*, Doc. 58.

130. *Ibid.*

131. *Ibid.*, Docs 59 and 60.

132. *Ibid.*, Doc. 61. See also *Judenverfolgung in Ungarn*, pp. 132–35, 141.

133. Statement by Lieutenant-General Jenő Rőder. *FAA*, 2:202–3.

134. *Ibid.*, pp. 395–98.

135. *RLB*, Docs. 54 and 56.

136. *FAA*, 1:279.

137. Interview given in Budapest on the occasion of his 90th birthday. *Uj Élet* (New Life), Budapest, October 15, 1972, p. 4.

138. *Ibid.*

139. *RLB*, Doc. 56.

140. *Ibid.*, Doc. 62.

141. *Ibid.*

142. *FAA*, 2:205.

143. Eck, "March of Death," p. 256. It is of course possible that the survivor confused this date with that of July 15.

144. *FAA*, 2:370–78.

145. A number of the Jewish labor servicemen on leave failed to report back to duty. Some of these simply went AWOL; others submitted "unacceptable excuses" for their action. A plan worked out in the Ministry of Defense called for the transfer of these "culprits," if apprehended, to the front lines. *Ibid.*, pp. 468–69.

146. *Ibid.*, p. 205.

147. *Oberbefehlshaber Südost* to OKW/WFSt/OP (H) (Generalmajor Horst Buttlar-Brandenfels), September 10, 1944. NOKW-981, as cited by Hilberg, *The Destruction of the Euro-*

pean Jews, p. 518. The bulk of the Hungarian Jewish labor servicemen was deployed in March 1944. See Zdenko Löwenthal, ed., *The Crimes of the Fascist Occupants and Their Collaborators Against Jews in Yugoslavia* (Belgrade: Federation of Jewish Communities of the Federative People's Republic of Yugoslavia, 1957), pp. 35 and 179.

148. Eck, "March of Death," p. 256.

149. *Ibid.,* p. 257.

150. Löwenthal, *The Crimes of the Fascist Occupants,* pp. 35 and 179–80.

151. *Ibid.,* p. 35. See also the personal testimony of Tibor Groner in *FAA,* 2:372–74. Some details about the cruelties perpetrated against the draftees were revealed at the trial of Károly Szaulich in May 1945. One of the officers at Bor, Szaulich, was condemned to 15 years' imprisonment. *Ibid.,* 2:580–84.

152. Löwenthal, *The Crimes of the Fascist Occupants,* p. 35.

153. The lot of the servicemen was at first eased through the packages (especially clothing) their relatives and friends were allowed to send in the fall of 1943. See *FAA,* 2:438, 493–94 and below.

154. For details on the suffering in Bor, the retreat, and rescue by partisans see, István György, *Fegyvertelenül a tüzvonalban* (Unarmed in the Line of Fire) (Budapest: Cserépfalvi, 1945), 204 pp.; György, *Halálraitéltek* (Condemned to Death) (Budapest: Kossuth, 1957), 238 pp.; László Szüts, *Bori garnizon* (The Garrison of Bor) (Budapest: Renaissance, 1945), 167 pp. See also *FAA,* 2:371–74.

155. Eck, "March of Death," p. 258. See also Tibor Groner's account cited below.

156. Eck, *ibid.,* p. 261. The horrors of the retreat from Bor to Cservenka and the mass executions at Cservenka are told by Zálmán Teichman, one of three men who, though gravely wounded, managed to crawl out of the mass grave and survive. Teichman was born in the village of Tuska in the Huszt District of Carpatho-Ruthenia. His account is reproduced with slight editorial changes in Eck's article. For a partially indirect account, see György Spira's statement in *FAA,* 2:632–35. See also the following personal narratives at the YIVO Institute for Jewish Research, New York: Tibor Groner (768/3583), Max Singer (769/841), Alexander Neumann (771/3485), George Engel (772/2356), Eugene Klein (772/2407), Nicholas Derera (773/1643), L. Benedek (773/1788), Ladislas Fischer (773/1902), and R. Rosenthal (775/3062).

157. Eck, "March of Death," p. 263.

158. Löwenthal, *The Crimes of the Fascist Occupants,* pp. 36 and 182–84.

159. *Ibid.,* pp. 36 and 184.

160. *Ibid.*

161. See Zálmán Teichman's account referred to above.

162. The approximate number of those massacred at Cservenka cannot be determined with certainty. The SS kept no record of their murderous actions. Teichman, who survived the execution, estimated the number of those killed as between 1,000 and 1,500. See Eck, "March of Death," p. 279. Yugoslav sources, however, established the number of those killed at 700. Löwenthal, *The Crimes of the Fascist Occupants,* pp. 36 and 185. See also Károly Gárdos (Dos), "Cservenka—1944 oktober 7" (Cservenka—October 7, 1944), in *Tanuk vagyunk!* (We Are Witnesses!), ed. Ervin G. Galili (Tel Aviv: The Editor, n.d.), pp. 108–115, and the personal accounts reproduced in *FAA,* 2:632–38, 640–41.

163. Löwenthal, *ibid.,* pp. 37 and 187.

164. Radnóti was born in Budapest on May 4, 1909. Although of bourgeois background, he dedicated his life to leftist causes. For details on his life and works see *Uj Magyar Lexikon* (New Hungarian Lexicon) (Budapest: Akadémiai Kiadó, 1961), 5:516; *Radnóti Miklós 1909–1944,* ed. Dezső Baróti. (Budapest: Magyar Helikon, 1959), 191 pp.; *Radnóti Miklós összes versei és műforditásai* (The Collected Poems and Translations of Miklós Radnóti) (Budapest: Szépirodalmi Könyvkiadó, 1956), 513 pp.; and Sándor Kocz-

kás, *Radnóti Miklós. Versek és műfordítások* (Miklós Radnóti. Poems and Literary Translations) (Budapest, 1954), 474 pp.

165. Lévai, *Zsidósors Magyarországon*, p. 153.

166. Veesenmayer telegram no. 1247, dated May 8, 1944. *NA*, Microcopy T-120, Roll 4665 (Serial K1509/K350109-). László Endre, the notorious anti-Semite who was then serving as Undersecretary of State in the Ministry of the Interior, claimed that only about 80,000 had been excluded from the deportation program because of their recruitment into the labor service system. Lévai, *Zsidósors Magyarországon*, p. 152.

167. *Der Kastner-Bericht*, p. 141.

168. *FAA*, 2:539.

169. *FAA*, 2:539–40.

170. Ferenczy Report No. 6 relating to the ghettoization program in Transylvania, dated May 10, 1944.

171. Ferenczy Report No. 2, dated May 29, 1944. The report mentions as an example the fact that 31 call-up notices were delivered to Jews in the Ungvár camp. It also notes that samples of the passes used by the labor servicemen were given to Eichmann and Endre.

172. *FAA*, 2:518–19.

173. Ferenczy Report No. 1 relating to the concentration of the Jews in Northern Hungary (Zone III), dated June 7, 1944. Hatvan was the headquarters of the dejewification squad in the area.

174. According to Imre Reiner, the legal advisor of the Orthodox Jewish Community of Hungary, 600 labor servicemen were deported from Hatvan. Statement by Imre Reiner, Israel Police, Bureau 06, Doc. No. 347. See also the following personal narratives by labor servicemen deported from Hatvan, which are available at the YIVO Institute for Jewish Research in New York: Endre Guttmann (File No. 768/3587), Dr. Alexander Puder (770/225), Tibor Nathan (772/2128), József Sprunz (772/2435), Alexander Ecker (773/2114), and Ernő Klein (774/2874).

175. See, for example, Ferenczy's Report No. 2 relating to the deportations from Northern Hungary, dated June 12, 1944.

176. Decree No. 151 158. eln. 42.-1944 repealing Decree No. 110 160. eln. KMOF.-1943. *FAA*, 2:548–52. The Decree also included a number of provisions relating to the conditions of employment and treatment of the Jews.

177. *Vádirat*, 3:268–69.

178. The National Superintendent of the Labor Service for Women in 1943 was Colonel Dénes Sturm. *FAA*, 2:837.

179. *Vádirat*, 3:53–54.

180. Decree No. 7200. eln. 6. k.-1944, dated August 11, 1944. *FAA*, 2:600–605.

181. See his *Hungarian Protestantism and the Persecution of Jews* (Budapest: Sylvester, n.d.), 47 pp.

182. Order dated October 21, 1944. *FAA*, 2:643–44.

183. Order No. 975. M. 42-1944. *Ibid.*, pp. 651–57.

184. Order No. 171 005 eln. 45.-1944. *Ibid.*, p. 658.

185. *Ibid.*, p. 659.

186. Lévai, *Fekete könyv*, p. 275.

187. About half of these were quartered in the Czeke Brickyards, the city brickyard, and the facilities of the Gulner Flour Mill. The other 4,000 were quartered in a brewery at the opposite end of the city. All of them were under the general command of a certain *Oberscharführer* Bauer. László Harsányi, *A kőszegi zsidók* (The Jews of Kőszeg) (Budapest: A Magyar Izraeliták Országos Képviselete, 1974), pp. 211–17.

188. Lévai, *Fekete könyv*, pp. 275–76.

189. Harsányi, *A kőszegi zsidók,* pp. 214–15.

190. *Mementó. Magyarország 1944* (Memento. Hungary 1944). Ödön Gáti, et al. (Budapest: Kossuth, 1975), pp. 54–55.

191. Decree No. 11 207/7.m.-1945. *FAA,* 2:669.

192. Decree No. 1031/1. kr. fővezérség-1945. *Ibid.,* p. 672. The Decree was forwarded by László Endre, who was then acting as the Commander of the Civilian Administration of Military Operational Territories (*a Hadműveleti területek polgári közigazgatási vezetője*), to the prefects of counties still under *Nyilas* control. *Ibid.,* p. 673.

193. For details on Fábián's activities in connection with the Veterans' Committee as well as with many other aspects of his political life, see *The Reminiscences of Béla Fábián.* New York: Columbia University Oral History Research Office, No. 79, November 1950–January 1951, 2 vols. (456 pp.), typewritten.

194. Decree No. 98 640. 1942-V of the Ministry of the Interior. Although the permit was issued only for two months, it was periodically renewed throughout the war. *FAA,* 2:107, 120, 305, 358–61. The text of the appeals for the extension of the campaign permits, like that of the appeals for donations of funds and clothing, is reproduced in the issues of *A Magyar Zsidók Lapja* (The Journal of Hungarian Jews).

195. Such appeals appeared in practically every issue of the journal after September 1942. For examples of such appeals see *ibid.,* pp. 106–7, 117–19, 352–54, 478–80, 493–94, 572–73, and 595–97.

196. According to the annual report of PIH for 1942–43, the following items were collected and shipped across the borders between November 17, 1942 and February 3, 1943: 8,174 blankets; 10,930 winter coats; 906 fur coats; 7,238 jackets; 3,354 fur vests; 5,334 vests; 16,306 pairs of pants; 26,944 warm caps; 27,970 pairs of gloves; 22,141 light weight jackets; 15,435 shorts; 40,381 shirts; 25,096 winter shorts; 70,224 socks; 34,022 foot clout; 25,338 scarfs; 7,766 knee warmers; 18,742 wrist warmers; 15,768 earmuffs; 42,958 handkerchiefs; 23,362 cakes of soap; 1,790 pairs of shoes; and 15,824 various other items. *Ibid.,* p. 200. The report also contains details about the results of the collection of clothes and funds during the subsequent periods.

197. *Ibid.,* p. 206.

198. *Ibid.,* pp. 227–30.

199. *Ibid.,* pp. 484–89, 491–93.

200. *Ibid.,* p. 405.

201. *A Magyar Zsidók Lapja,* March 16, 1944, p. 6.

202. See statement by Hillel Danzig, cited in fn. 125.

203. Nemeskürty, *Requiem egy hadseregért,* p. 212.

204. Lévai, *Fekete könyv,* p. 273.

205. Smaller groups of Hungarian Jews were held in many other camps in the Soviet Union. The information relating to the location and number of the camps was taken from the issues of the *Uj Élet* (New Life), Budapest, covering January 10, 1946 through September 26, 1947.

206. Although all four of these organizations operated for only a few years, so-called MUSZ organizations continue to exist in a number of countries where former labor servicemen resettled after the war, above all in Israel and the United States. In addition to the YIVO and Yad Vashem collections of personal narratives cited above, accounts by survivors of Soviet POW camps may also be found at the Historical Documentation Center on East-Central Europe of the University of Haifa, Israel.

207. Among the major speakers at this meeting were Dr. Zsigmond Perényi and Dr. Miklós Dániel and László Kádár, representing the National MUSZ Organization. *Uj Élet,* April 25, 1946, p. 6.

208. *Ibid.,* April 4, 1946, p. 7. In connection with their appeal to Szekfű, the National

MUSZ Organization launched a campaign for the acquisition of data relating to the labor servicemen in Soviet captivity. *Ibid.*, June 13, 1946, p. 3.

209. Shortly after the signing of the Peace Treaties, Foreign Minister János Gyöngyösi assured the leaders of Hungarian Jewry that the POW's were expected to return shortly under the provisions of Article 21 of the Treaties. *Ibid.*, March 6, 1947, p. 11.

210. The first labor serviceman to return from the Soviet Union was Ármin Benedek of Budapest, who claimed that Jews, Germans, and Hungarians were all well treated. *Ibid.*, August 22, 1946, p. 11.

211. *Ibid.*, June 19, 1947, p. 9. For further lists see subsequent issues of the paper.

212. For additional details on the labor servicemen, see the expanded version of this chapter: R. L. Braham, *The Hungarian Labor Service System, 1939–1945* (Boulder, Colorado: East European Quarterly and Columbia University Press, 1977), 159 pp.

CHAPTER ELEVEN

THE ROAD TO DESTRUCTION

Antecedents of the German Occupation

THE GERMANS' DECISION to occupy Hungary resulted from a series of complex political-military factors; the "unsolved" Jewish question, though important, was not the determining one. Following the extrication of Italy from the Axis Alliance in July 1943, coupled with the inexorable advance of the Red Army in the East and the victory of the Western Allies in North Africa, Sicily, and Southern Italy, the leaders of the Third Reich became extremely anxious to assure the absolute loyalty and subservience of their East European allies. They were particularly concerned with the political developments in Hungary, especially during the second year of Miklós Kállay's premiership.

The Germans were well aware of Kállay's attempts to establish contacts with the Western Allies through his own emissaries as well as the intermediary of neutral powers. They were upset about the failure of Hungary to contribute its full share to the war effort. They were further incensed by the dilatory tactics pursued by the Hungarians in response to their frequent requests to bring about a speedy "solution of the Jewish question" in Hungary.

The defiant position of the Hungarian government became quite evident after the crushing defeat of the Second Hungarian Army at Voronezh in January of 1943. Following the débacle, the Hungarians became ever more vocal in insisting that the remnant of their armed forces be returned from the Russian front for the defense of the Hungarian homeland.

In his desire to improve the atmosphere for meaningful negotiations with the Western Allies and possibly to prepare the country psychologically for eventual extrication from the war, Kállay in 1943 adopted a series of measures which clearly irritated the Germans. He allowed a partial relaxation of censorship, which resulted in open, and occasionally loud, demands by the opposition press and politicians for withdrawal from the war; he recognized the Badoglio government; he attempted to purge the foreign service of the openly pro-Nazi elements; he ordered a new investigation into the Délvidék massacres and brought the leading officers responsible for them to trial; he continued to physically protect the Jews, though he called for a radical solution "after the war"; and, last but not least, he decided to order the return of the Hungarian fighting forces "for the defense of the Carpathians."

The anti-German sentiment that was becoming increasingly discernible in the country, and the possible effect of the Hungarian government's policies on the national and security interests of the Third Reich were the subject of a series of dispatches of the German Minister in Budapest, Dietrich von Jagow. A comprehensive report on the situation in Hungary was prepared and submitted to the German Foreign Office on December 14, 1943, by SS-*Brigadeführer* Edmund Veesenmayer, then the assistant and special adviser to Wilhelm Keppler, the *Staatssekretär* (Secretary of State) in charge of special assignments in the German Foreign Office. In his report, Veesenmayer, who later became Hitler's representative in Hungary, not only identified the Jews of Hungary as "enemy no. 1" and as "Bolshevik vanguards," but openly suggested that the "Hungarian problem would be solved, for all practical intents and purposes, if Horthy were freed from his entourage" and "made a soldier of the Führer." He called for the replacement of Horthy's advisers "by the Führer, the Reich, and a delegate of the Reich who is up to his mission" (see chapter 7 for details about Veesenmayer's report).

Hitler later used Veesenmayer's analysis to justify the occupation of Hungary. The opening paragraph of Hitler's Order of March 12, 1944, relating to the occupation, states:

> For some time it has been known to me and to the Reich government that the Hungarian Kállay government has prepared Hungary's betrayal of the united European nations. The Jews, who control everything in Hungary, and individual reactionary or partly Jewish and corrupt elements of the Hungarian aristocracy have brought the Hungarian people, who were well disposed towards us, into this situation.[1]

Veesenmayer's bellicose report portending the occupation was made when the already precarious military situation of the Third Reich was becoming even more desperate. By the spring of 1944, the military pressures against Germany became both constant and overpowering. The Soviet forces had already cut the Lvov–Odessa rail line and crossed the Bug River and were about to enter Romania, (see map 11.1), while the Western Allies, having completed their successful landing on Anzio Beach, were marching toward Rome.

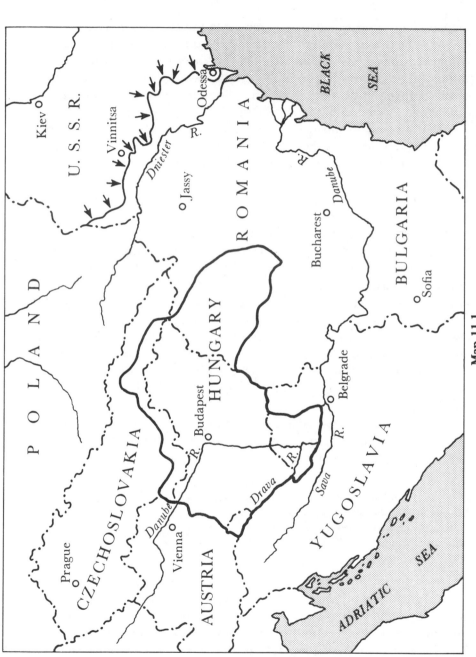

Map 11.1.

The Eastern front on the day of the German occupation of Hungary, March 19, 1944.

Kállay's ambiguous policy, though totally unrealistic in the pursuit of his twin objectives—the inducement of an Anglo-American presence in Hungary and the avoidance of a Soviet occupation—led to disaster, among other reasons, because he failed to take the necessary precautionary military measures against the eventuality of a German intervention.

Kállay tended to ignore the intelligence reports about German troop concentrations along the Hungarian border. He rejected the "rumors" of an imminent occupation, because he had been convinced that Germany would not risk losing its Hungarian lines of communication, which the Allies had tacitly agreed not to bomb as long as Hungary remained independent.[2] He dismissed the reports about the German troop movements, calling them "tactical threats" by the Nazis aimed at bringing about his resignation and the dismissal of such anti-German politicians as Ferenc Keresztes-Fischer, the Minister of the Interior.[3] One of the major sources of information concerning the German intentions in Hungary was the *Vaada*. The leaders of the Jewish relief and rescue organization were informed by Josef (Józsi) Winninger, one of the *Abwehr* agents in Budapest, almost a week before the occupation that "Hungary will cease to be an independent country."[4] Ironically, the national Jewish leaders also failed to take the necessary precautionary measures, even though they were already fully aware of what the Nazis had done to the Jews in occupied Europe (chapter 23).

No attempt was made to alert the armed forces to any possible resistance. The remnant of the Second Hungarian Army was left in the western parts of the Ukraine to perform occupation duties; the forces within the country were left practically at their peacetime preparedness level under the general command of mostly Germanophile officers. The fear of a possible Soviet occupation, which seemed more menacing in the long run than the immediate threat of a German occupation and the imposition of an openly Nazi-style totalitarian system, beclouded Kállay's thinking and virtually paralyzed his will. He steadfastly refused to heed the advice of men like Endre Bajcsy-Zsilinszky and General János Kiss, the two leaders of the minuscule resistance group later executed by the *Nyilas,* who demanded the "most resolute counteraction and the arming of the workers." He also rejected the request of the representatives of the Social Democratic Party that he openly and unmistakably break with the Axis and seek support of the Allies against the Nazi danger.[5] Had he followed the recommendations of these politicians of the Hungarian Left, whose views he often solicited but, as a

representative of the feudal conservative-aristocracy, was bound to reject, he might with some luck have extricated Hungary from the war
ahead of the Rofnanians and thereby incurred the political advantages
that were acquired by Hungary's traditional enemy. But the suggestions of the leftists, although noble, were to a large extent unrealistic,
for the remoteness of the fronts, geography, and domestic political-
military factors militated against such moves.[6]

While Kállay and some of the other leaders associated with his government had been genuinely concerned since the defeat at Voronezh
with the extrication of Hungary from the war, they consistently refused
the Allies' advice to turn against the Germans even to the extent of
declaring their readiness to defend their borders against a possible
German occupation. Their dealings with the representatives of the
Western Allies aimed not only to achieve Hungary's extrication from
the war, but also and above all to prevent any possible Russian occupation of the country.[7] Concerned with the preservation of the traditional
socioeconomic order and national political values, they were mortally
afraid of the rising specter of Bolshevik occupation. The military re-
verses notwithstanding, they were ready to continue the war on the side
of the Third Reich rather than surrender unconditionally to "the Allies," i.e., the Russians.

The immediate issue that triggered the chain of events which led to
the occupation was the Hungarian demand for the withdrawal of the
Hungarian forces from the Ukraine for the defense of the Carpathians. Acting in behalf of the Regent and Kállay, the Chief of the
General Staff, Ferenc Szombathelyi, raised the issue with both Keitel
and Hitler at the German headquarters on January 24, 1944. His formal oral request for the return of the Hungarian forces was reinforced
by a memorandum which he submitted to Keitel on February 14. The
request was echoed by Horthy in a personal letter to Hitler dated February 12, 1944.[8] Toward the end of the same month Kállay also contacted Keitel and presented his decision to withdraw his forces as a virtual ultimatum.

These demands (especially the one by Horthy, who until this point
had not been openly identified with the so-called Kállay line) and the
confirmed intelligence reports about the imminent arrival of an American mission in Budapest to work out the details of Hungary's surrender[9] reinforced Hitler's resolve to occupy Hungary and prevent it from
following the example of Italy.

The evidence now available indicates that these military and geopoli-

tical factors, rather than the unsolved Jewish question, were the determining elements underlying the occupation decision. At the Ministries
Trial in the summer of 1948, Karl Ritter, former Ambassador for Special Assignments in the German Foreign Office, quoted Ribbentrop in
stating the two basic reasons that moved Hitler to occupy Hungary: "A
short time previously Horthy had demanded that the Hungarian divisions be withdrawn from the Russian front. Simultaneously, we had
received news that the Hungarian Prime Minister, with Horthy's
knowledge, was negotiating with Britain concerning Hungary's giving
up the common struggle."[10] This assessment was also corroborated by
Colonel Walter Warlimont, Alfred Jodl's deputy at OKW, who claimed
that the occupation was ordered because of "Hitler's rage and thirst for
revenge against the Hungarian Regent" over his letter of February
12.[11]

Hitler's original idea was to bring about the total dismemberment of
Hungary with the aid of Romanian, Croatian, and Slovakian forces.
Marshal Ion Antonescu of Romania and President Josef Tiso of Slovakia, who visited Hitler on February 26–28, 1944, showed an interest in
Hitler's military plans. Hitler was particularly anxious to bring about
the expansion of Hungary's military effort in order to deprive the
Romanians of their excuse for their lagging war contributions since the
defeat at Stalingrad. The plan was apparently dropped in response to a
detailed memorandum prepared by SS-Sturmbannführer Wilhelm Höttl
(Walter Hagen), Head of the Intelligence Service of the Security Police
in Vienna (which covered Hungary) on March 11.[12] According to the
memorandum, the participation of the satellite forces would prove
counterproductive, for it would induce the formation of "a united
front, extending from the Communists to the Arrow Cross."

In addition, such a combined German-satellite occupation of
Hungary would

- Make it impossible to form a new government.
- Lead to the resignation of Horthy.
- Bring about military, political, and economic chaos and the de-
  velopment of a resistance movement.
- Tie down many German divisions for a long period of time.

Fearing that the military intervention would not necessarily result in
the achievement of the stated objectives, and might also lead to un-
foreseen strategical and foreign political difficulties, the author of the
memorandum suggested that "evolutionary methods" might be applied

under which political leaders and experts of the Right would be entrusted with the formation of a new Hungarian government. He identified Jenő Rátz, Jenő Ruszkay, Béla Imrédy, and László Baky among those to be included in such a new Right-oriented, pro-German regime. The advantages of the "evolutionary method," in Höttl's view, would have included:

- A domestically consolidated German-oriented Hungary.
- The continuation of Horthy as Hungary's Head of State.
- The guarantee that the Hungarian armed forces and security units would remain intact and at the disposal of the Reich.
- The total economic exploitation of the country.
- A greater military effort on the part of Romania, which would have lost the excuse to keep troops in Transylvania.
- The freeing of German troops for other purposes.

The memorandum—incorporating specific suggestions and recommendations concerning the approach to be followed in the attainment of the desired goals was submitted to Kaltenbrunner. The chief of the Reich Security Main Office revised it and submitted it to Hitler, who promptly approved it. The basic idea of the plan was to maneuver Horthy into acceptance and implementation, within the framework of a "restricted" occupation, of the German desire to align Hungary's policies with those of the Third Reich, augment its military contribution to the common war effort, and carry out an "unconditional program" to eliminate political undesirables and Jews.

In accordance with the provisions of the memorandum, Hitler signed and issued the order for Operation Margarethe I—the code name for the "restricted occupation"—on March 12.[13] The occupation was to be carried out under the general command of Field Marshal Maximilian von Weichs, and the inconspicuous deployment of the troops along the borders of Hungary was to be completed by March 15. As camouflage, the units were to disguise some of their preparations as guerrilla operations and the others as "exercises in preparation for a spring offensive in the East." The Führer also stipulated that in addition to the regular *Wehrmacht* and *Luftwaffe* units, the occupation forces include a number of SS units to be provided by the *Reichsführer-SS*. These were to be placed under the immediate control of Kaltenbrunner for the implementation of the Final Solution. These special SS detachments were to consist of an *Einsatzgruppe* of 500 to 600 Gestapo and SD men under the immediate command of *SS-Standartenführer* Hans Geschke and a 200 to 300 man *Sonderkommando* under the leadership of *SS-Obersturmbannführer* Adolf Eichmann, chief of Amt IV B 4 of the RSHA.[14]

With the preparations for the occupation completed, Hitler extended an urgent invitation to Horthy to come to Schloss Klessheim, near Salzburg, in order to discuss "the military situation in general and the question of the withdrawal of Hungarian troops" as requested in the Regent's letter of February 12.[15]

The Schloss Klessheim Conference

Although both Horthy and Kállay were at first inclined to decline the invitation, they were persuaded by Szombathelyi's arguments[16] and decided that Horthy should meet Hitler in the company of Szombathelyi, Minister of Defense Csatay, and Foreign Minister Ghyczy. The four-member Hungarian delegation left Budapest on the evening of March 17, 1944, leaving behind no instructions or contingency plans to guide the Prime Minister and the government in the event of a "negative" outcome of the conference. Apparently the only unofficial precautionary measure was adopted by the Foreign Minister, who agreed with Andor Szentmiklóssy, his deputy and former Chief of the Political Division of the Foreign Ministry, that if he wired back that "the visit is not to be communicated to the press" the German occupation was certain.

Horthy was received by Hitler soon after his arrival in the morning of March 18. The negotiations were conducted in a tense atmosphere and consisted basically of Hitler's attempt to rationalize the *fait accompli*. He invoked his responsibility to the German people to prevent Hungary from duplicating Italy's "treachery." Parallel "negotiations" were conducted between Ghyczy and Ribbentrop and between Csatay and Szombathelyi and Keitel.[17]

The "negotiations" were dragged out in order to keep the Hungarian delegation from returning home until the occupation was well under way, if not completed. The train left Salzburg at 9:30 P.M. just about 90 minutes before the German troops began to move into Hungary.

Horthy and his entourage left with no written agreement except for Hitler's "assurances" that the German troops would leave Hungary as soon as an "acceptable" government was formed and that no satellite troops would be involved in the occupation. No reference appears to have been made to the withdrawal of the SS units.

Horthy and his entourage arrived back in Hungary in the morning of March 19. While the train stopped at Bicske, just west of Budapest, von Jagow entered the Regent's compartment and introduced his successor, Dr. Edmund Veesenmayer, whom Hitler had appointed as German Minister and Reich Plenipotentiary in Hungary. Shortly thereafter Péter Hain, Horthy's own personal detective who had doubled as a paid German agent, introduced him to Ernst Kaltenbrunner.

The Crown Council Meeting
of March 19

A few hours after his arrival in Budapest at 11 A.M., Horthy called for a meeting of the Crown Council. Convened at 12:45 P.M., the meeting was attended by the five who had been to Klessheim (the four-member delegation from Budapest had been joined in Vienna by Döme Sztójay, the Hungarian Minister in Berlin), and by Miklós Kállay; Ferenc Keresztes-Fischer, Minister of the Interior; Lajos Reményi-Schneller, Minister of Finance; Dániel Bánffy, Minister of Agriculture; Géza Bornemissza, Minister of Industry; Ferenc Zsindely, Minister of Trade and Transportation; Jenő Szinyei-Merse, Minister of Cults and Education; László Radocsay, Minister of Justice; Lajos Szász, Minister of Supplies; and István Antal, Minister of Propaganda. István Bárczy, Secretary of State in the Council of Ministers, served as secretary.

Horthy reviewed his encounter with Hitler emphasizing the arguments he had advanced to dissuade the Germans from proceeding with the occupation. He had tried to persuade the Germans that the occupation would be counterproductive, for such a move would merely bring about an Anglo-American bombing of the industries serving the Axis war effort, the development of an anti-Nazi resistance movement, and worker strikes. The Germans, who had already finalized their occupation plans, had listened impassively, but insisted on the need to protect their security and national interests in view of the "treacherous" activities of the Kállay government. Specifically they cited, the activities of Professor Albert Szent-Györgyi of the University of Szeged and of the newspaperman Pál Szvatkó.

The allegations of the German leaders were, of course, not totally unfounded. Professor Szent-Györgyi, the Nobel-prize-winning scientist, had in fact been sent by Kállay to inform the British and the Americans in Istanbul about the anti-Nazi position and policies of the Hungarian people and government. He was accompanied to Istanbul by András

Frey, an editor of the *Magyar Nemzet* (Hungarian Nation), the highly respected daily of Budapest, and by Professor Gyula Mészáros. Szent-Györgyi was lured into a trap and instead of talking to the Anglo-Americans he in fact revealed the plans of the Prime Minister to German agents.[18] Szvatkó was a courageous journalist, who often echoed the aspirations of the anti-Nazi forces in Hungary. The article that especially irked the Germans appeared in the January 1, 1944 issue of *Magyarország* (Hungary). Hinting at the difficulty of extricating Hungary from the war, he wrote among other things:

The principle adopted at Teheran is beset by many contradictions and its application is in many cases a physical impossibility. For example, how can a country which is eager to end the war unconditionally surrender if there are no Allied forces by its borders or nearby to which the unconditional surrender could be offered?[19]

The Germans had been aware of the Hungarian emissaries' contacts with the British all along. According to a secret communication signed on July 16, 1943, by Counselor Grote of the German Foreign Office, Szent-Györgyi and Mészáros had established contact with the "enemy" in February–March of that year. In fact, Horthy was given some hints about these contacts during his first visit to Hitler at Schloss Klessheim in April 1943. It is quite possible that the Germans' source of information was Mészáros himself, who apparently acted as a double agent. German sources reveal that "the Foreign Office has found out by a strictly confidential route that at least Professor Mészáros has for a long time been in the service of the German Intelligence (Vienna Office) for which he received three hundred Turkish pounds per month."[20]

Horthy's account of Hitler's communications was corroborated by the others who had attended the conference. Kállay immediately submitted the resignation of his government and suggested that a new one consisting of the senior administrative state secretaries of the various ministries be established. Keresztes-Fischer informed the Crown Council of the police measures that the Germans had already effectuated and of his inability to continue even on a provisional basis. The Prime Minister urged Horthy to stay on, confirming the Regent's own arguments for continuing in office. Horthy rationalized that while he was in charge, the Germans would not absorb the Hungarian Army and "could not attempt putting the Arrow Cross Party into office to do their deadly work of murdering Hungarian patriots, of exterminating the 800,000 Hungarian Jews and the tens of thousands of refugees who sought sanctuary in Hungary."[21] In light of the fateful concessions he had made on the delivery of Jewish "workers" one can only wonder about the sincerity or veracity of Horthy's expressed concern over the safety of the Jews.

Although no formal agreement was signed at Klessheim,[22] there is absolutely no doubt that the question of the treatment of the Jews of Hungary was also discussed and that Horthy made certain concessions that proved disastrous for Hungarian Jewry.

In his report to the Crown Council Horthy made no reference to these concessions, but merely observed that Hitler had complained that "Hungary did nothing in the matter of the Jewish problem, and was not prepared to settle accounts with the large Jewish population in Hungary." In this connection, he also quoted Hitler's assertion with reference to the Jews of Finland. The Führer allegedly said: "Finland had only 6,000 Jews and what a subversive activity even these performed against Finland's standing her ground further."[23]

Laconic as the report was on the Jewish question, the minutes of the Crown Council meeting clearly reveal that the Regent, while anticipating many German demands, considered the Nazi occupation less of an evil than a possible Russian "invasion."

Apparently either Horthy deliberately failed to inform the Crown Council about the "agreement" to supply Germany with Jewish "workers" or the Council decided not to record this obviously controversial item in the minutes.[24] The evidence, however, reveals that Horthy in fact did agree—perhaps reluctantly and unwillingly—to the delivery of a considerable number of "Jewish workers for German war production purposes." Horthy's concurrence was important to the Germans, who were eager to maintain the façade of Hungarian sovereignty, to assure the cooperation of the new, pro-Nazi Hungarian government, and to provide legitimacy for the "limited" anti-Jewish operation.

Admiral Horthy's role during the German occupation in general and in the handling of the Jewish question in particular has emerged as one of the most controversial themes in postwar historiography. Marxist historians and journalists, especially those living in Hungary, tend to place ultimate responsibility for the catastrophe primarily on him and his bourgeois-aristocratic entourage. They indict the wartime leaders of Hungary for the failure to heed the warnings about the German troop concentrations along the borders, the reluctance to take any precautionary military countermeasures, the decision to accept Hitler's invitation to Schloss Klessheim, and finally for the decision to have Horthy continue as Head of State.[25]

By his failure to abdicate and by his subsequent decision to cooperate in the formation of the Sztójay government (see chapter 13), Horthy

- Legitimized the occupation and contributed to the placement of the entire Hungarian state apparatus at the service of the Germans without which they could not possibly have established or maintained an orderly occupation.
- Pacified the Hungarian masses and thereby assured the maintenance of law and order that the Germans desired, guaranteed the uninterrupted continuation of war production, and generated the development of a quisling spirit in the country.
- Contributed at least indirectly to the commission of the very mass crimes he feared the Arrow Cross people would perpetrate in his absence.

Among those who argued after the war that Hungary could have been saved the pains and horrors of the occupation era if only Horthy had resisted the German demands, including the appointment of Sztójay, was his former Minister of Defense, Vilmos Nagy, who maintains that had Horthy resisted the country would have followed his leadership and the world would have learned that Hungary too was a victim of Nazism rather than one of its satellites.[26]

On the other hand, there are many Jewish and non-Jewish historians and laymen, especially among those living in the West, who claim that Horthy and his subordinates followed the best possible course given Hungary's position. In their view, the Hungarian wartime leaders skillfully managed to maintain the country's independence for as long as they could while paying only lip service to the Axis Alliance. Moreover, they claim that the survival of about half of the Jews of Trianon Hungary (mainly those who had lived in Budapest) was due to Horthy's decision to continue as Head of State and to the actions he took in that capacity during July–October, 1944 (see chapter 25).

While there is considerable merit in both positions, objectivity requires that a differentiation be made between Horthy's original position of March through July and his changed attitude between July and October, 1944. While the Hungarians were perhaps powerless to prevent the German occupation, given the deployment of the bulk of the Army on the eastern front and the dispersal of the local military forces,[27] it was in retrospect a grave mistake for Horthy—once he decided to stay on—to withdraw himself from active leadership and give his newly appointed Prime Minister, Döme Sztójay, and the German-supported Hungarian government a free hand in the management of state affairs. This was particularly disastrous in the case of the Jews. The Sztójay government, installed over Horthy's signature on March 22, 1944, proceeded almost immediately with the implementation of the German-requested anti-Jewish program. At the Council of Ministers meeting of March 29, István Antal, the new Minister of Justice, declared that "Horthy left it to the government to order measures to be taken concerning the Jewish question. He gave a free hand on this issue and did not wish to exert any influence on these activities."[28]

Many of the wartime and postwar memoirists, including some of the leading figures of the Hungarian Jewish community,[29] tried to explain Horthy's withdrawal by asserting that the Regent was under virtual house arrest. While it was true that the Germans wanted to isolate him, Horthy appeared at public functions quite frequently to symbolize the retention of Hungarian sovereignty. On April 15, for example, he and his Minister of Defense, Lajos Csatay, signed an appeal to the troops calling on them to fight "shoulder to shoulder with the German comrades, the true and honorable allies." On May 5, he witnessed military maneuvers near Budapest and visited the Ludovika Military Academy when a new class of officers was graduated.[30] In addition, he continued to fulfill his functions as Head of State by adding his signature to most of the measures adopted by the Sztójay government, with the notable exception of those relating to the Jews.

The anti-Jewish measures were implemented by ministerial decrees and orders, which did not constitutionally require his countersignature. By adopting this attitude, Horthy, as Professor Macartney correctly observed, "went no further than Pontius Pilate: he washed his hands, but made no suggestion that any demand made by the Germans should be refused."[31] The record clearly shows that the German demands could have been refused or sabotaged—they were in Bulgaria and Romania as well as in the case of the Budapest Jews in July 1944—had Horthy and the Hungarian authorities really been concerned with their citizens of the Jewish faith. The Germans would have been quite helpless—as the post-July 1944 events demonstrated—without the wholehearted and effective cooperation of the Hungarian authorities.

Horthy's attitude was probably determined by his apparent conviction that the Germans were only interested in the "few hundred thousand Jewish workers" they then needed for their war industries and to whose delivery he had informally consented at Schloss Klessheim. Perhaps Horthy thought that with the delivery of the "Jewish workers" he would not only satisfy Germany's "legitimate" needs and hasten the end of the occupation, but would also get rid of the "Galician Jews" whom he openly detested. Finally, it is possible that he was merely following the advice of his former Prime Minister, whose judgment and friendship he greatly valued. Kállay advised him to stay on and save the integrity and unity of the Army and "possibly withdraw himself from the management of certain affairs."[32]

Horthy's apparent original decision to give the Sztójay government a free hand in the handling of the Jewish question was severely criticized by many both during and after the war. Among these was Miklós Mester, the Secretary of State in the Ministry of Cults and Public Education. A representative of Imrédy's Right radical party, Mester adopted a pronouncedly anti-German position during the summer of 1944 and maintained close contact with the leaders of the opposition, including Albert Bereczky and Ottó Komoly. In a discussion with Komoly on August 25, Mester openly declared: "One would have to condemn the Governor because the matter [of the Jewish question] did not interest him at the beginning, because he adopted the position that he would not deal with anything that happened against his will. This he should not have done."[33]

It is quite possible that Horthy simply did not realize the implications of what he had agreed to at Klessheim. At the time of his visit he was over 76, and according to several of his contemporaries he not only was politically inept but had also definitely shown many symptoms of senility. He suffered occasional lapses of memory, his thoughts tended to stray, and he often repeated himself. Some of his opponents, including Veesenmayer, exploited the Regent's weaknesses for the advancement of their own interests.

In his second report on Hungary, dated December 14, 1943, Veesenmayer characterized Horthy as basically a good soldier, but "a miserable politician," who "understands nothing about either domestic or foreign policy."[34] In one of his first telegrams after he had been appointed Reich Plenipotentiary in Hungary, Veesenmayer informed Ribbentrop about a discussion he had with Horthy on Germany's wishes in the formation of a new Hungarian government and included the following character evaluation:

Now that I have already had three longer meetings with the *Reichsverweser* within 24 hours, I have come more and more to the conclusion that either Horthy is lying to an incredible degree, or else he is just physically not up to his task any more. He repeats himself constantly, often contradicts himself within a few sentences, and sometimes does not know how to continue. What he has to say sounds like a memorized formula and I am afraid that he will be difficult to convince, much less to win over.[35]

Veesenmayer's own conclusions about the fullest exploitation of Hungary while maintaining Horthy as the nominal Head of State were reinforced by Ribbentrop who instructed him on April 2, 1944, to gradually remove Horthy from the management of state affairs until he was totally isolated and to deal only with the new Hungarian government.[36]

The impairment of Horthy's mental faculties was particularly noticeable in March 1948, when he appeared as a witness in the trial of Veesenmayer. Of course, this was four years after the Klessheim encounter with Hitler and Horthy may have become more senile—or perhaps he deliberately lied in order to conceal his own guilt. At any rate, when cross-examined by the defense, Horthy claimed that the ghettoization and entrainment of the Jews were carried out by the Gestapo and not by the Hungarian gendarmerie, which was under his command, and he claimed not to remember that Hungary had passed anti-Jewish legislation in 1938, 1939, and 1941. Neither did he remember that Hungary expelled "12,000 Jews" in August 1941,[37] most of whom were subsequently slaughtered at Kamenets-Podolsk.

Whatever the psycho-pathological explanation of Horthy's condition and whatever the line of reasoning or rationalization that he followed, the historical facts remain that during the crucial months of April, May, and June, when the ghettoization, concentration, and deportation of the provincial Jews was taking place, he did little, if anything, in behalf of the Jewish citizens of Hungary. And he could have done a lot, as the events of July–October amply demonstrated. In July, for example, he ordered the return of the Kistarcsa deportation train and put an end to further deportations from Hungary.

The currently available historical record indicates that it was beneficial, especially for the Jews of Budapest, that Horthy decided to stay on as Head of State. However, it was disastrous for the bulk of Hungarian Jewry—the provincial Jews—and for the Hungarian nation at large for Horthy to have consented or have chosen to remain merely a figurehead during the first four months of the German occupation. For during these months, through his consent to stay on and cooperate in the formation of the new government by the Germans, Horthy:

- Provided legitimization for the occupation.
- Assuaged the Hungarian masses and thereby assured the continuation of war production and the development of a pro-German spirit in the country.

- Contributed indirectly to the effectuation of the very mass crimes he feared the Arrow Cross would perpetuate.
- Expanded Hungary's military contribution and sacrifices in a losing war.
- Damaged the country's reputation and its political chances during the postwar period.

In addition to remaining as Head of State, dismissing Kállay, and appointing a new, pro-German government, Horthy also agreed to increase Hungary's contribution to the common war effort. In this context, he consented, among other things, to the delivery of "Hungarian Jewish manpower" for "German war production purposes."

The Jägerstab Project

Hitler had no difficulty in demonstrating his needs to Horthy. The Germans were suffering terrible losses on the eastern front and the German aircraft industry had been heavily damaged by the American Eighth and Fifteenth Air Forces. Field Marshal Erhard Milch, State Secretary in the Air Ministry and armaments chief of the *Luftwaffe,* approached Albert Speer, the Minister of Armaments and War Production, on February 23, 1944, with the idea that a Fighter Aircraft Staff (*Jägerstab*) be established for the purpose of pooling the talents and resources of their two ministries "in order to overcome the crisis in aircraft production."[38]

Milch apparently acted in response to a decision in this matter made by his superior, *Reichsmarschall* Hermann Göring. Citing the concurrence of Hitler, Göring asked Himmler, in a telegram dated February 14, 1944, to provide concentration camp labor for the building of underground aircraft factories. In his letter of March 9, 1944, Himmler assured Göring that plans were being implemented to allocate about 100,000 inmates for this purpose.[39]

The plan, as worked out in detail by Xaver Dorsch, a department head in Speer's ministry, called for the construction of six underground industrial sites, each with an area of over one million square feet, to be completed by November 1944. One of the sites was to be built in the Protectorates of Bohemia and Moravia with the aid of Jewish workers from Hungary. To head the Fighter Aircraft Staff, Hitler appointed Karl Saur, a department head in the Armaments Ministry, whom Milch and Speer also approved.[40]

On March 18, 1944—the day Horthy visited Hitler—Speer was convalescing in the Cloverleaf Palace, a curved pavilion in the park of

Schloss Klessheim.[41] The immediate labor needs for the project in the Protectorates were presumably discussed in light of Speer's communication and of the "Hungarian statesmen's" 1942 offers relating to 100,000 Jews as revealed by Wisliceny (see chapter 9). Hitler and Speer again reviewed the manpower needs of the *Jägerstab* project on April 6 and 7. They agreed, according to the notes made by Speer on April 9, that the Junkers Works (*Junkers-Werke*) would be expanded to build 1,000 ME-262s and 2,000 other fighter aircraft per month and that instead of following the original plan which called for the building of a second underground aircraft factory in either France, Belgium, or the Netherlands, one would be built in the more secure areas of the Protectorates. Since Hitler was dissatisfied with the performance of the *Industriegemeinschaft Schlesien* (the Silesian Industrial Association), he ordered that the Protectorates project be built by the *Todt* Organization with the 100,000 Jewish workers he would ask Himmler to deliver.[42]

In response to the decisions of April 6–7 and to Horthy's apparent concurrence with the request for Jewish labor, Hitler informed Milch on April 9 that 100,000 Hungarian Jews "were to be found for the construction of underground aircraft factories in the Reich."[43]

Duly appointed to his new position, Saur called a top-secret meeting of the Fighter Aircraft Staff on April 14, 1944, and revealed that the details relating to the employment of 100,000 Hungarian Jews in the Protectorates project were being finalized by Schlempp and Schmelter, two experts who were working under Dorsch. On the same day (less than one month after the occupation) Veesenmayer informed Ribbentrop that Sztójay had given him a "binding assurance" that 50,000 able-bodied Jews would be placed at the disposal of the Reich by the end of the same month, and that 50,000 more able-bodied Jews would be made available before the end of May. He further reported that the practical measures for the implementation of Sztójay's assurances were already under way through the action initiated by the SD and the Hungarian police. He also revealed that he had the concurrence of the Regent and that the Hungarian armed forces and Ministry of the Interior had expressed their readiness to cooperate.[44]

Horthy's Consent to the Delivery of "Jewish Workers"

Veesenmayer's assertion that he had the concurrence of the Regent is amply corroborated by evidence revealed after the war, especially at the war crimes trials.[45]

According to Ribbentrop, the Regent agreed that "a considerable number of Jewish workers were to be made available for German war production."[46] Otto Winkelmann, the Higher SS and Police Leader and Himmler's immediate representative in Hungary in 1944, stated in the Ministries Trial that there was a "legal agreement" with the Hungarian government "for the deportation of what was initially 100,000 Jews."[47] This was also corroborated by *SS-Hauptsturmführer* Ernst Kienast, Winkelmann's assistant in Budapest, who testified that according to his superior "the necessity for a solution of the Jewish question in Hungary was unequivocally established by Hitler at Klessheim and urgently pushed through," although "no agreement was reached on the form which the solution should take, nor on the extent of the program."[48]

In his testimony during his own trial in 1948, Veesenmayer stated:

Horthy himself told me that he was interested only in protecting those prosperous, the economically valuable Jews in Budapest, those who were well off. However, as to the remaining Jewry—and he used a very ugly term there—he had no interest in them and was quite prepared to have them go to the Reich or elsewhere for labor. He approved that; and he did not approve it after a demand made by me but he approved it after agreements and discussions with his premier and his ministries. The fact has been proved that he later—at first he moderated the deportations, and then later stopped them. Somebody who forbids something later on, must have given permission for it earlier.[49]

This assessment of Horthy was also corroborated by Baky. In his statement written while in prison, Baky claimed that he had issued the decree of April 7, 1944, which called for the ghettoization of the Jews, because László Endre had requested it on the basis that "the Regent agreed to the delivery of the Jews to the Germans for purposes of labor."[50] He believed this, he claimed, because during his own previous audience with the Regent, Horthy had told him:

Baky, you are one of my old Szeged officers. The Germans have cheated me. Now they want to deport the Jews. I don't mind. I hate the Galician Jews and the Communists. Out with them, out of the country! But you must see, Baky, that there are some Jews who are as good Hungarians as you and I. For example, here are little Chorin and Vida—aren't they good Hungarians? I can't allow these to be taken away. But they can take the rest.[51]

Baky's assessment of Horthy's attitude toward the Jews was also corroborated by Kurt Haller, Veesenmayer's secretary. In his view "Horthy considered the assimilated Jews of Budapest as Hungarians, but the poorer ones of the provinces only as rabble for whom he had done nothing for a long time."[52] The same view was expressed in an anonymous report on an interview with Horthy which was submitted to Himmler in July 1943. Horthy allegedly demonstrated a readiness to rid the country of the "little Jews, who originally came from Galicia," but was eager to protect those Jews who "had made contributions in the fields of science, industry, and finance."[53] Horthy's concern for the welfare of these "patriotic Jews" was recognized even by Hitler. Angered with the Regent's decision of July 7, 1944, to end the deportations, Hitler insisted that the "measures against the Jews of Budapest . . . be carried out . . . with the exceptions granted . . . in agreement with the proposals of the Hungarian Government." He coupled his demand to a warning that any departure from "the ways decided at Klessheim and instituted since then might jeopardize the very existence of the Hungarian nation."[54] Hitler's message clearly implies that Horthy consented at Klessheim to some of the measures the Führer had ordered in connection with the occupation of Hungary.[55]

Endre, the former Deputy Prefect of Pest County, who served after the German occupation as Secretary of State in the Ministry of the Interior in charge of Jewish affairs and as such was one of those chiefly responsible for the destruction of the Jews, also stated in his evidence that "the Regent raised no objection to the deportations, saying that the sooner the operation was concluded, the sooner the Germans would leave the country."[56]

Perhaps the most convincing evidence about Horthy's consent was offered by Bishop László Ravasz. He claims that when he was informed about the atrocities committed during the ghettoization of the Jews in Carpatho-Ruthenia and in northeastern Hungary—by Zsigmond Perényi, the president of the upper house[57]—he contacted Horthy to express his misgivings. At a meeting on April 28, Horthy told him that "a large number of labor draftees were requested of Hungary . . . A few hundred thousand Jews will in this manner leave the country's frontier, but not a single hair of their heads will be touched, just as is the case with the many hundreds of thousands of Hungarian workers, who have been working in Germany since the beginning of the war."[58]

An unidentified official spokesman of the Hungarian government, commenting on the deportations, informed the foreign journalists in June 1944 that:

The Hungarian authorities have placed Jewish manpower at the disposal of the Reich in order to meet the wish [for labor] of the German ally in the interest of the joint conduct of the war without prejudicing Hungarian war production. It is therefore a question not of deportation but of normal transfer of labor.[59]

This statement was in accord with Sztójay's memorandum of June 26, 1944, cabled to the Hungarian diplomatic representatives abroad, which aimed to "explain" the deportations:

In view of the position of the labor market in Hungary as well as of the full share this country takes in the war, the Hungarian Government has not been able to raise the contingent of Hungarian workers for Germany but has wished to comply with the requests of the Germans by placing Jews at their disposal. It was on the grounds of this agreement that Jews were sent to Germany for work. Experience having proved that in foreign countries the Jews' willingness to work diminishes when they are separated from their families, the members of their families were sent along with them.[60]

This telegram by Sztójay is the only official Hungarian confirmation that the Jews were delivered to the Germans on the basis of an "agreement."[61]

Another document of considerable historical importance in this respect is the one which Sándor Török, one of the leaders of the Jewish Council and of the Association of the Christian Jews of Hungary (*Magyarországi Keresztény Zsidók Szövetsége*), revealed to Ottó Komoly on September 2, 1944.[62] Török was anxiety-ridden over the plan Komoly, Bereczky, and some other leaders of the Hungarian opposition were then discussing with Lieutenant-Colonel László Ferenczy (the gendarmerie officer who was in charge of the deportations from the provinces), Captain Leó Lullay, his aide, and some officials of the Lakatos government. According to this plan the remaining Jews of Hungary, who were by then living almost exclusively in Budapest, were to have been placed in special concentration camps within Hungary "in order to satisfy the Germans" and as a means to prevent their deportation to Germany (see chapter 25). The document in Török's possession stipulated, among other things, that the Hungarian government had agreed with the German government eight days earlier to the effect that the Jews would be taken over from the Hungarian government in order to be put to work in Germany. The trains would be provided by the German government, and the people would be taken over not by name but in counted groups. The above document was signed by Krüger, the chief commander of an assault group (*főrohamcsoportvezető*). Upon studying the document, Komoly concluded that its date must have been either March or April, for the anti-Jewish measures that were carried out by the German and Hungarian authorities totally corresponded to the text of this agreement.

C. A. Macartney, who cannot be accused of being unsympathetic to

Hungary or Horthy, reached the following conclusion on the treatment of the Jewish question at Klessheim: "It seems established only that Horthy agreed to one specific step in this field: that a considerable number of Hungarian Jews should be sent to Germany for work in the German munitions factories."[63] In another context, in discussing Veesenmayer's request for 50,000 Jewish workers, Macartney very correctly identified that request as "an entirely *bona fide* demand . . . [for] Horthy had already, at Klessheim, agreed to supply the Reich with Jewish labor."[64]

The evidence is thus overwhelming that Horthy did indeed agree to the delivery of "Jewish workers" for the German war industry. This agreement was subsequently exploited by the German and Hungarian dejewification squads to bring about the Final Solution. Toward this end, they received not only the cooperation of the Hungarian instrumentalities of state power, but also that of the German occupation forces and authorities.

Notes

1. For further details on the Führer Order, see below. See also György Ránki, *1944. március 19* (March 19, 1944), 2nd ed. (Budapest: Kossuth, 1978), pp. 48–57.

2. Personal communication by Kállay in 1956. See also this author's review of Kállay's *Hungarian Premier* (New York: Columbia University Press, 1954) in *Jewish Social Studies*, 18, no. 3 (July 1956):226–27.

3. C. A. Macartney, 2:223.

4. Alex Weissberg, *Advocate for the Dead: The Story of Joel Brand* (London: Andre Deutsch, 1958), p. 65; *Der Kastner-Bericht*, p. 53.

5. C. A. Macartney, 2:231. As subsequent events clearly proved, most of these individuals contented themselves with the admonition of the government; they themselves made no adequate preparation for resistance either. For further details on this subject see chapter 29.

6. Kállay's irresoluteness during the war was criticized after the war even by some of his closest associates. Vilmos Nagy, Kállay's former Minister of Defense, for example, states in his memoirs that instead of pursuing a Janus-faced policy, Kállay could have saved the future of Hungary by taking a clear stand against continued participation in the war. Vilmos Nagy, *Végzetes esztendők, 1938–1945* (Fatal Years, 1938–1945) (Budapest: Körmendy, 1946), p. 157.

7. For an evaluation of the various contacts and negotiations with the representatives of the Western Allies, see C. A. Macartney, 2:209–18. One of the links for the possible establishment of direct contacts with the Western Allies was Colonel Charles Telfer Howie, a South African escapee from a German POW camp, who had somehow managed to find refuge in Hungary. For further details on the role of Howie, see Sándor Szent-Iványi, "A Howie-epizód" (The Howie Episode). *Menora*, Toronto, October 19, 1974, p. 6. See also chapter 7.

8. The text of the letter can be found in *Horthy Miklós titkos iratai* (The Secret Papers of Miklós Horthy), eds. Miklós Szinai and László Szücs (Budapest: Kossuth, 1963), pp. 408–10.

9. The agreement for sending the mission to Hungary was worked out in negotiations involving György Bakách-Bessenyey, the former Hungarian Minister in Paris and Berne, Allen W. Dulles, then Chief of the OSS in Switzerland, and Royall Tyler of the American Legation in Berne. The mission, led by a colonel, arrived on the night of March 16–17, but all its members were arrested a few days later together with Major-General István Ujszászy, then chief of the National Defense Center (*Államvédelmi Központ*) of the Ministry of the Interior, and Colonel Gyula Kádár, head of the counter-intelligence agency of the General Staff; both were involved in the receipt of the mission. C. A. Macartney, 2:255. See also Kállay, *Hungarian Premier,* pp. 219 and 386–87.

10. Transcript of the Ministries Trial (Court IV, Case XI), 1948, p. 12224, as quoted in C. A. Macartney, 2:223.

11. Walter Warlimont, *Inside Hitler's Headquarters, 1939–45* (New York: Praeger, 1964), pp. 412–13.

12. According to some sources, the memorandum originated from Ernst Kienast, then Director of the *Reichstag Büro.* C. A. Macartney, 2:225. The text of the memorandum is reproduced as Document No. D-679 in *IMT,* 35:358–65. For text in Hungarian consult *Magyarország és a második világháború* (Hungary and the Second World War), eds. László Zsigmond, Magda Ádám, Gyula Juhász, and Lajos Kerekes (Budapest: Kossuth, 1961), pp. 443–47. For Höttl's account, see Wilhelm Hoettl, *The Secret Front* (New York: Praeger, 1954), pp. 196–97. According to Höttl, his memorandum was submitted to Hitler by Walter Hewel, the Senior Liaison Officer of the Foreign Office at the Führer Headquarters. *Ibid.* For additional details on Höttl, see C. A. Macartney, 2:217–18.

13. A contingency plan for the total occupation of Hungary in case Horthy failed to cooperate was also prepared and code-named Operation Margarethe II. The March 12 order was issued by Hitler in his capacity as Supreme Commander of the Wehrmacht and is identified as "OKW/Wehrmacht Ops. Staff Op. No. 77683/44." The document was submitted by the defense in the Veesenmayer Trial and is identified as "Veesenmayer Document No. 167" in "Document Book V, a, Veesenmayer."

14. C. A. Macartney, 2:228.

15. Although the official name of the locality in Austria is Klesheim, it is rendered throughout this text as Klessheim in order to conform to the spelling used in most texts. The urgency and character of the invitation were reflected in Ribbentrop's telegram to Jagow of March 15. In it the Foreign Minister insisted that Horthy be informed that very day and that his answer be relayed no later than 1 P.M. the following day. Jagow's request for an audience with the Regent that evening was conveyed during the intermission of the opera *Petőfi,* which Horthy had attended in honor of Hungary's national holiday. For the text of Ribbentrop's telegram, see *A Wilhelmstrasse és Magyarország. Német diplomáciai iratok Magyarországról, 1933–1944* (The Wilhelmstrasse and Hungary. German Diplomatic Papers About Hungary, 1933–1944), compiled and edited by György Ránki, Ervin Pamlényi, Loránt Tilkovszky, and Gyula Juhász. (Budapest: Kossuth, 1968), pp. 781–82. See also C. A. Macartney, 2:232.

16. Szombathelyi argued that by meeting the Führer man to man, Horthy could persuade him to allow the return of the "Dead Army"—the remnant of the Hungarian forces in the East—and assure him of Hungary's resolve to defend the Carpathians. Ghyczy concurred, adding that refusal to meet the Führer would place Horthy's attitude in an unfavorable light in comparison with the position of Antonescu and Tiso, the Romanian and Slovak leaders. C. A. Macartney, 2:233.

17. In his order of March 12, Hitler clearly stated: "I have . . . decided to remove (the Kállay) clique of traitors forthwith. German troops will invade Hungary and occupy the country temporarily." For an account of the negotiations consult C. A. Macartney, 2:233–41; Nicholas (Miklós) Horthy, *Memoirs.* (New York: Robert Speller, 1957), pp. 212–17; Kállay, *Hungarian Premier,* pp. 412–22; Paul Schmidt, *Statist auf diplomatischer Bühne, 1923–1945* (Bonn: Athenaeum, 1950), pp. 551–52, 576–77. For the English trans-

lation of Schmidt's book, see *Hitler's Interpreter* (New York: Macmillan, 1951), pp. 270–72. See also Szombathelyi's account of the meeting in *Magyarország és a második világháború*, pp. 448–55. For the official account, see minutes of the Crown Council meeting of March 19 in *Horthy Miklós titkos iratai*, pp. 419–31.

18. Kállay, *Hungarian Premier*, p. 181.

19. *Horthy Miklós titkos iratai*, pp. 430–31.

20. *NA*, Microcopy T-120, Roll 688, Frames 311975-976.

21. Horthy, *Memoirs*, p. 215.

22. In anticipation of a favorable conclusion of the conference, the Germans prepared a draft communiqué, which, however, was not signed. For text see *A Wilhelmstrasse és Magyarország*, pp. 782–83.

23. For the minutes of the Crown Council meeting see *The Confidential Papers of Admiral Horthy*, pp. 278–90; for the original text, see *Horthy Miklós titkos iratai*, pp. 419–31.

24. C. A. Macartney has demonstrated that Horthy himself had prepared four different versions of his encounter with Hitler: (1) the version officially recorded at the Crown Council meeting; (2) the version given to Kállay and rendered in his *Hungarian Premier*, pp. 429–31; (3) the version included in his own *Memoirs;* (4) the version given to Macartney. Horthy's four accounts, according to Macartney, "are mutually inconsistent—less as regards substance than as regards number and time of conversations, and on which occasion which thing was said. *All of them pass over, practically entirely, the concessions to which Horthy undoubtedly agreed"* (Italics supplied). C. A. Macartney, 2:234.

25. According to many distinguished historians, the military forces of Hungary were at the time sufficient to withstand the German occupation, had the government taken the necessary measures to resist. For an evaluation of the German forces used in the occupation and of the available Hungarian forces, see Ránki, *1944. március 19*, pp. 65–72, and C. A. Macartney, 2:227–28.

26. Vilmos Nagy, *Végzetes esztendők* (Fateful Years) (Budapest: Körmendy, 1946), pp. 192–93. The failure of Hungary to take any precautionary measures to assure her national interests in the months before the German occupation is also emphasized by C. A. Macartney. See his *October Fifteenth*, 2:190.

27. The untenable military position of Hungary was reviewed before the Prime Minister by Szombathelyi. Kállay, *Hungarian Premier*, p. 410.

28. Jenő Lévai, *Eichmann in Hungary* (Budapest: Pannonia Press, 1961), p. 66.

29. See, for example, the account by Diámant, Freudiger, and Link in *HJS*, 3:78.

30. Mario D. Fenyo, *Hitler, Horthy, and Hungary* (New Haven: Yale University Press, 1972), pp. 178–79. See also *The New York Times*, April 16, 1944, p. 17.

31. C. A. Macartney, 2:275.

32. *Horthy Miklós titkos iratai*, p. 429.

33. See Komoly's diary entry of August 25, 1944, in *HJS*, 3:166.

34. *RLB*, Doc. 110.

35. *Ibid.*, Doc. 114.

36. *Ibid.*, Doc. 117.

37. Ministries Trial (Court IV, Case XI), Horthy's testimony of March 4, 1948, transcript pp. 2735 and 2745.

38. Albert Speer, *Inside the Third Reich* (New York: Macmillan, 1970), p. 395.

39. For the text of the correspondence between Göring and Himmler and their subordinates (including Brandt, Kammler, Pohl, and Fegelein) relating to this subject, see PS-1584-(I)-PS reproduced in *IMT*, 27:351–64. For Speer's interrogation in Nuremberg on this issue, see *ibid.*, 32:497–500.

40. Speer, *Inside the Third Reich*, p. 396.

41. *Ibid.*, p. 397.

42. R-124 (USA 179). See also *Vádirat*, 1:133–36, and Lévai, *Eichmann in Hungary*, p.

81. See also Elek Karsai, *A budai vártól a gyepüig, 1941–1945* (From the Fort of Buda to the Borderland, 1941–1945) (Budapest: Táncsics, 1965), p. 689.

43. C. A. Macartney, 2:280.

44. *RLB*, Doc. 134.

45. Perhaps Horthy had in mind only the shipment of labor servicemen or only of able-bodied "Galician" Jews from the territories acquired between 1938–41. He alludes to the former in his highly slanted *Memoirs*, p. 219. Kasztner claims that Horthy not only gave his consent to the delivery of "Jewish workers" for the German industry and thereby in fact sanctified the deportations, but also took cognizance of the fact that "German advisers (*das Judenkommando*)" would be assigned to help the Hungarian authorities in the solution of this task. *Der Kastner-Bericht*, p. 61.

46. This was revealed during the trial of Veesenmayer. See the Ministries Trial (Court IV, Case XI), testimony of July 22, 1948, transcript p. 13243.

47. Testimony by Winkelmann in the Ministries Trial involving Veesenmayer, October 18, 1948, transcript pp. 26172-173.

48. C. A. Macartney, 2:238–39. See also Ernst Kienast's statement of August 14, 1947 (NG-2528).

49. Veesenmayer's testimony on July 22, 1948, transcript p. 13260.

50. Lévai, *Fekete könyv*, p. 128.

51. *Ibid.*

52. Ránki, *1944. március 19*, p. 175.

53. Fenyo, *Hitler, Horthy, and Hungary*, p. 76.

54. *RLB*, Doc. 199.

55. See also Fenyo, *Hitler, Horthy, and Hungary*, p. 209.

56. C. A. Macartney, 2:283.

57. Perényi himself was informed by Samu Kahan-Frankl and Imre Reiner of the Jewish Council. Munkácsi, *Hogyan történt?* p. 142.

58. *Ibid.* Bishop Ravasz repeated this account during his testimony in the postwar war crimes trials in Budapest. According to his testimony, Horthy also mentioned that the families of the laborers were also to be sent out so that they could be together and that they should not have to be "supported by the nation when they [the laborers] are making a living out there." *Ibid.*, p. 168.

In contrast to Horthy's reference to the "many hundreds of thousands of Hungarian workers," Kállay, in discussing the readiness with which the other countries under German influence, including France and Italy, provided hundreds of thousands of workers to the Third Reich, asserted that before his assumption of the premiership on March 9, 1942, Hungary "had allowed only 24,000 workers to go." These, according to Kállay, were volunteers who earned good wages abroad. During his tenure, he claims, without providing any evidence, "not one went out." Kállay, *Hungarian Premier*, p. 114.

59. C. A. Macartney, 2:283.

60. Lévai, *Eichmann in Hungary*, p. 119.

61. See also Lévai's evaluation of this document in his *Fehér könyv. Külföldi akciók zsidók megmentésére* (White Book. Foreign Actions for the Rescuing of Jews) (Budapest: Officina, 1946), pp. 54–55.

62. *HJS*, 3:200–201.

63. C. A. Macartney, 2:239.

64. *Ibid.*, p. 280.

CHAPTER TWELVE

THE OCCUPATION FORCES AND AUTHORITIES

WHILE THE scenario was being played out at Schloss Klessheim, on March 18, 1944, the German forces were poised for the invasion scheduled for 11:00 P.M. and the various political and police agencies made ready to begin their respective tasks immediately. The German Foreign Office was informed at 5:00 P.M. by Major Kraussoldt of the *Wehrmacht* High Command that stringent censorship and travel restrictions had been imposed along the borders of Hungary.[1]

The Wehrmacht

The invading forces were spearheaded by a special parachute regiment of the Brandenburg Division, headed by Major-General von Pfuhlstein, which was dropped in the vicinity of Budapest and entrusted with the occupation of all key positions. The paratroopers were followed by the main occupation forces composed of 11 divisions under the overall command of Field Marshal von Weichs: four or five entered the country from the northwest, one from Eastern Slovakia, three or four from Syrmia, and one or two from the Romanian Banat. Most of these forces consisted of ethnic Germans. A few of the units, however, were composed of Swabians of Hungarian background and one unit, the Croat Mountain SS Division, included a number of Bosnian Muslims.[2]

During the first phase of the invasion, German troops occupied Hungary only up to the Tisza River; they entered Northern Transylvania toward the end of March. Except for a few isolated shots, the occupation was carried out on schedule without any interference or resistance by the Hungarian Army or masses. With the main objective of the occupation completed shortly after the invasion, the bulk of the *Wehrmacht* troops was assigned to front duties within a month; by April 25 Operation Margarethe I was officially completed. Field Marshal von Weichs returned to his headquarters on the Russian front and his place as the Plenipotentiary General of the *Wehrmacht* in Hungary was taken over by General Hans Greiffenberg, the former Military Attaché in Budapest. As revealed at the Conference of Army Group F chaired by General Foertsch, the *Wehrmacht* was not permitted to "mix into the Jewish question."[3] That was to remain the prerogative of the German Legation and of the SS acting in conjunction with their Hungarian counterparts.

Representation of the Führer and of the Foreign Office

The personal representative of the Führer and of the German Foreign Office was Dr. Edmund Veesenmayer, whom Hitler had appointed on March 19, 1944, as Plenipotentiary of the Greater German Reich and Minister in Hungary (*Bevollmächtigter des Grossdeutschen Reiches und Gesandter in Ungarn*).[4] The author of two ominous reports on Hungary based upon his on-the-spot investigations in 1943, Veesenmayer was called to Salzburg on the occasion of Horthy's visit and instructed to be ready for the mission.

Veesenmayer and his staff came to Hungary in Horthy's special train. He was introduced to the Regent during the stopover at Bicske, during which time he expressed his views concerning the formation of a new Hungarian government. Horthy's reaction to his ideas cannot be fully ascertained. In his first telegram to Ribbentrop, Veesenmayer claimed that Horthy's basic stance during the discussion was "positive."[5] Horthy, on the other hand, claims that he vehemently rejected Veesenmayer's idea of naming Béla Imrédy, "the Jew" as the possible head of a new government.[6]

Veesenmayer's powers and responsibilities were enormous, if not all-embracing. Under Hitler's special authorization, he was entrusted with or made responsible for[7]

- Overseeing the political development of Hungary and the formation of a new national government.
- Ascertaining that the country was administered so that all of Hungary's resources, especially in the economic field, were used for the common war effort.
- Guiding the activities of all German civilian agencies operating in Hungary and providing political directives to the Higher SS and Police Leader[8] to be appointed to his staff for purposes of performing "tasks of the SS and police to be carried out by German agencies in Hungary, and especially police duties in connection with the Jewish problem."

To assist him, Veesenmayer was provided with a formidable and zealous staff, including *Legationsrat* Gerhardt Feine, the chargé d'affaires and Veesenmayer's second in command; Dr. M. Boden, who succeeded H. Bunzler, the Legation's economic expert; *Legationsrat* Adolf Hezinger, the expert on the treatment of Jews of foreign citizenship, who was replaced toward the end of May 1944, by Theodor Horst Grell; Franz von Adamovic-Waagstaetten, an arthritis and sciatica victim, who served as the expert on anti-Jewish legislation; Counselors Kurt Brunhoff and Helmut Triska, in charge respectively of press and cultural affairs; *SS-Hauptsturmführer* Ballensiefen, the expert on anti-Jewish propaganda, who helped organize the Hungarian Institute for the Researching of the Jewish Question (*A Zsidókérdést Kutató Magyar Intézet*), headed by Zoltán Bosnyák (see chapter 15); and Carl Rekowski, Consul and Director of the German Legation in Budapest.[9]

In addition, there came four senior experts—Felix Benzler, Ruhle, Schmidt, and Franz A. Six[10]—with authority on questions relating to economics, the press, culture, and radio, respectively. Although technically independent, reporting directly to their own ministries in Berlin, they cooperated closely with Veesenmayer and the German Legation.[11]

Veesenmayer played a very important, if not decisive, role in the destruction of Hungarian Jewry. In addition to his two 1943 reports on Hungary, which were considered in Hitler's occupation decision, Veesenmayer was one of the major architects of the Jewish deportations in 1944. He constantly used the weight of his position and office to induce the Quisling Hungarian government to take ever-harsher measures against the Jews—measures which he regularly reported to his superiors in Germany.

Veesenmayer was born in Bad Kissingen on November 12, 1904. He became converted to Nazism early in life and joined the National Socialist German Workers' Party in 1932. Two years later he joined the SS, where he advanced rapidly. On September 13, 1938, he received the rank of *Untersturmführer,* from which he was subsequently promoted to *Haupsturmführer,* then to *Standartenführer,* and on January 30, 1942, to *Oberführer.* On March 15, 1944, just before his appointment to Hungary, he was promoted to his highest rank, *SS-Brigadeführer.* In the German Foreign Office, he was assigned to Wilhelm Keppler, who was an Under Secretary of State for Special Assignments. In this capacity, Veesenmayer was entrusted with special political assignments in Italy in

1940, in Zagreb and Belgrade in 1941, in France and Spain in 1942, and in Hungary in 1943.

In Croatia and Serbia Veesenmayer cooperated closely with his colleague Felix Benzler, the Minister to the puppet Serb government, in asking Ribbentrop for instructions to put pressure on the Military Commander for Serbia to bring about a quick and draconic solution of the Jewish question in Serbia.[12] He used his experiences there to deal with the Jews of Hungary.

Veesenmayer maintained cordial personal relations with many of the top leaders of the Reich, including Heinrich Himmler. He even took time from the hectic pace in Hungary, for example, to congratulate Himmler on his birthday, congratulations which Himmler acknowledged with thanks.[13]

Among those primarily responsible for the Hungarian Jewish catastrophe, Veesenmayer was found guilty at Nuremberg and sentenced in April 1949 to 20 years' imprisonment. His sentence was commuted early in 1951 by John Jay McCloy, U.S. High Commissioner for Germany, to 10 years; but he was released on December 16 of the same year.[14] He settled in Darmstadt, West Germany, where he worked until his death in December 1977 as the representative of the Pennel and Bulgomme perfumery firm.[15]

In reporting about his activities in Hungary, Veesenmayer normally corresponded with the Foreign Office through Karl Ritter, Ambassador for Special Assignments, and occasionally, on more important matters, directly with Ribbentrop. He also maintained constant and close contact with agencies of the RSHA, especially in cases involving Jews and other "enemies of the Reich."

Within the Foreign Office, the agency immediately concerned with the treatment of the Jewish question was *Abteilung Inland II*, headed by Horst Wagner and his associate Eberhard von Thadden. *Inland II* was especially entrusted with liaison functions with the RSHA. Historically, the agency can be traced back to *Referat Deutschland* (Section Germany), which was established in 1938. Nominally headed by Vicco von Bülow-Schwante, Protocol Chief of the Foreign Office, it was actually under the leadership of Dr. Emil Schumberg. *Referat Deutschland* was entrusted with the handling of the sensitive diplomatic problems that arose in consequence of the persecution of Jews, the dissemination of Nazi propaganda through German missions abroad, and collaboration with the Gestapo and the intelligence services of Himmler. In 1939,

Bülow-Schwante was replaced by Martin Luther, who had entered the Foreign Office in 1938 as Chief of *Referat Partei* (Party Section). On May 7, 1940, Luther was promoted by Ribbentrop to head the newly formed *Abteilung Deutschland* (Division Germany), superseding *Referat Deutschland*. The main functions of the new Division included collaboration with the RSHA and the Gestapo in the Final Solution, arrangement of diplomatic journeys abroad, and assassination plans.

With its offices removed to Rauchstrasse, a considerable distance from the headquarters of the Foreign Office at Wilhelmstrasse, the activities of *Abteilung Deutschland* after mid-1941 became shrouded in secrecy. In contrast to previous practice, incoming communications for the Foreign Office from the Gestapo, the SS, and the RSHA were now forwarded directly to Luther without first being sent to the State Secretary's office. As the war progressed, the collaboration between the RSHA and Luther's Division became increasingly close. This was made possible to a large extent by the ubiquity of the RSHA agents, who infiltrated the German embassies, legations, and consulates abroad, variously disguising themselves as trade attachés or scientific experts. This collaboration was especially close in the implementation of the Final Solution abroad. In 1942, for example, *Abteilung Deutschland* played a decisive role in facilitating negotiations with the Bulgarian, Hungarian, Romanian, and Slovakian governments that ultimately led to the deportation of Jews from these countries. In February 1943, Luther committed a fatal blunder: he wrote a memorandum for Himmler in which he discussed the mental infirmities of his boss, Ribbentrop. This act of disloyalty enraged even the otherwise ethically insensitive Himmler, who brought the memorandum to the attention of Ribbentrop.

The repercussions were swift and decisive. Luther was imprisoned in the Sachsenhausen "political bunker" and "died" there; Ernst von Weizsaecker, the State Secretary, was replaced by Steengracht von Moyland; many of the bureau, section, and division chiefs were reshuffled; and *Abteilung Deutschland* was replaced by a new agency—*Inland* (Home or Interior)—which was subordinated directly to the Foreign Minister and moved back to the Wilhelmstrasse.[16] The leadership of the new agency was entrusted to Wagner, a former youth leader and sports instructor.[17] The section dealing with Jewish and Freemason problems, racial policies, and the conscription of foreign "volunteers" for Germany's armies—*Inland II A*—was placed under the leadership of Thadden.[18]

Agencies of the RSHA

The entry of the SS and Gestapo units into Hungary was spearheaded by *SS-Obergruppenführer* Ernst Kaltenbrunner, the Chief of the RSHA. Like Veesenmayer, Kaltenbrunner also arrived in Hungary on Horthy's special train. He was introduced to Horthy at the Bicske stopover by Péter Hain, the Regent's personal detective, who, it turned out, had been in the Gestapo's service at least since 1938.[19] Kaltenbrunner returned to Germany three days later, after having played a determining role in the formation of the new Hungarian government and in launching the operation of the SS and Gestapo units in Hungary.

The Higher SS and Police Leader. After Kaltenbrunner's departure, *SS-Obergruppenführer* Otto Winkelmann, in his capacity as the Higher SS and Police Leader (*Der Höhere SS- und Polizeiführer*), became the representative of Himmler and the RSHA.

Winkelmann was born in Bordesholm, Schleswig-Holstein, on September 4, 1894.[20] By profession he was a policeman, who advanced rapidly in the ranks, especially after having joined the NSDAP in 1932 and the SS in 1938. During his interrogation by the Hungarian Police on May 17, 1946, Winkelmann provided the following autobiographical data:

My father was a town clerk. I was his only child. After learning at a private school I completed my secondary education, and passed the final examination at Kiel in 1914. I attended then a faculty of law for one term, when, on the outbreak of the First World War, I joined the Army. I was discharged as first lieutenant of the reserve in 1920. Before my discharge, already in 1919, I joined the *Staatliche Schutzpolizei* [State Security Police] at Sennelager, Westphalia. . . . From there I went to Altona whence I returned to Düsseldorf in April 1926. At the end of 1928, I was transferred to Dortmund, where I stayed until February 1, 1930. Here I was transferred to the communal police and holding a major's rank I was director of the municipal police at Görlitz until November 23, 1937. In 1937, I was transferred to the Ministry of the Interior in Berlin, where as major I was active in the *Hauptamt für die Ordnungspolizei* [Main Office for the Order Police]. My sphere of activities was extended gradually to the superintendence of the communal police, gendarmerie, state and communal security police, and the fire brigades. Later I was appointed chief executive of the *Kommandoamt* [Commando Office], and made a Lieutenant-General. This appointment I held until March 1944.[21]

As the representative of Himmler and of the RSHA, Winkelmann soon emerged as a bitter rival of Veesenmayer, the representative of the Führer and of the German Foreign Office. Their rivalry reflected to a large extent the animosity between Himmler and Ribbentrop. Although Veesenmayer, in his capacity as the Plenipotentiary of the Greater Reich, was undoubtedly more powerful and influential in the overall political sphere, Winkelmann enjoyed virtual autonomy in his particular area of competence, namely the Gestapo, the SS, and the German police forces in Hungary.

Unlike many of the other Higher SS and Police leaders in Nazi-occupied Europe, who were executed after the war, Winkelmann got away unscathed. He was captured by the Americans at Neukirchen on May 1, 1945, and was detained at Oberursel, the American Interrogation Center, until October 27, 1945. On that day, he was handed over to the Hungarians to serve as a witness in the trial of Hungarian war criminals. The several requests by the Hungarians for Winkelmann's extradition were rejected by the American authorities holding custody over him because "the charges . . . were found insufficient, and not of a war crimes nature." Winkelmann was handed back to the American authorities on September 1, 1948. He was never tried in Germany, where he lived until his death in September 1977 in his native town of Bordesholm, on a *Polizeioberst*'s pension of 1,705.82 German Marks a month.[22]

According to figure 12.1 prepared by Winkelmann on May 20, 1946, during his interrogation by the Hungarian police, he had jurisdiction over the following Gestapo, SS, and German police units in Hungary:[23]

- *Befehlshaber der Sicherheitspolizei (Politische Polizei und Kriminalpolizei)* [Commander of the Security Police (Political Police and Criminal Police)]—Dr. [Hans] Geschke;
- *Amt VI, Gruppe G (Politische Polizei; Politischer Nachrichtendienst)* [Office VI, Group G (Political Police; Political Intelligence Service)]—Dr. [Wilhelm] Höttl;
- *Amt IV (Politische Polizei—Judenfragen) Sonderkommando Eichmann* [Office IV (Political Police—Jewish Questions) [Adolf] Eichmann Special Commando;
- *Befehlshaber der Ordnungspolizei* [Commander of the Order Police]—Matros; succeeded by Hitschler;
- *Befehlshaber der Waffen-SS* [Commander of the Waffen-SS]—Keppler; succeeded by Pfeffer-Wildenbruch;
- *Pferdemusterungskommission, Ausrüstungsstab* [Commission for the Registration of Remount Horses, Armament Staff]—[Kurt A.] Becher;
- *SS-Wirtschaften (Intendant)* [SS-Economic Affairs (Superintendent)]—Dr. Bobermin; succeeded by Solleder;
- *Versorgungskommando Ungarn* [Supplies Commando Hungary]—Prescher;

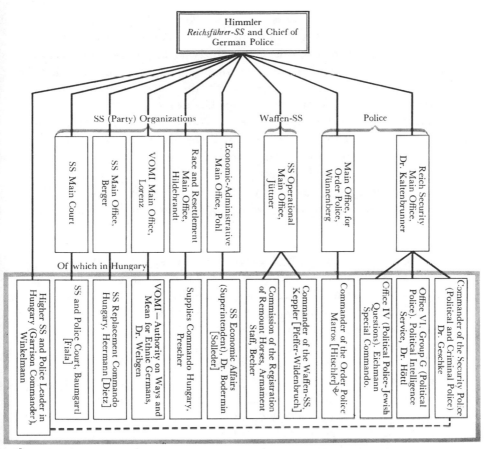

^a Names in brackets denote successor.

Figure 12.1.
Organizations of the *Reichsführer-SS* and Chief of the German Police (includes only those main offices which were active in Hungary).

- *VOMI* (*Volksdeutsche Mittelstelle*) [Authority on Ways and Means for the Ethnic Germans]—Dr. Weibgen
- *SS-Ersatzkommando Ungarn* [SS-Replacement Commando Hungary]—Heermann; succeeded by Dietz;
- *SS- und Polizeigericht* [SS and Police Court]—Baumgartl; suc-ceeded by Fiala.

The *Einsatzgruppe,* which entered Hungary along with the regular *Wehrmacht* troops, consisted of 500 to 600 Gestapo and SD men under the immediate command of *SS-Standartenführer* Hans Geschke. Geschke's chief lieutenant and head of the SIPO in Budapest was *SS-*

Obersturmbannführer und Oberregierungsrat Alfred Trenker.[24] The German police units under the command of Trenker were responsible for the mass arrest of the opposition and anti-German Hungarian leaders, members of the Hungarian Parliament (including Endre Bajcsy-Zsilinszky), and the Jews in and around the railway stations immediately after the German occupation (see chapter 15).

In this campaign, he enjoyed the full cooperation of the Hungarian police forces under the command of Péter Hain. Trenker served in Budapest until the end of July, when he was assigned to Berlin to round up those involved in the anti-Hitler coup attempt of July 20. His place in Budapest was taken over by SS-*Sturmbannführer* Gottstein.[25]

Winkelmann's staff included Ernst Kienast, his political adviser, and Wilhelm Höttl, his second in command and controller of political security and counterespionage.[26] Both were recognized Nazi experts on Hungary and, driven by ideological conviction and ambition, played a leading role in the formulation of German policy relating to the establishment of the post-occupation Hungarian government.

The Eichmann-Sonderkommando. For the Final Solution in Hungary, a special commando squad of around 150 to 200 men was organized under the immediate command of Adolf Eichmann.[27] Eichmann's office in the RSHA—Section IV.B.4.—was alerted in advance of the impending occupation and was instructed to make the necessary preparations. Eichmann himself must have felt highly gratified, for he finally had a chance to test his by now well-oiled death apparatus on a massive scale in a lightning operation. He must have felt totally vindicated for the position he took on September 25, 1942, when he had rejected the request of certain elements of the Hungarian radical Right, including József Heszlényi and Sándor Homlok, for the deportation of 100,000 "alien" Jews from Hungary. At that time he had argued that it did not pay to mobilize the entire deportation apparatus for only a fraction of Hungarian Jewry and that it would be better to wait until the Final Solution could be effectuated (chapter 9).

Eichmann's career was brought to a climax in Hungary, where The Master, as Heinrich Müller, his immediate superior in Berlin, had called him, proved to be at his best. Having the benefit of years of experience in the deportation and extermination program as directed centrally from Berlin, in Hungary he finally had the chance to test his efficiency in the field.

Eichmann's background and expertise in the implementation of the deportation program in Nazi-dominated Europe were revealed in full detail during his trial in Jerusalem in the early 1960s. Eichmann was born in Solingen on March 19, 1906, but grew up in Linz, Austria. His schooling included two years at a Technical Institute for Electrical Engineering, Construction, and Architecture. From 1925 to 1927 he worked as a salesman for *Oberösterreichische Elektrobau* and until 1933 as the representative for Upper Austria of the Vacuum Oil Company. He joined the NSDAP-Austria on April 1, 1932, and the SS shortly thereafter. On October 1, 1934, he was assigned to the SD Central Office, where he served as the agency's expert on the Jewish question. Following the annexation of Austria, he was active in the "promotion of emigration" from that country and after the establishment of the *Reichszentrale für jüdische Auswanderung* (Central Reich Office for Jewish Emigration) in 1939 he was also concerned with the emigration of Jews from the entire Reich territory, including the Protectorates. With the establishment of the RSHA in 1939, Eichmann was appointed to head the Department for Jewish Affairs, which was attached to Section IV of the Main Office, headed by Heinrich Müller. Eichmann's Department was known as "IV.D.4" between 1939–41, "IV.B.4" between 1941–44, and "IV.A.4" between 1944–45. Following the decision of the Nazi leaders to implement the Final Solution (as expressed in Göring's letter of July 31, 1941, to Reinhardt Heydrich, the then chief of the RSHA, and in the Wannsee Conference decision of January 20, 1942), Eichmann's Department was given the responsibility for rounding up and transporting the Jews to concentration camps. Despite his crucial role in the extermination of the Jews of Europe, Eichmann held a comparatively low rank in the Nazi hierarchy. His highest rank was that of *Obersturmbannführer* (Lieutenant-Colonel) to which he was promoted in 1941. Although within the RSHA he was technically subordinated to Müller, he often reported directly to Heydrich, and after his death to Kaltenbrunner, the chiefs of the RSHA.

Eichmann was captured by the Americans, but they did not discover his identity; he managed to escape from a POW camp and eventually to settle in Argentina. His last residence was in the San Fernando suburb of Buenos Aires, where he lived with his wife, Veronica (née Liebl), and three of his four sons under the assumed name of Ricardo Klement. When he was captured by Israeli agents on May 11, 1960, Eichmann was employed by the German-Argentine Mercedes-Benz Works at Suarez, a suburb of Buenos Aires. Following a lengthy and emotion-ridden trial in Jerusalem, Eichmann was found guilty and hanged at Ramla, Israel, on May 31, 1962.[28]

At the time of the German occupation of Hungary, Eichmann was at the prime of his life. The prospects of liquidating Hungarian Jewry at lightning speed must have enticed him, for they were the last large relatively intact Jewish community of Europe. The RSHA was alerted about the possible operations in Hungary even before Hitler had signed the order to occupy the country. Eichmann and his chief lieutenants met in Mauthausen from March 10 to 12, 1944, to work out a blueprint for the deportation and extermination program.[29] The *Sonderkommando* assigned to organize and direct the program included Eichmann's closest collaborators, with years of experience in the implementation of the Final Solution program in Europe. Among them were Hermann Alois Krumey, Otto Hunsche, Dieter Wisliceny, Theodor Dannecker, Franz Novak, Franz Abromeit, and Siegfried Seidl. Of lesser importance were Schmidtsiefen, Kryschak, Rau, Hartenberger, Girzick, Burger, Wolf, Ramberger, and Schmidt.[30]

The members of the *Sonderkommando* entered Budapest early in the morning of March 19, together with the advance guard of the German troops. (According to most reports, Eichmann himself did not arrive until March 21.) At first they established their headquarters at the Astoria Hotel in the heart of Pest. After a few days, they took over the Iron Workers Building on Magdolna Street. They finally settled in the Majestic Hotel, one of several resort hotels that the SS took over in the Svábhegy section of Buda. This area in Buda was not only more secluded, but also much more beautiful than the crowded and highly urbanized section of Pest. The *Sonderkommando* selected this area, according to Hunsche, because "around there it was green and one could sing a little."[31]

Administratively, Eichmann was subordinated to Winkelmann, who in his capacity as Higher SS and Police Leader was the senior SS officer in Hungary, but he had "plenipotentiary powers" in his own field of competence—Final Solution—on which he dealt to a large extent directly with the RSHA in Berlin.

Although a relatively small unit, the *Sonderkommando* successfully implemented its anti-Jewish program. This was due primarily to the support it received from the newly established Sztójay government, which showed its eagerness to solve the Jewish question by swiftly providing a legal basis for it, and by placing the instrumentalities of state power at the disposal of the German and Hungarian dejewification units.[32]

Notes

1. *RLB,* Doc. 111.

2. The troops were assembled under the direction of General Hermann Foertsch, who had his headquarters in Vienna. Although not all of these divisions were at full combat strength, they were highly mechanized. On reserve to assist them were the alerted units of the satellite armies. For identification of the divisions that took part in the occupation see C. A. Macartney, 2:227, 228.

3. NOKW-1912.

4. *RLB,* Doc. 113. Höttl claims that Veesenmayer's appointment was made at Ribbentrop's suggestion and at the recommendation of Keppler in order to prevent the appointment of General von Horstenau, the German Consul General in Zagreb, an expert on Hungary and a personal friend of Horthy, who had been recommended by the German Secret Service. Wilhelm Höttl, *The Secret Front* (New York: Praeger, 1954), p. 198.

5. *RLB,* Doc. 112.

6. Nicholas Horthy, *Memoirs* (New York: Robert Speller, 1957), p. 216.

7. *RLB,* Doc. 113.

8. At first there was considerable jurisdictional friction between Veesenmayer and Winkelmann, the Higher SS and Police Leader in Hungary. See *ibid.,* Docs. 116, 118. For some details on the Veesenmayer-Winkelmann dispute see below.

9. *Feine,* who succeeded Karl Werkmeister, was particularly involved in the initiation of economic measures against the Jews. After the war he served as the West German Ambassador in Copenhagen, where he died on April 9, 1959, at the age of 65. *Criminals at Large,* eds. István Pintér and László Szabó (Budapest: Pannonia, 1961), pp. 210–14. *Boden* was one of the few German economic experts in Hungary, who was instrumental in the transfer of the Weiss-Manfred Works to a German trusteeship in 1944 (see chapter 16). *Hezinger* was born February 3, 1905, in Esslingen-Mettingen. He had served in the *Inland II* section of the German Foreign Office since early February 1940. In Hungary, he claims that he sorted out about 100 to 200 Jews of foreign citizenship from the provincial ghettos. For his account on his activities in Hungary, see NG-4457. After the war, *Grell* settled in Heilbrunn, West Germany, where he started on a new career as a safety-box merchant. *Criminals at Large,* pp. 195ff. After the war, *Brunhoff* served as the Consul General of the Federal Republic of Germany in Sydney, Australia. *Criminals at Large,* p. 195. *Rekowski* was born on April 25, 1899. He was Veesenmayer's personal *Referent* in Hungary. For his affidavit signed on December 17, 1945, see NG-2054.

10. *Benzler* also served in Serbia, where he was active in the deportation of the Jews. He escaped punishment after the war. *Six* had the rank of *SS-Brigadeführer* and served as the chief of the Cultural Policy Division of the German Foreign Office from February 1943 to 1945. Earlier he had served as the head of *Amt VII* (Ideological Research) of the Reich Security Main Office.

11. C. A. Macartney, 2:228.

12. NG-2722 and NG-2723.

13. NG-2967.

14. *Criminals at Large,* p. 68.

15. *Ibid.,* p. 70. For his own biographical summary, see NG-1628. See also *NMT,* 14:858–59.

16. For further details, see *RLB,* pp. xxvii–xxviii, and Doc. 164. See also Chart of the German Foreign Office, *ibid.,* pp. 966–67, and Christopher R. Browning, "*Referat Deutschland,* Jewish Policy and the German Foreign Office (1933–1940)" in *YVS,* 12:37–73.

17. Horst Wagner was born on May 17, 1906. He entered the Nazi Party on May 1, 1937 and the SS shortly thereafter. He reached the rank of *SS-Standartenführer.* He was

arrested following the capture of Adolf Eichmann in May 1960, but was released on bail in 1961. His dossier is in the Berlin Document Center. For further details see chapter 32.

18. Eberhard von Thadden was captured after the war. He was released by the Allies in 1949, but charged by the Nuremberg Schwurgericht in December 1950. He fled, but was rearrested and charged again in Cologne in June 1952. The case was eventually quashed and Thadden became a factory manager in Düsseldorf. *Criminals at Large,* p. 195ff.

19. At his trial after the war, Hain confessed that while in Kiel with Horthy in 1938 he had met General Hubert of the Gestapo, "whom he had thereafter regularly informed of political events in Hungary." C. A. Macartney, 2:246.

20. NO-4139. The document also includes Winkelmann's assessment of Veesenmayer's role in Hungary.

21. *Criminals at Large,* p. 77. For an assessment of Winkelmann's role by Andor Jaross, László Ferenczy, Gábor Vajna, Emil Kovarcz, and other Hungarian war criminals, see *ibid.,* pp. 78–106.

22. *Ibid.,* pp. 107–16.

23. *Ibid.,* pp. 72–73.

24. *Geschke* died soon after the war and was never tried. *Trenker* was born in Zattig, a city that became part of Czechoslovakia after World War I, on July 2, 1905. From 1928 to 1938 he served in the Vienna police department and joined the Gestapo immediately after the Anschluss. He served in the Gestapo offices of Salzburg, Klagenfurt, Posen, and Munich. By the late 1960s he had still not been tried. He became a real estate agent in Munich. Jenő Lévai, "Biróság elé kell állitani Alfred Trenkert a budapesti zsidóság üldözőjét" (Alfred Trenker, the Persecutor of the Jews of Budapest, Must Be Brought Before a Court). *Menora-Egyenlőség,* Toronto, June 28, 1969, p. 8.

25. Péter Gosztonyi, "Aki 1944-ben élet-halál ura volt Budapesten" (He Who Was Master Over Life and Death in Budapest in 1944) *Menora-Egyenlőség,* December 23, 1978.

26. *Kienast* was born in Novaves bei Potsdam on May 30, 1910. He became somewhat of an expert on Hungary, having spent a number of years there even before his appointment to the Winkelmann staff. In 1935, he came to Hungary as an exchange student; five years later he was appointed to the German Legation in Budapest as an attaché. He joined the Waffen-SS in February 1941 and was transferred to the Southeast Section of the *SS-Hauptamt* on December 20, 1942. Kienast was reassigned to Hungary in 1943. Following the German occupation he was assigned by *SS-Obergruppenführer* Berger, the head of the *SS-Hauptamt,* to Winkelmann's staff. He was captured by the American forces in May 1945 and held as a POW for a few years. He testified in the trial against Veesenmayer in June 1948. See Ministries Case (Court 4, Case XI), June 2, 1948, transcript pp. 7143–7158. For his affidavit detailing Veesenmayer's activities in Hungary, see NG-2528.

Höttl was born in Vienna on March 19, 1915. He earned a Ph.D. in history, specializing in Southeastern Europe. He became the chief of Section VI of the RSHA for Southeastern Europe with headquarters in Vienna and as an expert on Hungary he entered it with the occupation forces. His rank in the SS was *Sturmbannführer.* He appeared as a witness in several war crimes trials, but was not charged. He settled in Alt Aussee, Austria, where he operates a private secondary school. *Criminals at Large,* pp. 117–49. For his own account see *Die Geheime Front* (Stuttgart: Veritas, 1953), 512 pp. (English translation: *The Secret Front* [London: Weidenfeld & Nicolson, 1953], 335 pp.) Both appeared under his pen-name, Walter Hagen. See also his statements made in Nuremberg: NG-2317, PS-2615, and PS-2738.

27. Eichmann's unit is variously referred to in the Holocaust literature as *Sondereinsatzkommando* (Special Strike Commando), *Sonderkommando* (Special Commando), or simply as *Kommando.* Its official name was *Einsatzkommando der Sicherheitspolizei und der SS* (Strike

Commando of the Security Police and of the SS). Technically, therefore, his immediate superior in Hungary was Hans Geschke.

28. The literature on the activities, capture, and trial of Adolf Eichmann is vast. For bibliographical references, see Randolph L. Braham, *The Eichmann Case: A Source Book* (New York: World Federation of Hungarian Jews, 1969), 186 pp. For a psychological profile of Eichmann, see Michael Selzer, "The Murderous Mind," *The New York Times Magazine,* November 27, 1977.

29. See Wisliceny's testimony at Nuremberg on January 3, 1946, in *IMT,* 4:355–73. See especially pp. 368ff.

30. For biographical notes on most of these members of the Eichmann *Sonderkommando* in Hungary, see *RLB.* Doc. 440 and 2:943–52. See also Doc. 440.

31. Originally, the SS toyed with the idea of using the Jewish community's main administrative center at 12 Sip Street as their headquarters. Munkácsi, *Hogyan történt?*, pp. 27–28.

32. The eagerness with which the radical rightists offered the services of the Hungarian state apparatus to the Nazis is reflected in Winkelmann's statement that upon his arrival in Hungary he was met at the German Legation by László Baky, the Jew-baiting officer in the service of the Germans, who placed the gendarmerie at his disposal. (C. A. Macartney, 2:245.) For further details on the occupation forces and the representatives of the German Reich in Hungary, see Ránki, *1944. március 19,* 2nd ed., pp. 154–60.

CHAPTER THIRTEEN

FORMATION OF THE SZTÓJAY GOVERNMENT

ALTHOUGH THE Kállay government for all intents and purposes came to an end with its formal resignation during the Crown Council Meeting of March 19, 1944, and the arrest of some of its members shortly thereafter, it was not officially dissolved until March 22.[1] In the interim feverish negotiations were conducted under the leadership of Veesenmayer for the establishment of a new government that would enjoy the confidence of the Third Reich.

The negotiations were at first handicapped by the conflicting interests of and power struggles within the various German and Hungarian party and governmental agencies. Himmler and the RSHA, expressing their wishes through Ernst Kaltenbrunner, insisted on the formation of a purely Nazi-type government composed of the leadership of the Hungarian National Socialist Party (*Magyar Nemzetiszocialista Párt*), organized and headed by Fidél Pálffy and László Baky. (See chapters 1 and 2 for information on the various political parties.) The German Foreign Office and Veesenmayer were more inclined toward a coalition government composed of the leaderships of the Hungarian National Socialist Party and the Party of Hungarian Renewal (*Magyar Megújulás Pártja*), headed by Béla Imrédy.

Horthy, although eager to bring about the formation of a new Hungarian government acceptable to the Germans "in order to end his country's military occupation," vehemently objected to the assignment of the premiership to Imrédy, who was Veesenmayer's first choice. Horthy despised Imrédy and continuously referred to him as "the Jew."[2] The Regent at first toyed with Kállay's original suggestion to form a government of experts, composed of the senior administrative state secretaries of the various existing ministries. This idea, however, Veesenmayer rejected outright.[3]

Although unflinching in his ideological commitment, Veesenmayer was primarily motivated by the desire to form a new government through which he could extract for the Third Reich the maximum economic and military contribution and bring about the Final Solution.[4] He was quite meticulous in his plan to preserve the façade of Hungarian independence and national sovereignty. He was convinced that he could best achieve these objectives by providing the cover of legitimacy through the signature and continued cooperation of the Regent. It was for these reasons that he originally rejected the recommendations of Kaltenbrunner for the introduction of pure National Socialism. And the events of March 19–October 15, 1944, and especially those relating to the annihilation of the Jews, sadly reveal that Veesenmayer was right in his assumption that the Reich would be better served by "working with Hungary, not against Hungary" and, above all, "with Horthy, not against Horthy."

It was for the same reasons that Veesenmayer rejected the candidacy of Szálasi, the leader of the Arrow Cross Party. Szálasi announced his readiness to take over power and to mobilize the nation in the struggle against Bolshevism if mandated by the "common will of the people and of the Head of State." His party, which consisted mostly of lower middle class and disgruntled military elements, emerged as a formidable political force after the occupation. It gained new adherents of working class background following the dissolution of the leftist opposition parties and tended to develop into a powerful mass movement.

Rejected for the premiership, Szálasi denounced the Sztójay government that was eventually established as "not Hungarian National Socialist, a transitory phenomenon brought into being without the wish or the will of the nation." On April 3, two days after this denunciation, Szálasi was received by Veesenmayer. Although Szálasi tried to persuade Veesenmayer that he and his movement were the only true friends of Hitler, the meeting left the Plenipotentiary very disappointed. The interview merely confirmed his earlier opinion of Szálasi as "a buffoon who alternately swaggers and grovels" and not suited for the immediate tasks ahead. As a realist, however, Veesenmayer realized that Szálasi represented a considerable force that had to be won over during the first phases of the occupation and held in abeyance for the future. His judgment was fully vindicated on October 15, 1944, when Szálasi was finally brought to power in the wake of Horthy's attempt to extricate Hungary from the war.[5]

At the beginning of the negotiations for the establishment of a new Hungarian government, Veesenmayer adopted a rather tough attitude toward Horthy. At a conference in the afternoon of March 20, the Plenipotentiary informed the Regent that "the time of eternal compromising was past" and that his desire to "gain time . . . was not in accordance with Hitler's will."[6]

The compromise that was finally hammered out in the early morning hours of March 22 reflected the triumph of Veesenmayer's position, although both the RSHA and Horthy had something to cheer about. The composition of the new government was as follows: [7]

Döme Sztójay served both as Prime Minister and Minister of Foreign Affairs. Sztójay had enjoyed very good relations with the Nazi hierarchy in Berlin, and his name was allegedly suggested by Ribbentrop, although Horthy also claimed credit for it. Sztójay (his original name was Sztojakovics) had the rank of Lieutenant-General in the Hungarian army. From 1925 to 1933 he had served as a Military Attaché in Berlin and from 1935 to 1944 as Minister to the Third Reich. The new Prime Minister's Cabinet consisted of Jenő Rátz, Deputy Prime Minister; Lajos Reményi-Schneller, Minister of Finance; Lajos Csatay, Minister of Defense; Antal Kunder, Minister of Trade and Transportation; Andor Jaross, Minister of the Interior; Lajos Szász, Minister of Industry; István Antal, Minister of Justice; and Béla Jurcsek, Minister of Agriculture. The Minister of Agriculture was also entrusted with the leadership of the Ministry of Supply, while the Minister of Justice was given provisional leadership of the Ministry of Cults and Public Education.

On the surface the composition of the new government was not radically pro-Nazi. Four of the members—Antal, Jurcsek, Reményi-Schneller, and Szász—belonged to the right wing of the traditional Government Party and actually had served in the Kállay government; three of them—Jaross, Kunder, and Rátz—belonged to Imrédy's party; and two were professional soldiers. Csatay was basically Horthy's man, appointed to ensure the integrity of the Hungarian armed forces; Sztójay, upon his appointment, was practically co-opted into the Government Party.

The interests of the RSHA were safeguarded, but the fate of the Hungarian Jews was practically sealed with the subsequent appointment of the notorious anti-Semites László Endre and László Baky as Secretaries of State in charge of the administrative and political departments respectively.

Endre was born in Abony on January 1, 1895. He grew up in Kiskunfélegyháza and obtained a doctorate in political science in 1918. As one of the leading figures of Hungarian Nazism since 1931, Endre emerged as the *spiritus rector* of the anti-Jewish measures during the German occupation. Before his rise to power he had served as the chief constable of Gödöllő and then as deputy prefect of the County of Pest.[8] He was tapped for the administrative leadership of the Ministry of the Interior by Andor Jaross on March 28, 1944, for his recognized expertise on Jewish affairs.

Eichmann, with whom he struck up a close personal friendship, claimed that Endre "wanted to eat the Jews with paprika." Indeed, when Jaross inquired whether he would be willing to undertake the "special handling of the Jewish question" in the Ministry of the Interior, Endre took a thick file out of his desk drawer, saying, "All the necessary draft laws can be found in this file; I have prepared everything."[9]

In the wake of the Crown Council meeting of June 26, 1944, Endre was removed from his position of authority over the Jewish question but was retained as Secretary of State. Early in September 1944 he was compelled to resign from this position as well by the Lakatos administration, but following the Szálasi coup he regained power. On November 29, he was appointed chief of civilian administration in the operational zones. Endre escaped when the Russians reached Budapest, but was caught in Austria in 1945. After a lengthy and sensational trial he was found guilty and condemned to death. He was hanged on March 29, 1946.[10]

Baky, who ranks with Endre as one of those mose clearly responsible for the tragedy of Hungarian Jewry, was born in Budapest on September 13, 1889. One of the most outspokenly anti-Semitic members of the Hungarian officers' corps, he made a career in the Gendarmerie from which he retired with the rank of Major-General in 1938 in order to devote his full time to the politics of the extreme Right. He joined the Arrow Cross Party, and in 1939 was elected to the lower house of Parliament, representing Abony. On September 12, 1941, he left the Szálasi party to reestablish the Hungarian National Socialist Party, which was nominally led by Fidél Pálffy. In his party's organ, the *Magyarság*, as well as in his speeches in Parliament and elsewhere, he emerged as one of the chief spokesmen for Nazism and anti-Semitism in Hungary. He was also secretly in the service of the Gestapo and the SS, whose leaders he regularly informed about political developments in Hungary. Like Endre, Baky was relieved of his duties relating to the Jewish question on June 30, 1944, following the Crown Council meeting of June 26, but was retained as a Secretary of State in the Ministry of the Interior. He resigned from this position during the Lakatos era; the resignation was accepted on September 2 but not made public until September 6, 1944.[11] He reacquired his power following the Szálasi coup on October 15, 1944. Like Endre, Baky was captured in Austria in 1945 and condemned to hang for war crimes. He was executed on March 29, 1946.

Baky was formally appointed to his position on March 24. Endre's appointment was not formally announced until April 9, although the Hungarian press had hailed his forthcoming appointment on March 31.[12] Two days earlier he had declared: "For the time being I cannot say anything about my functions. The important thing is that I do my work without any announcement or hullaballoo, as quickly as possible. The time will come when the public will know why I was appointed Secretary of State in the Ministry of the Interior."[13] The same day Baky was more specific, declaring: "I make my job dependent on the final and total liquidation of Left-wing and Jewish mischief in this country. I am sure that the government will be able to accomplish this overwhelming task which is of enormous historical importance."[14]

According to Jaross, Horthy gave his approval for the appointment of both Baky and Endre, remembering them as his former officers at Szeged. He apparently changed his mind about them a few months later, but by that time it was already too late for the Jews.[15]

The Sztójay government was sworn in at 6:00 P.M. on March 23 and shortly thereafter a communiqué was issued, with Horthy's concurrence, legitimizing the occupation.[16] The communiqué stated:

In order to assist Hungary in the common war waged by the European nations united in the Tripartite Pact against the common enemy, and in particular in effectively combating Bolshevism by the mobilization of all forces and by the giving of effective securities, German troops have arrived in Hungary as the result of a mutual agreement. . . . The two allied governments have agreed that the measures which have been taken will contribute towards Hungary's throwing into the scale every resource calculated to help in the final victory of the common cause, in the spirit of the old friendship and comradeship in arms between the Hungarian and German peoples.[17]

In addition to the explanation provided in the communiqué, the Hungarians were further enlightened about the "necessity" of the occupation. They were told that "the German Reich considered the unrestricted presence of some 1 million Jews and another 1 million Socialist and other refugees on Hungarian soil as a concrete threat to the safety of German arms in the Balkan Peninsula."[18]

As a compromise appointee, Sztójay was warned by Veesenmayer that his government was on trial and that it had to prove its sincerity especially by solving the Jewish question and by supplying Germany with desperately needed goods.[19]

The Police

As is the case in most countries with a centralized system of government, the police in Hungary operated within the framework of the Ministry of the Interior. Ultimate authority over the police was vested in the Minister of the Interior, who exercised it through his deputy, the National Chief Captain of the Police (*országos főkapitány*). Before the German occupation, the Ministry of the Interior had 18 departments, of which three were directly concerned with police matters:

- Department VI—Police Forces (*Karhatalmi osztály*), led by Dezső Horváth. It had two subdepartments: VI/a. Police (*Rendőrségi alosztály*), and VI/b. Gendarmerie Service (*Csendőrségi szolgálati alosztály*).
- Department VII—Public Safety (*Közbiztonsági osztály*), led by Ámon Pásztoy. It had three subdepartments: VII/a. Public Safety (*Közbiztonsági alosztály*), VII/b. Organizations (*Egyesületi alosztály*), and VII/c. The National Central Alien Control Office (*Külföldieket Ellenőrző Országos Központi Hatóság*), the nemesis of the Jewish refugees in the country.
- Department VIII—Police Penal Department (*Rendőri büntető osztály*), led by Jenő Tersztyánszky.[20]

It was through these departments that Minister of the Interior Keresztes-Fischer had exercised control over the police and the gendarmerie. His immediate subordinate in police matters was Sándor Eliássy, the Chief of the Budapest Police. As head of the Royal Hungarian Police Headquarters of Budapest (*Magyar királyi rendőrség budapesti főkapitánysága*), Eliássy had exercised control over a large network of police agencies of which by far the most important one with respect to the Jewish question was the Political Police Department (*Politikai rendészeti osztály*).

During the years before the German occupation, the Political Department was led by a number of relatively moderate individuals, including Gyula Kálnay and József Sombor-Schweinitzer.[21] Its primary concern during this time was not the Jewish question, but the protection of the aristocratic-gentry ruled semi-fascist regime from both the extreme Right and Left. It kept a careful eye not only on the members and sympathizers of the illegal Communist Party, but also on the legal Arrow Cross Party.

After the German occupation, the functions of some of these units in the Ministry of the Interior underwent a radical change; they were reoriented toward the solution of the Jewish question. A prominent role in this respect was assumed by Section VII/b, which acquired jurisdiction over the central Jewish Council and as such over Jewry as a whole. Previously under the leadership of János Páskándy, the section was headed after the occupation by Lajos Blaskovich, a personal friend and ideological-political associate of Endre. Among his closest collaborators in the so-called "Jewish Department" of this unit were István Vassányi, and Zoltán Bosnyák, a rabid anti-Semite. This unit worked closely with Dr. Lajos Argalás, a ministerial counselor in charge of preparing the anti-Jewish laws and decrees, and with Sections XX and XXI, which were also established after the occupation.[22]

The Political Department was reorganized under the leadership of Péter Hain. A detective inspector general (*detektivfőfelügyelő*), Hain had already served in the Political Department as the head of a sub-department in charge of the safety of state leaders, including Horthy—a position he had held since 1937. It was in this capacity that Hain accompanied Horthy on his many trips abroad and became the Governor's official counselor in 1939. While in Kiel, Germany, in 1938, Hain met General Hubert of the Vienna Gestapo, "whom he thereafter regularly informed of political events in Hungary."[23] It was as reward for his long and faithful services to the Gestapo that the Germans entrusted him with the Department's reorganization.[24]

In accordance with the plan worked out by Hain, the Political Department was removed from the jurisdiction of Police Headquarters and placed under the immediate control of Secretary of State Baky. Its name was changed to State Security Police (*Állambiztonsági Rendészet*)—i.e., the Hungarian counterpart of the Gestapo—and its headquarters moved to the Svábhegy, where the Gestapo and the Eichmann-*Sonderkommando* were also located. Of the four sections of the newly organized State Security Police, one was placed under the leadership of László Koltay and entrusted with "the implementation of the legal measures relating to persons considered as Jews."[25] Like the Eichmann-*Sonderkommando* this section also bore the number IV/4 and had its headquarters in the Majestic Hotel, one flight above Eichmann's.

The operations of Koltay's office were synchronized with Eichmann's. The cooperation between the two offices in the arrest of Jews and "politically unreliable" Hungarians was so close that often not even the members of the Sztójay government knew for certain which had effectuated a particular arrest or where the arrested individuals were.

During the period immediately after the occupation, Koltay's office participated in the drive against "anti-Nazi elements" and following the adoption of the anti-Jewish decrees it became particularly busy in implementing them. It took an especially active part in the expropriation of Jewish property and in satisfying the Germans' unceasing demands. It was Koltay's office that on its own initiative and in response to thousands of denunciations[26] prepared the many lists of Jewish newspapermen, lawyers, and other professionals, who were called to report to the "transient camp" of the National Theological Institute at 26 Rökk-Szilárd Street. (This proved to be the first stop to Auschwitz for many.) The lists were handed over to the Jewish Council, which was compelled to send out the military-type notices to the unfortunates on the lists. Though this function was imposed upon it, the Council was severely criticized for it both during and after the war (see chapter 14).

By the middle of May, when the mass deportations began, Hain's State Security Police carried out more than 7,000 "police investigations" and arrested 1,950 Jews. Of these, Hain handed 940 over to the Germans.[27] In addition, he expropriated a large quantity of jewelry and valuables as well as many art treasures, including paintings by El Greco, Goya, Rembrandt, Van Dyck, and Rubens, from his Jewish victims. Some of this confiscated property was taken over by Dénes Csánky, the appointee of the Sztójay government; the remainder was embezzled by Hain and his Hungarian and German colleagues.[28] Because of this as well as for political reasons, Baky replaced him in the summer of 1944 with Valér Nagy. However, with the ouster of Horthy in the wake of the *Nyilas* coup of October 15, 1944, Hain was rehabilitated and reappointed to head the State Security Police.

To supplement its activities, the new Szálasi government also established the National Unit for Accountability (*Nemzeti Számonkérő Különitmény*), which was particularly concerned with the investigation of the political views and attitudes of "suspected" individuals. For the short time it was in operation it was under the command of Lieutenant-Colonel Norbert Orendy of the gendarmerie.[29] By far the most important case handled by the Unit was that of the leaders of the weak Hungarian resistance, including Endre Bajcsy-Zsilinszky, János Kiss, Jenő Nagy, and Vilmos Tartsay. The latter three were executed on December 8, and Bajcsy-Zsilinszky on December 24.[30]

Departments XX and XXI

In addition to the three police-related departments, two others in the Ministry of the Interior were concerned with Jewish affairs during the German occupation. They were departments XX and XXI. The former was headed by László Baky, who thus acquired control over both the police and the gendarmerie. One of his closest associates in this department was Colonel Gyula Balázs-Piri. Department XX received, in accordance with Minister of the Interior Jaross' instructions of April 4, 1944, the reports Lieutenant Colonel László Ferenczy submitted daily on the progress of the ghettoization and deportation program. These documents, dating from May 3 through July 9, 1944, and addressed to Colonel Balázs-Piri, are among the most important ones relating to the catastrophe of Hungarian Jewry.

Department XXI was concerned more directly with the concentration, internment, and deportation of the Jews. Since the ghettoization of the Jews was camouflaged as "housing and relocation," the department was identified as "Housing Department" (*Lakásügyi Osztály*). Jewish affairs were the concern of Subsection b, a "special service unit" of Refugee Matters (*Menekültügyi alosztály*), whose functions were "the settlement of questions arising in connection with evacuation and internment of the Jews in camps, which do not fall under the jurisdiction of other departments, on the direct instructions of Secretary of State Dr. László Endre."

This special department was at first under the leadership of Dr. Zsigmond Székely-Molnár, a ministerial assistant secretary and Endre's close collaborator. He was replaced on May 30, 1944, by Dr. Gábor Ajtay, a ministerial department counselor, who, in turn, was replaced on June 24, 1944, by Dr. Albert Takács, the District Chief Constable who doubled as Endre's secretary.[31]

The Gendarmerie

The primary function of the gendarmerie was to maintain law and order and assure public safety throughout Hungary with the exception of the city of Budapest, the municipalities, and county seats, where the police were in charge. Although it operated under the jurisdiction of the Minister of the Interior, the gendarmerie was subordinated to both the Ministry of the Interior and the Ministry of Defense. In the former, it was placed under the jurisdiction of Section VI/b, which in the years immediately before the occupation had been headed by Gendarmerie Colonel István Vadászy.[32] The section was concerned with public safety and the pay and pension system of the gendarmes as well as with general economic and supply problems of the gendarmerie. It operated under the command of the Superintendent of the Royal Hungarian

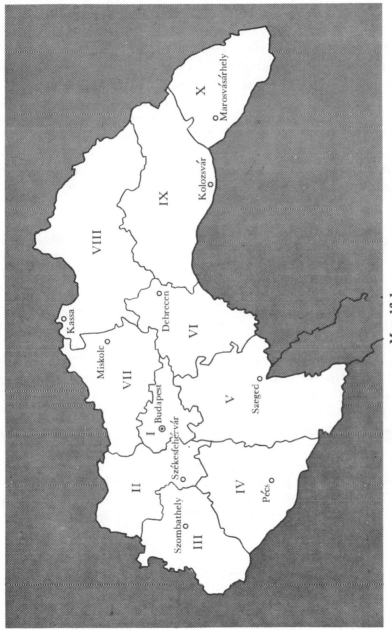

Map 13.1.
Gendarmerie districts and their headquarters, 1944.

Gendarmerie (*Magyar királyi csendőrség felügyelője*). Before the German occupation, the position of superintendent had been held by Lieutenant-General Márton Nemerey.[33] At the time of the occupation, it was held by Lieutenant-General Gábor Faraghó.[34] The Ministry of Defense exercised jurisdiction primarily in matters of training and discipline.

The gendarmerie, like the armed forces, operated on a territorial basis, with Hungary divided into 10 gendarmerie district commands (map 13.1). Each command was under the leadership of a colonel of the gendarmerie, who played a pivotal role in the planning and implementation of the ghettoization and deportation of the Jews in the territory under his jurisdiction. A list of the district headquarters and commanders is shown in table 13.1.[35]

The deportation of the Jews, which began on May 15, 1944, was planned and carried out on the basis of these territorial units, beginning with the Jews in District VIII. The district commanders took an active part in the roundup and deportation of the Jews, as did some top-ranking gendarmerie officers not in charge of any particular District Command. One of the most ferocious among these was Colonel Tibor Paksy-Kiss, the head of the Gendarmerie School Command of Nagyvárad.

A staff company (*törzsalosztály*) of the central investigative unit of the gendarmerie handled specifically political investigations. It had two subdivisions: *A*, State Police; *B*, Criminal. The former, in turn, had five sections, of which Section III had jurisdiction over the Zionist organizations and the Jewish communities and institutions.[36]

TABLE 13.1.
HEADQUARTERS AND COMMANDERS OF
GENDARMERIE DISTRICTS

District Number	Headquarters	Commander (Colonel)
I	Budapest	Lénárd Torzsay
II	Székesfehérvár	József Zirczy
III	Szombathely	Vilmos Poltáry
IV	Pécs	László Perey
V	Szeged	Vilmos Sellyey
VI	Debrecen	Artúr Sasady
VII	Miskolc	József Bátky
VIII	Kassa	Győző Tölgyesy
IX	Kolozsvár	Ferenc Vattay
X	Marosvásárhely	Aladár Pintér

The gendarmes constituted the major instrument through which the Jews of Hungary, excepting those of Budapest, were rounded up and deported in the course of less than two months. The number of gendarmes used for this purpose ranged from 3,000 to 5,000. Many of the gendarmes involved in the ghettoization, concentration, and deportation of the Jews were of Swabian background and particularly ferocious and pro-Nazi in sentiment. The testimonies of most of the survivors of the Holocaust in Hungary emphasize the cruel and barbarous behavior of the gendarmes during this catastrophic period. The "heroic actions" of the gendarmerie were later "explained" by a Hungarian exile in Canada in line with the position taken by most war criminals, namely that the gendarmes stood for law and order and merely carried out the orders of their superiors.[37]

To assure the effectiveness of the anti-Jewish operations, the dejewification high command provided for the rotation of the gendarme units involved. The ghettoization, concentration, and deportation of the Jews of a particular county were normally carried out with the participation of a unit from another part of the country so as to prevent possible corruption or leniency based on personal contacts with the local Jews. Thus, for example, in Dés the anti-Jewish drive was implemented with a special unit of 40 gendarmes from Zilah; in Beszterce there were 25 gendarmes from Nagydemeter; in Szászrégen there were 40 gendarmes from Szeged; and in Máramarossziget 50 gendarmes came from Miskolc.

The gendarmes were under the overall command of Lieutenant-Colonel László Ferenczy, who was also in charge of the anti-Jewish operations and had been appointed to this position following his return from the Russian front by Gábor Faraghó.[38] Nominally, he was the liaison officer in charge of coordinating the operations of the gendarmerie with those of the German Security Service and especially of the Eichmann-*Sonderkommando*. His headquarters were on the second floor of the Lomnic Hotel on the Svábhegy in Buda, not far from Eichmann's headquarters in the Majestic Hotel.

Ferenczy was a sinister figure whose political allegiance to the Germans was unswerving, though in the summer of 1944 he appeared for a while as a possible ally of the Regent. He was born at Felsővisó in 1898. Of Swabian background, he served from March 1940 to July 1942 as a commander of a gendarmerie investigative unit in Kassa, where he was also in charge of hunting down the Jewish refugees who had escaped from Slovakia into Hungary. The chief instrument in the roundup and deportation of close to 450,000 provincial Jews (April 16–July 8, 1944), he appeared to have second thoughts in the wake of the successful Allied landings in Normandy and the failure of Baky's coup attempt of July 8. In August, he established contact with the leaders of Hungarian Jewry, including Samu Stern, Ottó Komoly, Rezső Kasztner, and Miklós Krausz, purportedly "to save the remaining Jews" from the Germans, who, he claimed, had deceived him. His plan—really a search for an alibi—called for a meeting with the Regent in order to get official instructions relating to the halting of the deportations. To impress the Jewish leaders he even expressed his resolve to use the power of the gendarmerie against the Germans if they attempted to carry out the deportation of the Budapest Jews against the will of the Hungarians (see chapter 29).

Although the Jewish leaders accepted Ferenczy's search for an alibi at face value and even arranged for his meeting with Horthy, Ferenczy apparently never gave up his intimate association with the Germans. According to one source, he exploited his newly established contacts with the Jewish leaders and Horthy not only to keep the Germans fully informed but also to lay the groundwork for Szálasi's coup on October 15.[39] With Szálasi in power he once again openly assumed his leadership position in the anti-Jewish drive. As the head of the Hungarian dejewification squad, Ferenczy had the assistance of a loyal staff of gendarmerie officers, including Captain Leó Lullay, who served as his chief aide.[40]

Shortly before the Russians laid siege to Budapest, the gendarmerie and the public safety organs of the police were placed under the unified command of an inspector general for combat purposes. This Inspector General of the Gendarmerie and Police (*a csendőrség és rendőrség főfelügyelője*) was appointed by the Leader of the Nation (*Nemzetvezető*), Szálasi, on the recommendation of the Minister of the Interior and the Minister of Defense.[41] The combat assignments of the gendarmerie did not displace its preoccupation with the Jewish question. As earlier in the year, it continued to deal with this problem in close cooperation with the civil servants.

The Civil Service

As Veesenmayer and his superiors in the Reich well knew, the German occupation authorities could function effectively in Hungary only if they had the support of the Hungarian state apparatus. They were aware that in addition to securing the loyalty of the army, gendarmerie, and police, they would have to assure that the other central and local administrative and executive organs of the state remained loyal. With the establishment of the Sztójay government, the Germans insisted that the secretaries of state in charge of the administration of the various ministries as well as the heads of the major divisions and sections be replaced by pro-German elements. In the Ministry of the Interior, for example, purification of the ranks was assured through the appointment of Baky and Endre. In the Ministry of Foreign Affairs, the chief victims of the purge included Andor Szentmiklóssy, the Deputy Foreign Minister, and Aladár Szegedy-Maszák, the head of the Political Department. Both were arrested and deported to Dachau, where Szentmiklóssy died. Szegedy-Maszák survived the ordeal and was liberated there by American troops.[42] Also purged were the representatives of Hungary in the neutral countries who refused to recognize the legitimacy of the Sztójay government. Among these were Antal Ullein-Reviczky, the Minister to Stockholm,[43] and Ferenc Ambró, the Minister to Madrid.[44] They were also deprived of their Hungarian citizenship and of their property rights.

After the purge in the central organs of government, the Germans and their Hungarian hirelings turned their attention to the local ones. As stated in his report of April 14, 1944, addressed to the German Foreign Office, Veesenmayer had requested that Sztójay replace those county prefects and deputy prefects who were negatively disposed toward the Germans. By early May, Veesenmayer could report that 29 of the country's 41 prefects had been replaced, along with the mayors of two-thirds of Hungarian cities, including Budapest. Most of the new appointees came from the Right wing of the Government Party and especially from Imrédy's Party of Hungarian Renewal. The chief dispenser of patronage was Jaross, the Imrédyist Minister of the Interior.[45]

Among those purged or compelled to resign were Leó Deák, the Prefect of Újvidék and of Bács-Bodrog County, who was replaced by József Piukovics as County Prefect and by Péter Fernbach as Prefect of Újvidék; Andor Reők, the Prefect of Baja and Szabadka, who was replaced by Gyula Vojnits; Sándor Takáts, the Prefect of Szeged, who was replaced by Aladár Magyary-Kossa; Endre Széchenyi, the Prefect of Somogy County, who was replaced by Lajos Szathmáry; Árpád Siménfalvy, the Prefect of Ungvár and of Ugocsa and Ung Counties, who was replaced by Ferenc Réthy-Haszlinger; István Szücs, the Prefect of

Vas County, who was replaced by Ferenc Mesterházy; and Baron János Jósika, the Prefect of Szilágy County, who was replaced by Miskolci Szlávy László.[46]

Following the purification of the local governmental units it was the turn of the *Gleichschaltung* of all social organizations, associations, and institutions. To further assure the loyalty of the working class, the trade unions, which were already restricted in their operation, were placed under the leadership of Béla Marton. He was admirably suited for the new appointment as Ministerial Commissioner in charge of labor, having been involved in the 1930s in the organization of the workers in the Fascist-oriented National Labor Center (*Nemzeti Munkaközpont*).[47]

A few decent county and municipality leaders and even police officers resigned rather than get involved in the drive against the Jews. Among them were Baron János Jósika, the Prefect of Szilágy County;[48] and Count Béla Bethlen, the Prefect of Szolnok-Doboka County, who declared he would rather retire than become a mass murderer.[49] Dr. János Schilling, the Deputy Prefect of Szolnok-Doboka, who had actively participated in the preparations for the ghettoization and concentration of the county's Jewish population, changed his mind and, feigning illness, resigned on May 2—just one day before the beginning of the operation.[50] Another of those who resigned was Örményi, the chief of police of Gyergyószentmiklós.[51]

However, the overwhelming majority of the local, district, and county officials, including the civil servants, police, and gendarmerie officers, collaborated fully. Many of them were overzealous in implementing both the written instructions[52] and the oral communications given by László Endre at the various preparatory conferences—such as the one held at Munkács on April 12, 1944, in preparation for the anti-Jewish drive in Carpatho-Ruthenia, and the ones in Szatmárnémeti and Marosvásárhely on April 26 and 28, respectively, with respect to the ghettoization of the Jews of Northern Transylvania (see chapters 17 and 18). These conferences were attended by the top civilian, police, and gendarmerie officers of the appropriate regions, including the mayors and police chiefs of the municipalities and larger cities, the gendarmerie commanders, and deputy prefects of the various counties.

Following their return from these conferences, the city and county representatives of these three major instrumentalities of power coordinated their plans for the implementation of the anti-Jewish drive. At the headquarters of their city or county seat, they jointly decided on the location of the local ghetto and on details relating to the ghettoization. In fact, the so-called commissions for the round-up operations consisted almost entirely of representatives of the police, gendarmerie, and the civil service. The latter frequently included members of the local instructional staff. Occasionally, these commissions were joined by volunteers from all walks of life, who were normally members of the Arrow Cross Party.

The master plan for the liquidation of the Jewish community called not only for the subordination of the three major instrumentalities of the Hungarian state, but also for the creation of a Jewish Council that was envisioned to become, like those in all other Nazi-dominated countries, another tool for the smoothest possible implementation of the Final Solution program.

Notes

1. For the official documents relating to the resignation of the Kállay government and its individual members, signed by both Horthy and Sztójay, the new Prime Minister, see *Budapesti Közlöny* (The Gazette of Budapest), no. 67 (March 23, 1944), pp. 1–2.

2. In the summer of 1938, Károly Rassay, a Liberal politician, and Count Antal Sigray, a Legitimist leader—both members of the lower house of Parliament—discovered evidence that one of Imrédy's great-grandmothers had been a Jew baptized into the Catholic faith in 1814. This information was cleverly exploited by Imrédy's opponents, including Horthy, forcing him, among other things, to resign as Premier on February 15, 1939. C. A. Macartney, 1:327–28. His "Jewishness" was exploited by his political opponents even in 1944. On September 15, 1944, for example, Ministerial Counselor Perlaky of Section VII.a. of the Ministry of the Interior was compelled to issue an order to all administrative and police state organs to confiscate all copies of an illegal flyer directed against Imrédy. The text of the flyer was: "Jews! Co-religionists! Our last hope is Imrédy, pray for him! Published by the Akiba Printers of the Jewish Community." The flyer presumably was the product of the Baky group of National Socialists. For text of the order see *Vádirat*, 3:552.

3. *RLB*, Doc. 114. Interestingly enough, Horthy's proposal for the establishment of a government of experts was also supported by Imrédy, who claimed that the Regent was not in principle opposed to his own nomination as Prime Minister. *A Wilhelmstrasse és Magyarország, Német diplomáciai iratok Magyarországról, 1933–1944.* (The Wilhelmstrasse and Hungary. German Diplomatic Papers About Hungary, 1933–1944), compiled and edited by György Ránki, Ervin Pamlényi, Loránt Tilkovszky, and Gyula Juhász. (Budapest: Kossuth, 1968), p. 786.

4. For an evaluation of the military and economic exploitation of Hungary after the occupation, see György Ránki, *1944. március 19* (March 19, 1944), 2nd ed. (Budapest: Kossuth, 1978), pp. 186–237.

5. *RLB*, Doc. 119. See also C. A. Macartney, 2:290–91.

6. *RLB*, Doc. 114.

7. The formal appointments were made over Horthy's and Sztójay's signatures. See *Budapesti Közlöny*, no. 67 (March 23, 1944), p. 1.

8. Lévai, *Zsidósors Magyarországon*, p. 77.

9. Elek Karsai, *Itél a nép* (The People Judge) (Budapest: Kossuth, 1977), p. 200. Endre's anti-Semitic views were expressed in his *A zsidókról. A berni per tanulságai* (On the Jews: The Lessons of the Bern Trial) (Budapest: Kossuth, 1942), 71 pp.

10. C. A. Macartney, 1:186–87. See also Jenő Lévai, *Endre László a magyar háborús bünösök listavezetője* (László Endre, The Leader on the List of Hungarian War Criminals) (Budapest: Müller Károly, 1945), 112 pp.

11. *Budapesti Közlöny,* no. 203, p. 1.

12. *Budapesti Közlöny,* no. 70, March 28, 1944, p. 1; *Ibid.,* no. 80, April 9, 1944, p. 1; *Uj Magyarság* (New Magyardom), Budapest, March 31, 1944. The paper welcomed the appointment of Endre, hailing him as "an excellent expert on national-minded administration" and as "an energetic organizer." It emphasized that "the solution of the Jewish question" fell within the competence of the Ministry of the Interior.

13. *Magyarország* (Hungary), Budapest, March 29, 1944.

14. *Ibid.*

15. Munkácsi, *Hogyan történt?* pp. 168–69.

16. The Germans, of course, were the first to offer their congratulations. NG-5575.

17. C. A. Macartney, 2:252.

18. *The New York Times,* March 23, 1944.

19. C. A. Macartney, 2:252.

20. *Magyarország tiszti cim- és névtára* (Title and Name Register of Hungary (Budapest: A Magyar Királyi Állami Nyomda, 1942), 49:48–49.

21. Sombor-Schweinitzer was a follower of the political line of Keresztes-Fischer, and like him was arrested by the Gestapo soon after the occupation. He was taken to the Flossenburg concentration camp and liberated by the Americans in Heiligkrehnlen. After the liberation he assisted the American authorities in the interrogation of Hungarian war criminals. Ervin Hollós, *Rendőrség, csendőrség, VKF 2* (Police, Gendarmerie, VKF 2) (Budapest: Kossuth, 1971), pp. 43, 45–46.

22. Munkácsi, *Hogyan történt?,* pp. 72–74. Concerning Bosnyák's functions in the Ministry of the Interior, see also the testimonies of Drs. Argalás, Ernő Munkácsi, and József Nagy during the trial of Dr. Béla Berend in 1946. Berend Trial File NB 2600/1946, pp. 313, 342, and 354. For further details on Bosnyák, see chapter 14.

23. *Ibid.,* p. 385. See also C. A. Macartney, 2:246.

24. Allegedly neither Jaross, the Imrédyist, nor Baky, the National Socialist, were totally happy with the appointment of Hain, the representative of the Arrow Cross. Baky finally consented to the appointment, convinced that Hain was bound to commit mistakes that would give cause for his removal. The opportunity came in the summer of 1944, when gross irregularities were discovered in connection with the valuables, art treasures, and general property expropriated from the Jews. Conflict also arose over Baky's plan to have the police incorporated into the gendarmerie in anticipation of the coup he planned for July 8. While Hain visited Kaltenbrunner in search of assistance, Baky replaced him with Valér Nagy, a police counselor. Since this move had Winkelmann's support, Kaltenbrunner also concurred. Ervin Hollós, *Rendőrség, csendőrség, VKF 2,* pp. 385–96.

25. *Ibid.,* p. 390. Koltay (Kundics), whose wife was reportedly Jewish, had previously served as a detective inspector in charge of the forgeries section. Munkácsi, *Hogyan történt?,* p. 42.

26. According to Koltay there were about 35,000 denunciations against Jews and Leftists. Lévai, *Fekete könyv,* p. 106. According to the Germans themselves "in no other country did they encounter such a large number of denunciations as in Hungary." See Stern's statement in *HJS,* 3:12.

27. Lévai, *Fekete könyv,* p. 122.

28. *Ibid.,* p. 196.

29. Hollós, *Rendőrség, csendőrség, VKF 2,* pp. 400–16.

30. *Ibid.*

31. The unit was established under General Decree No. 3410/1944 of the Minister of the Interior dated May 13, 1944. *Vádirat,* 1:312–13. See also *Uj Élet* (New Life), Budapest, May 1, 1979.

32. *Magyarország tiszti cim- és névtára,* p. 48.

33. *Ibid.,* p. 633.

34. Lévai, *Fekete könyv,* p. 123.

35. *Magyarország tiszti cim- és névtára,* p. 633.

36. Section I was concerned with the rightist parties, Section II with the leftist parties, and Section IV with the national minorities. Section V was concerned with intelligence. Hollós, *Rendőrség, csendőrség, VKF 2,* pp. 99–100.

37. *Magyar Királyi Csendőrség. A csendőr békében, háborúban és emigrációban* (Royal Hungarian Gendarmerie. The Gendarme in Peace, War, and Exile), ed. Károly Kövendy (Toronto: Sovereign Press, 1973), 430 pp. The tragedy of the Hungarian Jews is "explained" on pp. 125–26.

38. During the war crimes trials of Budapest in 1945–46, Faraghó asserted that Ferenczy was in fact appointed by the Germans on László Baky's recommendation. Ferenczy insisted, however, that he was appointed by Faraghó. Lévai, *Fekete könyv,* p. 123.

39. Personal communication by Lévai, dated September 6, 1977.

40. Found guilty for his role in the deportations, Ferenczy was hanged in 1946. For a further characterization of Ferenczy, see Munkácsi, *Hogyan történt?,* pp. 156–60. See also chapters 17 and 32.

41. Decree No. 6.220/1944. M.E. *Budapesti Közlöny,* no. 280 (December 7, 1944), p. 1.

42. In January 1946, Szegedy-Maszák was appointed Hungarian Minister to Washington. He resigned that position in June 1947, but continued to live in Washington.

43. *New York Times,* March 23, 1944. For further details on the German occupation and the attitude of the Hungarian ministers abroad after the establishment of the Sztójay government as reflected in American diplomatic exchanges, see *Foreign Relations of the United States. Diplomatic Papers. 1944. Volume 3. The British Commonwealth and Europe* (Washington: Government Printing Office, 1965), pp. 847–983.

44. NG-5681.

45. Ránki, *1944. március 19,* pp. 119–21.

46. *Budapesti Közlöny,* no. 103 (May 7, 1944), p. 1.

47. Ránki, *1944. március 19,* pp. 121–22.

48. *Tribunalul Poporului, Cluj,* p. 116. See also chapter 18.

49. See Veesenmayer's telegram of May 8, 1944. *RLB,* Doc. 264.

50. *Tribunalul Poporului, Cluj,* pp. 133, 137–38. See also chapter 18.

51. *Ibid.,* p. 107.

52. See Decree No. 6163/1944. res. B.M. in chapter 16.

CHAPTER FOURTEEN

THE JEWISH COUNCIL

Guiding Principles

THE ESTABLISHMENT of the Jewish Council (*Zsidó Tanács; Judenrat*) was conceived by the SS as the first step in the Final Solution. In setting it up, the SS proceeded along the well-tested pattern they had employed elsewhere. They embarked upon the Final Solution program with the assumption that there was a Hungarian-German agreement to this effect and that the Jewish question was the exclusive responsibility of the SS. This assumption was fully corroborated by the attitude of the Hungarian authorities during the first few months of the occupation.

The Germans mostly followed the procedures outlined by Reinhard Heydrich, the head of the RSHA, on September 21, 1939. In a letter addressed to the chiefs of the *Einsatzgruppen* in Nazi-occupied Poland, Heydrich had identified the function of the Jewish Council[1] as ephemeral, a means for the achievement of "the ultimate goal (which requires a prolonged period of time)." The letter stipulated, among other things, that the Council

- Was to be composed of the influential personalities and rabbis of the particular community.
- Was to be "fully responsible for the exact execution . . . of all instructions . . ."
- Was to take a census of the Jews in its particular area.
- Was to be "made acquainted with the time and date of the evacuation . . ."
- Was to be made responsible "for the proper housing of the Jews" in the ghettos.[2]

The Nazis assigned a crucial role to the Jewish Councils, turning them into involuntary accessories to German crimes. And in fact they were trapped into outright though unwitting collaboration, although they did everything possible to gain time and to ease the suffering of their coreligionists.

In proceeding with their plan for the extermination of the Jews, the SS and their Hungarian hirelings had to consider the rapid advance of the Soviet forces in the East, the limited German forces available for the operation, the need to lull the large Jewish community into a false sense of security and optimism in order to minimize the risk of resistance, and the need "to make sure the Jews did not revolt as they had in the Warsaw Ghetto."[3]

These considerations required that the plan be implemented at lightning speed; therefore the establishment and subordination of the Jewish Council received immediate attention.

Although Jewish Councils were established in all the ghettos and/or concentration and entrainment centers of Hungary, the one of Budapest was the primary concern of the Nazis. In view of the swift ghettoization and deportation of the provincial Jews, those of the provinces were short-lived. They normally consisted of the traditional local community (*Kehillah*) leaders.[4] The Jewish Councils, and the provincial ghettos over which they exercised nominal jurisdiction, had little if any contact with each other and acted "independently" in response to the orders and directives they received from the central and local Hungarian and German authorities and to those issued by the Jewish Council of Budapest. The isolation that was imposed upon them was practically total, for the Jews were deprived of every means of communication soon after the occupation.

The Jewish Council of Budapest

On the fateful Sunday morning of March 19, 1944, when the Germans occupied Hungary, the Jewish Community of Pest (*Pesti Izraelita Hitközség*), the country's largest Neolog congregation, was holding its annual meeting under the chairmanship of President Samu (Samuel) Stern. Because of the anti-Jewish measures that the Germans had adopted immediately upon their entry into Budapest, the meeting was ended in a hurried fashion. That same afternoon, Hermann A. Krumey and Dieter Wisliceny of the Eichmann-*Sonderkommando* appeared at the Jewish community's headquarters at 12 Síp Street looking for Stern. They found only László Bánóczi conducting a program under the auspices of the OMIKE (*Országos Magyar Izraelita Közművelődési Egyesület;* National Hungarian Jewish Cultural Association), and made him personally responsible for convening the leadership of the community for the following day at 10:00 A.M. Shortly thereafter, Hugó Csergő, the chief recorder (*főjegyző*) of the community, called a meeting of some of the Jewish leaders for 6:00 P.M. The meeting, held in his home, was attended by Ernő Boda and Ernő Pető, the deputy chairmen, and Ernő Munkácsi, the secretary general of the Jewish Community of Pest, as well as by Béla Fábián, the head of the Veterans' Committee (*Hadviseltek Bizottsága*), and two other community officials.[5] It was decided that since they represented Hungarian citizens of the Jewish faith, they should consult the appropriate Hungarian authorities before taking up any contact with the Germans.

The authority having direct jurisdiction over the religious communities was the Minister of Cults and Public Education. Since he was not available, they contacted Kálmán Tomcsányi, Secretary of State in the Ministry of the Interior, and László Thuránszky,[6] Secretary of State in the Prime Minister's Office, who told them that their question on "whether or not to negotiate with the Germans" would be answered the following morning by the chief of police. The fateful answer when it came was terse: "The demands of the Germans must be obeyed!" It was transmitted by Bartha, the deputy police chief, who reflected the position of the Hungarian authorities. This order, which clearly demonstrated the understanding between the German and Hungarian leaders on the handling of the Jewish question, was the first in a long series of orders that resulted in the deportation of close to 450,000 Jews between May 15 and July 8, 1944.

That same morning the leaders of the Jewish community of Budapest gathered at their headquarters, expecting the worst. Some of them were so apprehensive that they brought their wives along, together with small valises with their essential things. Awaiting the Germans was János Gábor, one of the lawyers of the community, who spoke good German. In the months to come he emerged as the liaison between the Council and the *Sonderkommando*.

The meeting took place on the third floor of the community's building where Stern had his office. While they were waiting for a German stenographer to arrive to take minutes, Krumey, noticing the valises, reassured everybody that there would be no arrests. He further assured them that while there would be certain restrictions dictated by the war conditions, there would be no violation of personal and property rights and that there would be no deportations. After the arrival of the stenographer, the *Sonderkommando* representatives issued their first set of instructions.

The Jewish leaders were politely but firmly informed by Krumey that the Germans would from then on exercise exclusive control over all matters affecting the Jews. They were instructed that by noon of the following day they should establish a Jewish Council, which would exercise jurisdiction over all the Jews. To enable the members of the Council and its employees to carry out their functions properly, the SS would issue special immunity certificates that would exempt them from the anti-Jewish measures. They were further informed that no Jew would be permitted to leave his dwelling place and that all Jewish publications, including the official journal of the community, must undergo the censorship of the Gestapo. The Germans then requested a meeting for 5:00 P.M. of the following day with all the leaders of the Jewish organizations and institutions in the capital. The Jewish leaders were reassured once again that no one would be harmed simply because he was Jewish. Everyone was to continue his work and the community was permitted to perform its functions, including the religious ones. The leaders of Jewry were asked to calm the Jewish masses and prevent panic by informing them in their newspaper or through their rabbis about the reassurances given by the Germans.

To emphasize the Germans' exclusive jurisdiction in all matters affecting the Jews, Krumey and Wisliceny informed the Jewish leaders that the entire Jewish Community of Pest would come under the immediate jurisdiction of *SS-Obersturmbannführer* and *Oberregierungsrat* Alfred Trenker, the head of the Security Police (SIPO) in Budapest.[7]

One of the leaders of the Jewish community was so taken in by the reassurances of the Germans that immediately after the meeting he telephoned his wife informing her that "everything is all right, the Germans even want to help us."[8]

Shortly after the meeting, Samu Stern, who was not only the head of the Jewish Community of Pest but also of the National Bureau of the Jews of Hungary (*Magyarországi Izraeliták Országos Irodája*—MIOI), completed his plans for the composition of the Council. He devised a coalition of the representatives of the major Jewish communal organizations designed to share the burdens of, and the responsibility for, all the actions imposed upon the Council. Accordingly, the Council was to include the following eight leaders: Stern, President; Dr. Ernő Boda, Dr. Ernő Pető, and Dr. Károly Wilhelm, representing the Neolog community of Pest; Dr. Samu Csobádi, representing the Neolog community of Buda; Samu Kahan-Frankl and Fülöp Freudiger, representing the Orthodox community; and Dr. Nison Kahan, representing the Zionists.[9]

The composition of the Jewish Council was approved by the Germans at the meeting of March 21, which was attended by about 200 Jewish leaders, including some heads of the provincial Jewish communities who happened to be in Budapest at the time. The Jews were once again reassured about the safety of the Jewish community of Hungary. Wisliceny informed them that although there would be certain restrictions necessitated by the conditions of war, Jewish communal, cultural, and religious life would continue as before (*Alles geht weiter, wie vorher* . . .).[10]

Since the jurisdiction of the Jewish Council of Budapest was extended to cover the entire Jewish community of Hungary, it assumed the name of Central Council of Hungarian Jews (*Magyar Zsidók Központi Tanácsa*). The Central Jewish Council, like its successor organizations, held formal meetings only rarely. Most of its decisions were made on an emergency basis as events unfolded by a "presidential council" (*elnökség*) which included Stern and his two most intimate co-workers, Pető and Wilhelm.[11] The three leaders, however, held frequent discussions with many other officials of the Council on problems that confronted them.

The close cooperation between the three Neolog, assimilationist, traditional leaders of Hungarian Jewry throughout their tenure on the Council was based as much on their mutual trust and long-standing personal friendship as on their collective mistrust of some of the other members of the Council. It was further strengthened by the dictates of the constantly arising emergencies which required the speedy decisions that a larger "deliberative" body would have made more difficult.

The secrecy of their deliberations, however, chagrined several of their colleagues on the Council, who not only mistrusted their judgment but also resented the fact that they had to bear collective responsibility for decisions they had no part in making. The most prominent among these "rebels" were Béla Berend and Lajos Stöckler. They tended to oppose the "triumvirate" on both ideological-political and social-religious grounds. Berend and Stöckler claim to have tried to represent and defend the interests of the little, "unprotected" Jews, like the ones that lingered in the so-called "Yellow-Star Houses" and in the ghetto of Budapest (see chapters 24 and 25), in contrast to the "privileged" Jews, many of whom enjoyed special status because of their conversion or an exemption granted by the authorities.[12] They tended to look upon the members of the triumvirate as the elitist representatives of the propertied upper classes.

The Rationalizations of Samu Stern

In discussing his assumption of the Presidency of the Jewish Council, Stern claims that the Germans did not take him in and that he knew what they had done in all the Nazi-occupied parts of Europe. He also claims that he had "heard enough of the methods of the Gestapo's [Eichmann's] ill-famed Jewish department to know that they always shunned sensation, disliked creating panic and fear, worked noiselessly, coolly and in deepest secrecy, so that the listless, ignorant victims should be without an inkling of what was ahead of them even while the wagon was traveling with them toward death. [He] knew their habits, deeds, and terrifying reputation." He further asserts that the other members of the Council knew as much as he did when they consented to participate.[13]

Nevertheless, he accepted the role as leader of the Jewish Council, which technically had no legal basis since it was established under the orders of, and at the beginning at least was responsible exclusively to, the SS. He explains his decision as follows:

. . . A prisoner at the mercy of his jailer is not in a position to object to the cell into which he is thrown. . . . I had spent sixteen years as the head of the Jewish Community of Pest. . . . In my eyes, it would have been a cowardly, unmanly and unjustifiably selfish flight on my part to let down my brethren in the faith during the very instant they were in dire need of being led, when men having both experience and connections and ready to make sacrifices might prove useful to a certain extent. What would Jewry abroad have thought of me had I looked for some excuse to escape doing my duty? . . . I was aware that a race with time was on. It was anticipated that the war would end within months in a complete defeat of Germany. I calculated, though, that even these few months might prove too long a time for flight, that meanwhile other help might be required. I thought also of the possibility of claiming Governor Horthy's help for rescuing the Jews; that man whom I knew for two decades, whom I had assaulted with demands in Jewish affairs any time it had been necessary. I knew, as I had to, that in our state of utter helplessness only the Governor could be of help within the country, and no help could be forthcoming from outside . . .[14] I . . . kept concentrating all my thoughts on the stringent necessity to delay with the help of tactical moves that supreme danger, the annihilation of Hungarian Jewry in its entirety. For an aged man as I was, with health undermined by time already, it would certainly have been an easier alternative to step aside, and not take that onerous role on the Council upon my shoulders. But would not just stepping aside have been unscrupulous? . . . It is not good for the flock to change an experienced shepherd for an inexperienced one who just happened to be accepted in the midst of tempest.[15]

Just two months before the occupation, Stern had been honored throughout the country on the occasion of his 70th birthday.[16] He was a Counselor of the Hungarian Royal Court (*Magyar királyi udvari tanácsos*) and as a successful businessman had excellent relations with the aristocratic-conservative elements of Hungarian society. As head of the largest Jewish community in Hungary and of the central or national bureau of Hungarian Jewry, Stern was a highly respected leader. His generosity and ability to collect large amounts of money for Jewish causes earned him universal esteem. He was the representative and one of the chief spokesmen of the Neolog, assimilationist, and anti-Zionist strata of Hungarian Jewry. Yet he was always conscious of his deep Jewish roots and did everything *legally* possible to advance the cause and the interests of the Jews of Hungary. His tragedy and the tragedy of the Jewish Council in general lay partially in the fact that the aristocratic-conservative Christian leadership of Hungary to which they had good contacts was itself decimated. With the arrest of the leading members of this class during the first days after the occupation, the Jewish community became totally isolated and easy prey for the SS. This tragedy was compounded by the official Jewish leaders' insistence upon relying on the traditional legal methods, including the filing of appeals and petitions, methods which had proved highly effective during the pre-occupation semi-parliamentary era, but were totally insufficient during the extraordinarily perilous period of Nazi rule. Stern, for example, was so accustomed to the legalistic-formalistic approach in dealing with the authorities that even in the midst of the mass deportations of June 1944, he rejected the idea of a clandestine distribution of "an appeal to the Hungarian Christian society" (see below). While he displayed considerable personal courage and fearlessness and did everything possible to win the race with time, he and most other members of the Council had little, if any, direct contact with the Jewish masses of the country.

Perceptions and Policies of the Council

Although the central leaders of the Orthodox and conservative-assimilationist factions of Hungarian Jewry, like the national Zionist leaders, had been aware of what the Nazis had done in the neighboring countries in East Central Europe,[17] they kept neither the Jewish masses fully and accurately informed nor the country's Christian leadership up-to-date about the Final Solution program. Moreover, they failed to take any precautionary measures to forestall or minimize the possible catastrophe in the event of a German occupation. Consequently, although they lived in almost the immediate vicinity of Auschwitz, the masses of Hungarian Jewry had no idea of the gas chambers and of the mass murders committed in the German concentration camps. Those who heard something about them discounted the information as rumor or at best as anti-Nazi propaganda. They, like their leaders, deluded themselves that at any rate what had happened in Poland and elsewhere could not possibly happen in Hungary, where the destiny of the Jews had been intertwined with that of the Christian Hungarians for over a thousand years. The Jewish leaders, who were well informed, failed to keep the Jewish masses abreast of what was going on in the neighboring countries and, good law-abiding citizens that they were, they heeded all the strict censorship regulations and prohibited the use of the synagogues for such "propaganda" purposes.

Ilona Benoschofsky, who was an active member of the Jewish Community of Budapest and became director of the city's Jewish Museum after the war, argues that perhaps the Jewish Council members thought that since Hungarian Jewry could not be saved, it was better that it did not know its fate. And since the Germans threatened to execute those who spoke of deportation, the Council could not publicize that deportation was merely a euphemism for the gas chamber and the crematorium.[18] She further claims that if the "Jewish Council thought that there was no way out for the masses, there was one for itself." She asserts that since the anti-Jewish measures of the Horthy era, including the major anti-Jewish laws, affected primarily the lower strata of Jews—lower-ranking civil servants, small traders, and artisans—the members of the Jewish Council, "who knew of these restrictive measures largely only by hearsay, obviously hoped that they would be exempted this time as well."[19]

Although the members of the Jewish Council understandably tried to provide special protection and favors for their families and occasionally pressed the advancement of their own interests, it is stretching the argument too far to claim or assume that they did so consciously, and acted against the interests of the masses. Although they were shortsighted, too formalistic and legalistic in their attitude, and often mistaken in their judgment, they were nevertheless personally honorable men, who tried, however ineptly, to save what could still be saved given the unpreparedness and atomization of the Jewish community and the overwhelming power of the Nazis and their Hungarian allies.

Favors Granted to Council Members

Nevertheless, it is quite possible that the Hungarian Jewish leaders' perceptions of the policies and objectives of the Nazis was influenced to some extent by the personal favors the SS extended to them and their families. This was a standard SS approach in all the countries under Nazi occupation not only toward the Jewish leaders but also toward local officials. In this way the Nazis acquired their confidence and cooperation. In the case of the Jews, these favors consisted primarily of exempting the leaders and their immediate families from many of the anti-Jewish measures. However, these favors were normally ephemeral in character, for with the termination of the ghettoization and deportation program in a particular area the leaders themselves would also be picked up and subjected to the same treatment as the rest. This was obviously the intention of the Nazis in Hungary as well who, in fact, carried it out in the provinces; but Horthy's decision to put an end to the deportations on July 7, 1944, saved the leaders of the Central Council along with the Jews of Budapest from sharing the fate of their provincial counterparts.

It is both strange and surprising that the Hungarian Jewish leaders, who knew a considerable amount about the Nazi techniques, failed to act any differently from their counterparts elsewhere in Nazi occupied Europe, who had not had the benefit of this knowledge.

One of the first leaders of Hungarian Jewry to benefit from Nazi favors was Freudiger. His older brother, Sámuel, was arrested by the Gestapo on Tuesday, March 21, and taken together with many other hostages to the National Theological Institute (*Országos Rabbiképző Intézet*) at 26 Rökk-Szilárd Street, which was then serving as an internment camp under the control of Wisliceny. Freudiger, having received no word from Stern that the Council would intervene officially on behalf of his brother, decided to take matters in his own hands and looked up Wisliceny at the Astoria Hotel, which was then serving as the temporary headquarters of the Eichmann-*Sonderkommando*. He informed Wisliceny that, in view of his brother's arrest, he would not be able to attend the meeting the SS had scheduled with the Jewish leaders for that afternoon. Wisliceny, who recognized Freudiger as one of the leaders he had met the day before, assured him that his brother would be released. Freudiger's contact with Wisliceny was solidified toward the end of the same week, when the SS leader invited him, together with Nison Kahan and Baroness Edith Weiss, to visit him upon his return from a sudden trip to Bratislava. Wisliceny wanted to establish his credentials with the representatives of the Orthodox, Neolog, and Zionist factions with a "letter of reference" he had brought back from Rabbi Michael Dov Weissmandel of the Rescue Committee (*Va'adat Hatzala*) of Bratislava. Since Baroness Weiss could not be located, only Kahan and Freudiger went to the Institute. Wisliceny asked Kahan to wait in the lobby and when he was alone with Freudiger he handed him Weissmandel's letter, written in Hebrew. Weissmandel informed Freudiger that it was apparently the turn of Hungarian Jewry to suffer the same fate as the other Jews in German-occupied Europe, but that the Hungarian Jewish leaders should nevertheless try to continue the negotiations on the so-called "Europa Plan" with Wisliceny, "who could be trusted."[20]

Although Freudiger's contact with Wisliceny was shortly thereafter overshadowed by Rudolph Kasztner, who had taken over the direction of the negotiations with the SS, it remained solid enough to wrest additional favors from him. Whenever Wisliceny returned to Budapest after the completion of the ghettoization and deportation program in a particular province, Freudiger would visit him and take along boxes of sweets that contained not only bonbons, but also pieces of his family jewels. When he ran out of jewels, he replaced them with cash—including 50,000 *Pengős* on two occasions. Wisliceny, who found the "bonbons" to his taste, as a *quid pro quo* brought to Budapest about 80 (mostly Orthodox) Jews from a number of provincial ghettos, including Nagyvárad, Debrecen, Sopron, Pápa, and Székesfehérvár.[21] Practically all of these were saved by being included in the Kasztner transport that left Budapest on June 30 (see chapter 29). Wisliceny was also instrumental in the escape of Freudiger and his family to Romania on August 9, 1944.

Similar favors were also extended to many other leaders of Hungarian Jewry. When Imre Reiner, the Chief Legal Counselor of the Orthodox Community of Hungary and a leading official of the Jewish Council, found out that his aged parents were among those crowded together in the ghetto of Nyíregyháza, he rushed in the company of Freudiger to the Majestic Hotel on the Svábhegy, the permanent headquarters of the Eichmann-*Sonderkommando*, to lodge a complaint. There, Krumey assured him that since he belonged to the Jewish Council, his family would be exempted from ghettoization and could be brought to Budapest.[22] Similarly, Károly Wilhelm managed to have two of his sisters brought to Budapest from Kassa.[23] According to Freudiger, Eichmann instructed Krumey to have close relatives of the Central Jewish Council members brought to the capital.[24]

This privilege apparently was extended to the leaders of the provincial Jewish Councils as well. An order (*Verordnung*) was allegedly issued to the provincial Gestapo heads that the leaders of the local Jewish

Councils be taken to Budapest. Instructions to this effect were also issued to Wisliceny.[25] However, the local representatives of the Gestapo and of the *Sonderkommando* in accordance with Eichmann's interpretation that the order "was designed merely as an act of mercy for those Council members who helped and cooperated," often failed to carry out these orders. Those of the provincial Council leaders who were not brought to Budapest (and most of the provincial Jewish leaders were not) were deemed to have sabotaged the instructions of the Nazis and were deported together with the other Jews, usually in the last transports.[26] Before the deportations began, the local Council leaders were normally extended the privilege of living outside the ghetto.[27]

It is in this category that one may perhaps also include the "favor" extended by Eichmann to Rudolph Kasztner, enabling him to rescue 388 Jews from the ghetto of Kolozsvár, his home town. In his memoirs, published after the war, Eichmann claimed that he let Kasztner's group escape because he "was not concerned with small groups of a thousand or so Jews" and "because Kasztner rendered us a great service by helping keep the deportation camps peaceful."[28]

The Issue of the Immunity Certificates

In addition to saving the lives of many of their relatives, friends, and other members of their community, the Jewish leaders also enjoyed a few privileges that enabled them to serve the oppressed more effectively but which also made their own lives a little more tolerable. One of the privileges that caused great animosity among the Jews during the occupation and that became the subject of a heated debate after the war was the so-called Immunity Certificate (*Immunitäts-Ausweis*), which enabled the recipient to move about freely without being bound by many of the restrictions that were imposed upon the rest of the community. The certificates were, of course, absolutely essential for the leaders who acted in behalf of the community and had to be on the streets—often going from one German or Hungarian office to the other.

The certificates used in Hungary were modeled after the French *carte d'immunité,* a copy of which was brought back from Paris by Ernő Goldstein, the head of the Hungarian-Jewish colony in France who also worked as a secretary of the American Joint Distribution Committee there. Unlike the French model, however, the Immunity Certificates in

THE JEWISH COUNCIL 429

Hungary were bilingual and were signed by representatives of both the German security and the Hungarian police organs.[29]

The Jewish Council received about 250 such certificates;[30] thousands upon thousands of individuals who had anything to do with the Jewish community applied. The telephones rang incessantly and the offices of the Council were besieged by applicants eager to acquire a degree of security. It was under these circumstances that the Council had to undertake the onerous task of allocating the limited number of certificates. Using primarily the criterion of *current* service to the community, the certificates were allocated to the members of the Central Council, the leading officials of the Council, the members of the liaison group that maintained contact with the German and Hungarian authorities, and the members of the presidential section (*elnöki osztály*). Certificates were also given to the leaders and other important officials of the congregations, to the leaders of the legal, technical, housing, social, food supply, and labor servicemen's sections of the Council, and to the leaders of the Burial Society (*Chevra Kadisha*). Leading physicians received them, as did heads of the welfare organizations. Certificates were also supplied to the editor of *A Magyar Zsidók Lapja,* and to those leaders of the National Office (*Országos Iroda*) of Hungarian Jewry who did not belong in any of the above categories.[31]

The list was compiled by Dr. Zoltán Kohn, the executive officer of the Council, and put in its final form by Dr. János Gábor and Dr. Ernő Munkácsi. In view of the limited number of available certificates and the large number of applicants, the distribution was bound to evoke great controversy. The element of seniority, especially in nonessential functions, had to be subordinated to current needs, which were often more expertly satisfied by new recruits. The applicants who did not receive certificates emerged as the most vocal opponents of the Council. It is reasonable to assume that their complaints were not totally unjustified. It is quite possible that in some—probably a very limited number—of cases, the certificates were allocated on the basis of personal favoritism, recognition of past services, or political considerations.

The personal security conferred on the members of the Jewish Council by the Immunity Certificate was enhanced by their exemption from having to wear the telltale Star of David.[32] Although this privilege was also enjoyed by exempted Jews (chapter 25) and by those involved in dealing with the SS, including Rezső Kasztner and Joel

Brand (chapter 29), the members of the Jewish Council were subjected to special criticism for having "separated themselves from the community as a whole." One of the fiercest of these critics was Lajos Stöckler, the head of the Jewish Council during the *Nyilas* era, who together with the immediate members of his family defiantly continued to wear the Yellow Star.[33]

The natural instinct for the protection and advancement of personal interests was emboldened by the temporary easing of the deportation threat after Horthy's action of July 7. Some of the wealthier members of the Council became preoccupied with the protection of their property rights; Pető, Stern and Wilhelm applied in the summer for the exemption of their properties from the anti-Jewish measures then in effect. They not only filed the proper petitions, but also appeared personally before Miklós Mester, the State Secretary in the Ministry of Cults and Public Education. This concern with property matters in the midst of the great tragedy was a source of embarrassment to Ottó Komoly, who had almost daily contact with Mester at the time. Komoly's chagrin is reflected in his diary entry for September 6, covering his discussion with Mester: "I find it a bit strange when I think that the leaders of Jewry are thinking about the consolidation of their own property position in the midst of the dangers threatening Jewry."[34]

Atomization of the Community

In addition to the possibly distorted perception of the Jewish leaders caused, among other things, by the favors they had enjoyed, the tragedy of Hungarian Jewry must in part be traced also to the atomization of the community. The sudden occupation of the country found the Jews totally disunited. Few, if any, attempts were made to end the constant bickering within and between the Neolog, Orthodox, and Status Quo communities and the semi-illegal Zionist organization, which had characterized their activities during the interwar period.

One of the saddest aspects of this situation was that the bickering continued even after the German occupation. It was clearly discernible in the central Jewish Council, where the Neolog representatives generally insisted that the laws and instructions of the German and Hungarian authorities be strictly adhered to, while the Orthodox and Zionist leaders occasionally took bolder positions. The dimension of the conflicts within the Council also attracted the attention of the Nazis, who gleefully reported about them to their superiors in Berlin.[35]

Aside from the religion-related bickering Hungarian Jewry was plagued by political conflicts between the assimilated-acculturated groups and the Zionists (many of whom were also quite assimilated), the conflicting economic concerns of the rich and the poor, and rivalries among the larger and semi-autonomous congregations. All of these were compounded by the jealousy and personal animosity that motivated many of the leaders of these communities as they pursued narrow, parochial objectives.[36] The leaders of Hungarian Jewry, consequently, were totally unprepared to provide the kind of effective leadership that the extraordinarily perilous times required.

It was to lull the broad Jewish masses into submission by instilling in them a false sense of security that the SS assigned a special role to the Council, as they did to the Zionist leaders with whom they subsequently engaged in special "rescue" deals. Although these leaders were becoming increasingly aware of the function that was assigned to them, they were helpless and trapped. Power was in the hands of the Germans, who also enjoyed the enthusiastic support of the anti-Semitic elements of Hungary who placed at their disposal the country's instruments of coercion. The Hungarians, unlike the Danes and the West Europeans in general, were basically passive and many of them, intoxicated by the vicious anti-Semitic propaganda of the past two decades, were eager to share in the wealth expropriated from the Jews. Under these conditions, the members of the Council tried to save what could be saved by dilatory tactics and later by reestablishing contact with the Regent. The Zionist leaders, in turn, followed the so-called SS-line within the framework of the Europa Plan in an attempt to buy off the Germans (see chapter 29). Both approaches were equally futile from the point of view of the provincial Jews: with the exception of those in domestic internment camps, labor service companies, and approximately 18,000 others, they were deported to Auschwitz within a very brief period of time.[37]

Whatever the line of reasoning they followed and whatever the technique they employed, the historical fact remains that the members of the Jewish Council, helpless and deprived of their traditional contacts, unwittingly and unwillingly cooperated with the Nazis and their Hungarian henchmen in the implementation of at least some of the preliminary aspects of the Final Solution program in Hungary, constantly rationalizing their actions as being best for the community under the given conditions. As Itzhak Olshan, the Chief Justice of the Supreme Court of Israel, declared in a case involving the members of the *Ju-*

denrat in Bendzin, Poland, "no matter how the *Judenrat* acted, they served the Nazis. . . . Even those who served the interests of the Jewish communities assisted the Nazis. . . ."[38]

Because of their limited forces and eagerness to avoid antagonizing the local population unnecessarily, in Hungary as elsewhere in the German sphere of influence the Nazis used Jews and the local governmental authorities in carrying out the anti-Jewish measures. Although the Jewish leaders were motivated by the desire to maintain good relations with the Germans and gain time in order to save Jewish lives, they were the ones who lulled the masses into a false sense of security, issued the internment summonses, requisitioned apartments, distributed the Yellow Star badges, effectuated the moving of the Jews into special yellow-starred buildings, and surrendered large amounts of money. They had become despite themselves one of the instruments through which the Nazis carried out some aspects of the anti-Jewish program that led to the deportation of the provincial Jews.

The activities of the Jewish Council not only alarmed a considerable section of the Jewish community, but also incensed the small though increasingly assertive anti-Nazi faction of Hungarian society. According to some evidence, the Council was in fact warned by the Hungarian underground that it would be held accountable for its collaboration. Dezső Dán, a Transylvanian Jew who rendered great service to the *Vaada*,[39] claims that he was one of the conduits through which the Council was warned. In a document supplementing his testimony in the Eichmann Trial in 1962, Dán states that he and Dr. Imre Latkóczy had been entrusted by the Hungarian Independence Front (*Magyar Függetlenségi Front*) in May 1944 to warn Stern that the Hungarian resistance movement considered the Jewish Council a collaborator and that its members would be held responsible as war criminals. They allegedly further demanded of Stern that the Council cease all contacts with the SS command and issue no further summonses or telegrams for people to appear for work or to surrender money on the grounds that all their efforts were useless because the trains were continuing to roll toward Auschwitz.[40]

Could the Jewish leaders have acted differently? What would have happened if they had resigned from the Council? Like Horthy upon his return from Schloss Klessheim, the traditional legitimistic leaders of Jewry argued that by staying at the helm instead of escaping or resigning in a cowardly fashion they could mitigate if not avoid the losses of Jewry by continuing to provide experienced leadership. If they had resigned *en masse* there is no doubt that the Nazis and their Hungarian hirelings would have easily found another or yet a third set of Jewish leaders to serve them. And if they did not carry out the orders relating to internments and requisitioning of apartments, chances are that the German and Hungarian Gestapo units would have found a way to carry out these internments and requisitions in a much more cruel fashion.

On the other hand, while the resignation of Stern and his colleagues would certainly have brought about their immediate arrest and possible execution, the Jewish masses might have learned about the realities of the German occupation early and possibly would not have followed the orders of nonentities and Jewish quislings as subserviently as they followed those of the traditional leaders they trusted. It was exactly for this reason that the Germans insisted on retaining the old, traditional, and trusted leaders of the Jewish communities as members of the Jewish Councils.

Conversely, it is safe to assume that had Stern and his associates refused to undertake the task assigned to them by the Germans and by some miracle survived the ordeal while hundreds of thousands of Jews were massacred, they would certainly have been condemned by the survivors for only having stayed in power while prestige and honor were associated with it and for having abandoned the community during its darkest hour.

In spite of the obvious risks involved, the Council decided to accept its onerous task by adopting dilatory tactics designed to gain time. Moreover, at the time of the Council's formation, the pro-German Hungarian puppet government had not yet been formed. In the absence of any official Hungarian directives and not knowing the position of the Regent and the new government on the Jewish question, the Council tried to establish a *modus vivendi* with the Germans. The Council also hoped, during the early phase of the occupation at least, that the Germans intended to solve the Jewish question in Hungary by means different from those used in the other Nazi-occupied countries of Europe. Its hope was based on: the promises and declarations made by the SS officers during the first meetings with the Jewish leaders; the fact that the Regent, who had earlier concurred with Kállay's Jewish policy, was left at the helm; the realization that the military situation of the Germans was now much worse; the expectation that the Germans, aware of the unpopular character of the occupation, would wish to pacify rather than antagonize the country; the fact that in spite of the many anti-Jewish laws, the Jews were relatively well off in Hungary and that proposals for a radical solution in Hungary would bring forth a vocal political opposition in Parliament, as had been demonstrated during the adoption of the anti-Jewish laws in 1938–1942; and the realization that the Red Army was already at the edge of the Carpathians.[41]

Unfortunately, the Council's assumptions and expectations were ill-founded. The measures adopted by the Sztójay government in concert with the Germans after March 29, when the first batch of anti-Jewish decrees was issued, gradually dissipated these exceptions. But by that time the Council was already operating as an instrumentality of the Germans in deceiving the Jewish masses.

Lulling of the Jewish Masses

The lulling of the Jews began with an appeal the Central Jewish Council issued in the first Nazi-censored issue of the community's official journal, *A Magyar Zsidók Lapja* (The Journal of Hungarian Jews).[42] In its issue of March 23, 1944, the Council published the following "Appeal to Hungarian Jewry":

In these days, we must speak in an open and unmistakable fashion because serious and profound consequences attach to every attitude and action. Clear and open talk is also required because it provides an opportunity to dispel latent uncertainty and point resolutely to the way by which everyone can save himself and the community from problems. Today, more than ever, it must be clear that we are responsible not only for ourselves but also for any negative results for all that may follow from our attitude. With the publication of the definite instructions by the competent authorities, we identify the principles to be followed and the activities that are binding for us all.

In the future as at this time, the *A Magyar Zsidók Lapja* will promptly and accurately inform Hungarian Jews about official instructions and orders issued by the authorities.

Everybody must work, fulfill his duties, and devote his full energy to the work required of him by the authorities at the place where his duty puts him.

On the basis of the position taken by the competent authorities, we may point out that Jewish religious, cultural, and social life will continue. This should have a reassuring effect on all.

Jewry has been requested to establish a Central Council, which will, as the need arises, establish its own internal committees. The Central Council is the only authorized and responsible organ of all of Jewry, and is the competent organ to maintain contact with German authorities.

It has been declared that no one will be arrested because of his Jewishness, and that if arrests are necessary they will be for other reasons.

A Jew may not leave the territory of Budapest without permission, and it is also forbidden to change residence without permission. A Jew may not come to Budapest from the country. A Jew who has recently arrived in Budapest from the country must register immediately. Applications for travel and change of address must be submitted through the Central Council.

We emphasize the need for strict and conscientious adherence to all these regulations. Only by following the rules can it be possible for everyone to pursue his civilian life within the permitted framework.

The Central Council emphatically warns everybody that everyone must immediately appear and place himself at the disposal of the Council in response to requests made by the Council on orders of the authorities.

The lulling effect of the Central Council's appeal was reinforced a week later by the appeal of Rabbi Zsigmond Groszmann. He called on the Jews to "come to the synagogue" and not to listen "to the voice of the despairing or of those who make you despair." "It has been revealed at the most competent place," he continued, "that nothing and no one will disturb you in the exercise of your religious life." [43]

The scenario of March 21, in which the Jewish leaders of the capital were reassured, was replayed on March 28 for the benefit of the leaders of the provincial Jewish communities. The Central Council's invitation to the meeting was sent out on March 24 over the signature of Stern. It informed the provincial Jewish leaders that the Central Council had been in constant touch with the German authorities since March 20 and that these authorities "have placed great emphasis on the fact that the country's Jewish population should calmly and in a panic-free atmosphere continue not only its private life, but also its religious, social, and cultural activities." "It is for the achievement of these goals," the invitation continued, "that the Central Council of Hungarian Jews was established with jurisdiction over the entire country and will establish a National Committee [*Országos Bizottság*] as a subordinate organ. It is for this reason that the meeting announced in our introductory paragraph is to be held. We ask you to respond to our invitation without fail, because in these difficult days the life-and-death interests of all Jews depend on the suitable organization of Jewry and on the maintenance of a panic-free atmosphere." [44]

The meeting of March 28 began at 11:00 A.M. at the headquarters of the Jewish Community of Budapest. It was the last national meeting of the historic Jewish community of Hungary. [45] The SS was represented by Hermann A. Krumey, who repeated his earlier reassurances about the intentions of the Germans. When Dr. Imre Reiner, the legal counselor of the Orthodox community, inquired about those who had been arrested during the first days after the occupation, Krumey reassured all those present that he had already acted in this respect although his efforts were not yet successful. With Krumey's concurrence, the meeting adopted a resolution that in addition to the Central Council having overall jurisdiction, a national organization also be established.[46]

The attitude and mood of the Jewish leaders present at the meeting varied. One of the most optimistic during this early phase of the occupation was apparently Fülöp Freudiger, who had established personal contact with Wisliceny a few days earlier and had already managed to free his brother from the detention camp at Rökk-Szilárd Street by paying off the Nazi leader. Freudiger summarized his views on the possible fate of Hungarian Jewry under the German occupation to Alexander Leitner, the leader of the Orthodox community of Nagyvárad, who also attended the conference: "I do not believe that we shall suffer the same fate that befell the Polish Jews. We shall have to give up our wealth, we must be prepared for many sorrows and deprivations, but I am not worried for our lives. Finally even this war will end and we will start there, as in the year 1919."[47]

Dr. Nison Kahan, the Zionist representative in the Central Council, struck a more somber and prophetic tone: "Our fate is not only material ruin, and not even only a chain of physical and mental tortures and the beating down of the last fibers of our human dignity, but rather *certain physical annihilation.*"[48]

Leitner himself, upon his return to Nagyvárad, tended like most other local leaders to reflect Freudiger's position and did everything in his power to calm the local Jewish population in order to dissipate the prevailing mood of panic.[49]

The opinion of most of those present at the March 28 meeting was that since the Hungarian authorities refused to be of any assistance, the Jewish leaders should try to come to terms with the local SS commandos wherever they were stationed. Only a few of the delegates were skeptical about the idea of coming to terms with the local Nazis, and only the delegate from Munkács was definitely opposed to it. He suggested that the Jews engage in passive resistance, but this was decisively overruled.[50]

The First Meeting with Eichmann

On March 31, a delegation of the Jewish Council was received for the first time by Eichmann in his new headquarters in the Majestic Hotel in the Svábhegy section of Buda. By this time a series of drastic anti-

Jewish decrees had already been issued, including the one relating to the compulsory wearing of the Yellow Star, and thousands of Jews were already under arrest and imprisoned at Kistarcsa and elsewhere. The meeting was of a formal nature, with Ernő Boda taking shorthand notes. Eichmann's views and instructions were included in the following minutes:

Pro memoria relating to the meeting held at the Majestic Hotel of Svábhegy on March 31, 1944, from 8:30 to 9:45 A.M.

Present on the part of the German authorities: *Obersturmbannführers* Eichmann and Krumey, *Hauptsturmbannführer* Wisliceny and another officer. On our part: Samu Stern, president, Dr. Ernő Boda and Dr. Ernő Pető, deputy chairmen, and Dr. János Gábor, attorney.

First President Samu Stern presented the current requests included in a special memo. Thereafter *Obersturmbannführer* Eichmann responded, talking first of all about the Yellow Star. He declared that the Yellow Star must be issued by the Central Council. When we observed that this could not be done by the fifth [of April] he replied that it would have to be replaced by a temporary one, but that from the fifth everybody would have to wear a star and that the temporary star would have to be replaced later by the one to be officially issued by the Central Council. He then declared that everybody who was required to wear the Yellow Star fell under the jurisdiction of the Central Council irrespective of his religion. He advised us to make urgent arrangements with some factory, because we would have to provide about 3 million stars. He wanted the stars to be uniform throughout the country and to be factory-made. He said we should contact the Ministry of Supplies to have them issue the necessary materials, and to get in touch with Secretary of State László Endre who handled all such matters. In his view, we would need about 70,000 meters of fabric. He further advised that the Central Council should charge about 3 *Pengős* per star. To the counterargument that a poor family with many members could not pay that much, he answered that the rich should pay for them and that the Central Council would be able to raise some money through the sale of the stars.

Obersturmbannführer Eichmann then took up the requests submitted by Samu Stern, point by point:

With respect to travel, he declared that he would make no decision on long-distance travel for the time being (in the meantime, however, he acknowledged and favorably approved a number of such requests). As to provincial inhabitants who were in the capital to work and who had to commute between their working place and their home, he inquired how many would be involved and when he was told that there were several thousand he said that he would consider the question and respond in writing.

On the question of housing, he said that if somebody was evicted from his apartment without enough time to find another, he could go to his family or friends and that the Central Council would subsequently have to report the change of address for approval. If, however, somebody wanted to change residence on his own, he would first have to obtain approval from the Central Council.

He agreed that we should fill only requisitions submitted in writing and approved by him. In other words, a German-language order would have to be prepared and submitted for signature and seal, and would then serve as a certificate for us.

He would consider the matters relating to Kistarcsa,[51] but would not give a date; he said that if those there behaved, things would be expedited. At any rate, if a note were submitted he would free our employees, but we should see to it that nobody tried to deceive him.

With respect to the deliveries already made, we could prepare a bill and submit it to *Obersturmbannführer* Eichmann. We mentioned to him that we wanted to appear before the government. He acknowledged the request.

He declared in principle that his major concern was that industrial and war-industrial production be expanded, for which purpose he would set up workers' units. If Jews showed a proper attitude, no harm would befall them, and they would be treated like other workers. Perhaps they could go home at night. We raised the question whether those in the labor camps would remain in Hungary. He could not give a definitive answer at this time. We referred to the fact that Jewish men up to the age of 42 were in the labor camps. The Germans felt that men in the 45 to 56 age group were also suitable for the camps. For the time being, the Germans were requesting about 300 or 400 men. Eichmann would like to have them appear voluntarily; otherwise force would be used. These men would enjoy good treatment and good pay, just like other workers. We said that we would need authorization for this, and he answered that we should get rid of our liberal habits and that we should not request but order.

He wanted to place all the finances of Hungarian Jewry—including converts—under the jurisdiction of the Central Council. The converts were the richest, and we should collect greater amounts from them. This measure would be authorized by a forthcoming decree, and the structure of the Council should be such that it would include everything contained in it. The Council should have a section that would be familiar with the educational affairs of all the Jews of Hungary, know where the schools are, how many students there are, and in what buildings. For example, it should have a statistical and a technical section capable of action if there was a need for it. *Obersturmbannführer* Eichmann noted that he personally was very interested in Jewish historical artifacts and literature. He had been dealing with Jewish affairs since 1934 and knew Hebrew better than we did. We told him that we had a museum in which we kept our antiques, and that we had libraries; he would probably visit these on Wednesday and asked that we assign to him a person knowledgeable about these things.

He then mentioned that the Orthodox people had asked him to permit the publication of an Orthodox Jewish paper. He would not, wishing that only the *A Magyar Zsidók Lapja* appear; perhaps we could allot one or two pages of it for the Orthodox news.[52] He would order that the *A Magyar Zsidók Lapja* be sent to every Jewish family, and this would be one of the sources of income for the Community.

We also told him that if the Germans needed something it would be very difficult for us to select a particular source of supply, and that this would be extremely painful to us. He answered that the Germans would list everything they took to the smallest detail and either return the goods or compensate us, but that we were to handle the acquisition of the things the Germans needed.

In connection with organization, they requested the preparation of a map showing the cities in which there were Jewish institutions and the location of the institutions within the cities, with an appendix giving the name and nature of every one. Organizationally, every congregation was to remain intact, but all institutions belonging to the congregations would fall under the jurisdiction of the Central Council. However if, for example, somebody had set up a trust to have prayers said in the *Talmud Torah* for the salvation of his soul, was there any sense in letting such a trust continue? This money should be used for other purposes. The foundations would also come under the jurisdiction of the Central Council.

He emphasized that all these things would last as long as the war lasted. After the war, the Jews would be free to do whatever they wanted. Everything taking place on the Jewish question was in fact only for the wartime period, and with the end of the war the Germans would again become good natured and permit everything, as in the past.

He declared in general that he was no friend of force, and he hoped that things would go well without it. Personnel was written with a capital P to the Germans: they needed every man and could not possibly spare many guards. According to his experience so far, violence and executions had occurred only where the Jews took up opposition. Should it happen that Jews joined the Ruthenian partisans or Tito's bands, as in Greece, then he would mow them down mercilessly, because there was a war on and one could not proceed otherwise in a war. But if the Jews understood that he expected only order and discipline from them, and work in whatever area they were assigned to, not only would they not come to any harm but they would be protected from it and would enjoy the same treatment and pay as other workers. He emphatically wanted this idea of his to be propagated among the widest strata of Jewry, and for this reason the forthcoming decree would also provide that every Jewish household subscribe to the *A Magyar Zsidók Lapja*. He recommended that we establish a price that would enable the Jewish Council to derive some income from it.

Eichmann recognized that it was very natural that some among this large Jewish community would commit actions for which the Council could not be responsible. This fact would be taken into account. He reemphasized that he wanted to protect Jewry from all individual atrocities and, should such a thing happen anywhere—even by German soldiers—it should be reported to him immediately and he would deal harshly with the perpetrators. He would punish most severely anyone trying to enrich himself from Jewish wealth.

The organization of Jewry was to be unitary, and if we found it necessary we should raise the community (or congregation) tax; everyone was to obey the instructions of the Jewish Council, and he would see to it that this took place.

Moreover, he declared that he was a friend of plain speaking, and that we should tell him everything openly and honestly, and he would give an honest answer. He already had such great experience in handling Jewish matters that we should not believe that anybody could mislead him, and if someone were to attempt it he would have to face him.

Then a moving scene followed. Dr. János Gábor stood up and said that he was distressed by the introduction of the Yellow Star. His late father had taken part in the Great War as a Major Judge Advocate, and his grandfather had been a soldier in 1848. The wearing of the Yellow Star would encourage the riffraff to attack and mock Jews on the streets. In response, Eichmann declared that he would not tolerate the harming of Jews for wearing the Yellow Star, and that if any incident of this nature occurred it should be reported to him and he would deal with the attackers.[53]

The gullibility with which the Jewish leaders accepted Eichmann's explanations and reassurances was as surprising as it was tragic, for they, and especially Stern, were well aware by that time of the Nazis' techniques. Instead of taking effective precautionary measures, they naively proceeded with the implementation of the formal organizational measures suggested by Eichmann.

Plans for the Structural Reorganization of the Community

During the next few days, during which the Germans and their Hungarian hirelings were already finalizing their plans for the expropriation and ghettoization of the Jews as a prelude to their deportation, the Jewish leaders of Budapest were implementing the decisions adopted with Krumey's concurrence on March 28 and carrying out Eichmann's instructions of March 31.

The plans for the organization of the Hungarian Jews were worked out by Dr. Ernő Munkácsi, the Secretary General of the Jewish Community of Pest. According to his proposals, the work of the Central Jewish Council, which would retain its leading role, would be supplemented by that of a "Great Council of Budapest" (*Budapesti Nagytanács*). This was envisioned to be composed of 25 to 27 members, which, with the addition of the presidents of ten Neolog and two Status Quo communities, would constitute the "National Great Council" (*Országos Nagytanács*). Both Great Councils were to have only advisory powers. The country was to be divided into ten congregational or community districts, with the heads of the various communities at each district seat being responsible for the implementation of the Central Jewish Council's instructions.

In addition to working out the national structural plan for the administration of the communities, Munkácsi also completed a detailed administrative design for the Central Jewish Council. It called for the establishment of nine departments, each having distinct functions and responsibilities. Though they underwent some changes in response to the shifting requirements imposed upon them, most of these departments continued to operate relatively unchanged until shortly after the *Nyilas* coup in October.

By far the most important department was the "Presidential" (*Elnöki*) one, which was entrusted with responsibility for the implementation of the instructions issued to and by the Central Jewish Council. In accordance with a suggestion made by Wisliceny at a meeting with the leaders of the Council on April 20, the Council elected an executive secretary to assure the immediate and effective implementation of its orders. The choice fell on Zoltán Kohn, the superintendent of the schools of the Jewish community of Budapest. Though the appointment was meant to be only provisional, pending the recovery of Munkácsi, Kohn continued serving until early in June, when his functions were taken over by Rezső Müller, the head of the Housing Department (*Lakásügyi Hivatal*).[54] The presidential department's operations were shared among six major working groups. Perhaps the most important of these was the one entrusted with the maintenance of contact with the German and Hungarian authorities. It was first headed by Dr. József Vági, one of the attorneys of the Jewish community, and included Dr. János Gábor, Dr. György Gergely, Dr. Erzsébet Eppler, and Dr. László Pető as its leading officials.[55] After a short while, the chairmanship of this group was assumed by Gábor, primarily because of his excellent command of German. Another working group was in charge of translations. Headed by Dr. Dezső Kiss, it was primarily concerned with the translation of the materials designed for the *A Magyar Zsidók Lapja* into German to enable the SS authorities in charge of censorship to determine their suitability for publication. The group was also in charge of preparing the German-language petitions and correspondence. Kiss, who had formerly been associated with the *Pester Lloyd* of Budapest, was assisted by Ernő Bródy, Pál Bacher-Bodrogh, and Dr. József Turóczi-Trostler—all of whom were highly proficient in German.[56] The third working group was known as the "Provincial" Department (*Vidéki Osztály*) and was in charge of maintaining contact with the provincial districts, communities, and congregations. Headed by József Goldschmied, it had at its disposal a number of brave young *Halutzim* who went to several ghettos, gathering news about the conditions there and informing the leaders about the scope of the ghettoization.[57] Unfortunately, they were relatively few in number and able to get into only a limited number of ghettos. Although in several cases they managed to smuggle out their Zionist comrades, they were unable to persuade the ghetto leaders about the truth of their information. These leaders were more inclined to believe and trust in the traditional leaders of Budapest, whose instructions they received through official channels.

The three other working groups were of lesser importance. These were concerned with the dissemination of announcements through the press, the collection of statistical and demographic data, and the handling of personnel and legal aid matters.

The Financial Department (*Pénzügyi Osztály*) was in charge of communal tax matters as well as finances. It was headed by Bertalan Büchler, the financial officer of the Jewish Community of Pest, who was assisted by Arthur Szüsz.[58] The Social Department (*Szociális Ügyosztály*) took over the welfare responsibilities of MIPI. It was first headed by the former MIPI leader György Polgár. After Polgár left the country with the Kasztner group at the end of June, the leadership of this department was assumed by István Földes.

The most active department in terms of the demands made of it was the Economic and Technical Department (*Gazdasági és Műszaki Osztály*). It was in charge of all economic and technical matters involving Jewish institutions, including housing and food supplies, as well as of fulfilling the requisition demands imposed upon the Jewish community by the German and Hungarian authorities. For operational efficiency, its functions were divided among various specialized groups. The Department was under the overall charge of Miksa Domonkos, a dedicated and highly conscientious individual who—despite constant pressure—worked tirelessly in behalf of the persecuted community. His effectiveness was enhanced by the fact that he was exempted from the anti-Jewish measures, having been a highly decorated officer in World War I. In this capacity he was perhaps the most valuable and effective Jewish leader during the *Nyilas* era and the Soviet siege.[59]

The Education and Culture Department (*Oktatási és Kulturális Ügyosztály*) was only partially concerned with its nominal tasks during the occupation. While it operated a number of "progressive" and Orthodox educational institutions in Budapest, its primary function was to use the student body for facilitating the work of the Council. Students were used as messengers to compensate for the telephone restrictions imposed upon the Jews. They were also used, together with the employees of the Department, in the periodic drives for the requisitioning of apartments and for the relocation of the evicted Jews.

The Foreign Department (*Külföldi Ügyosztály*) was in charge of matters relating to emigration and theoretically handled the affairs of the Zionist organizations and of the Palestine Office (*Palesztina Hivatal*).

The Department of Religious Affairs (*Hitéleti Hivatal*) was established to handle all matters relating to the religious practices of the various congregations. One of its sections—the Office of Vital Statistics and Rites (*Szertartási Ügyosztály és Anyakönyvi Hivatal*)—became particularly busy during the occupation, for it also handled the question of conversions. The number of Jews desiring to convert as a means of saving their lives increased by leaps and bounds. For example, in the January 1–March 17, 1944, period there were 176 conversions; between March 20 and May 5 there were 1,072 Jews who decided to convert. The Vital Statistics Office was kept busy with the registration of deaths: during the first weeks of the occupation, there were 420 deaths in Budapest and only 39 births.[60]

The Housing and Travel Department (*Lakás- és Utazási Ügyosztály*) was one of the largest and busiest. The section dealing with housing was particularly active and always under great pressure, for it was constantly overwhelmed with demands and complaints concerning its operations. In satisfying the ever recurring requisition demands of the German and Hungarian authorities for Jewish apartments it was bound to chagrin many of the Jews affected. Its tasks became especially demanding after the Allied air-raids and almost superhuman in June, when the Jews were ordered to move into specially designated Yellow Star–marked buildings (chapter 24). The Department carried out its functions effectively, though occasionally with unavoidable ruthlessness, thanks to the energetic and efficient leadership of Müller. Among his closest collaborators were Miksa Trobits, the Department's administrator, Dr. Ármin Kun, Dr. István Kurzweil, and Dezső Bánó. The latter two had previously served with the Public Housing Department (*Közérdekű lakáshivatal*) of the Jewish Community of Pest, which was used as a basis for setting up the Jewish Council's Department.[61]

The Department on Converts (*Kitértek Ügyosztálya*) was established to handle the affairs of the converted Jews, who were placed by the Germans under the jurisdiction of the Jewish Council. It was short-lived, for after the representatives of the Christian Churches complained about the Germans' resolution to treat converts as Jews, the converts were placed under the jurisdiction of a new organization of their own: the Association of the Christian Jews of Hungary (*Magyarországi Keresz-tény Zsidók Szövetsége*).[62]

As a help to the large number of Jews who appeared at the Community's headquarters with a variety of complaints and inquiries, a special Information Office (*Tájékoztató Iroda*) was soon added to the organizational structure. It was in this office that later in the summer the so-called Kasztner group was set up under Zionist leadership.[63]

The workload of the various departments increased tremendously as time went on. Upon the news that the Gestapo had actually freed a number of people at the behest of the Jewish leaders, many thousands of Jews besieged the Council headquarters in search of individual favors. Some wanted the central organization to locate their relatives; others wanted to make sure that their interned family members or friends were adequately housed and fed; still others were eager to redress the injustices caused by the requisition of their apartments or to acquire travel permits. An increasingly large number of the visitors were interested in conversion in the hope of escaping the persecution.

In response to these pressures, the number of officials and clerical employees in the various departments of the Jewish Council increased dramatically. Many of these were volunteers who hoped to ease their own lot by being associated with, and thereby enjoying the "protection" of, the Council. Some of these worked tirelessly and devotedly in behalf of their persecuted brethren; others continued in the bureaucratic tradition of the pre-war period. However, there were also a few who acted in a dictatorial fashion, boasting about their direct contacts with the German and Hungarian authorities. All of them, including the leaders of the Council, had to act circumspectly because of the suspected presence of informers.[64]

Although employment by the Council continued to offer a degree of safety even after Horthy's halting of the deportations early in July, its attractiveness declined somewhat after the appearance of new opportunities for relief and rescue. These were the offices established in conjunction with the Swiss authorities for the registration of a limited number of Jews for emigration. The new centers of rescue activity attracted not only the young *Halutzim,* but also several council employees and volunteers who readily abandoned their positions and clients at 12 Síp Street. The switchover was engendered by the belief that the new centers offered greater opportunities for personal safety and above all the possibility of emigration.

The communal bylaws that guided the operation of the various departments of the Council and were designed to regulate the life of the entire Jewish community were completed by the Council lawyers and administrative experts within a few days after the meeting with Eichmann. Approved by the Council after a lengthy debate, they remained in effect, for all practical purposes, until the end of the Horthy era in October 1944. It is one of the ironies of history that the fragmented, disunited, and antagonistic Jewish communities of Hungary were united at last under Nazi tutelage! This "gift of the Danaides," as Munkácsi called it, reflects the deplorable organizational status of Hungarian Jewry before the occupation and the ease with which it could be manipulated. Ironically, even during the establishment of the Nazi-demanded organizational structure, the leaders of the various communal and Zionist organizations seem to have bickered over the allocation of functions. Nison Kahan interceded with Freudiger to have the Provincial Department and the Information Office assigned to the Zionists. Freudiger arranged this, because in his view only the Zionists were in a position to assure contact with the provincial Jews in the wake of the isolation of the communities by the Nazis.[65]

The draft bylaws were submitted on April 4 to Eichmann, who, having already finalized his extermination plans, returned them with his approval two days later.

With Eichmann's routine approval at hand, the leaders of the Council, failing to realize that they were merely playing out a charade, sent a letter to the heads of all the major Jewish communities together with an 18-point questionnaire. The ominous letter read as follows:

The Central Council of Hungarian Jews was instructed by the higher authorities to organize Hungarian Jewry on a national basis so that the instructions of the Central Council of Budapest can be received by the president of the community in the county seat or, in the case of two congregations, by the presidents of both congregations, who will be responsible for their implementation. The interests of the Jews of the particular counties are represented before the authorities by the president(s) of the congregation(s) operating in the county seat. We draw your attention to the fact that the Central Council of Hungarian Jews of Budapest implements the instructions received from the higher authorities and that the members of the Council are personally responsible for their immediate and thorough implementation under pain of drastic consequences. The same responsibility is borne by any person who does not carry out the instructions of the Central Council, which could have fatal results for all of Hungarian Jewry. Further instructions relating to the organization will be sent to you, Mr. President, in the near future. We ask you to acknowledge the content of this letter by return mail.[66]

Shortly after the Council mailed out its intimidating circular, it published an appeal in the official organ of Hungarian Jewry designed at once to reassure the Jews and cajole them into submission. It was planted to reassure the Jews that they were still being led by their traditional, trusted leaders and to advise them to obediently carry out the instructions of the Council and the authorities. It read as follows:

Brothers!

The Central Council of Hungarian Jews has been established on the instructions of, and on the basis of appointment by, the Hungarian authorities. Its members are those men whom the Jewish public trusts and has placed at the helm of the communal institutions during the peacetime years.

The Central Council is the only organ of Hungarian Jewry recognized by the authorities. It encompasses under its jurisdiction all those belonging to the Jewish religious community and those considered as Jews under the provisions of the newest regulations.

The Hungarian authorities deal exclusively with the Central Council, and it is to this body that they send all instructions relating to the Jews of the entire country. Each and every member of the Central Council is responsible with his life for the exact implementation of these instructions, as are all those who do not carry out exactly the instructions of the Central Council.

Brothers! Hungarian Jewry must carry out the instructions of the authorities through its own organs. Consequently, the Central Council is not an authority but only the implementing organ of the authorities.

The Central Council cannot allow some individuals' disobedience to frustrate the implementation of the instructions that were received, thereby precipitating a never before experienced misfortune for the entire community.

Following a request by the Central Council, whoever is called must appear at the requested place. The Central Council has received the responsibility as well as the absolute power to exercise control over the spiritual and material goods, as well as the labor capability, of every Jew. All of you, women, girls, men, and boys alike, are agents of the Central Council. Take note of the fact that the most serious measures of the Central Council are also undertaken on the basis of decisions by the authorities, and that the life of every individual as well of the entire community depends on their exact implementation.

May God be with us and give us strength and the ability to faithfully fulfill our task.[67]

The same issue of the journal carried an editorial entitled "Calm and Discipline, Self-Sacrificing Fulfillment of Duties" in which the Jews were warned again to remain calm and disciplined and work to the limit of their abilities. The Central Council assured them that on the basis of promises and definite assurances received from the competent authorities the Jews who fulfilled all their responsibilities would enjoy "the same treatment, food, and pay as other workers" and would be "protected."[68]

It is interesting to note that the Central Jewish Council's appeal of April 6 referred to the *Hungarian authorities* as the power that appointed it and whose instructions it must carry out. It is safe to assume that by then the Eichmann-*Sonderkommando* and its chief Hungarian supporters, including Baky, Endre, Hain, and Koltay, had already agreed on the details of the Final Solution and that for tactical reasons they decided to identify the Hungarian authorities as the ones having jurisdiction over Jewish matters. One of the intentions was, of course, to make the anti-Jewish measures more palatable to the Hungarian organs to be involved in their execution and more acceptable to Hungarian public opinion in general.

The actions that had already been taken by the German and Hungarian authorities clearly resembled those the Nazis had previously employed in other parts of Europe. To conceal the truth, the Jewish leaders were compelled to continue to lull the Jewish masses into a false sense of security. On April 13, Samu Stern issued an appeal titled "Work and Do Not Despair!" in which he informed Jewry that "all the instructions, orders, decisions, and decrees of the authorities will have to be carried out exactly and without any complaint or grumbling." He further informed them that the Central Jewish Council was in the process of building up its organizational structure "so that it will be in a position to carry out the tasks accruing to it in a more intense and dedicated fashion."[69] Concurrently, Dr. Ferenc Hevesi, the Chief Rabbi, urged the Jews in the patriotic tradition of his predecessors to "pray before God for yourself, your family, your children, but primarily and above all for your Hungarian Homeland! Love of homeland, fulfillment of duty, and prayer should be your life's guiding light!"[70]

Dr. Ernő Boda, deputy chairman of the Jewish Community of Pest and a Council member, who took the minutes at the conference with Eichmann on March 31, unwittingly reflected some of Eichmann's ideas in his appeal to the Jews. Entitled "The Word of the Law," Boda's appeal reminded the Jews that they were not only the people of the book, but also that of the law and therefore the Jews "must abide by all, even the most severe, measures without any deliberation and pondering." He further urged the Jews "to trust in their leaders and accept their instructions with resignation and the knowledge that the leaders are guided by brotherly love even in their severest instructions." In order that the Jews be acquainted with the laws and instructions affecting them, Boda insisted that everybody should subscribe and read the *A Magyar Zsidók Lapja*, by that time the only means of communication among the Jews of Hungary.[71]

The "Legalization" of the Council

Once the policies of the German and Hungarian authorities involved in the Jewish question were synchronized, the Jewish Council was given a legal basis for its operations. On April 19, 1944, the Cabinet adopted a decree (no. 1.520/1944.M.E.) "Concerning the Representation and Self-Government of the Jews," which went into effect three days later. This ended the "illegal" character of the Council, which the Germans had established by fiat on March 21. The draft of the decree, according to a historical source, was worked out by Béla Berend, the controversial member of the Council, and Zoltán Bosnyák, his sponsor for the Council seat.[72]

Bosnyák was one of the leaders of Hungarian anti-Semitism. The author of several anti-Semitic works,[73] he began his career as a public school teacher and managed to achieve an appointment as principal. Almost immediately after the German occupation he was tapped by his mentor, László Endre, and appointed to serve in the new Jewish Department of the Ministry of the Interior.[74] Because of his expertise in Jewish affairs, he was also appointed to serve as director of the Nazi-inspired Hungarian Institute for Researching the Jewish Question (*A Zsidókérdést Kutató Magyar Intézet*) and as editor of the Institute's vitriolically anti-Semitic organ called *Harc* (Battle).[75]

Under the original plan worked out by Berend and Bosnyák the Council was to have been called "Communal Organization of the Jews of Hungary" (*Magyarországi Zsidók Közösségi Szervezete*) and envisioned to have 10 members (5 religious and 5 lay), with Berend slated to serve as Secretary General.[76] Berend summarized the scope of his planned organization (identified by the acronym MAZSIOSZ) in a ten-point program appended to his letter to Endre dated April 12, 1944 (see below). He suggested the establishment within the Ministry of the Interior of a Jewish Department that would have direct and unitary jurisdiction over all of Jewry and whose head would work closely with the MAZSIOSZ directorate. He also suggested that the Jews be required to report all of their property to the new organization (with one copy to be forwarded to the Ministry) and that part of it be used for the state and part by the organization, under state supervision, for the agricultural and industrial retraining of Jewry. In his scheme, the leadership of Jewry was to consist exclusively of Zionists, whose identity he would reveal "after his negotiations in Pest." He assured Endre that "he and his brain-trust" were honestly considering the segregation of the Jews and their emigration after the war and offered him his own design for the Star of David to be worn by the Jews.

Endre did not bother to respond (he always tried to avoid any direct contact with Jews no matter what their positions were) though it is quite probable that he discussed the merits and implications of Berend's proposals with Bosnyák. They obviously decided against adopting them, for by that time the plans for the expropriation, ghettoization, and deportation of the Jews had already been completed. They consequently opted for the setting up of a Jewish Council whose organization and structure were not basically different from those in operation since March 20. The exception, which did not alter the role envisioned for the Council, was the addition of a few new members, including Berend.

The decree provided for the establishment of a nine-member Jewish Council to be known as Association of the Jews of Hungary (*Magyarországi Zsidók Szövetsége*). Its jurisdiction extended to all the Jews compelled to wear the Yellow Star. The Council operated under the direction of the Ministry of the Interior with immediate jurisdiction being exercised by Section VII/b, "Organizations" (*Egyesületi alosztály*). Headed before the occupation by János Páskándy, in 1944 the Section was led by Lajos Blaskovich, one of Endre's closest friends. Its secretary was István Vassányi, who was responsible for the inclusion of Dr. József Nagy in the Council.[77]

The Association was entrusted with:

- Guarding the behavior of the Jews under its jurisdiction and the issuance of instructions binding on them.
- Representation of the communal interests of the Jews under its jurisdiction.
- Advancement of the social, educational, and cultural interests of the Jews.
- Execution of all the tasks entrusted to it under law and by the authorities.

The Association was expected to fulfill these functions within an organizational framework specified under bylaws, not yet drafted, that would go into effect with the concurrence of the Minister of the Interior. In order to set up these bylaws and carry out the functions of the Association on an interim basis, the decree called for the establishment of a nine-man "provisional executive committee" (*ideiglenes intézőbizottság*).

The leaders of Hungarian Jewry tried to take advantage of the issuance of the decree to reestablish contact with the Hungarian authorities. They immediately contacted Albert Takács, Endre's secretary, who instructed them to get in touch with either Bosnyák or Lajos Argalás, the head of the Subsection on General Public Administration (*Általános közigazgatási alosztály*) of the Section for the Preparation of Laws (*Törvényelőkészítő osztály*) in the Ministry of the Interior and the author of the anti-Jewish draft laws. On April 23, Argalás received a delegation composed of Kahan, Munkácsi, and Pető. He explained the rationale for the decree and suggested that since he had merely prepared it, the Jewish leaders contact Endre's subordinate, Lajos Blaskovich, the head of the Jewish Department in the Ministry. Blaskovich received Munkácsi on May 1 in the company of Argalás, Bosnyák, and István Vassányi. The meeting was basically fruitless, for they merely reviewed the character of the new Provisional Executive Committee to be established and the suitability of the various candidates slated for membership.[78]

Argalás claimed that the basic reason for the decree was to provide a legal framework for the measures that had been adopted against the Jews since the German occupation and to assure that the interests of the Jews were represented.[79] It is safe to assume that, in addition, the Hungarians were eager to share with the Germans (whom they began to envy) in the expropriation of Jewish property and to reestablish the façade of sovereignty.

However, two days after the issuance of the decree and about two weeks before the members of the new "provisional executive committee" were appointed, the Central Jewish Council exposed itself to the charge of collaboration by consenting, however involuntarily, to the issuance and distribution of summonses that led to the internment and subsequent deportation of many journalists, lawyers, and other professionals who were identified on special lists prepared and handed over to the Council by the German and Hungarian dejewification units.[80]

The members of the Provisional Executive Committee were appointed on May 8 by virtue of a decree (no. 176.774/1944. VII.b. B.M.) of the Ministry of the Interior signed by Secretary of State László Endre.[81] They were: Samu Stern, Dr. Ernő Pető, Dr. Károly Wilhelm, Rabbi Dr. Béla Berend, Samu Kahan-Frankl, Fülöp Freudiger, Dr. Sándor Török, Dr. József Nagy, and Dr. János Gábor.

By this time, the ghettoization process was already in full swing in the provinces and the first transports had already left for Auschwitz from Kistarcsa and Topolya.

The members appointed to the Provisional Executive Committee convened to organize themselves on May 15—the very day the mass deportations began.[82] The meeting was attended only by six of the nine appointed members. Stern was ill, Berend excused himself, and Török could not be reached.[83] The meeting was chaired by Kahan-Frankl. Its business included the election of Stern as President of the Committee and the appointment of a committee in charge of drafting the bylaws.[84]

The replacement of the German-approved Central Jewish Council by the Provisional Executive Committee of the Association of the Jews of Hungary (*A Magyarországi Zsidók Szövetsége Ideiglenes Intézőbizottsága*) involved a change in the official leadership of Hungarian Jewry. Boda, Csobádi, and Kahan were replaced by Berend, Gábor, Nagy, and Török. Those replaced, however, were invited to continue to participate as counselors in the Provisional Executive Committee as were the counselors of the Central Council, including Dr. László Bakonyi, the Secretary General of MIOI, Dr. Hugó Csergő, Dr. Ernő Munkácsi, Dr. Zoltán Kohn, the superintendent of schools of the Jewish Community of Pest, and Dr. Imre Reiner, the legal counselor of the Orthodox community.[85] In fact, Nison Kahan was elected recording secretary (*jegyző*).[86]

The Basis for the Appointment of New Council Members

The basis for the appointment of the new members to the Provisional Executive Committee[87] became known only after the war. Dr. Nagy, who was a physician associated with the Jewish Hospital of Budapest, was appointed on the recommendation of one of his patients, Dr. István Vassányi, who worked under Endre in the section of the Ministry of the Interior which set up the new Jewish Council.[88] Török, a noted writer who was then under arrest, was appointed on the recommendation of Bosnyák following an intervention by someone acting for Mrs. Török, who was naturally eager to free her husband. A convert, he was appointed to represent the Christian Jews. Gábor's appointment was suggested by the Germans in order to assure the continuity of their contact with the Jewish leaders.

Berend and the Council. By far the most controversial appointment was that of Dr. Berend, the Chief Rabbi of the small town of Szigetvár, in the southwestern part of Hungary. Like Török, he was recommended by Bosnyák to whom he had been introduced, according to Lévai, as "a clearheaded nationalist Jewish clergyman" by Count Domonkos Festetics, the noted anti-Semitic landowner and ultra right-oriented deputy who represented his town in the lower house of the Hungarian Parliament.[89] Although in the course of his interrogation by the police just before his indictment for alleged crimes against the people (see below) Berend acknowledged that he had indeed approached Bosnyák at the recommendation of Festetics,[90] he claimed during and after his trial that it was on his own initiative following a resolution of a Zionist group. Citing the testimony of Imre Kálmán, one of his defense witnesses, Berend claims that at a *Betar* (right-wing Revisionist Zionist group) meeting in 1941 a number of concerned Jews, including Dénes Szilágyi, Imre Varga, and Ferenc Kauders, had decided to contact leading Right-radical figures in an effort to "Zionize" them and that he had been assigned Bosnyák for this purpose.

Béla Berend was born in Budapest on January 12, 1911, the son of Adolf Presser and Regina Márías. As a young rabbi, according to most of his contemporaries, he was a basically impetuous, somewhat compulsive nonconformist, who was politically motivated by certain idealistic and ideologically oriented concerns. According to Munkácsi, his attitude reflected a defiant, revolutionary posture directed against the traditional, capitalist Jewish leadership of the country.[91] Berend reportedly manifested the same disdain toward the communal leadership of Szigetvár as well.[92] His ire was directed especially against the rich, converted Jews, who in his view enjoyed special privileges at the expense of the poor. In contrast to the patriotic posture of the assimilationist establishment leaders (chapter 3), Berend advocated with conviction that Jewry had no place in Hungary and would have to emigrate.[93] His proclaimed opposition to the rich, the converts, and the patriotic orientation of the official leaders coincided with the views and interests of Bosnyák. Their views found a common denominator on two major issues. They agreed that conversion did not change the position of a Jew and that it could not provide advantages over those who clung to their faith. They also appear to have agreed on the desirability of the Jews' departure from Hungary. Although there is no evidence that Berend was ever formally affiliated with any Zionist group, Bosnyák and his entourage were presumably inclined to look upon him as a Zionist spokesman and encouraged him, as indeed they did all Zionists, to advocate the need for the Jews to emigrate. In this respect, the attitude of the Hungarian anti-Semites was identical with that of the German National Socialists prior to the launching of the Final Solution program. The Nazis also favored the Zionists (who advocated the need for the development of a national Jewish political consciousness) over the establishment assimilationists (who consistently adopted a patriotic stance).[94]

Motivated by ideological preconceptions, Berend was practically as active before the German occupation as after it, though the character of his activities naturally changed. Before the occupation he was particularly concerned with the alleged differential treatment of Jews and with the need to enlighten some of the Right radicals, including Bosnyák, about their "mistaken" or "distorted" views of the Talmud. He launched a kind of crusade to dissuade these rightists from accepting Count Alfonz Luzsenszky's interpretation of the Talmud.[95] Luzsenszky, a prolific author of anti-Semitic books and pamphlets, including the highly publicized *A talmud magyarul* (The Talmud in Hungarian), was a major propaganda source not only for the Hungarian anti-Semitic movements and parties, but also for those of other European countries, including the Third Reich.[96]

As to the alleged differential treatment of Jews, Berend, who was also a field chaplain, appears to have been particularly concerned with the perceived inequities in the labor service system. For example, in December 1940, when the system was still comparatively new and reasonably tolerable, he filed an appeal with the Ministry of Defense, which was cosigned by Imre Gyenes and László Fried, two labor servicemen from Pécs, complaining about the inequity inherent in the alleged preferential treatment of the rich converted Jews in the system.[97]

Berend's pre-occupation activities and contacts with rightists, which were unknown to the Jewish community at large, became the basis of his appointment to the reorganized Council. Berend claims that it was he who approached Bosnyák, exploiting his earlier contacts, after he discovered that the Hungarian anti-Semitic leader had been appointed to the Ministry of the Interior. He further claims that his intention was to safeguard Hungarian sovereignty by having the German-appointed Jewish Council replaced by a Hungarian-established Association of the Jews of Hungary—his and Bosnyák's design for the new Council. His objective was allegedly to bring about the transfer of the handling of the Jewish question from the Germans to the Hungarians.[98] It was his intention, he further argued, to persuade the new Nazi rulers of Hungary that their ultimate objective—to rid the country of its Jews— was similar to that of the Jewish leaders, who did not aspire to remain in Hungary but preferred to go to the Jewish homeland that would be established. The Jews should therefore not be deported, because they would emigrate anyway after the war.[99]

Berend's selection for a Council seat, allegedly to represent the provincial communities, was apparently decided even before the Decree (no. 1.520/1944) of April 19. In his testimony before the People's Tribunal, Berend asserted that he was freed by the Gestapo unit of Pécs soon after his arrest (allegedly for listening to the BBC) on April 17, because he had shown the SS interrogator a letter from Bosnyák to the effect that he was slated to become a Council member.[100] His quick release by the Gestapo and his ability to travel freely when practically all other Jews were subjected to severe restrictions gave rise to much speculation about the possibility that he had entered into deals. Berend's involvement in the preparatory work for the reorganization of the Council was also revealed in the two letters he sent to Endre prior to his formal appointment on May 8. These letters were subsequently used in his postwar indictment, which stated among other things:

The accused also aimed to acquire the confidence of László Endre, the then Secretary of State; this is reflected by the two letters he addressed to Endre from Szigetvár on April 12 and May 1, 1944, which also cast a sharp light on his personality; in these letters, he offered his services, demanded a strictly confidential private appointment, appended the plan for the Communal Organization of the Jews of Hungary together with the extract of the confidential proposal, offered methods for the dejewification of Buda and for the regulation of exemptions from wearing the badge, emphasizing in his second letter his successful activities in the course of the collection of the valuables of the deported Jews of Szigetvár and of the valuables of the Jewish community of Szigetvár.[101]

Although Endre never responded to the letters, he acknowledged them indirectly after the war. In the course of his interrogation by the American authorities in July 1945, Endre stated that "the separation and removal from the country (*kiszállítás*) of the Jews was recommended by the rabbi of Szigetvár. I represented the view that the Jews should have their own country; this view was also shared by the rabbi of Szigetvár."[102]

Berend's appointment to the Council was received by the traditional leaders of Hungarian Jewry with surprise and alarm. They were astonished to find in their midst a young rabbi of a small provincial community with no known record of prior service in any national communal or Zionist organization. Their surprise was soon replaced by apprehension and anxiety as they were apprised about Berend's connections with Bosnyák. Under the extraordinary perilous conditions of the time, the rumor that he had close connections also with other rightists, including possibly Endre, soon gained credence.[103]

Gergely, who was a member of the Council's liaison office that dealt with the SS, claims that he and János Gábor, a Council member, were actually tipped off by Krumey that Berend had been appointed to the Council on Endre's wishes.[104] The Council was aware of the possibility that Krumey's allegations might have been intended to exacerbate relations between the Council and the Hungarian authorities in order to protect and advance the interests of the Germans. Nevertheless, the Council took all the necessary precautionary measures in view of Berend's established close relationship with Bosnyák, Endre's intimate friend. Berend's mail was monitored and his movements were carefully followed. Acting on instructions from Stern, Gergely screened the letters left behind by Berend for mailing, occasionally coming across information which reinforced the Council's suspicions.[105] Because of these and other revelations, both real and imaginary, some of the leading Council members and officials became extremely apprehensive about the possible threat he represented to the community. Relations between them and Berend became so strained after a while that a plan was designed to eliminate him by arousing the Germans' suspicions toward him.[106] According to Gergely, contact was actually established with Franz Weinzinger, a lumber dealer who doubled as a German spy, informing him discreetly that Berend's activities were harming German interests.[107] The communication about Berend's alleged anti-German activities was duly forwarded to Eichmann, who promptly had him arrested, but allegedly had to let him go free at the request of Bosnyák and Endre.[108]

Unfortunately, Berend did nothing to dissipate the traditional Jewish leaders' assumptions about his dealings with Bosnyák and other rightists. Instead of exploiting his close contacts with the rightists in power by working closely and in harmony with the other members of the Council, he decided for reasons of his own to pursue his own independent line. Consequently, the initial distrust was further exacerbated.

The traditional Jewish leaders of the Council rarely if ever discussed matters of substance in his presence, fearing that he was an informer.[109]

As stated earlier, the reorganized Council first met on May 15, the very day the mass deportations began. While it is questionable whether a more harmonious and united Council would have had any impact on the speed and scale of the deportations, it is safe to assume that the morale and effectiveness of the Council would have been enhanced had Berend dissipated the distrust of his colleagues and consented to serve as a trusted conduit to the authorities. For, indeed, because of his close contacts with Bosnyák, he was practically a *persona grata* in the Ministry of the Interior, the center of the anti-Jewish measures, which he frequently visited. Although the substance of his discussions in the Ministry has been the subject of conjecture during and ever since the end of the war, it is safe to assume that it was often in support of certain Jewish causes or individual rescue efforts. These visits usually took place without the concurrence or prior knowledge of the other members of the Council. Occasionally, however, Berend also acted in behalf of the Council. At a time when Endre would not permit Jews to enter the Ministry (he reportedly feared that they would "infect" or have a detrimental influence on the Hungarian officials) Berend managed to acquire special permits for the other members of the Council to visit the Ministry during the course of their rescue efforts.[110]

In July 1944, when Horthy halted the deportations and promised the leaders of the Christian churches to exempt the converts from most anti-Jewish measures, Berend consented to give an interview for the *Harc,* the ultra anti-Semitic organ, emphasizing along the line pursued by the Right radicals that conversion did not change the status of a Jew.[111] Berend claimed after the war that his objective was to prevent mass conversions in order to retain the unity of the community and thereby assure its better protection. The radicals, on the other hand, opposed the conversions because they were eager to apply the Final Solution program to all Jews, including those who, like the Marranos, merely professed to accept Christianity in order to escape persecution.[112] The interview consequently caused great consternation among the Jews, both during and after the war, although some did not find it harmful.

According to some sources, Berend also suggested the article in the December 16, 1944 issue of *Harc,* which appeared shortly after the establishment of the ghetto of Budapest. Titled "The Great Separation" (*A nagy elkülönítés*), the article emphasized that the Jews were satisfied with the measures that were taken against them.[113]

Berend's activities during the *Nyilas* era, and especially in the ghetto of Budapest when the city was under Soviet siege, earned him both praise and scorn. According to many accounts he was quite fearless in the pursuit of his duties, when many of the other members of the Council, including Stern, Pető, and Wilhelm, were in hiding. He performed the ritual services for the dead, dealt with the authorities for the release of Jews or the supplying of the ghetto, and consoled the ill and the hungry. He undoubtedly saved many Jews from almost certain death during those trying weeks, often walking around dressed as a priest. However, there were also those who found Berend's activities not simply questionable but also clearly harmful. Some witnesses accused him of removing valuables from the dead before burial;[114] others accused him of participating in a *Nyilas* raiding party designed to extort money and valuables from Jews crowded in some "protected" buildings (see chapter 26). Specifically, he was accused of having been involved in the *Nyilas* raid on 49 and 52 Pozsonyi Road on January 7, 1945, which he never denied. However, the police and the trial records vary. In his signed police statement of May 8, 1945, he even confessed to having retained the valuables confiscated from the Jews.[115] Although the lower court had found that by participating in the raid he had rendered assistance to the violence perpetrated by an armed *Nyilas* military-type group, the higher court agreed with his contention that he had participated in the raid to prevent the use of force and to persuade the Jews to yield their valuables because these would be taken away anyhow upon their scheduled removal to the ghetto the following day. Some of the survivors accused Berend of having denounced Jews in hiding to the *Nyilas* authorities.[116]

Much of the suspicion surrounding Berend stemmed from his dealings with József Sarlosi, the *Nyilas* commander of the district in which the ghetto was located. His contacts with Sarlosi began on December 6, 1944, when he was arrested by some *Nyilas* who were not aware of his identity and taken to the "House of Vengeance" (*Megtorlás Háza*), Sarlosi's headquarters at 2 Szt. István Boulevard. Berend invoked his friendship with Bosnyák, which Sarlosi corroborated in a telephone conversation with Edith Sós, Bosnyák's secretary. She confirmed that Berend was Bosnyák's "confidential man" (*bizalmasa*).[117] Thereafter he visited the House of Vengeance six or seven times. Though some of these visits were undertaken with the knowledge of the active Council members, including Domonkos, Földes, Komoly, and Stöckler, in order to advance the cause of the beleaguered ghetto, others were allegedly for more questionable purposes. According to Ilona Hores, who was Sarlosi's secretary and took shorthand minutes of Berend's visits, Berend denounced Jews in hiding, including members of the Council.[118]

Berend left Budapest shortly after its liberation by the Red Army on January 17, 1945, and moved to Sátoraljaujhely, the home town of his second wife, Ilona Windt. His withdrawal from public life was short-lived, for he was soon denounced by survivors from both Szigetvár and Budapest, and arrested on suspicion of having been an informer.

The Trial of Berend. The post-liberation legal troubles of Berend began on April 16, 1945, when the Budapest Police addressed a request to its counterpart in Sátoraljaujhely for his arrest and transfer to the capital claiming that it had evidence that "he was an informer of the Gestapo."[119] He was brought to Budapest, where he was subjected to intensive interrogations. During the first half of May 1945, he signed several statements in which he confessed to many of the deeds catalogued in the earlier police reports.[120] Specifically, he confessed to having written Endre about his role in the collection of Jewish valuables in Szigetvár and having denounced Jews in hiding, to having joined the *Nyilas* in a raid on two "protected" houses, to having expropriated valuables found on those deceased in the ghetto, and to having taken advantage of five or six women by promising to help them.[121] The circumstances in which these confessions were made are not clear, though it is quite possible that at least some of them may have been extracted under duress.

Berend was taken into custody on May 18, 1945. For more than a year thereafter, the police and the prosecutor's office were busy rounding up witnesses and collecting evidence and sworn affidavits in preparation of the indictment. Statements were also collected from some of the major war criminals shortly before their execution early in 1946. All of them, including Endre, Baky, Ferenczy, Fidél Pálffy, and László Koltay, claimed that they either had not known or had not met Berend.[122] The People's Prosecutor's Office of Budapest (*Budapesti Népügyészség*), however, had no difficulty in preparing an indictment, which it submitted to the People's Tribunal of Budapest (*Budapesti Népbíróság*) on July 4, 1946. It charged Berend, among other things, with:

- Informing the gendarmes about the whereabouts of Jewish wealth in Szigetvár.
- Accompanying armed *Nyilas* guards during the January 7, 1945, raid on the "protected" buildings at 49 and 54 Pozsonyi Road and extracting money and valuables from the Jews.
- Informing the Gestapo unit in Pécs about the wealth and background of the Jews of Szigetvár.
- Collaborating with Bosnyák by supplying him with, among other things, valuable books, Torahs, and other Jewish ritual artifacts as well as the valuable library collection of Dr. Mihály Guttman.
- Collaborating with Sarlosi by denouncing Jews in hiding.
- Giving an interview to the *Harc*, discriminating against certain categories of people.
- Expropriating rings and other jewelry taken from the dead in the ghetto.[123]

The trial began on August 2, 1946. Berend was defended by Károly Dietz, a defense lawyer assigned by the Budapest Bar (*Budapesti Ügyvédi Kamara*). The prosecution was represented by Mihály Rhosóczy. The trial, one of the most sensational in postwar Hungary, continued with a few weeks' interruption until late in October.[124] In contrast to the assertions of many witnesses, Berend insisted that his actions were motivated by his desire to help the persecuted Jewish community. He summarized the political-philosophical theory that motivated him as follows:

In connection with the Jewish problem I wanted to advance the principle of the *Zionization of Anti-Semitism.* If the Fascists want to get rid of the Jews of Hungary, let them await the end of the war, for the Jewish question is a world problem. It must be solved so that the Jewry which lost its way for two thousand years can find a home. I was led by the desire to realize a truthful and honest emigration. I wanted to establish a certain state of toleration with the Fascists. I wanted to put an end to the [Jews'] fate as a minority, for as such Jewry is persecuted every 25 to 30 years.[125]

Berend insisted that it was the same concern for the welfare of his people that induced him to give the interview for the *Harc* and to participate in the raid. The People's Judges disagreed. In a wrathful decision made public on November 23, 1946, they found him guilty on two counts of the indictment and sentenced him to 10 years' imprisonment.[126] In a dissenting opinion, dated November 25, 1946, Dr. István Gálfalvy, the presiding professional judge, argued that the *Nyilas* would have robbed the Jews even in Berend's absence and that his presence possibly prevented the *Nyilas* from abusing the victims. In his view,

Berend was only guilty of his interview in the *Harc,* for which he should have received only one year in prison.[127]

Shortly after the judgment was rendered, Berend filed several appeals with the National Council of People's Tribunals (*A Népbíróságok Országos Tanácsa*—NOT), requesting a reversal of the lower court's decision.[128] The NOT panel, headed by Dr. Zoltán Szabó, concurred with the arguments advanced in the appeal. While upholding the lower court in the acquittal of Berend on four counts of the indictment "in the want of evidence" of criminal wrongdoing, the NOT reversed the lower court's judgment on the two other counts, including the charges of war crimes and crimes against the people, "in want of offense" (*bűncselekmények hiányában*). In its decision of April 11, 1947, NOT emphasized that Berend's activities had been generally helpful for the Jews and highlighted his positive deeds in the ghetto of Budapest during 1944 and January 1945.[129]

Shortly after his exoneration, he settled in the United States, where he changed his name to Albert B. Belton. His release after almost two years in custody did not end the controversy over his alleged role before and after the occupation. The suspicions and rumors relating to his wartime actions continued unabated for many decades in spite of the NOT decision, which was also viewed with some skepticism.[130] While those who were helped by him—and quite a few probably owed their survival during the last few months before the liberation to his assistance—continued to swear by him, many others continued to question the propriety of his wartime behavior. Especially bitter and critical in their assessment of Berend were the former leaders and officials of the Jewish Council, most of whom had, for some unknown reason, not been invited to testify at the trial. Perhaps this was because several Council members and officials had themselves been subjected to various legal proceedings and some of them were in fact held for a while in custody just a year earlier.[131] Several of them, including Stern, Eppler, and Gergely, prepared their statements about the Council's activities, assessing their own and Berend's allegedly detrimental role in it, *before* the NOT issued its final verdict.[132] Others, including Freudiger and Pető, revealed their critical assessment of Berend many years thereafter.[133] In writing their memoirs or statements, most of them depended upon their own experiences, although their judgments and perceptions may also have been influenced by the press reports of 1945–46 and the first documentary historical accounts published by some nationally known figures, which were equally condemnatory of Berend.[134] Two members of the Council, Nagy and Török, were less specific in their negative view, though the latter traced Berend's behavior to certain negative psychological traits.[135] Freudiger's assessment was reinforced by the periodic communications of Emil Bertl, the former editor of the parliamentary records of the lower house who was transferred after the occupation to serve with Endre and Bosnyák in the new Jewish Department of the Ministry of the Interior.[136] It received additional support during the Eichmann Trial in 1961–62, when the Israel Police unearthed a document stemming from Dieter Wisliceny, in which Eichmann's deputy identified Berend as "Endre's informer."[137] This section of the document was used by Freudiger in his testimony of May 25, 1961, describing how he was allegedly denounced to Endre and Eichmann as "the head of a Jewish conspiracy," compelling him to leave Hungary on August 9, 1944.[138]

Notwithstanding the NOT decision of 1947, Berend's public role during the Holocaust period continued, with a few exceptions,[139] to be viewed in a generally negative fashion in published memoirs,[140] histories,[141] and in full-length books[142] as well as articles.[143] Perhaps his critics have judged Berend too harshly, unmindful of the factors that may have driven him—a basically tragic figure—to emerge from the obscurity of a small provincial parish to the national notoriety engendered by his having been appointed by Endre to the central Jewish Council. While the instinct of survival may have played a role, as it indeed does in the behavior of practically all men, he may have also been motivated by a conviction that the approach followed by the establishment communal and Zionist leaders was counterproductive, if not fundamentally harmful. It appears that in contradistinction to Kasztner and his Zionist colleagues who pursued the SS-line of rescue (chapter 29) and to Stern and his Neolog and Orthodox associates, who preferred the bankrupt legalistic-formalistic approach to winning the race with time, Berend may have been convinced that the best way to save Hungarian Jewry was to deal directly with the Hungarian Right-radical leaders who were involved in the Final Solution program.

This approach might have yielded some results had Berend striven to gain the confidence of the other members of the Council instead of following a secretive, suspicion-arousing "Lone Ranger" approach in dealing with the Hungarian Right radicals. Moreover, although he may not have been aware of it in the midst of the tragic events of 1944, Berend's assumptions were historically disproven, for the Hungarian Nazis on whom he counted for some relief had outdone even the Germans in the eagerness with which they pushed the round-up, ghettoization, and deportation of the Jews. The SS were amazed by the speed and efficiency with which the Hungarian Nazis had acted, stating that in no parts of occupied Europe had they gotten such cooperation.

The Reorganized Council's Operations

Though the reorganized Jewish Council operated under the appointment of Endre, reflecting in a way the formal reestablishment of Hungarian jurisdiction over Jewish affairs, its functions continued to be identical with those of its predecessor, which was primarily under SS control. The beginning of its operations coincided with the launching of the mass deportations, involving the daily removal of approximately 12,000 Jews to Auschwitz. There was clear-cut evidence that the Jews were no longer simply being discriminated against and robbed; they were being destroyed. Nevertheless, the Council continued to help lull the Jews into submission. On May 19, when the Jews of Carpatho-Ruthenia and northeastern Hungary were already being gassed, the Council appealed to the Jews to trust in its activities. It called on them to "trust and believe" and to give the Council "unconditional and understanding confidence." The Council argued that some of the Jews "view the activities of the Council in an alien, nay inimical fashion" and that their criticism "normally leads to severe inferences not only at the expense of the Council but also of truth itself."[144]

Almost completely oblivious of the inferno around it, the Council continued to pursue bureaucratic technical details relating to its proposed bylaws. As the trains with their daily quota continued to roll toward the death camps, the Council agreed on a draft on May 22 and submitted it for approval to the Ministry of the Interior.[145] It was never formally approved because of the opposition of Bosnyák, who presumably favored the draft he had worked out in cooperation with Berend.[146] Nevertheless, the Council continued to operate under its provisions as though the Ministry of the Interior had approved it. With the Final Solution program in full swing, the Council's work was further complicated by the question of the increasingly large number of converts whose cause was being championed by the Christian churches.

The Association of the
Christian Jews of Hungary

The composition of the Provisional Executive Committee of the Jewish Council remained intact until the middle of July, when the Christians of Jewish origin were allowed to form their own organization. This came about largely as a result of the Christian churches' interventions against the inhuman treatment of the Jews and above all the inclusion of converts in the anti-Jewish measures. Unfortunately, the opposition of the Christian church leaders was expressed primarily in official communications to the various government leaders rather than in public statements or sermons. Nevertheless, their official pressure campaign became ever more intense during the summer, when the mass deportations were taking place. But it was only after Jusztinián Cardinal Serédi had decided to issue a pastoral letter on June 29 to be read in the Catholic churches that Prime Minister Sztójay reacted. Partially as a bargain under which the Prince Primate of Hungary agreed to withhold the distribution of the pastoral letter, Sztójay expressed a readiness to offer certain concessions relating to the deportations and the converts. The deal was hammered out at the Cardinal's summer home at Gerecs on July 7–8. Under its provisions Sztójay revealed that the converts had been allowed to form their own organization and that the deportation of the Jews of Budapest was suspended. He hastened to add that in case the deportations resumed, the converts would be exempted.[147]

By that time, of course, the deportations from the provinces had been completed and the Regent himself, under great pressure—at home and especially abroad—had decided against the continuation of the deportations. The news of the Serédi–Sztójay agreement leaked out, leading to a new wave of conversions among the Jews of Budapest, which the Nazis hoped to prevent or ignore in their anti-Jewish operations.

The establishment of a separate organization for the Christians of Jewish origin was also advanced by those who recognized the growing tension between the converts and the Jews, as well as their respective leaders. The leadership and bureaucracy of the Jewish Council were reportedly more concerned and preoccupied with the problems confronting the Jews who continued to cling to their religion than with those of the converts, who had many more protectors among the Christians. The tension that divided the two persecuted groups tended to become unbearable in spite of the tremendous efforts of Török, who went out of his way to secure help for both groups. These tensions were reflected in the letter Pastor József Éliás, the head of the Good Shepherd Mission (*Jó Pásztor Misszió*), wrote to Török on May 24, nine days after the beginning of the deportations:

It is the view of our Reformed Church, and all Christian denominations concur, that the congregants of Jewish origin to whom they minister should not in any connection come under the jurisdiction of another congregation, in this case the Jewish community. We are approaching the Royal Hungarian Government with a request that for the management of the affairs of the congregants of Jewish origin and Christian religion a special committee should be established or a government commissioner appointed on the basis of the suggestion of Church leaders. In other words, we cannot accept that an organization whose membership consists overwhelmingly of members of the Jewish community should deal with members of our church. It is unfair from the point of view of the ratio, and also from the point of view of the importance of the three historical churches of Hungary, that of the nine current members of the executive committee only one is of the Christian religion, but even if representatives of the three historical Christian churches [Catholic, Reformed, and Evangelical] were included—numbering a minimum of three—we could not agree that an authority having a majority of Jews should rule over those of the Christian religion. However, until the wishes of the churches can be realized, we take as a basis the situation—guided in this also by our respect for the laws—which His Excellency the Minister of the Interior determined by his Decree when he appointed you, sir, to the nine-member executive committee. In other words, as long as a better solution is not at hand, we shall support you, Sir, in your difficult work, but we expect and request you to represent our points of view and thus also the views of the individuals of Jewish origin in our Christian churches. It was the Central Council, which not only did not have a representative of the Christian churches but did not even have a member of the Christian religion, which vacated the apartments and imposed material burdens on the members of our churches also, but it is my definite experience that when those of Christian religion turned to them for support they were directed to the Christian churches. The Central Council did not inform the Christian churches about the measures affecting the converts, and for this very reason it never asked for their support, but took it for granted that it also had jurisdiction over members of the Christian churches. This situation was natural in terms of the regulations of the authorities, but not natural if one takes into account the view that if those of Jewish religion and those who persisted in remaining Jews had been placed under the jurisdiction of the Christian churches, the latter would officially have informed the Jewish community as well as each denomination. I would not have raised this issue if a government-appointed popular organ had been in operation and had offered equal social care to all those of Jewish origin, and not only an equal sharing of burdens. Since, however, it was appointed as a popular organ but in reality acted as a denominational organization, it is disheartening to observe the silence with which it treated the Christian churches and their competent spiritual and social organs. Since, however, these trying times are not appropriate for raising questions of this type, I merely emphasize that until the wishes of the Church leaders can be fulfilled, the current state of affairs must cease and the situation be relatively improved.[148]

Speaking in behalf of the churches Éliás suggested that:

- Török be in charge of all matters affecting those Jews of Christian religion.
- The ratio of the Jews of Christian religion be ascertained in order that they might share in the burdens as well as enjoy the care offered by the Council proportionately.
- Only Christians be assigned to implement decisions affecting Christians.
- Török be in charge of the funds collected by Christians for use in behalf of the new Christians.
- Representatives of the Good Shepherd Mission and of the Holy Cross Society (*Szent Kereszt Egyesület*) be liaisons.
- The converted Jews be represented in the Council by delegates of the three major Christian churches.[149]

Török brought these suggestions to the attention of the Council, but they were not implemented. The leaders of the Christian churches, however, kept up their pressure in the Ministry of the Interior. In response to these interventions, Albert Takács, Endre's confidant and secretary, received a delegation of the converted Jews on July 6, when the deportations from the provinces and the communities in the immediate vicinity of Budapest were being completed. One of the results of the meeting was that the delegation consisting of Török, Endre Somló, and András Sebestyén prepared a draft of the bylaws for the envisioned establishment of a separate Association of the Christian Jews of Hungary (*Magyarországi Keresztény Zsidók Szövetsége*).[150] The draft, consisting of 28 articles, was submitted to Takács the following day together with a cover letter in which Török and his colleagues requested that since the converted Jews would no longer belong to the Provisional Executive Committee of the National Association of the Jews of Hungary they be exempted, in accordance with the wishes of the churches, from wearing the Yellow Star.[151]

On July 11, Török sent a copy of the draft bylaws to Bishop László Ravasz. The same day, however, Török was informed by both Blaskovich and Takács that since the establishment of a separate organization would require a special government decree the questions affecting the converted Jews would be handled by a special unit of the Jewish Council. The leaders of the churches and of the Good Shepherd Mission and the Holy Cross Society were not easily deterred from their firm decision to have the converted Jews removed from the jurisdiction of the Association. The governmental legal hurdle was overcome on July 12, when Jaross recommended to the Cabinet that the decree establishing the Jewish Council be amended to make possible the establishment of an Association of the Christian Jews of Hungary to protect and advance the interests of the Christian Jews under the same provisions that were in effect for the Jewish Council.[152]

The decree establishing the new organization was issued on July 14[153] concurrently with Jaross' appointment of the members of its Provisional Executive Committee: Dr. György Auer, András Sebestyén, Sándor Antal, Pál Rózsa, Dr. Mihály Kádár, Sándor Török, Elemér Tamás, Endre Somló, and Sándor Balassa.[154]

Auer and Török were elected President and Vice President, respectively, but it was Török who remained the Association's actual executive leader.[155] Soon after the establishment of its headquarters in the Scottish Mission (*Skót Misszió*) in Vörösmarty Street, the new Association's leaders contacted the lay and religious leaders of the Christian churches, including Albert Radvánszky, the vice president of the upper house and Superintendent of the Evangelical Church, thanking them for their support and asking them for continued assistance.[156]

With the establishment of the new association, a number of organizations of converts requested that their members be admitted into it and removed from the jurisdiction of the Jewish Council. Among the most important of these organizations were the Christian Fraternal Congregations of Hungary (*A Magyarországi Keresztyén Testvérgyülekezetek*) and the Christ-Believing Jews (*Krisztus-hivő zsidók*). Their appeal was fully supported by Török's organization.[157]

Toward the end of July, the Association of the Christian Jews submitted a lengthy memorandum to Jaross requesting his assistance in easing some of the major problems affecting its members. It emphasized the plight of the very young and of the elderly and made a series of suggestions for the establishment of special homes and clinics and for allowing the neutral powers and the International Red Cross to assist the needy.[158]

The Association of the Christian Jews of Hungary continued to expand its operation until shortly after the Szálasi coup. At that time, it ceased to exist for all practical intents and purposes and the defense of the interests of the converts reverted back to the Provisional Executive Committee of the Association of the Jews of Hungary.[159]

Reorganization of the Provisional
Executive Committee

The vacancies created by the resignation from the Provisional Executive Committee of Török and Samu Kahan-Frankl, who decided to go into hiding, were filled on July 22, by the appointment of Ernő Boda and Lajos Stöckler, a lace manufacturer.[160]

Stöckler began his activities on the Committee on July 27, when the situation of the surviving Hungarian Jews, living by now almost exclusively in Budapest, had improved somewhat. He soon emerged as a gadfly on the Committee, challenging the secrecy with which the top leaders—Stern, Pető, and Wilhelm—tended to conduct their deliberations and reach decisions for which the entire Committee was normally made responsible.[161]

In the month that followed rumors were rampant about the "imminent" deportation of the Budapest Jews. During the Lakatos era, deportation rumors were replaced by those about the "secret plan" to concentrate the Jews somewhere in the countryside to "save" them from deportation. The secret negotiations for the prevention of the concentration, which was rightly viewed as a possible prelude to deportation, were conducted with Lieutenant-Colonel László Ferenczy, who had earlier directed the ghettoization and deportation program in the provinces. On the Jewish side, the negotiations were conducted by Ottó Komoly and the three top leaders of the Committee, who tried to take advantage of Ferenczy's search for an alibi at the time (see chapter 25). Those members of the Committee, including Stöckler, who were necessarily kept in the dark about the negotiations became restive and bombarded the top leadership with memoranda asking to become involved in the decision-making process.[162]

Stöckler emerged as the champion of the interests of the poorer strata of Jewry.[163] In his defense of the "little unprotected" Jews, he went as far as to oppose the establishment of so-called "protective houses" on Pozsonyi Road for the Jews that had obtained Swedish protective papers because that, he feared, would involve the relocation of the unprotected Jews in the affected buildings. Stöckler (and his family) also deviated from the other members of the Committee by refusing to take advantage of the opportunity not to wear the Yellow Star.

The attitude and the policies of the Jewish Council came under harsh criticism not only by its own gadflies but also by the Rabbinate of the Jewish Community of Pest. As its meeting of July 26, chaired by Rabbi Zsigmond Groszmann, the Rabbinate adopted the following statement aimed basically at the rejection of any responsibility for the catastrophe that befell the Jews of Hungary:

At the suggestion of Dr. Ferenc Hevesi, our Rabbinate has unanimously recorded before the tribunal of its own conscience, and also so that future generations and posterity will be able to see clearly, that our Rabbinate, which has faithfully fulfilled its tasks to the end, is in no way responsible for the grave ordeals that befell Hungarian Jewry and attacked our community from without and within. Even when in March the outside authorities empowered the leaders of our community to submit proposals for the nomination of a Central Jewish Council, not a single member of our Rabbinate was nominated for the Council by the denominational elements. Since then, the Jewish Council has never asked the opinion of our Rabbinate, even in religious matters; all its activities, procedures, and measures were taken without the knowledge of our Rabbinate, as if Jewry were not a religious community. We find it especially important to state that the use of our synagogues for profane purposes and thereby the prevention of our believers from worshiping there and of the holding of services contributed in no small measure to the spread of the sad epidemic of conversion. Moreover, a large number of the congregants revealed to us, both orally and in writing, the view that the Jewish Council, because of either impotence or indifference, left the believers in the lurch, so that in their desperation they tried to find safety by escaping from Judaism. The spread of this sad conversion movement was accelerated by the fact that an official conversion organ was operating in our communal building under the aegis of the Jewish Council. It required the intervention of our Rabbinate for this organ to cease its activities in the building. Our Rabbinate consequently disclaims all responsibility for the spiritual disintegration caused by these violations. We also disclaim any responsibility for the deportation of a part of Hungarian Jewry, partly because when we wanted to intervene with the leading clergymen of the churches and with high government officials our offers were rejected by the president of the Council, and partly because our denominational authorities gave our initiative no support or authority whatsoever; on the contrary they tried to prevent our activities of this type. Only recently, the leading denominational elements failed to accept the proposal of the Rabbinate that they intervene with the outside authorities to make possible the ritual burial of our dead, as if the burying of the dead were not a religious rite but only some kind of administrative act.[164]

The tension between the Rabbinate and both the Stöckler faction and the leading triumvirate increased considerably during the fear-ridden days before the planned deportation of the Jews of Budapest on August 26–27, and the subsequent weeks when plans were made for their concentration in the provinces. However, the situation eased considerably during the Lakatos era and some of the leading officials associated with the Council even began to set up special committees to aid the deported Jews. During the euphoric days just before October 15, when Horthy tried to extricate Hungary from the war against the Allies, they established a number of units designed, *inter alia,* to collect and classify the letters to be received from the deportees, to determine the place of the camps and the number of their inmates, to assure the acquisition or preparation of lists of the deportees, to collect food, clothing, and medicines for the deportees and to make general preparations for the returning deportees, including the identification of their apartments and the setting up of hospitals, homes, and other institutions for the young and the elderly.[165]

The naive optimism associated with these plans ended on October 15, when Szálasi came to power with German assistance. In the wake of these events the Jewish Council was once again reorganized. Lieutenant-Colonel László Ferenczy, who only a few months earlier had tried to play the savior of the Jews of Budapest, reemerged as the new regime's plenipotentiary in Jewish matters. He agreed to the establishment of a new Jewish Council[166] composed of Samu Stern as President, Lajos Stöckler as deputy, and Béla Berend, István Földes, Ottó Komoly, József Nagy, Miklós Szegő and Lajos Vas as members.[167] Although the new Council was never formally appointed, it acted as such until the end of the occupation of Budapest. Though not a formal member of the Council, Domonkos, the head of the Economic and Technical Department, emerged during the *Nyilas* era as one of the most courageous and effective Jewish leaders.

Shortly after his reappointment Stern decided to follow the example of Pető and Wilhelm and went into hiding. (The three had been warned that since they were among those actively involved in Ferenczy's earlier "rescue" schemes and knew too much, Ferenczy had decided to eliminate them.)[168] His place on the Council was taken over on October 28, 1944, by Stöckler, who in this capacity also came to head the Ghetto of Budapest, where he worked indefatigably.[169]

The members of the Council did their best during the few months before the liberation of Budapest on January 17, 1945, to care for the emaciated and disease-ridden Jews of the ghetto, still the largest concentration of Jews in Nazi-Europe (see chapter 26). They were witnessing the last phase of the process that led to the annihilation of close to 500,000 Hungarian Jews—a process that began ten months earlier with the establishment of the first Council. Few, if any, of them at the time had wanted to believe that the first anti-Jewish measures, including those designed to intimidate and isolate the Jews, were but a prelude to their ghettoization and deportation.

Notes

1. Heydrich, and the Germans generally, alternately referred to the Council as *Judenrat* (Jewish Council) or *Ältestenrat* (Council of Elders).

2. 3363-PS. The document is reproduced in *Nazi Conspiracy and Aggression* (Washington, D.C.: Government Printing Office, 1946), 6:97–101.

3. "Eichmann Tells His Own Damning Story," *Life*, 49, no. 22, (November 28, 1960):109.

4. Some of the local community leaders who were subsequently appointed to head their local Jewish Councils kept diaries of their work and experiences. See, for example, Alexander Leitner's manuscript, *Die Tragödie der Juden in Nagyvárad*, (Jerusalem: Yad Vashem, JM/2686), 96 pp. The English version is available in the Central Zionist Archives, Jerusalem, File No. S26/1469.

5. Munkácsi, *Hogyan történt?* p. 14.

6. Thuránszky was relieved of his position on April 8, 1944. *Budapesti Közlöny* (Budapest Gazette), no. 80 (April 9, 1944):1.

7. Krumey's and Wisliceny's instructions were identified in a nine-point "attendance list" distributed for all those present. For text see *Vádirat*, 1:25–28.

8. Munkácsi, *Hogyan történt?*, p. 17.

9. *Ibid.* See also Lévai, *Fekete könyv*, p. 89. In his statement of December 28, 1945, Stern mistakenly claims that the meeting was held on March 25, 1944, at which time the Germans demanded the establishment of a Jewish Council to be headed by him. *HJS*, 3:5.

The Zionists, who were co-opted into the leadership of the Jewish community, expressed their lack of confidence in the official leadership at the meeting of the Jewish Community of Pest of March 19, 1944. Munkácsi, *Hogyan történt?*, p. 12.

10. Lévai, *Fekete könyv*, p. 89.

11. Ernő Pető was born in Vámos, Veszprém County, on August 20, 1882. At the time of his election to the Jewish Council, he served as Deputy President of the Jewish Community of Pest. Shortly after the war, he and the two other lawyers on the Council, Boda and Wilhelm, were the subject of a disciplinary inquiry by the Chamber of Lawyers (*Ügyvédi Kamara*), the Budapest Bar, on suspicion of collaboration. All three were cleared, the Chamber having concluded that they did everything possible to help the Jews under the given circumstances. In March 1955, Pető settled in São Paulo, Brazil, where he died in the late 1960s. For his account of his activities on the Council, see *HJS*, 3:49–74. Károly Wilhelm was born in Kassa on February 17, 1886. After he received his doctoral degree in law, he became associated with the Budapest stock exchange. His law firm represented the Hatvan Sugar Factory and other industrial enterprises. At the time of his appointment to the Council, he was serving as one of the leaders of the Jewish Community of Pest. He survived the *Nyilas* era by hiding in the cellar of the Swiss Legation. After the liberation he became a general director of the Hungarian Sugar Industry Inc. (*Magyar Cukoripar*), a position he held until the industry's nationalization. He left Hungary in 1948 for Switzerland, where he died on September 20, 1951. Personal communication by Mrs. Magda Pastor, Wilhelm's daughter.

12. Berend outlined his views during his trial in Budapest in 1945–47 (see below). Stöckler reviewed his role in the Council in a series of articles published in 1947. See his "Gettó elött—gettó alatt" (Before the Ghetto—During the Ghetto), *Uj Élet* (New Life), Budapest, January 22, 30; February 6, 13, 20; March 6; April 17, 1947. (Referred to hereafter as Lajos Stöckler.) For more information on Berend and Stöckler, see below.

13. *HJS*, 3:6.

14. Stern and Pető claim that during the deportation of provincial Jewry, Horthy was isolated and was still inclined to believe Minister of the Interior Jaross, who misled him on the realities of the deportation. *HJS*, 3:17, 55.

15. *Ibid.*, pp. 6–7.

16. *A Magyar Zsidók Lapja* (*The Journal of Hungarian Jews*), Budapest, January 13, 1944, p. 4. Stern was born in Jánosháza on January 5, 1874, died in Budapest on June 9, 1946, and was buried two days later in the family plot in the Jewish Cemetery at Rákoskeresztur. *Uj Élet* (New Life), Budapest, June 13, 1946, p. 4.

17. For an evaluation of what the Hungarian Jewish leaders and the other Jewish and non-Jewish leaders of the world knew about the Final Solution program and when they learned its secrets, see chapter 23.

18. *Vádirat,* 2:44–45.

19. *Ibid.*

20. The leaders of the Bratislava *Vaada*, including Gisi Fleischmann and Rabbi Weissmandel, began their negotiation with Wisliceny late in May 1942—soon after the first deportation of a large number of Slovak Jews to Auschwitz—to halt the deportation of the European Jews to Poland against the payment of $2 million. The plan, which did not include the Polish Jews, came to be known as the "Europa Plan." For details see chapters 23 and 29.

21. Philip Freudiger, *Five Months.* Manuscript submitted to this author on November 21, 1972, p. 21.

22. Statement of Imre Reiner. Israel Police, Bureau 06, Eichmann Trial Document 347.

23. Reiner, statement.

24. Freudiger, *Five Months,* p. 10.

25. *Ibid.* This is probably the explanation of Wisliceny's "power" to meet the requests of Freudiger and of some of the other members of the Council.

26. *Ibid.*

27. See, for example, Leitner's *Die Tragödie der Juden in Nagyvárad,* p. 32. An Orthodox, Mr. Leitner was the leader of the Jewish Council in Nagyvárad. He was among those brought to Budapest in June, 1944.

28. "Eichmann Tells His Own Damning Story." *Life,* 49, no. 23 (December 5, 1960):146.

29. The text of the certificate read: ". . . der Inhaber dieses Ausweises ist Mitglied des Verbandes Ungarländischer Juden. Es ist von jeder Massnahme gegen diese Person und gegen mit ihm in gemeinsamen Haushalte wohnenden Familienangehörigen Abstand zu nehmen, bzw. ist mit der unterfertigten Dienststelle die Verbindung aufzunehmen." The German part was signed first by SS-*Obersturmbannführer* Krumey and later by SS-*Hauptsturmführer* Krieger. The Hungarian part was signed by Koltay in the name of the *Magyar királyi Állambiztonsági Rendészet* (Royal Hungarian State Security Police).

30. In addition to the certificates allocated to the Council, the German and Hungarian police authorities also sold such certificates to a few rich individuals.

31. *Beszámoló a Magyarországi Zsidók Szövetsége Ideiglenes Intéző Bizottsága munkájáról* (Report on the Work of the Provisional Executive Committee of the Association of the Jews of Hungary), by György Gergely (manuscript), 1945, p. 12. (Hereafter cited as *Beszámoló.*) Gergely's authorship was authenticated by Berend.

32. For further details on these issues, including the Council's rationalizations, see Stern's statement in *HJS,* 3:7–8.

33. Lajos Stöckler, *Uj Élet,* February 6, 1947. See also Munkácsi, *Hogyan történt?,* p. 218.

34. *HJS,* 3:212.

35. *RLB,* Doc. 248.

36. For an evaluation of the character of central and local Jewish leadership and of the structure of the Jewish communities before the occupation, see chapter 3.

37. Of the close to 18,000 provincial Jews, approximately 16,000 survived by being

taken to Strasshof and the others by being included in the Kasztner group (see chapters 21, 29).

38. The judgment in the Bendzin case was handed down on May 22, 1964. *The New York Times*, May 23, 1964.

39. For example, he helped Samuel Springmann penetrate Hungarian organizations, including the KEOKH. Béla Vágó, "The Intelligence Aspects of the Joel Brand Mission" in *YVS*, 10:119.

40. Police of Israel. Bureau 06. Eichmann Trial Document 367.

41. *Beszámoló*, p. 5.

42. With the launching of the anti-Jewish measures, the Jews were no longer considered "Hungarian Jews" but "Jews living in Hungary." Accordingly, the paper's name was changed on April 27, 1944, to *Magyarországi Zsidók Lapja* (The Journal of the Jews of Hungary).

43. *A Magyar Zsidók Lapja*, March 30, 1944, p. 1.

44. Munkácsi, *Hogyan történt?*, pp. 20–21.

45. Although the Germans issued special travel permits, the meeting was attended by only a few provincial Jewish leaders, among them Dr. József Greiner of Pécs, Imre Wesel of Szombathely, Dr. Ákos Kolos of Kassa, Dr. Gyula Unger of Győr, Dr. Miklós Szegő of Székesfehérvár, Dr. Samu Meer of Nagyvárad, Dr. Sándor Mandel of Szolnok, Dr. József Fischer of Kolozsvár, Dr. Róbert Pap of Szeged, Mór Feldmann of Miskolc, Sándor Leitner of Nagyvárad, and Jenő Ungár of Debrecen. *Ibid.*, p. 21.

46. Munkácsi, *Hogyan történt?*, pp. 21–22.

47. Leitner, *Die Tragödie der Juden in Nagyvárad*, p. 12.

48. *Ibid.*

49. *Ibid.*, p. 14. Interestingly, Freudiger, Kahan, and Leitner all survived: Freudiger by escaping to Romania and Kahan and Leitner by having been included in the Kasztner group.

50. Freudiger, *Five Months*.

51. Reference is to the Jews interned at the Kistarcsa camp following their arrest during the first days of the occupation.

52. The publishers of the *Orthodox Zsidó Ujság* (Orthodox Jewish Newspaper) informed the paper's readers on April 6 that due to reasons beyond their control the paper could no longer be published. *A Magyar Zsidók Lapja*, April 6, 1944, p. 8.

53. Munkácsi, *Hogyan történt?*, pp. 28–33.

54. *Ibid.*, p. 62.

55. Statement by Elizabeth Eppler, *Dokumentációs Ügyosztály* (Documentation Department) of the Jewish Agency for Palestine, Budapest. Protocol 3647, dated February 27, 1946. Available at the YIVO, Archives File 768.

56. *Ibid.*

57. Munkácsi, *Hogyan történt?*, p. 82.

58. Statement by Elizabeth Eppler cited above.

59. The nominal head of the Department was Dezső Székely. Statement by Elizabeth Eppler cited above. See also chapter 26.

60. *Magyarországi Zsidók Lapja*, May 11, 1944, p. 4. The rate of conversions increased dramatically during the summer months (chapter 25).

61. Statement of Elizabeth Eppler cited above.

62. Munkácsi, *Hogyan történt?*, pp. 35–36. For further details on the Association, see below.

63. Lévai, *Zsidósors Magyarországon*, p. 84. See also chapter 29.

64. Munkácsi, *Hogyan történt?*, pp. 24–25.

65. Freudiger, *Five Months*.

66. Lévai, *Fekete könyv*, p. 104. See also Munkácsi, *Hogyan történt?*, pp. 36–37.

67. *A Magyar Zsidók Lapja,* April 6, 1944, p. 1.
68. *Ibid.,* p. 2.
69. *Ibid.,* April 13, 1944, p. 1.
70. *Ibid.,* p. 2.
71. *Ibid.,* April 20, 1944, p. 1.
72. Lévai, *Black Book on the Martyrdom of Hungarian Jewry* (Zurich: The Central European Times, 1948), p. 103. See also item 20 in Appendix 3.
73. Among his major anti-Semitic tracts are: *Harc a zsidó sajtó ellen* (Struggle Against the Jewish Press) (Budapest: Held János, 1938), 95 pp.; *A zsidókérdés* (The Jewish Question) (Budapest: Stádium, 1940), 170 pp.; *A magyar fajvédelem úttörői* (Pioneers of Hungarian Racism) (Budapest: Stádium, 1942), 300 pp.; *Die Verjudung unserer Hauptstadt* (The Jewification of Our Capital) (Budapest: Berta, n.d.), 64 pp.; and *Szembe Judeával* (Face to Face with Judea) (Budapest: Centrum, 1943), 463 pp.
74. The importance of Bosnyák's role in the Ministry of the Interior was emphasized by Drs. Lajos Argalás, Erno Munkácsi, and József Nagy in their testimonies in the Berend Trial in 1946. NB. 2.600/1946, pp. 313, 342, and 354.
75. Unlike many of his associates, Bosnyák escaped punishment after the war. With the advance of the Red Army toward Budapest, he disappeared without a trace.
76. Document 96/1944. B. M. of the Ministry of the Interior as cited by Lévai in *Fekete könyv,* p. 109.
77. Munkácsi, *Hogyan történt?,* p. 73. On Páskándy, see *Magyarország tiszti cim- és névtára,* p. 48.
78. Munkácsi, *Hogyan történt?,* pp. 72–74.
79. *Ibid.,* p. 73.
80. See section "Internments through the Council" in chapter 17.
81. *Budapesti Közlöny,* no. 108 (May 13, 1944):3.
82. The appointment did not become official until its publication in the official gazette on May 13.
83. Decree no. 176.774/1944. VII. b. B.M. under which Török was appointed gave his address as 26 Rökk-Szilárd Street, i.e., the building of the National Theological Institute, which then served as an SS detention camp.
84. *Magyarországi Zsidók Lapja,* May 19, 1944, p. 2.
85. Lévai, *Fekete könyv,* p. 120. See also Munkácsi, *Hogyan történt?,* pp. 75–76.
86. Munkácsi, *ibid.,* p. 76.
87. For the sake of consistency the Provisional Executive Committee will continue to be referred to as the Jewish Council.
88. "Néptörvényszék a zsidó tanács felett" (Popular Tribunal on the Jewish Council) in *Fehér könyv* (White Book), eds. Sándor Bródy *et al.* (Budapest: Globus, 1945), p. 71.
89. Lévai, *Fekete könyv,* pp. 119–20.
90. Report of May 4, 1945, prepared by the Political and Police Division of the Budapest Headquarters of the Hungarian State Police (*Magyar Államrendőrség Budapesti Főkapitányságának Politikai és Rendészeti Osztálya*). Berend Trial File NB 2600/1946, p. 5.
91. Munkácsi, *Hogyan történt?,* p. 60.
92. Berend's failure to get along with the Jewish communal leaders of Szigetvár was revealed in the testimony of Ernő Kozári (Friedmann), the uncle of Berend's first wife, Rózsi Belák. NB. 2600/1946, p. 320.
93. Munkácsi, *ibid.*
94. In the 1930s, the Nazis in fact had advocated the separation of Jewry into these two categories. For example, in its issue of May 15, 1935, the *Schwarze Korps* (Black Corps), the official organ of the SS, stated: "The Zionists adhere to a strict racial position and by emigrating to Palestine they are helping to build their own Jewish state. . . . The assimilation-minded Jews deny their race and insist on their loyalty to Germany or claim

to be Christians because they have been baptized in order to subvert National Socialist principles." The Nazis insisted all along that the "attempts of the German-Jewish organizations to persuade Jews to remain in Germany" were not in the best interests of the Reich and were in opposition to National Socialist principles. Lucy S. Dawidowicz, *The War Against the Jews, 1933–1945*. (New York: Holt, Rinehart and Winston, 1975), p. 84.

95. Lévai, *Fekete könyv*, pp. 119–20.

96. Luzsenszky was tried after the war and condemned to 12 years in prison; his sentence was subsequently reduced to three years. *Uj Élet*, Budapest, March 28, 1946, p. 1.

97. "A Magyar Dreyfus-ügy" (The Hungarian Dreyfus Case), *Egyleti Élet* (Societal Life), New York, November 14, 1947.

98. Personal communication, December 3, 1972. See also "Néptörvényszék a Zsidó Tanács felett," pp. 71, 72.

99. "A Magyar Dreyfus-ügy."

100. Trial proceedings of October 21, 1946. NB. 2600/1946, p. 318.

101. *Ibid.*, p. 386. Although the prosecution identified only the letters of April 12 and May 1, Berend in fact wrote his first letter to Endre on April 1. He ended it by stating: "The goal is the same: why should we not do it together?!" He appended to this letter two appendices, containing details of his proposals. Copies of this letter and proposals are in possession of this author.

102. The Berend Trial File, NB. 2600/1946, p. 561. Incidentally, the prosecutor's office was alerted to this portion of Endre's answers to the Americans by Róbert Major, who was then the head of the press division of the Ministry of Justice.

103. Testimony of Miksa Domonkos at Berend's trial in 1946. *Ibid.*, p. 331.

104. From late July on, Gergely first worked for Raoul Wallenberg and then for the International Red Cross in connection with Ottó Komoly's scheme for saving children (chapter 29). After the war, Gergely settled in Sydney, Australia, under the name of George Emile Gregory.

105. According to Gergely, one of Berend's letters was addressed to a high-ranking gendarmerie officer in Szigetvár, his home town. In it he allegedly gave a progress report of his activities in the Council. Memorandum by Gergely (Gregory), dated September 25, 1978 in the author's possession. See also his *Beszámoló*.

106. Gergely claims the committee that worked out the details of the plan consisted of a number of young college graduates, including Erzsébet Windholz, and himself. *Ibid.*

107. The contact with Weinzinger was established through Erzsébet Windholz, whose husband had also been a lumber dealer. *Ibid.*

108. *Beszámoló*, pp. 21–22.

109. NB. 2600/1946, p. 332. See also Stern's statement in *HJS*, 3:21–22.

110. Munkácsi, *Hogyan történt?*, p. 60.

111. "Egy rabbi, a zsidók tömeges megkeresztelkedéséről . . ." (A Rabbi About the Mass Conversion of the Jews . . .), *Harc*, Budapest, July 29, 1944.

112. This point was also emphasized by Bosnyák in his lead article (*A zsidóság áttérése; The Conversion of Jewry*) in the same issue of *Harc:* "The Jews want to save themselves, they want to avoid the fate befalling them; they want to escape not from their Jewishness—we know that this is impossible anyway—but from the consequences of those legal enactments that affect Jewry." In their drive to include all Jews in their deportation program, the Nazis also used the censored Jewish organ to deter Jews from conversions. See, for example, the articles in *Magyarországi Zsidók Lapja* (Journal of the Jews of Hungary), Budapest, July 13, 1944, p. 1 and August 10, 1944, p. 1. Both articles are reproduced in *Vádirat*, 3:177 and 369–70.

113. Lévai, *Zsidósors Magyarországon*, pp. 389–90. This point was also emphasized in the June 4, 1975 judgment of the Court of the Capital (*Fővárosi Bíróság*) of Budapest in the suit launched by Dr. Albert B. Belton (formerly Berend) against the *Kortárs* (Contempo-

rary), a literary journal, and György Moldova, a noted Hungarian novelist, for having published in the February 1975 issue an extract from the novel *A Szent Imre-induló* (The Saint-Imre March) in which Berend's name was, among other things, linked to that of Endre (case no. 4.P.23.238/1975/6).

114. Berend admitted having done this in his confession to the police on May 11, 1945, though it is quite possible that he was at the time under some psychological or physical duress. During his trial, he denied having removed any valuables from the dead. One of Berend' major accusers on this issue, József Izsák, a former Jewish police commander in the ghetto, was discovered to have been an embezzler and it appears that his allegations concerning Berend's thefts were based on hearsay and circumstantial evidence. NB. 2600/1946, pp. 98–99, and 268.

115. *Ibid.,* pp. 264–65. In his police statement he also identified the addresses in Sátoraljaujhely where the valuables could be found.

116. Berend had also confessed to this in his statement of May 8, 1945, cited above.

117. Statement by Berend during the trial. *Ibid.,* pp. 275–76.

118. Statement by Ilona Hores dated May 14, 1945. *Ibid.,* pp. 13–14. In a statement signed before the police authorities on May 12, 1945, Berend, who was confronted with Hores that same day, admitted that Hores' assertions had been correct. *Ibid.,* pp. 6 and 271. However, in the course of the trial, both Berend and Hores asserted that those visits were primarily to help the cause of Jews.

119. *Ibid.,* p. 559. Berend's police file bears no. 3554/1945.

120. See, for example, the police reports of May 4 and 12, 1945, *ibid.,* pp. 5, 6.

121. For the several statements signed by Berend between May 8 and 12, see *ibid.,* pp. 264–71.

122. *Ibid.,* pp. 188–92, and 281. Ferenczy, who met him a few times, in fact emphasized Berend's anti-German stance. *Ibid.,* pp. 189–90. Appearing as a witness in Berend's trial, Dr. László Horti, a deputy people's attorney, declared on March 25, 1946—which was just four days before Endre's scheduled execution—that Endre had stated "that he had received Rabbi Berend and had a long conversation with him about the Jewish problem." Dr. Berend insisted that he had never met Endre. *Ibid.,* p. 296.

123. Indictment No. 1945 Nu. 2164/20. *Ibid.,* pp. 384–88.

124. For the text of the proceedings, including the statements by witnesses for the defense and prosecution, see *ibid.,* pp. 282–373.

125. "Nácibérenc rabbi a népbiróság elött" (A Nazi-Stooge Rabbi Before the People's Tribunal). *Világosság* (Light), Budapest, August 3, 1946.

126. He was found guilty of having participated in the *Nyilas* raid and having given the *Harc* interview. He was found not guilty on the other points of the indictment "in the want of evidence." For the text of the judgment, see NB. 2600/1946, pp. 389–404.

127. For Gálfalvy's dissenting opinion, see *ibid.,* pp. 374–76.

128. *Ibid.,* pp. 451–77.

129. NOT. V. 8293/1946-12. For text, see *ibid.,* pp. 405–24. The NOT decision was published on May 14, 1947, and went into effect on June 11, 1947.

130. According to several Jewish and non-Jewish communal and political leaders of postwar Hungary, the judicial authorities, including NOT, had been subjected to considerable pressure to reverse the lower court's decision allegedly "to prevent a rabbi from going down in history as a war criminal." Personal communication of Dr. Frederic Gorog, the former AJDC head in Budapest and former President of the World Federation of Hungarian Jews headquartered in New York, and public statements of Ödön Antl and Monsignor Béla Varga, former member and President of the postwar Hungarian Parliament, respectively. In a letter addressed to the World Federation of Hungarian Jews, dated November 18, 1976, and certified by Dudley G. Sipprelle, the American Consul in Vienna, on December 9, 1976, Robert Major, the former head of the Press Bureau of the

Hungarian Ministry of Justice, stated among other things: "I was aware that after the conviction of Dr. Berend and before his retrial, several leading personalities of Hungarian Jewish public life approached the judges to plead for Dr. Berend, because they wanted to prevent—after the extreme persecution of Hungarian Jews—the conviction of a Jewish priest." A number of sworn affidavits to this effect, including those of Dr. Frederic Gorog, Dr. Ervin Farkas, and Monsignor Béla Varga, the former President of the Hungarian Parliament, are in the possession of this author.

131. The three lawyer members of the Council—Boda, Pető, and Wilhelm—were summoned to account for their activities on the Council by the Budapest Bar or Chamber of Lawyers (*Ügyvédi Kamara*), but were eventually exonerated. Wilhelm was also arrested in the fall of 1945 together with Miklós Krausz and Hermann Krausz and accused of having accumulated and hoarded large amounts of funds in foreign currency. The authorities suspected that the funds were acquired through the sale of Swiss protective passes. Even Stern was for a while held in protective custody. All of them, however, were eventually freed and exonerated. For further details, see the series of articles in *Világ* (World), Budapest, November 20 and 27, 1945. For unknown reasons, many of the statements collected by the authorities for the possible indictment of the Council and other Jewish leaders, including those of the *Vaada,* were placed in the Berend Trial files. NB. 2600/1946.

132. Stern prepared his statement for the Documentation Section of the Budapest office of the Jewish Agency for Palestine on December 28, 1945. Identified as Protocol No. 3627, it is available at the YIVO (File 768) and the Yad Vashem Institute in Jerusalem (Archives 015). For its published version, see *HJS,* 3:1–47. For Eppler's assessment of Berend, see Protocol No. 3647, dated February 27, 1946, *ibid.* For Gergely's assessment, see his *Beszámoló,* pp. 21–22.

133. Freudiger, *Five Months,* cited above. For Pető's published statement, see *HJS,* 3:49–74.

134. See, for example, *A tizhónapos tragédia* (The Ten Months Tragedy), eds. Ervin Szerelemhegyi, István Gyenes, Károly Kiss, and Jenő Lévai. (Budapest: Müller Károly, 1945), p. 43, and Jenő Lévai, *A margitköruti vészbirák* (The Martial Law Court Judges of Margit Boulevard) (Budapest: Légrády, 1945), p. 70.

135. For Nagy's reference, see "Néptörvényszék a Zsidó Tanács felett," p. 72. See also Török's statement for the Jewish Agency for Palestine dated March 17, 1946, Protocol 3643 in the YIVO Archives, File 768.

136. According to Philip Freudiger, before the transfer Bertl, who had especially good relations with his brother Sámuel Freudiger, had gotten in touch with the Jewish leaders because he was apprehensive about its possible postwar implications. He was encouraged to accept the transfer and be of help to the Jews. Freudiger, *Five Months.*

137. "Bemerkungen des D. Wisliceny zum Bericht des Dr. Kastner" (Observations of D. Wisliceny About Dr. Kasztner's Report), dated March 25, 1947. Bureau 06 of Israel Police, Eichmann Trial Doc. 901.

138. Testimony of Freudiger, Eichmann Trial, Session 52, May 25, 1961. The following day, the *Uj Kelet* (New East), the Hungarian-language daily, ran a front-page account of this revelation under the headline "Berend, the Rabbi of Szigetvár, Was the Informer of the *Nyilas* and Eichmann." Berend's delayed reaction was to prepare a five-page typewritten exposé ("A Bird by Its Feather, Freudiger by His Friend . . . or Barons, When They Meet"), dated January 1970, purporting to demonstrate the mutuality of interests that existed between Freudiger and Wisliceny.

139. See, for example, the highly polemical pamphlet by Levi Ben Simon, a disgruntled Israeli of Hungarian background (formerly known as Lipót Péteri) directed against the Zionist establishment of Israel, *Miért nem lehetett megmenteni 6,000,000 zsidó testvérünket*

a megsemmisitéstől? (Why Was It Not Possible to Save Our 6,000,000 Jewish Brethren From Annihilation?) (Jerusalem: The Author, n.d.), pp. 36 ff.

140. Joel Palgi, . . . *és jött a fergeteg* (A Whirlwind Formed) (Tel Aviv: Neografika, n.d.), p. 374. Also available in Hebrew.

141. Bernard Klein, "The Judenrat," *Jewish Social Studies,* 22, no. 1 (January 1960):27–42. See also his MA Thesis "Hungarian Jewry in the Nazi Period" (New York: Columbia University, 1956), pp. 83–85.

142. György Moldova, "A Szent Imre-induló" (The Saint Imre March) *Kortárs* (Contemporary), 20, no. 2 (February 1975):274–75, 277–78, 292, 301. When this novel was published in book form, Berend's name was changed to Bárány.

143. To Berend's chagrin, several publications continued to link his name with leading Hungarian radical rightists even after the NOT's decision of 1947. Berend, who had changed his name to Albert Bruce Belton at the time of his naturalization, first took legal action in December 1973. At that time, he launched a suit against this writer, the World Federation of Hungarian Jews, and others, for having reproduced in Volume 3 of *Hungarian-Jewish Studies* (New York: World Federation of Hungarian Jews, 1973) the memoirs of Samu Stern and Ernő Pető, which he deemed libelous. He also objected to an editorial footnote relating to his background. After several postponements, a jury trial was held in New York Supreme Court on February 14–26, 1979, before Justice Martin Evans. Dr. Belton's request for $1 million in conpensatory damages and $10 million in punitive damages was dismissed by Justice Evans just before the case was to go to the jury. In his decision of February 26, Justice Evans stated among other things:

Keeping in mind this is a historical research, these are not factual statements by Dr. Braham, these are collections of materials for the purpose of serious study by other scholars, not personal allegations by Dr. Braham, it seems to me there is sufficient evidence here to show that Dr. Braham was not activated by any personal malice, although personal malice really isn't important in this case, it has to be shown by clear and convincing evidence he was activated by malice, which means complete, reckless disregard of the truth and acting in a grossly irresponsible manner. It seems to me there is no evidence in the case he did that. All his researches and studies before that show there was some serious question about the role of Dr. Berend. The reasons for that role in Hungarian Jewry probably have to be explored . . . . Under all these circumstances I think the plaintiff has failed to establish by clear and convincing evidence—or even by a preponderance—that there was in fact any malice in this case and, therefore, under all the circumstances of the case the motion by the defendant will have to be granted. (Supreme Court: State of New York, Part 29: County of New York, Index No. 3955/74.) Rabbi Belton appealed, but on January 22, 1980, the Appellate Division of the Supreme Court unanimously affirmed Justice Evans's judgment. (First Judicial Department in the County of New York, Case 7206.)

In 1975, Belton also sued the *Kortárs* (Contemporary), the literary and critical journal of the Hungarian Writers' League for having published in its February 1975 issue an excerpt from a novel by György Moldova, a well known Hungarian writer. In the novel, *A Szent Imre-induló* (The Saint Imre March), Berend's name is linked with that of Endre. The *Fővárosi Biróság* (Capital's Court) rejected Belton's request for retraction on June 4, 1975, holding that in light of the testimonies at the trial proceedings, the opinions expressed about the plaintiff "cannot be held as unfounded." Fővárosi Biróság, Budapest, File No. 4.P.23.238/1975/6.

144. *Magyarországi Zsidók Lapja,* May 19, 1944, p. 1.

145. *Ibid.,* May 25, 1944, p. 2.

146. Bernard Klein, "The Judenrat," p. 36. See also Ernő Munkácsi's article in *Uj Élet* (New Life), Budapest, April 11, 1946.

147. For the text of the agreement, see Jenő Lévai, *Szürke könyv magyar zsidók megmentéséröl* (Gray Book on the Rescuing of Hungarian Jews) (Budapest: Officina, n.d.), pp. 52–53. For further details on conversions and the attitude of the Christian Churches, see chapters 25 and 30.

148. Munkácsi, *Hogyan történt?*, pp. 152–53.

149. *Ibid.* For Éliás' account see Protocol no. 3652/a, Personal Testimonies File no. 768 at the YIVO.

150. The original name of the association was to be "Association of the Christians of Jewish Origin of Hungary" (*Magyarországi Zsidószármazású Keresztények Szövetsége*). *Vádirat*, 3:139.

151. *Ibid.*, pp. 139–40.

152. *Ibid.*, pp. 138–39, 147–50.

153. For text of Decree no. 2.540/1944. M.E. see *Budapesti Közlöny*, no. 157 (July 14, 1944):4. The text is also reproduced in *Vádirat*, 3:150–51.

154. For Jaross' Decree no. 190.031/1944.VII.b., dated July 14, 1944, see *ibid.*, pp. 152–53.

155. For Török's account see Protocol no. 3643, cited above.

156. For Török's letter to Radvánszky see *Vádirat*, 3:265–66. See also the follow-up letters by Auer and Török with specific requests, dated August 3 and September 15, *ibid.*, pp. 342–43, 553–55.

157. See letters of Dr. Ferenc Kiss of the Christian Fraternal Congregations of Hungary and of Aladár Ungár and Dr. Dezső D. Földes of the Christ-Believing Jews of July 13 and July 19, respectively, as well as that of Auer and Török of July 28 in *Vádirat*, 3:289–93.

158. *Ibid.*, pp. 317–25.

159. On November 28, 1944, János Solymossy, the Ministerial Commissioner in Charge of the Concentration of the Jews (*A zsidók összeköltöztetésére kirendelt miniszteri biztos*), planned to expand the eight-member Council to twelve by adding four Christian Jews, but nothing came of it. Lévai, *A pesti gettó* (The Ghetto of Pest) (Budapest: Officina, n.d.), p. 51.

160. Decree no. 191.449/1944.VII.b. signed by Minister of the Interior Jaross. *Budapesti Közlöny*, no. 169 (July 28, 1944):12.

161. Stöckler summarized his opposition to the "triumvirate" in his statement of May 14, 1946, before the Budapest Police, which was considering the possibility of action against the Council members. For Stöckler's statement, see NB. 2600/1946, pp. 111–14.

162. Interestingly enough Stöckler claims that he too had frequent contacts with Ferenczy and his staff. See his "Gettó elött—gettó alatt," and his memorandum addressed to Stern on August 28 in *Vádirat*, 3:485–87.

163. Lévai, *Fekete könyv*, pp. 203–4.

164. *Vádirat*, 3:266–68. In addition to Rabbis Groszmann and Hevesi, Rabbi Sándor Scheiber, Dr. Farkas, and Dr. Schwartz also attended the meeting, as did Drs. Bernath and Berkovits, as guests.

165. The plans, which were worked out on October 11 and 12, called for the cooperation of the International Red Cross and of the neutral countries, especially Sweden and Switzerland. Among the many officials and Jewish leaders that worked out these plans were Miklós Krausz, Ottó Komoly, Dr. Frigyes Görög, László Kluger, Andor Glücksthal, Ernő Hajek, Erzsébet Eppler, Dr. Imre Heller, Dr. József Nagy, Artúr Weisz, Andor Balog, Dr. Imre Reiner, and several members of the Jewish Council. *Vádirat*, 3:611–15.

166. Lévai, *Fekete könyv*, p. 222.

167. Following the departure of György Polgár on June 30 with the so-called Kasztner group (chapter 29), Földes was appointed to head the Social Department of the Coun-

cil. Komoly was the head of the Hungarian Zionist Association (*Magyar Cionista Szövetség*) and played a leading role after July in pursuing the Hungarian line of rescue (chapter 29). Szegő was the former head of the Jewish Community of Székesfehérvár. He was arrested and murdered by the *Nyilas* on January 5, 1945, when he was on his way home from the ghetto. Lévai, *Fekete könyv*, p. 253. See also E. M., "Dr. Szegő Miklós," *Uj Élet*, January 3, 1946, p. 6.

168. *HJS*, 3:44.

169. Stöckler remained an active, though highly controversial, leader even after the war. He became the head of the MAZOT (*Magyar Zsidók Országos Egyesülete*; National Association of Hungarian Jews) as well as of the Jewish Community of Pest and of the Central Board of Hungarian Jews. It was during his leadership that the Jewish community and its institutions were reorganized and placed under the control of the Communist state. He was arrested by the Secret Police in January 1953 at the height of the anti-Semitic campaign in the Soviet Bloc. On his controversial role during the postwar period, see Eugene Duschinsky, "Hungary," in Peter Meyer, et al., *The Jews in the Soviet Satellites* (New York: Syracuse University Press for the American Jewish Committee, 1953), pp. 373–489.

CHAPTER FIFTEEN

THE FIRST ANTI-JEWISH MEASURES

Arrests and Intimidations

THE SS and Gestapo units which entered Hungary with the *Wehrmacht* forces in the early morning hours of March 19, 1944, began their operations concurrently with the occupation, in accord with plans they had worked out in advance from the intelligence reports and enemy lists provided by the Budapest branch of Wilhelm Höttl's political security and counterespionage office. The enemy lists of persons slated for imprisonment identified Hungary's leading political and economic figures, including the aristocratic-conservative elite on which Jewry largely depended for its safety and the Jewish or Jewish-Christian leaders of business and finance. The lists also included a number of leading artists, journalists, and government officials—including some of the most prominent members of the police, diplomatic, and counterintelligence services—who were deemed actual or potential enemies of the Third Reich. The order of the arrests reflected the interests of the Reich as determined by the RSHA.

Among the leading political and financial-economic figures who were arrested soon after the occupation were Ferenc Keresztes-Fischer, the Minister of the Interior; Lajos Keresztes-Fischer, the head of the Regent's Military Office (*Magyarország Kormányzójának Katonai Irodája*); Counts Antal Sigray, Lajos Szapáry, Iván Csekonics, and György Apponyi, as well as Gusztáv Gratz, Károly Rassay, Dezső Laky, and Gyula Somogyváry, members of the lower house of Parliament; Endre Bajcsy-Zsilinszky, Lajos Szentiványi, and Ferenc Nagy, representatives of the Smallholders' Party; Manó Buchinger, Illés Mónus, Géza Malasits, and Károly Peyer, the leaders and representatives of the Social Democratic Party; György Parragi, I. Lajos, and Pál Szvatkó, journalists; Andor Szentmiklóssy and Aladár Szegedy-Maszák[1] of the Ministry of Foreign Affairs; Lipót Baranyai, Governor of the National Bank; József Sombor-Schweinitzer, a leader of the political police; and Lipót Aschner, Ferenc Chorin, Leó Goldberger, and Móric Kornfeld, leading Jewish financiers and industrialists.[2] The Germans also arrested the leaders of the Polish refugees as well as the representatives of Italy's Badoglio government to Hungary. Around the middle of April, the Germans arrested General István Ujszászy, the chief of the National Defense Center (*Államvédelmi Központ*) of the Ministry of the Interior, Colonel Gyula Kádár, head of the Counterintelligence Service of the General Staff, and Katalin (Varga) Karády, a noted actress.[3]

These arrests took place without any protest on the part of the Sztójay government or the Regent and without any resistance on the part of those affected; a notable exception was Bajcsy-Zsilinszky, who drew a revolver on his captors and was himself wounded. His was the only civilian blood spilled in Hungary on the day of the occupation.[4] Only one member of the lower house, József Közi-Horváth, dared to raise the issue of the arrests and of the violation of the constitutional order when the Hungarian Parliament met on March 22.[5] However, this representative of the city of Győr was ruled out of order by Speaker András Tasnádi-Nagy, and was shouted down by his colleagues.

Some of the leading anti-German political figures managed to get away in time. Among them were Count István Bethlen, who escaped via an underground tunnel in the Castle; Kállay, who found haven in the Turkish Legation;[6] Árpád Szakasits, Anna Kéthly, Zoltán Tildy, and Béla Varga of the Social Democratic and Smallholders' parties, as well as some leading Communists.

Concurrently with the arrests effectuated on the basis of the lists the Nazis brought along, the SS and the Gestapo also arrested a large number of Jews who happened to be in or around the railway stations and boat terminals.[7] When Himmler inquired in the early afternoon of the occupation day about the results of the campaign against the Jewish leaders and apparently found them wanting, Winkelmann ordered the arrest of 200 Jewish lawyers and doctors. Their names were picked out at random from the telephone book and soon after their arrest they were sent to Mauthausen.[8] The arrests were carried out by the organs of the Security Police of the SS under the command of SS-*Obersturmbannführer* Alfred Trenker.

The number of arrested Jews increased with each passing day, so that 3,364 Jews had been arrested in so-called "individual actions" (*Einzelaktionen*) by March 31.[9] On April 2, the Higher SS and Police Leader reported that 3,451 Jews had been arrested, not including "especially important persons." He also noted that in contradistinction to the Hungarian authorities, who felt that the population was not totally in agreement with the arrests effectuated by the Germans, the people welcomed the actions against the richer Jews and only sympathized with the "poor Jews" who were publicly manhandled or whose shops were looted by German military units.[10]

Concern about the possible reaction of the Hungarians to German-initiated anti-Jewish measures was also manifested on April 4, when a *Kommando* of one officer and 12 men of *Einsatzkommando 6* (SS Security Police) arrived from Szeged in Zombor, in the former Yugoslav-held territory of the Bácska, to "carry out an instantaneous arrest of Jews." Since *Obersturmführer* Hanke, the commander of the *Kommando,* had only an oral authorization from *Sturmbannführer* Blunk of the *Einsatzkommando 6* in Szeged, Combat Group Brauner of the 42nd Jäger Division refused to grant his request for men and vehicles, pointing out "the possible consequences for the Hungarian authorities."[11] Authorized individual arrests of Jews, however, continued unabated.

By April 16, when the systematic concentration of the Jews of the northeastern parts of Hungary began,[12] the number of Jews arrested in individual actions increased to 7,289.[13] In his telegram of April 18, transmitting the SS report of the same day, Veesenmayer relayed the communication of the Neumarkt (Marosvásárhely) Command of the Security Police according to which the Hungarian population in its area demanded, in view of the rapidly advancing front, a "quick and radical solution of the Jewish question since the fear of the Jews' revenge is greater than that of Russian brutality."[14]

Most of the Jews arrested in Budapest were temporarily interned in the facilities of the National Theological Institute (*Országos Rabbiképző Intézet*) at 26 Rökk-Szilárd Street. Formally transformed into an "auxiliary detention house" (*kisegítő toloncház*), the Institute in fact served as a Gestapo prison under the overall command of Wisliceny.[15] Its chief Hungarian officer was Pál Ubrizsi, László Baky's almost equally notorious cousin.[16] From here and the other auxiliary detention places, such as the one on Mosonyi Street, the Jews were usually taken to the internment camps at Kistarcsa, Topolya, or Csepel, from where they were among the first to be deported to Auschwitz.[17]

Perhaps the most important of the internment camps was Kistarcsa. The camp, located just northeast of Budapest, had served primarily as an internment camp for political prisoners before the occupation. With facilities for only about 200 persons, the camp was crowded during the occupation with close to 2,000 people. Of these, about 280 were the so-called "prominent" Jews and lawyers the Germans held as hostages after a week's stay at the Rökk-Szilárd detention house. Another category of prisoners consisted of those arrested by the Gestapo on a variety of excuses, including sabotage and espionage. The third group included the Jews who had been arrested by the Hungarian police at the railway stations during and soon after the occupation.

The internment camp was under the command of István Vasdényei, a decent police inspector who did everything possible to alleviate the plight of the inmates. He cooperated with the MIPI and other Jewish leaders to make life in the camp more bearable. Nevertheless, the treatment of the inmates was not uniformly satisfactory and in fact the first and last deportations from Hungary took place from the camp; but these were perpetrated either without the knowledge or against the will of Vasdényei.[18]

The feeding and general care of the prisoners were the responsibility of the MIPI, the agency which also took care of the Polish, Slovak, and other refugees and aliens interned at the Garany, Csörgő, Nagykanizsa, and Ricse camps. MIPI's chief representative at Kistarcsa was Miklós Gál and after his deportation Dr. Sándor Bródy. The feeding of the internees was to a large extent the responsibility of the Orthodox *Népasztal* (the Orthodox People's Table), the public kitchen that operated under the leadership of Mór Weisz. The success of this operation was due to the heroic activities of Sándor Boros. It was from Kistarcsa that the first train left for Auschwitz on April 28. Among the deportees on this train was János Vázsonyi, the former member of the lower house of the Hungarian Parliament. It was also from Kistarcsa that Eichmann succeeded in smuggling out the last group of deportees for Auschwitz.[19]

The arrests of the first few weeks after the occupation served many purposes. The Germans wished to eliminate the actual and potential leaders of the anti-German Hungarian opposition (including the political and aristocratic-gentry friends of the Jews), demonstrate their power in Hungary, intimidate the Jews, and capture hostages in order to blackmail the Jewish community or acquire control over various industries.

With the arrest of the Christian anti-German notables, Jewry became totally isolated and fell easy prey to the Nazis and their new Hungarian hirelings. Seeing the overwhelming power of the Germans, who also enjoyed the services of the Sztójay government (including those of the gendarmerie and the other instruments of coercion), the Jewish leaders thought, at the beginning at least, that their only hope was to gain time by cooperating with them. The hostages were cleverly exploited not only to wrest control over Hungary's major industrial concerns, including the Weiss-Manfréd Works (see chapter 16), but also to lull the Jewish leaders and masses into a false sense of security by occasionally freeing some of them voluntarily or at the specific request of the Jewish leaders.[20]

In order to ease the fears of the agitated Jews, Wisliceny and Krumey assured the Jewish leaders that nobody would be harmed simply because he was Jewish and that they would hold only the "scoundrels" and those who were politically prominent.[21] To give credence to their assertions, they did in fact act favorably on a petition handed in by the Central Jewish Council by releasing from Kistarcsa on March 24 all children under 16, all women over 50, and all men over 60.[22] In response to this favorable action, the news of which spread rapidly, many petitions were filed by the leaders of the provincial Jewish communities with the Central Jewish Council with the request that they be forwarded to the appropriate German authorities.[23] This time, however, practically all of these petitions were left unanswered. The notable exception was the permission granted to the Kasztner group to bring to the capital a few hundred Jews from the various provincial ghettos, especially from that of Kolozsvár, Kasztner's home town, as part of the SS-Kasztner deal, and to Freudiger, after he bought off Wisliceny, to bring to Budapest about 80 Jews, mostly Orthodox, from eight cities (see chapter 29).[24]

Demands and Requisitions

Simultaneously with the mass arrests carried out against the Jews and other opponents of the Third Reich, the SS began the expropriation of the Jewish community. During the first phase of the occupation, the demands and requisitions pertained to the plans of the various German units to set up their household in Budapest and other larger cities. No sooner had Wisliceny and Krumey "reassured" the Jewish leaders on March 20 than the first German demands were submitted to them. The first request, submitted on March 21, involved 300 mattresses, 600 blankets, and 30 printers. The printers were provided immediately and were taken to the printing shop of the Social Democratic Party—the *Világosság* (Light)—in order to make it operational for printing pro-Nazi leaflets and propaganda material.

When the Germans were informed about the difficulty of collecting the mattresses and blankets at such short notice, one of them pulled a revolver and stated that if the request were not fulfilled by 5:00 P.M., he would shoot the responsible leaders. The Jews had to learn that nothing was impossible. ("If one can execute 10,000 Jews in ten minutes, then one can satisfy such a request in one-and-a-half hours also." [25]) By 5:00 P.M. the Germans were given 300 mattresses, which had been taken from under the patients in the Jewish Hospital, and 600 blankets, which had been reserved for the Jewish labor service men. The Jewish leaders were also asked to provide a large number of buckets, mops, brooms, and other cleaning utensils.

That same day the Germans took over the headquarters of the Orthodox community at 31 Dob Street together with the adjacent synagogue and school [26] and transformed them into barracks and workshops. The demands, which strained the treasury of the Jewish community, continued each time an SS or Gestapo unit changed residence. The German demands were soon coupled with those of their Hungarian counterparts, who had set up their headquarters in the same area of the Svábhegy in Buda. [27]

The repeated demands of a variety of German units and organizations during the first few days of the occupation induced Krumey to protect the special interests of the *Sonderkommando*. He therefore concurred with the request of the Jewish leaders to prohibit entry into the premises of the Jewish Council at 12 Síp Street by unauthorized German personnel (figure 15.1).

In addition to ordinary bedding and household goods, the Germans soon began to ask for a variety of luxury items. Their demands included toiletries, perfumes, silverware, automobiles, and lingerie. To set up a household for a high-ranking German officer, for example, Samu Stern was requested to furnish original Watteau paintings. Characteristic of the extent to which the Jews were eager to satisfy the Germans' demands in order to gain their good will (at least this is what they thought at the beginning) was the response to Franz Novak's request. Novak, a music-loving transportation expert in the *Sonderkommando,* had asked for a piano; he was immediately offered eight of them, whereupon he remarked, "I do not desire to open a piano shop; I merely want to play the piano." [28]

Costly and nerve-racking as these demands were, they were soon overshadowed by the more drastic and demoralizing orders for the mass evacuation of apartments. Before the occupation, the Allies had a tacit agreement with the Kállay government to abstain from the bombing of Hungary; after the German occupation they no longer felt re-

Budapest, den 21. 3. 44

Das Betreten dieses Hauses VII., Sip u.12 durch Organe deutscher
Verbände bezw.Organisationen ist *strengstens* untersagt.

Der Chef der Einsatzgruppe I der
Sicherheitspolizei und des SD

i.A.

SS - Obersturmbannführer

N.S.: Bei allfälligen Unklarheiten ist die im Hotel "Astoria"
zuständige Dienststelle fernmündlich anzurufen bezw. aufzusuchen.

Fig. 15.1.
Krumey's order of March 21, 1944. *In English it reads:*

Budapest, 3/21/44

Organs of German societies and organizations are *most strictly* forbidden to
enter this house, VII., Sip u. 12. Infractions will be punished.

Chief, *Einsatzgruppe I* of the Security Police and Security Service
SS-*Obersturmbannführer*

N.B.—In case of doubt, telephone or visit the competent office in the Astoria
Hotel for clarification.

Source: *Vádirat,* 1:33.

strained. The first bombing of Budapest was by the Americans on April
2. British aircraft attacked on April 3 and 4; the targets were the rail
yards of Pest, the armaments works at Csepel, and the Thököl aircraft
components factory. These and subsequent bombings caused considerable damage; they also led to a further exacerbation of the anti-Semitic
fever in the country. The targets were industrial and working class
areas; there were relatively few Jewish casualties—a fact that the Nazis
exploited. They claimed that the Allied "Judaeo-terrorists" had inten-
tionally spared their "local fellow-gangsters."[29]

The first air attacks on Budapest brought forth a wave of anti-Jewish
feeling, which made it easier for the authorities to bring about the mass
evacuation of Jewish apartments for the benefit of the Christian raid
victims. Leaflets were scattered throughout the capital calling for the
execution of 100 Jews for each Hungarian killed by bombing. Rátz and

Kunder visited Veesenmayer about this matter and delivered Sztójay's message that there was danger of a revolution unless something drastic were done. Even Veesenmayer was taken somewhat aback by the severity of the proposed reprisals, for they would have involved the shooting of 30,000 to 40,000 Jews. However, he had no objection to the execution of 10 Jews for each Hungarian killed in any future raid. Rátz and Kunder impressed him with the readiness of the Hungarian government to carry out the reprisal measures.[30]

While the mass executions did not take place, primarily because the German and Hungarian Nazis had already decided on an "orderly" solution of the Jewish question, the Jews of Budapest were required to provide a large number of apartments on short notice. Shortly after the end of the air raid on April 4, Counselor József Szentmiklóssy asked Kurzweil of the Central Jewish Council's Housing Department to visit him at the City Hall (*Városháza*). He informed him in great confidence that Endre would in that same afternoon order the Council to provide 500 apartments within 24 hours to provide shelter for the Christian victims of the attack and as a reprisal measure for the bombings.

A few hours later, the order was officially transmitted by Koltay and Martinidesz (see chapter 6), who appeared in person at the Council's headquarters. There they found only Samu Kahan-Frankl and László Bakonyi, who were later joined by Imre Reiner.[31] Samu Stern, who was contacted by phone, suggested that the raid victims be given shelter in the gymnasium of the Jewish school in Wesselényi Street. Kahan-Frankl and Reiner were taken to the Svábhegy, where they met Eichmann for the first time. Upon being informed that Stern was ill with high fever in the hospital, Eichmann allegedly screamed that he would teach the Council a lesson (*"Ich werde mit Euch Schlitten fahren!"*). The Hungarian and German Nazis considered the offer of the school gymnasium as "another Jewish trick" and ordered that the Council provide 500 apartments within 24 hours by moving the Jews from Districts No. VIII and IX—the area near Pestszenterzsébet, which was hard hit—to Districts No. VI and VII. Szentmiklóssy, who was also present at the meeting, suggested that the requisitions be carried out under the auspices of the Jewish Council, for otherwise the authorities would simply throw the Jews out of their apartments together with their belongings.

The Council convened an emergency meeting for the same evening at 8:00, which, because of the continued air raids, was held in the headquarters' shelter. It continued until the early morning hours. Although some of those present, notably Samu Csobádi, expressed some concern about the tasks assigned to the Council, nobody was willing to assume responsibility for a refusal to carry out the order. That same evening the Council decided to assume the burden of the requisitions and entrusted the execution of the order to Rezső Müller. The requisition forms were printed in a hurry and the employees of the various communal organizations, including the Burial Society (*Chevra Kadisha*) and MIPI, as well as the teachers, were called to an immediate emergency meeting. Following a brief session at which Müller outlined their tasks and issued instructions for their fulfillment, they were dispatched to the Housing Department at City Hall. There they were organized into requisition groups each of which included two Jews, a policeman, and a Christian teacher.

The functions of the requisition groups and of the Christian teachers in particular were outlined in a decree (no. 619.926/1944.XVII.), signed by Szentmiklóssy on April 4. The decree identified the Jewish Council as the chief executive organ in charge of the housing requisitions. The Christian teachers were entrusted with the determination of the items the evicted Jews were expected to leave behind and with the supervision of the inventories that were taken. They were also made responsible, in conjunction with the building superintendents, for ensuring at the time of the actual eviction that all the items identified for retention were left in good order.

The essential provisions of the decree read as follows:

Instructions to the instructional staff assigned as governmental supervisors in the requisitioning of apartments for families made homeless by bombings:

In order to provide lodging for the families that became homeless as a result of air attacks, the Hungarian Royal Ministry of the Interior . . . has ordered the requisitioning at this time of 500 apartments with suitable furniture, to be selected by the Central Jewish Council.

The selection of the apartments is by a procedure whereby the inhabitants are requested to leave their apartments, together with the needed furniture as specified on an inventory, by 4 o'clock today.

In making the inventories, the Mayor of the Capital assigns the members of the teaching staff as representatives of the authorities.

One member of the teaching staff will appear in each apartment in the company of a policeman and two representatives of the Central Jewish Council. The inventory is to be prepared under the supervision of the assigned member of the teaching staff.

The cooperation of the members of the teaching staff will consist of the following:

1. They shall determine what furniture and necessary equipment must be

left in the apartment, i.e., beds and bedding, clothes cupboards, tables, chairs, lamps, clothing, linen, table and kitchen utensils, (plates, flatware, pots, etc.). All such items shall be in such quantities and to such an extent that those left homeless and without anything may continue their life . . . without requiring the most necessary furnishings. . . .

2. Upon the departure from the apartment of its residents, the members of the teaching staff shall ascertain, in the presence of the superintendent, whether the items listed in the inventory are actually left behind. They shall also check the electric and gas meters, and shall list the readings at the end of the inventory; further, they shall check that the fire has been put out in the oven, that water faucets are closed, that all equipment has been left in usable condition, and generally that the apartment has been left in livable condition. Afterwards the doors shall be carefully locked and sealed. . . . The departing resident shall turn over the sealed envelope [containing the inventory and the keys] to the Central Jewish Council.

3. The apartments shall then be assigned by the competent district authorities by turning over the abovementioned envelopes [to the new tenants]. Upon instruction, the members of the teaching staff shall once again appear in the individual apartments with the new tenants. In the presence of the superintendent, they shall determine whether the seal on the door has been left intact, and whether everything is in order inside and that all items on the inventory are present, and whether the gas and electric meters show the recorded readings. After this, the taking over of the apartment by the new tenant shall be certified, and this certificate shall be submitted to the head of the district.[32]

The 60 or 70 requisition groups left on their mission in the late morning of April 5, the day the compulsory wearing of the Yellow Star went into effect. Since the deadline for the submission of the keys and inventories was only a few hours away, many of the Jews were virtually thrown out of their apartments. No sooner had the requisition groups begun their work, than a new order was issued to the Jewish Council to provide an additional 1,000 apartments in retaliation for the bombing that took place in the afternoon of April 4. Because the 1,500 keys were not deposited by 4:00, Koltay arrested Kahan-Frankl and Wilhelm and had them taken to the Svábhegy. They were only released the following day at the intercession of Szentmiklóssy, who blamed the delay on the time required for the assignment of the Christian teachers and policemen. Endre granted an extension of two hours and by 6:30 P.M. 1,500 keys were deposited at the City Hall.[33]

Needless to say the requisition groups, working under the great pressure of an imminent deadline, often acted in an unjust and coarse manner, causing great anguish to the evicted and dispossessed Jews. The Housing Department of the Jewish Council, which was expanded in response to the requisitions, rapidly turned into one of the largest departments of the Council. Wielding considerable power, it operated with a series of subdepartments under the overall command of Müller (who was assisted by Max Trobits and Herman Kun, the department's administrative and legal officers), and by István Kurzweil, Dezső Bánó, György Bognár, and Imre Heller.[34] Rezső Müller, a strong-willed person who had been a private banker before he was mobilized by the Council, was dedicated to the successful completion of the tasks entrusted to him, but in the process often gave reasons for severe criticism of his actions.[35]

The barbarous, Council-assisted housing requisition drive was but the beginning of the avalanche that led to the destruction of the great majority of Hungarian Jewry. It was launched almost simultaneously with the issuance of a large number of decrees designed to bring about the isolation and pauperization of the Jews as a prelude to their ghettoization and deportation.

The Isolation of the Jews: The Anti-Jewish Decrees

The Nazis' approach to the isolation of the Jews of Hungary was similar to the one they had successfully employed elsewhere, with only minor adjustments to fit local conditions. The first measures involved arbitrary administrative actions, including the arrest of the conservative aristocratic-gentry elements and of the captains of industry and finance, many of whom were Jewish or of Jewish origin. They also involved the arrest of Jews in and around the railway stations and boat and bus terminals. Krumey and Wisliceny tried to explain the rationale of these measures during their first meeting with the Jewish leaders on March 20. As it turned out it was merely one of the gimmicks they used to gain the confidence of the Jews.

The prohibition to travel was "legalized" on April 7.[36] It was preceded by a number of measures that aimed at the same objective: the isolation of the Jews. The first major step toward this end was the adoption by the Sztójay government of Decree 1.140/1944. M.E. on March 27, which prohibited the ownership and use of telephones by Jews. Before the year was over, it was followed by over 100 other major decrees, which served as a "legal" cover to bring about the Final Solution (see Appendix 3).[37]

The issuance of anti-Jewish decrees even after the beginning of the mass deportations was in fact part of the strategy to deceive the Jewish leadership and the Jews in the areas not yet affected by deportation into believing that the anti-Jewish measures were directed only against the unassimilated Jews. A statement to this effect was reportedly issued by the Jewish Council, arguing that the continued issuance of anti-Jewish legislation was an indication that the Magyarized Jews would be treated differently. The propaganda campaign had its desired effect. As Eberhard von Thadden emphasized in his report of May 26, 1944, at the time of the deportations from Carpatho-Ruthenia, northeastern Hungary, and Northern Transylvania, "the Jews in the other parts of Hungary remained quiet, in spite of the deportations."[38]

The anti-Jewish measures of the Sztójay government were issued without the signature of Admiral Horthy, who was obviously aware of and perhaps even favored at least some of them, but prudently avoided any direct involvement in their issuance. Along with many other political and military figures, he had no doubt at the time about the final outcome of the war. Horthy's opportunistic posture was revealed during the fateful meeting of the Council of Ministers of March 29. When István Antal, the Minister of Justice, inquired about the procedure to be

---

66

Az igazságügyminiszter ur rámutat arra, hogy eddig az elöző kormányok alatt minden olyan M.E. kormányrendeleteket, amelyek előzőleg vagy utólag a 42-es illetve a 46-os bizottság elé kerültek, előzetes hozzajárulás végett be kellett mutatni a Kormányzó Ur Ő Főméltóságának. Mi erre nézve a kormány álláspontja?

A miniszterelnök ur szerint a Kormányzó Ur Ő Főméltósága az összes zsidó rendeletekre vonatkozólag szabad kezet adott az ő vezetése alatt álló kormánynak és ezek tekintetében nem akar befolyást gyakorolni.

Tudomásul vétetik.

Figure 15.2.
Sample of section 66 of the minutes of the meeting of the Council of Ministers of March 29, 1944, showing Admiral Horthy's attitude toward the issuance of anti-Jewish decrees. It reads in English:

The Minister of Justice pointed out that under previous governments all cabinet decrees requiring action by Committees 42 or 46, either initially or subsequently, had to be submitted for prior approval to His Excellency the Governor. What was the government's position on this matter?

According to the Prime Minister, His Excellency the Governor gave the government headed by him [Sztójay] a free hand with respect to all Jewish decrees, and did not want to exercise any influence in this connection.

Approved
Source: *Vádirat;* 1: Facing p. 72.

followed in the case of decrees normally requiring the prior approval of the Regent, the Prime Minister informed him and the entire Cabinet that Horthy had given the government a free hand in the issuance of anti-Jewish decrees and that he did not want to exert any influence in this sphere (see figure 15.2).[39]

At its session of March 29, the Council of Ministers adopted six major decrees. These related to the prohibition of the employment of non-Jews in Jewish households, the dismissal of Jewish civil servants and lawyers, the exclusion of Jews from the press and theater chambers,[40] and the requirement that Jews declare their motor vehicles, which proved the first step toward their expropriation. Restrictive as these measures were, they were overshadowed by the decree (no. 1.240/1944. M.E.) that provided for the compulsory wearing of the Yellow Star as of April 5—one of the first concrete steps adopted everywhere by the Nazis in the implementation of the Final Solution program.

Marking of the Jews

Conceived as the first in a series of measures leading to their annihilation, the marking of the Jews was clearly designed to separate and differentiate the Jews from the rest of the population. By being compelled to wear the telltale badge, the Jews became clearly identifiable and easily subjected to the subsequent steps in the annihilation process: ghettoization, concentration, and deportation.

The proposal for the introduction of the Yellow Star was submitted in the Council of Ministers by Minister of the Interior Andor Jaross, who argued that the badge was necessary because the nation's public security and military interests required that the "unreliable" Jews be clearly and easily identifiable. Such an identification, he further argued, would make it easier to check the actions and attitudes of the Jews and to keep them away from places where their presence might endanger the military interests of the nation. Since the emphasis was on national security and the military necessity for the introduction of the badge, a "legal" basis for the adoption of the decree was found (in Paragraph 2 of Article 141 of Law no. II of 1939 relating to national defense):[41]

If there is danger in delay, the Ministry may during a period of emergency take measures transcending the authorization specified in subsequent paragraphs by issuing decrees in the administrative, legal, procedural, and legislative spheres within its jurisdiction which are unavoidably necessary for national defense in a situation brought about by emergency conditions and for this purpose issue orders which deviate from laws currently in effect.[42]

The decree stipulated that beginning April 5, every Jewish person over six years of age must wear a 10×10 centimeter (3.8×3.8 inch) canary yellow six-pointed star made of cloth, silk, or velvet firmly sewn on the left chest side of the outer garment. The decree (Article 2) stipulated that Articles 9 and 16 of Law No. XV of 1941 (the "Racial Law"—an evaluation of which is in chapter 6) would be used to determine who was a Jew.

The decree (Article 3) also provided for exemptions for Jews who:

- Having manifested great bravery during World War I had earned either a gold or two silver, first class, medals.
- As company officers earned the sword-adorned iron cross order, third class, or higher medal.
- As field officers earned a sword-adorned medal higher than the sword-adorned iron cross order, third class, medal.
- Suffered 75 percent disability from war wounds.
- Were exempted under the provisions of Paragraph 6 of Article 2 of Law IV/1939, Article 66 of Decree No. 7720/1939. M. E., Article 3 of Decree No. 2.220/1941 M. E., and Article 2 of Decree No. 8.550/1941. M. E.[43]

The list of exemptions was extended a few days after the publication of the decree with the inclusion of the active and retired pastors and deacons of Christian religious communities; the wives, widows, and children of Jews decorated for heroism; the widows and orphans of soldiers who died in World War II; converts married to Christians; and Jews of foreign nationality with certification from the National Central Alien Control Office (KEOKH).[44]

Pastors, deacons, and deaconesses of Jewish origin and converts married to Christians were exempted after a petition submitted by the Holy Cross Society (*Szent Kereszt Egyesület*) to Prime Minister Sztójay. The petition was also supported by Prince Cardinal Jusztinián Serédi, who asserted that "the six-pointed star is not the sign of the Jewish race, but of the Jewish religion, which denotes a contradiction and apostasy for Christians." He urged the Prime Minister to exempt the pastors and the deacons, just as they had been exempted under all previous anti-Jewish legislation; otherwise he would reluctantly have to advise them not to wear the star. In his response of April 5, Sztójay drew Serédi's attention to a decree (no. 1.450/1944. M. E.) which has been published the same day and incorporated his wishes.[45] Serédi's special concern for the converts was shared by Bishop László Ravasz of the Reformed Church, who made similar appeals. He first appealed to the Minister of the Interior on April 3 and then to the Prime Minister on April 6.[46]

The exemption of the widows and orphans of those fallen in World War II was clarified a few days later; it was stipulated that only those widows and orphans whose husbands or fathers were certified by the Minister of Defense as killed in action were to be exempted.[47]

The decree (no. 1.240/1944. M. E.) stipulated that the Jews caught violating the provisions of the Yellow Star regulations were subject to certain fines as well as to an imprisonment of two months and in wartime of six months. The Nazi press considered these penalties too mild and the Prime Minister was also reproached by Veesenmayer to this effect. In response, on April 14 the Council of Ministers approved the Minister of the Interior's motion that Jews caught not wearing the badge be interned.[48]

Emboldened by these measures, the police and their *Nyilas* allies started a hunt. Many Jews were arrested and interned on the excuse that the color of the star was not the right canary yellow, or that it was not of the prescribed size, or that it was not sewn on the garment properly. For testing the latter, they used a pencil or a similar object. If they could push it through the stitches—and many a time they forced it through—the Jews were immediately interned.

To discourage Jews from trying to intervene in behalf of those arrested or interned, the police headquarters of Budapest issued an order signed by Deputy Police Commissioner György Petrányi, prohibiting all private contact between the employees of the Police Department and Jews wearing the Yellow Star.[49]

The leaders of the Council, like the Zionist leaders, were fully familiar with the ominous implications of the badge. The Zionist leaders had in fact been specifically warned against compliance by their colleagues in Istanbul. In letters dated September 25 and October 23, 1943, Menachem Bader instructed the Budapest *Vaada* leaders to desist from cooperating with the Germans even passively in the event of an occupation. He warned them specifically that the registration of the Jews and the wearing of the badge were "preparation for destruction." Nevertheless, the Hungarian Jewish leaders continued to cooperate with the authorities, calling upon the Jews to remain calm, disciplined, and law-abiding. In fact they issued special instructions relating to the wearing of the badge, relying on the provisions of the decree and on Eichmann's oral communications of March 31. They instructed the Jews that pending the availability of standard badges they should acquire their own Yellow Stars conforming to the specifications established by the authorities and warned them to wear the badge in all public places, including the streets, trolleys, trains, air-raid shelters, restaurants, and places of employment.[50]

On April 5, the Jews of Hungary began to wear the badge, unaware that it was but the prelude to their ultimate destruction. Most of the Jews wore it with a matter-of-fact resignation. Some wore it ostentatiously, reflecting a defiant pride in their Jewishness; others, mostly of assimilated-acculturated background, viewed it as a shameful stigma.

Events soon showed that in Hungary as everywhere else in German-occupied Europe the introduction of the Yellow Star was designed not simply to humiliate and degrade the Jews—though this objective was important—but primarily to isolate and easily identify them for the implementation of the subsequent steps in the Final Solution program.[51] The masses of Hungarian Jewry had been unaware of the sinister implications of the badge. Neither the members of the minuscule resistance movement nor the central or local Jewish leaders warned them of the consequences. The provincial community leaders were indeed as much in the dark as the masses were. The apparent domestic conspiracy of silence engendered by fear and naive political considerations had been reinforced by the inexplicable inaction of the Allies. The late Dr. A. Leon Kubowitzki, a former leader of the World Jewish Congress in New York, for example, claims that he had contacted the American authorities a number of times, pleading that in their broadcasts to Hungary they should warn the Jews against wearing the badge. On April 7, 1944, just two days after the Hungarian Jews were compelled to wear the badge, he addressed a letter to the War Refugee Board stating among other things: "We know from experience of other countries that . . . the yellow badges which the Jews are compelled to wear, are indispensable instruments for the execution of measures of deportation and extermination. May we therefore suggest that the broadcasts beamed to Hungary should urge the Jewish population to abstain from wearing yellow badges. . . ."

This suggestion, like the others that followed it, were according to Kubowitzki "rejected after consideration by several American governmental departments."[52]

The Kossuth Radio Hungarian-language broadcasts from Moscow,[53] in turn, while forcefully condemning the anti-Jewish measures and consistently calling on the population to aid the persecuted Jews, advised the Jews not to "let themselves be forced in a ghetto mood and to wear the yellow star proudly."[54]

The Jewish masses, who were deprived of all means of travel, contact, and communication, including radio and telephone service, depended almost exclusively on the news and instructions they received through their official, Nazi-censored, newspaper. And week after week, they were reminded and warned about the obligation to wear the badge. After the warnings of April 6 and 13, they were advised on April 20 that the badge be sewn firmly on both jackets and overcoats and that they should see to it that the badge was clearly visible and not covered by the collar or other objects.[55] The next issue, on April 27, again warned them that all the regulations relating to the badge were to be followed strictly and that the star was not to be covered by a scarf or any objects they might carry, including briefcases or musical instrument cases.[56] The warning of May 4, which was issued almost a week after the first transport had already left for Auschwitz from Kistarcsa and which coincided with the ghettoization process in Northern Transylvania and elsewhere, was practically a threat. It asserted that there were still some people who were not wearing the proper badge in the proper manner either because of carelessness or lack of information. They were requested to heed all the warnings and to remind all their friends and relatives about them.[57]

The repeated warnings by the Council added to the fear of the country's Jews, who were already terrorized by the frequent raids, internments, and denunciations. Escape, however, was impossible unless they abstained from wearing the telltale badge. And this kind of warning they received from nowhere.

While the Christian population at large received the news of the first anti-Jewish decrees and measures with the same passivity that they manifested during the ghettoization and deportation, the rightist elements and the Nazi press greeted them with great enthusiasm. According to the April 1 issue of the *Magyarság,* the organ of the Hungarian National Socialist Party of Pálffy and Baky, "the majority and the better strata of Hungarian society received the announcement of the decrees with the joy of liberation and feel that the struggle that was waged against Hungarian Jewry for years in the social, cultural, and political spheres was not in vain."[58] The same sentiment was expressed by the *Pester Lloyd* and the other mass circulation newspapers. All of them took advantage of Endre's radio interview of March 31 to identify him as the person in charge of the administration and implementation of all the measures adopted for the solution of the Jewish question.[59] Endre assured his audience that the governmental decrees adopted on March 29 constituted merely the beginning of the measures that would bring about the total solution of the Jewish question in Hungary.[60]

And Endre was right, for almost simultaneously with the atomization, separation, and isolation of the Jews, the Hungarian authorities began a drive for their further humiliation, under the guise of purifying the country's "social and spiritual-cultural" climate.

Social and Spiritual "Purification"

The drive that began in the 1930s for the reduction and eventual elimination of the Jews' influence in the social and cultural spheres of Hungarian society was radically intensified almost immediately after the German occupation. One of the first measures designed to ostracize the Jews from Christian society was the issuance of a decree that forbade Jews to wear military uniforms.[61] Subsequently they forbade Jewish students to wear school uniforms.[62] Jews were prohibited from using public baths and swimming pools[63] and could not frequent public restaurants, catering services, and all related establishments, including pastry shops, bars, espresso stands, and cafes.[64] They could use only certain specifically designated bathing facilities and food-dispensing establishments. In some localities, especially smaller cities and towns where Jews did not have their own facilities, they were allowed for a while at least to use the public facilities, but only under certain exceptional conditions and for a limited period—usually a few hours—specified by the local authorities.

The isolation of the Jews that began with the arrest of the leading representatives of the conservative-aristocratic stratum of Christian society on which Jewry largely depended for its protection was continued with the banning of the opposition parties and movements that might have acted as a mitigating force during the occupation.

Among the opposition parties and movements banned by the Council of Ministers on March 30, 1944, on the recommendation of Andor Jaross, the Minister of the Interior, were the Social Democratic Party, the Independent Smallholders' Party, and the Hungarian Peasant Union. The Hungarian Life Party, the official Government Party underwent an internal change with the resignation of many of its leading figures. Among them were Géza Bornemissza, Count Ferenc Hunyadi, János Makkai, Lajos Mezey, András Tóth, and Nándor Zichy, members of the lower house, and György Ottlik, a member of the upper house and the former chief editor of the *Pester Lloyd,* the German-language organ of the government. The situation was further aggravated when two new pro-Nazi political entities came to the fore, adding fuel to the anti-Jewish agitation of the older and more established Nazi parties. These were the People's Unity Party of the Ruthenians of Carpatho-Ruthenia (*Kárpátaljai Ruszinok Népi Egység Pártja*), headed by András Bródy, and the Bloc of German National Socialist Legislators (*Német Nemzeti Szocialista Törvényhozók Blokkja*), headed by Ferenc Hamm.[65]

The isolation of the Jews was coupled with a drive to protect the "spiritual purity" of Hungarian Christian society. Toward this end, the new government ordered the removal from the public and school libraries of all books by Jews or Christians of Jewish background. Following the issuance of the decree (no. 10.800/1944. M.E.) "Concerning the Protection of Hungarian Intellectual Life From the Literary Works of Jewish Authors,"[66] carefully staged book-burnings took place in Budapest and several other larger cities. Under the provisions of the decree of April 30, the works of both Hungarian and foreign Jewish authors, who were listed in an appendix,[67] could no longer be printed, published, or distributed.[68] Enterprises, institutions, and libraries in possession of copies of works by these authors were forbidden from selling or lending them out and were required to prepare a complete inventory of their possessions within 15 days. The inventory was to include the name(s) of the author(s), the title, language, and character of the works, and the number of copies available. The inventory was required to be submitted in quintuplicate to the Royal Hungarian Government Commissioner of the Press (*A sajtóügyek m. kir. kormánybiztosa*). He, in turn, was required to submit three copies to the Company for the Acquisition of Raw Materials for the Hungarian Paper Industry (*Magyar Papirosipari Nyersanyagbeszerző Kft.*). The company was empowered to order the enterprises, institutions, and libraries to deliver the stocks in their possession and at their own expense by June 15. Upon delivery, the books were to be shredded in the presence of the Government Commissioner or his appointee and the deliverers were to be compensated to the extent of the value of the scrap paper as determined by the government.

An exception was made only for scientific works specified by the authorities and for a number of institutions and libraries which were permitted to keep the literary works of Jewish authors for research and studies conducted under strict supervision.

The position of Government Commissioner of the Press was held by Mihály Kolosváry-Borcsa, a member of the lower house representing Pest-Pilis-Solt-Kiskun County and the President of the National Hungarian Press Chamber (*Országos Magyar Sajtókamara*).[69] He was appointed to this position on April 7, although the announcement was not made until April 15, when he was also named Secretary of State in the Prime Minister's Office.[70] Kolosváry-Borcsa was not new in this field. He had served as Chief of the Press Department in the Imrédy government in 1938–39, and was in charge of all agencies relating to the press and the media of mass communication, including the Hungarian Telephone News Service and Radio Corporation (*Magyar Telefonhirmondó és Rádió Részvénytársaság*). As a journalist, Kolosváry-Borcsa was in the forefront of the pro-Nazi group of propagandists responsible for fanning the flames of anti-Jewish psychosis in the country.

Kolosváry-Borcsa had an occasion to boast about his accomplishments as Government Commissioner a few weeks after his appointment. In a radio speech given under the auspices of the Ideological Academy (*Világnézeti Akadémia*) program, he claimed that the government had finally managed to "create a clear situation" in the cultural sphere by preventing Jewish authors from publishing their works and by closing down all Jewish-owned book stores and publishing houses.[71]

In addition to his drive against Jewish authors and Jewish-owned publishing houses and book stores, Kolosváry-Borcsa was also responsible for subordinating the press to the interests of the government by appointing his friends to leadership positions in various non-*Nyilas* organs. For example, he assigned Mátyás Nitsch to serve as editor-in-chief of the *Pester Lloyd,* and Jenő Gáspár, his deputy, to serve as editor-in-chief of *Új Idők* (New Times) as well as director of Singer & Wolfner, the prestigious Jewish-owned publishing concern. Endre Barabás was made editor-in-chief of *Magyarország* (Hungary). The total subservience of the press was assured by the silencing of the opposition organs. Among the major opposition (*ergo* deemed pro-Jewish) papers silenced were the *Mai Nap* (Today), *Népszava* (The People's Voice), the organ of the Social Democratic Party, *8 Órai Ujság* (The 8 O'clock Journal), *Esti Kurir* (Evening Courier), and *Magyar Nemzet* (Hungarian Nation), perhaps the most prestigious and reliable paper of the pre-occupation era.[72]

Kolosváry-Borcsa's moment of triumph came on June 16, when he presided over a bookburning ceremony in the company of Kurt Brun-hoff, the Press Attaché of the German Legation in Budapest. According to official reports, the ceremony involved the burning of the works of 120 Hungarian and 130 foreign authors of Jewish background. The festivity, which was filmed for propaganda purposes, included the destruction of 447,627 books, the equivalent of 22 fully loaded freight cars.[73]

The Hungarian Institute for the Researching of the Jewish Question. The day Kolosváry-Borcsa's reappointment was announced, a new institution was established for "the advancement of knowledge on the Jewish question." It was named the Hungarian Institute for the Researching of the Jewish Question (*A Zsidókérdést Kutató Magyar Intézet*). The founding members were László Endre, Mihály Kolosváry-Borcsa, Lajos Zimmermann, Géza Lator, Ákos Doroghi Farkas, Ferenc Réthy-Haszlinger, and Zoltán Bosnyák. Established with the advice and guidance of SS-*Hauptsturmführer* Ballensiefen, a Nazi expert on anti-Jewish propaganda, the Institute was put under the leadership of Bosnyák, who already had an office in the Jewish Department of the Ministry of the Interior. According to Article 3 of the bylaws, which were also adopted on April 15, the function of the Institute was "to study the Jewish question in Hungary in a systematic and scientific manner, to collect and scientifically process the related data, and to inform Hungarian public opinion about the Hungarian and general Jewish question."[74]

The Institute was formally inaugurated on May 12 at its new headquarters at 4 Vörösmarty Square, using the facilities of the Jewish-owned Unio-Club. Its educational resources consisted primarily of the ritual objects and books the authorities confiscated from the Jewish Museum in Budapest and from the various Jewish libraries and institutions. The inaugural speech was given by Endre, who, alluding to the mass deportations which were about to begin, declared that the government had decided to "bring about a final solution of the Jewish question within the shortest possible time given the present circumstances."[75] Bosnyák reviewed the importance of the Institute, emphasizing the predominant role the Jews had played in Hungary's economic life and in the professions. Ballensiefen spoke on the question of "world Jewry" and the alleged conspiracy to conquer the world in a style reminiscent of the *Protocols of the Elders of Zion*.[76]

The inaugural meeting saw the appearance of the first issue of the

Institute's organ, the *Harc* (Battle), which was modelled after *Der Stürmer*,[77] and heard plans about a permanent anti-Jewish exhibit. As the seemingly never ending stream of anti-Jewish decrees were being adopted, the Jews were urged and warned by both their Jewish and Nazi leaders to abide strictly by them. The Christian population, in turn, was constantly reminded that it was their patriotic duty to denounce Jews who tried to violate the measures adopted against them.[78] Confronted by an all-oppressive military-terror apparatus and surrounded by a basically passive and occasionally antagonistic population, the Jewish masses abided by the decrees enacted against them with the fatalism and submissiveness to which they had been accustomed through the ages. They were sustained by the hope that the advancing Red Army would frustrate the sinister plans of their enemies. But their hopes dissipated, as the dejewification squads were proceeding with the implementation of their plans at a faster rate than the Red Army was approaching. These plans called for the implementation of still another step toward the deportation and ultimate destruction of the Jews—the expropriation of the property of Hungarian Jewry.

Notes

1. Szegedy-Maszák was arrested in the middle of April, after having been accused of using the diplomatic service to transmit news and money for the Polish refugee organizations sent by the Polish Government-in-Exile in London. *RLB*, Doc. 251.

2. Baron Ferenc Hatvany, the head of important Hungarian sugar refining interests, who managed to escape, was found and arrested in July 1944, and was taken to a concentration camp. *The New York Times*, July 18, 1944, p. 5.

3. *RLB*, Doc. 251. For a highly informative personal account, see Kádár's *A Ludovikától Sopronkőhidáig* (From the Ludovika to Sopronkőhida) (Budapest: Magvető, 1978), 828 pp.

4. C. A. Macartney, 2:254, 256.

5. During the first days of the occupation, the Germans arrested nine members of the upper house and 13 members of the lower house of the Hungarian Parliament. *Ibid.*, p. 248.

6. Kállay remained in the Turkish Legation until October 25, 1944, when he surrendered to the *Nyilas*, who had threatened to break in and seize him by force. *Ibid.*, p. 255.

7. Dr. János Vázsonyi, the parliamentarian and son of Vilmos Vázsonyi, the former Minister of Justice, for example, was arrested with his entire family at the Eötvös Square steamer station from where he had wanted to travel to his wife's estate at Baja. Statement of Elizabeth Eppler, February 27, 1946. YIVO, Archives File 768, Doc. 3647. He was taken to Kistarcsa, from where he was deported on April 28, in the first transport from Hungary to Auschwitz.

8. C. A. Macartney, 2:255. See also György Ránki, *1944. március 19* (March 19, 1944) (Budapest: Kossuth, 1968), p. 92.

9. *RLB,* Doc. 246.

10. *Ibid.,* Doc. 247.

11. NOKW-1995.

12. Although the official order for the ghettoization of the Jews was not issued until April 27, the Jews of Carpatho-Ruthenia were ordered into the ghettos beginning on April 16. See chapter 17.

13. *RLB,* Doc. 251.

14. *Ibid.*

15. The Institute served as what was for all practical purposes a Gestapo prison until October 15, when the Szálasi regime transformed it into the jail of the Center for National Defense (*Államvédelmi Központ*). Lévai, *Fekete könyv,* p. 93. See also the personal narrative of Tibor Feldman at the YIVO: Archives No. 768/3620.

16. Just before the liberation Ubrizsi escaped to Switzerland. His equally sadistic deputy, János Kiss, XII, however, was arrested and condemned to 12 years in 1946. Endre Sós, "Ubrizsi," *Uj Élet,* (New Life), Budapest, October 31, 1946, p. 9.

17. The Germans planned to intern several thousand Jews in Csepel: About 850 in the various parts of the city, 750 in the Mauthner Factory, 500 to 600 "prominent Jews of Budapest" in the eastern wing of the Weiss-Manfréd Works, 600 Jews in the western wing of the Works, 450 in the northern part of the Works, 300 in Soroksár Street, and 600 in the Tsuck Fur Goods Plant. *RLB,* Doc. 252. For an account of life at the National Theological Institute and at the Kistarcsa camp, see Frigyes Bramer, "Koncentrációs tábor a Rabbiképző épületében" (Concentration Camp in the Building of the Theological Institute) in *Évkönyv, 1971/72* (Yearbook, 1971–72). (Budapest: Magyar Izraeliták Országos Képviselete, 1972), pp. 219–28. For the account of Mrs. Dezső Katz, née Ilona Ungár, who was arrested on March 20, 1944, at one of the railway stations of Budapest, taken to Kistarcsa and from there to Auschwitz on April 29, see *Vádirat,* 1:28–30. See also the following personal narratives available at the YIVO: Mrs. Joseph Weiser (771/3276), Mrs. A. Koltay (771/3523), Zoltán Lissauer (772/2122), Lewis Hamvai (773/1693), Ernest Löwy (773/1707), and Charles Reichard (773/1711).

18. Like many other decent Christians who interceded in behalf of the persecuted Jews, Vasdényei was awarded the highest honors by Yad Vashem on November 11, 1969: the Medal of Honour, a Certificate of Honour, and the right to plant a tree on the Avenue of the Righteous at Yad Vashem in Jerusalem.

19. Lévai, *Zsidósors Magyarországon,* pp. 236–37. See also Frigyes Bramer, Zsidó tuszok—"Kistarcsa 1944 'B' Pavilon" (Jewish Hostages—Kistarcsa, 1944, Pavilion "B"), in *Évkönyv, 1973/74* (Yearbook, 1973–74), ed. Sándor Scheiber. (Budapest: Magyar Izraeliták Országos Képviselete, 1974), pp. 340–51. For details on the last deportation from Kistarcsa see chapter 25.

20. For example, Károly Wilhelm, who was arrested in the afternoon of March 20, just after his meeting with the Nazi leaders, was freed by Krumey, who recognized him at the Astoria Hotel, which then served as the *Sonderkommando's* headquarters. Lévai, *Fekete könyv,* p. 92. Freudiger managed to free his brother from the detention house at 26 Rökk-Szilárd Street with the aid of Wisliceny. For the details on Freudiger's dealings with Wisliceny, see chapters 14, 23, and 29.

21. Lévai, *Fekete könyv,* p. 89.

22. *Ibid.,* p. 92. A delegation of the Central Jewish Council headed by Dr. József Vági appeared at the camp to accompany about 160 children and elderly to Budapest. Police Inspector István Vasdényei, the well-meaning commander of the Kistarcsa camp, begged Vági "not to send any more customers there." Munkácsi, *Hogyan történt?,* p. 38.

23. Individual petitions were filed on behalf of Jenő Lázár, a noted antique dealer, on March 26; Lajos Vajda and György Benedek, the presidents of the Jewish communities of Kecskemét and Nagykörös, on April 5; and Imre Wesel, the head of the Szom-

bathely communal district, on May 2. Similar petitions were subsequently filed in behalf of Miklós Szegő, the head of the Székesfehérvár communal district; Samu Meer, the head of the Nagyvárad Jewish community; Dr. József Fischer, the head of the Kolozsvár Jewish community; and many other Jewish leaders. For details see, *ibid.*, pp. 38–40.

24. Philip Freudiger, *Five Months* (manuscript submitted to this author on November 21, 1972), p. 21.

25. Lévai, *Fekete könyv*, p. 88.

26. Munkácsi, *Hogyan történt?*, p. 26.

27. For example, when the Eichmann-*Sonderkommando* and its Hungarian counterpart, László Koltay's unit, decided to use the Majestic Hotel as their headquarters, the Jews were asked to deliver 150 desks, 150 tables, 200 chairs, 300 beer glasses, 150 radio sets, 100 sets of tables and chairs for smoking purposes, 300 liqueur glasses, 300 wine glasses, 6 cocktail shakers, 150 waste-paper baskets, 150 writing desk-sets, and 150 desk lamps. Fifteen sets of the desks, tables, chairs, desk-sets, and lamps, probably designed for the leading officers of the commandos, were to be of especially good quality. Statement of Elizabeth Eppler.

28. Lévai, *Fekete könyv*, p. 93.

29. Budapest was bombed several times during 1944, suffering an especially severe attack on July 2. The Allies also bombed a number of other cities, including Bánhida, Győr, Szeged, Szolnok, Debrecen, Kolozsvár, and Nagyvárad. C. A. Macartney, 2:262–63.

30. *RLB,* Doc. 131.

31. For Reiner's account see Israel Police, Bureau 06, Doc. 347. Statement prepared on October 5, 1960, in preparation for the Eichmann Trial.

32. Munkácsi, *Hogyan történt?*, pp. 47–48.

33. *Ibid.,* pp. 42–50.

34. Statement of Elizabeth Eppler.

35. Lévai, *Fekete könyv*, p. 120.

36. Decree 1.270/1944. M.E. *Budapesti Közlöny. Hivatalos Lap* (Gazette of Budapest), no. 79, April 7, 1944, p. 4.

37. The German Foreign Office was kept regularly informed about the issuance of these laws and decrees. Many of these were also translated into German before submission. For a listing of the dispatches sent from Budapest to this effect, see *RLB,* 1:xix–xx.

38. *RLB,* Doc. 166.

39. Item 66 in the minutes of the March 29 meeting of the Council of Ministers. For text, see *Vádirat,* 1:150–51.

40. The press and theater chambers lost no time in implementing the decree. As a first step, the press chamber excluded 40 professional journalists and all technical writers of Jewish background; the theater chamber excluded 310 Jewish artists. Lévai, *Zsidósors Magyarországon,* p. 79.

41. Item 4 in the minutes of the Council of Ministers meeting of March 29. *Vádirat,* 1:51–52.

42. "1939. évi II. törvénycikk a honvédelemről" (Law No. II of 1939 on National Defense), in *1939. évi országos törvénytár* (Collection of Laws for the Year 1939) (Budapest, 1939), p. 62.

43. These provisions of the various anti-Jewish decrees stipulated that the exemptions granted for bravery were to be extended to family members as well. Jaross had originally wanted to amend this Article by adding the following text: "provided that their attitude was unimpeachable during the [Romanian, Czechoslovak, and Yugoslav] occupation as to their loyalty to the Hungarians." *Vádirat,* 1:112.

44. Decree no. 1.540/1944. M.E. *Budapesti Közlöny,* no. 77, April 5, 1944, p. 4. For the explanation and justification for its adoption offered by the Ministry of the Interior see *Vádirat,* 1:109–113. See also *A Magyar Zsidók Lapja,* April 6, 1944, pp. 7–8. For details on the KEOKH, see chapter 6.

45. Decree no. 1.450/1944. M.E. amended Article 3 of Decree no. 1.240/1944. M.E., broadening the category of exemptions by including the deacons and pastors as well as the Christian spouses and children of Jews. For text see *Budapesti Közlöny,* no. 77, April 5, 1944, p. 4. See also Lévai, *Fekete könyv,* pp. 98–99. Lévai mistakenly identifies the decree as no. 1.540/1944.

46. Lévai, *ibid.,* pp. 99–100.

47. *Magyarországi Zsidók Lapja,* April 27, 1944, p. 4. The exemptions from the provisions of the anti-Jewish laws and decrees were regulated by virtue of Decree no. 1.730/1944. M.E.

48. The fines were stipulated by Law No. X/1928 and Article 212 of Law No. II/1939. *Vádirat,* 1:163.

49. Decree No. 4689/fk/eln. 1944. For text see *Ibid.,* p. 165.

50. *A Magyar Zsidók Lapja,* April 6, 1944, pp. 3, 8; April 13, 1944, p. 3. For Bader's statement, see *RAH,* p. 442.

51. For a succinct survey of the Nazi use of distinguishing marks for Jews, see Philip Friedman, "The Jewish Badge and the Yellow Star in the Nazi Era," *Historia Judaica,* 17, no. 1 (April 1955): 41–70.

52. *Unity in Dispersion: A History of the World Jewish Congress* (New York: World Jewish Congress, 1948), p. 184.

53. It is claimed that the Kossuth Radio was established by the Foreign Committee of the Communists' Party in Hungary (*A Kommunisták Magyarországi Pártja Külföldi Bizottsága*) for the advancement of the interests of the Hungarian Independence Movement (*Függetlenségi Mozgalom*) and was in operation from 1941 to April 3, 1945. *Vádirat,* 1:21.

54. *Ibid.,* pp. 90–91.

55. *A Magyar Zsidók Lapja,* April 20, 1944, p. 3.

56. *Magyarországi Zsidók Lapja,* April 27, 1944, p. 4.

57. *Ibid.,* May 4, 1944, p. 3.

58. *Vádirat,* 1:96–98.

59. Endre's functions were spelled out semi-officially when he was formally appointed on April 9. The Hungarian Telegraphic Office (*Magyar Távirati Iroda*), the Hungarian official news agency, declared on April 11 that the function of Endre, "this fighting personality of Hungarian race-defense, who knows no compromise," was to solve "the technical aspect of the Jewish question." Lévai, *Fekete könyv,* p. 107.

60. *Vádirat,* 1:88–89.

61. Decree no. 26.666/Elnökség—1944. H.M. *Budapesti Közlöny,* no. 77, April 5, 1944, p. 4.

62. Decree no. 8.700/1944. V.K.M. *Ibid.,* No. 102, May 6, 1944, p. 4.

63. Decree no. 444/1944. B.M. *Ibid.,* No. 98, May 2, 1944, pp. 1–2.

64. Decree no. 500/1944. B.M. *Ibid.,* No. 113, May 20, 1944, p. 4.

65. For details on these parties, including their leading figures, consult *A tizhónapos tragédia* (The Ten Months Tragedy), eds. Ervin Szerelemhegyi, István Gyenes, Károly Kiss, and Jenő Lévai (Budapest: Müller Károly, 1945), 2:16, 24, and 32.

66. For text of the Decree, see *Budapesti Közlöny,* no. 97, April 30, 1944, pp. 5–6.

67. The list of names was supplemented on June 25 by virtue of Decree no. 11.300/1944. M.E. For text see *ibid.,* no. 142, June 25, 1944, pp. 14–15.

68. For the list of the Hungarian and foreign Jewish authors whose works were banned, see Appendix 4 to this book.

69. For the structure and composition of the Press Chamber immediately before the

occupation, when it was also under Kolosváry-Borcsa's leadership see *Magyarország tiszti cim- és névtára*, (Title and Name Register of Hungary), vol. 49 (Budapest: A Magyar Királyi Állami Nyomda, 1942), p. 32.

70. *Budapesti Közlöny*, no. 84, April 15, 1944, p. 1. During the Lakatos era, he was relieved of his position "at his own request" on September 9, 1944, and replaced by Endre Hlatky, a retired prefect. (*Budapesti Közlöny*, no. 206, September 10, 1944, p. 1). However, following the Szálasi coup, he was reappointed on October 31. (*Budapesti Közlöny*, no. 249, November 1, 1944, p. 1.). Found guilty of war crimes, he was executed in 1946.

71. Lévai, *Zsidósors Magyarországon*, p. 136.

72. *A tizhónapos tragédia*, 2:14.

73. *Ibid.*, p. 55. See also Sándor Scheiber, "Zsidó könyvek sorsa Magyarországon a német megszállás idején" (The Fate of Jewish Books in Hungary During the German Occupation) in *Magyar Könyvszemle* (Hungarian Review of Books) Budapest, 86, no. 3, 1970:233–35.

74. *Vádirat*, 2:166–69. The bylaws were approved by the Minister of the Interior under Decree no. 174.288/1944.VII.5.

75. Lévai, *Zsidósors Magyarországon*, p. 135. Lévai mistakenly identifies the inaugural date as May 15. Veesenmayer, who informed the German Foreign Office about the inaugural meeting in a telegram dated May 22, correctly identified the date as Friday, May 12. See *RLB*, Doc. 162.

76. Ballensiefen aroused the ire of Thadden, who visited Budapest that month, for his tactlessness and failure to invite any members of the German Legation to the opening ceremonies. *RLB*, Doc. 164.

77. According to the Hungarian Telegraphic Office, the Sztójay government banned the publication of the journal for one month (probably the June issue) "on the ground that it prejudiced the country's foreign policy." *The New York Times*, July 9, 1944.

78. Baky made a special appeal to the Hungarian population to this effect in the April 16 issue of the *Magyarság*. For text see *Vádirat*, 1:169–70. The April 9 issue of the *Magyarság* carried Ernő Abonyi's interview with Baky in which he spelled out the character and consequences of the anti-Jewish measures. *Ibid.*, pp. 136–40.

CHAPTER SIXTEEN

THE PROCESSES OF ECONOMIC DESTRUCTION

The Pauperization of the Jews

ONE OF the fundamental objectives of the Nazis' anti-Jewish program was the expropriation of Jewish property. On this the German and Hungarian National Socialists were of one mind and enjoyed the wholehearted support of the amoral strata of the Hungarian civilian population.

Although the property of the Hungarian Jews was confiscated only after the German occupation of March 19, 1944, the pauperization of the Jews had begun in 1938, when Hungary yielded to German pressure and internal radical rightist agitation and adopted the First Anti-Jewish Law. The drive continued with the adoption of a number of other major laws and decrees aimed at reducing and eventually eliminating the Jews' role in the national economy. The small upper layer of Hungarian Jewry, which played a leading role in the country's industrial, commercial, and financial life and was to some extent protected by its wealth and friends among the Christian aristocracy, managed, at least until the occupation, to absorb quite comfortably the increasingly severe restrictions imposed upon it. The masses of Hungarian Jewry, on the other hand, and especially the unassimilated Orthodox Jews of Carpatho-Ruthenia and Northern Transylvania, lived under crushing economic burdens and were virtually unable to make ends meet. In response to the rapidly deteriorating economic situation, MIPI (*Magyar Izraeliták Pártfogó Irodája;* Welfare Bureau of Hungarian Jews) and OMZSA (*Országos Magyar Zsidó Segítő Akció;* National Hungarian Jewish Assistance Campaign), two interrelated welfare organizations, were established in 1938 and 1939 respectively.

The German Expropriation Process

The systematic wholesale expropriation of the property of the Hungarian Jewish community began almost immediately after the German occupation. On Monday, March 20, 1944, the first business day after the occupation, Jews with bank accounts and safe deposit boxes staged a rush on the banks to remove their deposits and valuables. During their meeting with the leaders of Jewry the following day, Dieter Wisliceny and Hermann Alois Krumey, the two leading members of the Eichmann-*Sonderkommando,* found it necessary to point out that they laid great stress on the avoidance of panic. They urged the leaders to reassure the Jewish masses that everything would be all right and ask them to redeposit their money and valuables.[1] The Nazis, eager to lay their hands on Jewish wealth, not only approached the Jewish leaders, but also intervened with the Hungarian authorities. On March 20, *Legationsrat* Gerhardt Feine, the economic and legal expert in the German Legation and Edmund Veesenmayer's second in command, instructed Béla Csizik, the Secretary of State of the Ministry of Finance, to have the Hungarian authorities immediately limit bank withdrawals to 1,000 *Pengős* per day per person and seal all safe deposit boxes. That same evening, the Executive Committee of the Association of Savings and Commercial Banks (*A Takarékpénztárak és Bankok Egyesületének Végrehajtó Bizottsága*) as well as the Hungarian National Bank (*Magyar Nemzeti Bank*) instructed all their branches to this effect. Feine's request was duplicated the following day by *Hauptmannführer* Bruno Langbiehn, who approached Police Commissioner Ferenc Éliássy in the name of Krumey.[2]

At the meeting of the Council of Ministers of March 29, Minister of Finance Lajos Reményi-Schneller asked for a decision on whether the measures of March 20 should be continued in effect, since bank withdrawals had already declined from 207 million *Pengős* on March 20 to 70 million *Pengős* on March 21, and to only 19 million *Pengős* on March 22.[3] The measures taken by the banking authorities and the appeal by the Jewish leaders apparently had achieved the desired objectives.

The economic potential of the Jewish community declined drastically with the arrest of the most prominent Jewish industrialists and financiers almost immediately after the occupation. Some of them were deported to Mauthausen; others, including Ferenc Chorin and his family, were allowed to reach Portugal after they transferred control over the Weiss-Manfréd Works, Hungary's largest manufacturing complex, to the SS.

The treasuries of the Jewish communities all over Hungary, especially that of Budapest, were strained to the limit by the constant and ever more exorbitant demands of the German and Hungarian authorities. The illusion that the Jewish communities and the Jews in general were rich was fostered by the tendency of the anti-Semites to look at Jews through the perspective of the standards and life-styles of the relatively few very wealthy Jews who played a leading role in the country's economic life as well as in the affairs of the Jewish communities. This illusion was also nurtured by the financial dealings with the leaders of the *Sonderkommando* in Bratislava and Budapest through which representatives of the *Vaada* had hoped to buy off the Germans to save Jewish lives.

During the first two months of the occupation, when the Hungarian authorities refused to deal with the Jewish community and the Germans exercised *de facto* sovereignty, it was primarily the German authorities, including the SS and the *Wehrmacht,* that subjected the Jews to constant demands for a variety of goods and services (see chapter 14). On the Hungarian side, the "official" demands at this time were advanced almost exclusively by the offices of Péter Hain and László Koltay of the Royal Hungarian State Police (*Magyar Királyi Államrendőrség*).[4]

Acting as the complete masters that they were, the Germans simply confiscated whatever they needed from sequestered Jewish institutions and establishments. Following the selection of their headquarters, the various German authorities, and especially the SS, would usually order the Jewish Councils to provide the furniture and office equipment they needed. The Jews were also often ordered to provide furnished apartments for leading SS and *Wehrmacht* officers and to supply them with paintings, rugs, and musical instruments. When the Jewish Councils could no longer buy the goods the authorities needed, the Germans would simply take possession of appropriate Jewish stores which had already been closed by the Hungarian authorities.

The Jews of Budapest were particularly hard-hit by the exorbitant demands of the German and Hungarian authorities. In addition to the monetary and material sacrifices, they also had to absorb much of the damages caused by the Allied air raids on the capital. They were compelled after every major air raid to vacate a number of apartments for use by Christian victims of the raids. Eventually they were placed in special yellow-star buildings. Crushed as they were, however, they continued to sustain the sacrifices imposed upon them in hope that the Allied victory would come soon enough for them to avoid the fate of their brethren in the provinces. The latter not only saw their property expropriated, but were deported to Auschwitz after a few weeks' stay in their local ghettos.

The "Legislative" Measures of the Sztójay Government

The pauperization of the Jews of Hungary was also achieved through the Nazi-inspired "legislative" program of the quisling Sztójay government, which was issuing an avalanche of decrees toward this end. The relatively few Jews in the civil service and the public commissions were dismissed; Jewish lawyers were compelled to give up their practice; Jewish journalists and artists were expelled from their respective professional associations; and Jewish pharmacists were forced to surrender their licenses.[5] Jewish suppliers to state organizations or institutions were deprived of their licenses,[6] as were Jewish patent agents.[7] The Jewish officers and employees of the stock and commodity markets were dismissed.[8]

On April 6, the Ministry of the Interior issued a "strictly confidential" general decree (Körrendelet; no. 6138/1944. VI. res. B.M. signed by gendarmerie Colonel Gyula Károly), which instructed all police departments and organizations to take effective measures to prevent Jews from hiding jewelry and valuables, selling them privately, or giving them to Christian friends for safekeeping.[9] On April 14, the Council of Ministers heard a report from Minister of Finance Reményi-Schneller concerning the measures he intended to adopt for the dejewification of all financial, commercial, and related enterprises.[10] His proposals were incorporated in a decree (no. 1.600/1944. M.E.) Concerning the Declaration and Sequestration of the Wealth of the Jews, which was published two days later.[11] This sweeping measure went into effect the same day that the Jews of Carpatho-Ruthenia began to be driven into ghettos—almost two weeks before the issuance of the official ghettoization decree.

Under the decree, Jews were required to declare the current value of all their property by April 30 at the nearest state financial office, using officially provided forms. The property of minors and of wards had to be declared by their guardians or trustees. The Jews were required to declare all property with the exception of a maximum of 10,000 Pengős of household items and clothing; objects of art, rugs, and silverware could not be included among the household items. All legal transactions after March 22 by which Jews transferred property rights to non-Jews were considered invalid and these properties also had to be declared.

The property declarations had to include all jewelry and gold, securities, and savings and checking accounts. Jews were permitted to withdraw only 1,000 *Pengős* per month from banks, irrespective of the number of accounts they had.[12] Jewish-rented safe-deposit boxes were blocked and the respective institutions were required to take inventory of their contents. Jewish commercial and industrial establishments were ordered closed and inventory was taken of their stock and equipment.[13] Industrial enterprises that were deemed important for the general economy were reopened under Christian managers assigned by the Hungarian authorities.[14] The managers were formally appointed by "the Royal Hungarian Government Commissioner Appointed for the Solution of the Questions Relating to the Jews' Material and Property Rights" (*A zsidók anyagi és vagyonjogi ügyeinek megoldására kinevezett m. kir. kormánybiztos*). The appointments were published in the "Official Part" (*Hivatalos Rész*) of the official gazette, the *Budapesti Közlöny*.

As goods became ever scarcer in the wake of the dislocation of the economy caused by the frequent bombings, the anti-Jewish measures, the requirements of the armed forces, and the expropriations carried out by the Germans, the Hungarian authorities resorted increasingly to the use of goods and materials confiscated from the Jews. Jewish-owned retail stores were closed and sealed on April 21.[15] One of the reasons, according to Antal Kunder, Minister of Trade and Transportation, was that they were being systematically plundered to such an extent that protective measures were required to save the Jewish-owned goods for the economic needs of the country.[16]

The measures directed against Jewish businessmen and industrialists were gradually extended, in somewhat different form, to Jewish artisans, white-collar workers, and farmers. The avalanche of anti-Jewish decrees of an economic nature continued even after most of the provincial Jews of Hungary had already been deported. This reinforced the illusion of the predominantly assimilated Jews of Budapest and in the western parts of Hungary who had not yet been deported that they would be spared; "If the authorities intended to kill us, why would they pass decrees?" they rationalized.

Most Jews complied faithfully with the provisions of all the decrees. Some managed to hide some of their valuables or to "lend" them to Christian friends and neighbors. However, those suspected of such transactions were subjected to barbaric pressures and tortures when they were interrogated in the ghettos or prior to deportation. Occasionally the Christians involved, scared by the warnings of the regime and the extremely harsh penalties with which they were threatened, reported the transactions to the authorities.

Dispossessed and deprived of their livelihood, the Jews—already in the process of ghettoization—were also subjected to a curtailment of their food allowances. By virtue of a decree signed on April 22 by Béla Jurcsek, Minister of Agriculture and Minister of Supply, the sugar ration for Jews was reduced to 30 grams per month. They were prohibited from buying solid fats and were allowed only 300 grams of vegetable oil per month. They could not buy pork or veal and were entitled to only 100 grams of beef or horsemeat per week.[17] On April 27, the Minister of Supply issued a decree[18] requiring that "all persons considered Jews from the point of view of food supplies" must submit personal data to the mayor's office of their community by May 1, allegedly to obtain new ration cards and coupons. Unwarned and unguided, the Jews faithfully complied with this order, as they had with the earlier ones. This was on the eve of the large-scale ghettoization and the authorities used the data to supplement the lists prepared on Baky's orders earlier in the month for use by the Gestapo, the gendarmes, and their collaborators in the round-up of the Jews.

On June 4 the Jews were limited to only two hours daily for shopping, with the beginning and end of the period during which they would be allowed in stores determined by local authorities.[19]

In theory the houses and apartments of Jews who had been deported were to be sealed and their contents inventoried. The property of such Jews was to be administered or disposed of by various officially designated governmental authorities, including the Ministry of Finance and the Ministry of Trade and Communication. But no sooner were the Jews forcibly removed from their homes than their property began to be looted. Jewelry and money were often taken by officers assigned for the inventory; "sealed" apartments were broken into by German and Hungarian uniformed personnel, as well as the greedy and morally bankrupt among the general population. In the villages, Jewish-owned cattle, farm machinery, and equipment were grabbed by local peasants as soon as the Jews were concentrated into the major ghettos, which were usually in the county seats.

After the mass deportations began on May 15, a competition arose among Hungarians eager to acquire the professional offices, businesses, industrial establishments, farms, shops, and homes, which had either been confiscated from or left behind by the Jews.[20] To prevent the disruption of economic life, the governmental agencies assigned special Christian wardens, trustees (*gondnokok*), or managers to operate them. The assignment was usually based upon patronage considerations or petitions filed by the interested individuals.[21] In many cases, the management of Jewish firms was left in the hands of the non-Jewish "Strawmen" (*Strohmann*) the Jewish owners had originally taken in as "silent partners" to satisfy the requirements of the discriminatory acts of the late 1930s. This system of bypassing the letter of the law had at the time been popularly known as the Aladár system (*Aladár rendszer*).

Hungarian Reaction to German Expropriations

The Germans' continuing and ever more exorbitant confiscation of Jewish property during the first two months of the occupation alarmed the Hungarian authorities. Though they gave the Germans exclusive jurisdiction over the Jewish question during this period, they considered the wealth of the Jews to be part of the Hungarian national patrimony. While both the Germans and the Hungarians agreed on the desirability of expropriating the Jews they differed sharply over the distribution of the spoils. The rivalry which underlay the pursuit of their particular national economic interests was fierce, since according to one estimate the Jews' wealth was valued at between 7 and 9 billion gold *Pengős*.[22]

The first Hungarian official to check with the Jewish Council about the nature and scope of the German requisitions was Richárd Bodnár, the secretary of the Chamber of Commerce and Industry (*Kereskedelem és Iparkamara*), an agency associated with the Ministry of Trade and Communications. Following his first visit on May 17, he appeared at the Council's headquarters practically every day to scrutinize the German demands. The Jewish leaders welcomed this interest; they viewed it not only as additional evidence of the Hungarians' desire to reacquire jurisdiction over the handling of the Jewish question, but also as a means to retain the confiscated Jewish wealth within the country. Encouraged by Bodnár's initiative, the Jewish leaders expanded their contact with Hungarian officials in advancing what increasingly appeared to be their mutual interests. János Gábor and Miksa Domonkos were especially successful in establishing and expanding good relations with

Sándor Molitor and Gyula Kiss of the Ministry of Trade and Communications. As a consequence, the demands and acquisitions of the Germans were closely monitored from late May onward. The Hungarians were kept abreast of the German demands by Domonkos, who often risked his life in this endeavor.[23]

In pursuit of their national economic interests, the Hungarians took a number of countermeasures, which obviously irritated the Germans. In their desire to retain within the country as much Jewish wealth as possible, the Hungarian authorities would often go so far as to detach the baggage cars from the deportation trains. They were particularly concerned with the retention of artistic treasures that belonged to Jews. In the summer of 1944, Dénes Csánky, a well-known painter and director of the Hungarian National Museum of Fine Arts (*Országos Magyar Szépművészeti Múzeum*), was named Government Commissioner for the Evaluation and Protection of Works of Art Sequestered from Jews (*A zsidók zár alá vett műtárgyainak számbavételére és megőrzésére kirendelt kormánybiztos*). Late in July, Albert Turavölgyi was named Government Commissioner for the Solution of Problems Relating to the Jews' Material and Property Rights (*Kormánybiztos a zsidók anyagi és vagyonjogi ügyeinek megoldására*), a euphemistically named agency which was primarily concerned with the disposition of sequestered Jewish stores and the allocation of confiscated Jewish property.

Following Horthy's decision to halt the deportations and during the Lakatos era (July 7–October 15, 1944), the plundering of whatever Jewish property was left continued despite the easing of anti-Jewish pressures, although in an environment of greater legality. The government and many of its subordinated agencies periodically decided on the disposition of Jewish property, including the distribution of the clothing and linen left behind by deported Jews as well as the allocation of the goods and materials found in sequestered businesses and warehouses. These moves were often justified by the dire shortages caused by the war, which was coming ever closer to Hungary's borders.[24]

All semblance of legality was lost after the Szálasi coup of October 15, 1944, when the *Nyilas* gave vent to their anti-Jewish feelings. No more limits were placed upon the spoliation of Jewish property. Under the administration of Árpád Toldy, the former Prefect of Székesfehérvár who was named Government Commissioner for Jewish Affairs (*A zsidóügyek kormánybiztosa*), the seizure of Jewish property acquired unbelievable proportions. As Government Commissioner, Toldy also took over Turavölgyi's position and thus "legal" control over all seques-tered Jewish valuables. When the Red Army approached the capital in December 1944, a veritable "gold train" (*aranyvonat*) full of valuables left Budapest under the immediate command of László Avar, the former Mayor of Zenta.[25]

The countermeasures of the Hungarians notwithstanding, the Ger-mans also continued to lay their hands on whatever Jewish property they could get hold of. They had a special eye for valuable paintings, tapestries, precious stones, and Persian rugs. It was partially in pursuit of such valuables that the Germans occupied the houses belonging to rich Jews. They also looted the art treasures stored by wealthy Jewish collectors in bomb-proof cellars at Budafok. Among these were the collections of Jenő Káldi and the family of Baron Herzog, which in-cluded paintings by El Greco, Van Dyck, Rembrandt, Rubens, and Gauguin. The paintings were taken by Péter Hain and were first exhi-bited at the Svábhegy, near Eichmann's headquarters, amidst great anti-Jewish fanfare.[26] The SS also acquired large sums of local and foreign currency as well as large quantities of jewelry and precious stones through their dealings with the Zionist leaders, including Rezső Kasztner, who thought they could rescue the Jews by buying off the leading figures of the *Sonderkommando*.

The Germans aimed not only at achieving their ideologically defined goals—the extermination of the Jews—but also at maximizing the as-sociated economic advantages. As partial compensation for the dejewi-fication of the country, they demanded and received the food rations of the deported Jews as well as two billion *Pengős* to cover the trans-portation costs involved in the deportations. Even after deportation from Hungary the confiscation of Jewish property continued. On ar-rival in Auschwitz, the Jews were deprived of whatever they had man-aged to take along on what proved for most of them to be their final trip.

While the Hungarians were obviously annoyed by the removal of Jewish property from the country, they were particularly upset over the deal under which the SS acquired the Weiss-Manfréd Works, Hungary's largest industrial complex.

The SS Acquisition of the Weiss-Manfréd Works

One of the unpublicized objectives of the German occupation of Hungary was the maximum economic exploitation of the country and the subordination of its industrial and agricultural productive capacity to the interests of the Third Reich. In pursuit of these objectives the Germans resorted not only to the outright confiscation of Jewish wealth, but also to the bartering of a limited number of Jewish lives for goods and valuables. Such barters did not go counter to their Final Solution program, but were designed to obfuscate their sinister designs. They were usually negotiated by the SS officers in charge of the various field operations with the knowledge and consent of their superiors in Berlin.

Therefore, when the SS permitted close to 1,700 mostly prominent and well-to-do Hungarian Jews to leave the country on June 30, 1944, it was, under an agreement with the Kasztner-dominated *Vaada*, in exchange for a payment of one thousand dollars per capita. Since this agreement was reached without the involvement of the Hungarian authorities and the payment was met by the rescued individuals themselves and by some of the communal authorities, the official reaction to the affair was relatively muted. However, the Hungarian government became highly interested in and visibly chagrined over a deal under which four interrelated families who played a pivotal role in the country's industrial and financial life bought their freedom by transferring control of the Weiss-Manfréd Works to the SS. The families involved were those of Ferenc Chorin, Ferenc Mauthner, Baron Móric Kornfeld, and Baron Jenő Weiss, and included a number of Aryan members with links to the Hungarian aristocracy.[27] Most of the members of these families were associated with the aristocratic elite of Hungarian society and some of them, including Chorin, were on very close personal terms with Horthy. Several of them served in the upper house. Baron Kornfeld was also active in providing financial assistance to a number of liberal publications, including the *Magyar Nemzet* (Hungarian Nation), the *Magyar Szemle* (Hungarian Review), the *Nouvelle Revue de Hongrie* (New Review of Hungary), and the *Hungarian Quarterly*.[28]

The families owned not only the vast Weiss-Manfréd Works of Csepel, a diversified heavy-goods and armaments industrial complex employing over 40,000 workers, but also a large number of other industrial, mining, and banking enterprises which exerted considerable influence on Hungary's financial and economic life.[29]

With the exacerbation of the anti-Jewish political climate in the 1930s, the vast holdings of these families had been consolidated into a holding company known as the Labor Trust Corporation (*Labor Bizalmi Rt.*) originally formed on December 30, 1923, by the children and heirs of Manfréd Weiss;[30] 51 percent of the Trust's shares were registered in the name of the Aryan members of the family.[31] As a result, the Labor Trust Corporation, which incorporated the Weiss-Manfréd Works along with all other enterprises of the families, became an "Aryan" firm and as such immune to the anti-Jewish laws. Many of the enterprises, including the aircraft and munitions factories, were involved in war production serving not only the interests of the armed forces of Hungary but also those of the Third Reich.

Germany's preoccupation with Hungary intensified in the fall of 1943. Aware of the machinations of Prime Minister Miklós Kállay (chapter 7), Hitler became determined not only to prevent Hungary from following the example of Italy in extricating itself from the Axis Alliance, but also to bring about the intensification of Hungary's contribution to the war effort. This was especially important at the time since Germany was suffering staggering defeats on both the Eastern and Western fronts, and its domestic industries were being crippled by ever more devastating Western air raids. One of Germany's particular concerns at the time was the expansion of aircraft production with the aid of Hungary's manpower and industrial resources. One of the plans developed shortly before the occupation—the so-called *Jägerstab* (Fighter Aircraft Staff) plan—called for the building of six large underground aircraft factories, each with an area of over one million square feet, to be completed by November 1944. One of these was to be built in the Protectorate of Bohemia and Moravia with the aid of Jewish workers from Hungary. Horthy's consent at Schloss Klessheim on March 18, 1944, to the delivery of the "necessary Jewish workers" for this quixotic project was one of the foundation stones for Eichmann's deportation program (see chapter 11).

Another plan, effectuated shortly after the occupation, called for the intensification of aircraft and other war materiel production in the enterprises of the Labor Trust Corporation, including the Danube Aircraft Manufacturing Corporation (*Dunai Repülőgépgyár Rt.*), which produced Messerschmidt fighter planes. Several German agencies were actively and secretly involved in the acquisition of the plants for their own purposes. Hermann Göring, the head of the *Luftwaffe,* and his supporters wanted to acquire the Weiss-Manfréd Works and related enterprises and link them to the Steyr Works and the aircraft plants at Wiener-Neustadt, both associated with the Hermann Göring Works. The Hungarian government, when approached on the matter, gave its consent in principle on May 3, 1944. Neither the Göring group nor the Hungarian government were aware that private negotiations were then being conducted between the SS and the owners of the Weiss-Manfréd Works for the transfer of control over the plants to Himmler's group.[32]

Contrary to their behavior in other occupied countries, the Germans could not simply take over industrial plants in Hungary because, in accordance with the Schloss Klessheim agreement, the Germans' presence was not supposed to formally violate the country's sovereignty. Both the German and the Hungarian authorities scrupulously adhered to this agreement and were careful to retain the façade of Hungary's independence. Moreover, while the Germans received a free hand in the handling of the Jewish question during the first few months of the occupation, they could not openly take possession of what was legally an "Aryan" firm.

The chief negotiator for the four families, identified for purposes of the contract as the "family group" (*rokoni csoport*), was Ferenc Chorin, who was returned early in April from an internment camp near Vienna, where he had been taken together with many other prominent hostages arrested by the SS almost immediately after the occupation.[33] The interests of the SS were represented by SS-*Standartenführer* Kurt Becher, Himmler's economic agent in Hungary, who subsequently emerged as Kasztner's major negotiating partner in the grandiose scheme to rescue the surviving Jews of Europe. The intermediaries were Vilmos Billitz and Ferenc Máriássy, two of the top executive officers of the concern.

The negotiations dragged on for several weeks, for Becher, a careful and shrewd negotiator, was eager to have the cooperation of Otto Winkelmann, the Higher SS and Police Leader in Hungary and, above all, Himmler's consent to every aspect of the agreement. He was extremely prudent, because the issue also involved the rescuing of Jews, however few in number, by the top echelon of the SS. The offer involved the transfer of the 51 percent of the shares owned by the Aryan members of the families. (The 49 percent owned by the Jewish members were subject to the provisions of the decree, then in the process of adoption, which called for the declaration and eventual sequestration of the wealth of the Jews.) In return for the controlling majority of the shares, the SS was to make possible the departure of 45 to 47 members of the four families to Portugal, Switzerland, and Germany and to enable them to take along part of their valuables, including foreign currency. As worked out by the respective lawyers,[34] the major points of the agreement, consisting of four parts and a supplementary document, stipulated:

- The transfer to the SS group represented by Becher of the House Appraising and Management Corporation (*Házértéke-sitő és Kezelő Rt.; Hausverwertungs- und Verwaltungs A. G.*), a new holding company set up to facilitate the transaction.[35]
- The transfer of the controlling shares in the Weiss-Manfréd Works and all other associated industrial plants as well as the estates of the family group to the new holding company to be administered as a trusteeship for a period of 25 years.[36]
- The return by the SS of all the assets of the family group upon the expiration of the trusteeship period.[37]

The fourth part of the agreement, which was the most embarrassing section for the SS and which was never made public, made it possible for the members of the family group to leave Hungary and receive cash payments of $600,000 plus 250,000 German marks. Becher and the SS were to get 5 percent of the gross income of the concern for their services as trustees.

The agreement, having been approved by Himmler,[38] was signed on May 17, 1944, when the mass deportation of Jews was in full swing in the northeastern parts of the country. That same day, the family group was smuggled out of Hungary and taken temporarily to Vienna.[39] After a few weeks' stay in the Austrian capital, 32 members of the group, including Ferenc Chorin and his family and ten members of the Weiss family, were first taken by train to Stuttgart and then, on June 25, by two special Lufthansa planes to Lisbon via Madrid. A smaller group, including the Heinrich family, was taken to Switzerland. In accordance with one of Himmler's conditions for approving the agreement, nine members of the group[40] were retained in Vienna as hostages to assure the "good behavior" of the others in the free world.

Although the families reportedly managed to take along a large quantity of valuables, they were not successful in obtaining all the cash promised by the SS. The Chorin group received $170,000 en route to or upon arrival in Portugal, the Heinrich group obtained $30,000 in Switzerland, and 250,000 German Marks were placed at the disposal of Baron Alfonz Weiss in a Vienna bank. The remainder of the $400,000 was to be paid in several installments, but "circumstances" prevented the SS from making further payments.

The secrecy and speed with which the agreement was concluded and the potential impact of the direct involvement of the SS in Hungary's major industrial complex aroused, for varying reasons, the anger of both the Hungarian government and the German Foreign Office.

Reaction of the Hungarian Government

Almost immediately after he signed the agreement on May 17, Chorin wrote a personal note to the Regent of Hungary explaining its background and implications. He deplored the anti-Jewish measures of the Sztójay government, which placed severe restrictions upon the economy at the very time that demands were being made for its expansion, and which removed his effectiveness and that of the firms' other Jewish members. He pointed out that the family group did not want to negotiate with the government which had adopted the various anti-Jewish decrees and which—had it acquired control—would only have mismanaged the concern. Moreover, he claimed the transfer of control to the SS was bound to serve long-range Hungarian interests, for under the able administration of Becher, with whom he had concluded a "gentleman's agreement," the safety, integrity, and productive capacity of the plants were safeguarded.[41]

Horthy apparently was not totally convinced about the "positive features" of the agreement. He instructed Sztójay not to permit the transfer to a foreign power by a military or civilian authority of "agricultural, industrial or commercial enterprises, or the lands, buildings, equipment or raw materials necessary to maintain them" without his consent and the approval of the Council of Ministers and the appropriate Ministers.[42] Sztójay expressed his "astonishment" over the affair during his discussions with Veesenmayer on June 1.[43] He also discussed the affair and the issues raised by Horthy with Hitler on June 6, unaware that the Führer had also approved the agreement on Himmler's urging.[44] Sztójay's representations were counterbalanced by his communication relating to the German-Hungarian economic agreement which he and Veesenmayer had concluded on June 2 and under which Hungary's productive capacity was completely subordinated to the interests of the Reich.

The details and implications of the agreement for Hungary were outlined by Béla Imrédy, the former Prime Minister who was appointed on May 23 as Minister without Portfolio in Charge of Economic Coordination, at the Council of Ministers meeting of June 1.[45] It was at this Council meeting that questions pertaining to the transfer of the Weiss-Manfréd Works were first raised.

Although Imrédy held a number of meetings with the Germans with the aim of retaining Hungarian sovereignty over the concern, the Hungarians remained unaware of the fact that the deal involved Himmler and the SS rather than the Hermann Göring Works until July 5.[46]

Imrédy visited Veesenmayer on June 13 to express his and Sztójay's embarrassment over the transaction which, he complained, was concluded without the Hungarian government even having been informed. Veesenmayer suggested to Ribbentrop that Himmler be induced to make some concessions of a formal nature in order to settle the issue.[47] Imrédy objected especially to the duration of the trusteeship and the 5 percent of the gross income which the Germans were to receive for their services. He also insisted on the appointment of Hungarians as president and executive officer of the concern.[48] The discussions that involved Imrédy, Veesenmayer, Becher, and M. Boden, the economic expert of the German Legation, dragged on but led to no fundamental agreement. While Winkelmann was very optimistic in his report to Himmler, dated June 20, in which he heralded a six-point agreement,[49] Veesenmayer was more circumspect in his June 28 report to Ribbentrop. Veesenmayer related that the Hungarian government was opposed to the 25-year trusteeship, but that Imrédy expressed a willingness to cooperate toward a "satisfactory solution of the matter." He also transmitted the five-point position of the Hungarian government, which emphasized that, in connection with the laws then in force, the transaction could not be recognized. Veesenmayer intimated that a trusteeship for the duration of the war might be considered together with the appointment of a Hungarian as director of the concern.[50]

The position of the Hungarians was also summarized by Sztójay in a letter to Himmler dated July 7, shortly after the Imrédy-Becher negotiations reached an impasse. Sztójay suggested that the *Reichsführer-SS* receive Imrédy to work out a compromise.[51] This approach was also suggested by Imrédy himself at the July 12 meeting of the Council of Ministers. However, Becher and Winkelmann got wind of Imrédy's plans and managed to frustrate them by compelling the resignation of the former Prime Minister on August 7 by reviving the old controversy over his alleged Jewish origin.[52]

Becher and the SS were, of course, interested in getting the Hungarian government's swift approval of the agreements with the family group. The approval was necessary not only to assure complete SS control over the plants, but also, and perhaps more importantly, to protect the façade of Hungarian sovereignty. The problem was not so much with the 51 percent Aryan-held shares, but with the 49 percent Jewish-held ones, which came under the jurisdiction of the Hungarian state under Decree no. 1.600/1944. M. E. With regard to the former,

Becher was able to circumvent the restrictions of the decree (no. 1.970/1935. M. E.), under which foreigners could not acquire Hungarian securities without the approval of the National Bank, simply by identifying himself and some of his closest collaborators, including SS-*Obersturmbannführer* Hans Bobermin, as legal residents of Budapest.

At the Council of Ministers meeting of August 17, Becher's cause was championed by Minister of Finance Lajos Reményi-Schneller, one of Imrédy's rivals. Although the Council adopted no final decision in the case,[53] the SS obtained legal control over the concern when it was authorized by Reményi-Schneller and Lajos Szász, the Minister of Industry, to exercise voting rights for the Jewish shares as well for a period of one year.[54] The Hungarians were assuaged by the inclusion in the top management of the concern of a number of Hungarian nationals, including Andor Lázár, the former Minister of Justice (1932–1938) and Konstantin Takácsy. Of the 5,000 Aryan-held shares of the House Appraising and Management Corporation—the holding company—4,000 were held by Becher and 250 each by four Hungarians: Árpád Buzay, Lajos Koromzay, Tivadar Nemessányi, and Viktor Szmick. All six of the Hungarians had previously been associated with the concern in various capacities.

After the conclusion of the agreement with the Hungarians, Himmler proceeded with his plans to assure the total subordination of the concern to the interests of the SS. These included the establishment of a new holding company, the *Vereinigte Industrie-Werke (Manfred Weiss)—A.G., Budapest* (United Industrial Works [Manfréd Weiss] Corporation, Budapest). On Becher's advice, Himmler appointed *Generalfeldmarschall* Eberhard Milch of the *Luftwaffe* and three leading SS officials to represent his agency at the general meetings of the holding company—SS-*Brigadeführer* Baron Kurt Freiherr von Schroeder, SS-*Obergruppenführer* Hans Jüttner, and SS-*Obergruppenführer* Oswald Pohl.[55] While there is no evidence that the new holding company was ever formally established, the armaments and industrial plants associated with the Weiss-Manfréd Works continued their operations under Becher's overall leadership.

Although the SS managed to iron out their difficulties with the Hungarians thanks to the cooperation of their sympathizers in the government, including Reményi-Schneller and Szász, they continued to have some embarrassing encounters with the German Foreign Office, especially over the fourth part of the agreement with the family group.

Reaction of the German Foreign Office

Like the Hungarians, Veesenmayer and the German Legation in Budapest were informed about the deal only after it was concluded on May 17. Veesenmayer was contacted by Himmler shortly after the signing of the agreement with a request that he come to Berlin for a meeting. Since he felt that he could not leave Budapest, Veesenmayer sent Carl Rekowski, his personal *Referent* and director of the German Legation. Himmler explained the acquisition of the concern by emphasizing the contribution of the SS to the war effort and the need to assure for it a dependable supply of weapons during and after the war. Although he appreciated the importance to the SS of becoming self-sufficient, Veesenmayer, who had to break the news to the Hungarians, found himself in an embarrassing position, for he always believed that Hungary's maximum exploitation for Germany's interests could be assured only by retaining the goodwill of the country's leadership, including Horthy's, and by safeguarding the façade of its independence and sovereignty.

Veesenmayer informed Ribbentrop about Himmler's "purchase" of the Weiss-Manfréd Works on May 25, emphasizing that the transaction aimed primarily at making it possible to supply the SS with the necessary military equipment. To assuage the feelings of the Hungarians, Veesenmayer suggested that the purchase be justified by a number of weighty arguments, including the personal friendship of the Jewish owners of the concern with Horthy and the Hungarian upper class.[56]

Ribbentrop was angered not so much over the German acquisition of the concern as because the deal was concluded without his knowledge. He ordered an investigation, which resulted in a flurry of inter- and intradepartmental memoranda as well as a number of presumably uncomfortable meetings with Himmler and his subordinates.[57] The case added fuel to the rivalry between the *Reichsführer-SS* and the Foreign Minister. Ribbentrop forwarded copies of several of Veesenmayer's telegrams to Hitler only to learn to his great surprise and chagrin that the Führer had sided with Himmler by approving the agreement.[58]

Although Ribbentrop finally consented to the deal and even urged that Sztójay be given some concessions concerning the duration of the trusteeship,[59] the furor over the affair did not die down, primarily because of controversy over the fourth part of the agreement. The travel arrangements for the family group were the responsibility of SS-*Hauptsturmführer* Stapenhorst, one of Becher's closest adjutants, who often used the alias of Torstensen. The original plan called for the departure of the group by June 9; however, the date was changed several times because of difficulties associated with the receipt of the Portuguese and Swiss visas. The Chorin-Weiss group was to have been accompanied to Portugal by Becher, Stapenhorst, and *Haupsturmführer* Krell. The Germans were to travel in civilian clothes, ostensibly on an economic and diplomatic mission.[60] The SS eventually solved the problem of Portuguese and Swiss visas for the family group simply by falsifying them. The departure from Stuttgart was set for June 25, and on June 22 Lufthansa alerted German officials in Spain to expect the arrival of the planes in Madrid.[61]

From Madrid, the bulk of the group went to Lisbon by rail; a few arrived in Lisbon on June 26 by scheduled Spanish commercial flight. Stapenhorst, who had a genuine Portuguese visa himself but was responsible for the false visas in the group's passports, played it safe and traveled separately; Becher did not show up at all.[62]

The Swiss group, which included Ferenc Borbély and Antal Heinrich, left Stuttgart under equally dubious circumstances. On June 24, Stapenhorst persuaded the captain of a Swissair plane to take the passengers to Zurich without their passports, which allegedly had been delayed by some disturbance. The following day, the passports for all but one of them were forwarded as promised. However, they all contained falsified Swiss entry visas.[63]

In late June and July, the major news services, including the DNB and Reuters, unmasked the affair by reporting the arrival in Portugal of a number of "Hungarian millionaires" in possession of a great quantity of gold.[64]

Among those most embarrassed over the unexpected arrival of the millionaires in Lisbon was Ujpétery, the secretary of the Hungarian Legation who also doubled as *chargé d'affaires* following the resignation of Andor Wodianer. He expressed his anxiety to both Sztójay and the German authorities in Portugal, warning that these millionaires had valuable information concerning the industrial and military potential of Hungary and Germany, and that they might transmit it to the Anglo-Saxons. He noted that the only reason the millionaires might not talk would be their concern for the safety of the other members of the family who remained in Germany.[65] Sztójay summarized the background of the affair for him, emphasizing that the "internees," who, he claimed, had originally been arrested by the Germans to prevent them from interfering with "the normal evolution of the situation," would indeed remain silent.[66]

The mysterious arrival of the Chorin-Weiss group in Portugal not only bewildered Hungarian diplomats abroad, but also confused some of the Zionist leaders. Misled by reports in the British press, some of them contended that the Hungarian Jews "were released after intercession by the Hungarian government." In his letter addressed to Chaim Weizman on June 29, 1944, Leo Gestetner provided the following explanation: "The Lisbon report seems to bear out that the Hungarian leaders were not racial fanatics and that they might yet be of some use if they are given the impression that they themselves might be able to save their skins by helping the Jews."[67]

Gestetner also referred to a report in the *Manchester Guardian* of June 27 about the extermination of 100,000 Hungarian Jews. He cautioned Weizmann that the report was unconfirmed and "that it should not, perhaps, be taken at its face value." While it is quite possible that Gestetner had been in the dark about the realities of the catastrophe in Hungary, there is no doubt that Weizmann, like the other leaders of the free world, Jewish and non-Jewish alike, was familiar with most of its dimensions (chapter 23). By that time the dejewification squads were completing the deportation of the Jews from the Hungarian provinces, climaxing the process that begun with the isolation, expropriation, and ghettoization of the Jews.

Notes

1. Lévai, *Fekete könyv*, p. 89.

2. *Vádirat*, 1:59–63.

3. *Ibid.* The Council of Ministers acted in this respect on April 14.

4. Hain and Koltay compelled the Jewish Council of Budapest to provide them not only with automobiles, but also with expensive photographic equipment for their personal use. On occasion, other municipal or ministerial officials also submitted demands even during this phase of the occupation. However, they were less inclined to use terror than the police officials and on occasion also promised compensation. On May 3, 1944, for example, Dénes Szenkovich of the Mayor's Office and Kálmán Somogyváry of the Ministry of Defense submitted a request for "4,500 sheets, 4,500 blankets, 4,500 cooking utensils, and 100 bicycles against compensation." Lévai, *Fekete Könyv*, p. 308.

5. For the titles of all decrees relating to these measures see Appendix 3. For minutes of the discussions in the Council of Ministers relating to these decrees, see *Vádirat*, 1:63–66, 71–72. Over the signature of Deputy Mayor Bódy, the Mayor of Budapest also issued a decree of his own on March 31 relating to the dismissal of Jewish civil servants from the city administration. For text, see *Ibid.*, pp. 69–70.

6. Decree no. 1.580/1944. M. E. as implemented by Decree no. 1.204/1944. P.M. and Decree no. 74.187/1944. F.M. It was subsequently amended under Decree no. 7.700/1944. XIII.a.P.M. and Decree no. 100.100/1944. M.M.

7. Decree no. 24.200/1944. Ip. M. See also Announcement no. 418/1944. Eln. 107 of the President of the Patent Court.

8. Decree No. 1.870/1944. M. E.

9. For text see *Vádirat*, 1:120–21.

10. *Ibid.*, p. 164.

11. The decree was amended on April 29 (Decree no. 1.077/1944. P. M. VI fő), May 20 (Decree no. 1.252/1944. VI. P. M.) and on August 24 (Decree no. 3.050/1944. M. E.). The decree was implemented by virtue of Decree no. 1.252/1944. VI. P. M.

12. In the case of Jews with several bank accounts, all accounts but one were blocked. Article 7 of Decree no. 1.600/1944. M. E.

13. Business life came to a virtual standstill; in Budapest alone about 18,000 businesses were affected. Lévai, *Zsidósors Magyarországon*, p. 85.

14. The Christian managers were appointed by virtue of Decree no. 23.200/1944. Ip. M. and Decree no. 3.520/1944. M. E. as stipulated by Article 10, paragraph 4, of Decree no. 1.600/1944. M. E. Decree no. 23.200/1944. Ip. M. was abrogated during the Szálasi era by Decree no. 49.500/1944. Ip. M.

15. Decree no. 50.500/1944. K.K.M. This was amended by Decree no. 66.658/1944. K.K.M., dated May 25, 1944.

16. Lévai, *Zsidósors Magyarországon*, p. 85.

17. Decree no. 108.500/1944. K.M.

18. Decree no. 108.510/1944. K.M.

19. Decree no. 1.990/1944. M. E.

20. As an example see the petition filed by a resident of Gödöllő, Endre Szatmári, in *Vádirat*, 3:236–37.

21. See, for example, Announcement no. 418/1944. Eln. 107, and Decree no. 91.647/1944. K.K.M. in *Budapesti Közlöny*, no. 147 (July 2, 1944): 12, and no. 169 (July 28, 1944):11. The assignments in the case of larger Jewish firms were usually "legalized" through publication in the *Budapesti Közlöny*. See, for example, no. 206 (September 10, 1944):2.

22. Lévai, *Zsidósors Magyarországon*, p. 249.

23. Lévai, *Fekete könyv*, pp. 307–12.

24. For samples of related decisions, see *Vádirat*, 3:124–26, 214–15, 218–25, 367–68, 414–22, 433–45, 585–88.

25. The train apparently was first taken to Óbánya, near Zirc, and then to Brennbergbánya. Here, according to one account, Toldy rearranged the loot and on March 30, 1945, ordered the train to Austria. He fled to Innsbruck with three cars containing 44 crates filled with gold and jewelry and two boxes with diamonds. The remaining 61 crates laden with treasures were captured by the Americans. The detailed contents of the crates were allegedly as follows: 41 contained gold objects weighing 18.5 quintals (1 quintal = 220.46 pounds); 35 held men's and women's watches weighing 2 quintals; 18 held jewelry with precious stones weighing 7 quintals; eight crates held 114 kilograms of diamonds and 160 kilograms of genuine pearls (1 kilogram = 2.2046 pounds); and three crates contained various types of currency and gold bars weighing three quintals. Two large iron boxes contained choice diamonds and pearls. Lévai, *Fekete könyv*, p. 223.

26. Lévai, *Eichmann in Hungary* (Budapest: Pannonia Press, 1961), p. 227. The Hungarians were particularly resentful over the Germans' removal of the valuable paintings. See, for example, *Vádirat*, 3:166–67.

27. For an evaluation of the background of these families, see William O. McCagg, Jr., *Jewish Nobles and Geniuses in Modern Hungary*. (New York: Columbia University Press, 1972), 254 pp. On the Weiss family and the origins of the Weiss-Manfréd Works, see also I. Berend and Gy. Ránki, *Csepel története* (The History of Csepel) (Budapest: Kossuth, 1965).

28. C. A. Macartney, 2:287.

29. For a listing of the main industrial, mining, and banking enterprises owned by these families, see *Ibid.*

30. Elek Karsai and Miklós Szinai, "A Weiss Manfréd vagyon német kézbe kerülésének története" (The History of the German Acquisition of the Weiss Manfréd Fortune), *Századok* (Centuries), Budapest, 95 (nos. 4–5, 1961): 694. Hereafter referred to as Karsai and Szinai.

31. Among these were Baroness Jenő Weiss, neé Anna Geitler; Baroness György Kornfeld, neé Elza Kawalsky; Dr. Ferenc Borbély; and Dr. Antal Heinrich.

32. The rumor that the Weiss-Manfréd Works was to be consolidated with the Hermann Göring Works persisted not only during the negotiations with the Himmler group, but also after the conclusion of the agreement on May 17, 1944. See, for example, the report in the *New York Times*, April 30, 1944, and Veesenmayer's telegram to Ribbentrop, dated June 1, 1944. *RLB*, Docs. 408 and 411.

33. Also among those arrested were Baron Móric Kornfeld and Baron Jenő Weiss. The other members of the families had managed to escape in time.

34. The family group was represented by György Hoff, the legal counselor of the Weiss-Manfréd Works, and Zoltán Fenyvesi. The SS and Becher were represented by Wilhelm Schneider of Berlin and Friedrich Zabransky of Vienna. Hoff and Fenyvesi, along with several members of their families, escaped to Portugal together with a part of the family group.

35. This part of the agreement was signed by Baroness Jenő Weiss, neé Anna Geitler, an Aryan member of the family.

36. According to Becher, Himmler originally insisted on a trusteeship period of 33 years. This second part of the agreement was signed by 27 members of the family group, five of which were identified as pure Aryans and one, Dr. Antal Heinrich, as a *Mischling*. For their identification, see Karsai and Szinai, pp. 693, 697.

37. Under this agreement, signed by Baroness Jenő Weiss, the SS was given priority in the purchase of the concern upon the expiration of the trusteeship period. For the text of the agreements, see *Ibid.*, pp. 691–99.

38. NO-1254.

39. According to Becher, the members of the four families did not have valid Hungarian passports. The border crossing was facilitated, upon instructions from Vienna, by German passport and customs officials. Becher's statements to the Hungarian political police during the November 14–December 6, 1945, period are reproduced by Karsai and Szinai, pp. 707–18. See also NG-2972.

40. These were Alfonz Weiss, György Kornfeld, János Mauthner and their wives, the Kornfelds' son, and Vilmos Billitz and his wife. This group was subsequently joined by Ferenc Máriássy and his wife. *Ibid.*, p. 702. Although kept under close supervision in the Reich, they enjoyed, to the great chagrin of Ernst Kaltenbrunner, exceptionally good treatment.

41. For complete text, see Karsai and Szinai, pp. 700–701.

42. Minutes of the Council of Ministers meeting of May 22, 1944. *Ibid.*, pp. 686–87. See also C. A. Macartney, 2:288.

43. *RLB*, Doc. 411.

44. *Ibid.*, Doc. 421. See also Karsai and Szinai, p. 713.

45. For excerpts from the minutes, see *Vádirat*, 2:137.

46. *Ibid.*, p. 143.

47. *RLB*, Doc. 415.

48. Karsai and Szinai, p. 716.

49. *RLB*, Doc. 418.

50. *Ibid.*, Doc. 420.

51. *Ibid.*, Docs. 424–25.

52. For excerpts from Imrédy's October 9, 1945, statement before the Hungarian political police concerning the SS deal involving the Weiss-Manfréd Works, see Karsai and

Szinai, pp. 706–7. According to some observers, Imrédy was outmaneuvered by those eager to extricate Hungary from the war by exploiting the SS deal.

53. For excerpts from the minutes of the Council's meeting, see *Vádirat*, 2:143–44.

54. This was made possible under Decree no. 2.460/1944. M. E. of July 8, 1944, which authorized individual ministers to exercise voting rights with respect to shares owned by Jews in their spheres of jurisdiction. Karsai and Szinai, p. 690.

55. NO-601. See also NI-044, NI-045, and NO-603.

56. *RLB*, Doc. 409.

57. Among the Foreign Office personnel involved in these delicate contacts were Horst Wagner and Eberhard von Thadden of *Inland II* and Günther Altenburg, a member of Ribbentrop's Personal Staff. *Ibid.*, Docs. 413–14.

58. *Ibid.*, Docs. 420–21. The rivalry between the two ministers was paralleled by the animosity between Veesenmayer and Winkelmann in Budapest. For additional documents on the Weiss-Manfréd affair, see those originating from the archives of the *Reichsführer-SS* in *NA*, Microcopy T-175, Roll no. 59; for additional documentary materials emanating from the German Foreign Office, see Microcopy T-120, Roll no. 4203, Frames K209132, –138–141, –144–169, and –171–213.

59. *RLB*, 1:cxxxiv.

60. *Ibid.*, Doc. 416.

61. *Ibid.*, Doc. 419.

62. *Ibid.*, Docs. 422–23.

63. *Ibid.*, Doc. 435.

64. *Ibid.*, Doc. 422.

65. *Ibid.*, Doc. 423. See also *Vádirat*, 2:138–39 and 140–42.

66. *Ibid.*, pp. 139–40. For further details on the Weiss-Manfréd case, consult *Auswärtiges Amt, Inland II g., 213, Ungarn. Die Angelegenheit Manfréd Weiss 1944* (Foreign Office, Inland II g., 213, Hungary. The Weiss Manfréd Case, 1944) in the archives of the Foreign Office of the Federal Republic of Germany, Bonn.

67. Weizmann Archives, Rechovot, Israel.

CHAPTER SEVENTEEN

GHETTOIZATION: PHASE I

The Ghettoization Decision

ALTHOUGH THE decree for the relocation of Jews was not adopted until April 26, 1944, the German and Hungarian officials associated with the Final Solution program worked out the details of the ghettoization process as early as April 4. It was the day when the leaders and legal experts of the Jewish Council completed the draft of the new bylaws, naively acting out the tasks assigned to them by the SS.

The fateful meeting of the dejewification experts was held in the offices and under the chairmanship of László Baky in the Ministry of the Interior. It was attended by high-ranking officers of the *Wehrmacht* and of the *Honvédség* (Hungarian Armed Forces), by Eichmann and the other members of the *Sonderkommando,* and by László Endre, Colonel Győző Tölgyesy, the Commander of Gendarmerie District No. VIII with headquarters in Kassa—the first area destined to be cleared of Jews—and Lieutenant-Colonel László Ferenczy.

Appointed a few days earlier to serve as the gendarmerie's liaison to the German Security Service (*Sicherheitsdienst*), Ferenczy was assigned to direct and supervise the planned ghettoization and deportation program. His chief assistants for the implementation of the program included some of the most anti-Semitic and rightist-oriented commanders of the country's gendarmerie districts. Among these were Tölgyesy, in charge of operations in Carpatho-Ruthenia, Colonel Tibor Paksy-Kiss, entrusted with the anti-Jewish campaign in Gendarmerie Districts IX and X covering Northern Transylvania, Colonel László Orbán, the commander of the operations in the southern areas of the country, and Colonel Vilmos Sellyey, who was in charge of the operations in the country's other gendarmerie districts.[1]

Andor Jaross, the Minister of the Interior, who was formally responsible for all decisions adopted under the aegis of his Ministry, was kept fully informed about the deliberations of the dejewification experts. In fact, on the day of that fateful meeting Jaross wrote to Ferenczy, instructing him to submit daily reports about the campaign against the Jews to Section XX in the Ministry of the Interior.[2]

In launching the ghettoization and deportation program, the participants at the meeting were partially guided by the Nazi experience in
other parts of German-occupied Europe, which reflected the directives
of Reinhardt Heydrich of September 21, 1939.[3] Heydrich's directives,
addressed to the *Einsatzgruppen* in occupied Poland, stipulated that the
first prerequisite for the implementation of the "ultimate goal" was the
speedy "concentration of the Jews from the country to the larger cities." The number of concentration points was to be as low as possible
and care was to be taken that they be "located either at railroad junc-
tions or at least along a railroad." Temporary exemption was to be extended only to those Jews whose skills were needed by the army or for
the nation's security and economic interests. These "exempted" Jews
were to be removed immediately upon their replacement by competent
Aryans. For the implementation of his directives, Heydrich requested
that detailed numerical surveys of the Jews be prepared and that his office be informed about the timetable of the operations.

A document incorporating many of these ideas was prepared by
Endre and distributed to all those attending the April 4 meeting. Since
Endre would not be formally appointed Secretary of State until April 9,
the document (no. 6163/1944. res. of the Ministry of the Interior) was
issued secretly under the signature of Baky on April 7.[4] This most fateful document, addressed to the representatives of the local organs of
state power, spelled out the procedures to be followed in the ghettoization, concentration, and deportation of the Jews.

RE: *The Assignment of Dwelling Places for Jews*
The Royal Hungarian Government will soon have the country purged of Jews.
I order the purge to be carried out by regions. As a result of the purge,
Jewry—irrespective of sex or age—is to be transported to assigned concentration camps. In towns or large villages a part of the Jews are later to be accommodated in Jewish buildings or ghettos, assigned to them by the police authorities. Jewish experts and skilled workmen employed in factories engaged in war
production or in mines, large works, or landed estates, whose immediate replacement would endanger the production of the works in question are exempted. However, in factories, mines, or companies which are not earmarked
for war production, they must be replaced immediately by the most suitable
persons from the staff of the company, works, etc. in question. The persons
replacing the Jews must be given the full range of authority of their predecessors. Committees appointed by municipal or county authorities are to determine the persons concerned. The authorities are to proceed forthwith to provide for people to take their place. As soon as the replacement is feasible—and
the head of the administrative authority concerned must endeavor to achieve
this as soon as possible—an expert trustee must be immediately appointed and

placed at the head of the factory or company in question, with full responsibility. The rounding up of the Jews is to be carried out by the local police or by the Royal Hungarian Gendarmerie units concerned. If necessary, the gendarmerie will assist the Royal Hungarian Police in urban districts by providing armed help. The German security police will be on the spot as an advisory body. Special importance must be attached to achieving undisturbed cooperation with them. The administrative authorities of the counties must forthwith establish concentration camps in suitable places and numbers, corresponding to the number of Jews to be placed in them. The location of these camps is to be reported to the Secretary of State for Public Security. In every town or large village where the number of Jews necessitates the assignment of separate buildings for them, the police authorities are to take the necessary steps on their own initiative, since only Jews dangerous from the point of view of state security are to be detained in concentration camps, whereas the others are to be accommodated in Jewish buildings. Buildings where Jews have dwelt in large numbers are to be turned into Jewish buildings. People of non-Jewish origin living in such Jewish buildings are to be assigned residences of a similar value and similar rent within thirty days of the purge in the district concerned. They must be relocated there by the police authorities, so that on leaving the concentration camps the Jews can, when the time comes, immediately be accommodated in the Jewish buildings. Simultaneously with the rounding up and the transportation of the Jews the local authorities are to appoint committees which, in cooperation with the police and the gendarmerie, must lock up the residences and shops of the Jews and seal them separately. The sealed envelopes containing the keys and indicating the name and address of the Jew are to be handed over to the commander of the concentration camp. Perishable goods and live animals which do not serve the purpose of production must be handed over to the municipal and village authorities. They are to be used in the first place to cover the requirements of the army and public security organs, and secondly those of the local population. Money and valuables (gold, silverware, stock shares, etc.) must be taken into safe custody by the above bodies and, together with a short list specifying them, be handed over to the municipal or village authorities against a receipt and counter-receipt. The municipal authorities must deliver these valuables within three days to the branch of the National Bank at the center of the territory to be purged. The police bodies carrying out the purges shall determine these centers separately in each case.

Jews are to be transported as prisoners, by train or if necessary by relay coaches to be ordered by the municipal authorities. The Jews to be deported are allowed to take with them only the clothes they have on, at most two changes of underwear, and food sufficient for no more than 14 days. They will also be allowed luggage weighing not more than 50 kilograms, including the weight of the bedding, blankets, and mattresses. They are not allowed to take money, jewelry, gold or any other valuables. The rounding up of the Jews is to be carried out in the following sequence: Gendarmerie districts VIII, IX, X, II, III, IV, V, VI, VII, and I.

All armed companies and the training units subordinate to them are at the disposal of the district commanders of the gendarmerie and the police. However, when availing themselves of armed units, the commanders should bear in mind that closing the boundaries of a certain district must not cease before the rounding up of the Jews has been completed in the adjacent districts also. Headquarters of gendarmerie districts and police authorities are to establish contact with each other over the rounding up of the Jews, so that the purge may take place simultaneously and jointly. If a Jew cannot be found at his residence, the usual warrant must be issued against him with reference to my present order. The homes of such Jews are to be dealt with in the same way as those of Jews who are caught.

I draw the authorities' attention to the fact that all Jews who have fled here from the territories of foreign countries are to be given the same treatment as the Communists, i.e., they are to be taken without exception to concentration camps. People whose Jewish origin may be doubtful are also to be taken to concentration camps, where their origin is to be clarified.

My present order is to be treated as strictly confidential and the heads of the authorities or headquarters are responsible for seeing to it that no one will learn of it before the purges are started.

László Baky [5]

Although the Council of Ministers did not formally act on the issue of ghettoization until April 26,[6] many of the local authorities began to take immediate action on the basis of the decisions that were made on April 4. In some areas of the country, the overambitious local authorities had begun to round up the Jews on their own initiative even earlier. This was the case, for example, in the Enying District of Veszprém County and shortly afterward in the county's other districts, from where the Jews were reportedly taken to the city of Veszprém by the end of March.[7]

The speed with which the dejewification experts decided to implement the Final Solution program in Hungary is reflected by the fact that the Ministry of the Interior issued the first concrete directives for the implementation of Baky's confidential decree three days before the latter was issued. In a secret order (no. 6136/1944. VII. res.) dated April 4, the Minister instructed all the subordinated mayoral, police, and gendarmerie organs to bring about the registration of the Jews by the Jews. The order read as follows:

To All Mayors and Local Boards
  At Their Stations

Instruct the Jewish communal organizations to prepare a list in four copies of all Jews with their families, specifying their apartments and places of residence, and to submit it immediately to the mayor or the local boards.

The mayor or local board will send one copy of the list to the police authority of the first instance, another to the gendarmerie guard command, and a third by mail to the Royal Hungarian Minister of the Interior no later than April 8.[8]

While the unrealistic deadline set by the Minister of the Interior could not possibly be met, the local authorities lost no time in implementing the decision. Typical of the instructions issued by local officials are those that were issued by the Mayor of Nyíregyháza:[9]

9615/1944. F.J.   Subject: Registration of the Jews
DECISION
I hereby instruct the Jewish communal organs to prepare a list of all the Jews together with their family members, giving the address and apartment number, and to submit it in four copies to the City Clerk (City Hall, Room 3) within 48 hours from receipt of this Decision. The list should also include the name of the mother for all persons listed.

Nyíregyháza, April 11, 1944   *Pál Nyíregyházy*
                                                                Mayor

To make sure that no Jews would escape the net, another registration order was issued by the Minister of Supply, allegedly to regulate the allocation of food for the Jews. The order stipulated that the data relating to the Jews (including their names, the date and place of birth, occupation, and exact address), be submitted to the local governmental authorities by May 1, 1944.[10]

In response to the orders of Baky and Béla Jurcsek, who doubled as Minister of Agriculture and Minister of Supply, the mayors of the local communities asked the local Jewish communal leaders to prepare lists of all the Jews in their particular communities on the excuse that the sugar and soap ration coupons were being replaced by new ones.

The Jews, as they had with the decree ordering them to wear badges, complied with this ominous measure. Although the central Jewish leaders were aware that these two interrelated measures were designed to facilitate the isolation and ghettoization of the Jews—the Zionist leaders were specifically warned against compliance by the Istanbul *Vaada*—the local Jewish communal leaders were left in the dark. They faithfully prepared the lists. In smaller communities, it was usually the secretary or registrar of the congregation that prepared them; in larger ones, they were usually prepared by young men not yet mobilized for service in the military labor service system. They usually acted in pairs, conscientiously canvassing the entire city, eager not to leave out a single street or building. The lists included given name and surname, mother's name, address, occupation and age.[11]

On April 5, Baky issued a "strictly confidential" order (no. 6137/1944. VII. res.) instructing the head of the prosecutory-investigative section of the *Állumvédelmi Központ* (Center for State Defense)[12] to supervise, with the aid of the units subordinated to him, the implementation of the police measures enacted against the Jews. He was assigned to deploy his units to the field in order to "forestall any possible accusations or abuses in connection with the solution of the Jewish question."[13]

On April 7, the same day he sent out his ghettoization order, Baky held another conference in his office at the Ministry of the Interior. Participating were Endre, two SS officers, and a number of gendarmerie and police officers, including Colonel Tölgyesy, Captain Záhonyi, Police Counselors Thurzó and Meskó, and Ministerial Counselor Géza Halász. Baky announced the imminent evacuation of the Jews from the area of Gendarmerie District No. VIII, the area which encompassed Carpatho-Ruthenia and some parts of northeastern Hungary. He also revealed some of the operational techniques to be employed and the organizational structure to be set up.

Overall command was entrusted to a group of dejewification experts composed of members of the Eichmann-*Sonderkommando* and a number of Hungarians. Among the latter were Ferenczy and Meggyesi.

With respect to the operations in Carpatho-Ruthenia and northeastern Hungary, Munkács was selected as the headquarters of the command unit. In the other large Jewish centers of the area, including Huszt, Nagyszőllős, and Ungvár, the command was to be represented and assisted by special executive committees. The final detailed instructions relating to the planned anti-Jewish operations were spelled out by Endre in accordance with the general guidelines included in an order of April 7 (6163).[14] Endre identified the specific locations where the Jews were to be concentrated: empty warehouses, abandoned or nonoperational factories, brickyards, Jewish community establishments, Jewish schools and offices, and synagogues.[15]

The dejewification experts lost no time in implementing the guidelines. Among the first concrete steps they took were to place the areas slated for dejewification under special military rule and to organize the Hungarian dejewification headquarters.

The Military Operational Zones

Since the anti-Jewish operations could not be camouflaged and the mass evacuation of the Jews was bound to create dislocations in the economic life of the affected communities, the dejewification experts felt compelled to provide a military rationale for the operations. They assumed, it turned out correctly, that the local population, including some of the Jews, would understand the necessity for the removal of the Jews from the approaching frontlines "in order to protect Axis interests from the machinations of Judeo-Bolsheviks." The Council of Ministers proved cooperative and on April 12 adopted a measure under which Carpatho-Ruthenia and Northern Transylvania were declared to have become military operational zones as of April 1. The measure identified the counties of Bereg, Máramaros, Ugocsa, and Ung and the municipality of Ungvár in Carpatho-Ruthenia as well as the counties of Beszterce-Naszod, Csik, Háromszék, Kolozs, Maros-Torda, Szolnok-Doboka, and Udvarhely and the municipalities of Kolozsvár and Marosvásárhely in Northern Transylvania, as military operational areas.[16]

The Council appointed Dr. Vilmos Pál Tomcsányi to serve as Government Commissioner for the military operational zones in Carpatho-Ruthenia.[17] Probably realizing the implications of his appointment, Tomcsányi resigned shortly thereafter; his place was taken by Lieutenant-General András Vincze.[18] The position of Government Commissioner for Northern Transylvania was assigned to Béla Ricsóy-Uhlarik.[19]

The scenario for the removal of the Jews from the "military operational zones" was played out later in the month, when Veesenmayer conveyed the *Wehrmacht*'s request to that effect. It culminated in the deportation of the Jews following the revelation by Endre that the Germans were ready to accept the large number of Jews for whom there was no room in the country's interior (see chapter 19).

The Hungarian Dejewification Unit

The Hungarian dejewification unit acted under the guidance of the Baky-Endre group in the Ministry of the Interior and in close cooperation with the Eichmann-*Sonderkommando*. It was headed by Lieutenant-Colonel Ferenczy in his capacity as Liaison Officer of the Royal Hungarian Gendarmerie to the German Security Police (*Magyar királyi csendőrség összekötő tisztje a német biztonsági rendőrségnél*). The Hungarian dejewification unit had two headquarters: one was in Pest, at 6 Semmelweiss Street, in the County House (*Vármegyeháza*); the other was located in the Lomnic Hotel in Buda at 2 Evetke Road, immediately adjacent to Eichmann's headquarters in the Majestic Hotel.

Reflecting his callousness and his desire to camouflage his operations,

Ferenczy had the door plate of his Pest office inscribed with the name: "International Storage and Transportation Company, Inc." (*Nemzetközi beraktározási és szállitási kft.*).[20] His daily reports on the progress of the ghettoization and deportation operations were sent out from his Evetke Road headquarters.

Ferenczy's closest collaborators in the dejewification unit were Meggyesi, Márton Zöldi, Péter Hain, László Koltay (Hain's deputy), and the high-ranking gendarmerie officers in charge of the field operations in the various areas, including Tölgyesy, Paksy-Kiss, Sellyey, and Jenő Péterffy. Zöldi, who had escaped to Germany earlier in the year to avoid punishment for his role in the Délvidek massacres (chapter 6), returned as a member of the *Waffen SS* and served as Eichmann's liaison in the Hungarian dejewification unit.

Like their Nazi counterparts, the members of the Hungarian unit proceeded with cold-blooded precision to work out the details of the master plan that was to bring about the Final Solution.

The Ghettoization, Concentration, and Deportation Master Plan

The master plan worked out by the German and Hungarian dejewification experts called for the ghettoization and concentration to be effectuated in a number of distinct phases.

- Jews in the rural communities and the smaller towns were to be rounded up and temporarily transferred to synagogues and community buildings.
- Following the first round of investigation in pursuit of valuables, the Jews rounded up in the rural communities and smaller towns were to be transferred to the ghettos of the larger cities in their vicinity, usually the county seat.
- In the larger towns and cities Jews were to be rounded up and transferred to a specially designated area that would serve as a ghetto—totally isolated from the other parts of the city. In some cities, the ghetto was to be established in the Jewish quarter; in others in factories, warehouses, brickyards, or under the open sky.
- Jews were to be concentrated in centers with adequate rail facilities to make possible swift entrainment and deportation.

During each phase, the Jews were to be subjected to special investigations by teams composed of gendarmerie and police officials to compel them to surrender their valuables. The plans for the implementation of the ghettoization and deportation operations called for the launching of six territorially defined "mopping-up operations" (*tisztogatási akciók*). For this purpose, the country was divided into six operational zones, with each zone encompassing one or two gendarmerie districts (see table 13.1). The operations were to be launched according to the following territorial order of priority:

- Zone I. The Jews in Gendarmerie District VIII (Kassa)—Carpatho-Ruthenia and northeastern Hungary.
- Zone II. The Jews in Gendarmerie Districts IX (Kolozsvár) and X (Marosvásárhely)—Northern Transylvania.
- Zone III. The Jews of Gendarmerie Districts II (Székesfehérvár) and VII (Miskolc)—northern Hungary in the area extending from Kassa to the borders of the Third Reich.
- Zone IV. The Jews in Gendarmerie Districts V (Szeged) and VI (Debrecen)—the southern parts of Hungary east of the Danube.
- Zone V. The Jews of Gendarmerie Districts III (Szombathely) and IV (Pécs)—the southwestern parts of the country west of the Danube.
- Zone VI. The Jews in Gendarmerie District I (Budapest)—the capital and its immediate environs.

The order of priority, which mostly corresponded to the ideas expressed by the "personal secretary of Kállay" to Wisliceny early in October 1942 (see chapter 9), was established with an eye on a series of military, political, and psychological factors. Time was of the essence because of the fast approach of the Red Army. Politically it was more expedient to start in Carpatho-Ruthenia and Northern Transylvania, because the central and local Hungarian authorities and the local population had less regard for the "Galician," "alien," non-Magyarized, and Yiddish-oriented masses than for the assimilated ones. Their round-up for "labor" in Germany was accepted in many Hungarian rightist circles as doubly welcome: Hungary would get rid of its "alien" elements and would at the same time make a contribution to the joint war effort, thereby hastening the termination of the occupation and the reestablishment of full sovereignty.

This order of priority was adopted against the original objections of Endre, who would have preferred to start the ghettoization program in Budapest. He was won over by the Eichmann-*Sonderkommando* who convinced him of the desirability of launching the operations in the countryside beginning with the northeastern parts of the country. According to Höttl, the rationale behind this decision was to prevent the Jews of Budapest, the most sophisticated and assimilated in the country, from fleeing the capital and hiding in the countryside.[21] Following Horthy's decision of July 7 to halt the deportations, thereby saving the Jews of Budapest, Endre often reproached his colleagues for their failure to heed his advice.[22]

In deciding the order of operations, the dejewification squads considered not only the obvious political-military factors, but also the possible psychological impact upon the Jewish population.

The Rationalizations of the Jews

Many of the Jews in Zones I and II tended to rationalize their "removal from the military operational zone" as an understandable precautionary measure by an enemy that considered them as "allies of the Bolsheviks." According to the prevalent rumor encouraged by the authorities, they were to be taken to Kenyérmező,[23] an internment camp where they would be put to work and enabled to take care of their families. In many a ghetto, especially in Northern Transylvania, the gendarmes helped spread the rumor just before the deportations that the Jews were being relocated to Dunántul (Transdanubia), away from the front, to be employed in agricultural work. Another rumor, especially widespread in the Nagyvárad ghetto, had it that the Jews were being transferred for labor to Mezőtúr, the center of an agricultural region west of Nagyvárad just southeast of Szolnok.[24] In the ghettos of Carpatho-Ruthenia, the rumor was spread that the Jews would be taken for agricultural labor to the Hortobágy, the plains covering a large part of Hajdu County.[25]

The Jews in the larger towns and cities at first tended to believe that the ghettoization measures would affect only the rural Jews. When it became apparent that the drive in Zones I and II was in fact general, the Jews in Zones III, IV, and V rationalized that what happened to the non-Magyarized Jews in Carpatho-Ruthenia and Northern Transylvania could not possibly happen to themselves. After all, they were assimilated "Magyar Jews" who had a thousand-year history of coexistence with their Christian brethren. Finally, when these were concentrated and deported, the Jews of Budapest rationalized that what had happened in the provinces could not possibly happen to the large mass of cosmopolitan Jews who lived under the constant watch of Horthy and foreign diplomats.

This psychological state was fostered by the authorities through the information they supplied to the Jewish Council. Operations, they assured the Council, were being restricted to the eastern areas. To prove this the authorities adopted a series of anti-Jewish decrees, which were to be applicable in the areas of Hungary not yet dejewified; these were calculated to demonstrate that the Jews in these areas were destined to remain alive.[26] Many of the Jews, especially in Budapest, fell for this ploy: "If they wanted to annihilate us why would they pass these decrees?" they argued.

The complacency of the Jews was further encouraged by the propagation of the assurances Eichmann had given János Gábor a few weeks after the occupation. Agonized by some of the measures the Germans had taken, Gábor naively inquired whether the Jews were not really exposed to the danger of deportation. Eichmann disarmed him—and through him apparently many Jews—by his assurances that such drastic measures would not be taken if the Jews did not join the Ruthene partisans or Tito's units.[27]

Such "assurances" that only the unassimilated Jewish masses were going to be deported "for labor" and only from the military operational zones and that the Magyarized Jews would not be touched appear to have affected the attitude of the Jewish Council as well as that of the other leaders of Jewry.

The ghettoization and deportation of the provincial Jews were organized on an assembly-line basis. The Jews in Zones I and II were in the ghettos for an average of three to five weeks. It was only after the completion of the ghettoization and concentration process in these zones that the deportation was launched on May 15. From that date on, the concentration of the Jews into the entrainment centers took place just a few days before their scheduled deportation. These last days were usually exploited for a last gendarmerie-police search for hidden valuables.

Zone I: Carpatho-Ruthenia and Northeastern Hungary

The round-up and concentration of the Jews of Hungary began in Carpatho-Ruthenia and the northeastern parts of the country on Sunday April 16, 1944, the first day of Passover. The operation was based upon the decisions taken at the conference László Endre held at Munkács on April 12 with the top civilian, police, and gendarmerie officers from the cities, municipalities, and counties in the affected areas. The details of the operation in each county were worked out at local conferences held shortly after April 12, attended by the mayors, police chiefs, and gendarmerie commanders of the particular county. The local conferees worked from the written instructions of László Baky, and more importantly from the oral communications given by Endre at Munkács. It was the function of these local conferences not only to determine the location and administration of the local ghettos, but also to establish the commissions for the round-up of the Jews and the special teams for the identification and confiscation of Jewish wealth.

In order to mislead the masses and assuage the fears of the Jews elsewhere in Hungary, the public relations experts of the dejewification squad "justified" the operations launched on April 16 as necessary precautionary measures designed to protect the security of the country following the identification of the area as a military operational zone.

The ghettoization and concentration of the Jews of Carpatho-Ruthenia and of the northeastern parts of Hungary were formally illegal, as the decree calling for the ghettoization was not issued until April 28. Even after that date, the overzealous local officials often rounded up the exempted Jews and in many places Jewish labor servicemen, who were under the jurisdiction of the Ministry of Defense. Theoretically, the internment of children under six years of age was also illegal, as they were exempt from wearing the yellow Star of David and the anti-Jewish measures supposedly extended only to those compelled to wear it.

The day the anti-Jewish operations started, Ferenczy and his dejewification squad arrived to take command in Munkács, the area headquarters for the ghettoization, concentration, and deportation drive.

In addition to the German and Hungarian dejewification units, the local army units were also authorized to issue orders affecting Jews in their territories. In Carpatho-Ruthenia the Hungarian army units were under the immediate command of General Fehér (Weisz), who was recalled from the front for this purpose, allegedly because his predecessor, General Zoltán Álgya-Pap, had complained about the excesses of the gendarmes in the area.[28]

As was subsequently the case in all other parts of Hungary, the operation began with the round-up of the Jews in the hamlets and villages. The Jews were awakened by the gendarmes at the crack of dawn. They were usually given only a few minutes to pack essential clothes and food they happened to have in the house and then they were taken to their local synagogues. There they were robbed of their money, jewelry, and other valuables. Although their homes were "sealed" and the contents subsequently inventorized, they were soon plundered and poultry and farm animals removed. A few days after having been assembled, the Jews were marched to the nearest concentration centers, normally consisting of the brickyards of the larger cities, including Munkács, Ungvár, Beregszász, Nagyszőllős, Huszt, Técső, Sátoraljaujhely, Kassa, and Nyíregyháza.

In the assembly centers, the feeding of the Jews, including those transferred from the neighboring communities, became the responsibility of the local Jewish Councils. Although the main and frequently only meal consisted primarily of a little potato soup, the problem became acute after the first few days, when the supplies the rural Jews took along were consumed. The living conditions in the ghettos were extremely harsh, and often brutally inhuman. The terrible overcrowding in the apartments within the ghettos, with totally inadequate cooking, bathing, and sanitary facilities, created intolerable hardships as well as tension among the inhabitants. But deplorable as conditions were in the city ghettos, they could not compare to the absolutely cruel conditions that prevailed in the brickyards and the woods, where many of the Jews had to linger for several weeks under the open skies. The inadequate nutrition, the lack of sanitary facilities, the absence of bathing opportunities, as well as the inclement weather led to serious health problems in many places. Aside from minor illnesses and ordinary colds, which were prevalent, many people succumbed to serious diseases, including dysentery, typhoid, and pneumonia. All of these were compounded by the generally barbaric behavior of the gendarmes and police officers guarding the ghettos. Though in some communities there were local officials who endeavored to act as humanely as possible under those extraordinary conditions, their example was the exception rather than the rule.[29]

In Carpatho-Ruthenia and northeastern Hungary there were 13 major ghetto and entrainment centers. Their location, population, condition, and liquidation, on the basis of the available data, are summarized below.[30]

Munkács. This large center of Orthodoxy and Hasidism had two ghettos: one was for the Jews from the neighboring smaller towns and rural communities in Bereg County, including Berezska Roztoka, Bártháza, Ilosva, Irsava, Nagyrákoc, Opava, Szolyva, and Tárkány; the other was for the local Jews. The former was established in the facilities of the Sajovits Brickyards, which were totally insufficient for the approximately 14,000 rural Jews. As a consequence many of the Jews had to set up their makeshift households under the open sky in the factory yard, which was surrounded by planks.

The approximately 13,000 Jews of Munkács were ordered into the ghetto on April 18. It was located in the Jewish section of the city and encompassed Latorca, Dankó, Kálvin, Töltés, Zrinyi, Munkácsi, Szent Márton, Mikes Kelemen, Csokoli, Zenész, and Malom Streets. Both ghettos were under the internal administration of a Jewish Council composed of Sándor Steiner (President), Segelstein, Oszkár Klein, Ferenc Áron, János Morvai, and Mendel Eisenstätter.[31]

Like the homes of their village brethren, the homes of the city Jews were robbed soon after they had been vacated. The Jews of both the brickworks and the ghetto, increasingly emaciated by maltreatment and the hunger caused by the dwindling food supplies, were taken out to work in the course of which they were subjected to incessant cruelties and indignities. The special viciousness with which the Nazi-*Nyilas* gangs treated the unassimilated Hasidic Jews is illustrated by the use of these pious Jews to destroy a synagogue on a Saturday.

The deplorable conditions in the ghetto led to an outbreak of typhoid on April 23 in one of the sections. The ghetto commander, First Lieutenant Kiss, had this section quarantined until May 15, when the first trainload of Jews, ill as they were, were deported. In some of the rural communities in the area, typhoid broke out even before the Jews were transferred to Munkács. This was the case, for example, in Dombó from where the 1,006 quarantined Jews were eventually transferred to Técső for entrainment.[32]

On May 15, when the rural Jews were deported, the Jews of Munkács were transferred from their city ghetto to the Sajovits Brickyards for entrainment. The first transport of the city Jews left the brickyards on May 19; the last on May 24. As was the case in many other communities, the local authorities and dejewification units conspired to deport the exempted Jews as well. Among these were a number of Jews who had earned high military honors for bravery in World War I.[33]

Ungvár. About 18,000 Jews from the districts of Ungvár and Nagykapocs in Ung County, including those from the communities of Alsó-Pásztej, Csicser, Mircs, Nagyberezna, Poroszló, Szerednye, Turjaporoskő, and Ungdorocz, were concentrated in the Moskovits Brick Works on Minai Street and in the Glück Lumber Yard. They were joined there by the approximately 7,000 local Jews, who were rounded up on April 21–23.[34] As in Munkács, many of the Jews in the camps in

Ungvár had to set up a household under the open sky. The four-member Jewish Council was headed by a Dr. László.[35] The ghetto had an underground courier service to Budapest through which the representatives of the Hungarian and international Jewish organizations in Switzerland were kept abreast about developments in Carpatho-Ruthenia. On the basis of such information, for example, mail was sent to certain individuals in the ghettos addressed to the brickyards in which they were located. One of these couriers, Dr. Ackermann, a lawyer from Ungvár, was caught by the German Security Police. The documents in his possession revealed the humane attitude of Dr. Szendrődi, the deputy public notary who was assigned by the Major of Ungvár to handle food supplies and sanitation in the ghetto, and of Dr. Török, a Police Counselor. Upon Ferenczy's arrival at the scene these officials were promptly removed and the ghetto was placed under the overall command of Lieutenant Colonel Sándor Pálffy.[36]

Beregszász. The ghetto was located in the Kont and Vály Brick Works and the facilities of the so-called Weisz Farm. It contained approximately 10,000 Jews, including those of Ardod, Bátyú, Beregkővesd, Beregsurány, Bilke, Harangláb, Marosjánosi, Tarpa, and Vásárosnamény.[37] As in practically all the ghettos, no sooner were the Jews deported than the hunt for the money and valuables left behind by them began both in the ghetto and in the "sealed" homes. The extent of looting in Beregszász aroused the attention even of the Germans.[38]

Nagyszőllős. The Jews of the city and of the communities in Ugocsa County were concentrated in four streets around the synagogue and the so-called Magyar Sor. The ghetto held approximately 12,000 to 14,000 Jews, including those of the neighboring communities of Batarcs, Feketeardó, Halmi, Királyháza, Kőkényes, Nagytarna, Terebes, Tiszaszászfalu, Tiszaujlak, and Turc.[39] Of the ghetto's population, approximately 4,700 were from the city itself. The Jewish Council was composed of Mór (Moshe) Gutmann, Emil (Mendl) Würzburger, Lipót (Lippe) Friedmann, and Márton (Mordchay) Eisenberger.[40] Baron Zsigmond Perényi, the former Vice-President of the upper house of the Hungarian Parliament, and his son, who had their estate in the county, did their best to help alleviate the plight of the Jews in the ghetto by sending food.[41]

Huszt. In addition to the local Jews, about 5,000 rural Jews from the districts of Alsószinever, Gernyes, and Varjac—including those of the communities of Alsóhidegpatak and Eötvösfalva—were concentrated in Csőregréti, Izai, and Kossuth Streets. The Jewish Council was composed of Lazarovits (President), Rosenbaum, Dr. Hegedüs, Dr. Polgár, and Markovits.[42]

Iza. About 7,000 Jews from the districts of Alsóbisztra, Berezne, Felsőbisztra, Herincse, Kosolovó, Lisamező, Majdanka, Podoloc, and Vetéle were concentrated here under the leadership of the Jewish Council of Huszt.[43]

Técső. At one time approximately 10,000 Jews were concentrated in Técső. Among these were the close to 2,500 local Jews and the Jews from the neighboring communities in the districts of Kerekhegy, Pálosremete, Szaplonca, and Visk. Among the communities were Bedőháza, Brusztura, Dombó, Gánya, Kalinfalva, Királymező, Kőkényes, Körtvélyes, Nyéresháza, Oroszmokra, Taracköz, Tarackraszna, Visk, and Vulchovec. The original plan was to transfer the Jews gathered in Técső for entrainment to Mátészalka. At the end, however, they were deported directly from Técső, with the first transport leaving on May 22, 1944. The Jewish Council was headed by Jenő Roth and included Zoltán Kallos and Dr. Grünstein, a physician.[44] The ghetto was located in the town's Jewish section and in a special camp.

Sátoraljaujhely. About 15,000 Jews of Zemplén County, including those of Eötvösfalva, Mád,[45] Sárospatak,[46] and Taktaharkány, were concentrated in the local ghetto situated in the gypsy section around Rákoczy, Virág, Sziget, Vörösmarty, Zárda, Mészáros, Molnár, Széchenyi, Folkenstein, Apponyi, Árpád, Kisfaludy, Kölcsey, Zápolya, and Munkácsy Streets. They were under the leadership of a Jewish Council composed of Dr. Lajos Rosenberg (President), Dr. Sándor Glück, Sámuel Eisenberger, Henrik Szamek, and Mór Szofer.[47]

The deportation began on May 16 with a first transport of 3,500 Jews. The second transport of 3,500 left on May 22, and the third, involving 4,000 Jews, on May 25. The last group was deported on June 3.

The Mayor of Sátoraljaujhely, Indár Váró, and the gendarmerie captain in charge of the ghetto were condemned to death after the war for their cruel behavior toward the ghetto inhabitants.[48]

Máramarossziget. Although Máramaros County belonged geographically to Northern Transylvania, it was considered part of Carpatho-Ruthenia and northeastern Hungary for purposes of dejewification. As it contained one of the largest concentrations of Orthodox and Hasidic Jews in Hungary, the German and Hungarian officials were particularly anxious to clear the area of Jews.

The details of the anti-Jewish measures enacted in Máramaros County, as in Carpatho-Ruthenia as a whole, were adopted at the conference held at Munkács on April 12. Máramaros County and the municipality of Máramarossziget were represented in Munkács by the following officials: Dr. László Ilinyi, the deputy prefect, Dr. Sándor Gyulafalvi Rednik, the Mayor of Máramarossziget, Dr. Lajos Tóth, the chief of police, Colonel Zoltán Agy, the commander of the local legion of gendarmes, and Colonel Sárvári, the commander of District IV of the gendarmerie. On the morning of April 15, Ilinyi held a meeting in Máramarossziget with all the top officials of the county to discuss the details of the ghettoization process, including the selection of ghetto sites. That same afternoon, Tóth chaired a meeting of the civilian, police, and gendarmerie officials of Máramarossziget, in which the details of the operations were reviewed. This meeting also established the 20 commissions entrusted with the round-up of the Jews. Each commission was composed of a police officer, two policemen, two gendarmes, and one civil servant.

The ghetto of Máramarossziget was established in two peripheral sections of the city, inhabited primarily by the poorer strata of Jewry. They were located in and around Timár, Kigyó, and Ipar Streets up to Hajnal Street and included Kamarai Road between Timár and Ipar Streets. The ghetto included approximately 12,000 Jews, of whom a little over 10,000 came from the city itself. The remainder were brought in from the mostly Romanian-inhabited villages in the neighboring Drágomérfalva, Aknasugatag, and Felsővisó districts, including those of Barcánfalva, Bárdfalva,[49] Budfalva, Desenfalva, Farkasrev, Gyulafalva, Kracsfalva, Nánfalva, Szerbfalva, Szurdok, and Váncsfalva.

The ghetto was extremely crowded, with practically every room in every building, including the cellars and attics, occupied by 15 to 24 persons. The windows of the buildings bordering the ghetto had to be whitewashed, reportedly to prevent the ghetto inhabitants from communicating with non-Jews. To further assure the isolation of the Jews, the ghetto was surrounded by barbed wire and guarded not only by the local police but also by a special unit of 50 gendarmes assigned from Miskolc under the command of Colonel Sárvári. The commander of the ghetto was Tóth; József Konyuk, the head of the local firefighters, acted as his deputy. The ghetto was administered under the general authority of Sándor Gyulafalvi Rednik, whose expert advisor on Jewish affairs was Ferenc Hullman. It was Hullman who rejected practically all requests forwarded by the Jewish Council asking for an improvement in the lot of the ghetto inhabitants.

The Jewish Council was composed of Rabbi Dr. Samu Dánzig (the father of Hillel Dánzig, the noted Transylvanian journalist and Zionist leader), Lipót Joszovits, Jenő Keszner, Dr. Ferenc Krausz, Mór Jakobovits, and Ignátz Vogel.[50]

Like every other ghetto, Máramarossziget also had a "mint" (the place where Jews were tortured into confessing where they had hidden their valuables). It was directed by Tóth and Sárvári, who were assisted by János Fejér, a police commissioner, and by József Konyuk. The head of Máramaros County at the time of the anti-Jewish drive was László Szaplonczai, a leading member of Imrédy's *Magyar Megújulás Pártja* (Party of Hungarian Renewal).

The ghetto of Máramarossziget was among the first to be liquidated after the beginning of the deportations on May 15.[51] The Jews were deported in four transports. The local Jewish physicians and the few Jews who were caught after the departure of the transports were deported from the ghetto of Szlatina, near Máramarossziget. The Szlatina ghetto also held the Jews from the neighboring villages of Alsó Róna, Felső Róna, Hosszumező, Karácsonyfalva, Nagybocskó, Remetefalva, Rónaszék, and Szaplonca. The Jews of Felsővisó were transferred for entrainment to Alsóvisó from where they were deported together with the Jews from the villages of Alsóvisó, Botiza, Glod, Izakonyha, Izaszacsal, Jod, Rozália, Sajófalva, and Szelistye. The ghetto population of Felsővisó, which also included the Jewish communities of Borsa, Havasmező, Leordina, Majszin, Petrova, and Ruszkova was deported in two transports almost concurrently with those from the ghetto of Máramarossziget.[52]

Kassa. With one of the largest Jewish communities in Hungary, Kassa acquired the dubious distinction of becoming the transfer point from which the deported Jews were handed over to the Germans. German troops entered the city on the night of Hungary's occupation. As one of their first acts, they arrested approximately 100 prominent local Jews whom they held as hostages in the city's detention house. After the Germans exacted their demands, mostly monetary and material in nature, the hostages were released in smaller groups and taken into the local ghetto, which had been established in the meantime. The ghetto was set up in the three major "Jewish streets"—Zrinyi, Luzsenszky, and Pogány—which were isolated from the rest of the city by a fence put up under the direction of Grünwald, a local Jewish carpenter. Although the transfer of the Jews into the ghetto began in the first half of April, the major concentration drive was launched on April 28, the very day the government's ghettoization decree was issued. The

Jews brought in from the neighboring communities, like many from the city itself, were placed in the city's brickyards. The announcement of the ghettoization was posted throughout Abauj-Torna County the day before the round-up began. Typical of such announcements, it read:

With the exception of the brickworks camp area, no Jews may remain in the territory of the city of Kassa after 6:00 P.M. on April 28. Excepted are persons who were left in their apartments until further notice by the competent police or gendarme patrol and who were included on a special list. All other Jews must appear during this same day between 5:00 and 7:00 P.M. before the reception committee at the brickworks. Those Jews who are caught in the city after this hour will be arrested and interned by the authorities. The police captain once again strictly warns the city's population that those who hide Jews or their property after this hour, whether in their homes or elsewhere, will be arrested and interned.[53]

The ghettoization was carried out under the supervision of Mayor Sándor Pohl and Chief of Police György Horváth. The latter also served as the official commander of the ghetto, although his functions were often exercised by his deputy, a police officer by the name of Csatáry. Both Horváth and Csatáry gave vent to their sadistic inclinations during the searches for hidden valuables and during the entrainment of the Jews. The local Jewish Council was composed of a number of communal leaders, including Dr. Dezső Berger, Jenő Ungár, Ignác Spira, and Dr. Ákos Kolozs.

The Jews from the neighboring rural communities in Abauj-Torna County were concentrated in two brickyards on the outskirts of the city. Among these were the Jews of Bárcza, Kis Ida, Mindszent, Nagy Ida, Szepsi, Szikszó, Téhány, Tiszalők, and Torna. The brickyards, which also served as points of entrainment for the Jews in the local ghetto, were under the command of Gendarmerie Lieutenant Colonel Vasváry. Escape from either the ghetto or the brickyards was almost impossible. When a 17-year-old Jewish girl, whom everybody identified as Gizi, was killed in an attempt to flee from the brickyards, her nude body was displayed as a warning to other would-be escapees. A number of Jews committed suicide, including Dr. and Mrs. Zipser. Dr. Simkó, whose suicide attempt failed, was entrained wounded and in his bloodied clothes. The gendarmerie and police authorities were assisted by Schmidtsiefen, a member of the Eichmann-*Sonderkommando.*

A little over 12,000 Jews were concentrated in Kassa. Since Kassa was a railroad hub through which the deportation trains were scheduled to pass on the way to Auschwitz, the Jews concentrated in the city were among the first ones deported from the country. The deportations, which began on May 15, 1944, were brought to the attention of some of the most influential Hungarian notables. For example the gruesome details were brought to the attention of Mrs. Horthy on May 16 and 17 by Mrs. Sámuel Gotterer, the President of the local Jewish Women's Association, who was exempted because her husband was a 75 percent war invalid.[54] Many men and women were deprived of their clothes and compelled to enter the fright cars in their underwear and shoes, with one blanket each.[55]

The third and last transport left Kassa on June 2 with approximately 4,200 Jews. According to information revealed after the war during the war crimes trials, approximately 8,000 of the Jews deported from Kassa were taken straight to the gas chambers. Approximately 450 Jews returned from the camps.[56]

In the northeastern part of Hungary, just south of the Tisza River bend, major ghettos and concentration-entrainment camps were also established in the cities of Nyíregyháza, Mátészalka, and Kisvárda.

Nyíregyháza. As in Carpatho-Ruthenia, the concentration of the Jews in the northeastern parts of Trianon Hungary began in the middle of April. The ghettoization of the Jews in the villages and smaller towns of Szabolcs County began on April 14. After a few days in their local ghettos, which were almost always situated in and around the local synagogues and communal buildings, the Jews were transferred to Nyíregyháza, the county seat. The Jews of the city itself were ordered into the ghetto on April 24. By May 10, the ghetto population swelled to 17,580, of which close to 5,000 were from Nyíregyháza. The remainder were brought in from the neighboring communities in the county, including Apagy, Báj, Balkány, Balsa, Biri, Bököny, Büd-szentmihály,[57] Buj, Csobaj, Demecser, Encsencs, Gáva, Gelse, Geszteréd, Ibrány, Kállósemjén, Kemecse, Kenézlő, Kiskálló, Kótaj, Levelek, Máriapócs, Nagyhalász, Nagykálló,[58] Napkor, Nyíracsád, Nyíradony, Nyírbátor, Nyírbéltek, Nyírbogát, Nyírbogdány, Nyírgelse, Nyírlugas, Nyírmihálydi, Nyírtúra, Oros, Paszab, Pazony, Piricse, Pócspetri, Polgár, Prügy, Rakamaz, Ramocsaháza, Sényő, Szakoly, Székely, Tét, Timár, Tiszaadony, Tiszadada, Tiszadob, Tisza-Eszlár, Tiszaladány, Tiszalök, Tiszapolgár, Tiszarád, Tiszatardos, Ujfehértó, Vasmegyer, and Vencsellő.[59]

The ghetto for the local Jews was situated in and around Bessenyei

Square and Dohány, Kótaji, and Vay Ádám Streets. The Jews from the neighboring rural communities were concentrated in and around Kossuth, Körte, Epreskert, Nyírfa, and Keskeny Streets and at Varjúlapos, a plain (*puszta*) owned by Count Dessewffy. Supreme police command over the ghetto was exercised by Dr. Zoltán Horváth, who was assisted by two of his closest subordinates, Drs. Cziráky and Ujfalussy. The representative of the Eichmann-*Sonderkommando* in Nyíregyháza was *Sturmbannführer* Siegfried Seidl.

The Jewish Council was composed of Gábor Fischbein (who acted as its president), Samu Weinstock, Dr. Ignác Böhm, Dr. Mór Springer, Arnold Láng, Mór Weisz, László Kovács, Béla Ungár, Sándor Haas, Sándor Németi, and Kálmán Rosenwasser.[60] According to some chroniclers of the tragedy of the Jewish community, the local leaders of the Christian churches, including Miklós Dudás, the Greek Catholic Bishop, Zoltán Túróczy, the Bishop of the Evangelical Church, and Father Dezső Török, of the Roman Catholic Church, failed to live up to their mission. A similar accusation was directed against Dr. Károly Korompay, the local lay leader of Roman Catholicism.

In preparation of their deportation, the Jews were transferred toward the end of April and during the first half of May to three farm areas in the neighboring plains of Sima, Nyírjes, and Harangod. There, before their entrainment, the Jews were once again subjected to cruel investigations by the gendarmerie in search of valuables. By far the most cruel of the gendarmerie officers active in the concentration centers was József Trencsényi, whose methods of interrogation brought about the death of a number of Jews, including Sándor Németi, the President of the Orthodox Jewish Community of Nyíregyháza. Another among the martyred Jews of Nyíregyháza was Dr. Béla Bernstein, the Chief Rabbi and historian.

The deportations of the Jews of Szabolcs County began on May 17 with the entrainment at Nyíregyháza of the first transport from Nyírjes puszta. This was followed by the second transport from Harangod on May 23, and the third transport from Simapuszta on May 25. The fourth and fifth transports involved two groups from Nyírjespuszta; they were directed to Auschwitz on May 29 and June 6.

About two weeks after the completion of the deportation, all the exempted Jews, including those who had converted many decades earlier or had married non-Jews, were picked up one night and removed to an unknown destination. None of the 160 individuals arrested that night ever returned.[61]

Mátészalka. The ghetto was established in and around Kossuth and Tisza István Streets, Rákócz Road, and Temető and Hősök Squares. It contained approximately 18,000 Jews, including those of the city[62] and of the neighboring communities in northern Máramaros and Szatmár counties. Among these were the Jewish communities of Alsóresznice, Borkut, Bustyaháza. Csenger,[63] Fehérgyarmat,[64] Felsőapsa, Hodász, Kisbocskó, Kőkényes, Kőrösmező, Lonka, Nagybocskó, Nagykirva, Nitz, Rahó, Taracköz, Terebesfehérpatak, and Tiszabogdány.[65] One of the largest ghettos transferred to Mátészalka just before the beginning of the deportations was that of Szeklence.[66]

Kisvárda. The ghetto was located within Deák Ferenc, Petőfi, Horthy Miklós, Bessenyey, and Mátyás Király Streets. It included about 7,000 Jews of which approximately half were from the city.[67] The remainder were brought in from the neighboring communities, including Ajak, Anarcs, Dombrád, Gyulaháza, Jéke, Mándok, Nyírkárász, Nyírtas, Pátroha, Szabolcsbaka, and Tornyospálca. The ghettoization in some villages started as early as April 8. The relocation of the Kisvárda Jews began on April 15. The Jewish Council was composed of Dr. Sándor Katona (President), Miksa Lefkovics, Dr. Ignácz Lukács, Ernő Ellenbogen, Béla Friedmann, Samu Kun, Ignác Prerau, Mihály Steiner, Miklós Fischer, and Bertalan Guttmann. The ghetto population was deported in two transports, which left on May 29 and May 31, 1944.[68]

The "Emergency" Measures in Southern Hungary

Almost simultaneously with the identification of Carpatho-Ruthenia and Northern Transylvania as military operational zones, the Hungarian authorities, acting in conjunction with the German occupation forces, declared the southern parts of Hungary (neighboring Croatia and occupied Serbia) as operational zones. As a "precautionary" measure in the war against Tito's partisans, the Fascist authorities found it necessary to round up the Jews living in these territories. Among the Jews affected were not only those who had previously lived in the Yugoslav areas, but also many who had lived in Trianon Hungary. Among the latter, the great majority were those of Csáktornya, Nagykanizsa, and Perlak districts in Zala County. As was the case in Carpatho-Ruthenia, the round-up was undertaken several days before the official ghettoization decree had been issued. Along the Croatian border, 8,740 Jews were apprehended,[69] including those of the towns of Csáktornya and Nagykanizsa. The Jews of the latter community were concentrated on April 19 by policemen especially brought in from Szombathely.[70] The local ghetto was established in the local business school and in and around the synagogue and the neighboring communal buildings; it included approximately 3,000 Jews. On orders of Hörnicke, the local SS commander, Jewish men from 16 to 60 were separated on April 29 and taken "on an exceptional basis" to Auschwitz. Many among these had been in the Nagykanizsa labor camp, which had been established in 1942 for "criminals convicted of economic crimes." The rest of the ghetto population was deported on May 18, approximately six weeks before the scheduled deportation of the Jews in the southwestern parts of Hungary. The freight cars were so crowded that many people died before the train left the station. The dead were removed during a short stopover at Szombathely and buried under the supervision of Samu Halpert. Among those taken to Auschwitz were Jenő Haplhen, the head of the Jewish Council, and the community's last rabbi, A. Winkler.[71]

The emergency measures enacted in Zala County were coupled before the beginning of the mass deportations with a terror campaign designed not only to intimidate but also to pauperize the Jewish population. This campaign was especially intense in a number of communities where the German authorities used the "prominent" Jews as hostages. For example, on April 3, the Germans arrested 18 members of the Jewish community of Mezőberény and took them to Budapest. That same day, they also arrested 50 Jews of Székesfehérvár and held them as hostages pending the payment of a ransom of 100,000 Pengős.[72] These mass arrests paralleled the Einzelaktionen (individual operations) that had been rampant throughout the country since the occupation.[73]

Reaction of the Jewish Council

The leaders of the Council received an inkling of the impending disaster when they were instructed via János Gábor to appear at the 26 Rökk-Szilárd Street "detention house" at 3:00 P.M. on April 20. There they were received by Wisliceny, Novak, and Hunsche. While they were kept standing, Wisliceny inquired whether the requested maps and statistical data about the Jews and their institutions and organizations had been completed and suggested that the Council elect an executive officer in order to make its work more effective.[74] Bluffing the Jewish leaders once again into believing that the administrative "revitalization" reflected the Nazis' intention not to destroy the community, Wisliceny parenthetically remarked that the Jews would be permitted to live in communities with populations of over 10,000. He also informed them that he would go to the provinces together with Eichmann for about two weeks and that he would like the maps and statistical data ready by his return.[75]

Eichmann and Wisliceny were part of a mixed delegation composed of the leading members of the German and Hungarian *Sonderkommandos* that left on a tour of the major ghetto centers of Carpatho-Ruthenia and northeastern Hungary on April 24. The delegation also included Endre, Endre's secretary Albert Takács, the town clerk of Rákosliget Béla Rozsnyai, the police chief of Aszód Géza Czannik, Dr. Sándor Tardi (a physician from Budapest), Ferenczy, Leó Lullay, Lajos Meggyesi, Zöldi, and some lesser known figures. The first stop of these dejewification leaders was Kassa, where they were joined by Dr. Sándor Pohl, the city's Mayor and and old political friend of Endre, and by Ferenc Feketehalmy-Czeydner, "the hangman of Újvidék," who, like Zöldi, had returned to Hungary with the invading German forces.[76] From Kassa the delegation went on to inspect the ghetto of Sátoraljaujhely. The next stop was Ungvár, and then Nyíregyháza, Kisvárda, and Mátészalka. It is this group that discussed the details of the Final Solution program in Gendarmerie District VIII and decided on Kassa as the point where the Jews of Hungary would be handed over to the Germans.

Upon his return from this first inspection tour on May 2, Endre submitted a report to his superior, Minister of the Interior Jaross, in which he stated that he had "found everything in order. The provincial ghettos have a veritably sanatorium-like character. The Jews are finally getting fresh air and have changed their old lifestyle for a healthier one."

Jaross rushed a copy of the report to Horthy, who allegedly accepted its veracity at face value.[77] Horthy at the time was more inclined to believe the reassuring news of his government officials than the "horror propaganda" accounts of the "friends of the Jews." Among the latter was Bishop László Ravasz who approached Horthy on April 28 to express his concern about the anti-Jewish drive in Carpatho-Ruthenia and northeastern Hungary. Bishop Ravasz had been alerted about the horrors of this drive by Baron Zsigmond Perényi, the president of the upper house of the Hungarian Parliament, who in turn had been informed by Samu Kahan-Frankl and Imre Reiner, the president and legal counselor of the Orthodox Jewish Community of Hungary. The Bishop was assured by the Regent that since "a large number of labor draftees were requested of Hungary . . . a few hundred thousand Jews will . . . leave the country's frontier, but not a single hair of their heads will be touched. . . ."[78]

The leaders of the Jewish Council, who had learned some details about the horrors perpetrated in the course of the ghettoization,[79] tried to get in touch with Endre. He merely exchanged a few hurried words with them and referred them to his secretary, Albert Takács, who denied the "horror stories." Thereupon the Council sent a telegram to the Minister of the Interior on April 26 and expanded on its content in a detailed letter dated April 27. The letter is important for two reasons. It not only sheds light on the formalistic and utterly ineffective reaction of the Council to the anti-Jewish drives, but also provides historically valuable information relating to them. In contrast to Endre's "observations," the Council letter included a description of the real situation in the ghettos:

> In the name of the Central Council of Hungarian Jews, we take courage to reveal with great respect before Your Honor the extremely grave and critical situation of the Jewish population of the northeastern parts of the country in the wake of the measures adopted by the authorities.
> According to the information we have received, the Jews of the northeastern territories of the country, namely in the counties of Ung, Ugocsa, Bereg, Máramaros, Abauj-Torna, Zemplén, and Szabolcs, have in the past few days been taken irrespective of age or sex into the county seats or some of the larger district seats, where they are partly placed under the open sky and partly crowded in the outskirts of the cities, cut off from the rest of the world.
> Among other things, the following information reached us:
> *1. Ung County.* The Jews of Ung County were transported on the 16th to Ungvár, where they were placed in a brick factory and in a lumber yard. The Jews of Ungvár were taken to these same places on the 21st, the 22nd, and the 23rd. Both the Jews of Ungvár and those transported from the county to Ungvár were allowed to take only 30 *Pengős*, food for fourteen days, a change of underwear, the clothes they wore, and bedding. They had to leave the rest of their personal property in their homes. The number of Jews currently crowded in the brick factory and in the lumber yard is estimated at 20,000, who are camped outdoors, exposed to the vicissitude of the weather. Their daily nourishment is only one deciliter of soup. Bringing in food is prohibited. There is a water shortage in the area.
> Of course, under such conditions there cannot be proper attention to the feeding and health care of the great masses.

2. Szabolcs County. The situation is similar in Szabolcs County, from whose territory the Jews were taken to Nyíregyháza. According to the information received by us, these were only allowed to take along food for two days, 30 *Pengős,* and 50 kg. of luggage.

The people transported to Nyíregyháza were placed in private houses, but in view of the large number of people taken there they were crowded into apartments well beyond the latter's capacity. The feeding and nursing of the sick here is impossible.

3. Abauj-Torna County. The Jews of Abauj-Torna County, like a considerable number of the Jews of Kassa, were crowded together in the waterless brick factory of Kassa, where the most elementary needs for living could not be satisfied.

4. Bereg County. A similar procedure was followed for the Jews of Bereg County, where all valuables including wedding bands as well as all money above 1 *Pengő* were taken from the evacuated persons.

5. Máramaros County. The Jews living in this county were crowded together in Máramarossziget and some of the larger communities; in Máramarossziget, a considerable portion of the Jewish intelligentsia, about 140 people, were put into a small synagogue where they were kept without food or water for days.

From the above information, it can be seen that the great masses of the Jews from the northeastern part of the country—several hundred thousand—have come into this most dangerous situation for reasons beyond their control; because of their huge number and the brief period of time left, suitable provisions could not be made for their accommodation, sanitary arrangements, feeding, and medical and pharmaceutical care of the sick. Under these conditions it is to be feared that, in the absence of food, proper housing, and care for the sick, hunger will set in, contagious diseases will break out, and pregnant women, infants, children, the sick and aged will perish on a large scale.

For this reason we respectfully ask you to take measures so that the evacuated persons will receive suitable accommodations and food.

Our other respectful request is that you make it possible for our representatives to be deployed in the field, so that they will be able to help, in unison with the authorities and the local Jewish leadership, in the determination of the necessary measures.

In view of the great importance and urgency of the matter, we would respectfully ask Your Honor for quick action.

Please be assured, Your Honor, of our sincere respect.[80]

The Council provided additional details about the horrors in the various ghettos in Carpatho-Ruthenia and northeastern Hungary in its German-language appeal to Eichmann dated May 3. The Council obtained the data in a circuitous fashion, often through the services of young Zionists who braved the many travel restrictions. Occasionally, the local Jewish community leaders managed to send their own messengers to Budapest. These contacts and especially the communications conveyed in the Nazi-censored official Jewish journal had an unintended deleterious effect, for they reinforced the local leaders' conviction about the wisdom and effectiveness of the central leadership. Unaware of the realities in Budapest, they continued to follow the guidance of the central leaders "who had such good connections with the Hungarian and German authorities, and who had been so effective in the past." The central leaders, however, were still operating in a daze, trapped by their helpless positions, mesmerized by the "promises" of the Germans, and driven by the hope that they could buy off the Nazis or gain time by dilatory tactics.

The appeal to Eichmann read as follows:

With reference to our personal discussion with *Obersturmbannführer* Krumey on the 2nd of this month and at his urging, we submit our urgent request that the Jewish Council be permitted to send its representatives into the areas assigned for the Jews in the northeastern and southern parts of the country. We base our request on the fact that serious complaints have reached us from most of the concentration centers with respect to accommodations and food and health care. The function of the representatives would be to determine the visible serious shortcomings, with the concurrence of the local authorities and the cooperation of the local Jews, and make suitable recommendations to the Central Council in Budapest. In order to assure the success of the representatives, we ask you to grant them freedom of movement and travel and of contact with the local authorities and Jewry.

The petition continued with the concrete evaluation of the conditions in the various ghettos:

1. Nyíregyháza. The ghetto there has 4,120 local Jews and about 6,600 from the neighboring areas, a total of 10,759. These were placed into 123 houses, whose area, including kitchens and hallways, is 9,165 square meters. Under these circumstances, not even one square meter is allotted per person. It must be added that there is neither water nor sewerage in the area, which involves danger in regard to sanitation. In accordance with the general provisions, the concentrated individuals were allowed to take along food for 14 days, but the evacuation of the Jews from the villages was carried out at such speed that they were unable to gather this food. Thus, the Jews of Nyíregyháza are out of food and the local Jewish Council is unable to supply the ghetto.

2. Kisvárda. Here the accommodation and supplying of neighboring Jews is particularly difficult. They were gathered into the yard of the Jewish temple. They are out of food and their sanitary situation is desperate.

3. Ungvár. Most of the Jews concentrated here have no roof over their heads.

4. Kassa. The Jews were taken to the drying area of the local brick factory, which has no sidewalls; thus, the situation of the people there, who number 11,500, is desperate. They don't have enough food, and the communal kitchen that was set up cannot operate. There is no water system in the area.

5. *Munkács.* The number of Jews concentrated here is 18,000; they have been accommodated in the brick factory, but some of them could not be taken in and are in the open air.

6. From *Máramarossziget* the following report has been received: "Soldiers go from house to house and take everything removable. The ghetto is being prepared and all the Jews will have to move into it between the 20th and 30th of this month. The Jews collected from the villages suffer the most varied atrocities; women are raped, young girls are examined by midwives to check whether they have not hidden their jewelry."[81]

Eichmann was, of course, unmoved by these revelations and proceeded with the implementation of the predetermined Final Solution plans. The German Foreign Office was regularly informed about the progress of the ghettoization in Carpatho-Ruthenia and northeastern Hungary via the reports of the Higher SS and Police Leader, which were transmitted by Veesenmayer. Five days after the launching of the ghettoization drive, Veesenmayer reported that in addition to the arrest of 7,580 Jews in "individual actions" (*Einzelaktionen*), 100,038 Jews (about 50,000 in Máramaros County alone) were concentrated as a result of the "Special action" (*Sonderaktion*).[82]

On April 24, Veesenmayer reported that by the following day, April 22, the number of those arrested in individual and special operations had increased to 7,802 and 135,000 respectively, and that both the city and rural population "continue to welcome" the anti-Jewish measures.[83] By April 28, when the official ghettoization decree went into effect, the number of those arrested individually and collectively increased to 8,225 and 194,000 respectively.[84]

Internments through the Council

Frantic as the Jewish Council was about the ghettoization in Carpatho-Ruthenia and northeastern Hungary, it also became tragically and, of course, involuntarily involved in an internment program in Budapest. In the midst of the horrible news from the northeastern and southern parts of the country, the Council was asked by the German and Hungarian SS and police units to prepare and distribute summonses for the Jews identified on lists handed over to it, requesting them to appear "for work" at the detention camp at 26 Rökk-Szilárd Street. The lists were usually given to either Dr. Kohn or Dr. Gábor—the former in his capacity as Executive Secretary and contact man with the authorities at the detention house and the latter as the Council's liaison to the *Sonderkommando.* Occasionally some of the employees subordinated to them would pick up the sealed envelopes with the lists.

The first list of this type included the names of 133 Jewish journalists,[85] who by decree had been excluded from the Press Chamber.[86] It had been put together by Mihály Kolosváry-Borcsa and Jenő Gáspár, the president and the secretary of the National Hungarian Press Chamber, who handed it over to the Gestapo. In addition, the Council received two lists naming about 280 lawyers and three lists which included the names of about 300 "unreliable" Jews. The latter included the names of Jews who had died before the German occupation as well a large number of misspelled names, indicating that they had been compiled by German agents.[87] The list of lawyers was compiled with the cooperation of the National Association of Hungarian Lawyers (*Magyar Ügyvédek Nemzeti Egyesülete*—MÜNE).

The summons issued and distributed by the Central Jewish Council on April 24, 1944, read as follows:

ORDER

On higher order we call on you to appear personally tomorrow, Tuesday, April 25, at 9:00 A.M., before the authorities at 26 Rökk-Szilárd Street, Budapest VIII. In your own interest bring along a blanket, three changes of underwear, two suits, two pairs of shoes, a bowl, pot, or pan, a spoon, a metal cup, and food for three days. The weight of your personal luggage cannot exceed 50 kilograms. Failure to appear will result in grave consequences for the individual called in.[88]

The green-colored summonses were distributed immediately upon the receipt of the lists from the Gestapo by a special messenger service set up at the Council under the leadership of Kohn. The messengers were mainly Jewish high school students who were drafted or volunteered for the service. Most of the recipients of these summonses responded to the call and appeared "for labor service" at the specified place and time. Many of them had first gone to the Council's headquarters to inquire about the meaning of the summonses. There they were reassured that "only labor service was involved" and that failure would result in grave consequences not only for themselves but also for their families.[89] Instead of "labor service," however, the respondents were first transferred from the detention house at Rökk-Szilárd Street to Kistarcsa, Horthyliget, or some other internment camp in Hungary and from there shortly thereafter they were among the first ones to be deported in Auschwitz.

Most of the persons who failed to show up eventually escaped, primarily because the German and Hungarian Gestapo units simply did not have the necessary personnel to hunt for individual Jews. This was, reportedly, one of the basic reasons why these units asked for the "co-operation" of the Council. When some of the employees of the Council advised against assuming this task or actually suggested sabotaging it, Kohn allegedly admonished them and warned them that they "were exposing the entire Jewish Council to danger." In his thankless position Kohn, the legalistic-formalistic assimilationist leader, was bound to antagonize many of his coworkers. In the opinion of one of his contemporaries, this was due "not only to his ways, but also to his limitless cowardice."[90]

The leaders of the Council rationalized the acceptance of this onerous task by arguing that it was better for the victims to be forewarned by the Council than to be picked up without any advance notice by the Gestapo. Under the Council-issued summonses, they argued, the victims had at least 24 to 48 hours to settle their last-minute affairs, to obtain the necessary equipment, or to make up their minds to escape. The summonses were distributed immediately by messengers on bicycles to give the victims as much time as possible.[91]

While admitting that Koltay entrusted the Council with the distribution of the summonses because "the detectives could no longer cope with the task of laying hands on everybody who stood in somebody else's way," Stern rationalized the acceptance of this onerous role as follows:

. . . If we refused to carry out the order, unexpected arrests would go on as before, Jews being carried off without the least preparation. If we charged ourselves with the calling-up, one would have a fixed day for reporting to the Rökk-Szilárd camp and time to run away or go into hiding. But even those not so minded at least would have an opportunity to procure some equipment likely to render their bad situation more tolerable. A previous notice might even enable some to get into some clinic or to obtain a certificate from some medical officer. Thus we had no doubts whatsoever that even if we had to accept the criticism of our brethren about our part as postman, we had to take upon ourselves the handing over of the summons to report, and had to do this for the benefit of our brethren.[92]

Whatever the rationalization or explanation advanced by the Council members, the fact remains that with the exception of a few people on the lists who were advised by personal friends or acquaintances on the Council's staff not to accept or respond to the summons,[93] the victims were not given any inkling about the impending disaster. Whether the reason was plain naïveté, fear, or apprehension about possible greater immediate catastrophe, the fact remains that it was the Council that prepared and distributed the internment summonses, exposing itself to a charge of collaboration, which was advanced both during and after the war.

The Ghettoization Decree

Twelve days after the concentration of the Jews began—without legal authorization—in Carpatho-Ruthenia and northeastern Hungary, the government issued its ghettoization decree, camouflaged under the title "Concerning the Regulation of Certain Questions Relating to the Jews' Apartments and Living Places."[94] It went into effect on April 28, the day Bishop László Ravasz visited Horthy only to be misled about the intent of the anti-Jewish measures.

The Council of Ministers adopted the decree during its session of April 26. Its rationale and objectives were outlined by Minister of the Interior Jaross. He claimed that in view of their better economic status the Jews living in the cities had proportionally much better housing than non-Jews and therefore it was possible to "create a healthier situation" by rearranging the whole housing set-up. Jews were to be restricted to smaller apartments and several families could be ordered to move in together. National security required that Jews be removed from the villages and the smaller towns into larger cities, where the chief local official—the mayor or the police chief—would set aside a special section or district for them.[95]

The crucial provisions of the decree relating to the concentration of the Jews were included in articles 8 and 9. The former provided that Jews could no longer live in communities with a population of under 10,000, while the latter stipulated that the mayors of the larger towns and cities could determine the sections, streets, and buildings in which Jews were to be permitted to live. This legal euphemism in fact empowered the local authorities to establish ghettos.

By the time the official ghettoization decree was issued, the *de facto* ghettoization of the Jews of Carpatho-Ruthenia and northeastern Hungary was coming to an end. In fact, preparations were well under way for the first trains to roll toward Auschwitz from the internment camps at Kistarcsa and Nagykanizsa. The decree preceded the launching of the ghettoization drive in the other gendarmerie districts in the country, with the highest priority attached to the round-up in Gendarmerie Districts IX and X: Northern Transylvania, the area containing the last large concentration of Orthodox Jews.

Notes

1. Lévai, *Zsidósors Magyarországon*, p. 97.
2. *Ibid.*
3. PS-3363. For text see *Nazi Conspiracy and Aggression* (Washington, D.C.: Government Printing Office, 1946), 6:97–101.
4. Baky stressed this point in his defense after the war, and also in his statement to Dr. Endre Pollák, the prosecutor in the trial of Dr. László Gyapay, Dr. László Csoka, and Dr. László Vásárhelyi, the wartime mayors of Nagyvárad, Szatmárnémeti, and Kolozsvár, respectively. The trial of these mayors was held in Kolozsvár in 1946 (The original of the statement is in this author's possession.)
5. Jenő Lévai, *Eichmann in Hungary: Documents.* (Budapest: Pannonia Press, 1961), pp. 72–73. For the original Hungarian version of the text, see Lévai, *Zsidósors Magyarországon*, pp. 97–99 or *Vádirat*, 1:124–27.
6. Decree no. 1.610/1944. M.E., which went into effect on April 28. For details see below.
7. Lévai, *Zsidósors Magyarországon*, p. 96.
8. *Ibid.*
9. Aladár Király, *A nyíregyházi gettó története* (The History of the Ghetto of Nyíregyháza) (Nyíregyháza: The Author, 1946), p. 13.
10. Decree no. 108.510/1944. K.M. *Budapesti Közlöny*, no. 94 (April 27, 1944): 10–11.
11. In most towns and cities, the lists were usually prepared within three days. Dés was a typical case. In that town, the registration teams completed the listing of the 3,266 Jews living there within three days. For details on the procedures followed in this town, see *"Volt egyszer egy Dés . . ."* (There Was Once Upon a Time a Dés), ed. Zoltán Singer (Tel Aviv: A Dés és Vidékéről Elszármazottak Landsmannschaftja, n.d.), pp. 418–19.
12. The chief prosecutor of the Center for State Defense was Lajos Meggyesi. Lévai, *Zsidósors Magyarországon*, p. 101. In some sources Meggyesi's name is spelled as Medgyesy.
13. For text see *Vádirat*, 1:106–7.
14. According to a Yugoslav source, this conference was actually held on April 19, which is not plausible because the ghettoization of the Jews of Carpatho-Ruthenia had begun on April 16. It is quite possible that this official source intended to refer only to the conference held by the dejewification experts prior to the launching of the anti-Jewish drive in the former Yugoslav territories of the Bácska and Baranya region on April 26. See *The Crimes of the Fascist Occupants and Their Collaborators Against Jews in Yugoslavia*, ed. Zdenko Löwenthal (Belgrade: Federation of Jewish Communities of the Federative People's Republic of Yugoslavia, 1957), p. 169. (In Serbo-Croatian with the title and summary of chapters in English. Referred to hereafter as *Crimes of Fascist Occupants.*)
15. The notes of this April 7 meeting were taken by Géza Halász and recorded on May 27, 1944. *Vádirat*, 1:123–24.
16. Decree no. 1.440/1944. M.E. *Budapesti Közlöny*, no. 83 (April 14, 1944):1.
17. *Ibid.* Tomcsányi was a member of the upper house of the Hungarian Parliament and Government Commissioner for Carpatho-Ruthenia. He had previously served as Minister of Justice (1920) and Minister of the Interior (1921). *Magyarország tiszti cim- és névtára* (Title and Name Register of Hungary) (Budapest: A Magyar Királyi Állami Nyomda for the A Magyar Királyi Központi Statisztikai Hivatal, 1942), 49:4, 6, 12, 174.
18. *Budapesti Közlöny*, no. 96 (April 29, 1944):1.
19. Ricsoy-Uhlarik had been the head of the Production Division in the Ministry of Agriculture and represented the Ministry on a number of agencies, including the National Cinematography Committee (*Országos Mozgóképvizsgáló Bizottság*). *Magyarország tiszti cim- és névtára*, pp. 58, 217, 255, 289, and 300.

20. Lévai, *Zsidósors Magyarországon,* p. 101. For details on Ferenczy's background, see chapter 13.

21. Wilhelm Höttl, *The Secret Front* (New York: Praeger, 1954), p. 42.

22. *Der Kastner-Bericht,* p. 300.

23. The geographic name was basically fictional. During World War I, there was a military training camp near Esztergom that bore the name of Kenyérmező.

24. With respect to the Mezőtúr rumor see Andrei Paul, *Az északerdélyi zsidó lakosság deportálása 1944-ben* (The Deportation of the Jewish Population of Northern Transylvania in 1944). Manuscript (in author's possession) p. 35, and the personal account of István Marton in Béla Katona, *Várad a viharban* (Várad in the Storm) (Nagyvárad: Tealah Korháztámogató Egyesület, 1946), pp. 314–25.

25. László Gerend, "Kiűzettünk városunkból" (We Were Driven From Our City) in *Évkönyv 1977–78* (Yearbook 1977–78), ed. Sándor Scheiber (Budapest: Magyar Izraeliták Országos Képviselete, 1978), pp. 159–82.

26. See Eberhard von Thadden's report of May 26, 1944. *RLB,* Doc. 166.

27. Munkácsi, *Hogyan történt?,* p. 79. For a slightly different version of the same incident, see Lévai, *Zsidósors Magyarországon,* p. 162.

28. Lévai, *Zsidósors Magyarországon,* p. 102.

29. For personal narratives by survivors of the ghettos and concentration camps consult files 768–81 in the archives of the YIVO-Institute for Jewish Research In New York. They stem from the archives of the Documentary Section *(Dokumentációs Ügyosztály)* of the Jewish Agency for Palestine in Budapest, where they were recorded in 1945. Documents from the same source are also available at the Yad Vashem Institute in Jerusalem under Archives no. 0–15. For additional related narratives at Yad Vashem consult archives nos. 0–2, 0–3, 0–7, 0–11, 0–33, 0–37, and 0–39.

30. For details on the destruction of the Jews of Carpatho-Ruthenia and northeastern Hungary consult the following references: R. Aladár Vozáry, *Igy történt! 1944 március 19–1945 január 18* (This Is How It Happened! March 19, 1944–January 18, 1945). (Budapest: Halász, 1945), 160 pp.; Randolph L. Braham, "Untergang fun di Yidn in Karpatn-Rusland" (The Destruction of the Jews of Carpatho-Ruthenia), In *Algemeine Entsiklopedie* (General Encyclopedia) (In Yiddish. New York: Dubnoff-Fund, 1966), 7:386–91. For the English version see, *HJS* 1:223–35; *Karpatorus* (Carpatho-Ruthenia), ed. Y. Erez (In Hebrew. Jerusalem: Encyclopaedia of the Jewish Diaspora, 1959); Sh. Rosman, *Sefer zikhron kedoshim le'yehudei Karpatorus-Marmarosh* (Memorial Book of the Martyrs of Carpatho-Ruthenia and Máramaros) (In Hebrew. Jerusalem: Rehovot, 1969), 643 pp.; and *Sefer le'zikkaron kedoshei Ruskova ve-Soblas, Mehoz Marmarosh* (Memorial Book of the Martyrs of Ruskova and Soblas, Máramaros County), ed. Y.Z. Moskowits (In Hebrew and Yiddish. Tel Aviv: Former Residents of Ruskova and Soblas in Israel and in the Diaspora, 1969), 126 pp.

31. For personal narratives by survivors of these two ghettos see the following references at the YIVO (archive nos. within parantheses): Lajos Berman (769/1538), Edith Steinberg (772/2136), Eugene Markovits (772/2234), Mary Wachtenheim (722/2280), Samuel Katz (772/2389), Rose Holländer, et al. (772/2471), Rose Wachtenheim (772/2527), Fanny Weissmann (772/2532), Paula Klein (773/1646), Nicholas Harpuder (773/1745), M. Harpuder (773/1853), Rozsa Moskovics (773/1931), Serene and Helene Rochlitz (773/2065), G. Dachs (773/2067), Aranka and Regina Eisdorfer (773/2076), Emil Weisz (773/2077), L. Liberman, et al. (773/2088), N. Schonfeld (776/2), B. Hochmann, et al. (766/7), E. Rosenberg (776/8), H. and B. Stern (776/14), Dr. Terkeltaub, et al. (776/16), S. Braunstein and S. Meistlik (776/48), P. Grünfeld (776/50), J. Jelinek (776/68), and A. Hincel (776/80).

32. Lévai, *Zsidósors Magyarországon,* pp. 102, 106, and 407; Ferenczy Report of May 29, 1944, identified in the Eichmann Trial as Doc. 1319 of Bureau 06 of the Israel Police.

For a historical review of the Jewish community of Munkács, consult Shmuel Hakohen Weingarten, "Munkács," in *Arim ve-Imahot be-Yisrael* (Cities and Mothers in Israel), (Jerusalem: Mosad Harav Kuk, 1946), 1:345–71.

33. Gerend, "Kiűzettünk városunkból," cited above.

34. For personal accounts by Jews from Ungvár and the neighboring communities, including those mentioned in the text, see the following statements in the archives of the YIVO: R. and S. Keszler (770/126), S. and M. Jakobovics (770/161), Joseph Leifer (772/2272), Irene Lebovics (772/2277), Yolanthe Habermann (773/1743), Isidor Weisz (773/1750), Helene Herskovits (774/2880), I. Moskovics, et al. (776/6), I. Schönwirth (776/9), M. Braun (776/30), J. Deutsch (776/39), R. Herskovits and E. Schönberger (776/46), S. Grünwald (776/52), A. Schwimmer (776/70), Alexander Fraumovics (776/74), Helen Schwartz (776/82), Rose Rottmann (776/88), Béla Sztrulovits (776/95) and E. Bródy (776/98).

35. Lévai, *Zsidósors Magyarországon*, pp. 105, 106, 112, and 407.

36. Ferenczy Report of May 29, 1944. Israel Police. Bureau 06, Eichmann Trial Doc. 1319. For further details on Ungvár, see Yehuda Spiegel, "Ungvar," in *Arim ve-imahot be-Yisrael*, 4(1950):5–54.

37. Lévai, *Zsidósors Magyarországon*, p. 407. For personal narratives relating to the ghetto and deportation experiences by Jews from Beregszász and the neighboring communities, including those mentioned in the text, see the following statements in the YIVO archives: B. Lebovits (770/179), Sam Hoffmann (772/2137), Piroska Schwartz (773/1945), Menyhért Winkler (775/3085), A. Spitz (776/13), H. Katz (776/17), R. Klein, et al. (776/18), H. Holländer (776/19), L. Majerovits (776/54), and A. Lachs (776/100).

38. The looting was also noted by Veesenmayer in his telegram of June 27, 1944, addressed to the German Foreign Office. *RLB*, Doc. 285.

39. For personal accounts by Jews from Nagyszőllős and its environs, including the communities mentioned in the text, see the following documents at the YIVO: Ethel and Theresa Lébi (769/1450), Hédy Weisz, et al. (770/102), T. Alexander (772/2257), Joseph Schwarcz (772/2344), Fany Fuchs (772/2408), Charles Izsák (772/2531), Isaac Weisz (776/45), A. Salamon and I. Löwy (776/53), S. Markusz (776/76), and Ernő Glück (776/90).

40. Lévai, *Zsidósors Magyarországon*, p. 407. See also *Sefer zikaron le'kehilot Seljus ve'hasev-iva* (Memorial Volume of the Community of Seljus [Nagyszőllős] and Its Environs) (Tel Aviv: The Committee of Olei Nagyszőllős in Israel, 1976), pp. 183–84. For the list of the martyrs of Nagyszőllős and of the neighboring communities, see pp. 249–318.

41. *Ibid.*

42. Lévai, *Zsidósors Magyarországon*, p. 408. See also the following narratives at the YIVO: Charlotte Jutkovics (775/3178), Joseph Davidovics (775/3200), Hermann Jankelovits (776/12), S. Berkovits (776/72), M. Davidovits (776/78), M. Smilovits (776/38), W. Slamovits (776/62), and E. Berkovics (776/72).

43. *Ibid.* See also Rosman, *Sefer zikhron kedoshim le'yehudei Karpatorus-Marmarosh*, and the following personal narratives at the YIVO: Charlotte Jakobovits (769/1092), Joe Kaplovits (770/176), Alexander Lebovits (771/3510), and Charlotte Jutkovits (775/3178).

44. Personal communication by Dr. Ludvig Granát, a former inhabitant of Técső who settled in Jerusalem after the war. See also Lévai, *Zsidósors Magyarországon*, pp. 175 and 408 and the following personal narratives available at the YIVO: Esther Silber, et al. (769/1435), Edith Herskovits (774/2949), Esther Weiss et al. (774/2958), Lenke Indig (775/3090), A. Müller (776/4), and Ida Zelkovics et al. (776/262).

45. The beginnings of the Jewish community of Mád, a rural town located southwest of Sátoraljaujhely, can be traced to the early part of the seventeenth century. At the time of the ghettoization, the community numbered 230. They were first kept in the local syn-

agogue for three days, then concentrated in the ghetto of Sátoraljaujhely from where they were deported during the second half of May 1944. For details on the history of the community, see *Hakehila hayehudit shel Mád* (The Jewish Community of Mád), ed. Arieh Lewy. (English, Hebrew, Hungarian. Jerusalem: The Maad Memorial Committee, 1974), 154 + 31 pp. For the list of the martyrs and survivors see pp. 139–50.

46. The ghettoization of the approximately 1,000 Jews of Sárospatak began on April 18. After three days in the local synagogue and Jewish school, where they were subjected to the customary searches for property, they were transferred to Sátoraljaujhely. For details on the background of the community, see Fülöp Grünwald, "Sárospatak—Mátészalka—Paks" in *Évkönyv 1971/72* (Yearbook 1971–72), ed. Sándor Scheiber (Budapest: Magyar Izraeliták Orszagos Képviselete, 1972), pp. 130–34.

47. Lévai, *Zsidósors Magyarországon*, pp. 175 and 408.

In 1941, the city had a Jewish population of 4,160, representing 22.6 percent of the total. By 1946, the number had been reduced to 555 or 3.0 percent. In 1949, the local Jews still had two congregations, an orthodox one under the leadership of József Izsák and a Status Quo one under the chairmanship of Dr. Sándor Waller. In the late 1950s the community was reduced to 81 under the leadership of Lipot Klein and later of that of Bernát Menczel. *Zsidó Világkongresszus*, no. 4 (April 15, 1947):2–3; no. 13–14 (May 1949):19, 25; *Uj Élet* (New Life), Budapest, August 1957, April 1, 1958, June 15, 1958. See also *Pinkas ha'kehilot*, pp. 513–15, and the following personal narratives at the YIVO: H. Káhán (770/228), I. Révész and F. Müller (770/460), Stefania Winkler (772/2450), Árpád Stern (775/3150), and Gy. and S. Grünzweig (776/51).

48. *Mementó. Magyarország 1944* (Memento. Hungary 1944), Ödön Gáti et al. (Budapest: Kossuth, 1975), pp. 38–39.

49. According to one account, the ghetto of Bárdfalva included approximately 3,000 Jews before the transfer to Máramarossziget. Among those first taken to Bárdfalva were the Jews of Aknasugatag and 18 other smaller villages in Máramaros County. Lévai, *Zsidósors Magyarországon*, pp. 175 and 408. See also the following personal narratives at the YIVO: I. Berkovits (770/182) and Rose Szabó (770/307).

50. Personal communication, March 1, 1976, from Kálmán C. Kahán, the New York representative of the *Uj Kelet* (New East), the Hungarian-language daily of Tel Aviv.

51. *Tribunalul Poporului, Cluj*, pp. 109–15; Lévai, *Zsidósors Magyarországon*, p. 408.

52. The details concerning the deportations from Máramarossziget and the neighboring communities were supplied by Kálmán Kahán, cited above. See also Rosman, *Sefer Zikhron Kedoshim le'Yehudei Karpatorus-Marmarosh*. For personal accounts by survivors, see the following narratives at the YIVO in New York: M. Moskovits (770/168), M. Drummer (770/384), Helene Beck, et al. (774/2813), and A. Káhán (776/91). For a moving though somewhat fictionalized account of the community's destruction, see Elie Wiesel's *Night* (New York: Avon Books, 1969), 127 pp. The Jewish community of Máramarossziget was reestablished after the war. In 1947, it consisted of 2,308 members, many of whom had settled in the city after their return from the camps. *Aşezările evreilor*, p. 171.

53. Lévai, *Zsidósors Magyarországon*, pp. 104, 106, 142, 143, 407.

54. Munkácsi, *Hogyan történt?*, pp. 82–83.

55. György Ránki, *1944. március 19* (March 19, 1944) 2nd ed. (Budapest: Kossuth, 1978), p. 258; *Horthy Miklós titkos iratai* (The Confidential Papers of Miklós Horthy), eds. Miklós Szinai and László Szücs (Budapest: Kossuth, 1963), p. 447.

56. Personal communication by Tibor Farkas, a former resident of Kassa who settled in Israel after the war and became Executive Secretary of the *Hitachdut Olei Hungaria—H.O.H.*, an organization of Hungarian-Jewish immigrants. See also the following personal narratives available at the YIVO in New York: Andrew Horowitz (File No. 770/165), W. Wieder (776/3), Elizabeth Pollák (776/31), M. Kohn (776/42), E. Blau (776/44), B. Fuchs and M. Feuer (776/84), Paul Friedmann (776/86), and Ernő Gutt-

mann (776/93). See also Arthur Görög's *A kassai zsidóság tragédiája* (The Tragedy of Kassa's Jewry), manuscript at Yad Vashem Archives 015/17-4.

57. For details on the history and background of the community, which numbered 652 Jews on the eve of the Holocaust, see László Harsányi, "A büdszentmihályi hitközség története" (History of the Community of Büdszentmihály), in *Évkönyv 1975/76* (Yearbook, 1975–76), ed. Sándor Scheiber (Budapest: A Magyar Izraeliták Országos Képviselete, 1976), pp. 140–64.

58. For details on the community see László Szilágyi-Windt, *A kállói cádik. A nagykállói zsidóság története* (The Tsadik of Kálló. The History of the Jews of Nagykálló) (Tel Aviv: The Author, 1960; also available in a Hebrew edition published in 1970).

59. Király, *A nyíregyházi gettó története*, p. 17; See also Lévai, *Zsidósors Magyarországon*, pp. 106, 112, 114, and 409.

60. For the listing of the various units of the Jewish Council and of their personnel see Király, *A nyíregyházi gettó története*, pp. 12–16.

61. *Ibid.*, pp. 11–40; László Harsányi, "A nyíregyházi zsidók történetéhez" (Contributions to the History of the Jews of Nyíregyháza), in *Évkönyv 1973/74* (Yearbook 1973–74), ed. Sándor Scheiber. (Budapest: A Magyar Izraeliták Országos Képviselete, 1974), pp. 74–89. The dates and order of deportation given by Király (p. 40) are somewhat different from the ones given by Harsányi.

In 1941, Nyíregyháza had 4,993 Jews, representing about 8.4 percent of the total. In 1946, the city had 1,210 Jews, or around 2.0 percent of the total. In 1949, the Orthodox community had 325 and the Status Quo one had 675 members. *Zsidó világkongresszus*, no. 4(April 15, 1947):4–5; no. 13–14(May 1949):17, 24, 25, and 29. See also the personal account of Alexander Altmann (YIVO, 774/2987). For further details consult Király, *A nyíregyházi gettó története*. See also *Pinkas ha'kehilot*, pp. 379–81.

62. Lévai, *Zsidósors Magyarországon*, p. 410. In 1941, Mátészalka had 1,555 Jews representing 15.4 percent of the total population. By 1946, their number was reduced to 150, or 0.1 percent. Because of the influx of Jews from the neighboring rural communities their number increased to 238 by 1949. *Zsidó világkongresszus*, no. 4(April 15, 1947):6–7; no. 13–14(May 1949):15. See also *Pinkas ha'kehilot*, pp. 348–49, and Fülöp Grünwald, "Sárospatak—Mátészalka—Paks" in *Évkönyv 1971/72* (Yearbook 1971–72), ed. Sándor Scheiber (Budapest: Magyar Izraeliták Országos Képviselete, 1972), pp. 134–37.

63. The 602 Jews of Csenger headed by Samu Berger were first concentrated in the synagogue together with the Jews from the neighboring communities of Uraj and Ujfalu. The local Reformed (Protestant) High School served as the gathering point for the Jews of Sima, Géc, Tótfalu, and Szamosdara. All of the Jews concentrated in the city were shortly thereafter transferred to the ghetto of Mátészalka for deportation. For further details see Sh. Friedmann, *Sefer Yizkor le'kedoshei Csenger, Porcsalma ve'ha Seviva* (Memorial Book of the Martyrs of Csenger, Porcsalma and Vicinity) (Hebrew and Hungarian. Tel Aviv: The Author, 1966), 108 + 60 pp.

64. The Jews of Fehérgyarmat were concentrated in the local synagogue and Jewish school from where they were subsequently transferred to Mátészalka for deportation. For details on Fehérgyarmat, see J. Blasz, *Ayaratenu le'she'Avar Fehérgyarmat* (Our Former Town Fehérgyarmat) (Hebrew and Hungarian. B'nei B'rak; The Author, 1965), 44 + 52 pp.

65. For personal accounts by Jews from Mátészalka and the neighboring communities, including those mentioned in the text, see the following documents at the YIVO: Rose Feig (772/2277), Joseph and Ernest Ráth (772/2368), Mendel Herskovits (773/2066), Sam Fischer (773/2075), Anne Moskovitz (775/3204), R. Schweiger (776/56), J. Berger (776/69), Magda Brunnwasser (776/71), Mandel Gelbermann (776/79), A. Végh (776/83), and I. Lebovits, et al. (776/87).

66. The ghetto of Szeklence, according to one source, included approximately 5,000

Jews, among them those of the communities in the neighboring Száldobos, Ökörmező, Husztsófalva, and Mihálka districts. The ghetto operated under the leadership of the Jewish Council of Huszt. Lévai, *Zsidósors Magyarországon,* p. 408. See also the following personal narratives available at the YIVO: Charles Moskovits (774/2789), Salamon Neumann (776/73), and G. Lebovits (776/92).

67. In 1941, the total population of Kisvárda was 14,728, of which 3,770 or 25.5 percent were Jewish.

68. Király, *A nyíregyházi gettó története,* p. 46; Lévai, *Zsidósors Magyarországon,* p. 409. According to the Budapest Jewish Council report cited by Lévai, the Jewish Council of Kisvárda also included Dr. Miklós Schönwald, József Kain, and a certain Goldstein. See also the personal narrative by Béla Grünwald (YIVO, 772/2437). According to another source, the two transports left on May 25 and 27, respectively. *Pinkas ha'kehilot,* pp. 496–98.

69. *RLB,* Doc. 262.

70. Lévai, *Zsidósors Magyarországon,* p. 103.

71. *Pinkas ha'kehilot,* pp. 372–74.

72. Munkácsi, *Hogyan történt?,* pp. 40–41.

73. For details, see chapter 15.

74. The Council subsequently elected Dr. Zoltán Kohn, the Superintendent of the Jewish Schools, as its Executive Secretary. Ernő Munkácsi, the Executive Secretary of the Jewish Community of Pest, was ill at the time. Statement of Elizabeth Eppler, dated February 27, 1946, available at the YIVO (Protocol 3647, File 768).

75. Munkácsi, *Hogyan történt?,* pp. 61–62.

76. Lévai, *Zsidósors Magyarországon,* p. 104. See also, chapter 6.

77. *Ibid.,* p. 106.

78. Horthy had tried to assure Ravasz that the Jewish workers were to be treated in Germany the same way as the Hungarian workers were. For further details, see chapter 11.

79. The details about the ghettoization in Ung County and in Ungvár were given by an escapee to Budapest. They were included in a protocol taken by Dr. Zoltán Kohn on April 25, 1944. Munkácsi, *Hogyan történt?,* pp. 65–66.

80. Yad Vashem Archives 015/21-1. Reprinted in Munkácsi, *Hogyan történt?,* pp. 63–65.

81. Munkácsi, *Hogyan történt?,* pp. 67–68.

82. Telegram No. 127 of April 21, 1944. *RLB,* Doc. 254.

83. Telegram No. 133. *RLB,* Doc. 255.

84. Telegram No. 138. *RLB,* Doc. 258.

85. Lévai, *Zsidósors Magyarországon,* p. 128. György Gergely, who was at the time one of the Council's liaison officers with the Eichmann-*Sonderkommando,* claims that the list of journalists included only 60 names. See his *Beszámoló a Magyarországi Zsidók Szövetsége Ideiglenes Intéző Bizottsága munkájáról* (Report on the Work of the Provincial Executive Committee of the Association of the Jews of Hungary), 1945, pp. 16–17 (manuscript in this author's possession).

86. See item 4 in Appendix 3. See also chapter 15.

87. *Beszámoló a Magyarországi Zsidók Szövetsége,* p. 17.

88. *Vádirat,* 1:236–37.

89. Lévai, *Zsidósors Magyarországon,* p. 128.

90. Statement by Elizabeth Eppler of February 27, 1946.

91. These views were incorporated in the statement prepared by Dr. Ernő Pető, when he and his two lawyer-colleagues on the Council, Dr. Boda and Dr. Wilhelm, were called before the Chamber of Lawyers (*Ügyvédi Kamara*) soon after the liberation to explain their "cooperation" with the Nazi authorities. Dr. Pető claims that the lists were

handed over to the Council because the Council had lodged a complaint with respect to the arrests immediately after the occupation, when the victims were simply picked up without having been allowed to take along the barest essentials. The authorities "excused" themselves by claiming the detectives were overburdened and asked the Council to assist in order to avoid the early excesses. For excerpts from Pető's statement, see *Vádirat*, 1:237–39.

92. *HJS*, 3:12–13. See also the statement of Dr. Imre Reiner, which was prepared on October 5, 1960 for use by the prosecution in the Eichmann Trial. Israel Police, Bureau 06, no. 347, pp. 21–22.

93. This was, for example, the case of Géza Dach, a Budapest lawyer, whose summons was supposed to have been delivered by his own nephew. Statement of Elizabeth Eppler.

94. Decree no. 1.610/1944. M.E.. See item no. 26 in Appendix 3.

95. For the minutes of the Council of Ministers meeting on this issue, see *Vádirat*, 1:241–44.

CHAPTER EIGHTEEN

ZONE II: NORTHERN TRANSYLVANIA

THE GHETTOIZATION of the close to 160,000 Jews of Northern Transylvania—Gendarmerie Districts IX (Kolozsvár) and X (Marosvásárhely)—began on May 3 at 5:00 A.M.[1] The round-up of the Jews was carried out under Decree no. 6163/1944. res. B.M. (see chapter 17) as amplified by the oral communications given by László Endre and his associates at the two conferences on ghettoization plans in the region.

The Ghettoization Conferences

Details of the procedures for the ghettoization of the Northern Transylvanian Jews were discussed at two top-secret conferences. The first was held in Szatmárnémeti on April 26 and was devoted to the dejewification operations in the counties of Gendarmerie District IX, namely Bihar, Szatmár, Szilágy, Kolozs, Szolnok-Doboka, and Beszterce-Naszód. The second was held two days later in Marosvásárhely and was devoted to the concentration of the Jews in the so-called Székely Land, the counties of Gendarmerie District X: Maros-Torda, Csík, Udvarhely, and Háromszék (see map 13.1).

Both conferences were chaired by Endre. They were attended by the heads and representatives of the civil service, gendarmerie, and police of the concerned counties. Among these were the deputy prefects (in some cases the prefects themselves), the mayors of the cities and their top assistants, and the chief officers of the gendarmerie and police units.

Endre's personal entourage included Albert Takács, his secretary; Géza Szanik, the chief of police of Aszód, who was later appointed Prefect of Bereg County; Dr. Béla Rozsnyai, the supervisor of public welfare in Székesfehérvár; Dr. Ákos Simon, a military physician; and Dr. Sándor Tardi, the representative of the Ministry of Supply.[2] Among those present ex officio were the leading figures of the dejewification squad, including Lieutenant-Colonel László Ferenczy and Dr. Lajos Meggyesi.

The size of the delegations from the various Northern Transylvanian counties and cities varied. Nagybánya, for example, was represented by the Mayor of that city, Police Counselor Dr. Jenő Nagy, the head of the city's police department, and Gendarmerie Captain Tibor Várhelyi.[3]

Endre reviewed the procedures to be followed in the concentration of the Jews as detailed in Order no. 6163/1944, dated April 7. He informed the participants that the local Jewish Council was responsible for setting up the ghetto, but that drinking water, sanitary facilities, and hospital care had to be considered, and that the money and valuables of the Jews "constituting the property of the state" should be taken from them. He expressed the hope that the civil servants would cooperate in the implementation of "this work, which will perhaps only be appreciated by the succeeding generation."

Dr. Lajos Meggyesi emphasized that money, gold, silver, jewelry, typewriters, cameras, watches, rugs, furs, and valuable paintings taken from the Jews were to be listed in a form to be filled out in quadruplicate. One copy would remain with the city, the second would be given to the police, the third would be left in the apartment, and the fourth was to be given to the Jews concerned. Since he was sure that many of the Jews had placed their valuables for safekeeping with Christians, he urged that Christians be warned by town cryers, in newspaper announcements, and through posters to hand in those valuables under threat of internment. The mayors were made responsible for taking the inventories and the storing and safekeeping of the valuables until the job could be assumed by representatives of the postal savings bank system. Ecclesiastical objects could be confiscated from both homes and synagogues. Cash and valuables were to be placed in separate sealed envelopes. Meggyesi also suggested that women should be hired to help in the search for hidden valuables.

Livestock belonging to Jews was to be given into the care of neighboring Christian farmers, and the food supplies left by the Jews were to be removed from their apartments and—in theory—used to feed them in the ghettos at a later time. (For the first two weeks the Jews were to eat the supplies they brought into the ghettos themselves.)

Lieutenant-Colonel Ferenczy informed the participants about the beginning of the operation and announced the major concentration points in Gendarmerie District IX of Northern Transylvania: Nagyvárad, Szilágysomlyó, Szatmárnémeti, Kolozsvár, Szamosujvár, Dés, and Nagybánya. He advised them that in case of any difficulty they could telephone police headquarters in Kolozsvár between 10:00 and 11:00 A.M., where they could get instructions from himself, Dr. Meggyesi, or the German member of the Committee.

The conferees then learned about the composition of the ghettoization commissions and the areas from which the Jews would be transferred to the various ghettos. In Nagybánya, the conferees were told, the concentration would be carried out under the command of Jenő Nagy with the assistance of Captain Tibor Várhelyi and *SS-Haupsturmführer* Franz Abromeit. The ghetto in Nagybánya would hold not only the Jews of that city, but also those of Felsőbánya and of the districts of Nagybánya, Nagysomkut, and Kápolnokmonostor in Szatmár County.[4]

The final plans worked out under the guidance of Endre called for the concentration of the Jews of Northern Transylvania into 11 cities, of which only one, Nagyvárad, was to have a ghetto within the city proper. The 10 other cities with "suitable concentration camp areas" were identified as follows: Kolozsvár, Szamosujvár, Dés, Szilágysomlyó, Szatmárnémeti, Nagybánya, Beszterce, Szászrégen, Marosvásárhely, and Sepsiszentgyörgy.[5]

The Ghettoization Operation

In accordance with the decree and the oral instructions communicated at the two conferences, the chief executive for all the measures relating to the ghettoization of the Jews was the principal administrator of the locality or area. Under Hungarian law then in effect, this meant the mayor for cities, towns, and municipalities, and the deputy prefect of the county for rural areas. The organs of the police and gendarmerie as well as the auxiliary civil service organs of the cities, including the public notary and health units, were to be directly involved in the round-up and transfer of the Jews into ghettos.

The mayors, acting in cooperation with their subordinated agency heads, were empowered not only to direct and supervise the ghettoization operations but also to determine the location of the ghettos and to screen the Jews qualified for exemption. They were also responsible for seeing to the maintenance of essential services in the ghettos.

A few days before the scheduled May 3 start of the ghettoization drive in Northern Transylvania, the special commissions for the various cities and towns held meetings to determine the location of the ghettos and settle the logistics relating to the round-up of the Jews.

The commissions were normally composed of the mayors, deputy prefects, and heads of the local gendarmerie and police units. While nearly the same procedure was followed almost everywhere, the severity with which the ghettoization was carried out and the location of and the conditions within the ghetto depended upon the attitude of the particular mayors and their subordinates. Thus in cities such as Nagyvárad, Máramarossziget, and Szatmárnémeti, the ghettos were established in the poorer, mostly Jewish-inhabited sections; in others, such as Kolozsvár, Marosvásárhely, Szászrégen, Besztercc, and Szilágysomlyó, the ghettos were set up in brickyards. The ghetto of Dés was situated in the Bungur, a forest, where some of the Jews were put up in makeshift barracks and the others—the majority—under the open sky.

Late on May 2, on the eve of the ghettoization, the mayors issued special instructions to the Jews and had them posted in all areas under their jurisdiction. The text followed the directives of the decree, though it varied in nuances from city to city. Typical of such announcements was the one issued by László Gyapay in Nagyvárad:

Jews who are obliged to wear the yellow star are forbidden to leave their homes after the publication of this announcement. For the time being and until the issuance of other instructions, Jews will be permitted to leave their homes only between 9:00 and 10:00 A.M. With the exception of this period, all of them must stay at home. At the order of the Royal Hungarian Government, I am placing into a ghetto all the Jews compelled to wear the yellow star in Nagyvárad. I call upon all non-Jews holding Jewish valuables to report them to the mayor's office within three days from the publication of this announcement. I shall be in charge of the receipt of such reported valuables. I warn the non-Jewish inhabitants of the municipality that all persons holding Jewish property who fail to declare it within the period cited above will be prosecuted with the greatest severity and immediate measures will be taken for their internment in camps.[6]

The round-up of the Jews was carried out by special units composed of civil servants, usually including local primary and high school teachers, gendarmes, and policemen, which were organized by the mayoral commissions and operated under their jurisdiction.

Immediate and overall command over the ghettoization process in Northern Transylvania was exercised by Gendarmerie Colonel Tibor Paksy-Kiss, who delegated special powers in Nagyvárad to Lieutenant-Colonel Jenő Péterffy, his friend and colleague.

In some places, the Jews were collected at smaller centers before their transfer to the ghetto. At each stage they were subjected to an expropriation process which assumed an increasingly barbaric character. It became particularly vicious during the few weeks prior to the beginning of the deportations. The search for valuables was the task of special investigative units, which normally consisted of local detectives who knew the economic status of their victims, and of a few gendarmes and civil servants. These investigative units were legally under the immediate jurisdiction of the mayoral commissions.

May 3 was the first day of the ghettoization process in Northern Transylvania, and close to 8,000 Jews were rounded up in the territories of Gendarmerie District IX. During that day Paksy-Kiss visited the designated ghetto areas in Marosvásárhely, Szászrégen, Beszterce, Dés, and Szamosujvár. On May 5 and 6, he continued his tour by visiting the sites at Szatmárnémeti and Nagyvárad and spent some time observing the rounding up of the Jews in Nagykároly.

The ghettoization of the Jews was carried out smoothly, without major incidents of resistance on the part of either Jews or Christians. The Jewish masses, unaware of the realities of the Final Solution program, went to the ghettos resigned to their fate. Some of them rationalized their "isolation" as a logical step before the transformation of their territory into a battle zone. Others believed that they were being resettled at Kenyérmező in Transdanubia, where they would be employed on agricultural projects until the end of the war. Still others sustained the hope that the Red Army was not very far and that their concentration would be relatively short-lived. With the exception of some of the national leaders, none suspected that their ultimate destination would be Auschwitz (see chapter 23).

The Christians, even those friendly to the Jews, were mostly passive. Many cooperated with the authorities on ideological grounds or in the expectation of quick material rewards in the form of properties confiscated from the Jews. In practically every major community there were some Christians who denounced Jews in hiding.[7] On the other hand, there were also some Christians who helped either to hide Jews or to keep their valuables, although these cases were rare because of the fear instilled in the general population about helping Jews. Ferenczy was naturally impressed with the attitude of the Christian population. He noted in his report on the first day of the operations that the Christians were calm and in most places welcomed the campaign against the Jews. He also observed that the occasional expressions of sympathy came mostly from Romanians, who also suffered under the Horthy regime.[8] The smoothness with which the ghettoization and deportation program was effectuated in Northern Transylvania, as elsewhere, can be attributed in part to the absence of any meaningful resistance movement, let alone general opposition to the persecution of the Jews.

Neutrality and passivity were also the characteristic attitudes of the heads of the Christian churches in Transylvania, as reflected in the behavior of János Vásárhelyi, the Calvinist Bishop, and Miklós Józan, the Unitarian Bishop. The exemplary exception was Áron Marton, the Catholic Bishop of Transylvania whose official residence was in Alba-Iulia, in the Romanian part of Transylvania. In his sermon of May 18 in the St. Michael Church of Kolozsvár, Marton courageously condemned the ghettoization of the Jews and warned the Hungarians not to abandon the Jews to annihilation. He openly called on the Hungarian government to frustrate the intended deportation of the Jews. Unfortunately, his voice was echoed by only a few in the Catholic Church.[9]

The procedures for rounding up, interrogating, and expropriating property of the Jews, as well as the organization and administration of the ghetto, were basically the same in every county of Northern Transylvania. They were everywhere in accord with the instructions and the spirit of the central and local dejewification authorities.

The Ghetto of Kolozsvár.   The Jews of Kolozsvár and of the communities in Kolozs County were concentrated in a ghetto established at the Iris Brickyard on Kajántói Road, in the northern part of the city. The specifics of the concentration operation were worked out at a meeting held on May 2 under the leadership of László Vásárhelyi, the mayor,[10] László Urbán, the police chief, and Paksy-Kiss. The meeting, attended by approximately 150 officials of the municipality who were assigned to the round-up operations, was devoted to the details of the ghettoization process as outlined in the decree and during the conference with Endre held at Szatmárnenémeti on April 26.

The Hungarian officials received expert guidance in the anti-Jewish drive from SS-*Hauptsturmführer* Stroschneider, the local commander of the German security services.[11]

The ghettoization was carried out at a rapid pace. By May 10, the number of those concentrated in the brickyard reached 12,000.[12] At its peak just before the deportations, the ghetto population, including the Jews transferred from the ghetto of Samosujvár, reached close to 18,000.[13]

In addition to the officers cited above, József Forgács, the secretary general of Kolozs County representing the deputy prefect, Lajos Hollóssy-Kuthy, deputy police chief, Géza Papp, a high-ranking police official, and Kazmér Tarr, a top official in the mayor's office, were also heavily involved in the ghettoization of the Jews. Overall command of the ghettoization process in Kolozs County, excepting Kolozsvár, was exercised by Ferenc Szász, the deputy prefect of Kolozs County, and by József Székely, the Mayor of Bánffyhunyad. The Jews of the various towns and villages in the county were first concentrated in their localities, usually in the synagogue or a related Jewish institution. After a short while and a first round of expropriations, they were transferred to the ghetto in Kolozsvár.

In Bánffyhunyad, which had a Jewish community of considerable size, the ghettoization was carried out under the command and supervision of Székely, Pál Boldizsár, the city's supply official, József Orosz, the police chief, and police officers and detectives Ferenc Menyhárt, Andor Szentkúti, Andor Lakatos, and Elek Ojtozi.

The ghetto of Kolozsvár was under the direct command of Urbán. The overcrowding, shortage of washing and sanitary facilities, absence of hospitals, and tremendously inadequate food supply were typical of ghettos in Hungary.

The water supply for the ghetto's 18,000 inhabitants was provided by 15 faucets, many of which were often out of order for days on end. There was hardly enough water for drinking and cooking, let alone for washing. The brickyard consisted primarily of barns without walls, normally used as drying sheds for bricks and tiles. Four ditches were dug to serve as latrines for the entire ghetto—two for males and two for females. Each latrine was closed off on one side by a long board fastened to pillars.

A special building in the ghetto served as the "mint"—the place where Jews were tortured into confessing where they allegedly hid their valuables. Husbands were often tortured in full view of their wives and children; often wives were beaten in front of their husbands. The devices used were cruel and unusually barbaric. The victims were beaten on the soles of their feet with canes or rubber truncheons; they were slapped in the face, and kicked until they lost consciousness. Males were often beaten on the testicles; females, sometimes even young girls, were searched vaginally by collaborating female volunteers and midwives who cared little about cleanliness, often in full view of the male interrogators. Some particularly sadistic investigators used electrical devices to compel the victims into confession. They would put one end of such a device in the mouth and the other in the vagina or attached to the testicles of the victims. These inhuman tortures drove many of the well-to-do Jews to insanity or suicide.[14]

The internal administration of the ghetto was entrusted to a Jewish

Council consisting of the traditional leaders of the local Jewish community. In Kolozsvár, the Council was headed by Dr. Jozsef Fischer,[15] the head of the Neolog community and Dr. Kasztner's father-in-law, and included Rabbi Akiba Glasner, Dr. József Fenichel, Gyula Klein, Dr. Ernő Marton, editor-in-chief of the *Uj Kelet* (New East), Zsigmond Léb, and Rabbi Mózes Weinberger.[16] Its secretary general was József Moskovits, while Dezső Hermann served as secretary.[17]

Dr. Kasztner visited Kolozsvár on May 4–5 in the company of Dr. Rudolf Sedlacek, an SS officer, allegedly to meet Wisliceny, who directed the ghettoization in Northern Transylvania as adviser at the Kolozsvár headquarters of the Dejewification Committee. He also met the leaders of the Jewish community. (What he did or did not tell them then about the reality of the Jewish situation became the subject of a heated controversy after the war.) As a result of Kasztner's dealings with the SS, permission was given to select 388 Jews from the ghetto and take them on June 10 by special train to Budapest. There they were placed in a special camp at the Wechselmann Institute for the Deaf-Mute on Columbus Street. The Columbus Street Camp was a privileged camp: its inmates were treated humanely and it was protected by five SS guards under orders to prevent abuses. It is from here that the Kasztner-group, including 1,684 Jews, left Budapest on June 30, 1944, and eventually reached Switzerland via Bergen-Belsen (see chapter 29).

According to one source, the group of 388 Kolozsvár Jews was put together on the basis of a recommendation by Zsigmond Léb, the leader of the city's Orthodox community, who happened to be in Budapest at the time, and of selections made in the ghetto by a group of local leaders and Zionists, including József Fischer, Hillel Dánzig, Dr. Lajos Marton, Dr. Jenő Kertész, and Dr. Sándor Weisz.[18]

Szamosujvár. A small locality about 30 miles north of Kolozsvár, Szamosujvár had close to 1,600 Jews in its ghetto, which was located in the local brickyard. Nearly 400 of the ghetto inmates were from neighboring villages in Szamosujvár District, including Aranyszentmiklós, Bőd, Buza, Coptelke, Dengeleg, Derzse, Devecser, Feketelak, Iklód, Kecsed, Kékes, Kérő, Lozsárd, Mányik, Mátéfalva, Nószoly, Ördöngösfüzes, Pujon, Szamoskend, Szentmárton, Szék, Szentgothárd, and Veresegyháza. The Jewish Council consisted of Dr. Sándor Köves and Dr. Edmund (Ödön) Abel. The ghetto population was transferred on May 18 to the brickyard at Kolozsvár and shortly thereafter deported from there.[19]

The ghettoization and subsequent transfer of the Jews of Szamosujvár and its environs were carried out under the immediate command of Lajos Tamási, the mayor, and Ernő Berecki and Andor Iványi, the chief police officers of the city.[20]

Dés. The County of Szolnok-Doboka was represented at the April 26 conference with Endre in Szatmárnémeti by János Schilling, the deputy prefect, Jenő Veress, the Mayor of Dés, Lajos Tamási, the Mayor of Szamosujvár, Gyula Sárosi, the police chief of Dés, Ernő Berecki, the police chief of Szamosujvár, and Pál Antalffy, the commander of the gendarmerie in Szolnok-Doboka. The objectives and decisions of this conference were communicated to the chief civil service, gendarmerie, and police officers of the county at a special meeting convened and chaired by Schilling on April 30. At this meeting Dés and Szamosujvár were selected as the two major ghetto sites of the county.

Among the civilian officials at the meeting were Lajos Krämer, a pharmacist, Dr. Jenő Vékás, a physician, and Dr. Zsigmond Lehner (Lénárd), the health officer of Dés. Krämer's suggestion that the ghetto of Dés be set up in and around Kodor Street, the area of the city which was overwhelmingly Jewish, was vetoed on the insistence of Dr. Vékás, and above all of Dr. Lehner.[21] In accordance with the decision reached at this meeting, the ghetto was set up in Bungur forest, about two miles from the city, which was very close to a secondary railroad line that could be used for the later entrainment of the Jews. The local anti-Semitic organ, *Szamosvölgye* (Szamos Valley), edited by László Sztojka, had found even the forest too good for the Jews and would have preferred to see them placed "in a less beautiful area, in the open fields."[22]

Within a few days of the ghettoization drive, which was carried out under the overall command of Pál Antalffy, 7,800 Jews were brought into the Bungur.[23] Of these approximately half were from Dés.[24] Before their transfer to the Bungur, the Jews of Dés were concentrated at three centers within the city, where they were subjected to body searches for valuables. One of these centers was the large house of Miklós Bakay. The remainder of the ghetto population was brought in from the other communities in the county, many of whom were first concentrated in the district seats, including Bethlen, Magyarlápos, Nagyilonda, and Retteg.[25] The Jews in the county's rural communities were rounded up during May 3–5. At first the authorities toyed with the idea of transferring them to the much larger ghetto of Szamosujvár.[26] However, by May 6 enough materials, including planks from Jewish-owned lumber yards, were found to keep the Jews in Bungur.[27] The ghetto, surrounded by barbed wire, was guarded by the local police supplemented by a special unit of 40 gendarmes assigned from Zilah.[28] Supreme command over the ghetto was exercised by Emil Takács, a "government commissioner."

Sanitary conditions within the ghetto were miserable, as were the essential services and supplies. This was largely due to the malevolence of Veress and Lehner, the Mayor and the chief health officer of Dés. The investigative teams formed for the search of valuables were as cruel in Dés as they were everywhere else. Among those involved in the search who "distinguished" themselves by their cruelty were József Fekete, József Gecse, Margit Fekete, Jenő Takács, József Lakadár, and police officers Adalbert (Béla) Garamvölgyi, János Zomorjai, János Kassai, and N. Désaknai.[29] Abuses in the search for valuables also took place in the smaller towns of the county just before the transfer of the Jews to the Bungur. In Retteg, for example, Sándor Oláh and Rozália Jancsó were particularly zealous in their search, committing many brutal crimes. In Ciceu-Giurgeşti, Ferenc Lakatos acted viciously not only against the Jews, but also against the Romanians.[30]

Although he attended the Szatmárnémeti conference and convened the meeting of April 30 in Dés, Deputy Prefect János Schilling backed out just before the beginning of the ghettoization. Feigning illness, he resigned his position on May 2.[31] Needless to say, he failed to tip off the local Jewish leaders about the impending disaster. When he saw the columns of ragged Jews being driven into the ghetto, Schilling allegedly remarked to his subordinates: "Look, gentlemen, this is how thousand-year-old Hungary digs its grave."[32]

The internal administration of the ghetto was entrusted to a Jewish Council composed of the traditional leaders of the local community. The Council included Ferenc Ordentlich (chairman), Lázár Albert, Samu Weinberger, Manó Weinberger, and Andor Ágai. Dr. Oszkár Engelberg served as the ghetto's chief physician and Zoltán Singer as its economic representative in charge of supplies.[33]

The Jews were kept in the ghetto for about four weeks under the most miserable conditions. The wealthier ones were subjected to especially cruel treatment at the hands of police and gendarme investigators. During the short lifespan of the ghetto, 25 Jews died of natural and other causes. Among these were a number of newborn babies and Dr. Samu Biró of Magyarlápos, who was beaten to death. (Their bodies were transferred from the Bungur to the Jewish cemetery after the war.) A small number of able-bodied Jews were taken to the city daily under special escort to work on various projects; some of them were put to work in the city's main synagogue, which had been transformed into a warehouse. The ghetto was liquidated on June 6, when the third and last transport left the city.[34]

Szilágysomlyó. The ghettoization of the Jews of Szilágy County was carried out under the command and supervision of the officials who participated at the Szatmárnémeti Conference of April 26: Andor Gazda, deputy county prefect; János Schreter, Mayor of Zilah; József Udvari, Mayor of Szilágysomlyó; Lieutenant-Colonel György Mariska, commander of the gendarmerie unit of the county; Ferenc Elekes, police chief of Zilah; and István Pethes, police chief of Szilágysomlyó. Baron János Jósika, the Prefect of Szilágy County, resigned immediately when he was informed by Gazda about the decisions taken at the conference.[35] He was one of the few Hungarian officials who dared to take a public stand against the anti-Jewish actions, deeming them both immoral and illegal. His successor, László Szlávy, an appointee of the Sztójay government, had no such scruples and cooperated fully in the implementation of the anti-Jewish measures.

Soon after their return from Szatmárnémeti, the conferees met at the prefect's office with Béla Sámy, the chief county clerk, Drs. Suchi and Ferenc Molnár, the chief health officials of Szilágy County and of Szilagysomlyó respectively, László Krasznay, the head of Somlyó District, and István Kemecsey, the head of the technical services department of Szilágysomlyó, to select a site for the ghetto. They first thought of establishing it around Báthory Street and the synagogue in Szilágysomlyó, but eventually settled on the Klein Brickworks at Cehei, about three miles from the city.

The round-up of the Jews in Szilágysomlyó was carried out under the immediate command of István Pethes; in Zilah under the leadership of Ferenc Elekes; and in the other parts of the county under the direction of Gazda and the immediate command of Lieutenant-Colonel György Mariska. Among the sizable Jewish communities affected were those of Tasnád[36] and Kraszna. By May 6, there were 7,200 Jews in the ghetto, including 313 from Zilah.[37] At its peak, the ghetto had 8,500 inhabitants.

Despite the zeal of the commissions involved in the collection of the Jews, Ferenczy complained of some difficulties due to "the involvement of incompetent elements in the campaign." These were apparently ironed out soon after the assignment of a gendarmerie officer from Zilah. One of the difficulties Ferenczy mentioned was the discovery of a grenade in the luggage of one of the Jews.[38]

The brickyard was located in a marshy and muddy area. The brickdrying sheds in which the Jews were quartered had no walls and covered an area of only 700 by 200 meters. As a consequence, almost half of the ghetto population had to live outside. The ghetto was guarded by a special unit of gendarmes from Budapest and operated under the command of Krasznay, one of the most cruel ghetto commanders in Hungary. Under the guise of a search for valuables, he gave free rein to his sadistic instincts. In this and many other crimes, he had the full cooperation of many officials and *Nyilas* sympathizers: József Lázár, N. Sárközi, the gendarme commander of Zsibó, János Angya, László Petővári, Captain Sándor Horváth, János Vida, Ádám Kerekes, Sándor Nagy, Mihály Kovács, Sándor Farmati, Béla (Adalbert) Szabó, Irma (Irina) Duha, and Dezső Dénes. As a result of the tortures, poor feeding, and totally inadequate water supply in the ghetto of Szilágysomlyó, the Jews of Szilágy County arrived at Auschwitz in very poor condition, so that an unusually large percentage was selected for gassing immediately upon arrival.[39]

Szatmárnémeti. The Hungarian authorities decided to establish two ghettos in Szatmár County: one in Szatmárnémeti and the other in Nagybánya. Nagykároly was at first also used as a concentration center for its local Jews and those in the neighboring communities. The approximately 1,200 Jews gathered in Nagykároly were first housed in Hétsastoll, Debreceni István, Kazinczy, and Honvéd streets. The Jewish Council was composed of Dr. István Antal, Jenő Pfeffermann, Ernő Deutsch, and Lajos Jakobovics.[40] After a short while, the Jews concentrated in Nagykároly were transferred to the ghetto of Szatmárnémeti.

The county representatives at the Szatmárnémeti Conference of April 26 included László Csóka, the Mayor of Szatmárnémeti; Endre Boer, the deputy county prefect; Zoltán Rogozi Papp, the deputy mayor of Szatmárnémeti; Ernő Pirkler, the city's secretary general, and representatives of the local police and gendarmerie.

The commissions for the apprehension of the Jews of Szatmárnémeti and its environs were established at a meeting held shortly after the conference. The meeting was chaired by Csóka and attended by representatives of the police and gendarmerie—among them Károly Zegényi, Béla Sárközi, and Jenő Nagy of the police and N. Demény of the gendarmerie—and of the financial and educational boards of the city. The ghettoization in Szatmárnémeti was carried out under the direction of Csóka; in the rest of the county it was implemented under Boer.

The original plan called for the Jews to be concentrated at a special camp site. The final decision, however, was to establish the ghetto in and near Zrinyi, Petőfi, Báthory, and Tompa streets.[41] At its peak, the ghetto of Szatmárnémeti held approximately 18,000 Jews, including those of Erdőd, Nagykároly, and Szatmárnémeti districts. The larger Jewish communities involved were those of Apa, Aranyosmeggyes, Avasfelsőfalu, Avaslekence, Avasujváros, Batiz, Beltek, Bikszád, Erdőd, Huta, Kacs, Nagykároly, Sarkod, Szamoskrassó, Szatmárhegy, Szinerváralja, Terep, and Vámfalu.[42] Health care in the ghetto was organized and provided by a group of Jewish physicians, including Drs. Tibor Kőváry, László Sárkány, and Ármin Fenyves.[43]

The commander of the ghetto was Béla Sárközi, the police officer in charge of the local KEOKH office.[44] The Jewish Council[45] was headed by Zoltán Schwartz and included Sámuel Rosenberg, the head of the Jewish community, Singer, Lajos Vinkler, and József Borgida, all highly respected leaders of the Jewish commur ty of Szatmárnémeti.[46]

The searches for valuables were carried out with the customary cruelty by a team headed by Sárközi, Zegényi, and Demény. In the wake of the ghettoization and of the tortures within the ghetto, several Jews committed suicide.[47] As was the case everywhere else, the ghettoization took place without any noteworthy incidents. The smoothness of the operation was due, according to Ferenczy, to the participation of a special unit of 50 gendarmes stationed at Merk.[48] Ferenczy was also comforted by the fact that he had managed to bring about the internment of three families that had received special exemption from Csóka[49] and to capture some Jews who had gone into hiding.[50] Many of those in hiding were denounced by Christian neighbors.[51]

Nagybánya. The ghettoization of the Jews of Nagybánya and of the various communities in the southeastern districts of Szatmár County (Nagybánya, Nagysomkut, and Kápolnokmonostor) was based upon guidelines adopted a few days after the Szatmárnémeti Conference. The meeting of the local leaders was held at the headquarters of the Arrow Cross Pary in Nagybánya and was also attended by László Endre. The city was first represented by Károly Tamás, the deputy mayor, but he was soon replaced by István Rosner, an assistant mayor, who was more pliable. Among the others present were Jenő Nagy, the police chief; Sándor Vajay, the former secretary general of the mayor's office; Tibor Várhelyi, the commander of the gendarmerie unit; Gyula Gergely, the head of the Arrow Cross Party in Northern Transylvania; and József Horacsek, the president of the Baross Association, the highly anti-Semitic association of Christian businessmen.

The ghetto for the Jews of the city of Nagybánya was established in the vacant lots of the König Glass Factory; those from the various communities in Nagybánya, Nagysomkut, and Kápolnokmonostor districts were quartered in a stable and barn in Borpatak (Valea Burcutului), about two miles from the city.[52] The apprehension of the Jews and the searches for valuables were carried out under the command of Jenő Nagy and Gyula Gergely under the guidance of SS-*Hauptsturmführer* Franz Abromeit.[53] The ghettoization took place at high speed: the Jews were given no more than 10 minutes to get ready.

The ghetto of Nagybánya held approximately 3,500 Jews and that of Borpatak about 2,000.[54] Of the latter only 200 found room in the stable and the barn; the others had to be quartered outdoors. The commander in chief of the ghetto was Tibor Várhelyi. The Jews in the ghetto of Nagybánya were subjected to the tortures and investigative methods customary in all ghettos. Among those responsible, under the leadership of Nagy and Várhelyi, were Kornél Balogh and László Berentes, associates of the Phönix Factory of Nagybánya, as well as Horacsek, Péter Csisperger, Zoltán Osváth, and detectives József Orgoványi, Imre Vajai, and István Bertalan. Overall responsibility for the administration of the county at the time rested with Barnabás Endrődi, who was appointed Prefect of Szatmár County by the Sztójay government on April 25, 1944.[55]

Beszterce.   The approximately 8,000 Jews of Beszterce and of the other communities in Beszterce-Naszód County were concentrated at the Stamboli Farm, located about two to three miles from the city.[56] Close to 2,500 of the ghetto inhabitants were from Beszterce itself.[57]

The ghettoization of the city's Jews was carried out under the command of Mayor Norbert Kuales and Police Chief N. Debreczeni. In the other communities of the county, the round-up was guided by László Szmolenszki, the deputy prefect, and Lieutenant-Colonel Ernő Pásztohi of the gendarmerie. All four had attended the Marosvásárhely Conference with Endre on April 28.

The ghetto, consisting of a number of barracks and pigsties, was ill-equipped from every point of view. The inadequate water and food supply was due primarily to the vicious behavior of Henric Smolka, who was in charge. Among those who cooperated with Smolka in the persecution of the Jews was Gusztáv Órendi, a Gestapo agent in Beszterce. In addition to the local police authorities, the ghetto was also guarded by 25 gendarmes from Nagydemeter ordered to Beszterce by Paksy-Kiss.[58] After May 10, 1944, the prefect of the county was Kálmán Borbély.[59]

Nagyvárad.   The largest ghetto of Hungary—except for the Budapest

Ghetto, which was established only toward the end of November 1944—was that of Nagyvárad. Actually, Nagyvárad had two ghettos: one for the city's Jews, holding approximately 27,000 people and located in the neighborhood of the large Orthodox synagogue and the Great Market (*Nagypiac*), in the area surrounded by Mezei Mihály Street to the West, Kapucinus Street and Mussolini Square to the North, Frangepan K. Street to the East, and Szeptember 6 and Tompa Mihály Streets to the South. The other, for the approximately 8,000 Jews from the other communities in Bihar County, was at the city grange and in and around the Mezey Lumber Yards.[60]

Overall command over the ghettoization and spoliation process in Bihar County was exercised by Lieutenant-Colonel Jenő Péterffy of the gendarmerie, a close associate of Paksy-Kiss. Immediate command over the ghettoization in Nagyvárad was exercised by László Gyapay, the deputy mayor, who had just taken over for the Mayor of the city who had resigned. One of his closest assistants in this drive was Lajos Cser. In the other parts of the county, the ghettoization was carried out under the supervision of János Nadányi, the county's deputy prefect.

The ghettoization was carried out at great speed, and completed within five days. The Jews were first gathered in the courtyard of the synagogue, where they were subjected to the customary searches, and then directed into the ghetto through a narrow entrance. Among the Jews in the ghetto of Nagyvárad were a considerable number of labor servicemen, who, though exempted and under the jurisdiction of the Ministry of Defense, were illegally picked up on orders of Péterffy.

Among the Jewish communities concentrated at the Mezey Lumber Yard area were those of Élesd, Érmihályfalva, Margitta, and Székelyhid. As in the other smaller localities, the Jews of these communities were first concentrated in their local synagogues or other "suitable" locations, where they were subjected to a thorough body search for valuables,[61] and then transferred to Nagyvárad.

The ghetto of Nagyvárad was extremely overcrowded. The Jews of the city, who constituted about 30 percent of its population,[62] were crammed into an area sufficient for only $1/15$th of the city's inhabitants. The density was such that 14 to 15 Jews had to share a room.[63] The ghetto inhabitants also suffered from a shortage of food and essential services. The anti-Semitic city administration often cut off electric service and the flow of water to the ghetto.

The so-called Commissions for the Unearthing of Jewish Wealth were established on May 3 at a meeting in the Mayor's office chaired by

Gyapay and attended by the heads of the city agencies and the top officials of the city government, the police, and the gendarmerie. Ultimate power over the two ghettos was assigned to a Ghetto Commission consisting of Péterffy, Gyapay, and Nadányi, which also had jurisdiction over the exemption provisions of the anti-Jewish laws.

Internally, the ghettos were administered by a Jewish Council consisting of Sándor Leitner (President), Chief Rabbi István Vajda, Dr. Sándor Lörincz, a lawyer, Dr. René Osváth, a physician, and Sámuel Metzen, a manufacturer.[64]

Both ghettos were tightly guarded by special units of the police and gendarmerie. During the first week (until May 10), the Jews of Nagyvárad were under the immediate command of Imre Németh, a police captain. He acted under the guidance of Wennholz, the local Gestapo chief, and of Károly (Reiner) Rajnay, the newly appointed pro-Endre Prefect of Bihar.[65] Németh was assisted by István Kovács-Nagy, a fellow police officer. While the Jews were subjected to the customary searches and cruel treatment even during Németh's tenure, the real terror began after May 10, when Péterffy[66] and his gendarmes took control. Péterffy began his reign of horrors by issuing an announcement titled *Discipline in the Ghetto*, which included no less than 80 punitive and discriminatory provisions. They provided, *inter alia*, for the execution of Jews leaving the territory of the ghetto; for Jews to stand at attention and bareheaded in front of any Hungarian or German officers; and for the ghetto to be "enveloped in the silence of the grave" from early evening to early morning ("from taps to reveille"). One of Péterffy's immediate subordinates in the ghetto was Captain István Garay.

The search for Jewish wealth was entrusted to a special unit of 40 gendarmes, assisted by the local police and detectives. Acting under the immediate command of Péterffy, the gendarmes conducted their searches in the "mint" at the Dreher Breweries immediately adjacent to the ghetto. The "mint" of Nagyvárad achieved notoriety not only because of the large number of Jews abused there, but also because of the especially sadistic behavior of the gendarmes. The victims were usually stripped naked and whipped mercilessly by their tormentors. Many of them were subjected to electric-shock torture in full view of their families, which drove some to suicide.[67]

Among Péterffy's assistants who distinguished themselves by their cruelty were gendarmerie officers Lieutenant Gyula Petri, who also served as a liaison with Theodor Dannecker, the local Gestapo chief;

Lieutenant Ágoston Felegyházi Megyesi, one of the top leaders of the investigative teams; Lieutenant Béla Rektor; Captain István Garay; and Lieutenant Endre Bodolay. Among those active at the Dreher Breweries were Ferenc Sziklai, Andor Megyesi, Dezső Buss, Gyula Uri, György Fekete, Sándor Ilonka, János Teveli, István Szőllősi, Géza Szabados, József Tóth, Mihály Juhász, Sándor Pozsgai, Gábor Keresztesi, István Felföldi, Imre Garay, Sándor Fehér, Megyeri, Budai, Mihály Szabó, and József Horváth.[68] The investigative team in the mayor's office consisted of police officers Dr. Toperczer, Tapasztó, and Váradi.[69]

According to Péter Hain, the chief of the Hungarian Gestapo, Jewish wealth worth 41 million gold *Pengős* was "recovered" as a result of the "investigations," and suits were instituted against 2,004 Christians "for having concealed Jewish property."[70] As was the case in most ghettos, many of the policemen and gendarmes participating in the investigations succumbed to the temptation of easy loot and pocketed some of the confiscated valuables. So extensive was the practice in Nagyvárad that a special prosecutor of the Center for State Defense, Dr. Dénes Kovács, was called in to investigate.[71]

On May 17, Minister of the Interior Andor Jaross came to Nagyvárad to officiate at the inauguration of Dr. Károly (Reiner) Rajnay as the new Prefect of Bihar County.[72] Speaking two days after the beginning of the deportations in Carpatho-Ruthenia, Jaross declared:

Today I saw a new Nagyvárad emerge in the sunshine of May. I saw that here was the new nationalist Nagyvárad, where there are no Jews in the streets. I am convinced that there has been an appropriate segregation of the Jews in this city. Nagyvárad solved this problem and I notice with satisfaction that this solution is in accord with the requirements of the age. The Jewish problem, however, is not ended with this. One must remove from the nation's bloodstream every infecting material and the possibility of any infection. In this regard the Hungarian government marches on step by step. I don't want to make any declaration on this; please follow events carefully.[73]

Endre also expressed great satisfaction over the achievements in the ghetto when he returned to the city on May 18.[74] These "achievements" can be attributed largely to the advice the authorities received from Theodor Dannecker, the Eichmann-*Sonderkommando*'s representative in the city, who had already established his reputation in France and elsewhere in Nazi-occupied Europe.

The calvary of the Jews of Nagyvárad, which began on March 31,[75] came to a climax on May 24, when the first deportation train left the city.[76] The deportation of May 24 involved the rural Jews in the Mezey Lumber Yard. The first train from the ghetto proper left on May 27 and the last one on June 3.

The Székely Land

In Gendarmerie District X, the so-called Székely Land (Székelyföld), which covered Maros-Torda, Csík, Udvarhely, and Háromszék counties, the Jews were placed in three major ghettos: Marosvásárhely, Szászrégen, and Sepsiszentgyörgy.

The concentration of the Jews of the Székely Land counties was carried out in accordance with the decisions of a conference held in Marosvásárhely on April 28, 1944. The conference was chaired by Endre and attended by all prefects, deputy prefects, mayors of cities, heads of districts, and top police and gendarmerie officers of the area. As decided at this conference the ghetto of Marosvásárhely held not only the local Jews, but also those from the communities in Udvarhely County and the western part of Maros-Torda County. The ghetto of Szászrégen held the Jews of the communities in the eastern part of Maros-Torda County and in the northern part of Csík County. The ghetto of Sepsiszentgyörgy was established for the Jews of Háromszék County and the southern part of Csík County. As was the case everywhere else, the Jews of the various communities were first concentrated in the local synagogues, schools, or police headquarters, and then transferred to the assigned ghettos.[77]

Marosvásárhely. The ghetto of Marosvásárhely was located in a dilapidated brickyard at Koronkai Road. Encompassing an area of approximately 20,000 square meters, it had one large building, with a broken roof and cement floors; since it had not been in use for several years, it was also extremely dirty. The ghetto had a population of 7,380 Jews,[78] of which around 5,500 were from the city itself[79] and the remainder from the communities in the western part of Maros-Torda County and from Udvarhely County. Among these were the 276 Jews of Székelyudvarhely[80] and the Jews of Bözödújfalu, descendants of the Székely who had converted to Judaism in the early days of the Transylvania Principality. Allegedly these were given an opportunity to escape the ghettoization if they would declare that they were in fact Christian Magyars, but, according to one source, they refused to do so.[81]

In the brickyard, the largest ghetto in the area, approximately 2,400 of the 7,380 Jews found accommodation in the brickdrying barns.[82]

The others had to make do in the open. The commander of the ghetto was police chief Géza Bedő; his deputy was Dezső Liptai. The Jewish Council, which did its best to alleviate the plight of the Jews, included Samu Ábrahám, Mayer Csengeri, Mór Darvas, Ernő Goldstein, József Helmer, Dezső Léderer, Jenő Schwimmer, Ernő Singer, and Manón Szofer.[83]

Conditions in the ghetto were as miserable as everywhere else, the water supply being particularly bad. Responsibility for the failure of health and sanitary services in the ghetto must be borne by Dr. Ádám Horváth, the city health officer and his deputy, Dr. Mátyás Talos.

The Marosvásárhely Jews were concentrated under the overall guidance of Mayor Ferenc Májay, who had attended the conference with Endre. In fact, Májay proceeded with the implementation of Endre's directives the day after the conference, when he ordered that the main synagogue be converted into a makeshift hospital. The police and gendarmerie units directly involved in the ghettoization process were under the direct command of Colonel János Papp, the head of the Gendarmerie Inspectorate in the four counties of the Székely Land, Colonel János Zalantai, the commander of the Legion of Gendarmes of Maros-Torda County, and Géza Bedő. Leadership roles were also played by Colonel Géza Kőrmendy, the head of the *Honvéd* units in the city and the county, and General István Kozma, the head of the so-called Székely Border Guard (*Székely Határőr*) paramilitary organization. The involvement of these *Honvéd* officials was exceptional, inasmuch as regular military units were not normally involved in the ghettoization process. Kozma claimed that he had gotten involved at the personal request of Endre. Technical advice in the course of the anti-Jewish operations was provided by the local representative of the Gestapo, Major Schröder.[84]

The harshness and effectiveness of the local military-administrative authorities notwithstanding, Paksy-Kiss found much wanting in their operations and provided a special unit of gendarmes for their assistance.[85] The concentration of the Jews was carried out with the help of the local chapter of the Levente paramilitary youth organization. Several of its members were caught taking money from the Jews for forwarding letters and messages.[86]

Májay's immediate collaborators in the initiation and administration of the anti-Jewish measures in Marosvásárhely were Ferenc Hennel, the head notary in the Mayor's office, and Ernő Javor, the head notary of the prefecture. Within the county of Maros-Torda, the concentration was carried out under the direction of Andor Joós and Zsigmond Marton, prefect and deputy prefect respectively.

In Udvarhely County and the city of Székelyudvarhely, the county seat, the ghettoization was carried out under the general guidance of Dezső Gálfi, the prefect. Immediate command in the county was exercised by Deputy Prefect István Bonda and Lieutenant-Colonel László Kiss, the commander of the gendarmerie in the county. In Székelyudvarhely, the round-up was directed by Mayor Ferenc Filó, and Police Chief János Zsigmond.

As in all other major ghettos, the Marosvásárhely ghetto had a "screening commission" whose function was to evaluate petitions from Jews, including those claiming exemption status. The commission, whose position toward the Jews was absolutely negative, consisted of Májay, Bedő, and Colonel Loránt Bocskor of the gendarmerie. In Marosvásárhely also there was a "mint," located in a small building within the ghetto. Among the torturers active in the drive for Jewish valuables were Ferenc Sallós, and Captains Konya and Pintér of the gendarmerie. In one respect the "mint" of Marosvásárhely was unique: it had a Jewish informer working with the officials. He was József Lax, a jeweler with close ties to the local police and the counterintelligence service, and who reportedly had personal knowledge of the jewelry owned by the wealthier Jews. Occasionally he "intervened" with the authorities on behalf of Jews in return for large sums of money, which were then shared with the officials.[87] The first transport was entrained for Auschwitz on May 29. Within a week all the Jews had been deported from the three ghettos.[88]

Szászrégen. The ghetto of Szászrégen was established in a totally inadequate brickyard selected by Mayor Imre Schmidt and Police Chief János Dudás. Both of them had attended the Marosvásárhely Conference with Endre on April 28. They were assisted in this decision, as in the round-up of the Jews, by Major László Komáromi, the head of the _Honvéd_ forces in Szászrégen, Lieutenant G. Szentpáli Kálmán, the commander of the local gendarmerie unit, and Egon Csordacsics, a counselor in the Mayor's office and the local "expert" on the Jewish question.

Most of the Jews were housed in brick-drying sheds without walls. A number had to live in the open and a few were allowed to stay in houses at the edge of the city right next to the brickyard. At its peak, the ghetto population was 4,000,[89] approximately 1,400 from the city itself.[90] The remainder were brought in from the eastern part of Maros-Torda County and from the northern part of Csík County.

The Jews of Gyergyószentmiklós in Csík County were rounded up under the direction of Mayor Mátyás Tóth and Police Chief Géza Polonkai. (Polonkai's predecessor, Police Chief Ørményi, had resigned rather than become involved in such immoral activities.) Here even exempted Jews were picked up and held together with the others in a local primary school, where searches for valuables were conducted by Béla Ferenczi, a member of the local police department. After three days in the school, where they were given practically no food, the Jews were transferred to the Szászrégen ghetto.

The ghetto was guarded by a special unit of 40 gendarmes sent in from Szeged[91] in addition to the local police. The conditions in the ghetto were similar to those elsewhere. The searches for valuables were conducted by the police and gendarmerie officers mentioned above, assisted by Pál Bányai, Balázs Biró, András Fejér, and István Gosi, members of a special gendarme investigative unit. To help with the "interrogation" of the Jews from Gyergyószentmiklós, Béla Ferenczi was summoned from that city. Vaginal searches were performed primarily by Irma Lovász. Immediate command in the ghetto was exercised by János Dudás, though two others vied for a while for this infamous position—Komáromi and György Feleki Kugler, a leader of the local Arrow Cross Party. As a consolation for their defeat by Dudás, they were allowed to participate in the "search parties," during which they gave vent to their sadistic instincts.[92]

During the short lifetime of the ghetto, a number of the men were put to work in the construction of a nearby airport. About 20 Jewish women were assigned every day to the Germans for kitchen and household work.[93]

Sepsiszentgyörgy. The ghetto of Sepsiszentgyörgy held the local Jews as well as those from the small communities in Háromszék County and the southern part of Csík County. The total ghetto population numbered only 850.[94]

The ghettoization of the few hundred Jews of Sepsiszentgyörgy differed from the procedure followed elsewhere. On May 2, the Jews were informed by the police to appear the following morning at 6:00 at police headquarters with all members of their families. One member of each family was then allowed to return home in the company of a policeman to pick up the essential goods permitted by the authorities. After this operation, the Jews were transferred to an unfinished building that had neither doors nor windows. The commission for the selection of the ghetto site consisted of Dr. Gábor Szentiványi, the prefect of

Háromszék County, who behaved quite decently toward the rural population; Dr. András Barabás, the deputy prefect; Dr. András Virányi, the mayor; Dr. István Vincze, the chief of the Sepsiszentgyörgy police; and Lieutenant-Colonel Balla, the commander of the gendarmes in Háromszék County. All of them had attended the Marosvásárhely Conference with Endre.

The Jews of Csík County, including those of Csíkszereda, were rounded up under the general command of Ernő Galli, the prefect of Csík County; Dr. József Ábrahám, the deputy prefect; Gerő Szász, the Mayor of Csíkszereda; Pál Farkas, the city's chief of police; and Lieutenant-Colonel Tivador Loór, the commander of the gendarmes at Csíkszereda. Like the city and county leaders of Háromszék County, these leaders also attended the Marosvásárhely Conference.

The conditions in the Sepsiszentgyörgy ghetto, which was under the immediate command of an unidentified SS officer, were harsh. The Jews from this ghetto were transferred to the ghetto of Szászrégen after a week. On this occasion they had a foretaste of the kind of transportation they would be subjected to later in the month during their deportation to Auschwitz, for they were packed 70 to a freight wagon without regard to sex, age, or state of health.[95]

Endre's Second Tour

During the first half of May 1944, László Endre undertook a second inspection tour, visiting some of the major ghettos in existence at the time. Shortly after the Szatmárnémeti and Marosvásárhely Conferences of April 26 and 28, respectively, Endre inspected Mátészalka. From there he went to Marosvásárhely, where he reviewed the local ghettoization details with the perfect, the deputy prefect, and the Mayor. In Sepsiszentgyörgy, he inspected the unfinished structure holding the Jews, in the company of the prefect of Háromszék, Dr. Gábor Szentiványi. Next he went to Kolozsvár, where he reviewed the ghettoization plans with Lieutenant-General Lajos Veres, Mayor László Vásárhelyi, and deputy police chief Hollóssy. The next stop was Nagyvárad, where he dealt with László Gyapay and deputy prefect János Nadányi.[96]

Upon his return to Budapest Endre gave an interview to a staff reporter of the Nazi-oriented *Uj Magyarság* (New Magyardom) in which he declared that the conclusion of the dejewification campaign represented a gigantic step calculated to defend the life of the Hungarian nation "by ridding it of the Jewish poison, a self-defense which will end Jewish predominance." He further asserted that in his view "the population in all cities and communities hailed the government measures with genuine delight." This was especially true, he claimed, in the cities of Munkács, Ungvár, Beregszász, and Máramarossziget, "which had borne the brunt of the flood of eastern Jews [and where] the population rejoiced and frequently supplied means of transportation to speed resettlement and get rid of the Jews."

Endre then proceeded to assuage the concern of the Hungarians by declaring:

We adopted measures that were always carried out humanely and with consideration for moral factors. Really, no harm is befalling them. They can live among themselves in one group within the borders of the ghetto in accordance with their own folk and racial laws. We made it possible for them to cook with sesame oil, which enables them not to violate one of their important religious tenets. The ghettoization was carried out humanely with the avoidance of all rough conduct. I issued instructions that good care be taken for their safety.[97]

The Ghettoization in
Northern Transylvania: An Overview

The campaign for the concentration of the Jews in Gendarmerie Districts IX and X of Northern Transylvania, which began on May 3, 1944, was generally completed within one week. By noon of May 5, 16,144 Jews had been concentrated; their number increased to 72,382 by May 6, and to 98,000 by May 10.[98]

The effectiveness of the anti-Jewish drive was assured not only by the cooperation of the local administration and police authorities and the direct involvement of the gendarmerie, but also by the guidance provided by the SS-*Sonderkommando* and the central Hungarian authorities, especially those under the direct command of Baky and Endre. Contact between the dejewification field offices in Northern Transylvania and the central organs in Budapest was provided by two special gendarmerie courier cars that traveled daily in opposite directions, meeting in Nagyvárad—the midpoint between the capital and Kolozsvár, the headquarters for the ghettoization and deportation program in Northern Transylvania.[99]

A few days after the completion of the ghettoization and the transfer of the Jews from the smaller communities into the larger ghetto centers, the dejewification authorities turned their attention to the finalization of deportation plans.

The top administrative, police, and gendarmerie officers of the various counties and county seats in Northern Transylvania were informed about the details of the planned deportations at a conference chaired by László Endre, held in Munkács on May 8. The participants were told the procedures to be used in the entrainment of the Jews and the schedule of the transports from the various ghettos. More detailed instructions were also given "in the field," normally by Lieutenant-Colonel László Ferenczy, the gendarmerie officer in charge of the ghettoization operations throughout Hungary. During May 18–20, for example, he held a conference with the civilian and police and gendarmerie leaders of the counties around Kolozsvár, giving them final instructions relating to the deportations from Gendarmerie Districts IX and X.[100] A few days later, the liquidation of the Jewish communities of Northern Transylvania began.[101]

Notes

1. For a statistical evaluation of the Jews of Northern Transylvania, see chapter 5.

2. Statement by László Endre given on December 17, 1945, in connection with the preparation of the prosecution by Dr. Endre Pollák of the cases against László Gyapay, László Csóka, and László Vásárhelyi, the mayors of Nagyvárad, Szatmárnémeti, and Kolozsvár, respectively. The original Endre statement is in the possession of this author.

3. Endre statement cited above.

4. Ferenczy Report F. I. Israel Police, Bureau 06, Eichmann Trial Doc. no. 1314.

5. Ferenczy Report dated May 3, 1944. Israel Police Bureau 06, Eichmann Trial Doc. no. 1315. Ferenczy sent his reports on the operations in Northern Transylvania to Department XX of the Ministry of the Interior with copies to Secretaries of State Baky and Endre, the head of Department VII of the Ministry of the Interior, the commander of the investigative unit of the gendarmerie, and Béla Ricsóy-Uhlarik, the Government Commissioner for Northern Transylvania.

6. *Tribunalul Poporului, Cluj*, p. 21.

7. For incidents of denunciations, see *Tribunal Poporului, Cluj*, pp. 58–65, 81–88.

8. Ferenczy Report of May 3. Israel Police. Bureau 06, Eichmann Trial Doc. no. 1315. For further details on the attitude of the Jewish and non-Jewish masses, see chapters 23 and 30, respectively. For details on the treatment of the Romanians during the Hungarian era, consult *Tribunalul Popurului, Cluj. Completul de judecată. Hotărîrea No. 1. Şedinţa Publică din 13 Martie 1946* (Judgment. Decision No. 1. Public Session of March 1, 1946), 59 p. Judgment rendered against 63 individuals accused of war crimes. See also Ion Spalatelu, "The Horthyist Occupation of Northern Transylvania (1940–1944)" in *Romanian News*, Bucharest, 4, no. 8 (May 9, 1978):8–9.

9. Marton's stand in behalf of the Jews was rebuked by the government. He returned to Alba Iulia at the end of May and was not allowed back to Kolozsvár until after the war. Béla Vágó, "The Destruction of the Jews of Transylvania" in *HJS*, 1:192–93.

10. Vásárhelyi, a city councillor, was appointed Mayor early in April after Tibor Keledy was assigned to serve as Mayor of Budapest. Lajos Marton, *A Svájcba 1944 augusztusban és decemberben érkezett bergen-belseni csoport eseményeinek rövid kronográfiája* (A Short

Chronology of the Bergen-Belsen Group That Arrived in Switzerland in August and December 1944) (Geneva, 1945), p. 6 (Manuscript).

11. The German security police unit arrived in Kolozsvár on March 30, 1944, and established its headquarters in the Péter-Pál villa at 24 Apácai Csere János Street. *Ibid.*

12. Ferenczy Report of May 10. Israel Police. Bureau 06, Eichmann Trial Doc. no. 1317.

13. Kasztner claims that 18,000 Jews were in the ghetto of Kolozsvár. *Der Kastner-Bericht*, p. 107. According to the census of 1941, the city had a total population of 110,956 of which 16,763 were Jews. In 1947, the city had a Jewish population of about 6,500 consisting not only of the local survivors of the Holocaust, but also of persons who moved in from neighboring rural communities and from such Southern Transylvanian towns as Turda and Uioara. *Aşezările evreilor*, p. 167.

14. *Tribunalul Poporului, Cluj*, pp. 74–92.

15. Fischer was born in 1887 in Tiszaújhely. He came to Kolozsvár in 1913. In 1920, he was elected head of the Zionist Association of Transylvania and the Banat (*Erdély-Bánáti Cionista Szövetség*). Shortly thereafter he was also elected President of the Neolog community and as a Jewish Party representative in the Romanian Parliament. He headed the so-called Kasztner group both in Bergen-Belsen and in Switzerland. He died in Israel in 1952. *A kolozsvári zsidóság emlékkönyve* (The Memorial Book of Kolozsvár's Jewry), ed. Mózes Carmilly-Weinberger (New York: The Author, 1970), pp. 86–88.

16. *A kolozsvári zsidóság emlékkönyve*, p. 223. Following the Council's reorganization late in April, the membership included Fischer, Marton, Léb, and the following new members: Ernő Kasztner (Rudolph Kasztner's brother), Pál Klein (Joel Brand's brother-in-law), and Dr. Jenő Weisz (Fischer's brother-in-law). *Ibid.*, p. 225. Zoltán Glatz claims that the Council was composed of Fischer, Endre Balázs, and Sándor Weisz. See his statement in Yad Vashem, Archives M-20/95.

17. Marton, *A Svájcba 1944 augusztusban.*

18. Report of Zoltán Glatz. Yad Vashem, Archives M-20/95. For further details on the fate of the Jewish community of Kolozsvár and its environs see *A kolozsvári zsidóság emlékkönyve*. See also *Zikkaron netsah le'kehila ha'kedosha Kolozhvar-Klauzenburg asher nehreva ba'shoa* (Everlasting Memorial to the Martyred Community of Kolozsvár Which Perished in the Holocaust), eds. Sh. Zimroni and Y. Schwartz (Tel Aviv: Former Residents of Kolozsvár in Israel, 1968), 118 pp. Mimeographed in Hebrew and Hungarian. See also the personal accounts of Ester Pollák (YIVO, 770/184), Ferdinand Salamon (774/2872), and S. Weisz (775/3115).

19. Personal communication by Michael Bar-On. For further details see *Szamosujvár, Iklód és környéke* (Szamosujvár, Iklód, and Environs), ed. Michael Bar-On (Deutsch) (Tel Aviv: Izsák Efrájim és Fia, 1971), 90 + 190 pp. Pages 157–82 contain the lists of the martyred Jews of the various communities in Szamosujvár District.

20. *Tribunalul Poporului, Cluj*, p. 142.

21. *"Volt egyszer egy Dés . . ."* (There Was Once Upon a Time a Dés . . .), ed. Zoltán Singer (Tel Aviv: A Dés és Vidékéről Elszármazottak Landsmannschaftja, n.d.), pp. 426–27, 432. Vékás committed suicide after the war.

22. *Ibid.*

23. Ferenczy Report of May 10. Israel Police, Bureau 06, Eichmann Trial Doc. no. 1317.

24. In 1941, Dés had a total population of 16,353, of which 3,719 were Jews. In 1947, there were 1,020 Jews in the city, including those who moved in from the neighboring villages and from elsewhere in Romania. *Aşezările evreilor*, pp. 201–7. At the time of the ghettoization, the community consisted of 3,266 people. (Several hundred additional males were serving in labor service companies.) A list of the 3,266 Jews (a copy is in possession of this author) was prepared by order of the authorities shortly before the

beginning of the anti-Jewish operations. Only 239 of them returned after the war. *"Volt egyszer egy Dés . . . ,"* p. 459. For a partial list of the martyred Jews of Dés, see *Ibid.*, pp. 465–542.

25. For details on the Jewish communities of these district seats and of the neighboring villages, including Alőr, Alső-Ilosva, Apanagyfalu, Domokos, Felőr, Galgó, Ispánmező, Kaczkó, Kosály, Mikeháza, Somkerék, and Szőcs, see *Ibid.*, pp. 291–459, 616–25. The same source lists all the Jewish settlements of Szolnok-Doboka (Szamos) County with some statistical data for 1857, 1886, 1891, 1930, 1944, and 1946 (pp. 178–86), and gives the names of the martyred Jews of Bethlen, Magyarlápos, Nagyilonda, Retteg, and some neighboring smaller communities (pp. 543–90).

26. Ferenczy Report of May 5, 1944.

27. *Ibid.*, May 6, 1944.

28. *Ibid.*, May 7, 1944.

29. For details on the activities of these individuals, see *Tribunalul Poporului, Cluj,* pp. 135–40.

30. *Ibid.*, pp. 140–42.

31. Ferenczy Report of May 6, 1944. In his telegram dated May 8, 1944, Veesenmayer claimed that Count Béla Bethlen, the Prefect of Szolnok-Doboka County, had also resigned. *RLB,* Doc. 264. Ferenczy, however, does not mention Count Bethlen at all. Singer, in turn, mistakenly asserts that Bethlen had cooperated with the authorities and been condemned by a postwar People's Tribunal to ten years of forced labor. (*"Volt egyszer egy Dés . . . ,"* p. 422). In fact it was Schilling rather than Bethlen who was condemned to 10 years' imprisonment. *Tribunalul Poporului, Cluj,* p. 173.

32. *"Volt egyszer egy Dés . . . ,"* p. 422.

33. *Ibid.*, p. 432, and personal communication to this author by Singer dated January 11, 1973.

34. The first transport left on May 28, and the second on June 4. *Ibid.*, pp. 446 and 450. For further details on the fate of the Jews of Szolnok-Doboka County see Singer's account cited above and the statements of Andreas Havas (Yad Vashem, Jerusalem, 015/17-3, 1016/55) and Ephraim (Ferenc) Singer (Yad Vashem, 0-3/1756).

35. Andrei Paul [Endre Pollák], *Az északerdélyi zsidó lakosság deportálása 1944-ben* (The Deportation of the Jewish Population of Northern Transylvania in 1944). Manuscript, pp. 9 and 48. Andrei Paul was one of the chief prosecutors in the war crimes trials held in Kolozsvár in 1945–46.

36. For an account of the Jewish community of Tasnád, which numbered about 800 in 1941, see Abraham Fuchs, *Tasnád* (Jerusalem: The Author, 1973), 276 pp. (Hebrew).

37. Ferenczy Report of May 6, 1944.

38. *Ibid.*, May 5, 1944.

39. For further details on the ghetto and the activities of the Hungarian officials active in the drive against the Jews of Szilágy County, see *Tribunalul Poporului, Cluj,* pp. 115–33. See also statement by Dr. Joseph Szerényi, YIVO Institute for Jewish Research, New York, Archives 772/2593.

40. Lévai, *Zsidósors Magyarországon,* p. 410.

41. Ferenczy Report of May 3, 1944. Israel Police, Bureau 06, Eichmann Trial Doc. 1315. See also Lévai, *Zsidósors Magyarországon,* p. 410.

42. *Ibid.* Also personal communication by Lea Merksamer (*neé* Lili Markovits), a former clerk of the Jewish Council in Szatmárnémeti, who settled in Israel after the war.

43. Communication by Lea Merksamer cited above.

44. Sárközi surfaced during the Hungarian Uprising of October–November 1956. Recognized by survivors of the Holocaust, he was arrested, brought to trial, and hanged in Budapest in 1960. Communication by Lea Merksamer, who served as one of the witnesses in the trial.

45. The composition of the Council is based on a personal communication from József Borgida, who served as deputy head of the Council.

46. Szatmárnémeti had a large Jewish community before the war. According to the census of 1941, the city had a population of 52,011, of which 12,960 were Jews. In 1947, the city had 7,500 Jews, including those who moved there from other parts of Romania after World War II. *Aşezările evreilor,* p. 194. See also Lévai, *Zsidósors Magyarországon,* p. 410.

47. Ferenczy reported the suicides of Dr. Oszkár György and his mother, and of Mr. and Mrs. Albert Weisz. Ferenczy Report of May 6, 1944.

48. *Ibid.,* May 7, 1944.

49. The Mayor of Szatmárnémeti had exempted Sámuel Engel and nine members of his family because they were raising 250 pigs, which were deemed economically essential for the country. Ferenczy, however, saw to it that the task was entrusted to a Christian by the name of Géza Papler, and Engel and his family were interned. Ferenczy Report of May 9, Israel Police, Bureau 06, Eichmann Trial Doc. 1316.

50. Among these was András Wohl, a converted university student, who had sought refuge in the local Roman Catholic Seminary. Ferenczy Report of May 10. Israel Police, Bureau 06, Eichmann Trial Doc. 1317.

51. For further details on the Szatmárnémeti ghetto and the officials associated with its establishment and operation, see *Tribunalul Poporului, Cluj,* pp. 51–65. On the denunciation of Jews, see pp. 58–65. See also the following personal narratives available at the YIVO Institute for Jewish Research in New York: Eugene Sernthal (Archives, 768/3637), Mirjam Perl (770/133), Béla Rosenberg (774/2716), and H. Moskovits (776/40).

52. *Tribunalul Poporului, Cluj,* p. 63.

53. Israel Police, Bureau 06, Eichmann Trial Doc. 1314.

54. *Tribunalul Poporului, Cluj,* p. 64; Ferenczy Report of May 10, 1944. Among the Jews at Borpatak were the 246 Jews of Felsőbánya. Ferenczy Report of May 6, 1944.

55. *Tribunalul Poporului, Cluj,* pp. 51, 63–74. See also the personal narrative of Herman Jeger at the YIVO Institute for Jewish Research, New York, Archives 775/3172. For further details, see *Baia-Mare. Nagybánya mártirjainak emlékkönyve* (Memorial Book of the Martyrs of Nagybánya), ed. Naftali Stern (B'nei B'rak, Israel: The Editor, 1979), 245 pp. (mimeographed).

56. *Tribunalul Poporului, Cluj,* pp. 142–43. In his report of May 10, 1944, Ferenczy claims that the number of Jews in the ghetto was approximately 6,000 and that the ghetto was established in a brickyard located at Borgó Prund, about 4 miles from the city.

57. In 1941, Beszterce had a population of 16,282, of which 2,358 were Jews. The city's Jewish population in 1947 was 1,300, including those relocated there from the neighboring communities and from elsewhere after the war. *Aşezările evreilor,* p. 178.

58. Ferenczy Reports of May 5 and 7, 1944.

59. *Tribunalul Poporului, Cluj,* pp. 142–45.

60. Ferenczy Reports of May 7 and 10, 1944. For a copy of the Nagyvárad ghetto map, see University of Haifa, Center of Historical Studies, File H3h23–A.M.E.1/25.

61. One of the women involved in the search for valuables at the Érmihályfalva ghetto was Rozália Zeffer Kiss. *Tribunalul Poporului, Cluj,* pp. 50–51. The Jewish women of Margitta were searched vaginally by Erzsébet Valkó and Erzsébet Mutza Megyesi. The latter was especially cruel, violating virgin girls. *Ibid.,* pp. 49–50.

62. In 1941, 21,337 of the city's population of 92,942 identified themselves as Jewish. (If one includes converts, the number of Jews was much larger.) In 1947, the city had a Jewish population of 8,000, including those who moved in from other parts of Romania. *Aşezările evreilor,* pp. 159–64.

63. *Tribunalul Poporului, Cluj,* p. 27.

64. For details on the Jewish Council and the ghetto of Nagyvárad, see Alexander

(Sándor) Leitner, *Die Tragödie der Juden in Nagyvárad* (The Tragedy of the Jews of Nagy-várad). Manuscript, Yad Vashem, Jerusalem, Archives JM/2686. The English version is available at the Central Zionist Archives, Jerusalem, File No. S26/1469.

65. Rajnay was relieved of his position by the Lakatos government on September 5, 1944, and replaced by Dr. Károly Barcsay, the county's chief prosecutor. *Budapesti Közlöny*, no. 204, September 7, 1944, p. 1.

66. Pétterffy was associated with the Royal Hungarian Gendarmerie Cadet School of Nagyvárad (*Magyar Királyi nagyváradi csendőriskola*), which was headed by Paksy-Kiss. He was arrested soon after the war and held for trial at the Markó Street prison of Budapest. He hanged himself shortly before his scheduled extradition to Romania to stand trial for his crimes in Northern Transylvania. Paul, *Az északerdélyi zsidó lakosság deportálása 1944-ben*, p. 47.

67. One of those who committed suicide in the wake of the tortures was Dr. Osváth of the Jewish Council.

68. For details on their background and activities in the ghetto, see *Tribunalul Poporu-lui, Cluj*, pp. 26–51.

69. *Ibid.*

70. Lévai, *Zsidósors Magyarországon*, pp. 108 and 409.

71. Ferenczy Report of May 6, 1944. Among those suspected was Pál Krasznay, the Police Chief Counselor of Nagyvárad. Ferenczy Report of May 7, 1944.

72. For details on Rajnay's culpability in the destruction of the Jews of Nagyvárad and Bihar County, see *Tribunalul Poporului, Cluj*, pp. 41–47.

73. Lévai, *Zsidósors Magyarországon*, pp. 137–38.

74. *Egyedül Vagyunk* (We Are Alone), an anti-Semitic organ, satirically observed that although Endre walked in the ghetto in the company of only one gendarme, none of the ghetto's 30,000 Jews dared touch him. Lévai, *Fekete könyv*, pp. 134–35.

75. On this date the SS entered the city and immediately confiscated the Jewish Hospital. The Jewish leaders were asked to have it refurbished within two days for transformation into a German military hospital. Alexander Leitner, *Die Tragödie der Juden in Nagy-várad*, pp. 14–16.

76. For details on the Nagyvárad ghetto see Alexander Leitner's *Die Tragödie der Juden in Nagyvárad*. Leitner and his family were taken to Budapest early in June and included in the Kasztner group that left the country on June 30, 1944. For further details, consult the personal narratives of Frida and Ella Leser (YIVO, 772/2487), Thomas Bárdi (775/311), and B. Eisenberg (776/5), as well as Béla Katona, *Várad a viharban* (Várad in the Storm) (Nagyvárad: Tealah Korháztámogató Egyesület, 1946), 363 pp.

77. *Tribunalul Poporului, Cluj*, pp. 93–94.

78. *Ibid.*, p. 94. In his report of May 10, 1944, Ferenczy claims that 6,050 Jews were interned by that day.

79. In 1941, the city had a population of 44,933, of which 5,693 were Jews. In 1947, Marosvásárhely had 2,420 Jewish inhabitants. *Aşezările evreilor*, p. 173.

80. Ferenczy Report of May 6, 1944.

81. Jicchak Perri (Friedmann), *Prakim be'toldot ha'yehudim be'Transylvania b'et hehadasha. Korot yehudei Marosvásárhely ve'hasviva* (Chapters From the History of the Jews of Transylvania in Modern Times. History of the Jews of Marosvásárhely and Environs) (Tel Aviv: Bet Lohamei Hagetaot, 1977), 2:207.

82. Perri claims that in addition to the brickyard at Koronkai Road, the synagogues of the Orthodox and Status Quo communities also served as ghettos. *Ibid.*, p. 204.

83. *Ibid.*, p. 203. This source—with one volume in Hungarian and one in Hebrew—contains a detailed, though not fully documented, history of the Jewish communities of Marosvásárhely and its environs. The Hungarian volume includes a partial list of the martyrs of Marosvásárhely (pp. 213–55) and 34 neighboring communities, including

Bergenye, Mezőbánd, Erdőszentgyörgy, Nyáradszereda, Parajd, Székelyudvarhely, Szováta, and Székelykeresztur (pp. 256–64). According to Dr. Adalbert (Béla) Charap, the Council was composed of Abrahám, Szofer, and Krausz, representing the Orthodox, and of Darvas, Léderer, and Rabbi Ferenc Loewy, representing the Status Quo. See his statement signed in Bucharest on February 9, 1945, at the University of Haifa, Center of Historical Studies, File H3h17–A.M.E.1/5.

84. *Tribunalul Poporului, Cluj,* p. 97. According to Dr. Charap, the commander of the SS units in Marosvásárhely was Captain Sotzki.

85. Ferenczy Report of May 7, 1944.

86. *Ibid.,* May 5, 1944. See also *RLB,* Doc. 263.

87. *Tribunalul Poporului, Cluj,* pp. 94–102. See also the personal narrative of M. Grün at the YIVO-Institute for Jewish Research, New York, Archives 776/10.

88. Perri, *Prahim be'toldot,* p. 209. According to Dr. Charap, whose statement was cited above, the deportations took place between May 25 and 27.

89. Ferenczy Report of May 10, 1944. Israel Police, Bureau 06, Eichmann Trial Doc. no. 1317.

90. In 1941, 1,635 of the city's 10,165 inhabitants were Jewish. In 1947, there were 820 Jews in Szászrégen. *Aşezările evreilor,* p. 173.

91. Lévai, *Zsidósors Magyarországon,* p. 410.

92. *Tribunalul Poporului, Cluj,* pp. 103–8.

93. Lévai, *Zsidósors Magyarországon,* p. 410.

94. Ferenczy Report of May 9, 1944. In the same report, Ferenczy noted that the one Jewish family authorized to remain in Sepsiszentgyörgy—that of Izsó Silberstein—was also placed in the ghetto at his insistence.

95. *Tribunalul Poporului, Cluj,* pp. 108–9.

96. Endre's statement of December 17, 1945.

97. *Uj Magyarság,* May 15, 1944. The interview was reproduced in the *Völkischer Beobachter* of May 17, 1944. See also *NMT,* 13:351–52.

98. Ferenczy Reports of May 6, 7, and 10. The figures for Northern Transylvania do not include the Jews of Máramaros and the neighboring counties of the Northeast, which were administratively considered to belong to Gendarmerie District VIII, i.e., to Carpatho-Ruthenia and northeastern Hungary.

99. Ferenczy Report of May 3, 1944. Israel Police, Bureau 06, Eichmann Trial Doc. 1315.

100. *Tribunalul Poporului, Cluj,* pp. 146–47.

101. In addition to the references cited for the various communities discussed in this chapter, see *Toldot ha'kehilot b'Transylvania* (History of the Communities of Transylvania), ed. Yehuda Schwarz (Tel Aviv: Ha'aguda yad Le'Kehilot Transylvania, 1976), 294 pp. The book contains brief historical review notes on a large number of communities, including Alőr, Bánffyhunyad, Bárdfalva, Beszterce, Betlen, Biharnagybajom, Borsa, Csárda, Derecske, Dés, Érmihályfalva, Felsővisó, Halmi, Havasmező, Hidalmás, Iklód, Ilonda, Kiskalota, Kissármás, Kolozsvár, Kraszna, Magyarlápos, Máramarossziget, Margitta, Marosvásárhely, Mezőtelegd, Mócs, Nagybánya, Nagykároly, Nagysomkut, Nagyszalonta, Nagysármás, Nagyvárad, Naszod, Náznánfalva, Retteg, Sepsiszentgyörgy, Szamosujvár, Szaplonca, Szászrégen, Szatmárnémeti, Szilágycseh, and Szilágysomiyó. Of these communities, Kissármás and Nagysármás—both in Southern Transylvania—were affected in the wake of the Hungarian invasion of the Romanian-held territories in September 1944.